COUNSELLING PSYCHOLOGY RESOURCES DIRECTORY

7th Edition (1994)

Edited by Isobel Palmer
BAC Information & Publications Manager

© **Copyright 1993**

All rights reserved. No part of this publication may be reproduced or incorporated in any publication to be sold for profit without the written prior permission of the British Association for Counselling.

We have taken great care in compiling this directory but cannot be held responsible for any mistakes or omissions. BAC has printed information about individuals and organisations, supplied by those individuals and organisations in good faith and cannot vouch for its truth and accuracy, except insofar as, where stated, membership of and accreditation by BAC were accurate at time of going to press.

ISBN 0 946181 42 X

CONTENTS

Section	Page
Introduction to the Directory	iii
How to use the Directory	vii
BAC Code of Ethics & Practice for Counsellors	viii
BAC Accreditation Criteria	xiv
Acceptable Codes/training organisations	xv
List of Abbreviations	xix

National Organisations
- Specialist Counselling 1
- Professional Organisations 7
- Charities, Voluntary Organisations & Self-Help Groups 15

London
- Central 25
- East 37
- North 53
- North West 93
- South East 127
- South West 151
- West 181

	Page
Avon	209
Bedfordshire	223
Berkshire	229
Buckinghamshire	239
Cambridgeshire	249
Cheshire	261
Cleveland	271
Cornwall	275
Cumbria	277
Derbyshire	279
Devon	283
Dorset	291
Durham	297
Essex	299
Gloucestershire	321
Greater Manchester	327
Hampshire	339
Hereford & Worcester	357
Hertfordshire	363
Humberside	385
Kent	389
Lancashire	411
Leicestershire	419
Lincolnshire	427
Merseyside	431
Middlesex	437
Norfolk	457
Northamptonshire	465
Northumberland	469
Nottinghamshire	471
Oxfordshire	477
Shropshire	487
Somerset	491
Staffordshire	497
Suffolk	501

Surrey
- North East (Postcodes CR, SM) 509
- North West (Postcodes KT, TW) 519
- South (Postcodes GU, RH) 539

Sussex
- East 559
- West 571

	Page
Tyne & Wear	581
Warwickshire	585
West Midlands	593
Wiltshire	611

Yorkshire
- North 617
- South 625
- West 631

	Page
Scotland	645
Wales	661
Northern Ireland	671
Channel Islands	673

Index
Organisations
Individuals Practitioners

INTRODUCTION

All of us feel worried or depressed now and again and most of us have known times when we feel like saying "I can't cope any more" or "I don't know which way to turn". When we look back on these periods it's easy to see that they're part of life and that it's quite normal to feel this way at some time or another. But at the time we may feel sad, hurt or frightened and ill at ease. It's at difficult, painful times like these, facing personal problems or periods of crisis, that many of us would welcome the chance to talk things over in confidence with an understanding and objective outsider.

Friends, of course, can be wonderful but we may feel we don't want to or else can't burden them with our problems, or they may simply not be there when we need them. A counsellor, or psychotherapist, is a person trained to listen actively while you talk through your personal problems, to support you through your bad patch and to help you find your own answers to your troubles. They can help you see the overall picture. And you don't need to worry about overburdening them - their job is to offer this kind of help and to give you the concentrated time and objectivity that friends can't give.

Hundreds of thousands of people seek help from a counsellor or psychotherapist at some time in their lives. They may be suffering the death of a loved one, or not getting on with their partner, they may have lost their job or be worrying about coping with a new one, they may be finding the strain of work or exams too much, they may be at the end of their tether, anxious about the kids, their parents or themselves, or simply down in the dumps. Many people also seek guidance when they come to points in their lives when nothing seems to be seriously wrong but they just don't know which way to go next; they may have just retired or their children have left home or they may feel suddenly, for no apparent reason, that life seems to lack a purpose for them.

This directory lists counsellors, psychotherapists and organisations throughout the UK, but before you start using the directory here are some answers to the most frequently asked questions about counselling and psychotherapy. These will also help guide your choice.

What is Counselling?

> Counselling is a process which involves the helping skills of caring, listening and reflecting. It's based on listening to the client and a trusting relationship between the client and the counsellor. It's not the same as the advice giving service of, say, the Citizen's Advice Bureaux. A counsellor will be supportive but give little or no direct advice since the aim of counselling is to help us develop our own insight into our problems. They help us re-find our own resources within (resources we often forget we've got) and so enable us to approach our lives and problems in a fresh way.

Counselling is also rather different from self-help groups where a group of people with the same problems talk together and try to help each other. Self-help groups can be very supportive and often go well with counselling - but one-to-one sessions with a trained counsellor offer a more concentrated kind of help.

Counselling involves very human skills - like knowing how to ask the right questions and when - and these are highly developed through training and experience. The counselling relationship is used to explore personal problems, to enable us to make sense of our unhappiness. By getting to know ourselves we can understand our feelings and motives better and this can reduce anxiety and ease depression in a deep way.

One of the main aims of counselling is to guide us from feeling victims of circumstances to feeling we have some control over our lives. So in the course of counselling we can reassess our 'coping skills' - how we deal with problems, challenges, relationships, work - and learn ways that are more effective. Counselling also looks at how we communicate with each other, guiding us to be more clear and direct - saying what we mean and asking for what we want, being assertive without being aggressive.

Sessions usually last 50-60 minutes, once a week for a period of weeks or months, depending on the need and how the counsellor works. Setting some sort of goal together with the counsellor (e.g. not feeling panicked by work at the end of, say, eight sessions) is often a part of counselling.

Confidentiality is of major importance in counselling and would only be breached after discussion with the client in circumstances where the client or others (particularly children) were at risk.

What is the difference between counselling and psychotherapy?

It is not easy to give a brief answer as both terms cover a wide variety of practice. Certainly, there is considerable overlap in that much psychotherapy is about overcoming personal difficulties and facilitating change in the ways already described in relation to counselling. The methods used in psychotherapy are similar and in some instances identical to those used in counselling. If there are differences, then they relate more to the individual psychotherapists's or counsellor's training and interests and to the setting in which they work, rather than to any intrinsic difference in the two activities. A psychotherapist working in a hospital is likely to be more concerned with severe psychological disorders than with the wide range of problems and predicaments about which it is appropriate to consult a counsellor. In private practice, however, a psychotherapist is more likely to accept clients whose need is less severe. Similarly, in private practice a counsellor's work will overlap with that of a psychotherapist. Those counsellors, however, who work for voluntary agencies or in educational settings such as colleges and schools usually concentrate more upon the 'everyday' problems and difficulties of life than on the more severe psychological disorders; though many are qualified to offer, and do in fact engage in, therapeutic work which in any other context would be called psychotherapy. Both psychotherapists and counsellors are capable of deciding whether or not they should seek further medical and psychiatric advice, and are normally able to make referrals to appropriate specialists, though frequently this can only be done in consultation with the client's own GP (doctor).

Psychoanalysis, created by Freud at the turn of the century, is the 'grandfather' of all psychotherapy. Nowadays it's best considered as one form of psychotherapy on offer. Analysis is very intense, typically hourly sessions four days a week for years, however the 'popular' image of the analyst's couch and the anonymous analyst you never see is a bit outdated now. You can still go for traditional analysis but most analysts have incorporated newer, person-centred techniques into their working method. Analysis is just one form of psychotherapy. Depending on their training a psychotherapist may use a whole range of techniques, not just talking: guided imagery work, drama techniques or role playing, etc.

Fortunately, the distinction between counselling and psychotherapy is not a matter which need greatly concern anyone seeking help. Most practitioners of either activity, before any commitment on either side is made, will want to be sure that the help they can offer is appropriate for the individual concerned. If a counsellor or psychotherapist is not prepared to discuss this, then it would be wise for the prospective client to seek help from someone else.

Many of the people who seek psychotherapy are not going through a crisis but are looking for a way to get to know themselves better, to understand their relationships better or to get more out of life. For lots of people this can be an exciting and rewarding adventure.

Who goes for counselling and psychotherapy?

All sorts of people. Counselling and psychotherapy are not just for the rich or for those who are seriously disturbed, and going for counselling does not mean one is self-indulgent or has gone mad! It is a very natural and healthy response to seek help when we can't sort things out on our own. In the old days we might have gone to the local priest or family doctor, to a 'wise woman' or favourite aunt, when we needed to talk over our feelings or get help in an emotional crisis. Nowadays, with communities split up and everyone leading busier lives, for most of us these characters have faded from the scene and in many ways counsellors and psychotherapists have filled the gap. Men and women of all ages and from every kind of background go to counsellors with problems ranging from depression or anxiety to addictions, phobias, stress at work, trouble at home or in a relationship to sexual difficulties.

As an example of the numbers of people who now make use of counselling and psychotherapy, in 1990 some 70,000 people went to just one of the organisations, Relate, which provides specialist counselling.

How long will it take and how much will it cost?

How long it takes depends on you, the counsellor/therapist and the problem. While deep-rooted problems will need longer, say one hour a week for several months, short term counselling for a specific problem may take only a few weekly sessions. Some people begin this way and then decide to make deep changes to their lives and enter therapy for a year or more. Mostly you might expect to go for one hour a week, but the question of how many sessions, how frequently and the length of each session should be discussed with the counsellor/therapist you choose.

Within the NHS counselling/psychotherapy (if available) is free. Otherwise the average range of fees is £15-40 but they can range from free to as high as £50 or more per hour.

Many counselling/psychotherapy centres and individuals try to offer a sliding scale of fees which takes ability to pay into account. Also most of the training institutes offer low cost sessions with trainees. There is some therapy on the NHS but the waiting lists at hospitals tend to be long. More GP practices are including counsellors as part of the primary care team, so enquire if counselling is available at your surgery.

How to choose the right person for you

The final judge of whether a counsellor/therapist is 'right' for you can only be yourself, and in the end you must trust your own instincts and how you feel about them. Ask yourself if you would feel comfortable telling this person intimate details of your life, do you feel safe with them, do you like their manner towards you and their attitude to your questions, do you trust them and feel able to be completely open with them? The more open you can be the more you will gain from the counselling.

Word of mouth from someone you respect is one of the best recommendations, but you may also prefer just to choose someone from the Directory. The entries for individual counsellors summarise their qualifications and training. Length of experience is an obvious thing to think about. Supervision is considered to be equally important; this means that the counsellor/therapist meets regularly with a colleague to talk over their work, for support and discussion of problems. Many people consider that personal therapy is the most important qualification: this means that the therapist/counsellor has been a client in their own therapy, which helps them to understand themselves and others better. These two factors are often an indication of high standards.

Finally, all individual counsellors and therapists in this directory are members of either the British Association for Counselling (BAC), the Institute of Psychosexual Medicine (IPM) or a member organisation of the United Kingdom Council for Psychotherapy (UKCP). These organisations all have a code of ethics and practice to which their members are expected to adhere. BAC is the main national membership body for counselling and we include in this introduction the BAC Code of Ethics

& Practice for Counsellors as an example of the principles a code should contain. Some training institutes and some organisations offering counselling services have their own codes too, but many belong to an umbrella organisation such as BAC or use the code of the counsellors/psychotherapists working in the service.

We have highlighted BAC Accredited members as we feel that as producers of this Directory we ought to be promoting **our members** who have successfully submitted their work for consideration by BAC. This is a voluntary scheme which means that non-accredited members can be equally highly trained and experienced. Other organisations also have accreditation schemes or different categories of membership. It is important, therefore, when choosing a counsellor to check their training and qualifications as there is a wide range contained in this Directory.

Some therapist specialise (e.g. sexual, addictions, marriage) so if your problem is very specific you may want to see a specialist, although most therapists will deal with a wide range of problems.

However you make your choice, we suggest you shop around: see two or three counsellors/therapists for a first interview before deciding, and don't be afraid to ask questions. How does the therapy work, what will a session involve, what sort of supervision does the therapist/counsellor have, how much of their own therapy have they done, what is their professional qualification and what kind of training did they do?

HOW TO USE THIS DIRECTORY

The Directory lists organisations, counsellors and psychotherapists in England, Northern Ireland, Scotland, Wales, Isle of Man and Channel Islands. It is laid out for you in two sections and you should use both of them to find a therapist.

A. National Organisations

1. **Specialist Counselling Services** many of which offer Employee Assistance Programmes and workplace counselling to companies (some take self-referrals) or deal with particular client groups.

2. **Professional Organisations** such as the counselling and psychotherapy training bodies can also be contacted directly for a counsellor or therapist. Contact the office number listed.

3. Organisations such as the Samaritans, Relate or Cruse are listed under the head office in the section for **Charities, Voluntary Organisations & Self-Help Groups**. Once you find an organisation that you think may suit you, look up your local branch in the telephone directory or contact the head office and they will give you the address of your nearest local branch.

B. Local Information is divided into two sections within each area

1. Organisations which may include statutory bodies, charities and private centres. You are most likely to find free or low cost counselling in this section.

2. Individual practitioners, including those who are BAC Accredited counsellors or BAC Recognised Supervisors, which have been shaded. Each entry contains details on the organisation to whose code of ethics and practice they work; the counsellor's qualifications/training, the kind of therapy they do, whether they have undergone therapy themselves, what kind of clients they see and any specialisations, their theoretical approach and fee structure.

   The listing in each section is not strictly alphabetical.

   London is divided by postcode, e.g. Central, East, North, etc., and numerically within each area, e.g. E1 - E18, N1 - N22, etc.

   Entries for the counties are listed alphabetically by town, so that in the West Midlands, for example, Birmingham is listed before Coventry, which is before Wolverhampton. This is done to make life easier for those who use the Directory for regular referral purposes, particularly in response to telephone enquiries when the caller is likely to want a counsellor in a specific locality. For this reason we have divided Surrey into 3 areas by postcode.

BAC CODE OF ETHICS & PRACTICE FOR COUNSELLORS

1. **Status of this code**
1.1 In response to the experience of members of BAC, this code is a revision of the 1992 code.

2. **Introduction**
2.1 The purpose of this code is to establish and maintain standards for counsellors who are members of BAC, and to inform and protect members of the public seeking and using their services.
2.2 All members of this Association are required to abide by existing codes appropriate to them. They thereby accept a common frame of reference within which to manage their responsibilities to clients, colleagues, members of this Association and the wider community. Whilst this code cannot resolve all ethical and practice related issues, it aims to provide a framework for addressing ethical issues and to encourage optimum levels of practice. Counsellors will need to judge which parts of this code apply to particular situations. They may have to decide between conflicting responsibilities.
2.3 This Association has a Complaints Procedure which can lead to the expulsion of members for breaches of its Codes of Ethics & Practice.

3. **The Nature of Counselling**
3.1 The overall aim of counselling is to provide an opportunity for the client to work towards living in a more satisfying and resourceful way. The term 'counselling' includes work with individuals, pairs or groups of people often, but not always, referred to as 'clients'. The objectives of particular counselling relationships will vary according to the client's needs. Counselling may be concerned with developmental issues, addressing and resolving specific problems, making decisions, coping with crisis, developing personal insight and knowledge, working through feelings of inner conflict or improving relationships with others. The counsellor's role is to facilitate the client's work in ways which respect the client's values, personal resources and capacity for self-determination.
3.2 Only when both the user and the recipient explicitly agree to enter into a counselling relationship does it become 'counselling' rather than the use of 'counselling skills'.
3.3 It is not possible to make a generally accepted distinction between counselling and psychotherapy. There are well founded traditions which use the terms interchangeably and others which distinguish them. Regardless of the theoretical approaches preferred by individual counsellors, there are ethical issues which are common to all counselling situations.

4. **The Structure of this Code**
This code has been divided into two parts. The Code of Ethics outlines the fundamental values of counselling and a number of general principles arising from these. The Code of Practice applies these principles to the counselling situation.

A. CODE OF ETHICS

A.1 Counselling is a non-exploitative activity. Its basic values are integrity, impartiality, and respect. Counsellors should take the same degree of care to work ethically whether the counselling is paid or voluntary.

A.2 **Client Safety:**
All reasonable steps should be taken to ensure the client's safety during counselling.

A.3 **Clear Contracts:**
The terms on which counselling is being offered should be made clear to clients before counselling commences. Subsequent revisions of these terms should be agreed in advance of any change.

A.4 **Competence:**
Counsellors shall take all reasonable steps to monitor and develop their own competence and to work within the limits of that competence. This includes having appropriate and ongoing counselling supervision/consultative support.

B. CODE OF PRACTICE

B.1 **Introduction:**
This code applies these values and ethical principles to more specific situations which may arise in the practice of counselling.

B.2 **Issues of Responsibility:**
B.2.1 The counsellor-client relationship is the foremost ethical concern, but it does not exist in social isolation. For this reason, the counsellor's responsibilities to the client, to themselves, colleagues, other members of the Association and members of the wider community are listed under separate headings.

B.2.2 **To the Client:**
Client Safety
2.2.1 Counsellors should take all reasonable steps to ensure that the client suffers neither physical nor psychological harm during counselling.
2.2.2 Counsellors do not normally give advice.
Client Autonomy
2.2.3 Counsellors are responsible for working in ways which promote the client's control over his/her own life, and respects the client's ability to make decisions and change in the light of his/her own beliefs and values.
2.2.4 Counsellors do not normally act on behalf of their clients. If they do, it will be only at the express request of the client, or else in the exceptional circumstances detailed in B.4.
2.2.5 Counsellors are responsible for setting and monitoring boundaries between the counselling relationship and any other kind of relationship, and making this explicit to the client.
2.2.6 Counsellors must not exploit their clients financially, sexually, emotionally, or in any other way. Engaging in sexual activity with the client is unethical.

2.2.7 Clients should be offered privacy for counselling sessions. The client should not be observed by anyone other than their counsellor(s) without having given his/her informed consent. This also applies to audio/video taping of counselling sessions.

Pre-Counselling Information

2.2.8 Any publicity material and all written and oral information should reflect accurately the nature of the service on offer, and the training, qualifications and relevant experience of the counsellor (see also B.6).

2.2.9 Counsellors should take all reasonable steps to honour undertakings offered in their pre-counselling information.

Contracting

2.2.10 Clear contracting enhances and shows respect for the client's autonomy.

2.2.11 Counsellors are responsible for communicating the terms on which counselling is being offered, including availability, the degree of confidentiality offered, and their expectations of clients regarding fees, cancelled appointments and any other significant matters. The communication of terms and any negotiations over these should be concluded before the client incurs any financial liability.

2.2.12 It is the client's choice whether or not to participate in counselling. Reasonable steps should be taken in the course of the counselling relationship to ensure that the client is given an opportunity to review the terms on which counselling is being offered and the methods of counselling being used.

2.2.13 Counsellors should avoid unnecessary conflicts of interest and are expected to make explicit to the client any relevant conflicts of interest.

2.2.14 If records of counselling sessions are kept, clients should be made aware of this. At the client's request information should be given about access to these records, their availability to other people, and the degree of security with which they are kept (see B.4).

2.2.15 Counsellors have a responsibility to establish with clients what other therapeutic or helping relationships are current. Counsellors should gain the client's permission before conferring with other professional workers.

2.2.16 Counsellors should be aware that computer-based records are subject to statutory regulations under the Data Protection Act 1984. From time to time the government introduces changes in the regulations concerning the client's right of access to his/her own records. Current regulations have implications for counsellors working in social service and health care settings.

Counsellor Competence

2.2.17 Counsellors should monitor actively the limitations of their own competence through counselling supervision/consultative support, and by seeking the views of their clients and other counsellors. Counsellors should work within their own known limits.

2.2.18 Counsellors should not counsel when their functioning is impaired due to personal or emotional difficulties, illness, disability, alcohol, drugs or for any other reason.

2.2.19 It is an indication of the competence of counsellors when they recognise their inability to counsel a client or clients and make appropriate referrals.

B.2.3 To Former Clients:
2.3.1 Counsellors remain accountable for relationships with former clients and must exercise caution over entering into friendships, business relationships, sexual relationships, training and other relationships. Any changes in relationship must be discussed in counselling supervision. The decision about any change(s) in relationship with former clients should take into account whether the issues and power dynamics present during the counselling relationship have been resolved and properly ended.

2.3.2 Counsellors who belong to organisations which prohibit sex with all former clients are bound by that commitment.

B.2.4 To Self as Counsellor:
2.4.1 Counsellors have a responsibility to themselves and their clients to maintain their own effectiveness, resilience and ability to help clients. They are expected to monitor their own personal functioning and to seek help and/or withdraw from counselling, whether temporarily or permanently, when their personal resources are sufficiently depleted to require this (see also B.3).

2.4.2 Counsellors should have received adequate basic training before commencing counselling, and should maintain ongoing professional development.

2.4.3 Counsellors are encouraged to review periodically their need for professional indemnity insurance and to take out such a policy when appropriate.

2.4.4 Counsellors should take all reasonable steps to ensure their own physical safety.

B.2.5 To other Counsellors:
2.5.1 Counsellors should not conduct themselves in their counselling-related activities in ways which undermine public confidence in either their role as a counsellor or in the work of other counsellors.

2.5.2 If a counsellor suspects misconduct by another counsellor which cannot be resolved or remedied after discussion with the counsellor concerned, they should implement the Complaints Procedure, doing so without breaches of confidentiality other than those necessary for investigating the complaint (see B.9).

B.2.6 To Colleagues and Members of the Caring Professions:
2.6.1 Counsellors should be accountable for their services to colleagues, employers and funding bodies as appropriate. The means of achieving this should be consistent with respecting the needs of the client outlined in B.2.2.7, B.2.2.13 and B.4.

2.6.2 Counsellors are encouraged to increase their colleagues' understanding of the counselling role. No colleague or significant member of the caring professions should be led to believe that a service is being offered by the counsellor which is not, as this may deprive the client of the offer of such a service from elsewhere.

2.6.3 Counsellors should accept their part in exploring and resolving conflicts of interest between themselves and their agencies, especially where this has implications for the client (see also B.2.2.13).

B.2.7 **To the Wider Community:**
Law
2.7.1 Counsellors should work within the law.
2.7.2 Counsellors should take all reasonable steps to be aware of current law affecting the work of the counsellor. A counsellor's ignorance of the law is no defence against legal liability or penalty including inciting or 'counselling', which has a specific legal sense, the commission of offences by clients.
Social Context
2.7.3 Counsellors will take all reasonable steps to take account of the client's social context.

B.3 **Counselling Supervision/Consultative Support:**
B.3.1 It is a breach of the ethical requirement for counsellors to practise without regular counselling supervision/consultative support.
B.3.2 Counselling supervision/consultative support refers to a formal arrangement which enables counsellors to discuss their counselling regularly with one or more people who have an understanding of counselling and counselling supervision/consultative support. Its purpose is to ensure the efficacy of the counsellor-client relationship. It is a confidential relationship (see also B.4).
B.3.3 Counsellors who have line managers owe them appropriate managerial accountability for their work. The counselling supervisor role should be independent of the line manager role. However where the counselling supervisor is also the line manager, the counsellor should also have access to independent consultative support.
B.3.4 The volume of supervision should be in proportion to the volume of counselling work undertaken and the experience of the counsellor.
B.3.5 Whenever possible, the discussion of cases within supervision/consultative support should take place without revealing the personal identity of the client.
B.3.6 The ethics and practice of counselling supervision/consultative support are outlined further in their own specific code: the Code of Ethics & Practice for the Supervision of Counsellors (see also B.9).

B.4. **Confidentiality: Clients, Colleagues and Others:**
B.4.1 Confidentiality is a means of providing the client with safety and privacy. For this reason any limitation on the degree of confidentiality offered is likely to diminish the usefulness of counselling.
B.4.2 Counsellors treat with confidence personal information about clients, whether obtained directly or indirectly or by inference. Such information includes name, address, biographical details, and other descriptions of the client's life and circumstances which might result in identification of the client.
B.4.3 Counsellors should work within the current agreement with their client about confidentiality.
B.4.4 Exceptional circumstances may arise which give the counsellor good grounds for believing that the client will cause serious physical harm to others or themselves, or have harm caused to him/her. In such circum-

stances the client's consent to a change in the agreement about confidentiality should be sought whenever possible unless there are also good grounds for believing the client is no longer able to take responsibility for his/her own actions. Whenever possible, the decision to break confidentiality agreed between a counsellor and client should be made only after consultation with a counselling supervisor or an experienced counsellor.

B.4.5　Any breaking of confidentaility should be minimised both by restricting the information conveyed to that which is pertinent to the immediate situation and to those persons who can provide the help required by the client. The ethical considerations involve balancing between acting in the best interests of the client and in ways which enable clients to resume taking responsibility for their actions, a very high priority for counsellors, and the counsellor's responsibilities to the wider community (see B.2.7 and B.4.4)

B.4.6　Counsellors should take all reasonable steps to communicate clearly the extent of the confidentiality they are offering to clients. This should normally be made clear in the pre-counselling information or initial contracting.

B.4.7　If counsellors include consultations with colleagues and others within the confidential relationship, this should be stated to the client at the beginning of counselling.

B.4.8　Care must be taken to ensure that personally identifiable information is not transmitted through overlapping networks of confidential relationships. For this reason, it is good practice to avoid identifying specific clients during counselling supervision/consultative support and other consultations, unless there are sound reasons for doing so (see also B.2.2.14 and B.4.2).

B.4.9　Any agreement between the counsellor and client about confidentiality may be reviewed and changed by joint negotiations.

B.4.10　Agreements about confidentiality continue after the client's death unless there are overriding legal or ethical considerations.

B.4.11　Counsellors hold different views about whether or not a client expressing serious suicidal intentions forms sufficient grounds for breaking confidentiality. Counsellors should consider their own views and practice and communicate them to clients and any significant others where appropriate (see also B.2.6.2).

B.4.12　Special care is required when writing about specific counselling situations for case studies, reports or publication. It is important that the author either has the client's informed consent, or effectively disguises the client's identity.

B.4.13　Any discussion between the counsellor and others should be purposeful and not trivialising.

B.5　Confidentiality in the Legal Process:

B.5.1　Generally speaking, there is no legal duty to give information spontaneously or on request until instructed to do so by a court. Refusal to answer police questions is not an offence, although lying could be. In general terms, the only circumstances in which the police can require an answer about a client, and when refusal to answer would be an offence, relate to the prevention of terrorism. It is good practice to ask police personnel to clarify their legal right to an answer before refusing to give one.

B.5.2 Withholding information about a crime that one knows has been committed or is about to be committed is not an offence, save exceptionally. Anyone hearing of terrorist activities should immediately take legal advice.

B.5.3 There is no legal obligation to answer a solicitor's enquiry or to make a statement for the purpose of legal proceedings, unless ordered to do so by a court.

B.5.4 There is no legal obligation to attend court at the request of parties involved in a case, or at the request of their lawyers, until a witness summons or subpoena is issued to require attendance to answer questions or produce documents.

B.5.5 Once in the witness box, there is a duty to answer questions when instructed to do so by the court. Refusal to answer could be punished as contempt of court unless there are legal grounds for not doing so. (It has been held that communications between the counsellor and client during an attempt at 'reconciliation' in matrimonial cases are privileged and thus do not require disclosure unless the client waives this privilege. This does not seem to apply to other kinds of cases).

B.5.6 The police have powers to seize confidential files if they have obtained a warrant from a circuit judge. Obstructing the police from taking them in these circumstances may be an offence.

B.5.7 Counsellors should seek legal advice and/or contact this Association if they are in any doubt about their legal rights and obligations before acting in ways which conflict with their agreement with clients who are directly affected (see also B.2.7.1).

B.6. Advertising/Public Statements:

B.6.1 When announcing counselling services, counsellors should limit the information to name, relevant qualifications, address, telephone number, hours available, and a brief listing of the services offered.

B.6.2 All such announcements should be accurate in every particular.

B.6.3 Counsellors should distinguish between membership of this Association and accredited practitioner status in their public statements. In particular, the former should not be used to imply the latter.

B.6.4 Counsellors should not display an affiliation with an organisation in a manner which falsely implies the sponsorship or verification of that organisation.

B.7. Research:

B.7.1 The use of personally identifiable material gained from clients or by the observation of counselling should be used only after the client has given consent, usually in writing, and care has been taken to ensure that consent was given freely.

B.7.2 Counsellors conducting research should use their data accurately and restrict their conclusions to those compatible with their methodology.

B.8. Resolving Conflicts between Ethical Priorities:

B.8.1 Counsellors will, from time to time, find themselves caught between conflicting ethical principles. In these circumstances, they are urged to consider the particular situation in which they find themselves and to discuss the situation with their counselling supervisor and/or other experienced counsellors. Even after conscientious consideration of the salient issues, some ethical dilemmas cannot be resolved easily or wholly satisfactorily.

B.8.2 Ethical issues may arise which have not yet been given full consideration. The Standards & Ethics Sub-Committee of this Association is interested in hearing of the ethical difficulties of counsellors, as this helps to inform discussion regarding good practice.

B.9. The Availability of other Codes and Guidelines Relating to Counselling:

B.9.1 The following codes and procedures have been passed by the Annual General Meetings of the British Association for Counselling:

Code of Ethics & Practice for Counselling Skills applies to members who would not regard themselves as counsellors, but who use counselling skills to support other roles.

Code of Ethics & Practice for the Supervision of Counsellors exists to guide members offering supervision to counsellors and to help counsellors seeking supervision.

Code of Ethics & Practice for Trainers exists to guide members offering training to counsellors and to help members of the public seeking counselling training.

Complaints Procedure exists to guide members of BAC and their clients resolving complaints about breaches of the Codes of Ethics & Practice.

Copies and other guidelines and information sheets relevant to maintaining ethical standards of practice can be obtained from the BAC office.

BAC INDIVIDUAL ACCREDITATION CRITERIA

These criteria apply only to counsellors working with individuals or couples. They do not apply to group counselling.

There are three routes to Accreditation. The successful applicant will be one who prior to application:

1. i. Has undertaken a total of 450 hours of counselling training comprising of two elements:
      a) 200 hours of skills development
      b) 250 hours of theory
      AND
      Has had at least 450 hours of counselling practice supervised in accordance with paragraph 2. below, over a minimum period of three years.
      OR
   ii. Has completed a BAC Recognised Counsellor Training Course
       AND
       Has had at least 450 hours of counselling practice supervised in accordance with paragraph 2. below, over a minimum period of three years.
       OR
   iii. Has had no formal training in counselling, or whose training does not meet the above criteria, but can provide evidence of ten years experience in counselling as understood by BAC with a minimum of 150 hours per year practice under formal supervision.

   In addition to the above, the applicant is required to meet the following criteria:

2. Has an agreed formal arrangement for counselling supervision, as understood by BAC, of a minimum of one and a half hours monthly on the applicant's work, and a commitment to continue this for the period of the accreditation.
3. Gives evidence of serious commitment to ongoing professional and personal development such as regular participation in further training courses, study, personal therapy, etc.
4. Is a current individual member of BAC and undertakes to remain so for the accreditation period.
5. Has a philosophy of counselling which integrates training, experience, further development and practice. Evidence of at least one core theoretical model should be demonstrated.
6. Demonstrates practice which adheres to the BAC Code of Ethics & Practice for Counsellors and undertakes to continue working within this Code.

Applicants are asked to give evidence of the above in the form of a written application including two case studies. Assessors will be looking for congruence between all parts of the application as well as checking that the above criteria have been and are being met.

ENTRY REQUIREMENTS

In order to gain entry into this Directory, individual practitioners must be a member of one of the following organisations.

1. British Association for Counselling
2. Institute of Psychosexual Medicine
3. One of the member organisations of the United Kingdom Council for Psychotherapy

UNITED KINGDOM COUNCIL FOR PSYCHOTHERAPY (UKCP)
071 487 7554
Regent's College, Inner Circle Regent's Park, LONDON NW1 4NS

Service:	UKCP is a federation of psychotherapy orgs. Aims to protect the public by promoting high standards of training, research & educ; fostering knowledge & availability of psychotherapy
Area served:	Nationwide
Training of workers:	The first National Register of Psychotherapists was launched on 20 May 1993 & is available from UKCP office
Code of Ethics:	UKCP
Management by:	The UKCP is a Registered Charity managed by a Governing Board

Members of UKCP:

ARBAS	Arbours Association	081 340 7646
	46 Westbere Road, LONDON NW2 3RU	
AGIP	Association for Group & Individual Psychotherapy	
	1 Fairbridge Road, LONDON N19 3EW	
ANLP	Association for Neuro-Linguistic Programming	0384 443935
	75A Castellain Road, LONDON W9 1EU	
AUTP	Association of University Teachers of Psychiatry	
	Dept of Mental Health, 41 St Michael's Hill, BRISTOL BS2 8DZ	
ACP	Association of Child Psychotherapists	
	30 Regents Park Road, LONDON NW1	
AJA	Association of Jungian Analysts	071 794 8711
	c/o Flat 3, 7 Eton Avenue, Hampstead, LONDON NW3 3EL	
AHPP	Association of Humanistic Psychology Practitioners	
	14 Mornington Grove, LONDON E3 4NS	081 983 1492
BCPC	Bath Centre for Psychotherapy & Counselling	0225 62835
	Openings, Bluecoat House, Saw Close, BATH BA1 1EY	
BTC	The Boyesen Training Centre	081 743 2437
	Acacia House, Centre Avenue, Acton Park, LONDON W3 7SX	
BAAP	Brighton Association of Analytic Psychotherapists	
	10 Withdean Road, BRIGHTON BN1 5BL	
BAP	British Association of Psychotherapists	
	37 Mapesbury Road, LONDON NW2 4HJ	
BASMT	British Association for Sexual & Marital Therapy	
	Maudsley Hospital, Denmark Hill, LONDON SE5 8AZ	071 703 6333

BABCP	British Association for Behavioural & Cognitive Psychotherapy	0690 710647
	Green Oak, Pentre Dy, Betws-y-coed, BETWS-Y-COED LL24 0BU	
BPDA	British Psychodrama Association	
	8 Rahere Road, Cowley, OXFORD OX4 3QG	
BPS	British Psychological Society	0533 549568
	St Andrews House, 48 Princes Road East, LEICESTER LE1 7DR	
CambSP	Cambridge Society for Psychotherapy	0234 345553
	c/o 70 Cavendish Avenue, CAMBRIDGE CB1 4UT	
CCPE	Centre for Counselling & Psychotherapy Education	
	21 Lancaster Road, LONDON W11 1QL	
CPCP	Centre for Personal Construct Psychology	071 834 8875
	132 Warwick Way, LONDON SW1V 4JD	
CPP	Centre for Psychoanalytical Psychology	081 600 8329
	99 Holmleigh Road, Stamford Hill, LONDON N16 5QG	
CSPK	Centre for the Study of Psychotherapy	0227 764000 x 3691
	Rutherford College, University of Kent, CANTERBURY CT2 7NX	
CCHP	Chiron Centre for Holistic Psychotherapy	081 997 5219
	26 Eaton Rise, Ealing, LONDON W5 2ER	
CCC	Creative Counselling Centre	
	7 Park Road, Dun Laoghaire, Co Dublin	
-	Forum for the Advancement of Educational Therapy & Therapeutic Teaching	
GC	The Gestalt Centre	0727 864806
	188 Old Street, LONDON EC1V 9UP	
GPTI	Gestalt Psychotherapy Training Institute	0272 411619
	PO Box 620, BRISTOL BS99 7DL	
GAPPS	Group for the Advancement of Psychodynamics 7 Psychotherapy in Social Work	081 846 6494
	21 Malbrook Road, LONDON SW15 6UH	
-	Guild of Psychotherapists	081 947 0730
	19b Thornton Hill, LONDON SW19 4HU	
GCSP	Guildford Centre & Society for Psychotherapy	
	3 Hillicr Road, GUILDFORD GU1 2JG	0483 504554/61313
-	Hallam Institute of Psychotherapy (Sheffield)	
	Whitley Wood Clinic, Whiteley Wood Close, Woofindin Road, SHEFFIELD S10 3TL	
IGAP	Independent Group of analytical Psychologists	
	20 Woodriffe Road, LONDON E11 1AH	081 556 3180
ISF	Institute for Self Analysis	071 794 4306
	12 Nassington Road, LONDON NW3 2UD	
IFT	Institute of Family Therapy	
	43 New Cavendish Street, LONDON W1M 7RG	
IGA	Institute of Group Analysis	
	1 Downs Road, BECKENHAM BR3 2JY	
IPC	Institute of Psychotherapy & Counselling	081 340 3324
	71 Umfreville Road, LONDON N4 1RZ	
IPS	Institute of Psychosynthesis	081 959 2330
	The Barn, Nan Clark's Lane, LONDON NW7 4HH	
IPSS	Institute of Psychotherapy & Social Studies	071 284 4762
	18 Laurier Road, LONDON NW5 1SG	
ITA	Institute of Transactional Analysis	071 404 5011
	BM Box 4104, LONDON	
-	Joint Training in Educational Therapy	071 263 4671
	13 Highbury Terrace, LONDON N5 1UP	

KI	Karuna Institute	
	Natsworthy Manor, Widecombe-in-the-Moor, NEWTON ABBOT TQ13 7TR	
KCC	Kensington Consultation Centre	071 793 0148
	47 South Lambeth Road, South Lambeth, LONDON SW8 1RH	
LCP	London Centre for Psychotherapy	071 435 0873
	19 Fitzjohn's Avenue, LONDON NW3 5JY	
MPTI	Metanoia Psychotherapy Training Institute	081 579 2505
	13 North Common Road, LONDON W5 2QB	
MC	The Minster Centre	071 435 9200
	57 Minster Road, LONDON NW2 3SH	
-	NAFSIYAT	071 263 4130
	Inter-Cultural Therapy Centre, 278 Seven Sisters Rd, Finsbury Park, LONDON N4 2HY	
NCHP	National College of Hypnotherapists & Psychotherapists	
	12 Cross Street, NELSON BB9 7EN	0282 699378
NRHP	National Register of Hypnotherapists & Psychotherapists	
	12 Cross Street, NELSON BB9 7EN	0282 699378
NSHAP	National School of Hypnosis & Psychotherapy	
	28 Finsbury Park Road, LONDON N4 2JX	071 226 6963, 071 359 6991
NWDIP	North West Institute of Dynamic Psychotherapy	061 276 5355
	Dept Psychiatry, Rawnsley Building, Oxford Road, MANCHESTER M13 9BX	
NAAP	Northern Association for Analytical Psychotherapy	
	10 West Lawn, Ashbrooke, SUNDERLAND SR2 7HW	
PA	Philadelphia Association	071 794 2652
	4 Marty's Yard, 17 Hampstead High Street, LONDON NW3 1QW	
PPA	Psychology & Psychotherapy Association	
	c/o 29B Kings Road, RICHMOND TW10 6EX	
PET	Psychosynthesis & Education Trust	071 403 2100
	92/94 Tooley Street, LONDON SE1 2TH	
-	Re•Vision	081 451 2165
	8 Chatsworth Road, Cricklewood, LONDON NW2 4BN	
-	Regent's College School of Psychotherapy & Counselling	
	Inner Circle, Regent's Park, LONDON NW1 4NS	071 487 7406
RCP	Royal College of Psychiatrists	071 235 2351
	Psychotherapy Section, 17 Belgrave Square, LONDON SW1X 8PG	
SIP	Severnside Institute for Psychotherapy	0272 562049
	45 Quakers Road, Downend, BRISTOL BS16 6JF	
SHPTI	Sherwood Psychotherapy Training Institute	0602 603137
	London & South East, 2 Hyde Park Gardens, LONDON W2 2LT	
SAP	Society of Analytical Psychology	071 435 7696
	1 Daleham Gardens, LONDON NW3 5BY	
STTDP	South Trent Training in Dynamic Psychotherapy	
	Nottingham Psychotherapy Unit, 114 Thorneywood Mount, NOTTINGHAM NG3 2PZ	
STPTI	Stockton Psychotherapy Training Institute	0642 611292
	77 Acklam Road, Thornaby-on-Tees, STOCKTON-ON-TEES TS17 7BD	
-	Tavistock Clinic	071 435 7111
	120 Belsize Lane, LONDON NW3 5BA	
TIMS	Tavistock Institute of Marital Studies	071 435 7111
	120 Belsize Lane, LONDON NW3 5BA	
-	Therapy North Staffordshire	

ULDP	University of Liverpool Diploma in Psychotherapy	
		051 794 5529, Fax 051 794 5537
	Dept of Clinical Psychology, Whelan Building, PO Box 147, LIVERPOOL L69 3BX	
WMIP	West Midlands Institute of Psychotherapy	021 442 4545
	Uffculme Clinic, Queensbridge Road, BIRMINGHAM B13 8QD	
SPF	Westminster Pastoral Foundation	071 937 6956
	23 Kensington Square, LONDON W8 5HN	
WTC	Women's Therapy Centre	071 263 6200
	6-9 Manor Gardens, Holloway, LONDON N7 6LA	
YAPP	Yorkshire Association for Psychodynamic Psychotherapy	0532 439000
	Dept. of Psychology, Southfield House, 40 Clarendon Road, LEEDS LS2 9PJ.	

ABBREVIATIONS

For members of UKCP, see pages xviii-xx

AAPP	Association of Accredited Psychospiritual Psychotherapists
ABC	Association of Black Counsellors
Acc	Accredited
ACPP	Association of Core Process Psychotherapy
ADMT	Association of Dance Movement Therapists
AEP	Association of Educational Psychology
AFBPsS	Associate Fellow of the British Psychological Society
AFT	Association of Family Therapy
AHP	Association of Humanistic Psychology
AIPM	Associate of the Institute of Personnel Management
APMT	Association of Professional Music Therapists
APP	Association of Psychosynthesis Practitioners
APPNHS	Association of Psychoanalytic Psychotherapists in the NHS
APSW	Association of Psychiatric Social Workers
APT	Association of Professional Therapists
ASC	Association for Student Counselling [Division of BAC]
ASIP	Adlerian Society for Individual Psychology
Assoc	Association
AssocCPP	Association for Child Psychology & Psychiatry
ASSP	Association of Short Term & Strategic Psychotherapists
BAAT	British Association of Art Therapists
BABP	British Association of Behavioural Psychotherapy
BAFAT	British Association for Autogenic Training
BAPCA	British Association for the Person-Centred Approach
BADT	British Association of Drama Therapists
BAOT	British Association of Occupational Therapists
BASP	British Association for Social Psychiatry
BASW	British Association of Social Workers
BAThH	British Association of Therapeutic Hypnotists
BCHE	British Council of Hypnotist Examiners
BCPA	Bath Counselling & Psychotherapy Association
BHMA	British Holistic Medical Association
BHR	British Hypnotherapy Research
BIBA	British Institute for Bioenergetic analysis
BICA	British Infertility Counselling Association
BIIP	British Institute of Integrative Psychotherapy
BIM	British Institute of Management
BPA	British Psychodrama Association
Brit	British
BSS	Bachelor of Social Studies
CAC	Centre for the Advancement of Counselling
CAH	Corporation of Advanced Hypnotherapy
CAP	Centre for Analytical Psychotherapy
CAT	Cognitive Analytical Therapy
CBT	Cognitive Behavioural Therapy
CCBT	Centre for Cognitive Behavioural Therapy
CHP	Certificate in Hypnotherapy & Psychotherapy

CMAC	Catholic Marriage Advisory Council
CNAA	Council for National Academic Award
CPN	Community Psychiatric Nurse
CPsychol	Chartered Psychologist
CRAH	Central Register of Advanced Hypnotherapists
CSCT	Central School for Counselling & Therapy (see CAC)
CPCP	Centre for Personal Construct Psychology
CQSW	Certificate of Qualification in Social Work
CTA	Clinical Theology Association
CTP	Centre for Transpersonal Psychology
Cert	Certificate
DHA	District Health Authority
Dip	Diploma
DipCPC	Diploma in Clinical & Pastoral Counselling
DST	Diploma in Systemic Therapy
EAPA	Employee Assistance Professionals Association
EATA	European Association for Transactional Analysis
EGI	English Gestalt Institute
FBPsS	Fellow of the British Psychological Society
FDI	Facilitator Development Institute
FMA	Family Mediators Association
FoH	Federation of Hypnotherapists
FWA	Family Welfare Association
GAN	Group Analysis North
GAS	Group Analytic Society
GAUK	Gestalt Association UK
GMC	General Medical Council
GRTA	Group Relations Training Association
IACT	International Association of Colour Therapists
IAH	International Association of Hypnoanalysts
IATE	Institute of the Arts in Therapy & Education
ICM	Institute for Complementary Medicine
IDHP	Institute for Development of Human Potential
IIP	Institute for Individual Psychology
IP	Institute of Psychosynthesis
IPA	Institute for Psycho-analysis
IPM	Institute of Psychosexual Medicine
IRTAC	International Round Table for the Advancement of Counselling
ISA	Institute for Self-analysis
ISM	Institute of Stress Management
ISMA	International Stress Management Association
ITAA	International Transactional Analysis Association
ITEC	International Therapeutic Examining Council
ITHP	Institute of Traditional & Humanistic Psychotherapy
IWO	Institute of Welfare Officers
Inst	Institute
Int	International
LCIP	Lincoln Clinic & Institute for Psychotherapy
LicSW (USA)	Licensed Social Worker (United States of America)
MCHC	UK College qualification
Memb	Member

MIMgt	Member of the Institute of Management
MITD	Member of the Institute of Training & Development
MIWO	Member of the Institute of Welfare Officers
MTI	Massage Training Institute
NAFMACS	National Association of Family Mediation & Conciliation Services
NAHP	National Association of Hypnotists & Psychotherapists
Nat	National
NCH	National Children's Homes
NLP	Neuro-Linguistic Programming
OU	Open University
PCAI	Person Centred Approach Institute
PCATA	Person Centred Art Therapy Association
PCPC	Personal Construct Psychotherapy Centre
PGCE	Post Graduate Certificate in Education
Poly	Polytechnic
PPS	Psychologists Protection Society
PTSD	Post Traumatic Stress Disorder
RAT	Registered Art Therapist
RET	Rational Emotive Therapy
RF	Richmond Fellowship
RGN	Registered General Nurse (formerly SRN)
RMN	Registered Mental Nurse
RSH	Royal Society of Health
RWTA	Redwood Women's Training Association
SAPP	Society for Advanced Psychotherapy Practitioners
SCODA	Standing Conference on Drug Abuse
SEA	Society for Existential Analysis
SPCAH	Society for Primary Cause Analysis by Hypnosis
SPOD	Association to Aid the Sexual & Personal Relationships of People with a Disability
SRN	State Registered Nurse
Soc	Society
TA	Transactional Analysis
UKCP	United Kingdom Council for Psychotherapy
Univ	University

NATIONAL ORGANISATIONS

1. SPECIALIST COUNSELLING SERVICES

ALBANY TRUST 081 675 6669
SUNRA Centre, 16 Balham Hill, Clapham South, LONDON SW12 9EB
Service:	Help for people with relationship, psychosexual & sexuality issues, especially sexual minorities, through individual counselling sessions
Area served:	Nationwide
Referral:	Self or others
Training of workers:	All trained counsellors. Regular supervision
Code of Ethics:	BAC
Management by:	Trustees
Fees:	£30 negotiable

ASHLEY CAREER COUNSELLING 061 927 7299
The Graftons, Stamford New Road, ALTRINCHAM WA14 1DQ
Service:	Career and redeployment counselling for individuals & groups, stress & PTSD counselling for individuals & groups. Also couns training
Area served:	UK & overseas
Referral:	Self, Companies
Training of workers:	Work counselling training, personal therapy, regular case discussion
Code of Ethics:	BAC
Management by:	Managing Director
Fees:	Negotiable

CANCER HELP CENTRE BRISTOL 0272 743216
Grove House, Cornwallis Grove, Clifton, BRISTOL BS8 4PG
Service:	Offers holistic therapy (nutrition, stress management)/ psychotherapy/visualisation/healing for anyone with cancer (16+). General/crisis cllg for those facing mortal disease.
Area served:	Anywhere
Referral:	GP, Self
Training of workers:	Trained counsellors appointed. Peer group co-operation
Code of Ethics:	BAC
Management by:	Board of Trustees
Fees:	£450 patient week (resid)

CAREASSIST GROUP LTD (STRESSCARE) 021 233 0202
Brittania House, 50 Great Charles Street, Queensway, BIRMINGHAM B3 2LP
Service:	Telephone & face to face counselling service for companies, trades unions & affiliation groups for emotional, work- related, relationship, bereavement & other personal problems
Area served:	UK
Referral:	Organisations
Training of workers:	Experienced, qualified counsellors/chartered clinical psychologists. Regular case conferences & individual supervision
Code of Ethics:	BAC
Management by:	Sandra Ridley
Fees:	Negotiable

NATIONAL ORGANISATIONS

CAREER AND EDUCATIONAL COUNSELLING   Ansaphone 071 794 1309
The Tavistock Centre, 120 Belsize Lane, Hampstead, LONDON NW3 5BA

Service:	Career problem counselling (working relationships, career choices, motivation) considered from psychodynamic perspective
Area served:	London, Cambridge, Reading, Brighton
Referral:	Self
Training of workers:	All are therapists & qualified psychologists with extensive personal therapy
Code of Ethics:	BPS
Management by:	Co-operative with a co-ordinator
Fees:	£40 (£75 1st 90 min consultation)

CAROLE SPIERS ASSOCIATES   fax 081 907 9290
Gordon House, 83-85 Gordon Avenue, STANMORE HA7 3QR

Service:	Crisis intervention, post traumatic stress, divorce, bereavement, stress management, redundancy, harassment - all work related problems
Area served:	UK
Referral:	Self, Organisations
Training of workers:	Appropriate professional qualification; regular supervision
Code of Ethics:	BAC
Management by:	Carole Spiers
Fees:	By arrangement

CHILD & CHILCOTT - EMPLOYEE COUNSELLING PROGRAMMES
0306 741698
83 South Street, DORKING RH4 2JU

Service:	Counselling for employees; general, stress, racial and sexual harassment; training in counselling skills, stress management and sexual and racial awareness
Area served:	UK
Referral:	Self, Employer
Training of workers:	All professionally qualified; personal therapy; regular supervision
Code of Ethics:	BAC
Management by:	Directors: Melanie Child and Diana Chilcott
Fees:	£50

EAR EMPLOYEE ADVISORY RESOURCE   0895 271155
Brunel Science Park, Kingston Lane, UXBRIDGE UB8 3PQ

Service:	Employee Assistance Program - counselling & referral service for management, employees & their families for any problem - emotional, relationship, addiction, career, employment, etc
Area served:	UK, Europe and USA
Referral:	
Training of workers:	Relevant professional training, qualifications & experience. Regular monthly casework meetings
Code of Ethics:	BAC
Management by:	Mike Megranahan
Fees:	Negotiable

NATIONAL ORGANISATIONS

GODALMING COUNSELLING SERVICES   0483 420759
140A High Street, GODALMING GU7 1RG

Service:	Eclectic, Humanistic, Person-centred counselling drawing on a range of training & experience including Transpersonal work & TA. Other services include training courses/facilitation for self-help groups/workshops
Area served:	Surrey, Hants, W Sussex & London
Referral:	Self
Training of workers:	All hold Certs Couns & have experience in many areas; pers-onal therapy & regular supervision
Code of Ethics:	BAC
Management by:	The Co-operative
Fees:	£15 - £20 Training fees on application

HERONBROOK HOUSE INTERNATIONAL THERAPEUTIC CENTRE FOR CLERGY   0564 776214, Fax 0564 779504
Bakers Lane, Knowle, SOLIHULL B93 8PW

Service:	**Residential therapeutic community, non-residential psychotherapy & counselling mostly dealing with emotional difficulties of clergy & religious people**
Area served:	International
Referral:	Self or others
Training of workers:	Personal therapy & at least Masters level with good clinical experience of individual and group therapy
Code of Ethics:	BAC, BPS, BMA
Management by:	Board of Governors and Trustees
Fees:	Professional fees charged

HUMAN PERSPECTIVE LTD   081 349 9399
5th Floor, Grosvenor Gardens House, 35/37 Grosvenor Gardens, LONDON SW1W 0BS

Service:	**Organisational Development Consultancy, Research and Management Training, Executive & Outplacement Counselling**
Area served:	International
Other languages:	French, German
Referral:	
Training of workers:	All consultants are qualified in organisational development consultancy, research and counselling
Code of Ethics:	Agency's own code
Management by:	Board of Directors
Fees:	By arrangement

ICAS LTD   0908 281128
Radlett House, West Hill, Aspley Guise, MILTON KEYNES MK17 8DT

Service:	**Major provider of EAPs appropriate to UK organisations, offering personal & career counselling; support/training etc for in-house counsellors; selection/recruitment of counsellors for organisations**
Area served:	UK
Referral:	Self, Organisations
Training of workers:	Appropriate professional qualification
Code of Ethics:	BAC, BPS, EAPA, IPM
Management by:	Dr M Reddy (Chief Executive) and board
Fees:	By arrangement with employer

NATIONAL ORGANISATIONS

IDENTITY COUNSELLING SERVICE — 071 487 3797
Marylebone Counselling Centre, 17 Marylebone Road, LONDON NW1 5LT

Service:	Counselling people with personal, relationship, and identity difficulties
Area served:	London area, SE & other major towns
Referral:	Self
Training of workers:	Workers must be trained and accredited by recognised agency (eg WPF, BAP, Guild of Psychotherapists)
Code of Ethics:	IPC, BAC
Management by:	The Viva Trust
Fees:	£18 - £25 assess; contribution sought up to £25

LAMBOURN COURT INTERNATIONAL — 0234 708848, Fax 0234 708702
The Manor Barn, Keysoe, BEDFORD MK44 2HR

Service:	An In-house Team of Stress Management Consultants who offer services to the general public and to companies
Area served:	UK wide
Other languages:	German, Iranian, Danish, Main Asian
Referral:	Self
Training of workers:	1 year In-house Diploma; some personal therapy; regular supervision. Director is a Chartered Psychologist
Code of Ethics:	Agency's own code
Management by:	Board of Directors
Fees:	Vary according to problem

MERSEYSIDE PRIVATE COUNSELLING — 051 722 0401
122 Bowring Park Road, Broadgreen, LIVERPOOL L14 3NP

Service:	Individual/family/group therapy for a wide range of problems from depression/anxiety to emotional, bereavement, alchohol & drug abuse
Area served:	UK
Referral:	Self, Health/Soc Work Professional
Training of workers:	Qualified psychotherapist & BAC Acc counsellor; experienced personal therapy; ongoing supervision
Code of Ethics:	BAC
Management by:	Local Executive Committee
Fees:	By negotiation

RAPHAEL CLINIC — 071 794 5328
211 Sumatra Road, West Hampstead, LONDON NW6 1PF

Service:	Psychodynamic & Humanistic counselling & psychotherapy, RET, Psychosynthesis, Analytical Psychology & Hypnotherapy. Support groups for bereavement, addictions, cancer, relationships, sexual/spiritual
Area served:	Mostly London & South East
Other languages:	Norwegian, Danish, Swedish, French, German
Referral:	Self
Training of workers:	Group of highly qualified therapists w various backgrounds & different specialisations; personal therapy & regular supervision
Code of Ethics:	BAC
Management by:	A therapist
Fees:	£1 - £30 sliding scale

NATIONAL ORGANISATIONS

ROLE MANAGEMENT LTD　　　　　　　　　　　　　　0908 678114
Meridian House, 57 North 12th Street, MILTON KEYNES MK9 3BS
Service:	Counselling in a work context: career change & evaluation, life crises, stress management, org & team development, redundancy, outplacement, trauma counselling
Area served:	UK
Referral:	Employer, Self
Training of workers:	Mainly relationship counselling background with wide commercial/industrial experience; ongoing supervision
Code of Ethics:	BAC, Institute of Management Consultants
Management by:	Executive Directors
Fees:	Negotiable

TENOVUS - CANCER INFORMATION CENTRE
Freefone 0800 526 527, Admin 0222 619 846
142 Whitchurch Road, CARDIFF CF4 3NA
Service:	Free telephone helpline for information and support for cancer. Drop in centre and one to one counselling
Area served:	UK
Other languages:	Welsh
Referral:	Self
Training of workers:	All trained nurses or counsellors
Code of Ethics:	BAC
Fees:	None

VECTOR CENTRE FOR EATING DISORDERS　　　　　071 485 8257
12 Boscastle Road, Kentish Town, LONDON NW5 1EG
Service:	Workshops, support groups and individual therapy for people with eating disorders
Area served:	Within reach of London
Referral:	Self or others
Training of workers:	Fully trained counsellors and psychotherapists
Code of Ethics:	BAC, AGIP, Guild of Psychotherapists
Management by:	Partners
Fees:	Individual negotiable: Workshop £35; Support Group £11

WHITEHOUSE TRUST　　　　　　　　　　　　　　0296 613475
Terrick House, Terrick, AYLESBURY HP22 5XP
Service:	Counselling individuals suffering from financial stress and hardship. Runs financial workshops to educate the public on related subjects. Main project title 'Financial Concern'
Area served:	England & Wales
Referral:	Self or others, GP
Training of workers:	Only counsellors with financial expertise recruited and training is provided by the trust. Supervision
Code of Ethics:	BAC
Management by:	D S Whitehouse - Director
Fees:	Donations (Fees for Wkshps)

NATIONAL ORGANISATIONS

WINNICOTT CLINIC OF PSYCHOTHERAPY 081 868 1611
11a Acacia Avenue, Eastcote, RUISLIP HA4 8RQ
Service:	**Initial consultations for individuals, then onward referral for long or short term treatment either within clinic or outside**
Area served:	London & Home Counties
Referral:	Self or others
Training of workers:	All are qualified analysts
Code of Ethics:	Therapists' Professional body
Management by:	Board of Trustees
Fees:	According to means

NATIONAL ORGANISATIONS

2. PROFESSIONAL ORGANISATIONS

ADLERIAN SOCIETY FOR INDIVIDUAL PSYCHOLOGY (ASIP)
081 858 7299

55 Mayhill Road, Charlton, LONDON SE7 7JG

Service:	Promotion of Adlerian Counselling and Psychotherapy through lectures, workshops, training. Offers referral to accredited Adlerian counsellors/therapists from lists held
Area served:	UK
Referral:	Self or others
Training of workers:	Fully trained Adlerian counsellors/therapists
Code of Ethics:	BAC
Management by:	Elected Council of Full Members
Fees:	By arrangement

ASSOCIATION FOR RATIONAL EMOTIVE THERAPISTS 021 427 7292

49 Wood Lane, Harbourne, BIRMINGHAM B17 9AY

Service:	Provides information/support to its members including maintenance of professional standards of practice & via its journal. Holds register of trained RET counsellors/psychotherapists for referrals/professional contact
Area served:	UK & Eire
Referral:	Self or others
Training of workers:	All members are required to have completed an approved training in RET delivered by rec Trainers. Membership reflects degree competency; Full/Fellow Membs are rec competent pract
Code of Ethics:	AOC
Management by:	ARET elected Council
Fees:	Set by therapist

ASSOCIATION FOR NEURO- LINGUISTIC PROGRAMMING (ANLP)
0384 443935

75A Castellain Road, LONDON W9 1EU

Service:	General counselling and psychotherapy for individuals, couples, groups, families and organisations. Member of UKCP
Area served:	No restriction
Referral:	Self or others
Training of workers:	Training is undertaken by independant, commercial training institutes
Code of Ethics:	NLP
Management by:	*Elected Officers
Fees:	Negotiable

ASSOCIATION OF SHORT-TERM & STRATEGIC PSYCHOTHERAPISTS

194 Emlyn Road, LONDON W12 9TB

Service:	To promote awareness of short-term & focal/strategic psychotherapy & provide a network for those interested in this method
Area served:	UK
Training of workers:	At least 5 years experience (post-training) & 1 year equivalent full time training
Code of Ethics:	BAC, AHPP
Management by:	Board of Management
Fees:	Set by individual therapist

NATIONAL ORGANISATIONS

ASSOCIATION OF COGNITIVE ANALYTIC THERAPISTS (ACAT)
071 955 4822

Munro Clinic, Guys Hospital, LONDON SE1 9RT

Service:	Brief integrated psychotherapy for individuals, couples and groups. Generally 16 session contracts of therapy integrating cognitive psychology with analytic therapy
Area served:	Available at centres throughout UK. Also Finland & Greece
Other languages:	French
Referral:	Self or others
Training of workers:	Own 4 year training programme with personal therapy, regular supervision
Code of Ethics:	BAC
Management by:	Council of the Association with liaison to Dept of Psychiatry of Guys Medical School
Fees:	NHS, private - sliding scale

ASSOCIATION OF HUMANISTIC PSYCHOLOGY PRACTITIONERS (AHPP)
081 983 1492

14 Mornington Grove, LONDON E3 4NS

Service:	Accrediting organisation with list of members (psychotherapists, counsellors, group and dramatherapists, educators, organisational consultants etc.) for referral
Area served:	UK
Other languages:	French, Italian, German, Spanish, Hebrew, Czech
Referral:	Self or others
Training of workers:	All members accredited by AHPP in line with UKCP. Members' qualifications renewed 3 yearly. Regular supervision
Code of Ethics:	AHPP
Management by:	Board, membership committee & general meetings
Fees:	By arrangement

BRITISH ASSOC FOR BEHAVIOURAL & COGNITIVE PSYCHOTHERAPIES
081 715 1812

The Old Church Hall, 89a Quicks Road, Wimbledon, LONDON SW19 1EX

Service:	Member of the UK Council for Psychotherapy

BRITISH ASSOCIATION OF ANALYTICAL BODY PSYCHOTHERAPY
0273 303382

c/o The Secretary, 47 Dean Court Road, Rottingdean, BRIGHTON BN2 7DL

Service:	Analytical body psychotherapy, work with individuals, groups, couples, families
Area served:	London, South East England, Belfast, Glasgow, Belgium
Other languages:	French, Spanish
Referral:	Self
Training of workers:	5 year part-time programme in analytical body psychotherapy
Code of Ethics:	ABP
Management by:	Executive Committee
Fees:	Negotiable

NATIONAL ORGANISATIONS

BRITISH ASSOCIATION FOR SEXUAL & MARITAL THERAPY
PO Box 62, SHEFFIELD S10 3TL

Service:	Please send SAE for information on availability of sexual/relationship therapy both NHS & private. BASMT promotes & maintains high standards thro' approved courses & accred.
Area served:	UK
Training of workers:	Varies. An accreditation scheme has been implemented
Code of Ethics:	BAC, BASMT
Management by:	Elected executive

BRITISH ASSOCIATION OF PSYCHOTHERAPISTS (BAP)
081 452 9823, fax 081 452 5182

37 Mapesbury Road, LONDON NW2 4HJ

Service:	The Clinical Service offers consultations & placements for individual psychoanalytic psychotherapy for adults, adolescents and children. Members of UKCP and BCP
Area served:	Mainly London, also Brighton, Cambridge, Oxford, Bristol
Other languages:	Various
Referral:	Self or others
Training of workers:	Own training course for adult and child psychotherapists including personal therapy throughout training
Code of Ethics:	BAP
Management by:	BAP Elected Council
Fees:	£30 assessment then by arrangement

BRITISH PSYCHODRAMA ASSOCIATION (BPA)   0865 715055
8 Rahere Road, Cowley, OXFORD OX4 3QG

Service:	National Association for psychodrama practitioners, trainers and trainees holding registers and details of those trained, training and therapy groups available. Member of UKCP
Area served:	UK
Training of workers:	All must have completed minimum 1,200 hours training before qualification and registration
Code of Ethics:	BPA
Management by:	Executive committee with external moderator
Fees:	For private work

BRITISH PSYCHOLOGICAL SOCIETY (BPS)   0533 549568
St Andrews House, 48 Princes Road East, LEICESTER LE1 7DR

Service:	Professional & Learned Society of Psychologists within the United Kingdom, Incorporated by Royal Charter. Member of the UK Council for Psychotherapy

NATIONAL ORGANISATIONS

CENTRE FOR COUNSELLING AND PSYCHOTHERAPY EDUCATION (CCPE)
071 221 3215
21 Lancaster Road, Notting Hill, LONDON W11 1QL

Service:	Individual, couple & family counselling & psychotherapy. Spiritual perspective on psychotherapy also provided. Member of UK Council for Psychotherapy
Area served:	No restrictions
Other languages:	French, German, Portuguese, Greek, Spanish
Referral:	Self or others
Training of workers:	4 years, weekly ongoing supervision
Code of Ethics:	BAC
Management by:	Management Committee
Fees:	£8 - £35 depending on income

CENTRE FOR TRANSPERSONAL PSYCHOLOGY (CTP)
7 Pembridge Place, Paddington, LONDON W2 4XB

Service:	Referral service and counselling network covering most spheres of counselling
Area served:	South & Midlands, NE Eng, Edinburgh & Ireland
Other languages:	Please enquire
Referral:	Self or others
Training of workers:	Part-time, 3-5 yr Cert & Dip stages. Dip requires personal therapy & regular supervision
Code of Ethics:	BAC
Management by:	Ian Gordon-Brown & Barbara Somers
Fees:	By arrangement with counsellor

CLINICAL THEOLOGY ASSOCIATION
0993 830209
St Mary's House, Church Westcote, Oxford, CHIPPING NORTON OX7 6SF

Service:	A pastoral counselling referral service to tutors throughout the UK, although this is primarily a training organisation. Tutors will see individuals, couples, group
Area served:	Nationwide
Referral:	Self
Training of workers:	All are trained in clinical theology, most will have other training and experience too; all have ongoing supervision
Code of Ethics:	AOC
Management by:	By Council
Fees:	Negotiable

GUILD OF PSYCHOTHERAPISTS
081 947 0730
19b Thornton Hill, LONDON SW19 4HU

Service:	Analytical psychotherapy
Area served:	Nationwide
Other languages:	French, German, Spanish, Hebrew
Referral:	Self or others
Training of workers:	Own 4 yr training in analytical psychotherapy; personal therapy; ongoing supervision
Code of Ethics:	Guild of Psychotherapists
Management by:	Management committee
Fees:	£18 - £25 Varies with therapist

NATIONAL ORGANISATIONS

INSTITUTE OF FAMILY THERAPY (IFT)   071 935 1651, Fax 071 224 3291
43 New Cavendish Street, LONDON W1M 7RG

Service:	Family therapy: working with families experiencing psychological, behavioural and relationship problems. Member of UKCP
Area served:	London, Home Counties, SE region
Referral:	Self
Training of workers:	Therapists have normally completed formal training at Institute or another equivalent course
Code of Ethics:	IFT
Management by:	Council of members through the directorate
Fees:	Sliding scale based on family income.

INSTITUTE OF PSYCHOTHERAPY AND SOCIAL STUDIES (IPSS)
071 281 5193
18 Laurier Road, LONDON NW5 1SG

Service:	Individual, couple, family and group psychotherapy in psychodynamic/psychoanalytic tradition. Member of UKCP
Area served:	London, Home Counties & Midlands
Other languages:	Hungarian, Hebrew, German, French, Spanish
Referral:	Self or others
Training of workers:	3 year Diploma course in psychotherapy, personal therapy and ongoing supervision. All members included on Register of UKCP
Code of Ethics:	IPSS
Management by:	Staff council
Fees:	£5 + according to means of client

INSITUTE OF PSYCHOSEXUAL MEDICINE (IPM)   071 580 0631
11 Chandos Street, Cavendish Square, LONDON W1M 9DE

Service:	Holds national information on location of clinics and times of sessions in respect of full Members of the Institute - nationwide
Area served:	United Kingdom
Referral:	Self or others
Training of workers:	Training by Institute of qualified doctors over at least 4 years leading to assessment & Cert of Accreditation
Code of Ethics:	IPM, GMC
Management by:	Elected Council
Fees:	NHS free; private variable

LONDON ASSOCIATION OF PRIMAL PSYCHOTHERAPISTS
071 267 9616
18a Laurier Road, Kentish Town, LONDON NW5 1SH

Service:	Individual, couple and group psychotherapy based on work of A Janov & A Miller
Area served:	No specific catchment area
Other languages:	German, Italian, French, Finnish, Norwegian, Swedish
Referral:	Self or others
Training of workers:	Theoretical and clinical training
Code of Ethics:	BPS
Management by:	Co-operative
Fees:	£35

NATIONAL ORGANISATIONS

LONDON CENTRE FOR PSYCHOTHERAPY (LCP)   071 435 0873
19 Fitzjohns Avenue, LONDON NW3 5JY

Service:	Psychotherapy and counselling for individuals, couples and groups. Member of the UK Standing Conference for Psychotherapy
Area served:	Nationwide
Other languages:	French, German, Spanish, Italian
Referral:	Self or others
Training of workers:	Theoretical and clinical training in analytical psychotherapy, personal therapy required
Code of Ethics:	AOC
Management by:	Council/Training Committee with sub-committees made up of members
Fees:	By arrangement

METANOIA   081 579 2505
13 North Common Road, Ealing, LONDON W5 2QB

Service:	Provides general couns & psychotherapy and psychosexual couns for individuals, couples, groups & families. Member of UKCP
Area served:	National - associated counsellors throughout Britain
Referral:	Self or others
Training of workers:	3 to 4 years of advanced training plus personal therapy & supervision
Code of Ethics:	BAC, BPS, ITA, GPT
Management by:	Board of Directors
Fees:	£5 - £45 depending on income

MINSTER CENTRE   071 435 9200
57 Minster Road, West Hampstead, LONDON NW2 3SH

Service:	General counselling & psychotherapy offered by students (low cost) & graduates for individuals, couples & groups aged 17 or over. Member of UK Conference for Psychotherapy
Area served:	In and around London
Other languages:	German, Italian, French
Referral:	Self or others
Training of workers:	4 years training plus 2 years supervised practice after graduation. Regular supervision
Code of Ethics:	BAC, ITHP
Management by:	Minster Centre
Fees:	£10 - £30 low cost with students

NATIONAL COUNCIL OF PSYCHOTHERAPISTS   0932 227772
46 Oxhey Road, WATFORD WD1 4QQ

Service:	Holds a list of practitioners around the country who offer psychotherapy/counselling for help with emotional, behavioural & relationship problems. Register of hypnotherapists
Area served:	Nationwide by 185 members
Referral:	Self or others
Training of workers:	Therapists must have proof of competence via casework & examination. Personal therapy & ongoing supervision are required for accreditation
Code of Ethics:	BAC, AOC
Management by:	Elected Committee
Fees:	£10 - £40 less in cases of hardship

NATIONAL ORGANISATIONS

NATIONAL REGISTER OF HYPNO THERAPISTS & PSYCHOTHERAPISTS   0282 699378
12 Cross Street, NELSON BB9 7EN
Service: Therapeutic use of hypnosis, counselling, psychotherapy; addresses of members provided by Head Office. Member of the UK Council for Psychotherapy
Area served: Nationwide
Referral: Self, GP
Training of workers: All are graduates of the National College of Hypnosis and Psychotherapy
Code of Ethics: NRHP
Management by: Representatives of the College and Members of the Register
Fees: By negotiation with counsellor

PSYCHOSYNTHESIS & EDUCATION TRUST (PET)
071 403 7814, 071 403 2100
92/94 Tooley Street, London Bridge, LONDON SE1 2TH
Service: Counselling service, short courses in personal growth, courses in professional development, youth programme, prof dip courses in psychosynthesis counselling & therapy
Area served: National
Training of workers: 3 year Diploma Course at PET
Code of Ethics: BAC, UKCP
Fees: On application

RE-VISION   081 456 2165
8 Chatsworth Road, LONDON NW2 4BN
Service: Counselling & psychotherapy to individuals, couples & families. Member of the UKCP
Area served: London & Home Counties
Referral: Self or others
Training of workers: 3-5 years part-time training
Code of Ethics: BAC, TPB
Management by: Ewa Robertson & training committee
Fees: £15 - £30 negotiable

SOCIETY FOR PRIMARY CAUSE ANALYSIS   081 657 3624
13 Beechwood Road, Sanderstead, SOUTH CROYDON CR2 0AE
Service: General, marital & sexual counselling, psychotherapy, crisis intervention, relaxation therapy, habit control and termination
Area served: Home Counties, Hampshire, South Yorkshire
Referral: Self
Training of workers: Qualified counsellors/therapists plus in-house training; regular supervision
Code of Ethics: BAC, AOC
Management by: Standing Committee
Fees: By arrangement

NATIONAL ORGANISATIONS

TAVISTOCK CLINIC   071 435 7111
120 Belsize Lane, Hampstead, LONDON NW3 5BA

Service:	NHS out-patient assessment and psychotherapy service for adults, young people, children and their parents. Individual, couple, group and family therapy
Area served:	National
Referral:	GP, Health/Soc Work Professional, Self - young people only
Training of workers:	Recognised training in psychotherapies; regular supervision
Code of Ethics:	TPB
Management by:	NHS
Fees:	None

TAVISTOCK INSTITUTE OF MARITAL STUDIES (TIMS)   071 435 7111
Tavistock Centre, 120 Belsize Lane, LONDON NW3 5BA

Service:	Professional psychotherapy for couples, married or not, who are experiencing difficulties in their relationship. Also consultation service. Member of UKCP
Area served:	No restriction
Referral:	Self or others
Training of workers:	All trained in Institute after prior professional training, regular supervision, most have had personal therapy
Code of Ethics:	AOC
Management by:	An elected staff Directorate
Fees:	£25 minimum

WESTMINSTER PASTORAL FOUNDATION (WPF)   Minicom 071 937 6956
23 Kensington Square, LONDON W8 5HN

Service:	Counselling for individuals, couples, families & groups inc young people and the physically ill. Facilities for the disabled. Member of UKCP.
Area served:	London HQ, associated centres throughout UK
Referral:	Self or others
Training of workers:	Counsellors trained by WPF, or equivalent training elsewhere
Code of Ethics:	BAC
Management by:	Directory & Senior Management Team responsible to a Council of Management
Fees:	£8 - £25 according to means

NATIONAL ORGANISATIONS

3. ORGANISATIONS & SELF-HELP GROUPS

ADFAM NATIONAL   **071 405 3923**
1st Floor, Chapel House, 18 Hatton Place, LONDON EC1B 8ND
Service:	Telephone helpline for carers, relations & friends of drug users
Area served:	UK
Referral:	Self
Training of workers:	Various & ADFAM training. Supervision
Code of Ethics:	CH
Management by:	ADFAM National Executive Committee and Director
Fees:	None

AIDS AHEAD   **voice 0270 250736, text 0270 250743, Fax 0270 250742**
Unit 17, Macon Court, Herald Drive, CREWE CW1 1EA
Service:	Health Education & Advisory Service to deaf people with or without AIDS; AIDS counselling; befriending service; Advice with sexuality issues; some grant aid.
Area served:	UK
Other languages:	British Sign Language
Referral:	Self or others
Training of workers:	Cadre of deaf workers receiving ongoing training
Code of Ethics:	AOC
Management by:	A department of the British Deaf Association, Carlisle
Fees:	£25 negotiable

BACUP (British Association of Cancer United Patients)
    couns 071 696 9000, med info 071 613 2120, freefone 0800 181199
3 Bath Place, Rivington Street, LONDON EC2A 2JR
Service:	Cancer counselling at head office for people with cancer, their families & friends; also information service on all aspects of cancer
Area served:	UK tel, anyone who can travel to London-based office
Other languages:	French, Italian, German, Swahili, Gujerati, Hindi, Urdu
Referral:	Self
Training of workers:	Intensive introductory & in-service training; ongoing supervision; own psychotherapy
Code of Ethics:	BAC
Management by:	BACUP
Fees:	None

BEAUMONT TRUST   **0606 871984, 0325 382878, partners 071 730 7453**
B M Charity, LONDON WC1N 3XX
Service:	Confidential befriending service & helpline for gender dysphoria, transvestites, transexuals, their wives and partners
Area served:	UK and overseas
Referral:	Self
Training of workers:	All have received at least basic training
Code of Ethics:	BAC
Management by:	Thirteen trustees, committee of 8
Fees:	Donations

NATIONAL ORGANISATIONS

BOARDING SCHOOL SURVIVORS 081 341 4885
128a Northview Road, LONDON N8 7LP
Service:	Specialises in Boarding school educated men & women. Runs workshops for those who wish to consider its effects on their lives, and look for ways to heal the wounds
Area served:	National
Referral:	Self
Training of workers:	4 years psychosynthesis training - Family Therapy, on-going training, personal therapy, regular supervision
Code of Ethics:	BAC
Management by:	Sole proprietor
Fees:	£25 (£95 weekend workshop)

BRITISH PREGNANCY ADVISORY SERVICE 0564 793225
Austy Manor, Wootton Wawen, SOLIHULL B95 6BX
Service:	Offers information, counselling, operations & a wide range of services linked with pregnancy/contraception in complete confidence. Consult phone book for local branches.
Area served:	England Wales & Scotland
Referral:	Self or others
Training of workers:	Appropriate training & qualifications
Code of Ethics:	TPB
Management by:	Reg charity. Each branch run by a manager
Fees:	Kept to min, no-one refused

CATHOLIC MARRIAGE ADVISORY COUNCIL 071 371 1341
Clitherow House, 1 Blythe Mews, Blythe Rd   West Kensington, LONDON W14 0NW
Service:	Education for family life, marriage counselling, psycho-sexual counselling and a natural family planning service. For local branches consult 'phone book
Area served:	England, Wales, Scotland
Referral:	Self
Training of workers:	Initial training, in-service training, regular supervision
Code of Ethics:	AOC
Management by:	Local Management Committees
Fees:	App donation encouraged

CHILD DEATH HELPLINE 071 829 8685
Hospital for Sick Children, Great Ormond Street, LONDON WC1N 3JH
Service:	A telephone helpline for anyone affected by the death of a child. The telephone volunteers are all bereaved parents and offer non-directive, listening skills (not counselling)
Area served:	Nationwide
Referral:	Self
Training of workers:	Selection interview & training according to model of good practice for telephone helplines
Code of Ethics:	CH
Management by:	Project Co-ordinator, Social Work Team Manager, GreatOrmond Street
Fees:	None

NATIONAL ORGANISATIONS

CHILD GROWTH FOUNDATION — 081 994 7625
2 Mayfield Avenue, Chiswick, LONDON W4 1PW

Service:	Support and information for parents & professionals involved with growth disorders. Service for individuals, couples, groups, families
Area served:	UK
Referral:	Self
Training of workers:	None
Code of Ethics:	-
Management by:	Child Growth Foundation
Fees:	Free, but donations welcome

CHILDLINE — Helpline 0800 1111, Office 071 239 1000
Freepost 1111, LONDON N1 0BR

Service:	24 hour telephone counselling to children and young people in trouble or danger
Area served:	Natiowide
Referral:	Self or others
Training of workers:	Trained volunteer counsellors supported by professional staff
Code of Ethics:	AOC
Management by:	Board of Trustees, Executive Director
Fees:	None - Freephone

COMPASSIONATE FRIENDS — Helpline 0272 539 639, Admin 0272 665 202
53 North Street, BRISTOL BS3 1EN

Service:	Support offered to bereaved parents by other bereaved parents. Special groups; SOS -shadow of suicide, POMC - parents of murdered children
Area served:	Nationwide
Referral:	Self or others
Training of workers:	Minimum 2 years since their bereavement
Code of Ethics:	-
Management by:	Registered Charity run by National Committee
Fees:	None

COT DEATH RESEARCH & SUPPORT FOR BEREAVED PARENTS
0836 219010, 0934 613333/41333, 0934 510230

29A Orchard Street, WESTON-SUPER-MARE BS23 1TQ

Service:	A full counselling service to newly bereaved parents and their families following the unexpected death of their baby (Mobile phone 0831 611811)
Area served:	UK
Training of workers:	Personal experience, trained counsellors
Code of Ethics:	BAC
Management by:	Welfare & Support Committee

NATIONAL ORGANISATIONS

COUNSELLING & ADVISORY SERVICE FOR NURSES   071 409 3333
Royal College of Nursing, 20 Cavendish Square, LONDON W1M 0AB

Service:	Confidential counselling, help and information on personal problems, stress, Home Office difficulties, disablement, bereavement, AIDS, relationships, distress, retirement
Area served:	Based in London but available at various venues through UK
Referral:	Self
Training of workers:	Appoint counsellors who are accredited or eligible for accreditation with BAC
Code of Ethics:	BAC
Management by:	For administration - Royal College of Nursing
Fees:	None

CRUSE - BEREAVEMENT CARE   081 940 4818, Brvmt line 081 332 7227
Cruse House, 126 Sheen Road, RICHMOND TW9 1NR

Service:	Counselling, advice on practical problems & opportunities for social contact for all bereaved people. For local branches - contact Cruse House
Area served:	UK
Referral:	Self or others
Training of workers:	Training organised locally - introduction & basic counselling skills then ongoing and work supervised
Code of Ethics:	CRU
Management by:	A reg charity run by Director and Council
Fees:	Cllg free (Membership £10)

DYMPNA CENTRE   071 286 6107
60 Grove End Road, St John's Wood, LONDON NW8 9NH

Service:	Counselling, marital therapy, psychotherapy for all ministers of religion, religious orders & religious communities of all Judeo-Christian denomination
Area served:	Great Britain, Ireland, Missions
Referral:	Self, Health Practitioner
Training of workers:	Selection by interview with professional committee; regular supervision
Code of Ethics:	AOC
Management by:	Professional Committee and Board of Governors
Fees:	Negotiable

EATING DISORDERS ASSOCIATION   0603 621414
Sackville Place, 44 Magdalen Street, NORWICH NR3 1JU

Service:	On a national basis offers information on a telephone help-line. Locally, self-help groups & counselling for anorexia & bulimia nervosa. Youth helpline 0603 765050
Area served:	Nationwide
Referral:	Self
Training of workers:	Pre & in-service training; regular supervision
Management by:	Council & paid Director
Fees:	£15 (£5 concessionary)

NATIONAL ORGANISATIONS

FAMILY PLANNING ASSOCIATION   071 636 7866
27-35 Mortimer Street, LONDON W1N 7RJ
Service:	Information on sexuality & family planning. Professional training/consultancy on sexuality & personal relationships. Info on FPA Clinics & related organisations.
Area served:	Nationwide
Referral:	Self
Training of workers:	Appropriate to service offered
Code of Ethics:	VPS
Management by:	Director and management team & National Executive Committee
Fees:	Info none, consultancy by neg.

FAMILY SERVICES UNITS   071 402 5175
207 Old Marylebone Road, LONDON NW1 5QP
Service:	Aims to promote the welfare of families & communities which are seriously disadvantaged through lack of personal social or economic resources. See also local sections
Area served:	England and Scotland
Other languages:	Please enquire
Referral:	Self or others
Training of workers:	Relevant qualifications, mainly CQSW
Code of Ethics:	SW
Management by:	Registered charity with Director local/national management committees

GENDER DYSPHORIA TRUST INTERNATIONAL
0323 641100, Fax 0323 417817
BM Box 7624, LONDON WC1N 3XX
Service:	For individuals, couples, families, transexuals and their partners
Area served:	UK & Europe
Referral:	Self or others
Training of workers:	Accredited by the Trust; varies according to the individual. Regular supervision
Code of Ethics:	BAC
Management by:	Board of Directors
Fees:	According to income

ISSUE (THE NATIONAL FERTILITY ASSOCIATION) LTD   021 359 4887
St George's Rectory, Tower Street, BIRMINGHAM B19 3UY
Service:	**Informal self-help counselling service for infertile couples provided by 'contacts'**
Area served:	United Kingdom
Referral:	Self
Training of workers:	Basic weekend training course
Management by:	Issue
Fees:	Enrolment £30, renewal £15

NATIONAL ORGANISATIONS

LESBIAN & GAY CHRISTIAN HELPLINE
Couns 071 587 1235, Office 071 739 1249
Oxford House, Derbyshire Street, LONDON E2 6HG

Service:	Helpline for those finding conflicts between their sexuality and their spirituality. Helpline staffed Wed 7-10pm & Sun 4-10pm. One to one counselling available
Area served:	Nationwide
Referral:	Self
Training of workers:	Qualified counsellors and counsellors in training; personal therapy and regular supervision
Code of Ethics:	BAC
Management by:	Institute for study of Christianity & Sexuality Trustees
Fees:	1st meeting free, then by arr.

LIFE
24 hrs 0926 311511, 0926 421587, 0926 311667/316737
Life House, Newbold Terrace, LEAMINGTON SPA CV32 4EA

Service:	Non-directive pregnancy & post abortion counselling. Specialises in unsupported pregnant women. Call head office for local branch or see telephone directory.
Area served:	Nationwide
Referral:	Self or others
Training of workers:	Basic counselling skills - in-service training
Code of Ethics:	AOC
Management by:	Management Committee
Fees:	Donations accepted

MATCH (MOTHERS APART FROM THEIR CHILDREN)   None stated
c/o BM Problems, LONDON WC1N 3XX

Service:	Self-help group offering encouragement/support through the sharing of experiences. No formal couns offered. All clients in need of couns encouraged to consult a trained counsellor
Area served:	UK
Referral:	Self
Training of workers:	Some trained counsellors in own right
Code of Ethics:	CH
Fees:	None, donations welcomed

MEDIATION UK
0272 241234, Fax 0272 441387
82a Gloucester Road, Bishopston, BRISTOL BS7 8BN

Service:	A network of mediation schemes and of persons interested in promoting constructive methods of conflict resolution. National Office provides advice & information to anyone
Area served:	UK, many local schemes, but not all areas
Other languages:	Various
Referral:	Self or others
Training of workers:	Local schemes run training courses for mediators, developing own standard courses and training modules
Code of Ethics:	AOC
Management by:	Elected Committee
Fees:	None

NATIONAL ORGANISATIONS

NATIONAL ASSOCIATION FOR GIFTED CHILDREN 0604 792300
Park Campus, Boughton Green Road, NORTHAMPTON NN2 7AL
Service: General counselling for members of families who have a gifted child
Area served: UK - counsellors at branches
Referral: Self
Training of workers: Counsellors interviewed & selected by trained counsellor; training & supervision ongoing
Code of Ethics: BAC
Management by: Counselling Co-ordinator - May MacKay
Fees: Donations encouraged

NATIONAL FRIEND LTD
B M National Friend, LONDON WC1N 3XX
Service: Information, advice, befriending, counselling to people with concerns about homosexuality. Has many branches throughout UK, look in local telephone directory
Area served: UK
Referral: Self
Training of workers: Varies from group to group
Code of Ethics: BAC
Management by: National Friend has annually elected committee. Each group manages itself

NORCAP 0865 750554
3 New High Street, Headington, OXFORD OX3 7AJ
Service: Counselling for adopted adults seeking their origins, their adoptive parents & for birth parents hoping to be found. Contact leaders around the country with similar experience
Area served: Nationwide
Referral: Self, Agencies
Training of workers: CQSW &/or personal experience of adoption plus training by NORCAP
Code of Ethics: AOC
Management by: Trustees
Fees: Subscriptions

OUTSIDERS CLUB 071 837 3559
PO Box 4ZB, Westminster, LONDON W1A 4ZB
Service: Welcomes socially & physically disabled people into a network where they can contact each other, meet at social events, gain confidence & become emotionally secure
Area served: UK, network of local groups
Referral: Self
Training of workers: Doctor has Diploma in Human Sexuality, will refer to other therapists
Code of Ethics: BAC
Management by: Management Committee
Fees: £15 Membership; unwaged £6

NATIONAL ORGANISATIONS

PARENTLINE   0268 757077
Westbury House, 57 Hart Road, Thundersley, BENFLEET SS7 3PD
Service:	A network of Telephone Helplines for parents experiencing difficulties with their children. Contact Central office for local helpline numbers
Area served:	UK
Referral:	Self
Training of workers:	Training in local groups based on principles of PARENTLINE Training Pack provided
Code of Ethics:	AOC
Management by:	Management Committee
Fees:	None

PARENTS' FRIEND   Helpline 0532 674627
c/o V A Leeds, Stringer House, 34 Lupton St, Hunslet, LEEDS LS10 2QW
Service:	For parents with gay/lesbian/bi-sexual children; counselling for individuals, couples, groups, families
Area served:	Country-wide
Referral:	Self or others
Training of workers:	Degree standard course & RSA Cert; Mental Health/Therapy + Groupwork (Leeds Metro Univ); personal therapy; supervision
Code of Ethics:	BAC, TPB
Management by:	Founder Secretary, Assistant Secretary & Treasurer
Fees:	Donations welcome

POST-ADOPTION CENTRE   071 284 0555
8 Torriano Mews, Torriano Avenue, LONDON NW5 2RZ
Service:	Counselling, family & group work for any of the participants in adoption
Area served:	No restriction
Other languages:	French
Referral:	Self or others
Training of workers:	Social workers with adoption experience or trained counsells
Code of Ethics:	BAC, SW
Management by:	Management Committee
Fees:	Local Authority/Donations

PREGNANCY ADVISORY SERVICE   071 637 8962
11-13 Charlotte Street, LONDON W1P 1HD
Service:	Provides advice & treatment for women in the fields of pregnancy, abortion & fertility
Area served:	Not restricted
Other languages:	Spanish, French, German, Italian
Referral:	Self
Training of workers:	Counsellors selected & trained by Pregnancy Advisory Service Training Team
Code of Ethics:	AOC
Management by:	Charitable Trustees
Fees:	£45 counselling only

NATIONAL ORGANISATIONS

RELATE (NATIONAL MARRIAGE GUIDANCE)   0788 573241
Herbert Gray College, Little Church Street, RUGBY CV21 3AP
Service:	Counselling for problems of personal relationships, principally marital; es therapy at some branches. For local branches see under RELATE or Marriage Guidance in phone book
Area served:	England, Wales, N.Ireland, Channel Islands
Referral:	Self
Training of workers:	Volunteers undergo 2 years basic training; additional training for sex therapy; regular supervision
Code of Ethics:	BAC
Management by:	A registered Charity with Director & Management Team
Fees:	Contributions to running costs

SAMARITANS   0753 532713
10 The Grove, SLOUGH SL1 1QP
Service:	Offers emotional support & befriending to the lonely, suicidal & despairing in complete confidence at any time of the day or night. See telephone directory for local number
Area served:	UK, Eire, Channel Islands, Isle of Man
Other languages:	Welsh, Japanese
Referral:	Self or others
Training of workers:	Preparation largely experiential. Regular supervision
Code of Ethics:	AOC
Management by:	Council of Management consisting of one representative from each branch
Fees:	None

SEAHORSE SOCIETY
BM Seahorse, LONDON WC1N 3XX
Service:	Helpline for the heterosexual transvestite and transexuals
Area served:	Nationwide
Referral:	Self
Training of workers:	Training with Beaumont Trust
Management by:	Elected Committee
Fees:	None

STEPFAMILY   071 372 0844
72 Willesden Lane, Kilburn, LONDON NW6 7TA
Service:	Provides a telephone counselling service, local self-help groups, publications and newsletters for all members of step families
Area served:	UK
Referral:	Self
Training of workers:	In-service training
Code of Ethics:	AOC
Management by:	Director
Fees:	None, donations accepted

NATIONAL ORGANISATIONS

VICTIM SUPPORT 071 735 9166
Cranmer House, 39 Brixton Road, LONDON SW9 6DZ
Service:	**Practical help & advice & basic emotional support to victims following crime. Leaflets in Asian Languages in preparation**
Area served:	Many local schemes, see local phone book
Other languages:	Please enquire
Referral:	Police, Self or others
Training of workers:	Training organised locally
Code of Ethics:	AOC
Management by:	National: Council elected by membs; Local: Management
Fees:	None

VICTIMS' HELPLINE 071 729 1252
St Leonard's, Nuttall Street, LONDON N1 5LZ
Service:	**24 hour confidential telephone helpline for victims of crime or those in a crisis. Limited spaces for face to face couns**
Area served:	National
Referral:	Self or others
Training of workers:	Professional counselling qualifications & telephone couns skills; regular personal therapy
Code of Ethics:	BAC
Management by:	Management committee and staff
Fees:	Donations

London - Central

Organisations

GESTALT CENTRE LONDON apptments 0727 864806
Gestalt Centre, 66 Warwick Road, ST. ALBANS AL1 4DL
Service:	Referral to practitioners trained by the centre. Individual psychotherapy, group therapy & general counselling. Member of UK Council for Psychotherapy
Area served:	UK
Other languages:	German, French
Referral:	Self
Training of workers:	Min 5 yrs part-time training. Regular supervision
Code of Ethics:	AHPP
Management by:	Three directors
Fees:	£14 - £30 depending on therapist

BISHOP R O HALL CHINESE CNTRE, BISHOP HO MING WAH ASSOCIATION 071 925 0755, 071 839 5581
Under the Courtyard, St Martin in the Fields Church, Trafalgar Square, LONDON WC2N 4JJ
Service:	General counselling to Cantonese speaking Chinese people
Area served:	London
Other languages:	Cantonese
Referral:	Self or others
Training of workers:	Social work training
Code of Ethics:	BASW
Management by:	Council of management of Bishop Ho Ming Wah Association
Fees:	None

LONDON CLINIC OF PSYCHOANALYSIS 071 436 1177
Mansfield House, 63 New Cavendish Street, LONDON W1M 7RD
Service:	Psychoanalysis 5 times per week (1 50-minute session, Mon-Fri) for 2-3 yrs. Adult, Child and Adolescent Depts
Area served:	No restrictions
Referral:	Self
Code of Ethics:	British Psycho-analytical society
Management by:	Clinical Directorate
Fees:	By arrangement

CHOICE FWA (Islington) 071 490 7740
143 Central Street, LONDON EC1V 8AR
Service:	Individual & couple counselling. Informal drop-in. Support for carers of the frail elderly & people with Alzheimers Disease Befriending for people w long term emotional difficulties
Area served:	Islington & City
Referral:	Self or others
Training of workers:	CQSW or relevant mental health experience, in regular supervision
Code of Ethics:	Agency's own code
Management by:	Area committee answers to parent body
Fees:	None

London - Central

Individuals

*Every individual is a **member of** one or more organisations eligible for entry into this directory. BAC Accredited Counsellors and Recognised Supervisors are shaded*

ALBERY-SPEYER Josephine   081 208 2853
Neal's Yard Therapy Rooms, 2 Neal's Yard, Covent Garden, LONDON WC2H 9DP
Member of:	AHPP
Quals/training:	Cert Psychotherapy Chiron Centre 1985
Personal Therapy:	Yes
Supervision:	Ongoing
Counselling offered:	**Psychotherapy, Massage, Grief**
Service for:	Individuals
Theoretical Approach:	Integrative
Other languages:	German
Fees:	£28 concessions negotiable

AMBROSE Tony   ansaphone 081 542 5930
Consulting room in EC1, LONDON
Member of:	**BAC, Gestalt Centre**
Quals/training:	BA; Practitioner Training in Gestalt psychotherapy (Gestalt Centre)'87-present; Human Relations & Group Dynamics(Morley College); Memb GAUK
Personal Therapy:	Yes
Supervision:	Ongoing
Counselling offered:	**General, Bereavement, Personal growth, Psychotherapy**
Service for:	Individuals
Theoretical Approach:	Gestalt
Fees:	£16 - £25 sliding scale

BENTLEY Charles   071 834 0193
607 Howard House, Dolphin Square, LONDON
Member of:	**AHPP, Memb of UKCP Register**
Quals/training:	MA; PhD Psychol; Acc Group Facilitator (AHPP)
Personal Therapy:	Yes
Supervision:	Ongoing
Counselling offered:	**General, Psychotherapy, Supervision**
Service for:	Individuals, Groups, Organisations
Theoretical Approach:	Humanistic, Integrative
Fees:	£30

BOLLINGER Charmain   071 935 6743 (24 h)
124 Montagu Mansions, LONDON W1H 1LE
Member of:	**BPS, BASMT, BABCP**
Quals/training:	MA; AFBPsS; Chartered Clinical Psychol; Dip Human Sexuality (St George's); trained in Behavioural Therapy (Middx Hosp Med School); Cognitive Therapy (PA); Memb BSECH
Personal Therapy:	Yes
Supervision:	Ongoing
Counselling offered:	**General, Sexual, Relationship**
Service for:	Individuals, Couples
Theoretical Approach:	Behavioural, Cognitive/Behavioural, Hypnotherapy
Other languages:	French
Fees:	£45 Sliding scale in rare cases

London - Central

BROWN Revd Ian B 071 487 3551
38 Nottingham Place, LONDON W1M 3FD
Member of:	BAC
Quals/training:	BA; Dip Th; Cert in Couns Skills (WPF) & (AGIP); intro courses at LCP & IGA
Personal Therapy:	Ongoing
Supervision:	Ongoing
Counselling offered:	**General, Sexuality**
Service for:	Individuals, Groups
Theoretical Approach:	Analytical
Fees:	Sliding scale

CASSIDY Janis 071 222 1522
78 Buckingham Gate, LONDON SW1E 6PD
Member of:	NRHP, NCHP
Quals/training:	Assoc member of NRHP, NCPHR
Personal Therapy:	Ongoing
Supervision:	Ongoing
Counselling offered:	**General, Hypnotherapy, Relationship, Eating disorders**
Service for:	Individuals, Couples
Theoretical Approach:	Behavioural, Cognitive/Behavioural, NLP, RET
Fees:	£20 - £30 sliding scale

CRAWFORD Audrey 071 487 3766
The Counselling Partnership, 5 Albert Mansions, Luxborough Street, LONDON W1M 3LN
Member of:	BAC
Quals/training:	Dip Soc Admin; NMGC Trained 1977 (inc sex therapy & group training)
Personal Therapy:	Ongoing
Supervision:	Ongoing
Counselling offered:	**General, Marital, Sexual**
Service for:	Individuals, Couples, Groups
Theoretical Approach:	Psychodynamic
Fees:	£25 - £40

CROSBY Simon ansaphone 034 282 4545
4 Sandringham Court, Dufour's Place, LONDON W1V 1FE
Member of:	BAC
Quals/training:	BSc (London) 1966; Cert Couns (LCIP) 1989; Cert PCP 1991
Personal Therapy:	Ongoing
Supervision:	Ongoing
Counselling offered:	**General, Relationship, Crisis**
Service for:	Individuals, Couples, Families
Specific to:	Parents
Theoretical Approach:	Eclectic, Constructivist
Fees:	£30

London - Central

CURRA Jenny   081 940 2046
88 Denbigh Street, Pimlico, LONDON SW1V 2EX
Member of: BAC, IPC/WPF
Quals/training: BA; Dip Memb IPC(WPF); currently working for Dip Supervision (WPF); ACAT
Personal Therapy: Yes
Supervision: Ongoing
Counselling offered: General, Relationship, Bereavement, Short-term, Long-term, Supervision
Service for: Individuals
Theoretical Approach: Eclectic, CAT
Fees: £18 - £28

ENTWISTLE Christine-Anne   071 833 1595
Holborn, LONDON WC1X
Member of: BAC
Quals/training: Dip Couns (CSCT)
Personal Therapy: Yes
Supervision: Ongoing
Counselling offered: General, Divorce, Midlife, Personal growth, Self-understanding
Service for: Individuals, Groups
Theoretical Approach: Humanistic, Psychodynamic
Fees: Negotiable

ENTWISTLE Paul Andrew   071 636 6540
The Rodney Clinic, 10 Harley Street, LONDON W1N 1AA
Member of: BAC
Quals/training: M Phil; Dip Clinical Chemistry; Consultant Reproductive Biologist; Hypnotherapist, Memb BICA, NARP & BHMA
Personal Therapy: Ongoing
Supervision: Ongoing
Counselling offered: Infertility, Psychosexual, Hypnotherapy
Service for: Individuals, Couples
Theoretical Approach: Eclectic
Fees: £50

FAIRHURST Irene   071 240 0695
The Gym at the Sanctuary, 11 Floral Street, LONDON WC2E 9DH
Member of: BAC Acc
Quals/training: BAC(Acc); Dip Client-centred Psychotherapy & Counselling & applications of the Person-centred Approach(PCAI)
Personal Therapy: No
Supervision: Ongoing
Counselling offered: General, Psychotherapy, Eating disorders, Phobias
Service for: Individuals
Specific to: Women only
Theoretical Approach: Client-centred
Fees: £30

London - Central

GLADSTONE Guy 081 549 9583
The Open Centre, 188 Old Street, LONDON EC1V 9FR
Member of:	BAC, AHPP, IPSS
Quals/training:	BA;Dip IDHP; IPSS; AHPP Acc
Personal Therapy:	Ongoing
Supervision:	Ongoing
Counselling offered:	**General, Psychotherapy, Bodywork**
Service for:	Individuals, Groups
Theoretical Approach:	Psychodynamic, Bioenergetic, Psychodrama
Fees:	£30 a few concessions in groups

GORNEY Carry 071 583 2652
43 Spencer Rise, LONDON NW5 1AR
Member of:	BAC
Quals/training:	BA(Hons); Adv Dip Systemic Therapy
Personal Therapy:	No
Supervision:	Ongoing
Counselling offered:	**General**
Service for:	Individuals, Couples, Families
Specific to:	Children
Theoretical Approach:	Systemic
Other languages:	German
Fees:	£20 - £40

GREEN Fiona 071 580 9223
28 Tottenham Street, LONDON W1P 9PN
Member of:	BAC, GPTI
Quals/training:	Dip couns (SW London College) 1981; MSc (Cranfield) 1981; Fellow College of Preceptors 1987; training in Gestalt (metanoia); London Marriage Guidance Training 1991
Personal Therapy:	Ongoing
Supervision:	Ongoing
Counselling offered:	**General, Sexual, Relationship, Bereavement**
Service for:	Individuals, Couples, Groups
Theoretical Approach:	Gestalt
Other languages:	French
Fees:	£25 - £45 sliding scale

HARPER Suzanne 071 637 3377, 071 631 0156
The Hale Clinic, 7 Park Crescent, LONDON W1N 3HE
Member of:	ANLP (PCS)
Quals/training:	Master Practitioner NLP; Hypnosis training with Richard Bandler
Personal Therapy:	Ongoing
Supervision:	Ongoing
Counselling offered:	**Personal growth, Hypnotherapy, Relationship**
Service for:	Individuals, Couples
Theoretical Approach:	NLP
Fees:	Up to £50

London - Central

HEADON Christopher ansaphone 081 777 6422, ansaphone 081 675 6669
Albany Associates, 12 Harley Street, LONDON W1N 1ED
Member of:	BAC Acc, BASMT
Quals/training:	BAC(Acc); MA(Oxford); PhD(McGill)'74; Cert Couns(LCIP)'83; Cert in Psychosexual Couns(Albany Trust)'84; Dip in Human Sexuality(St George's Hosp Med Sch)'89
Personal Therapy:	Yes
Supervision:	Ongoing
Counselling offered:	General, Relationship, Substance abuse
Service for:	Individuals, Couples
Theoretical Approach:	Psychodynamic, Humanistic
Fees:	£35 - £45

HORDER Daphne 071 828 5398
88 Denbigh Street, LONDON SW1V 2EX
Member of:	BAC, IPC
Quals/training:	Dip Advanced Psychodynamic Couns WPF
Personal Therapy:	Ongoing
Supervision:	Ongoing
Counselling offered:	General, Relationship, Bereavement, Eating disorders
Service for:	Individuals
Theoretical Approach:	Psychodynamic
Fees:	£22 - £30

JACKSON Roderick 071 935 1900, Fax 071 224 1528
148 Harley Street, LONDON W1N 1AU
Member of:	IPC/WPF
Quals/training:	Dip Advanced Psychodynamic Couns(WPF); Cert Transpersonal Couns(CTP)
Personal Therapy:	Yes
Supervision:	Ongoing
Counselling offered:	General, Stress
Service for:	Individuals
Specific to:	Executives
Theoretical Approach:	Psychodynamic, Transpersonal
Fees:	Negotiable

JANE-PATMORE Tanya 071 631 0156
Hale Clinic, 7 Park Crescent, LONDON W1N
Member of:	BAC
Quals/training:	CQSW 1977; Cert Brief Psychotherapy 1990; currently training for Dip Couns Skills & CAT accreditation; Memb BICA
Personal Therapy:	Yes
Supervision:	Ongoing
Counselling offered:	General, Fertility
Service for:	Individuals, Couples
Theoretical Approach:	Integrative
Other languages:	Swedish
Fees:	£30 negotiable

London - Central

LEDERMANN Eric 071 935 8774
121 Harley Street, Mayfair, LONDON
Member of: RCPsych, Memb of UKCP Register
Quals/training: Training analysis 1951-53; Experience in Psychotherapy at Psychiatric Day Hospital 1951-80; FRCPsych 1986
Personal Therapy: Yes
Supervision: No
Counselling offered: Psychotherapy
Service for: Individuals, Couples
Theoretical Approach: Existential
Other languages: German
Fees: £20 - £50 sliding scale

LEWIS David evening 071 734 1911
12 Harley Street, LONDON W1N 1AA
Member of: NRHP
Quals/training: Qualified 1985-6; Memb of International Inst of Hypnotherapists, World Federation of Hypnotherapists
Personal Therapy: Ongoing
Supervision: Ongoing
Counselling offered: General, Hypnotherapy, Psychotherapy, Phobias, Stop smoking, Obsessions, Relationship, Stress, Weight, Unwanted habits
Service for: Individuals, Couples, Groups, Families
Theoretical Approach: Freudian, Jungian, Rogerian, Gestalt
Fees: £35 variable for group therapies

LILLIE Mr Francis 071 323 2370
10 Harley Street, LONDON W1N 1AA
Member of: BPS, BABCP
Quals/training: BA Psychol; MA(Hons) Psychol; C Psychol; AFBPsS
Personal Therapy: No
Supervision: Yes
Counselling offered: Depression, Phobias, Sexual
Service for: Individuals, Couples, Groups, Families
Theoretical Approach: Cognitive/Behavioural
Fees: £80

LLOYD Patricia 071 224 6872
3 De Walden Street, Marylebone, LONDON W1M 7PJ
Member of: BAC, BASMT
Quals/training: NMGC Trained; BASMT Acc
Personal Therapy: Ongoing
Supervision: Ongoing
Counselling offered: General, Relationship, Sexual
Service for: Individuals, Couples
Theoretical Approach: Psychodynamic, Eclectic
Fees: £35 - £50

London - Central

MASON Richard   071 437 7118
Centre for Health & Healing, 197 Piccadilly, LONDON W1V 9LF
Member of:	BAC, PET
Quals/training:	Dip Psychosynthesis Couns & Therapy (PET)
Personal Therapy:	Yes
Supervision:	Ongoing
Counselling offered:	**General, Anxiety, Stress, Redundancy**
Service for:	Individuals, Groups, Organisations
Theoretical Approach:	Psychosynthesis, Gestalt
Fees:	£25

PATERSON Sheila   ansaphone 071 515 6310, Wed-Fri 081 746 8725
LONDON SW1V
Member of:	BAC, ACP
Quals/training:	Dip (Occupational therapy); Dip Couns; training in Core Process Psychotherapy (Karuna); Memb BAOT
Personal Therapy:	Yes
Supervision:	Ongoing
Counselling offered:	**General, Crisis, Eating disorders, Psychotherapy**
Service for:	Individuals, Groups
Theoretical Approach:	Humanistic, Integrative
Fees:	£25 negotiable

PRICE Kit   071 834 7081
Pimlico, LONDON SW1V 2HA
Member of:	BAC, MPTI
Quals/training:	BA & MA Eng Lit; Dip in Rogerian Counselling (metanoia); Trained at Centre for Transpersonal Psychology; Cert Person-Centred Art Therapy
Personal Therapy:	Ongoing
Supervision:	Ongoing
Counselling offered:	**General, Transition, Change, Loss, Bereavement, Personal growth, Creative potential**
Service for:	Individuals
Theoretical Approach:	Rogerian, Transpersonal, Gestalt
Fees:	£18 - £22 sliding scale

QUINN Asher   071 834 7081
21a Denbigh Place, LONDON SW1V 2HA
Member of:	BAC, CCPE
Quals/training:	BA(Hons) '77; Dip in Couns & Psychotherapy '89, Dip Couns '92 & Advanced training in Psychotherapy (CCPE) ongoing
Personal Therapy:	Ongoing
Supervision:	Ongoing
Counselling offered:	**Crisis, Relationship, Eating disorders, Incest, Abuse, Dream**
Service for:	Individuals
Theoretical Approach:	Transpersonal, Humanistic, Spiritual, Analytical
Fees:	£23 - £30

London - Central

RAMAGE Margaret   071 935 0616, 081 674 6522
82 Harley Street, Regent's Park, LONDON W1N 1AE
Member of:	**BAC Acc RSup, BASMT, AFT**
Quals/training:	BAC Acc & Recognised Supervisor; RGN 1964; Trained at St George's Hospital Dept Adult Psychiatry; Sex Therapy trainer; Dip Family Therapy; BASMT Acc
Personal Therapy:	Ongoing
Supervision:	Ongoing
Counselling offered:	**General, Relationship, Sexual, Family, Hypnotherapy**
Service for:	Individuals, Couples, Families
Theoretical Approach:	Integrative
Fees:	£35 - £60 dependent on income

REBUCK Gerald   071 636 7628
University of London Health, 20 Gower Street, LONDON WC1E 6DP
Member of:	**BAC**
Quals/training:	Senior Psychotherapist(St George's Hospital); Senior Psychotherapist(Univ of London Health Service); Memb GAS
Personal Therapy:	Yes
Supervision:	Ongoing
Counselling offered:	**General, Marital, Psychotherapy**
Service for:	Individuals, Couples, Groups
Theoretical Approach:	Analytical
Fees:	£25 - £35

ROBINS Julia   071 630 6326
Flat H, 58 St Georges Square, Pimlico, LONDON SW1V 3QT
Member of:	**BAC**
Quals/training:	Cert Hynotherapy & Counselling (UK Training Coll in Hyp & Couns); Teaching Cert Ed
Personal Therapy:	Ongoing
Supervision:	Ongoing
Counselling offered:	**General, Relationship, Addiction, Psychotherapy**
Service for:	Individuals
Theoretical Approach:	Rogerian
Fees:	£35

ST JOHN AUBIN Beverley   071 486 4207
2 Spring Mews, Crawford Street, LONDON W1H 1PQ
Member of:	**BAC**
Quals/training:	Cert Couns(WPF); Cruse Bereavement Couns Course; various Gestalt workshops
Personal Therapy:	Ongoing
Supervision:	Ongoing
Counselling offered:	**General, Bereavement, Stress**
Service for:	Individuals, Couples, Families, Groups
Theoretical Approach:	Rogerian, Person-centred
Fees:	£15 - £25

London - Central

SPURR Pamela   071 823 6018
Victoria, LONDON SW1W
Member of:	BPS
Quals/training:	BSc (Hons) Psychol; Adult placement of MSc Clin Psychol completed
Personal Therapy:	Yes
Supervision:	Ongoing
Counselling offered:	**Personal growth, Crisis, Communication skills**
Service for:	Individuals, Couples
Specific to:	Women
Theoretical Approach:	Cognitive, Behavioural, Dynamic
Fees:	£20 - £40 sliding scale

STRUTHERS Cassandra   071 834 3475
31 Cambridge Street, LONDON SW1V 4PR
Member of:	BAC, AGIP
Quals/training:	Qualified in Psychotherapy AGIP 1981
Personal Therapy:	Yes
Supervision:	Ongoing
Counselling offered:	**Psychotherapy**
Service for:	Individuals, Groups
Theoretical Approach:	Analytic
Fees:	£45

STYLE Hinda   071 638 9537
303 Gilbert House, Barbican, LONDON EC2Y 8BD
Member of:	BAC
Quals/training:	CQSW; Cert in Couns, LCP; trained in Family Therapy, IFT; trained in group work
Personal Therapy:	Yes
Supervision:	Ongoing
Counselling offered:	**General, Bereavement, Personal growth, Marital**
Service for:	Individuals, Couples, Families
Theoretical Approach:	Eclectic
Fees:	£15 - £35 sliding scale

WARREN Steven   Appts 081 870 7353
LONDON SW1
Member of:	BAC Acc
Quals/training:	BAC(Acc); BA(Hons) Psychol; Cert Couns
Personal Therapy:	Yes
Supervision:	Ongoing
Counselling offered:	**General, Bereavement, Loss, Transition, Change, Divorce, Separation, Health, Stress management**
Service for:	Individuals, Couples, Groups, Organisations
Theoretical Approach:	Analytical, Eclectic
Fees:	£45 negotiable, groups on application

London - Central

WEST Antonia   071 387 4509
20 Tavistock Court, Tavistock Square, LONDON WC1H 9HE

Member of:	BAC, IGA
Quals/training:	BA Art & Languages; Dips Psychosynthesis Couns & Psychotherapy; Shamanism; Dip Anatomy, Physiology & Body Massage (ITEC); Reiki 1st Degree
Personal Therapy:	Yes
Supervision:	Ongoing
Counselling offered:	**Stress, Addiction, Dependency, Creative potential, Sexuality, Relationship, Spiritual, Massage**
Service for:	Individuals, Couples, Groups
Theoretical Approach:	Psychosynthesis, Shamanistic, Reiki & Seichim healing, Holistic
Other languages:	French, Italian, Spanish, Portuguese
Fees:	£30 - £40

WHITE Mary   071 251 6348
9 Fortune House, Fortune Street, LONDON EC1Y 0RY

Member of:	BAC
Quals/training:	SRN; Dip Couns'85; Int Therapists Exam Cert; Memb British Psychosocial Oncology Group
Personal Therapy:	Yes
Supervision:	Ongoing
Counselling offered:	**General, Relationship, Chronic illness**
Service for:	Individuals, Couples, Families
Theoretical Approach:	Rogerian, TA
Fees:	£25 sliding scale

WRIGHT Patricia   071 935 3073
22 Upper Wimpole Street, LONDON W1M 7TA

Member of:	BAC Acc, BPS
Quals/training:	BAC(Acc); SRN'58; BA Psychol(London Univ)'69; Dip Couns & Pastoral Care(CNAA); Chartered Occupational Psychologist; trained in TA '81-'87
Personal Therapy:	Yes
Supervision:	Ongoing
Counselling offered:	**General, Marital, Stress, Career, Retirement, Redundancy**
Service for:	Individuals
Specific to:	Executives, Managers, Professionals
Theoretical Approach:	Eclectic, Humanistic, Person-centred
Fees:	£45

Organisations

ROYAL LONDON HOSPITAL SEXUAL PROBLEMS CLINIC
071 377 7044

The Royal London Hospital, Fielden House, 4th Floor, Whitechapel, LONDON E1

Service:	Psychosexual problems, reproductive health & menopausal problems for individuals and couples
Area served:	Tower Hamlets Health District
Referral:	Health Practitioner
Training of workers:	Dr M Griffin is a member of IPM
Code of Ethics:	IPM, GMC
Management by:	NHS
Fees:	None

TOWER HAMLETS YOUTH COUNSELLING SERVICE
071 739 3082

Oxford House, Derbyshire Street, LONDON E2 6HG

Service:	Non-directive counselling for people aged 12-25. Staff team includes white, Afro-caribbean & Bangladeshi members and both male & female counsellors
Area served:	Tower Hamlets
Other languages:	Bengali
Referral:	Self
Training of workers:	CNAA PG Dip Couns (Univ E London); Dip Couns (Goldsmiths' Coll). Regular supervision
Code of Ethics:	BAC
Management by:	Voluntary Management Committee
Fees:	None

JUST ASK ADVISORY & COUNSELLING SERVICE
071 628 3380

46 Bishopsgate, LONDON E2 3JA

Service:	Individuals 17-35 who need short or long term counselling or can be helped by analytic work. Walk-in service remains at all times concordant with the aims of the YMCA
Area served:	London & others
Referral:	Self
Training of workers:	All paid staff qualified psychotherapists. Sessional staff in training or trained counsellors. Supervision is weekly
Code of Ethics:	Agency's own code
Management by:	Director and Management Committee
Fees:	Donation system

ROYAL LONDON PSYCHOLOGY DEPARTMENT
071 377 3954

The Royal London Hospital, St Clements, LONDON E3 4LL

Service:	Individual analytical and cognitive/behavioural therapy, social skills, stress management, group, family, marital & child therapy
Area served:	Tower Hamlets
Other languages:	Bengali, Gujerati, Hindi, Punjabi, German
Referral:	GP, Health/Soc Work Professional
Training of workers:	Postgraduate clinical psychology, BAP, Tavistock Clinic
Code of Ethics:	BPS
Management by:	Royal London Trust via District Psychologist
Fees:	None

ASSOCIATION FOR PSYCHOTHERAPY IN EAST LONDON (APEL)
081 556 5089

36 Richmond Road, Leytonstone, LONDON E11 4BU
Service: Individual, group and marital psychotherapy for a wide range of problems including depression, anxiety, emotional and relationship difficulties
Area served: East London and Essex
Referral: Self, GP
Training of workers: Minimum of 3 yrs psychotherapy training at BCP or UKCP approved institutions
Code of Ethics: IPC, LCP, AGIP, BPS, BAP
Management by: Elected management committee and consultant psychiatrist
Fees: £20 - £30 assessment £40

UNIVERSITY OF EAST LONDON DEPARTMENT OF PSYCHOLOGY
081 590 7722 ex 4501

Dept of Psychology, Romford Road, Stratford, LONDON E15 4LZ
Service: Short or medium term for individuals
Area served: North East London & West Essex
Referral: Self or others
Training of workers: Psychologists and counsellors, all highly trained & experienced trainee Dip/MSc students; regular supervision
Code of Ethics: BAC
Management by: Diploma Course staff - contact Ian Horton
Fees: None (Donations)

WALTHAM FOREST HIV/AIDS COUNSELLING SERVICE 081 520 3766

Thorpe Coombe Hospital, Forest Road, Walthamstow, LONDON E17 3HP
Service: Confidential pre and post test counselling and support to anyone with concerns about HIV and AIDS including HIV people, their partners, families and friends
Area served: Forest Health Care NHS Trust
Referral: Self, GP
Training of workers: Qualified counsellors
Code of Ethics: BAC
Management by: Forest Health Care NHS Trust
Fees: None

WALTHAM FOREST YOUTH COUNSELLING SERVICE 081 509 1219

Chestnuts House, 398 Hoe Street, Walthamstow, LONDON E17 9BR
Service: Individual counselling for young people aged 16-25
Area served: Waltham Forest
Other languages: Serbo-Croat
Referral: Self
Training of workers: Dip Couns (WPF/IPC); Child and Adolescent Psychotherapy
Code of Ethics: ACP, IPC
Management by: Local Authority Education Dept, Youth & Community Service
Fees: None

London - East

BARNET HEALTHCARE NHS TRUST SEXUAL/RELATIONSHIP THERAPY CLINIC
081 440 5111 x 4603
Psychiatric Unit, Barnet General Hospital, Wellhouse Lane, BARNET EN5 3DT

Service:	Individual and couple counselling for a wide range of sexual dysfunctions and difficulties, paraphilias and relationship difficulties and issues around HIV
Area served:	Barnet Healthcare NHS Trust area and others by negotiation
Referral:	GP
Training of workers:	BASMT Accredited therapist
Code of Ethics:	BAC, BASMT
Management by:	Barnet Healthcare NHS Trust
Fees:	None

Individual Practitioners

*Every individual is a **member of** one or more organisations eligible for entry into this directory. BAC Accredited Counsellors and Recognised Supervisors are shaded.*

BOULTON Anthony John   071 265 0091
39 Shearsmith House, Hindmarsh Close, Cable Street, LONDON E1 8HT

Member of:	**BAC, CAP**
Quals/training:	BSc; MA; CAP trained
Personal Therapy:	Ongoing
Supervision:	Ongoing
Counselling offered:	**General, Sexual, Addiction, Bereavement, Psychotherapy**
Service for:	Individuals, Couples
Theoretical Approach:	Psychodynamic, Kleinian
Fees:	£18 - £30 Sliding scale

JENNINGS Anne   071 265 9354
Stepney, LONDON E1

Member of:	**BAC Acc**
Quals/training:	BAC Acc; CNAA Dip Couns (Univ of E London) 1989; MSc Psychol Couns (Roehampton Inst) 1991
Personal Therapy:	Ongoing
Supervision:	Ongoing
Counselling offered:	**General, Relationship, Bereavement**
Service for:	Individuals
Theoretical Approach:	Integrative, Psychodynamic
Fees:	£18 - £30 sliding scale

BRADY Kate   071 737 5188
Bodywise Clinic, 119 Roman Road, LONDON E2 0QN

Member of:	**BAC, IPS**
Quals/training:	Diploma in Psychosynthesis Counselling; BA; PGCE
Personal Therapy:	Ongoing
Supervision:	Ongoing
Counselling offered:	**General, Relationship, Bereavement, Addiction**
Service for:	Individuals
Specific to:	Recovering addicts/alcoholics
Theoretical Approach:	Psychosynthesis, Psychodynamic
Fees:	£28 negotiable

London - East

BANNISTER Gill 081 981 2244
78 Lichfield Road, Bow, LONDON E3 5AL
Member of: BAC, IPC
Quals/training: IPC/WPF (Full)
Personal Therapy: Yes
Supervision: Ongoing
Counselling offered: Psychotherapy, Supervision
Service for: Individuals
Theoretical Approach: Psychoanalytic
Fees: £28 sometimes negotiable

CHEW Elisabeth 081 981 1553
50 Blondin Street, Bow, LONDON E3 2TR
Member of: BAC Acc
Quals/training: BAC Acc; Dip in Couns, PET
Personal Therapy: Ongoing
Supervision: Ongoing
Counselling offered: General
Service for: Individuals
Specific to: Women
Theoretical Approach: Psychosynthesis, Person-centred, Humanistic
Fees: £28 negotiable

HAWKINS Jan 081 531 9760
376 Hale End Road, Highams Park, LONDON E4 9PB
Member of: BAC Acc, BPS
Quals/training: BAC(Acc); BSc(Hons) Psychol; Cert LCIP; Cert Ed; Dip PCAI
Personal Therapy: Yes
Supervision: Ongoing
Counselling offered: General, Abuse, Bereavement, Crisis, Disability, Psychotherapy
Service for: Individuals, Couples, Families, Groups, Organisations
Specific to: Survivors of sex abuse, People w learning difficulties, People with disabilities
Theoretical Approach: Client-centred
Fees: £15 - £30 sliding scale

MARTIN Margaret 081 524 3795, 0831 25 9292
20 Queens Grove Road, Chingford, LONDON E4 7BT
Member of: BAC Acc
Quals/training: BAC Acc; Dip Dramatherapy (Hertfordshire College of Art); Post Grad Dip Guidance & Couns (Poly of East London)
Personal Therapy: Yes
Supervision: Ongoing
Counselling offered: General, Crisis, Bereavement, Stress management, Drama therapy, Supervision
Service for: Individuals, Families, Groups
Specific to: Young adults, Adolescents, Children with special needs
Theoretical Approach: Egan
Fees: £5 - £20 negotiable

London - East

SAGGERS Andrew   081 524 5045
84 Ainslie Wood Road, Chingford, LONDON E4 9BY

Member of:	BAC
Quals/training:	Dip Couns; currently training for Dip Psychotherapy
Personal Therapy:	Ongoing
Supervision:	Ongoing
Counselling offered:	**General, Addiction, Eating disorders, Psychosexual**
Service for:	Individuals
Specific to:	Women
Theoretical Approach:	Existential, Rogerian
Fees:	£8 - £20

HUXTABLE Pamela   081 529 4120
55 Hurst Avenue, Chingford, LONDON E4 8DL

Member of:	AGIP
Quals/training:	Training member (AGIP) 1989
Personal Therapy:	Yes
Supervision:	Ongoing
Counselling offered:	**Psychotherapy, Midlife**
Service for:	Individuals
Theoretical Approach:	Eclectic, Psychoanalytic
Fees:	£15 - £20

HARLING Biljana   081 806 9508
57 Clapton Terrace, Clapton, LONDON E5

Member of:	BAC, MPTI
Quals/training:	Grad Psychologist(Yugoslavia); Adv training in TA(metanoia)
Personal Therapy:	Ongoing
Supervision:	Ongoing
Counselling offered:	**General, Psychotherapy, Bereavement**
Service for:	Individuals, Groups
Theoretical Approach:	TA, Rogerian
Other languages:	Serbo-Croat
Fees:	£25 indivs, £15 group

HASLAM Deidre   ansaphone 081 986 3051
85 Rushmore Road, Clapton, LONDON E5 0EX

Member of:	BAC, IPC
Quals/training:	BEd; MA; Dip Couns (WPF/Roehampton); Cert in Supervision (metanoia)
Personal Therapy:	Yes
Supervision:	Ongoing
Counselling offered:	**General, Child abuse**
Service for:	Individuals, Couples
Specific to:	Women, Gays, Ethnic minorities, Survivors of sex abuse, Families of alcoholics
Theoretical Approach:	Integrative
Other languages:	French, German
Fees:	£15 - £30 sliding scale

London - East

JONES Cerys Ms 081 806 7752
52 Reighton Road, Hackney, LONDON E5 8SG

Member of:	BAC
Quals/training:	Dip HE; BA(Hons) Psychotherapy/Counselling; dip Client-centred Psychotherpy/Counselling; Memb BAPCA
Personal Therapy:	Yes
Supervision:	Ongoing
Counselling offered:	**General, Psychotherapy**
Service for:	Individuals, Couples
Specific to:	Women
Theoretical Approach:	Person-centred
Fees:	Negotiable

KEENE Linda 081 470 6638
38 Norfolk Road, East Ham, LONDON E6 2NJ

Member of:	BAC
Quals/training:	BA; Cert Couns (Highgate Couns Centre)
Personal Therapy:	Yes
Supervision:	Ongoing
Counselling offered:	**General, Bereavement, Eating disorders, Infertility**
Service for:	Individuals
Theoretical Approach:	Psychodynamic
Fees:	£10 - £25 sliding scale

BARKER Jocelyn 081 555 7853
6 Cranmer Road, Forest Gate, LONDON E7 0JW

Member of:	BAC, BPS, MPTI
Quals/training:	BSc Hons (Psych); Dip Couns; TA Foundation Course (metanoia)
Personal Therapy:	Ongoing
Supervision:	Ongoing
Counselling offered:	**General**
Service for:	Individuals
Theoretical Approach:	Person-centred
Fees:	£20 - £25 sliding scale

BRION Marion 081 534 5494
59 Osborne Road, LONDON E7 0PJ

Member of:	BAC, ANLP (PCS)
Quals/training:	PhD; Cert Ed; NLP Practitioner; Dip British Hypnosis Research
Personal Therapy	Ongoing
Supervision:	Ongoing
Counselling offered:	**General, Psychotherapy, Stress management, Personal growth**
Service for:	Individuals, Groups, Organisations
Theoretical Approach:	Integrative, Systemic
Fees:	£15 - £30

London - East

LUMSDEN Barbara   081 519 7777
62 Osborne Road, Forest Gate, LONDON E7 0HP
Member of:	BAC
Quals/training:	BSc; MA; CQSW 1978; Dip Gestalt & Contribution Training (Pellin Inst)
Personal Therapy:	Ongoing
Supervision:	Ongoing
Counselling offered:	**Psychotherapy, Crisis, Work, Relationship, Self-understanding**
Service for:	Individuals, Couples
Specific to:	Women, Incest survivors
Theoretical Approach:	Alice Miller, John Bowlby
Fees:	£18 - £25 sliding scale

ROBERTS Laurence   appts 081 472 2430
Ty'ny Doed, 40 Boleyn Road, Forest Gate, LONDON E7 9QE
Member of:	BAC
Quals/training:	BEd(Hons); Cert Ed; Southwark Pastoral Care & Couns; North London Poly; IGA; TC; WPF; Member GAS
Personal Therapy:	Ongoing
Supervision:	Ongoing
Counselling offered:	**General, Long-term, Short-term, Bereavement, Loss, Crisis, Cancer, AIDS, Abuse, Supervision**
Service for:	Individuals, Groups, Organisations
Specific to:	People with language problems
Theoretical Approach:	Psychodynamic, Analytical
Fees:	£25 - £30 (£11-£16 groups)

ADAMS Martin   071 254 2707
84 Middleton Road, Hackney, LONDON E8 4LN
Member of:	BAC
Quals/training:	BSc Psychol; Dip Couns & Supervision, Roehampton 1986; MA Couns (Hatfield) 1992
Personal Therapy:	Yes
Supervision:	Ongoing
Counselling offered:	**General, Short-term, Long-term**
Service for:	Individuals
Theoretical Approach:	Psychodynamic
Fees:	£18 - £25 Sliding scale

FORSTER Kay   ansaphone 071 249 7627
Dalston, LONDON E8
Member of:	BAC, BPS
Quals/training:	BSc(Hons) Psychology with Visual Arts (Middlesex) '89; PG Diploma in Couns Psychol (East London)
Personal Therapy:	Ongoing
Supervision:	Ongoing
Counselling offered:	**General, Anxiety, Abuse, Bereavement, Crisis, Mental health**
Service for:	Individuals, Groups
Specific to:	Survivors of child abuse, Mentally ill
Theoretical Approach:	Integrative, Humanistic
Fees:	£15 - £30 few £5 places (income support)

MOTHERSOLE Geoff   071 249 3519
18 Horton Road, Hackney, LONDON E8 1DP
Member of:	**BAC Acc**
Quals/training:	BAC Acc; 1980 BSc Psychology; 1984 MA (Social Work); CPsychol; Memb ITAA
Personal Therapy:	Ongoing
Supervision:	Ongoing
Counselling offered:	**General, Psychotherapy**
Service for:	Individuals, Couples, Groups
Theoretical Approach:	Integrative, TA
Fees:	£35 negotiable (£15 group)

MORRISON Barbara   071 923 1096
57 Parkholme Road, LONDON E8 3AQ
Member of:	**ITHP**
Quals/training:	Cert Ed; training in Traditional & Humanistic Psychotherapy, Minster Centre 1984
Personal Therapy:	Yes
Supervision:	Ongoing
Counselling offered:	**General, Bereavement, Crisis, Relationship, Psychotherapy**
Service for:	Individuals, Couples, Groups
Theoretical Approach:	Psychodynamic, Integrative
Fees:	£20 - £30

PIXNER Stef   071 254 6216
94 Colvestone Crescent, Hackney, LONDON E8 2LJ
Member of:	**ITHP**
Quals/training:	BA Psychol/Sociology; MSc Social Psychol; Training in Humanistic & Analytic Psychotherapy (Minster Centre)
Personal Therapy:	Ongoing
Supervision:	Ongoing
Counselling offered:	**General, Psychotherapy**
Service for:	Individuals
Specific to:	Women, Gays, Ethnic minorities, Survivors of sex abuse
Theoretical Approach:	Object relations, Neo-Reichian
Fees:	£15 - £30

JACQUES Glenys   081 533 2948
15 Kemeys Street, Homerton, LONDON E9 5RQ
Member of:	**BAC Acc**
Quals/training:	BAC Acc; BEd; Dip Couns; training in Gestalt Psychotherapy (metanoia)
Personal Therapy:	Ongoing
Supervision:	Ongoing
Counselling offered:	**General, Relationship, Sexual, Bereavement, Crisis, Psychotherapy**
Service for:	Individuals, Couples, Groups
Theoretical Approach:	Client-centred, Rogerian, Gestalt, Existential
Fees:	£18 - £30 negotiable

London - East

SANDELSON Adam 081 985 7955
9 Meynell Crescent, Hackney, LONDON E9 7AS
Member of:	BAC
Quals/training:	BA (Hons); Cert Couns (City Univ); Facilitator & Couns Experiential Training & Supervision Programme; courses at Workshop Associates & Spectrum
Personal Therapy:	Ongoing
Supervision:	Ongoing
Counselling offered:	**General, Crisis, Relationship, Sexual abuse, PTSD**
Service for:	Individuals
Specific to:	Survivors of sex abuse
Theoretical Approach:	Humanistic, Client-centred
Fees:	£22 negotiable(some £5 Inc Supp)

BELL Angela 081 530 6516
75 Belgrave Road, Wanstead, LONDON E11 3QP
Member of:	BAC
Quals/training:	Dip Couns(SW London Coll)'83; Supervision Skills training '90; Art Therapy training '89; Counsellor, London Univ
Personal Therapy:	Yes
Supervision:	Ongoing
Counselling offered:	**General, Bereavement, Relationship, Psychotherapy**
Service for:	Individuals
Specific to:	Students, Young adults
Theoretical Approach:	Psychodynamic, Eclectic
Fees:	£15 - £25

DARLING Nick 081 518 8180
84 Halstead Road, Wanstead, LONDON E11 2AZ
Member of:	BAC
Quals/training:	MSc Counselling Psych; RELATE trained counsellor; Diploma of the College of Occupational Therapists
Personal Therapy:	Yes
Supervision:	Ongoing
Counselling offered:	**Loss, Relationship, General**
Service for:	Individuals, Couples, Organisations
Theoretical Approach:	Psychodynamic
Fees:	Negotiable

JONES David 081 989 6565
8 Forest Glade, Leytonstone, LONDON E11 1LU
Member of:	BAC Acc, AHPP
Quals/training:	BAC Acc; BA(Hons); Cert Couns (Minster & Lincoln Centres NE London Poly) 1984-6; Qualified Psychotherapist; AHPP Acc; Dip (Minster Centre)
Personal Therapy:	Ongoing
Supervision:	Ongoing
Counselling offered:	**General, Relationship, Career, Psychotherapy**
Service for:	Individuals, Couples
Specific to:	Caring professions, Creative people
Theoretical Approach:	Humanistic, Jungian, Transpersonal
Fees:	£15 - £25

London - East

LAMPRELL Michael   081 556 5089
36 Richmond Road, Leytonstone, LONDON E11 4BU
Member of:	BAC Acc, IPC
Quals/training:	BAC Acc; Full memb IPC/WPF
Personal Therapy:	Yes
Supervision:	Ongoing
Counselling offered:	Psychotherapy
Service for:	Individuals
Theoretical Approach:	Psychodynamic
Fees:	£20 - £30

RITTER Sandie   081 502 9232
87 Whipps Cross Road, Leytonstone, LONDON E11 1NJ
Member of:	BAC, AHPP
Quals/training:	BA(Hons); Transpersonal Psychol; MA (Consciousness Studies); CQSW; Dip PET; Memb Inst of Logotherapy and Inst of Transpersonal Psychol
Personal Therapy:	Yes
Supervision:	Ongoing
Counselling offered:	General, Relationship
Service for:	Individuals, Couples, Families, Groups
Theoretical Approach:	Existential, Transpersonal
Fees:	£15 - £25 sliding scale

SHEARMAN Christine   081 989 5206
Hawthorn, 24 Hollybush Hill, Leytonstone, LONDON E11 1PP
Member of:	BAC, ITA, MPTI, GPTI, Member of UKCP Register
Quals/training:	MA; PGCE; Dip Hypnotherapy(GPTI); Dip Couns Skills; Integrative Psychotherapist; Dip Gestalt; Assistant Teaching Memb GPTI; Clin Teaching & Supervising Transactional Analyst
Personal Therapy:	Yes
Supervision:	Ongoing
Counselling offered:	General, Psychotherapy, Supervision
Service for:	Individuals, Couples, Groups
Theoretical Approach:	Systemic, Integrative, TA, Gestalt
Other languages:	German, French
Fees:	£40 negotiable

WILLISON Sandra   081 989 0222
40 Colebrooke Drive, Wanstead, LONDON E11 2LY
Member of:	BAC, IPC/WPF
Quals/training:	Assoc Memb GAS; Adv Dip(IPC/WPF)'86; Cert in Systemic Therapy for couples '89
Personal Therapy:	Yes
Supervision:	Ongoing
Counselling offered:	General, Relationship, Marital
Service for:	Individuals, Couples
Theoretical Approach:	Analytic
Fees:	£25 - £35

London - East

HARDING Celia
081 556 5089
36 Richmond Road, Leytonstone, LONDON E11 4BU
Member of:	IPC
Quals/training:	IPC/WPF
Personal Therapy:	Yes
Supervision:	Ongoing
Counselling offered:	**Psychotherapy**
Service for:	Individuals
Theoretical Approach:	Psychoanalytic
Fees:	£25 - £35

RATOFF Tamar Ms
081 558 0622
80 Melford Road, Leytonstone, LONDON E11 4PS
Member of:	LCP
Quals/training:	Training with London Centre for Psychotherapy
Personal Therapy:	Ongoing
Supervision:	Ongoing
Counselling offered:	**Psychotherapy, Long-term, Eating disorders, Bereavement**
Service for:	Individuals
Theoretical Approach:	Psychodynamic
Fees:	£20 - £30

JELFS Martin
081 981 0480
14 Chesterton Road, Plaistow, LONDON E13 8BA
Member of:	BAC Acc RSup, AHPP
Quals/training:	BAC Acc & Recognised supervisor; BSc; Dip -Biodynamic Psycho therapy (Boyesen Centre) 1983; Integrative Pscyhotherapy (metanoia) 1988
Personal Therapy:	Ongoing
Supervision:	Ongoing
Counselling offered:	**General, Psychotherapy**
Service for:	Individuals, Couples
Specific to:	Access for disabled people
Theoretical Approach:	Integrative
Fees:	£20 - £30 sliding scale

MACDONALD Laurie
081 472 3137
Flat 6, Helen Seymour House, Florence Road, Plaistow, LONDON E13 0DW
Member of:	BAC, ANLP (PCS)
Quals/training:	NLP Master Practitioner Cert; dip Ericksonian Hypnotherapy & Psychotherapy; BSc(Hons) Clinical Communications Studies
Personal Therapy:	Yes
Supervision:	Ongoing
Counselling offered:	**General, Bereavement, Obsessions, Mental health, Psychotherapy, Educational, Social skills**
Service for:	Individuals, Couples, Families, Groups, Organisations
Specific to:	Carers
Theoretical Approach:	NLP, Ericksonian, Cognitive/Behavioural
Fees:	Negotiable

London - East

JUSTICE Patricia 071 538 8228
14 Landons Close, Prestons Road, Poplar, LONDON E14 9QQ
Member of:	**BAC Acc**
Quals/training:	BAC Acc; Adv Cert Psychodynamic Couns (WPF) 1986; Group Co-ordinator Parent Network; trainer & supervisor
Personal Therapy:	Yes
Supervision:	Ongoing
Counselling offered:	**General, Bereavement, Relationship, Stress, Transition, Psychotherapy, Supervision**
Service for:	Individuals, Couples, Groups
Specific to:	Ethnic minorities, People with language problems
Theoretical Approach:	Psychodynamic, Client-centred
Fees:	£15 - £30 sliding scale

MALKIN Julius 071 987 2805
Professional Development Found, 21 Limehouse Cut, Morris Road, LONDON E14 6NQ
Member of:	**BAC**
Quals/training:	BEd (Hons) & MPhil (London); Dip Couns & Health Care (RSH) 1985
Personal Therapy:	Ongoing
Supervision:	Ongoing
Counselling offered:	**General, Educational, Children's problems, Career**
Service for:	Individuals, Couples, Families, Groups
Theoretical Approach:	Rogerian, Behavioural
Fees:	£10 - £50 sliding scale

SADEGHIAN Arsalan 071 476 7117
118 Hilda Road, Canning Town, LONDON E16 4NN
Member of:	**BPS**
Quals/training:	BSc (Hons) Psychol Hypnotherapy 1988; training Rogerian Couns 1990, ongoing training in NLP
Personal Therapy:	Yes
Supervision:	Yes
Counselling offered:	**General, Psychotherapy**
Service for:	Individuals, Couples
Theoretical Approach:	Rogerian, NLP, Hypnotherapy
Other languages:	Persian
Fees:	£30 negotiable

DAVIES Joy 081 521 5932
56 Coleridge Road, LONDON E17 6QU
Member of:	**BAC Acc**
Quals/training:	BAC Acc; Dip Couns & Interpersonal Skills (SW London College) 1985; Dip Gestalt & Contribution Training (Pellin Inst '89)
Personal Therapy:	Ongoing
Supervision:	Ongoing
Counselling offered:	**General, Inner child**
Service for:	Individuals
Theoretical Approach:	Rogerian, Gestalt, Alice Miller
Fees:	£30

London - East

HOANG Astrid   081 527 7258
Gratton Lodge, 40 Spruce Hills Road, Walthamstow, LONDON E17 4LD
Member of:	BAC
Quals/training:	Lic.es Psych (Sorbonne, Paris); Dip Couns (Middx Poly); Dip Analytic Group Psychotherapy (WPF)
Personal Therapy:	Ongoing
Supervision:	Ongoing
Counselling offered:	**General, Bereavement, Crisis, Work**
Service for:	Individuals, Couples, Groups
Specific to:	Adolescents, Young adults
Theoretical Approach:	Analytic, Psychodynamic
Other languages:	French, German
Fees:	£20 - £30 sliding scale

NELSON Denise
216 Carr Road, Lloyd Park, Walthamstow, LONDON E17 5EW
Member of:	BAC Acc, BASMT
Quals/training:	BAC Acc; BASMT Acc; Dip Human Sexuality 1989; Dip Theology 1974; Training in Personal Development & Group Skills; Cert Couns (LCIP); Cert Psychosynthesis
Personal Therapy:	Ongoing
Supervision:	Ongoing
Counselling offered:	**General, AIDS, HIV, Sexual, Spiritual**
Service for:	Individuals, Couples, Groups
Specific to:	Gays
Theoretical Approach:	Psychosynthesis, Rogerian
Fees:	£27 £35 couples, negotiable

PENNINGTON Adrian   081 521 3982
CCAPS, 9 Russell Road, Walthamstow, LONDON E17 6QY
Member of:	BAC, AHPP
Quals/training:	Adv Dip Couns; Hons degree Psychol; MA Couns & Psychol; Accredited Sports Psychologist; Memb BASS
Personal Therapy:	Yes
Supervision:	Ongoing
Counselling offered:	**General, Stress, Sexual, Relationship, Sport**
Service for:	Individuals, Couples, Groups
Specific to:	Ethnic minorities, Athletes
Theoretical Approach:	Developmental, Integrative, Cognitive/Behavioural
Fees:	£10 - £35 sliding scale

PERSIGHETTI Teresa   ansaphone 081 556 1245
3 Ivy Road, Walthamstow, LONDON E17 8HX
Member of:	BAC Acc
Quals/training:	BAC Acc; Dip Couns (E London Univ) 1991; CQSW; BA Soc Studies 1976
Personal Therapy:	Yes
Supervision:	Ongoing
Counselling offered:	**General**
Service for:	Individuals, Groups
Specific to:	Women, Adolescents, Ethnic minorities
Theoretical Approach:	Humanistic, TA
Fees:	£15 day; £17.50 after 5pm

London - East

RENWICK John
081 521 2364
48 Hillside Gardens, Walthamstow, LONDON E17 3RJ
Member of:	BAC
Quals/training:	BA; Cert Couns(Roehampton Institute)1982; Cert Youth & Community Work; T A Psychotherapist
Personal Therapy:	Yes
Supervision:	Ongoing
Counselling offered:	**General, Psychotherapy**
Service for:	Individuals, Couples, Groups
Theoretical Approach:	Rogerian, TA, Gestalt
Fees:	£30 ind/cpl(£15/2hr grps negot)

TURNER Pauline
081 523 1051
22 Fleeming Road, Walthamstow, LONDON E17 5ES
Member of:	BAC
Quals/training:	CQSW; Psychotherapy Training (LCIP)
Personal Therapy:	Yes
Supervision:	Yes
Counselling offered:	**General, Psychotherapy**
Service for:	Individuals, Groups
Theoretical Approach:	English school
Fees:	£18 some negotiation

WALTON Patricia
081 523 3582
68 Fleeming Road, Walthamstow, LONDON E17 5ES
Member of:	BAC
Quals/training:	Dip Couns/Psychotherapy; BA Psychol; Memb BHMA
Personal Therapy:	Yes
Supervision:	Ongoing
Counselling offered:	**Psychotherapy, Sexual abuse, Bereavement**
Service for:	Individuals, Groups
Theoretical Approach:	Analytical
Fees:	£18 negotiable

COX Philip
081 520 9391
63 Somerset Road, Walthamstow, LONDON E17 8QN
Member of:	AGIP
Quals/training:	Associate member of AGIP; member of Analytic Psychology Club
Personal Therapy:	Yes
Supervision:	Ongoing
Counselling offered:	**General, Psychotherapy**
Service for:	Individuals, Couples
Theoretical Approach:	Jungian
Fees:	Negotiable

London - East

ELLWOOD Jane　　　　　　　　　　　　　　　　　　081 520 9727
Ground Floor Flat, 46 Upper Walthamstow Road, LONDON E17 3QQ
Member of:	**LCP, ACP**
Quals/training:	BA(Hons) Psychol; Postgraduate Course Child, Adolescent & Family Psychotherapy Tavistock Clinic; Adult Psychotherapy Training (LCP); Leicester Group Relations Conferences
Personal Therapy:	Yes
Supervision:	Ongoing
Counselling offered:	**Psychotherapy**
Service for: Individuals, Specific to:	Groups Adolescents, Staff
Theoretical Approach:	Kleinian
Fees:	£25 low fee £8-12

ANGEL Rita　　　　　　　　　　　　　　　　　　081 530 4422
Flat 7, Half Acre, 67/69 Woodford Road, LONDON E18 2EX
Member of:	**BAC, IPC/WPF**
Quals/training:	NMGC trained 1979-85; 1984-6 CTP
Personal Therapy:	Ongoing
Supervision:	Ongoing
Counselling offered:	**General, Bereavement, Marital, Psychotherapy**
Service for:	Individuals
Theoretical Approach:	Analytic
Fees:	£24 - £26 negotiable

FARUKI Shirley　　　　　　　　　　　　　　　　　081 989 6734
38 Pulteney Road, Woodford, LONDON E18 1PS
Member of:	**BAC, NRHP**
Quals/training:	BA Psychol; Cert Ed; Adv Cert Couns CAC; Dip Hypotherapy & Psychotherapy; Brit Register Complementary Practitioners (Hypnotherapy); Memb APT & BCHE
Personal Therapy:	Unknown
Supervision:	Ongoing
Counselling offered:	**General, Bereavement, Cancer, Hypnotherapy, Stress management, Sexual abuse**
Service for:	Individuals
Theoretical Approach:	Rogerian, Gestalt, Cognitive
Fees:	£30

CLOWES Brenda　　　　　　　　　　　　　　　　081 505 8328
176 Princes Road, BUCKHURST HILL IG9 5DJ
Member of:	**BAC RSup**
Quals/training:	RELATE trained; counsellor and tutor
Personal Therapy:	Yes
Supervision:	Yes
Counselling offered:	**General, Relationship**
Service for:	Individuals, Couples
Theoretical Approach:	Psychodynamic, Person-centred
Fees:	£25 - £35

London - East

Organisations

JEWISH BEREAVEMENT COUNSELLING SERVICE
Ansaphone 081 349 0839, Office 071 387 4300 x 227
1 Cyprus Gardens, Finchley, LONDON N3 1SP

Service:	Bereavement counselling to members of the Jewish community. Counsellors visit bereaved in their own homes
Area served:	NW- SW London & Redbridge
Referral:	Self or others
Training of workers:	Introductory & ongoing group training; regular individual and group supervision
Code of Ethics:	LABS
Management by:	Visitation Committee
Fees:	None

NORTH LONDON PERSONAL CONSULTATION PRACTICE
081 349 9399
17a Templars Crescent, Finchley, LONDON N3 3QR

Service:	Diagnostic assessment and psychoanalytic psychotherapy for people of all ages
Area served:	London & Home Counties
Referral:	Self or others
Training of workers:	Psychotherapists are all members of qualifying professional assocs in individual, marital, family or group psychotherapy
Code of Ethics:	Varies with professional seen
Management by:	Psychotherapists are self-managing independent contractors
Fees:	On application

SPECTRUM
081 341 2277
7 Endymion Road, Finsbury Park, LONDON N4 1EE

Service:	Personal and professional development courses. Individual, couples & family therapy, a full sexuality programme for men & women & an incest project which is a registered charity
Area served:	London
Other languages:	Italian, French
Referral:	Self or others
Training of workers:	Variously qualified, regular supervision, ongoing profess-ional work
Code of Ethics:	BAC
Management by:	Terry Cooper, Jenner Roth, Maggie McKenzie & Rex Bradley
Fees:	£20 - £50 & low-cost programme

NATIONAL SCHOOL OF HYPNOSIS & PSYCHOTHERAPY 071 226 6963
28 Finsbury Park Road, LONDON N4 2JX

Service:	Referrals to N-SHAP graduates who are members in good standing of Central Register of Advanced Hypnotherapists (CRAH)

MIND IN HARINGEY, COUNSELLING SERVICE 081 347 8507
Station House, 73c Stapleton Hall Road, LONDON N4 3QF
Service:	Counselling service for people living in Haringey
Area served:	Haringey
Referral:	Self
Training of workers:	Trained/in training counsellors/psychotherapists. Regular group supervision with external supervisors
Code of Ethics:	BAC
Management by:	Counselling Development Worker, Director & ExecutiveCommittee
Fees:	Contributions negotiated

GROUP ANALYTIC NETWORK 081 340 9597
132 Stapleton Hall Road, Finsbury Park, LONDON N4 4QB
Service:	Group for those with emotional & inter-personal difficulties Following initial consultation, session people are placed in a group or given appropriate individual or couple therapy
Area served:	North, East, Central London
Referral:	Self, Health/Soc Work Professional
Training of workers:	Group Analysts, 4 year training including regular supervision & group therapy. Psychotherapy training (2 members)
Code of Ethics:	IGA
Management by:	Self-management
Fees:	£20 - £25 Cons £25;group £10 - £12.50

ASSOCIATION OF INDEPENDENT PSYCHOTHERAPISTS 071 266 3340
PO Box 1194, LONDON N6 5PW
Service:	Psychotherapy for individuals, couples, groups. Psychotherapy training.
Area served:	UK
Referral:	Self or others
Training of workers:	Various, minimum 3 yrs of training & 4 yrs of personal therapy, 3 times per week. Regular supervision
Code of Ethics:	Agency's own code
Management by:	Members
Fees:	£30 assessment then by arrangement

PROJECT FOR ADVICE, COUNSELLING & EDUCATION, LESBIAN & GAY CENTRE 071 700 1323
c/o London Lesbian & Gay Centr, 2 Shelburne Road, LONDON N7 6DL
Service:	Individual, group, couple & HIV/AIDS couns, art therapy. A couns service for lesbians & gay men provided by lesbians & gay men. Referral to private psychotherapists.
Area served:	London mainly
Referral:	Self
Training of workers:	Counsellors all have basic training & regular supervision, most have had personal therapy
Code of Ethics:	BAC
Management by:	Management Committee
Fees:	Sliding scale, some free

London - North

WOMEN'S THERAPY CENTRE 071 263 6200
6-9 Manor Gardens, Holloway, LONDON N7 6LA

Service:	Individual & group psychotherapy from a feminist perspective Some groups focus on eating disorders, childhood sexual abuse Service for women on low income, lesbians, black/ethnic, disab
Area served:	Islington women given priority but no catchment area
Other languages:	French, German
Referral:	Self or others
Training of workers:	All therapists analytically trained eg Tavistock, Arbours etc Regular supervision
Code of Ethics:	Varies with professional seen
Management by:	Management Committee
Fees:	Negotiable on a sliding scale

HIGHGATE COUNSELLING CENTRE 081 883 5427/8
Tetherdown Halls, Tetherdown, Muswell Hill, LONDON N10

Service:	Short and long term counselling based on psychdynamic model for individuals, couples, groups, families
Area served:	North London
Referral:	Self or others
Training of workers:	By centre (Highgate Certificate), ongoing supervision
Code of Ethics:	BAC
Management by:	Council of management elected at AGM
Fees:	Contribs, guidlines offered

ASSOCIATION FOR ANALYTIC AND BODYMIND THERAPY/TRAINING
081 883 5418
Princes House, 8 Princes Avenue, Muswell Hill, LONDON N10 3LR

Service:	Psychoanalytically oriented psychotherapy, bodymind, hypnoprimary & Gestalt therapy, hypnotherapy, couple & group therapy
Area served:	No restriction
Other languages:	French, German
Referral:	Self or others
Training of workers:	2 year Diploma; personal therapy, weekly group and individual supervision
Code of Ethics:	BAP
Management by:	The Director G Seaborn-Jones PhD, BA(Oxon) Psych
Fees:	£12 - £28 dependent on therapist

COUNSELLING IN NORTH LONDON 081 368 2144
2 Hemington Avenue, Friern Barnet, LONDON N11 3LR

Service:	General & relationship counselling & psychotherapy; specialises in young people, alcohol dependence and eating issues
Area served:	Greater London & Herts
Referral:	Self or others
Training of workers:	All are qualified in counselling and/or psychotherapy; all have had personal therapy & have ongoing supervision
Code of Ethics:	BAC, IPSS
Management by:	Four Associates
Fees:	£25 - £35 negotiable for lower income

NORTH LONDON CENTRE FOR GROUP THERAPY 081 440 1451
138 Bramley Road, Oakgate, Southgate, LONDON N14 4HU
Service: Group analytic psychotherapy, once & twice weekly groups. Individual, marital & family therapy. Centre also offers supervision & organises workshops
Area served: Essentially North London, NW London, Herts
Other languages: German
Referral: Self or others
Training of workers: All therapists graduate members of Institute of Group Analysis, London
Code of Ethics: IGA
Management by: Management jointly by the psychotherapists
Fees: £63 group/per month.Please enquire

LONDON IRISH WOMEN'S CENTRE 071 249 7318
59 Stoke Newington Church St, Hackney, LONDON N16 0AR
Service: Free short-term client-centred counselling to Irish women. Depending on waiting list, contract may be extended up to 6 months. Evening sessions available
Area served: Greater London
Other languages: Irish
Referral: Self, Agencies
Training of workers: Trainee at metanoia. In Diploma preparation year, final year of training
Code of Ethics: BAC
Management by: Voluntary management committee
Fees: Donations, 50p - £6

NE LONDON PSYCHOTHERAPY & COUNSELLING ASSOCIATION
071 249 3110
51 Evering Road, Stoke Newington, LONDON N16 7PU
Service: Long & short term for individuals, couples, groups for a wide range of problems inc emotional crisis, relationships, transcultural issues. Service for all. Initial assessment.
Referral: Self or others
Training of workers: Fully trained psychotherapists (min 3 year training); personal therapy, regular supervision
Code of Ethics: BAC, ITHP, IGA
Management by: Founder members
Fees: £20 - £30 assess £25;grp £45;cpl £40-50

NORTH MIDDLESEX HOSPITAL PSYCHOSEXUAL CLINIC
081 889 4311 x 57
North Middlesex Hospital, Sterling Way, Upper Edmonton, LONDON N18 1QX
Service: Sexual, marital, relationship counselling, brief psycho-therapy
Area served: North London
Referral: Self, Health Practitioner
Training of workers: Institute of Psychosexual Medicine (IPM)
Code of Ethics: IPM, BAC
Management by: NHS

London - North

NORTH LONDON PSYCHOTHERAPY & COUNSELLING ASSOCIATION
071 272 4133
15 Gresley Road, LONDON N19 3LA

Service:	Individual & family couns & psychotherapy for a wide range of problems from depression & anxiety to sexual abuse, marital & relationship difficulties. Clin sup & groupwork
Area served:	North & Central London
Other languages:	Greek
Referral:	Self or others
Training of workers:	Counselling Psychol (BPS) and 4 yr Psychoanalytic Psychotherapy training (GIP).Personal Therapy. Regular Supervision
Code of Ethics:	BAC, Guild of Psychotherapists
Management by:	Group Practice
Fees:	Sliding scale up to £35

CHOICE FWA (Islington)   071 272 1551, 071 263 1181
608 Holloway Road, LONDON N19 3PH

Service:	Individual & couple counselling. Informal drop-in. Support for carers of the frail elderly & people with Alzheimers Disease Befriending for people with long term emotional difficulties
Area served:	Islington & City
Referral:	Self or others
Training of workers:	CQSW or relevant mental health experience. In regular supervision
Code of Ethics:	Agency's own code
Management by:	Area committee answers to parent body
Fees:	None

INDEPENDENT PSYCHOLOGY SERVICE   071 272 3311
17 Lambton Road, Upper Holloway, LONDON N19 3QJ

Service:	A group of chartered clinical psychologists offering psychoanalytic psychotherapy, cognitive-behavioural therapy & counselling to individuals, couples, families & groups
Area served:	North London
Referral:	Self
Training of workers:	All chartered, experienced professional clinical psychologists with NHS & additional psychotherapy training. Regular supervision
Code of Ethics:	BPS
Management by:	Referral group with central co-ordinator
Fees:	£25 - £35 by negotiation

ISLINGTON WOMEN'S COUNSELLING CENTRE   071 281 2673
Eastgate Building, 131B St John's Way, Holloway, LONDON N19 3RQ

Service:	Multicultural feminist agency offering psychodynamic couns for inds & groups. The service has counsellors for Irish & black women & unemployed who have not had couns previously
Area served:	Borough of Islington
Referral:	Self, Health/Soc Work Professional
Training of workers:	Dip Psychodynamic Couns, one trainee counsellor
Code of Ethics:	BAC
Management by:	Management Committee
Fees:	None

London - North

CARE CONCERN 081 446 5418
Counselling Svce League of Jewish Women
120 Oakleigh Road North, Whetstone, LONDON N20 9EZ
Service:	General, bereavement & marital counselling on a regular weekly basis.
Area served:	Greater London
Referral:	Self or others
Training of workers:	Counselling training, regular supervision
Code of Ethics:	BAC
Management by:	Chairman & League of Jewish Women
Fees:	Donations

AIDSLINE 081 366 9187
Highlands Hospital, Worlds End Lane, Winchmore Hill, LONDON N21 1PN
Service:	Counselling, advice, information, support to people affected by HIV/AIDS
Area served:	Enfield and District
Referral:	Self
Training of workers:	All have counsellor training with peer supervision
Code of Ethics:	BAC
Management by:	NHS
Fees:	None

Individual Practitioners

*Every individual is a **member** of one or more organisations eligible for entry into this directory. BAC Accredited Counsellors and Recognised Supervisors are shaded.*

SHATTOCK Avril 081 449 4810
87 Westpole Avenue, Cockfosters, BARNET EN4 0BA
Member of:	BAC
Quals/training:	RELATE Trained 1980; Course (Tavistock Inst) 1986-7; Introductory Groupwork course (IGA) 1990
Personal Therapy:	Ongoing
Supervision:	Ongoing
Counselling offered:	**General, Marital, Relationship, Bereavement**
Service for:	Individuals, Couples
Theoretical Approach:	Psychodynamic, Rogerian
Fees:	£25 negotiable

WHITESON Riva 081 449 2489
93 Westpole Avenue, Cockfosters, BARNET EN4 0BA
Member of:	BAC
Quals/training:	RELATE/NMGC Trained 1980
Personal Therapy:	Ongoing
Supervision:	Ongoing
Counselling offered:	**General, Bereavement, Relationship, Marital, Sexual**
Service for:	Individuals, Couples
Theoretical Approach:	Client-centred, Psychodynamic, Object relations
Fees:	£25

London - North

GORDON Mrs Loekie　　　　　　　　　　　　　　081449 2077
11 Warwick Road, BARNET EN5 5EE
Member of:	BAC, BPS
Quals/training:	BSc(Hons) Psychol (Middx Univ) 1987; Adv Cert Couns (CSCT) 1989; Bereavement training (CSCT)
Personal Therapy:	Yes
Supervision:	Ongoing
Counselling offered:	**General, Bereavement, Trauma, Alcohol, Drugs, HIV, AIDS, Mental health**
Service for:	Individuals, Couples
Specific to:	Adolescents
Theoretical Approach:	Rogerian, Cognitive/Behavioural, Humanistic
Other languages:	French, Dutch
Fees:	£18 - £30 Sliding scale

HUISH Margot　　　　　　　　　　　　　　081 440 4092
96 Hadley Road, New Barnet, BARNET EN5 5QR
Member of:	BAC, BASMT
Quals/training:	BA(Hons); Dip Human Sexuality; Dip Couns (Univ of Herts); HIV Couns Cert; ITEC; BASMT Acc
Personal Therapy:	Yes
Supervision:	Ongoing
Counselling offered:	**General, Sexual, Relationship, Sexual dysfunction**
Service for:	Individuals, Couples
Specific to:	Survivors of sex abuse
Theoretical Approach:	Eclectic, Psychodynamic, Humanistic
Fees:	£30 NHS free

LEROY Eric　　　　　　　　　　　　　　071 278 9740
109 Cloudesley Road, Islington, LONDON N1 0EN
Member of:	BAC
Quals/training:	BA Social Science; Dip Couns (WPF)
Personal Therapy:	Ongoing
Supervision:	Ongoing
Counselling offered:	**General, AIDS, Psychotherapy**
Service for:	Individuals
Specific to:	Gays
Theoretical Approach:	Eclectic
Fees:	£30

KEELING David　　　　　　　　　　　　　　071 278 0869
116 Barnsbury Road, LONDON N1 0ES
Member of:	BAC
Quals/training:	MA Philosophy; Dip Couns (CAC)
Personal Therapy:	Ongoing
Supervision:	Ongoing
Counselling offered:	**General**
Service for:	Individuals
Theoretical Approach:	Jungian, Humanistic, Psychodynamic
Fees:	£24 Negotiable

London - North

VELLACOTT Julia　　　　　　　　　　　　　　　　　　　　071 359 2831
4 Compton Terrace, LONDON N1 2UN
Member of:	LCP
Quals/training:	Psychotherapy training (LCP)
Personal Therapy:	Yes
Supervision:	Ongoing
Counselling offered:	**General, Psychotherapy**
Service for:	Individuals
Theoretical Approach:	Eclectic
Fees:	Negotiable

ISAAKS Cath　　　　　　　　　　　　　　　　　　　　　071 254 0673
97C Mildmay Road, LONDON N1 4PU
Member of:	BAC Acc
Quals/training:	BAC Acc; Dip Ed; Adv Cert (WPF); Adv Course Consultancy (Tavistock Inst)
Personal Therapy:	Ongoing
Supervision:	Ongoing
Counselling offered:	**General, Bereavement, Crisis, Relationship, Educational, Employment, Career, Rape**
Service for:	Individuals, Groups
Specific to:	Parents, Gays, Survivors of sex abuse
Theoretical Approach:	Psychodynamic, Eclectic
Fees:	£25 negotiable

OAKLEY Madeleine　　　　　　　　　　　　　　　　　　071 226 2391
Islington, LONDON N1
Member of:	BAC, Member of UKCP Register, IPSS
Quals/training:	BA(Hons); Cert Ed; training in Psychoanalytic Psychotherapy (IPSS)
Personal Therapy:	Yes
Supervision:	Ongoing
Counselling offered:	**General, Short-term, Long-term, Psychotherapy**
Service for:	Individuals, Couples
Specific to:	Women
Theoretical Approach:	Psychoanalytic
Fees:	£20 - £30

SAMUELS Carole　　　　　　　　　　　　　　　　　　　081 883 7823
14 Deansway, East Finchley, LONDON N2 0JF
Member of:	BAC, LCP
Quals/training:	4 year training in individual adult psychotherapy, LCP accredited; 1 year introductory course, IGA
Personal Therapy:	Yes
Supervision:	Ongoing
Counselling offered:	**Psychotherapy**
Service for:	Individuals
Theoretical Approach:	Jungian, Winnicottian, Psychoanalytic
Fees:	£20 - £30 sliding scale, some reductions

London - North

BARON Yvonne 081 458 2340
47 Holne Chase, East Finchley, LONDON N2 0QG
Member of: BAC Acc
Quals/training: BAC Acc; BA '49; Educational Therapy (Tavistock Clinic) '76; Dip Counselling '81; currently GP counsellor/therapist - Camden FHSA
Personal Therapy: Yes
Supervision: Ongoing
Counselling offered: General, Medical, Educational, Bereavement, AIDS
Service for: Individuals, Couples
Specific to: Children with special needs
Theoretical Approach: Psychodynamic
Other languages: German, Russian
Fees: £30 negotiable

HARNESS Jennifer 081 883 2724
50a Manor Park Road, East Finchley, LONDON N2 0SJ
Member of: BAC Acc
Quals/training: BAC Acc; Dip Couns Skills (SW London College) 1988; MA Couns (Hatfield Poly) 1991
Personal Therapy: Yes
Supervision: Ongoing
Counselling offered: General, Bereavement, Relationship
Service for: Individuals, Groups
Theoretical Approach: Psychodynamic
Fees: £22 negotiable

COHEN Renee ansaphone 081 883 8968
27 Beresford Road, East Finchley, LONDON N2 8AT
Member of: BAC
Quals/training: BA Psychol (Cape Town) 1960; Dip Applied Social Studies - CQSW (London) 1978
Personal Therapy: Ongoing
Supervision: Ongoing
Counselling offered: Psychotherapy, Depression, Anxiety, Shyness, Stress
Service for: Individuals, Couples, Families
Theoretical Approach: Psychoanalytic
Fees: £15 - £25 sliding scale

ROSENFIELD Maxine ansaphone 081 883 5870
10 Elmfield Road, East Finchley, LONDON N2 8EB
Member of: BAC
Quals/training: Dip Therapy (College of Radiographers); Cert Cancer Couns (CAC); Couns Problem Drinkers (Accept); Dip Couns (CSCT); Relapse Prevention Workshop
Personal Therapy: Yes
Supervision: Ongoing
Counselling offered: General, Cancer, Chronic illness, Drinking problems
Service for: Individuals
Specific to: Women
Theoretical Approach: Psychodynamic, Person-centred
Fees: £15 - £25 sliding scale

London - North

GOLDZWEIG Jack   081 883 0454
65 Durham Road, East Finchley, LONDON N2 9DR
Member of: BAC
Quals/training: NMGC/RELATE Acc; CAT Brief Psychotherapy Acc
Personal Therapy: Yes
Supervision: Ongoing
Counselling offered: General, Marital, Anxiety, Depression
Service for: Couples, Individuals
Theoretical Approach: Psychodynamic, Cognitive
Fees: £20 - £30 sliding scale

COHEN Ruth   081 346 5302
14 Church Crescent, Finchley, LONDON N3 1BG
Member of: BAC
Quals/training: Dip Couns Skills SW London College 85
Personal Therapy: Yes
Supervision: Ongoing
Counselling offered: General, Bereavement
Service for: Individuals
Theoretical Approach: Psychodynamic
Fees: £20 negotiable

COOPER Howard   081 349 3891
37 Lansdowne Road, Finchley, LONDON N3 1ET
Member of: AGIP
Quals/training: 11 years experience; 1985 Associate Member AGIP
Personal Therapy: Unknown
Supervision: Ongoing
Counselling offered: Psychotherapy
Service for: Individuals
Specific to: Jewish
Theoretical Approach: Analytical
Fees: £25 - £35 negotiable

COOPER Sara   081 349 3891
37 Lansdowne Road, Finchley, LONDON N3 1ET
Member of: Guild of Psychotherapists
Quals/training: Trained with Guild of Psychotherapists
Personal Therapy: Yes
Supervision: Ongoing
Counselling offered: Psychotherapy, Supervision
Service for: Individuals, Couples
Theoretical Approach: Eclectic, Analytical
Fees: £30 negotiable

London - North

DELROY Dr Sandra   081 346 4010
3 Northumberland House, 237 Ballards Lane, Finchley, LONDON N3 1LB
Member of:	BAC, BPS
Quals/training:	BS; MA Psychol; 1984 PsyD; 1988 Reg C Psychol, Graduated from Illinois School of Professional Psychol (USA); Memb NHS
Personal Therapy:	Ongoing
Supervision:	No
Counselling offered:	**General, Bereavement, Assertiveness, Stress management, Psychotherapy**
Service for:	Individuals, Couples, Families, Groups
Specific to:	People with disabilities, Ethnic minorities
Theoretical Approach:	Psychoanalytic
Fees:	£60

GILDEBRAND Katarina   081 349 9827
25 Grove Avenue, LONDON N3 1QS
Member of:	BAC Acc, ITA
Quals/training:	BAC Acc; Dip Occupational Therapy 1980; 6 yrs training in TA
Personal Therapy:	Ongoing
Supervision:	Ongoing
Counselling offered:	**General, Psychotherapy, Short-term, Long-term**
Service for:	Individuals, Couples, Groups
Theoretical Approach:	TA, Person-centred
Other languages:	Swedish
Fees:	£25 indivs, £15 groups

DAVID Ann   081 349 9827
25 Grove Avenue, Finchely Central, LONDON N3 1QS
Member of:	BAC, ITA, Member of UKCP Regiser
Quals/training:	BSc; MA; Dip Couns Skills (SWLondon Coll) '81; CTA (ITAA)
Personal Therapy:	Ongoing
Supervision:	Ongoing
Counselling offered:	**General, Psychotherapy, Bereavement, Crisis, Personal growth**
Service for:	Individuals, Couples, Groups
Theoretical Approach:	Integrative, TA, Gestalt, Psychodrama
Fees:	£28 individuals; £15 groups

HARLEY Ki   081 349 9827
25 Grove Avenue, Finchley Central, LONDON N3 1QS
Member of:	BAC Acc, ITA
Quals/training:	BAC Acc; Cert Ed; Dip Couns; TA Psychotherapist (EATA)
Personal Therapy:	Ongoing
Supervision:	Ongoing
Counselling offered:	**Psychotherapy, Supervision**
Service for:	Individuals, Couples, Groups
Theoretical Approach:	Integrative
Other languages:	Swedish
Fees:	£30

London - North

MARKS Lesley ansaphone 081 346 2263
13e St Mary's Avenue, Finchley, LONDON N3 1SN
Member of:	BAC
Quals/training:	Post Grad Dip; BA
Personal Therapy:	Ongoing
Supervision:	Ongoing
Counselling offered:	**General, Adoption, Fostering, Bereavement, Crisis**
Service for:	Individuals, Groups
Theoretical Approach:	Person-centred
Other languages:	Hebrew
Fees:	£15 - £30 Sliding Scale

PARKS Val 081 349 1214
18 Rosemary Avenue, LONDON N3 2QN
Member of:	IPC
Quals/training:	Full memb IPC/WPF 1985
Personal Therapy:	Yes
Supervision:	Ongoing
Counselling offered:	**General, Psychotherapy**
Service for:	Individuals
Theoretical Approach:	Psychodynamic
Fees:	£20 negotiable

SINGH Tony 081 449 7433
3 Cumberland Court, Cyprus Road, LONDON N3
Member of:	BAC, BPA
Quals/training:	FACETS training programme for Couns (City Univ) 1988-92; Adv Group Dynamics (Inst of Group Dynamics) 1991-2
Personal Therapy:	Ongoing
Supervision:	Ongoing
Counselling offered:	**General, Depression, Phobias**
Service for:	Individuals, Couples
Specific to:	Adolescents, Ethnic minorities
Theoretical Approach:	Holistic, Existential, Gestalt
Fees:	£15 - £30 sliding scale

HOLLINGS Avril 081 341 7214
Spectrum, 7 Endymion Road, LONDON N4 1EE
Member of:	BAC
Quals/training:	BA; PGCE; Spectrum 1 yr course in Psychotherapy; Practitioner Cert in Holistic Massage
Personal Therapy:	Ongoing
Supervision:	Ongoing
Counselling offered:	**General, Bodywork, Abuse, Co-dependency, Self-esteem, Stress management**
Service for:	Individuals, Groups, Organisations
Specific to:	Women, Gays, Teachers
Theoretical Approach:	Humanistic, Integrative
Fees:	£30 some concessions

London - North

DRIVER Christine 081 340 3324
71 Umfreville Road, Harringay, LONDON N4 1RZ
Member of:	**BAC, IPC, Member of UKCP Register**
Quals/training:	BSc; Memb (Psychotherapy) IPC/WPF 1982; Dip in Supervision (WPF)
Personal Therapy:	Ongoing
Supervision:	Ongoing
Counselling offered:	**General, Bereavement, Psychotherapy**
Service for:	Individuals
Theoretical Approach:	Jungian, Kleinian
Fees:	£25 negotiable

MAYNES Paddy (Ms) 081 809 1230
48 Gloucester Drive, Finsbury Park, LONDON N4 2LN
Member of:	**BAC Acc**
Quals/training:	BAC Acc; BA Lib; Cert Couns (Lincoln Centre) 1988; Dip Adult Couns (London Univ) 1990
Personal Therapy:	Ongoing
Supervision:	Ongoing
Counselling offered:	**General**
Service for:	Individuals, Couples
Theoretical Approach:	Psychodynamic, Analytical
Fees:	£20 - £25 sliding scale

BRATERMAN Eleanor 081 802 9206
36e Portland Rise, LONDON N4 2PP
Member of:	**CRAH**
Quals/training:	MA; Dip EHP NLP; MCRAH
Personal Therapy:	Yes
Supervision:	Ongoing
Counselling offered:	**Hypnotherapy, General**
Service for:	Individuals, Couples, Groups, Organisations
Theoretical Approach:	Ericksonian, NLP, Holistic
Fees:	£35 Concessions

MHLONGO Anne 071 354 0436
126a Wilberforce Road, LONDON N4 2SU
Member of:	**IGA**
Quals/training:	IGA 1981
Personal Therapy:	Ongoing
Supervision:	Ongoing
Counselling offered:	**General, Relationship, Psychotherapy**
Service for:	Individuals, Couples, Groups
Theoretical Approach:	Analytic, Group analytic
Fees:	£18 - £25 (£11-£14 grps)

London - North

HEWSON Jan Ms 071 359 7671
Finsbury Park, LONDON N4
Member of:	BAC, AHPP
Quals/training:	Dip in Couns, CSCT; ongoing training in Humanistic therapies
Personal Therapy:	Yes
Supervision:	Ongoing
Counselling offered:	General, Crisis, PTSD, Personal growth
Service for:	Individuals
Theoretical Approach:	Person-centred
Fees:	£20 negotiable

LISTER Patricia 071 281 3646
23 Wray Crescent, Islington, Finsbury Park, LONDON N4 3LN
Member of:	BAC
Quals/training:	BA (London); MSc (Surrey); Adv Dip Couns & Health Care (RSH, London); PhD Couns, Psychol & Educational Therapy (Clayton Univ, Missouri)
Personal Therapy:	Yes
Supervision:	Ongoing
Counselling offered:	General, Bereavement, Anxiety
Service for:	Individuals, Couples, Groups, Families
Specific to:	Children
Theoretical Approach:	Humanistic, Cognitive, Behavioural
Fees:	£25 - £40

FLINSPACH Elisabeth 071 263 2098
LONDON N4
Member of:	BAC, ITHP, BPA
Quals/training:	Trained in Humanistic & Analytic Psychotherapy(Minster Centre); Assertiveness Trainer(Redwood)
Personal Therapy:	Ongoing
Supervision:	Ongoing
Counselling offered:	General, Relationship, Crisis, Bereavement, Assertiveness
Service for:	Individuals, Couples, Groups
Specific to:	Women
Theoretical Approach:	Psychodynamic, Eclectic
Other languages:	German
Fees:	£18 - £25 negotiable

KELLY Michael 081 340 9597
132 Stapleton Hall Road, Finsbury Park, LONDON N4 4QB
Member of:	ARBAS, IGA, AFT
Quals/training:	Group Analyst Memb (IGA); Qualified Psychotherapist (Arbours Assoc)
Personal Therapy:	Yes
Supervision:	Ongoing
Counselling offered:	General, Marital, Bereavement, Phobias
Service for:	Individuals, Couples, Groups, Families
Theoretical Approach:	Psychodynamic, Group analysis
Fees:	£20 negotiable, Groups £12

London - North

HERSHMAN Claire Odeon　　　　　　　　　　　　　　071 226 9218
9 Aberdeen Road, Highbury, LONDON N5
Member of:	BAC
Quals/training:	BA (Hons); Dip Couns (CNAA) 1989; NELP St Thomas Hospital; Post Grad Dip Couns (Univ East London) 1992
Personal Therapy:	Ongoing
Supervision:	Ongoing
Counselling offered:	**General, Psychotherapy, Communication skills, Relationship**
Service for:	Individuals, Families, Groups
Theoretical Approach:	Psychodynamic, Jungian, Cognitive, Analytic
Fees:	Sliding scale, negotiable

HOPE Joyce　　　　　　　　　　　　　　071 226 2251
28 Highbury Hill, Highbury, LONDON N5 1AL
Member of:	BAC
Quals/training:	BA; Dip Soc Sci & Pub Admin; Mental Health Cert
Personal Therapy:	Yes
Supervision:	Ongoing
Counselling offered:	**General, Cancer, Problem solving, Short-term, Relationship**
Service for:	Individuals
Specific to:	Parents, Children
Theoretical Approach:	Humanistic
Fees:	£15 - £25 sliding scale

YOUNG Margot　　　　　　　　　　　　　　071 704 8876
132 Highbury Hill, Highbury, LONDON N5 1AT
Member of:	**BAC, ITHP, Member of UKCP Register**
Quals/training:	BA; Dip Psychotherapy (Minster Centre) 1990
Personal Therapy:	Yes
Supervision:	Ongoing
Counselling offered:	**General, Psychotherapy**
Service for:	Individuals, Couples, Organisations
Theoretical Approach:	Integrative
Fees:	Negotiable

MEREDEEN Shirley　　　　　　　　　　　　　　071 359 9859
Flat 3, 4 Highbury Place, Highbury, LONDON N5 1QZ
Member of:	BAC
Quals/training:	BA; Dip Couns Skills (SW London College) 1986; Cert Conciliation in Divorce & Separation (Poly North London)
Personal Therapy:	Ongoing
Supervision:	Ongoing
Counselling offered:	**General, Crisis, Redundancy, Marital, Conciliation**
Service for:	Individuals, Couples, Groups
Theoretical Approach:	Humanistic, Eclectic
Fees:	£15 - £25

London - North

NAISH Julia 071 354 0612
45 Highbury Hill, Highbury, LONDON N5 1SU
Member of: BAC
Quals/training: PhD; 1 yr course in Psychotherapy 1986, Postgrad Course in Psychotherapy 1989, Relationship Skills Training 1990 (Spectrum); currently training with Gestalt Inst of Miami
Personal Therapy: Ongoing
Supervision: Ongoing
Counselling offered: **General, Relationship, Work, Career, Psychotherapy**
Service for: Individuals, Couples, Groups
Theoretical Approach: Humanistic
Fees: £40

HEMMING Judith 071 359 3000
79 Ronalds Road, LONDON N5 1XB
Member of: **GPTI, AHPP, Member of UKCP Register**
Quals/training: Dip Psychotherapy (GPTI) 1992; Dip Gestalt Therapy & AHPP Acc 1991; MA(Oxon) 1970; PGCE 1972; RELATE trained 1990
Personal Therapy: Ongoing
Supervision: Ongoing
Counselling offered: **Psychotherapy, Marital, Supervision**
Service for: Individuals, Couples, Groups, Organisations
Theoretical Approach: Gestalt
Fees: £30 - £40 sliding scale

WIGHAM Avril 071 354 1603
Highbury, LONDON N5
Member of: PET
Quals/training: BA(Hons)Psychol; Dip Psychosynthesis; Dip Art Therapy
Personal Therapy: Yes
Supervision: Ongoing
Counselling offered: **General, Art therapy, Relaxation**
Service for: Individuals, Groups
Theoretical Approach: Psychosynthesis, Art therapy, Rebirthing
Fees: £30

TIMBER Jennifer 071 359 8979
90b Petherton Road, LONDON N5 2RG
Member of: BAC
Quals/training: BA Eng; Dip Careers Service Training Board; Dip Couns London Univ
Personal Therapy: Ongoing
Supervision: Ongoing
Counselling offered: **General**
Service for: Individuals
Theoretical Approach: Psychoanalytic
Fees: £20 - £30 negotiable

London - North

BERGER Noemi 081 341 0071
37 High Sheldon, Sheldon Avenue, Highgate, LONDON N6 4JR
Member of:	BAC
Quals/training:	BA Social Work; MSW Psychiatric Social Work; training in Marital Therapy, Art therapy, Groupwork, Short Term Therapy
Personal Therapy:	Yes
Supervision:	Ongoing
Counselling offered:	**General, Relationship, Marital, Mixed faith marriages**
Service for:	Individuals, Couples, Groups
Theoretical Approach:	Person-centred, Eclectic
Other languages:	Hebrew
Fees:	£25 Sliding scale

BALFOUR Joan 081 348 4331
17b North Grove, Highgate, LONDON N6 4SH
Member of:	BAC
Quals/training:	BA; NMGC trained 1976-9; Licentiate of College of Traditional Chinese Acupuncture (UK)
Personal Therapy:	No
Supervision:	Ongoing
Counselling offered:	**General, Marital**
Service for:	Individuals, Couples
Theoretical Approach:	Analytical
Fees:	£30

BULMAN Brian 081 348 6211
8 Melisa Court, 21 Avenue Road, Highgate, LONDON N6 5DH
Member of:	BAC, MPTI
Quals/training:	Training in Person-Centred Couns (metanoia) 1992-3
Personal Therapy:	Yes
Supervision:	Ongoing
Counselling offered:	**General**
Specific to:	Managers, Gays
Theoretical Approach:	Person-centred, Rogerian
Fees:	£15 - £30 Sliding scale

MONTUSCHI Olivia 081 341 0406
32 Cholmeley Crescent, Highgate, LONDON N6 5HA
Member of:	BAC
Quals/training:	BEd(London); Dip Couns (AEB); Intro courses (IGA & TIMS)
Personal Therapy:	Yes
Supervision:	Ongoing
Counselling offered:	**General, Parenting problems, Bereavement**
Service for:	Individuals, Couples, Groups
Specific to:	Parents, Women
Theoretical Approach:	Psychodynamic, Integrative
Fees:	£15 - £30 Sliding Scale

London - North

SIMMONDS Gail   081 340 4837
58 Priory Gardens, Highgate, LONDON N6 5QS
Member of:	BAC
Quals/training:	BA; MA, CQSW; Pre-clinical Child Psychotherapy Training (Tavistock Clinic)
Personal Therapy:	Yes
Supervision:	Ongoing
Counselling offered:	**General, Relationship, Work, Bereavement**
Service for:	Individuals
Theoretical Approach:	Psychodynamic
Fees:	£25

NIGHTINGALE Eileen   071 794 0321
Flat 1, 60 Shepherds Hill, Highgate, LONDON N6 5RN
Member of:	BAC
Quals/training:	Dip Psychosynthesis Counselling & Therapy; training in Gestalt & Bio-energetics
Personal Therapy:	Yes
Supervision:	Ongoing
Counselling offered:	**General, Abuse, Bereavement, Inner child, Substance abuse, Co-dependency**
Service for:	Individuals
Theoretical Approach:	Psychosynthesis, Gestalt, Bioenergetic
Fees:	£15 - £25 sliding scale

BRAVE Anna   081 340 9137
59 Holmesdale Road, Highgate, LONDON N6 5TH
Member of:	ISF, IPSS
Quals/training:	BEd; Couns Skills(N London Poly); 3 Year training (IPSS); Registered Psychanalytic Psychotherapist ISA; IPSS Assoc
Personal Therapy:	Ongoing
Supervision:	Ongoing
Counselling offered:	**Psychotherapy**
Service for:	Individuals
Theoretical Approach:	Analytic
Fees:	£15 - £30 sliding scale

SMITH Jonathan   081 340 9137
59 Holmesdale Road, Highgate, LONDON N6 5TH
Member of:	IPSS
Quals/training:	1976 CQSW; 1987 completed 3 year training (IPSS); 1988 Registered Inner Child acvocate (ISA)
Personal Therapy:	Ongoing
Supervision:	Ongoing
Counselling offered:	**General, Psychotherapy**
Service for:	Individuals
Theoretical Approach:	Psychodynamic
Fees:	£20 - £25 negotiable

London - North

ANKER Ofra   081 341 4413
13 Oldfield Mews, Highgate, LONDON N6 5XA
Member of:	BAC, Member of UKCP Register
Quals/training:	Qualified in Psychosynthesis Couns 1986-89; qualified in Psychosynthesis Psychotherapy 1990
Personal Therapy:	Ongoing
Supervision:	Ongoing
Counselling offered:	**General, Relationship, Crisis, Depression**
Service for:	Individuals, Couples, Groups
Theoretical Approach:	Psychosynthesis
Other languages:	Hebrew
Fees:	£25 - £30 negotiable

PALMER-BARNES Fiona   081 340 1493
4 Pond Square, Highgate, LONDON N6 6BA
Member of:	BAC, IPC, AJA
Quals/training:	BA(Hons); PGCE; Prof Memb IPC/WPF; AJA trained
Personal Therapy:	Yes
Supervision:	Ongoing
Counselling offered:	**General, Psychotherapy, Analysis, Midlife**
Service for:	Individuals
Specific to:	Young people
Theoretical Approach:	Jungian, Analytical, Psychodynamic
Fees:	£30 negotiable according to means

CLOUTTE Penny   071 607 7095
40A Huddleston Road, LONDON N7 0AG
Member of:	BAC
Quals/training:	BA (Hons) Soc Studies; Dip Couns; 6 yrs in self-help therapy group; Feminist Psychodynamic input from WTC
Personal Therapy:	Yes
Supervision:	Ongoing
Counselling offered:	**General, Abuse**
Service for:	Individuals, Groups, Organisations
Specific to:	Women, Mothers
Theoretical Approach:	Rogerian, Psychodynamic
Other languages:	French, Spanish, Portuguese
Fees:	£15 - £30 sliding scale

WOOLFENDEN Jennifer   071 607 5339
36 Huddleston Road, Holloway, LONDON N7 0AG
Member of:	BAC
Quals/training:	BA(Hons)German & Italian (London Univ); CQSW (Nottingham Univ)1967; Dip Adult Couns (London Univ)1990
Personal Therapy:	Ongoing
Supervision:	Ongoing
Counselling offered:	**Depression, Loss, Eating disorders, Assessment**
Service for:	Individuals
Theoretical Approach:	Analytic
Fees:	£15 - £25 sliding scale

London - North

GRAY Nigel   071 607 1823
The Garden Flat, 65 Anson Road, Tufnell Park, LONDON N7 0AS
Member of:	CCHP
Quals/training:	BSc(Hons) Psychol; Cert Holistic Psychotherapy (Chiron); Cert Biodynamic Massage
Personal Therapy:	Ongoing
Supervision:	Ongoing
Counselling offered:	**General, Relationship, Sexual, Psychotherapy, Bodywork**
Service for:	Individuals
Theoretical Approach:	Eclectic
Fees:	£25 negotiable

O'CONNOR Noreen   071 700 2625
125 Tufnell Park Road, LONDON N7 0PS
Member of:	PA
Quals/training:	MA; PhD; Dip Analytical Psychotherapy
Personal Therapy:	Yes
Supervision:	Ongoing
Counselling offered:	**Psychotherapy**
Service for:	Individuals, Couples
Theoretical Approach:	Psychoanalytic
Fees:	£25 - £30

YORKE Kathy   081 881 1871
18 Alexandra Road, Hornsey, LONDON N8 0PP
Member of:	BAC
Quals/training:	Cert Psychotherapeutic Couns(Highgate Couns Centre)
Personal Therapy:	Ongoing
Supervision:	Ongoing
Counselling offered:	**General, Bereavement, Loss, Relationship**
Service for:	Individuals
Theoretical Approach:	Psychodynamic
Fees:	£18 - £26

NOBLE Jane   081 348 2801
54 Redston Road, Hornsey, LONDON N8 7HE
Member of:	**Guild of Psychotherapists**
Quals/training:	Trained with RELATE & WPF; Memb Guild of Psychotherapists
Personal Therapy:	Yes
Supervision:	Ongoing
Counselling offered:	**General, Psychotherapy**
Service for:	Individuals, Couples
Theoretical Approach:	Psychoanalytic
Fees:	£20 - £30

London - North

DUFFELL Nicholas 081 341 4885
128a Northview Road, Hornsey, LONDON N8 7LP
Member of:	IPS
Quals/training:	BA Oxon; Dip Psychotherapy IP Acc; Family Conciliator
Personal Therapy:	Ongoing
Supervision:	Ongoing
Counselling offered:	General, Relationship, Psychotherapy, Management, Supervision
Service for:	Individuals, Couples, Families, Organisations
Theoretical Approach:	Psychosynthesis, Family therapy
Fees:	£30

CRIDDLE Felicity 081 340 4515
7 Edison Road, LONDON N8 8AE
Member of:	BAC
Quals/training:	Dip Occupational Therapy; BA (Hons) Soc Psychol; Cert Couns (Analytic); Dip Couns (Eclectic); training in Analytical Psychotherapy
Personal Therapy:	Ongoing
Supervision:	Ongoing
Counselling offered:	General, Bereavement, Relationship, Crisis, Cross/multi-cultural
Service for:	Individuals
Specific to:	Women, Students, Young people, People with disabilities
Theoretical Approach:	Eclectic
Other languages:	French
Fees:	Negotiable

GOODRICH Diana 081 340 6397
16 Clifton Road, Hornsey, LONDON N8 8JA
Member of:	BAC, IPC
Quals/training:	BA(Hons); Cert Ed; Dip Advanced Psychodynamic Couns (WPF)
Personal Therapy:	Yes
Supervision:	Ongoing
Counselling offered:	General, Short-term, Long-term
Service for:	Individuals
Theoretical Approach:	Psychodynamic
Fees:	£25 average

ELSON Melinda 081 340 4340
64D Rokesly Avenue, LONDON N8 8NH
Member of:	Minster
Quals/training:	BA Psychol; BA Fine Arts; Dip Art Ed; Spectrum Psychotherapy Course 1987; Post-grad Course 1989; The Minster Centre 1990-present
Personal Therapy:	Ongoing
Supervision:	Ongoing
Counselling offered:	General, Relationship
Service for:	Individuals, Groups
Specific to:	Women
Theoretical Approach:	Humanistic, Psychodynamic
Fees:	£10 - £30 sliding scale

London - North

CHAMLEE-COLE Laurena　　　　　　　　　　　　　081 340 8156
38 Middle Lane, Crouch End, LONDON N8 8PG
Member of:	**BAC, ANLP (PCS)**
Quals/training:	NLP Master Practitioner; Cert California State Hypnotherapist; Dip Adv Ericksonian Hypnotherapy
Personal Therapy:	Ongoing
Supervision:	Ongoing
Counselling offered:	**General, Obsessions, Phobias, Hypnotherapy, Relationship**
Service for:	Individuals, Couples, Groups, Organisations
Theoretical Approach:	Eclectic, Client-centred, Cognitive
Fees:	£40 negotiable

HESSEL Susan　　　　　　　　　　　　　　　　　081 340 1465
10 Ivy Gardens, Hornsey, LONDON N8 9JE
Member of:	**BAC**
Quals/training:	BSoc Sc; MSc; CQSW 1980; Cert Psychotherapeutic Couns (Highgate Couns Centre)
Personal Therapy:	Yes
Supervision:	Ongoing
Counselling offered:	**General, Relationship**
Service for:	Individuals
Fees:	£20

RAM Elizabeth　　　　　　　　　　　　　　　　　081 340 4240
12 Uplands Road, Hornsey, LONDON N8 9NL
Member of:	**BAC, LCP**
Quals/training:	In-service Training RF '78; Dip Art Therapy '81; Cert Analytical Psychotherapy(LCP)'86
Personal Therapy:	Yes
Supervision:	Ongoing
Counselling offered:	**Art therapy, Psychotherapy**
Service for:	Individuals
Theoretical Approach:	Eclectic, Analytical
Fees:	£22 - £28 sliding scale

BAUGHAN Richard　　　　　　　　　　　　　　　081 342 9040
Flat B, 13B Weston Park, Crouch End, LONDON N8 9SY
Member of:	**BAC**
Quals/training:	BSc; Dip Couns; Dip Humanistic Psychol; Cert Couns Skills & Attitudes
Personal Therapy:	Yes
Supervision:	Ongoing
Counselling offered:	**General, Psychotherapy**
Service for:	Individuals
Theoretical Approach:	Humanistic, Client-centred
Fees:	£15 - £35

London - North

MORDECAI Aslan   081 883 9665
76 Grove Avenue, Muswell Hill, LONDON N10 2AN
Member of:	BAP
Quals/training:	PhD Psychol; AFBPsS
Personal Therapy:	Yes
Supervision:	No
Counselling offered:	**Psychotherapy, Analysis**
Service for:	Individuals
Theoretical Approach:	Eclectic, Freudian, Kleinian
Fees:	£25 - £30

MORDECAI Kay   081 883 9665
76 Grove Avenue, Muswell Hill, LONDON N10 2AN
Member of:	BAP
Quals/training:	PhD Psychol (Lond Univ); AFBPsS.
Personal Therapy:	Yes
Supervision:	Ongoing
Counselling offered:	**Psychotherapy, Analysis**
Service for:	Individuals
Theoretical Approach:	Eclectic, Freudian, Kleinian
Fees:	£20 - £25

ELDER Penny   081 883 3399
24 Muswell Road, Muswell Hill, LONDON N10 2BG
Member of:	LCP
Quals/training:	BA(Hons) Sociol; Dip Ed Couns Skills 73-81; Cert Analytic Psychotherapy LCP '87; Supervisor/Trainer at Counselling Centre & for Cruse
Personal Therapy:	Yes
Supervision:	Ongoing
Counselling offered:	**Psychotherapy**
Service for:	Individuals, Couples
Theoretical Approach:	Psychoanalytic, Kleinian
Fees:	£20 - £30 sliding scale

YENDELL Bridget   081 883 0343
Heathside Counselling Service, 4 Coniston Road, Muswell Hill, LONDON N10 2BP
Member of:	BAC
Quals/training:	MA Oxon; Qualified teacher; Dip Hum Psych (IDHP); Dip in Individual & Relationship Couns
Personal Therapy:	Yes
Supervision:	Ongoing
Counselling offered:	**General, Supervision**
Service for:	Individuals, Couples, Families, Groups
Theoretical Approach:	Person-centred, Integrative
Fees:	£25 (Initial session £5)

London - North

MARSHALL Antoinette   081 444 9357
73 Alexandra Park Road, LONDON N10 2DG
Member of:	BAC, IPSS
Quals/training:	1984 Diploma in Psychotherapy (IPSS)
Personal Therapy:	Ongoing
Supervision:	Ongoing
Counselling offered:	Psychotherapy, Bodywork, Relaxation
Service for:	Individuals, Couples, Groups
Specific to:	Ethnic minorities
Theoretical Approach:	Psychodynamic, Analytical, Existential, Integrative
Other languages:	French
Fees:	£18 - £25 sliding scale

ENGEL-MADISON Rachel   081 444 8790
314 Dukes Mews, Muswell Hill, LONDON N10 2QP
Member of:	BAC Acc
Quals/training:	BAC Acc; trained in Rogerian, Egan, Person-centred and Psychodynamic counselling
Personal Therapy:	Ongoing
Supervision:	Ongoing
Counselling offered:	General, Bereavement, Stress, Relationship, Abuse
Service for:	Individuals, Couples
Theoretical Approach:	Person-centred, Egan, Rogerian
Other languages:	Afrikaans, Italian
Fees:	Negotiable

CROSS Vara   081 883 7607
Curzon Road, Muswell Hill, LONDON N10
Member of:	BAC
Quals/training:	Cert Couns(LCIP)'82; Dip Couns (SW London College)'85; Cert Psychodynamic Couns(Highgate Couns Centre)'88
Personal Therapy:	Yes
Supervision:	Ongoing
Counselling offered:	General, Bereavement
Service for:	Individuals
Specific to:	Women, Ethnic minorities
Theoretical Approach:	Analytical, Existential
Other languages:	Italian
Fees:	£15 - £18

TILLER Brenda Leo   081 883 3218
82a Cranley Gardens, Muswell Hill, LONDON N10 3AH
Member of:	NSHAP, CRAH
Quals/training:	MCAHyp; 1983 Dip Therapeutic Hypnosis & Advanced Psycotherapy (SHAP); ICM Reg; Corp of Advanced Hypnotherapy
Personal Therapy:	Yes
Supervision:	Ongoing
Counselling offered:	Hypnotherapy, Psychotherapy, Hypnohealing
Service for:	Individuals
Theoretical Approach:	Ericksonian, Elman
Fees:	£35

London - North

COWLING Sue 081 444 8084
28 Cranley Gardens, Muswell Hill, LONDON N10 3AP
Member of:	BAC
Quals/training:	Dip Couns; training in TA, Gestalt (metanoia)
Personal Therapy:	Ongoing
Supervision:	Ongoing
Counselling offered:	**General, Adoption, Bereavement**
Service for:	Individuals, Couples, Families
Specific to:	Adoptees, Adoptors
Theoretical Approach:	Rogerian, TA, Gestalt
Fees:	£20 sliding scale

CHRISTOPHER Elphis Dr 081 883 0085
Muswell Hill, LONDON N10
Member of:	BAC, Institute of Psychosexual Medicine, BAP
Quals/training:	MB.BS; Psychotherapist (BAP)
Personal Therapy:	Ongoing
Supervision:	Ongoing
Counselling offered:	**General, Marital, Sexual, Psychotherapy**
Service for:	Individuals, Couples
Theoretical Approach:	Analytical, Jungian
Fees:	£25 - £30

RENTOUL Lynette 081 883 3687, 071 872 3021
27 Pages Hill, Muswell Hill, LONDON N10 1PX
Member of:	BPS, BAP, Member of UKCP Register
Quals/training:	BSc; MSc Clinical Psychology; C Psychol; Cert Seminars in Psychotherapy (Tavistock Clinic); Cruse counsellor/ supervisor; BAP (Student Member); C Health Psychol; AFBPsS
Personal Therapy:	Ongoing
Supervision:	Ongoing
Counselling offered:	**General, Crisis, Bereavement, Psychotherapy**
Service for:	Individuals, Couples, Families, Groups
Theoretical Approach:	Psychodynamic
Other languages:	French
Fees:	£25 - £30 sliding scale

SHAPIRO Ilona 081 444 6211
7 Muswell Hill Road, LONDON N10 3JB
Member of:	BAC
Quals/training:	BA; Secondary Teachers Dip; Cert Couns (Highgate Counselling Centre) 1981
Personal Therapy:	Yes
Supervision:	Ongoing
Counselling offered:	**General**
Service for:	Individuals, Couples
Theoretical Approach:	Eclectic
Fees:	Negotiable

London - North

FAGIN Anthony　　　　　　　　　　　　　　　　　　　　　081 883 6885
31 Onslow Gardens, Muswell Hill, LONDON N10 3JT
Member of:　　　　　　BAC Acc
Quals/training:　　　　　BAC Acc; 1979-84 training at ITA; 1984 course in Group Work (IGA)
Personal Therapy:　　　Yes
Supervision:　　　　　　Ongoing
Counselling offered:　General
Service for:　　　　　　 Individuals, Couples
Theoretical Approach:　Rogerian, TA
Fees:　　　　　　　　　 £18 per hour

SEABORN-JONES Glyn　　　　　　　　　　　　　　　　　081 883 5418
8 Princes Avenue, Muswell Hill, LONDON N10 3LR
Member of:　　　　　　BAP
Quals/training:　　　　　BA Oxon; PhD Psychol & Philosophy; Director Assoc for Analytic & Bodymind Therapy & Training
Personal Therapy:　　　Ongoing
Supervision:　　　　　　Ongoing
Counselling offered:　General, Sexual, Relationship, Psychotherapy
Service for:　　　　　　 Individuals, Couples, Families, Groups
Theoretical Approach:　Gestalt, Hypnotherapy
Other languages:　　　 French, German
Fees:　　　　　　　　　 sliding scale

SHAER Madeleine　　　　　　　　　　　　　　　　　　　081 883 2651
Flat 2, Woodside, Fortis Green, Muswell Hill, LONDON N10 3NY
Member of:　　　　　　BAC
Quals/training:　　　　　NMGC/RELATE Trained; Psychosexual Couns Dip (London Inst for Study of Human Sexuality) 1985; Cert AIDS/HIV Couns (THT) 1989
Personal Therapy:　　　Yes
Supervision:　　　　　　Ongoing
Counselling offered:　General, Sexual, Relationship, AIDS
Service for:　　　　　　 Individuals, Couples, Groups
Theoretical Approach:　Rogerian, TA, Eclectic
Fees:　　　　　　　　　 £20 - £35 sliding scale

KESHET-ORR Judi　　　　　　　　　　　　　　 ansaphone 081 444 9217
Lancaster House, 583 High Road, Tottenham, LONDON N17
Member of:　　　　　　BAC, AHPP, BASMT
Quals/training:　　　　　Dip Hum Psyche (IDHP); Dip Hum Sex (St George's Hosp); Cert Couns (Middx Poly); PG Cert Psychotherapy (Spectrum) & CSS (W London); Wkshp leader's training (WTC); Memb ICM
Personal Therapy:　　　Yes
Supervision:　　　　　　Ongoing
Counselling offered:　Psychosexual, Personal growth, Sexuality, Psychotherapy
Service for:　　　　　　 Individuals, Couples, Families, Groups, Organisations
Specific to:　　　　　　 Survivors of sex abuse
Theoretical Approach:　Humanistic, Behavioural
Fees:　　　　　　　　　 £25 - £50 indivs & couples

London - North

NAIK Raman   081 368 8633
15 Lower Maidstone Road, New Southgate, LONDON N11 2RU

Member of:	BAC
Quals/training:	MA; Cert Couns (LCIP) 1980; Mental Health Theories & Therapies (Goldsmith's) 1979; Dip School of Psychotherapy & Hypnotherapy, IMP (Bombay) '82; PGCE (Leicester)
Personal Therapy:	Yes
Supervision:	Ongoing
Counselling offered:	**General, Marital, Sexual, Bereavement, Psychotherapy**
Service for:	Individuals, Couples, Groups, Families
Theoretical Approach:	Cognitive/Behavioural, Psychodynamic
Other languages:	Gujerati, Hindi, Urdu, Punjabi
Fees:	£20 - £25

CONSTANTINOU Lydia   081 881 1063
5 Deanswood, Maidstone Road, Bounds Green, LONDON N11 2TQ

Member of:	BAC
Quals/training:	FACETS training programme for counsellors (City Univ) 1988- 92
Personal Therapy:	Ongoing
Supervision:	Ongoing
Counselling offered:	**General**
Theoretical Approach:	Eclectic, Person-centred
Fees:	Negotiable, below £20

REGIS Steve   081 361 1693
11 St Johns Avenue, Friern Barnet, LONDON N11 3BX

Member of:	BAC Acc, BPS
Quals/training:	BAC Acc; BPs (Affil); British Association of Social Functioning; BD; CQSW; Lecturer/Practitioner Human Social Functioning (HSF)
Personal Therapy:	Yes
Supervision:	Ongoing
Counselling offered:	**General, Disability, Stress management, Psychotherapy**
Service for:	Individuals, Couples, Groups, Organisations
Theoretical Approach:	Person-centred
Fees:	£20 - £30 negotiable

OVERTON David   081 368 2144
2 Hemington Avenue, Friern Barnet, New Southgate, LONDON N11 3LR

Member of:	BAC, AHPP
Quals/training:	NMGC/RELATE Trained; Dip Couns (SW London College) 1983
Personal Therapy:	Yes
Supervision:	Ongoing
Counselling offered:	**General, Marital, Relationship, Alcohol**
Service for:	Individuals, Couples, Groups
Specific to:	Young people
Theoretical Approach:	Psychodynamic, Person-centred
Fees:	£25 - £30 reduced in cases of need

London - North

LEWIN Susan 071 320 1370, 081 349 3236
43 Bow Lane, Finchley, LONDON N12 0JL
Member of: BAC
Quals/training: MA; Dip Couns; training in Family Therapy
Personal Therapy: Yes
Supervision: Ongoing
Counselling offered: **General, Bereavement, Marital, Psychotherapy**
Service for: Individuals, Couples, Families
Specific to: Asian, Students, Women
Theoretical Approach: Integrative, Systemic, Transpersonal
Fees: £30 negotiable

KLEIN Valentina 081 446 1157
2 The Garth, Holden Road, North Finchley, LONDON N12 7DL
Member of: BAC, BPS
Quals/training: BSc(Hons); MSc; Dip Psychol Couns; Practitioner Memb BPS
Personal Therapy: Ongoing
Supervision: Ongoing
Counselling offered: **Psychotherapy, Vocational**
Service for: Individuals, Couples
Specific to: Police
Theoretical Approach: Analytical
Fees: £25 - £30

STOLZENBERG Jenny 081 446 5574
4 Steynings Way, North Finchley, LONDON N12 7LN
Member of: BAC Acc
Quals/training: BAC Acc; RELATE trained; Dip Creative Arts Therapy; Cert in Advanced Gestalt Therapy; studying for MA (Couns)(Herts Univ)'93-'04
Personal Therapy: Ongoing
Supervision: Ongoing
Counselling offered: **General, Short-term, Long-term**
Service for: Individuals, Couples, Groups
Theoretical Approach: Rogerian, Gestalt
Fees: £25 negotiable

MAUGER Benig 081 446 4854
27 Westbury Road, Finchley, LONDON N12 7NY
Member of: BAC, AGIP
Quals/training: Humanistic psychotherapy training; Rebirthing; Sesame training in Drama & Movement therapy; training memb AGIP (Psychoanalyitical Psychotherapy)
Personal Therapy: Ongoing
Supervision: Ongoing
Counselling offered: **General, Psychotherapy, Eating disorders, Peri-natal, Depression**
Service for: Individuals, Couples
Specific to: Women
Theoretical Approach: Jungian, Eclectic
Other languages: French
Fees: £20 - £30 sliding scale

London - North

BOURNE Ruth   081 445 5128
2 Greenbank, Woodside Avenue, North Finchley, LONDON N12 8AS

Member of:	BAC
Quals/training:	Cert Ed (London Univ); Cert Educational Psychol; Cruse Training; 1 yr Couns course (WPF); Dip & Acc Adlerian Counsellor (3 yr training Adlerian Soc of GB); IIP
Personal Therapy:	Yes
Supervision:	Ongoing
Counselling offered:	**Work, Crisis, Loss, Short-term, Long-term, Anxiety**
Service for:	Individuals, Families
Specific to:	Jewish
Theoretical Approach:	Dynamic, Eclectic, Adlerian, Art therapy
Fees:	£20 - £25 concessions negotiable

PASSER Sadie   081 445 2417
3 Vicarage Court, 38/40 Holden Road, North Finchley, LONDON N12 8HT

Member of:	BAC
Quals/training:	BA; NMGC/RELATE Trained 1965; Dip Couns (LCIP) 1974
Personal Therapy:	Yes
Supervision:	Ongoing
Counselling offered:	**General, Relationship, Bereavement, Psychotherapy**
Service for:	Individuals, Couples, Families
Theoretical Approach:	Psychodynamic, Jungian, Freudian, Rogerian
Fees:	£30 negotiable

HARRIS Rowena   081 446 6401, 081 446 8431
Rowlandson House, 289-293 Ballards Lane, LONDON N12 8NP

Member of:	BAC
Quals/training:	Couns course (Harrow CHE) 1981-2; Cert Couns Skills (CSCT) 1987
Personal Therapy:	Yes
Supervision:	Ongoing
Counselling offered:	**General, Bereavement, Cancer, Relationship**
Service for:	Individuals
Theoretical Approach:	Rogerian, Eclectic
Fees:	£25

CRACE Gay   081 446 7497
125 Ashurst Road, North Finchley, LONDON N12 9AD

Member of:	BAC
Quals/training:	Adv Cert in Couns (CAC) 1986-87; Cruse Bereavement Couns training 1991; student member of Assoc of Independent Psychotherapists 1992-
Personal Therapy:	Yes
Supervision:	Ongoing
Counselling offered:	**Psychotherapy**
Service for:	Individuals
Theoretical Approach:	Analytical
Fees:	£12 - £25 sliding scale

London - North

BAKER Celia 081 886 1521
7 Lipton Court, 196 Chase Side, Southgate, LONDON N14 5HG
Member of: BAC
Quals/training: Speech Therapist; NMGC/RELATE Trained 1979
Personal Therapy: Yes
Supervision: Ongoing
Counselling offered: General, Marital, Bereavement
Service for: Individuals, Couples
Theoretical Approach: Psychodynamic
Fees: £25 negotiable for special cases

KUBEL Patricia 081 361 4527
60 Shamrock Way, Southgate, LONDON N14 5RY
Member of: BAC
Quals/training: Combined Cert Couns Skills & Theory (CSCT) 1990; SEN 1979
Personal Therapy: Ongoing
Supervision: Ongoing
Counselling offered: General, Bereavement, Crisis
Service for: Individuals, Couples
Theoretical Approach: Rogerian, Adlerian
Fees: £15 negotiable

SHARON Linda 081 886 6324
76 Queen Elizabeths Drive, Southgate, LONDON N14 6RD
Member of: BAC
Quals/training: RELATE trained
Personal Therapy: Yes
Supervision: Ongoing
Counselling offered: General, Relationship, Bereavement, Crisis
Service for: Individuals, Couples
Theoretical Approach: Psychodynamic, Client-centred
Fees: £20

WILKINSON Linda 081 882 0124
12 The Green, Southgate, LONDON N14 7EH
Member of: BAC Acc
Quals/training: BAC(Acc); trained as RELATE counsellor & supervisor; additional training at Tavistock Inst of Marital Studies
Personal Therapy: Ongoing
Supervision: Ongoing
Counselling offered: General, Relationship, Marital, Eating disorders, Supervision
Service for: Individuals, Couples
Theoretical Approach: Psychodynamic
Fees: £26 negotiable for low income

London - North

BANNERMAN Afrakuma ansaphone 081 800 3771
LONDON N15
Member of:	BAC, BAP
Quals/training:	Infant Observation (SAP) '86-89; Assoc Memb BAP '92; Full Memb Internat Assoc for Analytical Psychol (IAAP) '92
Personal Therapy:	Yes
Supervision:	Yes
Counselling offered:	**Psychotherapy, Analysis, Bereavement, Stress, Anxiety, Depression, Identity crisis, Supervision, Dream, Abuse**
Service for:	Individuals, Groups
Specific to:	Ethnic minorities, Teachers, Actors
Theoretical Approach:	Jungian, Analytic, Psychodynamic
Fees:	approx £30, negotiable

BROWN Ursula 081 809 0355
26 South Grove, South Tottenham, LONDON N15 5QD
Member of:	BAC
Quals/training:	BA (Hons); trained in Psychotherapy (Gestalt Studio)
Personal Therapy:	Ongoing
Supervision:	Ongoing
Counselling offered:	**General, Psychotherapy, Bereavement**
Service for:	Individuals, Couples, Groups
Theoretical Approach:	Gestalt
Fees:	£27 negotiable

SIMON Gail 081 809 7218
41 Lealand Road, South Tottenham, LONDON N15 6JS
Member of:	BAC Acc
Quals/training:	BAC Acc; CQSW 1980; Further Training at Tavistock & Portman Clinics & IFT; Counselling Supervision (Kensington Consultation Centre)
Personal Therapy:	Yes
Supervision:	Ongoing
Counselling offered:	**General**
Service for:	Individuals, Couples, Families, Groups
Specific to:	Women
Theoretical Approach:	Eclectic, Systemic, Psychodynamic
Other languages:	French, German
Fees:	£18 - £28 sliding scale

BUSH Sandra 081 800 9540
23 Leweston Place, Stamford Hill, LONDON N16 6RJ
Member of:	BAC, IPC
Quals/training:	Dip Adv Psychodynamic Couns (IPC/WPF) 1992
Personal Therapy:	Yes
Supervision:	Ongoing
Counselling offered:	**General, Bereavement, Crisis, Depression, Relationship**
Theoretical Approach:	Psychodynamic
Fees:	£20 Negotiable

London - North

MARX Philippa 071 624 1775, 071 275 8002
Newington Green, Hackney, LONDON N16
Member of:	**IPC**
Quals/training:	Dip CQSW; Dip Group Analytic Psychotherapy/Couns; Training in creative groupwork, group analytic psychotherapy & family therapy
Personal Therapy:	Ongoing
Supervision:	Ongoing
Counselling offered:	**General, Relationship, Psychotherapy**
Service for:	Individuals, Groups
Theoretical Approach:	Group analytic, Psychodynamic, Systemic
Fees:	£18 - £20 £10-12 grps, also in Kilburn

PALMER Helen 071 249 5477
13 Oldfield Road, Stoke Newington, LONDON N16 0RR
Member of:	**BAC**
Quals/training:	Dip Couns Gestalt Therapy 1989; Women's Therapy Centre 1990
Personal Therapy:	Ongoing
Supervision:	Ongoing
Counselling offered:	**eneral, Psychotherapy**
Service for:	Individuals, Couples
Specific to:	Women, Lesbians, Gays
Fees:	£20

KENNY Angela 071 254 8558
128 Nevill Road, Stoke Newington, LONDON N16 0SX
Member of:	**BAC, AGIP**
Quals/training:	Dip Couns 1981 NE London Poly; Trained in Psychoanalytic Psychotherapy '82-85 AGIP
Personal Therapy:	Yes
Supervision:	Ongoing
Counselling offered:	**General, Psychotherapy**
Service for:	Individuals
Specific to:	Women
Theoretical Approach:	Object relations
Fees:	£30 - £45 Sliding Scale

MANN David 081 800 4992
Flat 6, 164 Lordship Road, LONDON N16 5HB
Member of:	**Guild of Psychotherapists**
Quals/training:	BSc (Hons) Psycho; Dip Art Therapy; training in Psychoanalytic Psychotherapy (Guild of Psychotherapists)
Personal Therapy:	Yes
Supervision:	Ongoing
Counselling offered:	**General, Supervision**
Service for:	Individuals
Theoretical Approach:	Psychoanalytic
Fees:	£20 - £30 sliding scale

London - North

GROTE Janie   ansaphone 081 806 5961
167 Kyverdale Road, Stoke Newington, LONDON N16 6PS
Member of:	**BAC, MPTI, GPTI**
Quals/training:	PhD; 1st Adv Dip in Gestalt (Pellin); currently training at metanoia; student member GPTI
Personal Therapy:	Ongoing
Supervision:	Ongoing
Counselling offered:	**General, Psychotherapy, ME**
Service for:	Individuals
Specific to:	Women, Lesbians
Theoretical Approach:	Gestalt
Fees:	£18 - £25 sliding scale

EISEN Susan   081 806 8703
53 Benthal Road, Stoke Newington, LONDON N16 7AR
Member of:	**Guild of Psychotherapists, BPS**
Quals/training:	SRN; BSc Psychol; Trained in Analytical Psychotherapy
Personal Therapy:	Ongoing
Supervision:	Ongoing
Counselling offered:	**Psychotherapy**
Service for:	Individuals
Theoretical Approach:	Analytic, Jungian
Fees:	£15 - £30 sliding scale

DALAL Farhad   071 249 5118
51 Evering Road, Stoke Newington, LONDON N16 7PU
Member of:	**BAC Acc, ITHP, IGA**
Quals/training:	BAC Acc; Qualified psychotherapist (Minster Centre); Member ITHP; Qualified Group Analyst (IGA)
Personal Therapy:	Ongoing
Supervision:	Ongoing
Counselling offered:	**General, Bereavement, Marital, Psychotherapy, Supervision**
Service for:	Individuals, Couples, Groups
Theoretical Approach:	Psychodynamic, Group analysis
Fees:	£20 - £30

HENDERSON Pauline   071 249 5118
51 Evering Road, Stoke Newington, LONDON N16 7PU
Member of:	**BAC, ITHP**
Quals/training:	Accredited by Minster Centre; Full Member ITHP
Personal Therapy:	Ongoing
Supervision:	Ongoing
Counselling offered:	**General, Marital, Bereavement, Psychotherapy, Supervision**
Service for:	Individuals, Couples, Groups
Theoretical Approach:	Psychodynamic
Fees:	£18 - £25 dependant on income

London - North

PRESANT Fern 071 241 0611
112A Farleigh Road, LONDON N16 7TF
Member of:	**BAC, ITHP**
Quals/training:	Dip Psychotherapy (Minster Centre)
Personal Therapy:	Yes
Supervision:	Ongoing
Counselling offered:	**General, Cross/multi-cultural, Psychotherapy**
Service for:	Individuals, Couples
Theoretical Approach:	Integrative
Fees:	£15 - £25 sliding scale

TAYLOR Meg 071 254 0597
76A Farleigh Road, Stoke Newington, LONDON N16 7TQ
Member of:	**BAC, BPS**
Quals/training:	BSc Soc Psychol 1974; MSc Psychopathology 1977; RM 1980; IPSS 1983-7; Dip Couns (Inst of Educ) 1990
Personal Therapy:	Ongoing
Supervision:	Ongoing
Counselling offered:	**General, Peri-natal**
Service for:	Individuals
Theoretical Approach:	Psychodynamic
Fees:	£20 negotiable

KENNY Brigid 071 254 4975
105 Clissold Crescent, Stoke Newington, LONDON N16 9AS
Member of:	**BAC, PET**
Quals/training:	Dip Psychosynthesis Couns & Therapy; CQSW; Dip Appl Soc Studies
Personal Therapy:	Ongoing
Supervision:	Ongoing
Counselling offered:	**General**
Service for:	Individuals, Couples, Groups
Theoretical Approach:	Psychosynthesis
Fees:	£18 - £35 sliding scale

PICKSTOCK Keith 071 254 4975
105 Clissold Crescent, Stoke Newington, LONDON N16 9AS
Member of:	**BAC, PET**
Quals/training:	Dip Psychosynthesis Couns & Therapy
Personal Therapy:	Ongoing
Supervision:	Ongoing
Counselling offered:	**General, Relationship**
Service for:	Individuals, Couples, Groups
Theoretical Approach:	Psychosynthesis
Fees:	£20 - £35 sliding scale

London - North

BARKER Gina 071 275 8002
50 Burma Road, Stoke Newington, LONDON N16 9BJ
Member of:	**BAC Acc, AHPP, Member of UKCP Register**
Quals/training:	BAC Acc; AHPP Acc Psychotherapist, UKCP Registered; Psychosynthesis Psychotherapy (IP) 1990; ext training therapist for ISA
Personal Therapy:	Ongoing
Supervision:	Ongoing
Counselling offered:	**General, Abuse, Inner child**
Service for:	Individuals
Specific to:	Women, Lesbians
Theoretical Approach:	Humanistic, Analytical, Attachment
Fees:	£27.50

FOX Susan 071 275 8002
50 Burma Road, Stoke Newington, LONDON N16 9BJ
Member of:	**BAC**
Quals/training:	BSc Psychology; 1988 Dip Couns & Psychotherapy (Pellin Inst); training in Psychosynthesis (Re-Vision); Terrence Higgins Trust Cert in HIV/AIDS Couns
Personal Therapy:	Ongoing
Supervision:	Ongoing
Counselling offered:	**General, Child abuse**
Service for:	Individuals
Fees:	£22

WOODER Bernie 081 207 3457
8 Glaserton Road, Stamford Hill, LONDON N16 5QX
Member of:	**KI**
Quals/training:	Cert Couns (Herts & Beds Past Found); In Core Process Psycho-therapy(Karuna Inst)
Personal Therapy:	Ongoing
Supervision:	Ongoing
Counselling offered:	**General, Bereavement, Crisis, Self-esteem, Psychotherapy**
Service for:	Individuals, Organisations
Specific to:	Trade Union members, Managers
Theoretical Approach:	Humanistic, Transpersonal
Fees:	£19 - £30 sliding scale

FERNANDES Jennie 081 801 3865
22 Fairbourne Road, Tottenham, LONDON N17 6TP
Member of:	**BAC**
Quals/training:	FACET training programme (City Univ)
Personal Therapy:	Yes
Supervision:	Ongoing
Counselling offered:	**General, Crisis, Sexual abuse, Physical abuse**
Service for:	Individuals, Couples, Families, Children
Specific to:	Women, Children
Theoretical Approach:	Person-centred, Integrative
Fees:	£15 - £35 sliding scale

London - North

NIGHTALL Celia   081 801 5707
28 Baldewyne Court, Lansdowne Road, Tottenham, LONDON N17 9XH
Member of:	BAC, IPC
Quals/training:	Dip Couns (IPC/WPF)
Personal Therapy:	Yes
Supervision:	Ongoing
Counselling offered:	General, Psychotherapy, Bereavement, Crisis, Eating disorders, Chronic illness, Terminal illness
Service for:	Individuals
Theoretical Approach:	Analytical, Psychodynamic
Fees:	£20 - £25 negotiable

GOSLING Peggy   071 281 1741
20a Ashley Road, Upper Holloway, LONDON N19 3AE
Member of:	BAC
Quals/training:	BA Psychol; MSc Human Communication; Dip Couns; Training in Personal Construct Psychology
Personal Therapy:	Yes
Supervision:	Ongoing
Counselling offered:	General, Learning difficulties, Supervision
Service for:	Individuals, Families, Groups
Specific to:	Children, Young people, Women
Theoretical Approach:	Integrative, Cognitive, Behavioural, Humanistic
Fees:	£15 - £30

KLEANTHOUS Dina   071 263 7270
41 Cheverton Road, Upper Holloway, LONDON N19 3BA
Member of:	BAC
Quals/training:	BA(Hons) Soc; PGCE; Cert (UK Coll Couns & Hypnotherapy); Cert (Inst Training & Development); currently training with Arbours Association; memb BHMA, BHR, PPS
Personal Therapy:	Ongoing
Supervision:	Ongoing
Counselling offered:	General, Hypnotherapy
Service for:	Individuals, Couples, Families, Groups
Theoretical Approach:	Humanistic, Integrative, Ericksonian, NLP
Other languages:	Greek
Fees:	£20 negotiable

LAND Patricia   ansaphone 071 272 6077
4 Scholefield Road, Islington, LONDON N19 3EX
Member of:	GAPPSW, Member of UKCP Regoster
Quals/training:	CQSW; Dip in Applied Behavioural Science 1976; Cert of Qualification in Psychotherapy with Young People, Families & Groups (Tavistock Clinic)1988
Personal Therapy:	Yes
Supervision:	Ongoing
Counselling offered:	General, Brief, Psychotherapy, Supervision
Service for:	Individuals, Couples, Groups, Families, Organisations
Specific to:	Women, Incest survivors, Parents, Young people
Theoretical Approach:	Psychoanalytic, Kleinian, Eclectic
Other languages:	French
Fees:	£20 - £25 concessions, £30 couples

London - North

LONCELLE Marie-Jose   071 281 2639
36 Warrender Road, LONDON N19 5EF
Member of:	BAC Acc
Quals/training:	BAC Acc; General Course (IGA); Training with Centre for Psycho-analytical Psychotherapy
Personal Therapy:	Ongoing
Supervision:	Ongoing
Counselling offered:	**General, Psychotherapy**
Service for:	Individuals, Couples
Theoretical Approach:	Analytical, Kleinian
Other languages:	French
Fees:	£20 negotiable

STEINER Monika   071 272 8473
Flat 3, 25 Hornsey Rise Gardens, Crouch End, LONDON N19 3PP
Member of:	IPSS
Quals/training:	BA Psychol(Haifa Univ)'81; Dip in Dance & Movement Therapy (Haifa Univ)'83, Dip Psychotherapy(IPSS)'88; Memb ADMT
Personal Therapy:	Unknown
Supervision:	Ongoing
Counselling offered:	**Psychotherapy, Movement therapy**
Service for:	Individuals, Groups
Theoretical Approach:	Psychodynamic, Existential
Other languages:	German, Hebrew
Fees:	£20 - £30 sliding scale

SEALE Donna   071 272 3311
17 Lambton Road, Upper Holloway, LONDON N19 3QJ
Member of:	BPS
Quals/training:	Dip Clinical Psychol 1983; C Psychol; AFBPsS; Assoc Memb APPNHS
Personal Therapy:	Ongoing
Supervision:	Ongoing
Counselling offered:	**General, Psychotherapy, Marital, Chronic illness, Disability, Life threatening illnesses**
Service for:	Individuals, Couples
Specific to:	People with disabilities
Theoretical Approach:	Psychoanalytic
Fees:	£25 - £35 negotiable

GRANOWSKI Margaret   071 485 5274
191 Brecknock Road, Tufnell Park, LONDON N19 5AB
Member of:	ITHP
Quals/training:	BA; Dip Social Work (Sydney) 1957; qualified Psychotherapist (Minster Centre) 1987
Personal Therapy:	Yes
Supervision:	Ongoing
Counselling offered:	**General, Bereavement, Relationship, Psychotherapy**
Service for:	Individuals, Couples
Theoretical Approach:	Psychodynamic, Integrative
Fees:	£30 negotiable

London - North

OPPENHEIMER Diana 071 281 0806
Flat A, 7 Tremlett Grove, Upper Holloway, LONDON N19 5LA
Member of:	BAC
Quals/training:	Dip Couns (CSCT) 1992
Personal Therapy:	Yes
Supervision:	Ongoing
Counselling offered:	General, Short-term, Long-term, Chronic illness
Service for:	Individuals
Theoretical Approach:	Psychodynamic
Fees:	£15 - £20 sliding scale

ROGNERUD Tove 071 263 0397
12 Francis Terrace, LONDON N19 5PY
Member of:	BAC
Quals/training:	BSc; Psychotherapy training (IPSS)
Personal Therapy:	Ongoing
Supervision:	Ongoing
Counselling offered:	General
Service for:	Individuals, Couples, Groups
Theoretical Approach:	Analytic
Other languages:	Norwegian
Fees:	Negotiable

STOKES Tania 081 281 5174
Basement Flat, 20a St John's Grove, Upper Holloway, LONDON N19 5RW
Member of:	BAC
Quals/training:	Memb of London Co-Couns Commun 78; Cert Couns Theory (Middx Poly)84; Foundat Cse in Couns & Interpersonal Skills & Dip Couns Skills 87 (SW London Coll); Dip Assert Trng CAI
Personal Therapy:	Yes
Supervision:	Ongoing
Counselling offered:	General, Relationship, Depression, Assertiveness, Eating disorders
Service for:	Individuals, Couples
Theoretical Approach:	Eclectic, Rogerian, Cognitive, Behavioural, Psychodynamic
Fees:	£15 - £20

SIMMONS Gloria 081 361 3740
Timbers, 64 Manor Drive, Whetstone, LONDON N20 0DU
Member of:	BAC, KCC
Quals/training:	Dip Couns (RELATE); Dip Brief Solution-focused Therapy (Marlborough); KCC Dip Family Therapy (Surrey Univ); Conciliation/Mediation (NAFMACS); Comp Mediation (FMA)
Personal Therapy:	Yes
Supervision:	Ongoing
Counselling offered:	General, Marital, Family, Mediation
Service for:	Individuals, Couples, Families
Theoretical Approach:	Psychodynamic, Rogerian, Systemic
Fees:	£30 - £40

London - North

STEIN Avril   081 445 7879
131 Friern Barnet Lane, Friern Barnet, LONDON N20 0XZ
Member of:	**BAC**
Quals/training:	Dip/Acc in Adlerian Couns (Adlerian Soc for Individual Psychol); qualified dental surgeon
Personal Therapy:	Yes
Supervision:	Ongoing
Counselling offered:	**General, Bereavement, Crisis, Phobias**
Service for:	Individuals, Couples, Groups
Theoretical Approach:	Adlerian
Fees:	£15 - £30 sliding scale

STONE Rosalind   081 446 4912
New House, Totteridge Green, Whetstone, LONDON N20 8PB
Member of:	**BAC**
Quals/training:	Cert Couns (WPF) 1983; Dip Psychol (London Univ) 1985; 1985 to date Psychotherapy Training (Gestalt Centre)
Personal Therapy:	Ongoing
Supervision:	Ongoing
Counselling offered:	**General, Marital, Bereavement, Eating disorders**
Service for:	Individuals, Groups
Theoretical Approach:	Gestalt
Fees:	£25 sliding scale

STOVELL Joy   081 446 2434
42a Athenaeum Road, Whetstone, LONDON N20 9AH
Member of:	**BAC Acc, IPSS**
Quals/training:	BAC Acc; RELATE Acc; Dip IPSS
Personal Therapy:	Yes
Supervision:	Ongoing
Counselling offered:	**General, Psychotherapy, Eating disorders, Relationship, Supervision**
Service for:	Individuals, Couples, Groups
Theoretical Approach:	Existential, Psychodynamic
Fees:	£25 negotiable

FENTON Judy   081 360 5128
4 Bush Hill, Winchmore Hill, LONDON N21 2DA
Member of:	**BAC Acc**
Quals/training:	BAC Acc; RELATE Acc; 1981 Dip Guidance & Couns (Middx Poly)
Personal Therapy:	Yes
Supervision:	Ongoing
Counselling offered:	**General, Marital**
Service for:	Individuals, Couples, Groups
Theoretical Approach:	Rogerian, Gestalt, Integrative
Fees:	£25 some concessions

London - North

SHAPLEY Bernard   081 889 4069
111 Willingdon Road, Wood Green, LONDON N22 6SE
Member of:	BAC Acc, BAP
Quals/training:	BAC Acc; Dip Student Couns 1985; currently training in Adult Psychotherapy (BAP)
Personal Therapy:	Ongoing
Supervision:	Ongoing
Counselling offered:	General, Learning difficulties
Service for:	Individuals, Couples
Theoretical Approach:	Psychodynamic
Fees:	£22 negotiable

HOBBS Janet   081 881 5585
12 Vallance Road, Wood Green, LONDON N22 4UB
Member of:	BAC
Quals/training:	NMGC trained
Personal Therapy:	Yes
Supervision:	Ongoing
Counselling offered:	Marital, Relationship
Service for:	Couples
Theoretical Approach:	Psychodynamic
Fees:	£20 dependent on income, unwaged negotiable

McGEE Colin   081 889 5965
95 Woodside Road, Wood Green, LONDON N22 5HR
Member of:	BAC
Quals/training:	Cert Ed; Schools Psychol Service Couns Cert; Psychotherapy training (IPSS)
Personal Therapy:	Ongoing
Supervision:	Ongoing
Counselling offered:	General, Relationship, Psychotherapy
Service for:	Individuals, Couples, Groups, Families
Theoretical Approach:	Existential, Humanistic
Fees:	Negotiable

LEA Claire J   081 888 2197
40 Page High, 4 Lymington Avenue, Wood Green, LONDON N22 6JQ
Member of:	BAC
Quals/training:	BSc(Hons) Psychol:Cert Couns; independent psychotherapy practice since 1984; tutor in Couns & Psychol
Personal Therapy:	Yes
Supervision:	Ongoing
Counselling offered:	General, Psychotherapy, Relationship, Social skills, Bereavement
Service for:	Individuals, Couples, Groups
Specific to:	Refugees, Trauma victims
Theoretical Approach:	Psychodynamic, Existential, Humanistic
Fees:	£20 - £25

London - North West

Organisations

BRANDON CENTRE 071 267 4792
26 Prince of Wales Road, Kentish town, LONDON NW5 3LG
Service:	Counselling & psychotherapy for young people, inc brief consultation, short & long term psychotherapy (once/week), group therapy for sexual abuse survivors; creche
Area served:	London
Referral:	Self, Agencies
Training of workers:	Training in psychotherapy, psychiatry and medicine
Code of Ethics:	Therapists' Professional body
Management by:	Council of Management
Fees:	None, contributions welcome

HEALING CENTRE 071 284 4143
91 Fortess Road, Tufnell Park, LONDON NW5 1AG
Service:	General, relationship and child psychotherapy for individuals, couples, families and groups. Counselling & Basic Couns Skills Trainings
Area served:	London & South-East
Referral:	Self
Training of workers:	Therapists include an Educational Psychologist trained in Child Guidance & Clin Psychol. All hold Dip Couns
Code of Ethics:	BAC
Management by:	Administrator
Fees:	£30

RAPHAEL CENTRE 081 428 3568, 24 hr ansa 081 203 9881
100 Ashmill Street, Marylebone, LONDON NW1 6RA
Service:	Counselling for people who wish to see a Jewish professional for help with a wide range of issues eg relationships, family, depression, anxiety, stress & bereavement
Area served:	All areas of London
Other languages:	German, Hebrew
Referral:	Self, GP, Rabbi
Training of workers:	Counsellors need to have completed an advanced counselling or psychotherapy training; ongoing supervision
Code of Ethics:	BAC
Management by:	Management
Fees:	Sliding scale

ANNA FREUD CENTRE 071 794 2313
21 Maresfield Gardens, Hampstead, LONDON NW3 5SH
Service:	Full analytic treatment for children up to 18 years of age, 5 days/week
Area served:	London
Other languages:	Please enquire
Training of workers:	Own training course
Code of Ethics:	ACP
Management by:	Mrs A M Sandler
Fees:	None

London - North West

GESTALT STUDIO   071 485 2316, (Bristol) 0272 661100
49 Croftdown Road, LONDON NW5

Service:	Gestalt psychotherapy for individuals, couples, women's groups, mixed groups looking at male/female relationships relationships
Area served:	N & W London, Surrey, Bristol
Referral:	Self or others
Training of workers:	Qualified Gestalt therapists, personal therapy, regular supervision
Code of Ethics:	Agency's own code
Management by:	Partners
Fees:	£12 - £30 groups £45-100/w.e negotiable

PHILADELPHIA ASSOCIATION LTD (PA)   071 794 2652
4 Marty's Yard, 17 Hampstead High Street, LONDON NW3 1PX

Service:	Individual, couple, group & family psychoanalytic psycho therapy. Therapeutic communities
Code of Ethics:	Agency's own code

NETWORK 6 COUNSELLING & THERAPY   071 482 4537
c/o 95b Leighton Road, Kentish Town, LONDON N15 6TA

Service:	Long/short term for indivs, couples, groups, workshops, case supervision. Working with anxiety, depression, bereavement, relationships, sexuality, adult children of alcoholics, etc
Area served:	Greater London
Referral:	Self or others
Training of workers:	Humanistic & traditional approaches at the Minster Centre; personal therapy; regular supervision
Code of Ethics:	BAC
Management by:	Women's collective
Fees:	£15 - £25

LONDON ASSOCIATION OF BEREAVEMENT SERVICES   071 288 2153
68 Charlton Street, LONDON NW1 1JR

Service:	Bereaved people can contact the LABS to find the name of a local group for bereavement counselling. Offers support, training & guidelines to all London Bereavement
Area served:	Greater London
Referral:	Self
Training of workers:	Each group varies, but a minimum would be weekly sessions over two months, counsellors are in supervision
Management by:	Members of the group
Fees:	None

HEATHSIDE COUNSELLING SERVICE   081 883 0343
17 South Hill Park, LONDON NW3 2ST

Service:	Individual, couple and family counselling. Supervision, Groups and Trainings
Area served:	London
Referral:	Self
Training of workers:	CQSW & MA (Oxon). Both counsellors hold Dip in Individual & Relationship Counselling and are qualified teachers. They have regular supervision and personal therapy
Code of Ethics:	BAC
Management by:	Therapists
Fees:	£25 (£5 initial consultation)

London - North West

WEST HAMPSTEAD PSYCHOTHERAPY & COUNSELLING 071 794 5308
21 Mill Lane, LONDON NW6 1NT
Service:	Psychotherapy and counselling, couples sessions (all sexual orientations), group therapy, consultancy for parents and guardians, supervision
Area served:	North West London
Other languages:	German
Referral:	Self or others
Training of workers:	All members have training in both Humanistic & Psychodynamic approaches. Personal Therapy and Regular Supervision
Code of Ethics:	BAC
Management by:	Members
Fees:	£20 - £40

ASIAN COUNSELLING SERVICE 071 387 0401, 071 387 5972
Camden Family Service Unit, 25 Bayham Street, Camden Town, LONDON NW1 0EY
Service:	General, marital and family counselling for the Asian community in their native languages
Area served:	Camden
Other languages:	Main Asian
Referral:	Self or others
Training of workers:	Asian co-ordinator is fully trained, volunteers have basic counselling skills
Code of Ethics:	BAC
Management by:	Management Committee of Camden Family Service Unit
Fees:	None

BIOENERGETIC PARTNERSHIP 071 435 1079
22 Fitzjohn's Avenue, LONDON NW3 5NB
Service:	Movement & body based psychotherapy. Individual & supervision sessions along psychodynamic lines with a body orientation
Area served:	London based
Other languages:	French
Referral:	Self, Other counsellors/therapists
Training of workers:	BIBA, Couns Course (SW London College); MA Couns (Hatfield) Personal therapy. Regular supervision
Code of Ethics:	BAC, AGIP
Management by:	Partnership
Fees:	£25 - £36 £46 for day group/foundation

WOMENS THERAPY LINK 071 916 0123
PO Box 2704, LONDON NW1 0EP
Service:	Counselling and psychotherapy for women, by women. Our approach includes Gestalt therapy and Contribution Training counselling
Area served:	London
Referral:	Self or others
Training of workers:	Pellin Institute/Pellin Centre
Code of Ethics:	BAC
Management by:	Co-Directors
Fees:	Sliding scale

London - North West

BOTTLEFED: THERAPY SERVICES FOR ADULT CHILDREN OF ALCHOLICS   071 284 2497
c/o 53 Shirlock Road, Gospel Oak, LONDON NW3 2HR

Service:	Introductory workshops, ongoing groups and individual psychotherapy for adults who grew up with parent(s) who drank too much. Some women only workshops available
Area served:	Greater London
Referral:	Self
Training of workers:	Traditional and Humanistic Psychotherapy from the Minster Centre
Code of Ethics:	BAC
Management by:	Collective responsibility
Fees:	£20 £55w/end w/shop;£120 10 wks

CHURCH ARMY COUNSELLING SERVICE   071 723 0573
London Centre, 10 Daventry Street, Marylebone, LONDON NW1 5NX

Service:	Individual counselling for emotional & spiritual problems, depression, marital & sexual difficulties in strict confidence for those of any creed or none
Area served:	Any
Referral:	Self or others
Training of workers:	Professionally accredited psychotherapists and counsellors
Code of Ethics:	BAC
Management by:	Church Army
Fees:	Dependent on personal circumstances

HAMPSTEAD COMMUNITY COUNSELLING   071 794 2238
1 Christie Court, 3 Aspern Grove, LONDON NW3 2BX

Service:	Adult general counselling service for individuals. Not a drop-in or crisis service
Area served:	In and around NW3
Referral:	Self
Training of workers:	Four women counsellors trained at SW London College; fortnightly supervision
Code of Ethics:	BAC
Management by:	Management Committee
Fees:	Realistic regular donation

ST MARYLEBONE HEALING & COUNSELLING CENTRE   071 935 6374
St Marylebone Church, 17 Marylebone Road, LONDON NW1 5LT

Service:	Counselling offered to those wishing to deal with choice, change or confusion in their lives, in a spiritual and non-judgemental setting
Area served:	London and surrounding area
Referral:	GP, Church, Self
Training of workers:	Mostly WPF trained; continued in-service training; regular supervision
Code of Ethics:	BAC
Management by:	Committee of PCC of St Marylebone Church
Fees:	Donations welcomed

NETWORK FOR PSYCHOTHERAPY & CONSULTATIVE SERVICES
081 340 4837
58 Priory Gardens, Highgate, LONDON N6 5QS

Service:	Individual and group analytic psychotherapy for adults and young people and those in further and higher education
Area served:	London
Referral:	Self, Health/Soc Work Professional
Training of workers:	Recognised training in psychotherapy and group analysis including personal therapy; ongoing supervision
Code of Ethics:	BAC
Management by:	Network
Fees:	£25 sliding scale

ADLERIAN COUNSELLING CENTRE
081 789 8086
Swiss Cottage CAB, LONDON NW3

Service:	General counselling service provided by Adlerian counsellors under supervision
Area served:	Greater London
Training of workers:	Adlerian Society or Inst for Individual Psychology accredited courses
Code of Ethics:	BAC, IIP
Management by:	Adlerian Society
Fees:	£12 negotiable by appointment

NORTH END ROAD PRACTICE
24 hours 081 905 5937
18b North End Road, Golders Green, LONDON NW11 7PH

Service:	Counselling, psychotherapy & personal development for individuals, couples & families. Group therapy. Divorce mediation. Supervision of other professionals
Area served:	Central, north & west London & suburbs
Referral:	Self, GP, Health/Soc Work Professional
Training of workers:	Min 4 years Psychosynthesis, analytical bodywork, family therapy. Ongoing supervision & personal therapy
Management by:	Partnership
Fees:	Average £30

ASSOCIATION OF WOMEN PSYCHOTHERAPISTS
081 202 0816
46 Westbere Road, LONDON NW2 2HR

Service:	Consultations & referrals for individuals & couples seeking psychoanalytical psychotherapy, with a particular interest in women's issues
Area served:	N, NW & W London
Other languages:	French, Hebrew, Italian, Polish
Referral:	Self or others
Training of workers:	Fully trained psychoanalyitc psychotherapists, including personal therapy & ongoing supervision
Code of Ethics:	Varies with professional seen
Management by:	Consensus
Fees:	£25 - £35 £30 1st consultation/placement

London - North West

NETWORK FOR PSYCHOTHERAPY & CONSULTATIVE SERVICES
081 965 5872

60 All Souls Avenue, LONDON NW10 3BG
Service:	Individual & group analytic therapy for adults & young people & those in H & FE. Organisational/educational consultancy offered to institutions on a sessional basis.
Area served:	Greater London
Referral:	Self, Professional workers
Training of workers:	Recognised training in psychotherapy and group analysis
Code of Ethics:	BAC, BASW, IGA, BPS
Management by:	Members of group
Fees:	Negotiated individually

LINK PSYCHOTHERAPY CENTRE
081 349 0111

110 Cholmley Gardens, Fortune Green Road, Kilburn, LONDON NW6 1UP
Service:	Professional psychotherapy service to Jewish community as well as forum for education and dialogue between Judaism and psychotherapy
Area served:	London
Other languages:	Spanish, Hebrew, German
Referral:	Self or others
Training of workers:	All are analytically trained in recognised organisations - BAP, AGIP, LCP, Guild of Psychotherapists, IP
Code of Ethics:	Varies with professional seen
Management by:	Council of Management
Fees:	£35 initial consultation, then by arrangemt

Individual Practitioners

*Every individual is a **member of** one or more organisations eligible for entry into this dierctory. BAC Accredited Counsellors and Recognised Supervisors are shaded*

MASON Lindy
081 341 2889

89 St Augustine's Road, LONDON NW1
Member of:	BAC, IPC
Quals/training:	Dip Adv Psychodynamic Couns (IPC/WPF & Roehampton Inst)
Personal Therapy:	Yes
Supervision:	Ongoing
Counselling offered:	**General, Bereavement**
Service for:	Individuals
Theoretical Approach:	Psychodynamic
Fees:	£20 - £30

BONNEFIN Valerie
071 486 6367

83 Nottingham Terrace, LONDON NW1 4QE
Member of:	BAC Acc
Quals/training:	BAC Acc; CQSW; Dip Couns Skills; Dip Applied Social Studies
Personal Therapy:	Yes
Supervision:	Ongoing
Counselling offered:	**General, Relationship, Autogenic training**
Service for:	Individuals
Specific to:	Women
Theoretical Approach:	Rogerian, Psychodynamic
Fees:	£25 Reviewed annually

London - North West

KAPLAN Myron　　　　　　　　　　　　　　　　071 724 3062
1 Clarence Gate Gardens, Glentworth Street, Marylebone, LONDON NW1 6AY
Member of:	AGIP
Quals/training:	1959 BA Psychol; Psychotherapy training (AGIP) '82-86 Training in sexual/marital therapy (London Inst for Study of Human Sexuality) '82-84
Personal Therapy:	Ongoing
Supervision:	Unknown
Counselling offered:	**Psychotherapy, Marital, Sexual**
Service for:	Individuals, Couples
Theoretical Approach:	Analytical
Fees:	£25 - £35 Sliding Scale

COGHAN Tony　　　　　　　　　　　　　　　　071 722 1612
120 Regents Park Road, LONDON NW1 8XL
Member of:	BAC, PET
Quals/training:	BA; Dip Couns; Psychosynthesis (PET) 1992
Personal Therapy:	Yes
Supervision:	Ongoing
Counselling offered:	**General, Crisis, Sexuality**
Service for:	Individuals, Couples
Specific to:	Gays
Theoretical Approach:	Humanistic, Psychosynthesis, Gestalt
Fees:	£15 - £30 sliding scale

MANDER Gertrud　　　　　　　　　　　　　　　071 722 0033
24 Chalcot Crescent, LONDON NW1 8YD
Member of:	BAC RSup
Quals/training:	Full Member of IPC; supervisor & tutor at WPF; BAC recognised supervisor
Personal Therapy:	Yes
Supervision:	Ongoing
Counselling offered:	**General, Psychotherapy**
Service for:	Individuals, Groups
Specific to:	Elderly, Gays, Lesbians, Artists, Professionals
Theoretical Approach:	Psychodynamic, Analytical
Other languages:	German
Fees:	£20 - £25 sliding scale

AHRENDS Liz　　　　　　　　　　　　　　　　071 485 7570
16 Rochester Road, LONDON NW1 9JH
Member of:	BAC Acc
Quals/training:	BAC(Acc), BA Soc. Sci.; MPhil; Cert in Couns, WPF
Personal Therapy:	Ongoing
Supervision:	Ongoing
Counselling offered:	**General**
Service for:	Individuals
Theoretical Approach:	Psychodynamic, Eclectic
Fees:	£20 Negotiable

London - North West

GABLE Judith 071 794 0373
Cricklewood, LONDON NW2
Member of:	BAC
Quals/training:	Training in Person-centred Couns (metanoia)
Personal Therapy:	Yes
Supervision:	Ongoing
Counselling offered:	**General**
Service for:	Individuals
Theoretical Approach:	Rogerian
Fees:	£20 negotiable

VICKERS Kate 081 452 7876
8 Oman Avenue, LONDON NW2 6BG
Member of:	BAC Acc, IPS
Quals/training:	BAC(Acc); Dip in Psychosynthesis Psychotherapy; BA; MA
Personal Therapy:	Yes
Supervision:	Ongoing
Counselling offered:	**General, Crisis, Psychotherapy**
Service for:	Individuals, Groups
Theoretical Approach:	Integrative, Psychosynthesis, Psychodynamic, Person-centred
Fees:	£30

PREISINGER Kristiane 081 452 6703
14 Richborough Road, LONDON NW2 3LU
Member of:	BAC, AHPP
Quals/training:	AHPP(Acc); Psychology Graduate (Germany); Humanistic Couns training (Boyesen Centre); training in Psychodynamic Supervision (WPF)
Personal Therapy:	Ongoing
Supervision:	Ongoing
Counselling offered:	**General, Psychotherapy**
Service for:	Individuals
Theoretical Approach:	Integrative
Other languages:	German
Fees:	£20 - £30

GRANVILLE Marion Ansaphone 081 452 0308
Flat 2 Davina House, 59a Fordwych Road, LONDON NW2 3TN
Member of:	CPCP
Quals/training:	Teacher training; Cert Ed (English, Psychology); Personal Construct Psychology Courses; Dip PCP
Personal Therapy:	Unknown
Supervision:	Ongoing
Counselling offered:	**General**
Service for:	Individuals, Couples
Theoretical Approach:	PCP
Fees:	£20

London - North West

ROBERTSON Ewa   081 451 2165
Re-vision, 8 Chatsworth Road, Cricklewood, LONDON NW2 4BN
Member of: IPS
Quals/training: BA Psychol; Dip Couns; trained in Psychosynthesis Psychotherapy(IP)'83
Personal Therapy: Ongoing
Supervision: Ongoing
Counselling offered: **General, Psychotherapy, Women's issues**
Service for: Individuals, Groups
Theoretical Approach: Psychosynthesis, Transpersonal
Other languages: Polish, Italian
Fees: £30

MENEZES Evette   081 450 3669
1 Westly Court, 155 Dartmouth Road, Cricklewood, LONDON NW2 4EL
Member of: BAC
Quals/training: Dip Couns (CSCT)
Personal Therapy: Yes
Supervision: Ongoing
Counselling offered: **General**
Service for: Individuals
Theoretical Approach: Integrative
Fees: £15

ILJON FOREMAN Elaine   081 459 3428
21a Dean Road, Cricklewood, LONDON NW2 5AB
Member of: BPS, BABCP
Quals/training: BA(Hons) Psychol; MSc Clinical psychol; C Psychol; AFBPsS; Trained in Clinical Hypnosis (BABP)
Personal Therapy: Ongoing
Supervision: Ongoing
Counselling offered: **General, Phobias, Panic attacks, Stress management, Fear of flying**
Service for: Individuals, Groups, Couples
Theoretical Approach: Cognitive/Behavioural
Fees: £50

KADISH Faigie, Mrs   081 451 1559
1b Alverstone Road, LONDON NW2 5JS
Member of: LCP
Quals/training: LCP Course in Psychotherapy 1983-87; LCP Assoc
Personal Therapy: Yes
Supervision: Ongoing
Counselling offered: **Psychotherapy**
Service for: Individuals
Theoretical Approach: Eclectic, Kleinian, Analytical
Fees: £20 - £30

London - North West

ALBERY Nicholas 081 208 2853
20 Heber Road, LONDON NW2 6AA
Member of:	IPSS
Quals/training:	Dip Psychotherapy IPSS 1985
Personal Therapy:	Yes
Supervision:	Ongoing
Counselling offered:	**Psychotherapy, Creative potential**
Service for:	Individuals, Groups
Specific to:	Schools
Theoretical Approach:	Gestalt, Grofian, Rebirthing
Other languages:	French
Fees:	Negotiable

ROTH Ruth 081 452 7376
16 Oman Avenue, Cricklewood, LONDON NW2 6BG
Member of:	BAC, ITHP, Member of UKCP Register
Quals/training:	MA; Dip HIP; UKCP Registered
Personal Therapy:	Yes
Supervision:	Ongoing
Counselling offered:	**General, Relationship, Psychotherapy**
Service for:	Individuals, Couples, Groups
Theoretical Approach:	Humanistic, Integrative
Fees:	£30 - £35 negotiable

BURNS Alex 071 435 5369
Garden Flat, 31 Denning Road, Hampstead, LONDON NW3
Member of:	BAC, IPSS
Quals/training:	BA(Hons); Dip Psychotherapy (IPSS)
Personal Therapy:	Ongoing
Supervision:	Ongoing
Counselling offered:	**Psychotherapy**
Service for:	Individuals, Couples, Groups, Families
Theoretical Approach:	Psychodynamic
Fees:	£28 - £35

SCARLETT Jean 071 435 2362
3 Byron Villas, Vale of Health, LONDON NW3 1AR
Member of:	BAP, LCP, BPS
Quals/training:	BA (Hons) Psychol 1961; AFBPsS; BAP Mem (Assoc) 1967; BAP Full Memb 1970
Personal Therapy:	Yes
Supervision:	Yes
Counselling offered:	**General, Psychotherapy**
Service for:	Individuals, Groups
Theoretical Approach:	Eclectic, Freudian, Winnicottian, Analytical
Fees:	£20 - £26 sliding scale

London - North West

HODSON Phillip 071 794 2838
179c Haverstock Hill, Hampstead, LONDON NW3
Member of: BAC, BASMT
Quals/training: MA (Oxon); Dip (LCIP) 1984; Trained with NMGC/RELATE
Personal Therapy: Yes
Supervision: Ongoing
Counselling offered: General, Marital, Sexual, Psychotherapy
Service for: Individuals, Couples, Families
Fees: £60 a few clients at £35

McKENNELL Vivienne 071 794 6839
56 The Pryors, East Heath Road, Hampstead, LONDON NW3 1PB
Member of: BAC
Quals/training: 1976 CQSW; Psychiatric Social Worker; further training TIMS; IGA; BAP; Inst Psycho-Analysis
Personal Therapy: Ongoing
Supervision: Ongoing
Counselling offered: General, Marital, Divorce, Bereavement, Stress, Family, Alcohol, Relationship
Service for: Individuals, Couples, Families
Theoretical Approach: Eclectic
Fees: £25 dependent on income

ROBERTSON Judith 071 794 1049
7 Rudall Crescent, Hampstead, LONDON NW3 1RS
Member of: BAC
Quals/training: Cert Ed'72; BA Psychol'78; Dip Couns Skills 81-84; IFT'85; SHAP'86; LCP'90; Tavistock'92; Guild of Psychotherapists'93
Personal Therapy: Ongoing
Supervision: Ongoing
Counselling offered: General, Sexual abuse, Psychotherapy
Service for: Individuals, Couples, Groups
Theoretical Approach: Rogerian, Gestalt, Analytical
Fees: £23

NEWSOME Marjorie 071 435 7647
3 Carlingford Road, Hampstead, LONDON NW3 1RY
Member of: BAC
Quals/training: Assoc Memb BAP; Assoc Memb & Charter Member BPS
Personal Therapy: Yes
Supervision: Ongoing
Counselling offered: Psychotherapy, Long-term
Service for: Individuals
Theoretical Approach: Psychoanalytic, Winnicottian
Fees: £20 - £25

London - North West

CONWELL James   071 435 8679
2 Kemplay Road, Hampstead, LONDON NW3 1SY
Member of: BAC Acc, ITHP
Quals/training: 3 yr training in Psychotherapy(Minster Centre); 9 yrs post-grad working experience in various settings
Personal Therapy: Ongoing
Supervision: Ongoing
Counselling offered: General, Addiction
Service for: Individuals
Specific to: Creative people
Theoretical Approach: Psychodynamic
Fees: £25 sliding scale

MACHADO Danuza   071 722 7383
14 Eton Hall, Eton College Road, Hampstead, LONDON NW3 2DW
Member of: BPS, CFAR
Quals/training: Clinical Psychologist; qualified Psychotherapist 1974; trained in Lacanian Psychoanalysis 1982
Personal Therapy: Yes
Supervision: No
Counselling offered: General, Analysis
Service for: Individuals, Children
Specific to: Children
Theoretical Approach: Lacanian
Other languages: Portuguese, Spanish, French
Fees: Negotiable

DUNN Nicola   071 284 2497
53 Shirlock Road, Gospel Oak, LONDON NW3 2HR
Member of: BAC, ITHP
Quals/training: 3 yr training in Humanistic & Traditional Psychotherapy Minster Centre; 1 yr Intro course in Family Therapy (IFT)
Personal Therapy: Yes
Supervision: Ongoing
Counselling offered: General, Relationship, Crisis, Psychotherapy, Pregnancy, Bereavement
Service for: Individuals, Groups
Specific to: Performing artists, Adult children of alcoholics
Theoretical Approach: Humanistic, Psychodynamic
Fees: £20 - £32 sliding scale

MILLER Alison   071 485 9559
108 Fleet Road, Hampstead, LONDON NW3 2QX
Member of: BAC, AHPP
Quals/training: BA; Dip Psych; Psychotherapy Training (Serpent Inst)
Personal Therapy: Ongoing
Supervision: Ongoing
Counselling offered: General, Psychotherapy
Service for: Individuals
Theoretical Approach: Humanistic, Integrative
Fees: £10 - £22 Sliding Scale

London - North West

HANCOCK Alan   081 883 0343, 071 794 4836
Heathside Counselling Service, Flat 5, 17 South Hill Park, LONDON NW3 2ST
Member of:	BAC
Quals/training:	Dip in Individual & Relationship Couns; CQSW; Qualified teacher
Personal Therapy:	Yes
Supervision:	Ongoing
Counselling offered:	**General, Crisis**
Service for:	Individuals, Couples, Families, Groups
Theoretical Approach:	Person-centred, Eclectic
Fees:	£25 (initial £5)

STONE Miriam   071 435 6072
39 Parliament Hill, Hampstead, LONDON NW3 2TA
Member of:	BAC, IPC
Quals/training:	Dip in Advanced Psychodynamic Couns
Personal Therapy:	Yes
Supervision:	Ongoing
Counselling offered:	**General, Psychotherapy**
Service for:	Individuals
Theoretical Approach:	Psychodynamic, Analytical
Fees:	£20 - £30 negotiable

JACKSON Roderick   071 794 5184
49 Parliament Hill, LONDON NW3 2TB
Member of:	IPC/WPF
Quals/training:	Dip Advanced Psychodynamic Couns(WPF); Cert Transpersonal Couns(CTP)
Personal Therapy:	Yes
Supervision:	Ongoing
Counselling offered:	**General, Stress**
Service for:	Individuals
Specific to:	Executives
Theoretical Approach:	Psychodynamic, Transpersonal
Fees:	Negotiable

SOUTHGATE John   071 794 4306
12 Nassington Road, Hampstead, LONDON NW3 2UD
Member of:	BAC, ISF
Quals/training:	MA; Cert Ed; Dip Applied Behavioural Science (N London Poly); Founder Memb ISA
Personal Therapy:	Yes
Supervision:	Ongoing
Counselling offered:	**Psychotherapy, Inner child**
Service for:	Individuals, Groups
Theoretical Approach:	Alice Miller, Karen Horney, John Bowlby
Fees:	£25 negotiable

London - North West

O'GORMAN Mary Pat 071 794 5468
17 Lambolle Road, Hampstead, LONDON NW3 4HS
Member of:	BAC, ITHP
Quals/training:	Dip Integrative Psychotherapy (Minster Centre)'93
Personal Therapy:	Yes
Supervision:	Ongoing
Counselling offered:	**General, Cross/multi-cultural, Eating disorders, Psychotherapy**
Service for:	Individuals
Theoretical Approach:	Integrative
Fees:	£15 - £25 sliding scale

TEPER Mrs Gay 071 794 8488
63 Ornan Road, Hampstead, LONDON NW3 4QD
Member of:	BAC Acc
Quals/training:	BAC Acc; Dip HE Couns & Humanistic Psychotherapy 1987; BA(Hons) Client-Centred Couns & Psychotherapy (Poly E London) 1988; Memb BAPCA
Personal Therapy:	Yes
Supervision:	Ongoing
Counselling offered:	**General, Psychotherapy**
Service for:	Individuals, Couples
Theoretical Approach:	Client-centred
Fees:	£20 individuals, negotiable

CAMPBELL Elizabeth 071 722 7573
2 Provost Road, Hampstead, LONDON NW3 4ST
Member of:	**BAC, Guild of Psychotherapists**
Quals/training:	BA (Hons); trained Marriage Guidance Counsellor; trained in Psychoanalytic psychotherapy (Guild of Psychotherapists)
Personal Therapy:	Yes
Supervision:	Ongoing
Counselling offered:	**General, Relationship, Infertility, Psychotherapy**
Service for:	Individuals, Couples
Theoretical Approach:	Psychoanalytic
Fees:	£20 - £37 sliding scale

FITZGERALD Maura 071 435 4174
Flat 12, 31 Daleham Gardens, Hampstead, LONDON NW3 5BU
Member of:	BAC
Quals/training:	Cert Couns Skills & Attitudes (WPF); Dip Couns (SW London College); training in Supervision in Alcohol Couns (Alcohol Concern)1992
Personal Therapy:	Ongoing
Supervision:	Ongoing
Counselling offered:	**General, Addiction, Eating disorders, Stress management**
Service for:	Individuals, Organisations, Groups
Theoretical Approach:	Psychodynamic
Fees:	£15 - £25 orgs by arrangement

London - North West

ARTHUR Andrew 071 388 6990
23 College Crescent, Hampstead, LONDON NW3 5LL
Member of:	BPS, WMIP
Quals/training:	BA; MSc; associate fellow BPS; C Psychol; full member W Midlands Institute of Psychotherapy; Chartered Clinical Psychologist
Personal Therapy:	Ongoing
Supervision:	Ongoing
Counselling offered:	Psychotherapy
Service for:	Individuals
Theoretical Approach:	Psychoanalytic
Fees:	£30

GOODMAN Diana 071 435 1079
22 Fitzjohns Avenue, Hampstead, LONDON NW3 5NB
Member of:	BAC
Quals/training:	Dip Couns Skills (SW London College); ASC Acc; MA Couns (Univ of Herts); Training in Psychotherapy (AIP)
Personal Therapy:	Ongoing
Supervision:	Ongoing
Counselling offered:	General, Relationship, Sexual, Stress management, Bodywork
Service for:	Individuals, Couples, Groups
Theoretical Approach:	Psychodynamic, Bioenergetic
Fees:	£22 - £30

MILLER John Andrew 071 435 1079
22 Fitzjohn's Avenue, Hampstead, LONDON NW3 5NB
Member of:	AGIP
Quals/training:	1982-7 training in Bioenergetic Analysis (BIBA); '82-89 post-doctoral research in occupational psychology; AGIP Affil; GAS Assoc
Personal Therapy:	Yes
Supervision:	Ongoing
Counselling offered:	Psychotherapy, Career, Transition, Life planning, Occupational, Consultation
Service for:	Individuals, Couples, Groups
Theoretical Approach:	Bioenergetic, Psychodynamic, Group analytic
Other languages:	French
Fees:	£35 - £40 (£45 groups)

STRASSER Dr Freddie 081 455 0118
99 West Heath Road, LONDON NW3 7TN
Member of:	BAC Acc
Quals/training:	PhD; MA Psychotherapy
Personal Therapy:	Ongoing
Supervision:	Ongoing
Counselling offered:	General, Psychotherapy, Supervision
Service for:	Individuals
Theoretical Approach:	Existential
Fees:	£35

London - North West

WITKIN Colleen 071 794 8347
Flat 6, No 1 Lyndhurst Gardens, Hampstead, LONDON NW3 5NS
Member of: BAC Acc, IPC/WPF
Quals/training: BAC(Acc); IGA trained; CTP; Assoc Memb ASMT; Dip Advanced Psychodynamic Couns(IPC/WPF)'89
Personal Therapy: Ongoing
Supervision: Ongoing
Counselling offered: General, Bereavement, Psychotherapy
Service for: Individuals
Theoretical Approach: Psychodynamic
Fees: £15 - £30 negotiable

FORSYTH Tom 071 435 3640
39 Belsize Court, Lyndhurst Gardens, Hampstead, LONDON NW3 5QP
Member of: BAC
Quals/training: Group psychotherapist; Psychotherapist Tutor (LCIP)
Personal Therapy: Yes
Supervision: Yes
Counselling offered: General, Psychotherapy
Service for: Individuals, Couples, Groups
Fees: £25 dependent on income

PHILLIPS Marian 081 458 2772
7 Sandy Road, Hampstead, LONDON NW3 7EY
Member of: BAC Acc, BPS, AFT
Quals/training: BAC Acc; CPsychol; BPS Practitioner Memb Couns Psychol; BSc Psychol 1979; MSc Couns Psychol 1992; Trained with NMGC 1966-84, IGA, IFT & TIMS
Personal Therapy: Yes
Supervision: Ongoing
Counselling offered: General, Marital, PTSD
Service for: Individuals, Couples, Groups, Families
Theoretical Approach: Analytical, Psychodynamic, RET
Fees: £25 - £35 sliding scale

LEFTON Mildred 071 435 2009
43a Redington Road, Hampstead, LONDON NW3 7RA
Member of: BAC
Quals/training: Dip Couns & Community Skills; Cert Stages of Emotional Development (London Univ)
Personal Therapy: Yes
Supervision: Ongoing
Counselling offered: General, Crisis
Service for: Individuals
Theoretical Approach: Rogerian
Fees: £15 - £20

London - North West

LOEWE Eva ansaphone 071 431 1515, direct 071 435 7112
43 Redington Road, Hampstead, LONDON NW3 7RA
Member of: IPC
Quals/training: Full Memb IPC/WPF 1987 (Counsellor Psychoanalytic Psychotherapist)
Personal Therapy: No
Supervision: Ongoing
Counselling offered: Psychotherapy
Service for: Individuals, Couples, Groups
Specific to: Artists, Musicians
Theoretical Approach: Jungian, Archetypal
Other languages: German, French, Spanish
Fees: £30 negotiable

GOLDENBERG Harriett 071 586 5431
Flat 2-6 Upper Park Road, Belsize Park, LONDON NW3 9SY
Member of: BAC, BPS
Quals/training: BA Psychol; MSc Psychol Couns (Roehampton); Memb SEA & BICA; C Psychol
Personal Therapy: Ongoing
Supervision: Ongoing
Counselling offered: **General, Psychotherapy, Infertility, Bereavement, Adoption, Sexual abuse**
Service for: Individuals, Couples
Theoretical Approach: Existential
Fees: £20 - £30 s

NEWSON Mary 081 202 4525
Inst of Psychosynthesis Couns, & Psychotherapy Service, 65a Watford Way Hendon, LONDON NW4 3AQ
Member of: BAC Acc
Quals/training: BAC(Acc); Dip Couns; Psychosynthesis Psychotherapy(IP)'92; Dip Psychotherapy '93
Personal Therapy: Yes
Supervision: Ongoing
Counselling offered: **General, Psychotherapy**
Service for: Individuals
Theoretical Approach: Psychosynthesis
Fees: £30

HUNTER Norma 081 202 9279
16 Linfield Close, LONDON NW4 1BZ
Member of: BAC
Quals/training: BA(Hons)(London); PG Dip Soc St(London);Dip Couns SW London
Personal Therapy: Ongoing
Supervision: Ongoing
Counselling offered: **General, Relationship, Bereavement**
Service for: Individuals
Theoretical Approach: Rogerian, Psychodynamic
Fees: £15 - £30

London - North West

HILDEBRAND Miki Mrs   081 203 0332
67 Parson Street, Hendon, LONDON NW4 1QT
Member of:	BAC
Quals/training:	Dip in Couns
Personal Therapy:	Yes
Supervision:	Ongoing
Counselling offered:	**General, Bereavement**
Service for:	Individuals, Couples
Theoretical Approach:	Rogerian, Psychodynamic
Fees:	£25

FRANKLYN Frank   081 202 7546
26 Sydney Grove, Hendon, LONDON NW4 2EH
Member of:	BAC, IPSS
Quals/training:	BSc (Dunelm); MA (Antioch Univ); Dip IPSS; Certified Practitioner NLP (USA 1981); Certified Practitioner "Hypnosis & NLP" (USA 1983)
Personal Therapy:	Yes
Supervision:	Ongoing
Counselling offered:	**Psychotherapy, Hypnotherapy, Brief**
Service for:	Individuals
Theoretical Approach:	Humanistic, Ericksonian, Eclectic
Fees:	£30

MARTIN Anne   081 203 1041
43 Hillview Gardens, Hendon, LONDON NW4 2JJ
Member of:	BAC, NRHP
Quals/training:	BA; Dip Stress Management; NRHP(Affil) Memb ISM; Trained in Individual Psychodynamic Psychotherapy (LCP); Relationship & Psychosexual Couns (Albany T)
Personal Therapy:	Yes
Supervision:	Ongoing
Counselling offered:	**General, Hypnotherapy, Gender dysphoria, Depression, Psychotherapy**
Service for:	Individuals, Couples, Families, Groups
Specific to:	Gays, Lesbians, Performing artists, Minorities
Theoretical Approach:	Eclectic, Kleinian, Jungian, Freudian, Ericksonian
Other languages:	German
Fees:	Negotiable

HARRIS Michael   081 202 8643
18 Shirehall Gardens, Hendon, LONDON NW4 2QS
Member of:	BAC
Quals/training:	RELATE trained
Personal Therapy:	No
Supervision:	Ongoing
Counselling offered:	**Marital**
Service for:	Individuals, Couples
Theoretical Approach:	Psychodynamic
Fees:	£20

London - North West

COPEMAN Ann　　　　　　　　　　　　　　　　　081 202 6477
17 Foscote Road, Hendon, LONDON NW4 3SE
Member of:	BAC
Quals/training:	MA in Couns (Univ of Hertfordshire)
Personal Therapy:	Ongoing
Supervision:	Ongoing
Counselling offered:	**General, Bereavement, Addiction, Eating disorders, Depression**
Service for:	Individuals, Couples
Theoretical Approach:	Psychodynamic, Person-centred
Fees:	£15 - £25 sliding scale

DOGMETCHI Geraldine　　　　　　　　　　　　　071 485 2883
18 Spencer Rise, Kentish Town, LONDON NW5 1AP
Member of:	BAC, IPSS
Quals/training:	BA Social Sciences; CQSW; IPSS Trained Psychotherapist
Personal Therapy:	Yes
Supervision:	Ongoing
Counselling offered:	**General, Psychotherapy**
Service for:	Individuals, Couples
Theoretical Approach:	Psychoanalytic
Fees:	Negotiable

DOBBS Wendy　　　　　　　　　　　　　　　　　071 485 8257
12 Boscastle Road, Kentish Town, LONDON NW5 1EG
Member of:	BAC Acc, AGIP
Quals/training:	BAC Acc; Slade Dip Fine Art 1952; Cert Ed Psychol '70; Cert Student Couns London Univ '86; AGIP
Personal Therapy:	Ongoing
Supervision:	Ongoing
Counselling offered:	**General, Eating disorders, Art therapy, Psychotherapy**
Service for:	Individuals, Groups
Theoretical Approach:	Jungian, Winnicottian
Fees:	£18 - £24

ELLIS Mary Lynne　　　　　　　　　　　　　　　071 485 5266
49 Croftdown Road, LONDON NW5
Member of:	PA
Quals/training:	Dip Art Psychotherapy 1983; MA Art Psychotherapy; Group Analysis 1 yr (IGA); Dip Psychotherapy (Philadelphia Assoc)
Personal Therapy:	Yes
Supervision:	Ongoing
Counselling offered:	**General, Psychotherapy, Art therapy**
Service for:	Individuals, Couples, Groups
Specific to:	Women, Lesbians, Gays
Theoretical Approach:	Psychoanalytic, Existential
Fees:	£25

London - North West

GREENBERG Harry — 071 485 4825
19 Parliament Hill Mansions, Lissenden Gardens, LONDON NW5 1NA
- **Member of:** BAC
- Quals/training: BA (Hons); Dip Ed Malad Child; courses at the Tavistock & IGA
- Personal Therapy: Yes
- Supervision: Ongoing
- **Counselling offered:** **General, PTSD, Crisis, Bereavement**
- Service for: Individuals, Couples
- Specific to: Refugees
- Theoretical Approach: Psychoanalytic
- Fees: Sliding scale

OWEN Christopher — 071 284 2553
20 Parliament Hill Mansions, Lissenden Gardens, Kentish Town, LONDON NW5 1NA
- **Member of:** BAC, NRHP
- Quals/training: Dip Nat College of Hypnosis & Psychotherapy 1986
- Personal Therapy: Yes
- Supervision: Ongoing
- **Counselling offered:** **Psychotherapy, Hypnotherapy**
- Service for: Individuals, Couples
- Theoretical Approach: Eclectic, Ericksonian, Adlerian
- Fees: £20

TAYLOR Mary — 071 485 5719
The Hillside Practice, 1 Hillside, Highgate Road, LONDON NW5 1QT
- **Member of:** BAC, AFT
- Quals/training: Dip Couns; Systemic Therapy with Individuals, Couples & Families
- Personal Therapy: Yes
- Supervision: Ongoing
- **Counselling offered:** **General, Bereavement, Brief, Crisis, Sexual abuse, Mental health, Cross/multi-cultural, Sexuality**
- Service for: Individuals, Couples, Families, Groups, Organisations
- Theoretical Approach: Systemic, Integrative
- Fees: £20 minimum

LA TOURELLE Maggie — 071 485 4215
58 Leverton Street, Kentish Town, LONDON NW5 2NU
- **Member of:** **BAC Acc, ANLP (PCS), Member of UKCP Register**
- Quals/training: BAC Acc; training in Couns Skills; Master Practitioner NLP
- Personal Therapy: Ongoing
- Supervision: Ongoing
- **Counselling offered:** **General**
- Service for: Individuals
- Theoretical Approach: Rogerian, NLP
- Fees: £30

London - North West

FAWCETT Jane   071 485 4591
34 Patshull Road, LONDON NW5 2UY
Member of:	BAC
Quals/training:	B Ed; Dip in Adv Couns; Cert Art Therapy
Personal Therapy:	Ongoing
Supervision:	Ongoing
Counselling offered:	**General, Work, HIV**
Service for:	Individuals
Theoretical Approach:	Person-centred, Psychodynamic
Fees:	By arrangement

McGINNIS Sylvia   071 485 0437
Kentish Town, LONDON NW5
Member of:	BAC
Quals/training:	Dip Psychodynamic Couns (Manor House Centre); tutor Nat Childbirth Trust
Personal Therapy:	Yes
Supervision:	Ongoing
Counselling offered:	**General, Bereavement, Crisis, PTSD, Relationship, Peri-natal, Parenting problems**
Service for:	Individuals, Couples
Theoretical Approach:	Psychodynamic
Other languages:	French
Fees:	£15 - £30 Sliding Scale

CARAPETIAN Rosemarie   071 794 7608
15 Ingham Road, West Hampstead, LONDON NW6 1DG
Member of:	NRHP
Quals/training:	Dip ED CHP DHP (NC) training in Educational Therapy (FAET) (MIVRHP) 1989
Personal Therapy:	No
Supervision:	Ongoing
Counselling offered:	**General, Bereavement, Hypnotherapy, Psychotherapy, Divorce, Learning difficulties**
Service for:	Individuals, Groups, Families
Specific to:	Children
Theoretical Approach:	Eclectic
Fees:	£30

BARNETT Ruth   071 431 0837
73 Fortune Green Road, Kilburn, LONDON NW6 1DR
Member of:	LCP
Quals/training:	1980 Graduated from LCP
Personal Therapy:	Yes
Supervision:	Ongoing
Counselling offered:	**Psychotherapy, Supervision**
Service for:	Individuals, Couples
Theoretical Approach:	Freudian, Object relations
Fees:	Negotiable

London - North West

LUCKS Cecilia   071 435 9130
32 Marlborough Mansions, Cannon Hill, LONDON NW6 1JR
Member of:	BAC
Quals/training:	Cert Couns 1989 & Dip Counse 1990 (CSCT)
Personal Therapy:	Ongoing
Supervision:	Ongoing
Counselling offered:	**General**
Service for:	Individuals
Theoretical Approach:	Rogerian, RET
Fees:	£25

LEDER Catherine   071 794 2995
12A Ravenshaw Street, West Hampstead, LONDON NW6 1NN
Member of:	BAC, AHPP
Quals/training:	BA Cult Anthropol; training in Neo-Reichian Therapy (Boyesen Inst); short course IGA; various seminars
Personal Therapy:	Ongoing
Supervision:	Ongoing
Counselling offered:	**Psychotherapy, Bodywork**
Service for:	Individuals, Couples, Groups, Organisations
Theoretical Approach:	Psychodynamic
Fees:	£20 - £30 sliding scale

GLOGER Estela
167 Sumatra Road, West Hampstead, LONDON NW6 1PN
Member of:	BAC
Quals/training:	MA Couns; Qualified psychoanalytic psychotherapist (LCIP)
Personal Therapy:	Yes
Supervision:	Ongoing
Counselling offered:	**Psychotherapy**
Service for:	Individuals
Theoretical Approach:	Psychoanalytic
Other languages:	Spanish, Hebrew
Fees:	£18 - £30 sliding scale

GOMEZ Lavinia   071 794 5308
21 Mill Lane, Kilburn, LONDON NW6 1NT
Member of:	BAC Acc, ITHP
Quals/training:	BAC Acc; MA (Cantab); Full member ITHP; 4 yr course (Minster Centre) APP; IGA
Personal Therapy:	Yes
Supervision:	Ongoing
Counselling offered:	**General, Crisis, Psychotherapy, Rape, Eating disorders, Depression, Sexuality**
Service for:	Individuals, Couples, Organisations
Specific to:	Young adults, Survivors of child abuse, Survivors of sex abuse, Parents, Caring professions
Theoretical Approach:	Integrative
Fees:	£20 - £30 sliding scale

London - North West

SMITH Carole　　　　　　　　　　　　　　　　　　　　　071 624 5271
86 Canfield Gardens, South Hampstead, LONDON NW6 3EE
Member of:　　　　　　　IPSS
Quals/training:　　　　　BA; Dip Ed; General Cert IGA; Dip IPSS
Personal Therapy:　　　Yes
Supervision:　　　　　　Ongoing
Counselling offered:　Psychotherapy
Service for:　　　　　　Individuals
Theoretical Approach:　Psychoanalytic, Existential
Fees:　　　　　　　　　£25 negotiable

WANLESS Peter　　　　　　　　　　　　　　　　　　　　071 328 7641
Flat 1, 170 Goldhurst Terrace, Kilburn, LONDON NW6 3HN
Member of:　　　　　　　BAC Acc, ITHP
Quals/training:　　　　　BAC(Acc); Dip Assoc Bodymind Therapy '82; CQSW; qualified as practising psychotherapist (Minster Centre) '91
Personal Therapy:　　　Yes
Supervision:　　　　　　Ongoing
Counselling offered:　Psychotherapy, Consultation, Relationship, Co-dependency
Service for:　　　　　　Individuals, Couples, Groups
Theoretical Approach:　Integrative
Fees:　　　　　　　　　£15 - £30 negotiable

VAL BAKER Jess　　　　　　　　　　　　　　　　　　　081 960 1079
28 Milman Road, Queens Park, Kilburn, LONDON NW6 4HT
Member of:　　　　　　　BAC Acc, BPS
Quals/training:　　　　　BAC Acc '87; BSc(Hons) Psychol (London Univ) '78; MSc Psychol Couns (Surrey Univ); Dip Couns Skills (SW London Coll) '87
Personal Therapy:　　　Yes
Supervision:　　　　　　Ongoing
Counselling offered:　General, Psychotherapy
Service for:　　　　　　Individuals, Couples
Theoretical Approach:　Rogerian, CAT
Fees:　　　　　　　　　£25 negotiable

MOJA-STRASSER Lucia　　　　　　　　　　　　　　　　071 372 6407
144A Abbey Road, Kilburn, LONDON NW6 4SR
Member of:　　　　　　　BAC, Member of UKCP Register
Quals/training:　　　　　Adv Dip Existential Psychotherapy; Memb SEA; MA Psychol of Therapy & Counselling; Cert Couns (LCIP); BA
Personal Therapy:　　　Ongoing
Supervision:　　　　　　Ongoing
Counselling offered:　Psychotherapy, General
Service for:　　　　　　Individuals, Couples
Theoretical Approach:　Existential
Other languages:　　　　French, Spanish, Hungarian, Romanian
Fees:　　　　　　　　　£30

London - North West

ROBINSON Hazel 071 624 0877
75a Hartland Road, LONDON NW6 6BH
Member of:	**Guild of Psychotherapists**
Quals/training:	MSc; CQSW; Memb Guild of Psychotherapists
Personal Therapy:	Yes
Supervision:	Ongoing
Counselling offered:	**Psychotherapy, Supervision**
Service for:	Individuals, Groups
Theoretical Approach:	Analytic
Fees:	£25 - £30

SVIRSKY Orit 071 372 3588
Flat 1, 126 Goldhurst Terrace, South Hampstead, LONDON NW6 3HR
Member of:	**BAC, IPSS**
Quals/training:	BA Psychol; Memb Grupo del Salud; trained in Clinical Psychol; also in Psychoanalytical Psychotherapy (IPSS)
Personal Therapy:	Ongoing
Supervision:	Ongoing
Counselling offered:	**Long-term, Short-term**
Service for:	Individuals
Theoretical Approach:	Psychodynamic
Other languages:	Portuguese
Fees:	£20 - £30

JOFFE Riva 081 969 0288
6 Peploe Road, Queens Park, LONDON NW6 6EB
Member of:	**BAC, IPSS**
Quals/training:	IPSS Trained; NAFSIYAT Dip
Personal Therapy:	Ongoing
Supervision:	Ongoing
Counselling offered:	**Brief, Long-term**
Service for:	Individuals, Couples, Groups
Specific to:	Women, Adoptees, Adoptors, Ethnic minorities
Theoretical Approach:	Analytic, Humanistic, Eclectic
Fees:	£15 - £35 sliding scale

ISAACSON Zelda ansaphone 081 960 5121
LONDON NW6 6LP
Member of:	**BAC**
Quals/training:	BEd; MA (Ed); training in Psychosynthesis (IP) 1989; Humanist and Integrative Psychotherapy (Minster Centre) '90-1; Currently:MA in Couns & Psychotherapy (Regent's Coll)
Personal Therapy:	Yes
Supervision:	Ongoing
Counselling offered:	**General, Psychotherapy**
Service for:	Individuals, Groups
Specific to:	Women, Gays, Jewish, Teachers
Theoretical Approach:	Integrative
Fees:	£15 - £27

London - North West

GORDON Paul   071 624 4529
16 Kenilworth Road, Kilburn, LONDON NW6 7HJ
Member of: IPSS
Quals/training: LLB(Hons); IPSS trained psychotherapist
Personal Therapy: Ongoing
Supervision: Ongoing
Counselling offered: Psychotherapy
Service for: Individuals, Couples
Theoretical Approach: Psychoanalytic
Fees: £25 negotiable

RICHARDS Diana   081 459 3180
71 The Avenue, LONDON NW6 7NS
Member of: BAP
Quals/training: AMBAP; CQSW; Couns training (CTA); Dip Applied Social Studies; Dip Social Studies; Dip Sociology
Personal Therapy: Yes
Supervision: Ongoing
Counselling offered: General, Abuse, Bereavement, Cross/multi-cultural, Consultation, Psychotherapy
Service for: Individuals, Couples, Groups
Specific to: Social workers, Ethnic minorities
Theoretical Approach: Psychodynamic, Psychoanalytic
Fees: Negotiable

SCHILD Maureen   081 451 4772
11/f Christchurch Avenue, Kilburn, LONDON NW6 7QP
Member of: BAC
Quals/training: BEd; Dip Psychosynthesis Couns & Psychotherapy (IP); Supervisor (IP)
Personal Therapy: Ongoing
Supervision: Ongoing
Counselling offered: General, Addiction, Dependency, Women's issues, Midlife, Spiritual
Service for: Individuals, Couples, Groups
Specific to: Women
Theoretical Approach: Psychosynthesis, Psychodynamic
Fees: £30

DRYDEN Windy   071 624 0732
14 Winchester Avenue, Brondesbury Park, Kilburn, LONDON NW6 7TU
Member of: BAC Acc
Quals/training: BAC Acc; Dip Couns (Univ of Aston) '75; MSc Pychotherapy (Warwick Univ) '80
Personal Therapy: Yes
Supervision: Ongoing
Counselling offered: General, Marital, Psychotherapy
Service for: Individuals, Couples
Theoretical Approach: Eclectic, RET
Fees: £60

London - North West

SIMMONS Rochelle   081 959 1065
59 Hale Lane, Mill Hill, LONDON NW7 3PS
Member of:	BAC
Quals/training:	Dip Couns; Memb Nat Coun Psychotherapists; Ac Dip Ed Psychol
Personal Therapy:	Yes
Supervision:	Ongoing
Counselling offered:	General, Psychotherapy, Stress management, Relaxation, Assertiveness
Theoretical Approach:	Existential, Humanistic, Gestalt
Fees:	£25 negotiable, groups by arrangement

PLATT Sue   081 959 6560
6 Marion Road, Mill Hill, LONDON NW7 4AN
Member of:	BAC
Quals/training:	Cert Couns & Psychotherapy (Minster Centre) 1988
Personal Therapy:	Ongoing
Supervision:	Ongoing
Counselling offered:	General, Crisis, Relationship, Sexuality, Short-term, Long-term
Service for:	Individuals, Couples
Specific to:	Women, Lesbians
Theoretical Approach:	Psychodynamic, Object relations
Fees:	£20 some concessions

CONROY Ruth   081 959 3456
7 Lawrence Street, Mill Hill, LONDON NW7 4JJ
Member of:	BAC
Quals/training:	Dip Couns & Community Skills; Adv Dip in Psychodynamic Couns; AIDS; Bereavement
Personal Therapy:	Yes
Supervision:	Ongoing
Counselling offered:	AIDS, General, Bereavement
Service for:	Individuals, Groups
Specific to:	Parents, Children with special needs, Bereavement
Theoretical Approach:	Psychodynamic
Fees:	£25 negotiable

JACKSON Val   081 959 7691
22 Bedford Road, Mill Hill, LONDON NW7 4LU
Member of:	BAC
Quals/training:	BA Psychol 1980; Child Guidance Training, Play Therapy, Groupwork, Drama Psychotherapy 1972-80; Post Grad trainee in Human Sexuality
Personal Therapy:	Yes
Supervision:	Ongoing
Counselling offered:	General, Crisis, Victimisation, Sexual dysfunction, Sexual abuse, Eating disorders
Service for:	Individuals, Groups, Families
Specific to:	Children, Young people, People with language problems
Theoretical Approach:	Gestalt, Play therapy
Fees:	£30 negotiable

London - North West

WARREN Madeline 081 959 1463
51 Victoria Road, Mill Hill, LONDON NW7 4SA
Member of: BAC Acc
Quals/training: BAC Acc; Dip Couns (Stevenage CHE) '87; Memb ICM
Personal Therapy: Yes
Supervision: Ongoing
Counselling offered: General, Bereavement, Depression, Alcohol, Abortion
Service for: Individuals, Couples, Groups
Theoretical Approach: Psychoanalytic
Fees: £20 - £22 negotiable

HOWARD Angela 071 624 1709
37 Loudoun Road, St John's Wood, LONDON NW8 0NE
Member of: Guild of Psychotherapists
Quals/training: Member of Guild of Psychotherapists; RELATE trained 1982
Personal Therapy: Yes
Supervision: Ongoing
Counselling offered: Psychotherapy
Service for: Individuals, Couples
Theoretical Approach: Analytical, Freudian, Object relations
Fees: £14 - £24 sliding scale

LEVY Colette 071 624 4777
52 Springfield Road, St John's Wood, LONDON NW8 0QN
Member of: IPC
Quals/training: Full memb IPC/WPF
Personal Therapy: Yes
Supervision: Ongoing
Counselling offered: Psychotherapy, Marital
Service for: Individuals, Couples
Theoretical Approach: Analytical
Fees: £25 negotiable

POTTER Val 081 802 3582
Consulting Room, 38 Circus Road, St Johns Wood, LONDON NW8
Member of: BAC, BPS
Quals/training: BA(Hons) Psychol (OU); Cert Supervision of Psychodynamic Couns (WPF) 1989
Personal Therapy: Yes
Supervision: Ongoing
Counselling offered: General, Psychotherapy
Service for: Individuals
Theoretical Approach: Analytical
Fees: £27 negotiable

London - North West

OKIN Sandra   071 722 7798
58a Viceroy Court, Prince Albert Road, LONDON NW8 7PS
Member of:	BAC
Quals/training:	Dip Couns (Outreach) 1990; Adv Dip Counselling (Outreach) 1993; working towards BAC Acc
Personal Therapy:	Ongoing
Supervision:	Ongoing
Counselling offered:	**General, Bereavement, Crisis**
Service for:	Individuals, Groups
Theoretical Approach:	Psychodynamic
Fees:	Negotiable

SOBERS Marlene   081 204 5272
4 Hillside, Hay Lane, Kingsbury, LONDON NW9 0NE
Member of:	BAC
Quals/training:	Dip Couns (CSCT); SRN; City & Guilds Teaching Cert
Personal Therapy:	Ongoing
Supervision:	Ongoing
Counselling offered:	**General, Cancer**
Service for:	Individuals, Couples
Specific to:	Substance abusers
Theoretical Approach:	Freudian, Rogerian, Jungian
Fees:	£10 - £25 sliding scale

COOPER Cassie   081 204 8693
34 Fryant Way, Kingsbury, LONDON NW9 9SB
Member of:	BAC, BPS, CPCP
Quals/training:	BSc Applied Social Studies '50; BSc Special Degree in Psychol '69; trained at Birkbeck College & Tavistock Inst; ASC Acc
Personal Therapy:	Ongoing
Supervision:	Ongoing
Counselling offered:	**General, Bereavement, Sexual, Psychotherapy**
Service for:	Individuals, Groups
Theoretical Approach:	Eclectic
Other languages:	French, German
Fees:	£30 sliding scale

ANDERSON Linda   081 965 5872
60 All Souls Avenue, Willesden, LONDON NW10 3BG
Member of:	IGA
Quals/training:	1971 CQSW; 1981 Group Analyst IGA; Member GAS
Personal Therapy:	Yes
Supervision:	Ongoing
Counselling offered:	**Psychotherapy, Analysis**
Service for:	Individuals, Groups
Specific to:	Students, Lecturers
Theoretical Approach:	Psychoanalytic
Fees:	£22.50-£45, low student fees

London - North West

O'CALLAGHAN Lesley   081 459 8571
53 Okehampton Road, Willesden, LONDON NW10 3EN
Member of: BAC
Quals/training: Humanistic & Traditional Psychotherapy (Minster Centre)
Personal Therapy: Ongoing
Supervision: Ongoing
Counselling offered: **General**
Service for: Individuals
Theoretical Approach: Humanistic
Fees: £15 - £22

SMITH Christine   081 969 5313
15 Wrentham Avenue, Willesden, LONDON NW10 3HT
Member of: BAC Acc
Quals/training: BAC Acc; Dip Couns Skills (SW London College) 1979
Personal Therapy: Yes
Supervision: Ongoing
Counselling offered: **General**
Service for: Individuals
Theoretical Approach: Psychodynamic
Fees: £20 - £25 negotiable

SEGAL Julia   081 453 2337
Central Middlesex Hospital, Multiple Sclerosis Unit, Acton, LONDON NW10 7NS
Member of: BAC
Quals/training: NMGC Trained
Personal Therapy: Yes
Supervision: Ongoing
Counselling offered: **MS**
Service for: Individuals, Couples, Families
Theoretical Approach: Kleinian
Other languages: German, French
Fees: Funded by clients' local HA

BODGENER Sue   081 961 2763
9 Brownlow Road, Harlesden, LONDON NW10 9QN
Member of: BAC, MPTI, GPTI
Quals/training: Dip Couns; Cert Art Therapy; trainee Gestalt Psychotherapist
                        (metanoia)
Personal Therapy: Ongoing
Supervision: Ongoing
Counselling offered: **General, Eating disorders, Incest**
Service for: Individuals, Groups
Theoretical Approach: Rogerian, Gestalt
Fees: £20 - £25

London - North West

SILVERSTONE Liesl   081 455 8570
17 Cranbourne Gardens, Golders Green, LONDON NW11 0HS
Member of:	BAC Acc
Quals/training:	BAC Acc; Dip Couns (SW London Coll)'79; Dip Art Therapy (St Albans)'81; Cert Transpersonal Psychol '86; Memb Brit Assoc for Person-Centred Approach
Personal Therapy:	Ongoing
Supervision:	Ongoing
Counselling offered:	General, Supervision
Service for:	Individuals, Groups
Specific to:	Holocaust survivors
Theoretical Approach:	Person-centred, Art therapy, Gestalt, TA
Other languages:	German, Czech, French
Fees:	£30

REECE Rosalind   081 455 0562
24 Saffron Close, Hendon Park Row, Golders Green, LONDON NW11 0PY
Member of:	BAC
Quals/training:	Dip Sociol(LSE); CQSW; ex psychiatric hospital worker; psycho-analytical training(Tavistock Clinic)
Personal Therapy:	Yes
Supervision:	Ongoing
Counselling offered:	Supervision
Service for:	Individuals, Groups
Theoretical Approach:	Jungian
Fees:	£25 (negotiable for students)

WATKINS SEYMOUR Eileen   ansaphone 081 455 3743
The Ravenscroft Centre, 6 Ravenscroft Avenue, Golders Green, LONDON NW11 0RY
Member of:	ANLP (PCS)
Quals/training:	BA Lib Arts; MA(ABT) Humanistic Psychol; 3 yrs TA training; 2 yrs Social Psychiatry (Bierer, Harley St); NLP(Co-founded UKTC)1981; NLP Trainer (EINLP) 1986
Personal Therapy:	Yes
Supervision:	Ongoing
Counselling offered:	General, Psychotherapy, Anxiety, Phobias, Learning difficulties, Psychosomatic, Relationship, Unwanted habits, Stress
Service for:	Individuals, Couples, Organisations
Theoretical Approach:	NLP
Fees:	£50 + VAT (payment programmes)

STONE Anthony   081 455 0794
7 Westholm, Golders Green, LONDON NW11 6LH
Member of:	BAC, AHPP
Quals/training:	Couns & Psychotherapy at Spectrum; Essentials of Psychosynthesis etc
Personal Therapy:	Ongoing
Supervision:	Ongoing
Counselling offered:	General, Depression, Work, Relationship
Service for:	Individuals, Couples
Theoretical Approach:	Rogerian, Gestalt, Existential
Fees:	£20 - £30

London - North West

DELL Judith 081 455 8737
45 Litchfield Way, Golders Green, LONDON NW11 6NU
Member of:	BAC RSup, AHPP
Quals/training:	BAC; AHPP; RELATE Acc; training in Couns & Psycotherapy; Group Analysis, Psychodrama, Marital & Family Therapy, 1969-90; BAC Recognised Supervisor '89
Personal Therapy:	Yes
Supervision:	Ongoing
Counselling offered:	**General, Short-term, Long-term, Psychotherapy, Supervision**
Service for:	Individuals, Couples, Families, Groups
Theoretical Approach:	Psychodynamic
Fees:	£30 ind; £40 group & families

KELLY Kathleen 081 458 1695
15 Stowe House, Emmott Close, Golders Green, LONDON NW11 6QA
Member of:	BAC
Quals/training:	Dip in Psychosynthesis Couns & Therapy, PET; BSc; Cert Ed; RN
Personal Therapy:	Yes
Supervision:	Ongoing
Counselling offered:	**General, Health**
Service for:	Individuals
Theoretical Approach:	Psychosynthesis
Fees:	£30 Negotiable

PHILLIPS Wendy 081 458 0306
5 Turner Drive, Golders Green, LONDON NW11 6TX
Member of:	BASMT
Quals/training:	NMGC Trained
Personal Therapy:	Yes
Supervision:	Ongoing
Counselling offered:	**Marital, Relationship, Eating disorders, Bereavement**
Service for:	Individuals, Couples, Groups
Theoretical Approach:	Psychodynamic, Eclectic
Fees:	£30 negotiable

BRAIN Sara 081 455 9024
50 Waterlow Court, Heath Close, LONDON NW11 7DT
Member of:	BAC Acc
Quals/training:	BAC Acc; 1977-9 training with WPF; Couns Course (CTP); seminars in Psychotherapy (Tavistock Clinic)
Personal Therapy:	Yes
Supervision:	Ongoing
Counselling offered:	**General, Bereavement, Psychotherapy**
Service for:	Individuals, Couples
Theoretical Approach:	Psychodynamic
Fees:	£35 sliding scale

London - North West

BROIDO Isabelle 081 458 3979
34 Park Drive, Golders Green, LONDON NW11 7SP
Member of:	BAC
Quals/training:	Dip Couns
Personal Therapy:	Yes
Supervision:	Ongoing
Counselling offered:	**General, Bereavement, Brief**
Service for:	Individuals
Specific to:	Women, Ethnic minorities
Theoretical Approach:	Egan, Cognitive/Behavioural
Fees:	£15 - £25 Sliding scale

CHANDWANI Lilian 081 458 8204
18 Park Drive, Golders Green, LONDON NW11 7SP
Member of:	BAC
Quals/training:	BA; Dip Couns; training in psychotherapy (IPSS)
Personal Therapy:	Ongoing
Supervision:	Ongoing
Counselling offered:	**General, Bereavement, Cross/multi-cultural, Psychotherapy**
Service for:	Individuals
Theoretical Approach:	Psychodynamic
Fees:	£20 - £30 sliding scale

ORLANS Vanja 081 458 6937
The Hillside Practice, 1 Hillside, Highgate Road, LONDON NW5 1EF
Member of:	BAC, BPS, GPTI, MPTI
Quals/training:	C Psychol; AFBPsS; PhD on Stress 1987; training in Gestalt Psychotherapy (GPTI/metanoia) since 1988
Personal Therapy:	Ongoing
Supervision:	Ongoing
Counselling offered:	**General, Psychotherapy**
Service for:	Individuals, Couples, Groups
Theoretical Approach:	Gestalt, Humanistic
Fees:	£30

JACKSON Diana 081 458 5791
26 Willifield Way, Golders Green, LONDON NW11 7XT
Member of:	BAC, ITHP
Quals/training:	Dip Couns Skills (London College) 1987; Dip in Integrative Couns (Minster Centre) 1991; Foundation year in working with couples (TIMS) 1992
Personal Therapy:	Ongoing
Supervision:	Ongoing
Counselling offered:	**General, Bereavement, Crisis, AIDS, Terminal illness, Eating disorders**
Service for:	Individuals, Couples
Theoretical Approach:	Psychodynamic, Object relations
Fees:	£25, £40.00 couples

London - North West

SUGARMAN John   081 455 7438
11 Golders Green Crescent, LONDON NW11 8LA
Member of: BAC
Quals/training: Int Assoc Hypnotists '52; Psychol Soc GB '59; Brit Coll Naturopathy
                       & Osteopathy '60; Lond Soc Ericksonian Psychotherapy & Hypno-
                       sis; Assoc Holistic Hypnotherapists
Personal Therapy: Ongoing
Supervision: Ongoing
Counselling offered: **General, Hypnotherapy, Psychotherapy**
Service for: Individuals, Couples, Families
Theoretical Approach: Eclectic, Holistic
Fees: £40 intl cons; £25 thereafter

CLAYTON Zena   081 458 1461
Flat 1, 1 Helenslea Avenue, Golders Green, LONDON NW11 8NE
Member of: BAC
Quals/training: 1981 Counselling courses (Middx Poly); '83-4 introduction to Family
                       &Marital Therapy (IFT); ongoing bereavement training (Jewish
                       Bereavement Counselling Service)
Personal Therapy: Ongoing
Supervision: Ongoing
Counselling offered: **General, Bereavement**
Service for: Individuals
Theoretical Approach: Eclectic
Fees: £27.50 negotiable

HAMILTON Irene   081 458 6021
27 Sandringham Road, Golders Green, LONDON NW11 9DR
Member of: BAC, IPC, BPA
Quals/training: Dip Adv Psychadynamic Couns (WPF); CAT Training (Guy's Hos-
                       pital); Introductory Course (IGA); Dip Psychodrama & Group Ana-
                       lytic Psychotherapy (London)
Personal Therapy: Yes
Supervision: Ongoing
Counselling offered: **General, Eating disorders**
Service for: Individuals, Groups
Theoretical Approach: Psychodynamic, Analytical, Psychodrama
Fees: £25 - £35 groups from £10/person

ULLMANN Jacqueline   Ansaphone 081 458 4490
19 Highfield Gardens, Golders Green, LONDON NW11 9HD
Member of: BAC
Quals/training: Law Degree (France); Dip Ed; Dip Couns (CSCT)
Personal Therapy: Yes
Supervision: Ongoing
Counselling offered: **General, Bereavement, Stress, Cancer**
Service for: Individuals, Couples
Specific to: Adolescents, Carers
Theoretical Approach: Person-centred, Psychodynamic
Other languages: French, Hebrew
Fees: £25

London - North West

McGEE Colin   **081 889 5965**
95 Woodside Road, Woodgreen, LONDON N22 5HR
Member of: **BAC, IPSS**
Quals/training: Cert Ed, Schools Psychol Service Couns Cert; IPSS Psychotherapy Training
Personal Therapy: Ongoing
Supervision: Ongoing
Counselling offered: **General, Relationship, Psychotherapy**
Service for: Individuals, Couples, Families, Groups
Theoretical Approach: Existential, Humanistic
Fees: Sliding scale

London - South East

Organisations

PSYCHOSYNTHESIS & EDUCATION TRUST (PET)
071 403 7814, 071 403 2100
92/94 Tooley Street, London Bridge, LONDON SE1 2TH
Service: Counselling service, short courses in personal growth, courses in professional development, youth programme, prof dip courses in psychosynthesis couns & therapy
Area served: National
Training of workers: 3 year Diploma Course at PET
Code of Ethics: BAC, UKCP
Fees: On application

WATERLOO COMMUNITY COUNSELLING PROJECT   071 928 5921
5 Murrio House, Murfly Street, LONDON SE1 7AJ
Service: General counselling
Area served: For those living/working/studying in Lambeth & Southwark
Other languages: French
Referral: Self or others
Training of workers: Dip Couns & psychotherapy and various specialist courses. Regular supervision
Code of Ethics: BAC
Management by: Management Committee
Fees: Donations welcome

CENTRE FOR STRESS MANAGEMENT   081 293 4114
156 Westcombe Hill, Blackheath, LONDON SE3 7DH
Service: Stress & anxiety counselling & therapy, phobias & panic disorders, PTSD, stress management, relaxation, assertion training. REBT cognitive/behavioural therapy; multimodal ther.
Area served: London & south; UK for training & in-house courses
Referral: Self or others
Training of workers: Appropriate qualifications in psychology, counselling or health education; ongoing supervision
Code of Ethics: BPS
Management by: Director
Fees: By arrangement

MAUDSLEY HOSPITAL, PSYCHOSEXUAL CLINIC   071 703 6333
Denmark Hill, LONDON SE5 8AZ
Service: Sexual and marital therapy for people with sexual dysfunction, psychiatric and marital problems
Area served: South East England
Referral: GP
Training of workers: All fully qualified or in training, with individual and group supervision
Code of Ethics: BASMT
Management by: NHS
Fees: None

London - South East

SOUTH EAST LONDON COUNSELLING 071 403 4854
4 Elliscombe Road, Charlton, LONDON SE7 7PY
Service:	General counselling to individuals, couples & groups using a variety of approaches
Area served:	SE & Central London
Referral:	Self or others
Training of workers:	Appropriate professional qualification in counselling & psychotherapy; ongoing supervision
Code of Ethics:	BAC
Management by:	Partnership
Fees:	£20 - £30 some concessions

GREENWICH MIND NETWORKS 081 305 2388, 081 853 1473
N Charlton Community Project, 38 Floyd Road, Greenwich, LONDON SE7 8AN
Service:	Offers casework counselling to individuals and families within the African-Caribbean community. Also a mental health telephone advice line from 10am - 1pm
Area served:	Greenwich and surrounding areas
Referral:	Self
Training of workers:	BA (Social Science), Foundation course in counselling, RSA Cert in Cllg, Post grad Dip in Personnel Management. Supervision
Code of Ethics:	BAC
Management by:	Management Committee
Fees:	None

EQUILIBRIUM COUNSELLING SERVICES appointmts 081 870 8761
Meridian House, Royal Hill, Greenwich, LONDON SE10
Service:	Person-centred counselling for stress-related problems, couples, gender issues. Available daytime & evenings
Area served:	South East London
Referral:	Self
Training of workers:	Cert Prof Couns(Albany Trust); personal therapy & regular supervision
Code of Ethics:	BAC
Management by:	The Agency
Fees:	£25 day(£31 eve with concessions)

SOUTH LONDON PSYCHOTHERAPY CENTRE 081 659 8486
6 Owen Walk, Sycamore Grove, Anerley, LONDON SE20 8BY
Service:	Analytical psychotherapy for individuals (adults and young people), couples, groups, families; consultancy to groups
Area served:	South London
Other languages:	Dutch, German, French, Maltese
Referral:	Self or others
Training of workers:	AGIP trained, except affiliate members
Code of Ethics:	AGIP
Management by:	Committee of entire membership. Centre is part of Penelope,Lady Balogh Psychotherapy Trust
Fees:	£20 - £30 lower fees negotiable

London - South East

**CASSEL CENTRE
(COUNSELLING & SOCIAL WORK SE LONDON)   081 291 3436**
4 Waldram Park Road, Forest Hill, LONDON SE23 2PN
Service: Individual, couple and family counselling for a wide range of problems: depression, anxiety, stress, relationship, bereavement, mental health, crisis, transcultural, dom. viol
Area served: London Borough of Lewisham
Other languages: French, Spanish
Referral: Self or others
Training of workers: CQSW, Psychodynamic counselling; Psychotherapist in training; Humanistic
Code of Ethics: BAC, IPC
Management by: Management Committee of local residents, ex users, members of other voluntary or statutory services
Fees: None

LONDON THERAPY CO-OPERATIVE   081 299 4587, 081 674 6937
18 Berwyn Road, LONDON SE24 9BD
Service: Wide range of problems both long and short term for individuals, couples and groups
Area served: South London
Other languages: German
Referral: Self or others
Training of workers: CQSW; PCGE; Humanistic Dips Couns & Adv Dip Gestalt & Contrib Train (Pellin Inst); Personal therapy, regular supervision
Code of Ethics: BAC
Management by: Co-operative
Fees: £16 - £30 negotiable

ISIS COUNSELLING & THERAPY SERVICE   071 737 5188
22 St Luke's Close, LONDON SE25 4SX
Service: Network of counsellors and psychotherapists working at different locations throughout South London and East London
Area served: Mainly South and East London
Referral: Self
Training of workers: Minimum of 3 yrs training & 2 yrs experience in counselling and/or psychotherapy; Personal therapy & regular supervision
Code of Ethics: BAC
Management by: Directors
Fees: £20 - £30

**PSYCHOTHERAPY REFERRAL SERVICE SOUTH & WEST LONDON
081 771 2311**
West Side Row, 222 South Norwood Hill, LONDON SE25 6AS
Service: Individuals seeking analytic psychotherapy are placed with qualified & experienced therapists following an initial consultation; group work also available
Area served: South & West London
Other languages: Finnish, German
Referral: Self or others
Training of workers: Qualified members of recognised psychotherapy training orgs
Code of Ethics: Therapists' Professional body
Management by: Management Committee
Fees: £25 - £35 negotiable, consultation £36

London - South East

Individual Practitioners
*Every individual is a **member of** one or more organisations eligible for entry into this directory. BAC Accredited Counsellors and Recognised Supervisors are shaded.*

HART Chris   0728 688134
Psychosynthesis & Education Trust, 92-94 Tooley Street, London Bridge, LONDON SE1 2TH
Member of:	BAC
Quals/training:	Dip Psychosynthesis Couns (PET)
Personal Therapy:	Ongoing
Supervision:	Ongoing
Counselling offered:	**Psychotherapy**
Service for:	Individuals
Theoretical Approach:	Humanistic, Transpersonal
Fees:	£25

PLOWMAN Polly   ansaphone 071 403 4854
Flat 2, 14 Trinity Church Square, LONDON SE1 4HU
Member of:	BAC
Quals/training:	BA '74; Cert Ed '76; Dip Couns (IP); Dip Therapy (Re-vision) IDHP Facilitator Styles (Bath Univ); Memb AAPP; Supervision Course (metanoia)
Personal Therapy:	Ongoing
Supervision:	Ongoing
Counselling offered:	**General, Psychotherapy**
Service for:	Individuals, Couples, Groups
Theoretical Approach:	Psychosynthesis, Transpersonal
Fees:	£28 - £30 Some concessionary rates

ROBSON Barbara   071 633 0447
77 Falcon Point, Hopton Street, Bankside, LONDON SE1 0JP
Member of:	BAC Acc
Quals/training:	BAC(Acc); Dip Couns(WPF)'78
Personal Therapy:	Yes
Supervision:	Ongoing
Counselling offered:	**General, Sexual, Bereavement, Psychotherapy**
Service for:	Individuals, Groups
Theoretical Approach:	Psychoanalytic
Fees:	£35 negotiable

GARDINER Margaret   081 318 1693
3 Collins Square, off Tranquil Vale, Blackheath, LONDON SE3 0BT
Member of:	BAC, AGIP
Quals/training:	MA; PGCE; Cert Couns; currently training with AGIP
Personal Therapy:	Yes
Supervision:	Ongoing
Counselling offered:	**General**
Service for:	Individuals, Couples
Theoretical Approach:	Analytic
Fees:	Negotiable

London - South East

McMAHON Gladeana 081 852 4854
11 Streetfield Mews, Blackheath Park, Blackheath, LONDON SE3 0ER
Member of:	BAC Acc RSup
Quals/training:	Couns Skills Course (SWLC); Cert Couns Skills (LCIP) 1989; Cert Behavioural Psychother (Inst Psychiat) 1989; Sup & Consult Course (Maudsley): Prim Cert Pers Constr Psychol
Personal Therapy:	Ongoing
Supervision:	Ongoing
Counselling offered:	**General, Addiction, Stress management, Trauma, Supervision**
Service for:	Individuals, Couples
Fees:	£25 - £30 (assessment £25)

HOWARD Heather 081 852 6564
83 Blackheath Park, Blackheath, LONDON SE3 0EU
Member of:	BAC
Quals/training:	BA (Hons); Dip (IPSS) Psychodynamic section'82; Gestalt Training'78-'81; Psychosynthesis Humanistic Training'79-'82; Supervision '82-'92 by qualified Therapist (Tavistock Inst)
Personal Therapy:	Ongoing
Supervision:	Ongoing
Counselling offered:	**General, Psychotherapy**
Service for:	Individuals
Theoretical Approach:	Psycho-developmental
Fees:	£25 negotiable

KERR Anna 081 852 1751
3 Talbot Place, Blackheath, LONDON SE3 0TZ
Member of:	Guild of Psychotherapists
Quals/training:	Psychiatric Social Worker; trainee psychotherapist
Personal Therapy:	Ongoing
Supervision:	Ongoing
Counselling offered:	**General, Family**
Service for:	Individuals, Couples, Families
Specific to:	Stepfamilies, Adoptees
Theoretical Approach:	Psychodynamic
Other languages:	French
Fees:	£25 (£30 couples)

PALMER Stephen 081 852 6165
3 Southvale Road, Blackheath, LONDON SE3 0TP
Member of:	BAC
Quals/training:	BA Psychol; CPCP Trained '86; Cert Couns (LCIP) '88; Fellow RSH; PG Cert Behavioural Therapy (Inst Psychiatry) '90; Cert RET '90; Dip RET & Couns '92, Memb Assoc RET (Acc) & ISMA
Personal Therapy:	Yes
Supervision:	Ongoing
Counselling offered:	**General, Stress, Anxiety, Work, Panic attacks, PTSD, Phobias**
Service for:	Individuals, Couples, Families, Groups, Organisations
Theoretical Approach:	Eclectic, RET, Cognitive/Behavioural, Multimodal
Fees:	£40 dependent on income

London - South East

BISHOP Patricia   081 293 1995, 081 692 9260
156 Westcombe Hill, Blackheath, LONDON SE3 7DH
Member of:	**BAC, IPSS**
Quals/training:	BA(Hons) First class (OU); Dip Psychotherapy (IPSS) 1985-88
Personal Therapy:	Ongoing
Supervision:	Ongoing
Counselling offered:	**Psychotherapy**
Service for:	Individuals
Theoretical Approach:	Psychoanalytic
Fees:	£40 consultation, then negotiable

SULLIVAN Mary   081 858 5960
60 Humber Road, Blackheath, LONDON SE3 7LU
Member of:	**BAC**
Quals/training:	BEd (RS); Found Cert Psych, Adv Dip Integ Couns
Personal Therapy:	Ongoing
Supervision:	Ongoing
Counselling offered:	**General, Psychotherapy**
Service for:	Individuals
Specific to:	Young adults
Theoretical Approach:	Psychoanalytic, Existential
Fees:	£10 - £18

KILBURN Andrew   081 853 5467, 081 659 2151
Blackheath, LONDON SE3
Member of:	**BAC**
Quals/training:	BA(Hons); RMN; Cert Psychodynamic Couns (WPF)
Personal Therapy:	Yes
Supervision:	Ongoing
Counselling offered:	**General, Relationship, Personal growth**
Service for:	Individuals
Theoretical Approach:	Psychodynamic
Fees:	£20 - £30

BOHL Yvonne   081 852 0405
70 The Hall, Foxes Dale, Blackheath, LONDON SE3 9BG
Member of:	**BAC, IPC**
Quals/training:	BA; Dip Sociology; Dip Adv Psychodynamic Couns (IPC/WPF) 1991
Personal Therapy:	Ongoing
Supervision:	Ongoing
Counselling offered:	**General**
Service for:	Individuals
Specific to:	Women
Theoretical Approach:	Analytic
Fees:	£18 - £25 Sliding scale

London - South East

WHYTE Elizabeth 081 852 5287
2 Pond Road, Blackheath Park, LONDON SE3 9JL
Member of: BAC
Quals/training: Dip Couns (Kingston Coll)
Personal Therapy: Ongoing
Supervision: Ongoing
Counselling offered: General, Relationship, Pastoral
Service for: Individuals
Theoretical Approach: Psychodynamic
Fees: £20 - £26 sliding scale

CLOUGH Andrea 081 691 5303
37 Harefield Road, Brockley, LONDON SE4 1LW
Member of: BAC, Member of UKCP Register
Quals/training: Accredited by UKCP; Dip Couns (IP); Dip Psychotherapy (IP)
Personal Therapy: Ongoing
Supervision: Ongoing
Counselling offered: General, Bereavement, Relationship, Psychotherapy, ME
Service for: Individuals, Couples
Specific to: Women, Students
Theoretical Approach: Eclectic, Integrative
Fees: £25 - £30 negotiable

EDWARDS Linda 081 691 5419
65 Manor Avenue, Brockley, LONDON SE4 1TD
Member of: BAC
Quals/training: Dip & Adv Dip (Pellin Inst)
Personal Therapy: Ongoing
Supervision: Ongoing
Counselling offered: General, Psychotherapy
Service for: Individuals, Couples
Specific to: Gays, Lesbians
Theoretical Approach: Analytic, Person-centred, Gestalt
Fees: £20 (£15 low waged)

CLEMINSON Dorel 071 358 9661
36 Seymour Gardens, Brockley, LONDON SE4 2DN
Member of: BAC
Quals/training: RGN; Cert CPN, RMN; Combined Cert in Couns; RSA Cert; Dip Couns; taking MA in Psychotherapy & Counselling
Personal Therapy: Ongoing
Supervision: Ongoing
Counselling offered: General, Bereavement, Psychotherapy
Service for: Individuals, Couples
Specific to: Women, Ethnic minorities
Theoretical Approach: Rogerian, Psychodynamic
Fees: £18 - £25 sliding scale

London - South East

ROSE Suzanna 071 703 5411 x3123
Traumatic Stress Project, Institute of Psychiatry, De Crespigny Park, LONDON SE5 8AF
Member of:	BAC
Quals/training:	MA (Counselling); RGN; RHV; UKCC
Personal Therapy:	Ongoing
Supervision:	Ongoing
Counselling offered:	General, Crisis, Crit. incident debriefing
Service for:	Individuals, Groups, Organisations
Specific to:	Trauma victims, Victims of crime, Victims of violence
Theoretical Approach:	Psychodynamic, Cognitive/Behavioural
Other languages:	Dutch
Fees:	No charge at present

WILSON Sally 071 703 5977
White Lodge, 67 Grove Lane, Camberwell, LONDON SE5 8SP
Member of:	BAC Acc
Quals/training:	BAC(Acc); MA(Oxon); Dip Couns Skills(SW London Coll)'83
Personal Therapy:	Yes
Supervision:	Ongoing
Counselling offered:	General
Service for:	Individuals, Couples
Specific to:	Teachers, Young people, Women
Theoretical Approach:	Rogerian, Psychodynamic
Fees:	£20

EDGE Jon 081 698 3205
29 Rosenthal Road, Catford, LONDON SE6 2BX
Member of:	BAC, Guild of Psychotherapists
Quals/training:	MA & BEd (London Univ); Cert Couns (LCIP) 1981; Dip Student Couns 1988; & Adv Student Couns Practice (London); Tutor & supervisor in Couns at Goldsmiths'
Personal Therapy:	Ongoing
Supervision:	Ongoing
Counselling offered:	General, Bereavement, Relationship, Personal growth
Service for:	Individuals
Theoretical Approach:	Psychoanalytic, Psychodynamic
Fees:	£25 - £45

LEYGRAF Bernd 081 291 7808
Flat 9, Rutland Lodge, 81 Perry Hill, Catford, LONDON SE6 4LL
Member of:	BAC, AHPP, BASMT, GPTI
Quals/training:	BSc Couns Psychol (German equiv); Dip Couns (IIP); AAHPP Acc; Other training: Gestalt Centre, metanoia, RET, Client-centred Therapy
Personal Therapy:	Ongoing
Supervision:	Ongoing
Counselling offered:	General, Sexual abuse, Alcohol, Substance abuse, Dependency, Men's issues
Service for:	Individuals, Couples, Families, Groups
Specific to:	Survivors of sex abuse, Offenders
Theoretical Approach:	Humanistic, Gestalt, Rogerian
Other languages:	German, Italian, Spanish
Fees:	£25 - £35 some burseries

London - South East

ALLMAN David 081 690 8215
Third Floor Flat, 7A Catford Broadway, Catford, LONDON SE6 4SP
Member of: BAC Acc, ITA
Quals/training: BAC(Acc); Dip Couns Skills(S W London College); BA; training in TA (metanoia)
Personal Therapy: Ongoing
Supervision: Ongoing
Counselling offered: General, Psychotherapy
Service for: Individuals
Theoretical Approach: TA
Fees: £25 negotiable

LUSTY Robert 081 883 3687
LONDON SE6
Member of: BAC Acc
Quals/training: BAC(Acc); BSc; MSc; Dip Couns & Psychotherapy(PCAI) '87; Memb BAPCA
Personal Therapy: Yes
Supervision: Ongoing
Counselling offered: General, Psychotherapy, Relationship
Service for: Individuals, Couples, Groups
Theoretical Approach: Person-centred
Fees: £15 - £30 sliding scale

TYRWHITT Stephen 081 858 1767
161 Charlton Church Lane, Charlton, LONDON SE7 7AA
Member of: BAC
Quals/training: Dip Hypnosis & Psychotherapy 1986; Dip Adlerian Couns (IIP) 1989; Memb AHP & Adlerian Soc
Personal Therapy: Yes
Supervision: Ongoing
Counselling offered: General, Marital, Analysis, Psychotherapy
Service for: Individuals, Couples
Theoretical Approach: Adlerian, Holistic
Other languages: French
Fees: £25 negotiable

SHARMAN Roslyn 081 858 7299
55 Mayhill Road, Charlton, LONDON SE7 7JG
Member of: BAC
Quals/training: BEd (Hons); Dip RSA; WPF Cert Pastoral Counselling 1983; Dip Adlerian Couns 1991 & Accredited Adlerian Counsellor 1992 (IIP)
Personal Therapy: Yes
Supervision: Ongoing
Counselling offered: General, Bereavement, Relationship, Assertiveness
Service for: Individuals, Couples
Specific to: Teachers, Single parents
Theoretical Approach: Adlerian, Humanistic
Fees: £15 - £25 sliding scale

London - South East

MYERS Dania 081 858 1722
4 Elliscombe Road, Charlton, LONDON SE7 7PX
Member of:	BAC Acc
Quals/training:	BAC Acc; Dip in Adult Couns, London Univ; Dip in Applied Social Studies, CQSW, Surrey Univ
Personal Therapy:	Yes
Supervision:	Ongoing
Counselling offered:	**General, Anxiety, Bereavement, Substance abuse, Relationship**
Service for:	Individuals, Couples
Theoretical Approach:	Psychodynamic
Fees:	£18 - £25 Sliding Scale

STUART Lilly 081 854 3606
106 Heathwood Garden, Charlton, LONDON SE7 8ER
Member of:	BAC, BPS, ITA
Quals/training:	Dip Clinical Psychol (Hamburg) 1969; Chartered C Psychol; TA Practitioner Level 1 (Clinical) since 1980
Personal Therapy:	Yes
Supervision:	Ongoing
Counselling offered:	**General, Depression, Stress, Relationship**
Service for:	Individuals, Couples, Families
Specific to:	Women
Theoretical Approach:	TA, Gestalt, Rogerian, Systems
Other languages:	German
Fees:	£25 - £40 sliding scale

MEIGS Melinda 081 691 7519
261 Grove Street, Deptford, LONDON SE8 3PZ
Member of:	BAC Acc
Quals/training:	BAC Acc 1992; BA(Hons) 1975; Jungian Training Analysis 1976- 84; Seminars in Couns (WPF) 1985-6; Dip Couns (London Univ) 1991
Personal Therapy:	Ongoing
Supervision:	Ongoing
Counselling offered:	**General, Marital, Career, Voice work**
Service for:	Individuals, Couples, Groups
Theoretical Approach:	Eclectic
Other languages:	French, German
Fees:	£30 negotiable

CREAMER Mary 081 850 8357
21 Archery Road, Eltham, LONDON SE9 1HF
Member of:	BAC
Quals/training:	Dip in Gestalt & Contribution Therapy (Pellin Inst); Dip Applied Social Studies; CQSW; Dip in Management
Personal Therapy:	Yes
Supervision:	Ongoing
Counselling offered:	**General**
Service for:	Individuals, Couples, Families
Specific to:	Caring professions, Managers
Theoretical Approach:	Client-centred, Holistic
Fees:	£15 - £30

London - South East

SQUIRE Sheila
081 8503641
114 Well Hall Road, Eltham, LONDON SE9 6SL
Member of: NRH
Quals/training: CQSW; NRHP (Assoc); MIIR (Reflexology)
Personal Therapy: Yes
Supervision: Ongoing
Counselling offered: General, Health, Hypnotherapy, Psychotherapy
Service for: Individuals
Theoretical Approach: Eclectic
Fees: £20

MUMFORD Susan
081 853 0713
38 Crooms Hill, Greenwich, LONDON SE10 8HD
Member of: BPS, BABCP
Quals/training: BA(Hons) Psychol; CPsychol; Clinical Psychol; BPS (Assoc) Cognitive therapy course (Inst Psychiatry)
Personal Therapy: No
Supervision: No
Counselling offered: General, Relationship, Bereavement, Stress, Obsessions, Psychotherapy
Service for: Individuals
Theoretical Approach: Cognitive
Other languages: French
Fees: £25 - £55

DALTON Helen
081 293 5906
60 Brand Street, Greenwich, LONDON SE10 8SR
Member of: BAC Acc
Quals/training: BAC Acc; Dip Applied Social Studies; Cert Couns (WPF); training in psychoanalytic psychothrapy (Tavistock, LCP & BAP); training in family & marital therapy
Personal Therapy: Yes
Supervision: Ongoing
Counselling offered: General
Service for: Individuals
Theoretical Approach: Psychodynamic
Fees: £20 - £30

BLOMFIELD Val
081 853 0772
12 Woodlands Park Road, Greenwich, LONDON SE10 9XD
Member of: BAC, Member of UKCP Register
Quals/training: BEd(Hons); Dip Couns Skills (SW London Coll)'78; Psycho S
Personal Therapy: Ongoing
Supervision: Ongoing
Counselling offered: Psychotherapy, Creative potential, Educational
Service for: Individuals, Couples, Groups
Specific to: Gays, Ethnic minorities, Students
Theoretical Approach: Psychosynthesis, Rogerian, Gestalt
Fees: £20 - £35 sliding scale

London - South East

MUIR Margaret 071 735 7049
St Anne's Community Centre, 46 Harleyford Road, Vauxhall, LONDON SE11 5AY
Member of:	BAC Acc
Quals/training:	BAC(Acc); Couns Course (Tavistock Inst) '75; Dip Couns (SW London Coll) '80
Personal Therapy:	Ongoing
Supervision:	Ongoing
Counselling offered:	**General**
Service for:	Individuals, Couples
Theoretical Approach:	Rogerian, Gestalt, TA, Psychosynthesis
Fees:	No charge under 18s & families

LANGDON Monica 081 318 0110
6 Upwood Road, Lee, LONDON SE12 8AA
Member of:	AGIP
Quals/training:	BA Psychol; MSc Couns; CQSW; trained with AGIP
Personal Therapy:	Ongoing
Supervision:	Ongoing
Counselling offered:	**General, Psychotherapy**
Service for:	Individuals, Couples, Groups
Theoretical Approach:	Analytical
Fees:	Negotiable

HANCHEN Tomasz fax 081 318 3102, 081 318 3102
55 Cressingham Road, Lewisham, LONDON SE13 5AQ
Member of:	ANLP
Quals/training:	BA Soc Studies; CQSW; Post Qualifying Award in SW Educ; Practitioner NLP
Personal Therapy:	No
Supervision:	Ongoing
Counselling offered:	**General, Change, Career, Personal growth**
Service for:	Individuals, Groups, Organisations
Theoretical Approach:	Humanistic, NLP
Other languages:	Polish
Fees:	£20 - £30 sliding scale

DONOVAN Marlyn 081 314 0019
211 Algernon road, Ladywell, LONDON SE13 7AG
Member of:	BAC, PET
Quals/training:	Dip Psychosynthesis Counselling & Therapy
Personal Therapy:	Ongoing
Supervision:	Ongoing
Counselling offered:	**General, Psychotherapy**
Service for:	Individuals
Theoretical Approach:	Psychosynthesis, Client-centred
Fees:	£25 some concessions

London - South East

KOWSZUN Graz 081 690 0395
39 Ellerdale Street, Lewisham, LONDON SE13 7JX
Member of:	BAC Acc
Quals/training:	BAC Acc; BA Sociol, Phil & Psychol 1980; Dip couns (SW London College) 1985; Memb of AHP, MIND & Alcohol Concern
Personal Therapy:	Yes
Supervision:	Ongoing
Counselling offered:	General, Alcohol, Drugs, Identity crisis, Oppression, Relationship, HIV, AIDS, Psychotherapy, Supervision
Service for:	Individuals, Couples, Groups
Specific to:	Women, Lesbians, Gays, Ethnic minorities
Theoretical Approach:	Humanistic, Integrative
Other languages:	Polish
Fees:	£25 - £35 sliding scale for reg clients

CARUANA Charles 071 277 7402
46 Erlanger Road, New Cross, LONDON SE14 5TG
Member of:	AGIP, BAC Acc
Quals/training:	BAC Acc; BSc Psychology 1984; AGIP Associate; Dip in Supervision (WPF)
Personal Therapy:	Yes
Supervision:	Ongoing
Counselling offered:	Psychotherapy
Service for:	Individuals
Theoretical Approach:	Analytical
Fees:	£18 - £25 sliding scale acc to income

SEEAR Louise 071 635 5809
153 Pepys Road, New Cross, LONDON SE14 5SG
Member of:	IPC
Quals/training:	Dip Member IPC/WPF 1989
Personal Therapy:	Ongoing
Supervision:	Ongoing
Counselling offered:	General, Psychotherapy, Supervision
Service for:	Individuals
Theoretical Approach:	Psychodynamic
Fees:	£25

PUCKETT Jane 071 639 1472
244 Ivydale Road, Nunhead, LONDON SE15 3DF
Member of:	BAC, ANLP (PCS), NRHP
Quals/training:	Cert Hypnotherapy; NRHP (Assoc)
Personal Therapy:	Ongoing
Supervision:	Ongoing
Counselling offered:	Hypnotherapy, Psychotherapy
Service for:	Individuals, Organisations
Specific to:	Adult survivors of abuse
Theoretical Approach:	Cognitive, Ericksonian, NLP
Fees:	£25

London - South East

GRANT Nigel   081 769 2766
50 Conyers Road, Streatham, LONDON SE16 6LT
Member of: BAC, ITA
Quals/training: CQSW 1978; Dip Couns & Supervision (Roehampton Inst) 1986; Dip Humanistic Psychology - IDHP (Guildford) 1990
Personal Therapy: Yes
Supervision: Ongoing
Counselling offered: **General, Supervision**
Service for: Individuals, Couples, Groups, Families
Specific to: Young people, Managers
Theoretical Approach: Person-centred, Humanistic
Fees: £25 Unwaged £8

NEWBIGIN Alison   071 703 9544
48 Surrey Square, LONDON SE17 2JX
Member of: BAC, ITHP
Quals/training: RGN; SCM; HV Cert; trained (CTA)'81 & (Minster Centre)'88; Assoc Memb ITHP; experienced in Primal Therapy; Intro to Groupwork (IGA)
Personal Therapy: Ongoing
Supervision: Ongoing
Counselling offered: **General, Psychotherapy, Art therapy, Drama therapy, Perinatal**
Service for: Individuals, Groups
Specific to: Nurses
Theoretical Approach: Analytic, Gestalt, Primal therapy, Psychodrama
Fees: £18 - £25

JONES Sue   ansaphone 081 316 2070
58 Admaston Road, Plumstead, LONDON SE18 2TX
Member of: BAC
Quals/training: One yr training in Rogerian Couns; Dip & Adv Dip Gestalt & Contribution Training (Pellin) 1986 & 1988
Personal Therapy: Yes
Supervision: Ongoing
Counselling offered: **General, Sexual abuse**
Service for: Individuals, Couples, Groups
Specific to: Women, Survivors of sex abuse
Theoretical Approach: Rogerian, Gestalt, Contribution training
Fees: £30

GILMORE Ian   081 316 0378
93 John Wilson Street, LONDON SE18 6QL
Member of: BAC Acc
Quals/training: BAC Acc; BA(Hons) (Leeds)'78; Dip Couns (Aston Univ)'81; Cert RET; Cert Ed(FE); Memb ITAA
Personal Therapy: Yes
Supervision: Ongoing
Counselling offered: **General, Marital, Sexual, Bereavement, Psychotherapy**
Service for: Individuals, Couples, Groups, Families
Theoretical Approach: Integrative
Fees: £30

London - South East

LE DUC-BARNETT Roger　　　　　　　　　　　　　　　　　　　　　　　　081 771 9244
338 Grange Road, Upper Norwood, LONDON SE19 3DQ
Member of:　　　　　　　　BAC Acc, BASMT
Quals/training:　　　　　　　BAC Acc; Dip Guidance; Human Sexuality; Marital & Sexual A
Personal Therapy:　　　　　Ongoing
Supervision:　　　　　　　　Ongoing
Counselling offered:　　　General, Relationship, Sexual, PTSD
Service for:　　　　　　　　Individuals, Couples, Families
Theoretical Approach:　　　Jungian, Analytical, Behavioural
Fees:　　　　　　　　　　　　£20 - £35 negotiable in hardship cases

COTTRELL Sue　　　　　　　　　　　　　　　　　　　　　　　　　　　　081 771 5309
50 Orleans Road, Upper Norwood, LONDON SE19 3TA
Member of:　　　　　　　　BAC
Quals/training:　　　　　　　BA Social Science; Dip & Advanced Dip in Gestalt; Contribution training & Feminist Psychotherapy (Pellin)
Personal Therapy:　　　　　Ongoing
Supervision:　　　　　　　　Ongoing
Counselling offered:　　　General, Psychotherapy
Service for:　　　　　　　　Individuals, Couples
Specific to:　　　　　　　　Women, Gays, Lesbians, Survivors of sex abuse
Theoretical Approach:　　　Integrative, Gestalt, Rogerian
Fees:　　　　　　　　　　　　£25 indivs; £40 couples

FOX Joshua　　　　　　　　　　　　　　　　　　　　　　　　　　　　　081 778 7942
129 Croydon Road, Anerley, LONDON SE20 7TT
Member of:　　　　　　　　BAC, BPS
Quals/training:　　　　　　　MA; MSc Occ Psychol
Personal Therapy:　　　　　Yes
Supervision:　　　　　　　　Ongoing
Counselling offered:　　　Career
Service for:　　　　　　　　Individuals, Organisations
Theoretical Approach:　　　Eclectic
Fees:　　　　　　　　　　　　Negotiable

NKUMANDA Rachel　　　　　　　　　　　　　　　　　　　　　　　　　081 778 2929
6 Kelso Court, 94 Anerley Park, Anerley, LONDON SE20 8NZ
Member of:　　　　　　　　BAC
Quals/training:　　　　　　　RGN; RM; RSCN; Dip Psychol Couns
Personal Therapy:　　　　　Yes
Supervision:　　　　　　　　Ongoing
Counselling offered:　　　General
Service for:　　　　　　　　Individuals
Specific to:　　　　　　　　Women, Ethnic minorities
Theoretical Approach:　　　Psychodynamic
Other languages:　　　　　Xhosa
Fees:　　　　　　　　　　　　£20

London - South East

GOTTSCHALK Margaret   081 693 5112
9 Court Lane Gardens, Dulwich, LONDON SE21 7DZ
Member of:	BAC
Quals/training:	BA (Hons)1965; Psychotherapist (Minster)
Personal Therapy:	Ongoing
Supervision:	Ongoing
Counselling offered:	**General, Psychotherapy**
Service for:	Individuals
Theoretical Approach:	Psychodynamic, Eclectic
Fees:	£25 negotiable

BLACK Sandra   081 693 6656
112 Friern Road, Dulwich, LONDON SE22 0AX
Member of:	BAC, IPSS
Quals/training:	Dip in Speech, Drama & Teaching; Dip Psychotherapy (IPSS)
Personal Therapy:	Yes
Supervision:	Ongoing
Counselling offered:	**Psychotherapy, Marital**
Service for:	Individuals, Couples, Groups
Theoretical Approach:	Analytical, Existential, Object relations
Fees:	£23 Sliding scale

NEUSTEIN David   071 693 5288
24 Rye Court, 214 Peckham Rye, LONDON SE22 0LT
Member of:	BAC, ITA
Quals/training:	Cert Transactional Analyst (Clinical Speciality); ASC Acc 1987
Personal Therapy:	Ongoing
Supervision:	Ongoing
Counselling offered:	**General, Relationship, Crisis, Psychotherapy**
Service for:	Individuals, Couples
Theoretical Approach:	TA
Fees:	£20

ROHRIG Angelika   081 299 4587
168 Overhill Road, LONDON SE22 0PS
Member of:	BAC
Quals/training:	CQSW '86; Dip Couns (St Patrick's College)'87; Adv Dip Gestalt Psychotherapy and Contribution Training (Pellin Inst) '91
Personal Therapy:	Yes
Supervision:	Ongoing
Counselling offered:	**General, Bereavement, Health**
Service for:	Individuals, Couples
Specific to:	Women
Theoretical Approach:	Humanistic, Gestalt
Other languages:	German
Fees:	£20 - £25 negotiable

London - South East

### RYLEY Brigitte					081 693 6953
Flat 1, 39a Glengenny Road, Dulwich, LONDON SE22 8QA
Member of:	BAC, AHPP
Quals/training:	Qualified Biodynamic Psychotherapist(Gerda Boyesen Inst)'83
Personal Therapy:	Yes
Supervision:	Ongoing
Counselling offered:	General, Psychotherapy, Bodywork
Service for:	Individuals, Groups
Specific to:	Women
Theoretical Approach:	Neo-Reichian, Transpersonal, Psychodynamic
Other languages:	French
Fees:	£20 - £25 sliding scale

### THOMAS Mary					081 693 8316
East Dulwich, LONDON SE22
Member of:	BAC, IPC
Quals/training:	BA; MA; Dip Adv Psychodynamic Couns (WPF)
Personal Therapy:	Ongoing
Supervision:	Ongoing
Counselling offered:	General, Bereavement
Service for:	Individuals, Couples, Groups
Theoretical Approach:	Psychodynamic, Analytic
Fees:	£20 - £30 sliding scale

### THOMAS Peter			Work 081 693 4715, Home 081 302 8187
The Surgery, The Gardens, East Dulwich, LONDON SE22 9QD
Member of:	BAC Acc
Quals/training:	BAC(Acc); MSc Couns Psychol; PG Dip Guidance & Couns '87
Personal Therapy:	Yes
Supervision:	Ongoing
Counselling offered:	General, Bereavement, Relationship, Depression, Anxiety, Eating disorders, Supervision
Service for:	Individuals
Theoretical Approach:	Integrative
Fees:	£27.50

### STEPHENS Elyan P				ansaphone 081 299 2213
57 Oakhurst Grove, East Dulwich, LONDON SE22 9AH
Member of:	BAC
Quals/training:	BA (Hons) English; PGCE; Cert Couns (Personal & Pastoral); Member Radionics Register (MRR) of ICM; MRR(ICM); BCMA; BAPCA
Personal Therapy:	Yes
Supervision:	Ongoing
Counselling offered:	General, Bereavement, Crisis
Service for:	Individuals, Groups
Specific to:	Women, Lesbians, Gays, Ethnic minorities, Health care professionals
Theoretical Approach:	Person-centred, Transpersonal
Fees:	£20

London - South East

SMALL Juliette 081 299 2832
62 Ulverscroft Road, East Dulwich, LONDON SE22 9HG
Member of:	BAC
Quals/training:	Dip Couns (SW London Coll) 1987
Personal Therapy:	Ongoing
Supervision:	Ongoing
Counselling offered:	General, Addiction, Alcohol, Relationship, Bereavement
Service for:	Individuals
Specific to:	Women, Black people
Theoretical Approach:	Person-centred, Psychodynamic
Fees:	£15 - £25 negotiable

HARGADEN Helena 081 690 3175
39 Duncombe Hill, Forest Hill, LONDON SE23 1QY
Member of:	BAC Acc, MPTI, Member of UKCP Register
Quals/training:	BAC Acc; BA; Dip Couns (metanoia)
Personal Therapy:	Ongoing
Supervision:	Ongoing
Counselling offered:	General, Bereavement, Relationship, Psychotherapy, Supervision
Service for:	Individuals, Couples, Groups
Specific to:	Gays
Theoretical Approach:	Rogerian, Gestalt, TA
Fees:	£30 negotiable

PEARCE Peter 081 690 6265
52 Montem Road, Forest Hill, LONDON SE23 1SJ
Member of:	BAC
Quals/training:	FACETS Training Programme (City Univ); further training in Psychotherapy & Mental Health Handicap (Tavistock)
Personal Therapy:	Yes
Supervision:	Ongoing
Counselling offered:	General, Psychotherapy
Service for:	Individuals
Specific to:	People with learning difficulties
Theoretical Approach:	Person-centred, Existential
Fees:	£15 - £30 sliding scale

DE IONNO Christine 081 291 5070
71 Sunderland Road, Forest Hill, LONDON SE23 2PS
Member of:	BAC
Quals/training:	Dip Couns
Personal Therapy:	Ongoing
Supervision:	Ongoing
Counselling offered:	General, Relationship, Bereavement, Cross/multi-cultural, Cancer
Service for:	Individuals, Couples, Families, Groups
Theoretical Approach:	Psychodynamic
Fees:	Negotiable

London - South East

CHAPMAN Trudy 081 693 3116
Forest Hill, LONDON SE23 3DS
Member of: BAC Acc
Quals/training: BAC Acc; Dip Adult Couns & Adv Couns Practice Course (Univ of London); (WPF); training in group process (IGA) 1990-92; Dip Couns Supervision (WPF)
Personal Therapy: Yes
Supervision: Ongoing
Counselling offered: General, Anxiety, Depression, Relationship, Supervision
Service for: Individuals, Couples, Groups, Organisations
Theoretical Approach: Psychodynamic
Fees: £20

MARTIN Edward 071 699 2303
17 Honor Oak Rise, Forest Hill, LONDON SE23 3QY
Member of: BAC RSup, SAP
Quals/training: NMGC trained; BAC Recognised Supervisor; Jungian Analyst
Personal Therapy: Yes
Supervision: Ongoing
Counselling offered: General, Analysis
Service for: Individuals
Theoretical Approach: Jungian, Analytic
Fees: Individually negotiated

BUCKROYD Julia 071 274 6157
15 Fawnbrake Avenue, LONDON SE24 0BE
Member of: Guild of Psychotherapists
Quals/training: MA; PhD; Dip in Counselling, Birkbeck College;
Personal Therapy: Yes
Supervision: Ongoing
Counselling offered: General, Eating disorders
Service for: Individuals, Couples, Groups
Theoretical Approach: Psychodynamic
Fees: £35

HALL Jan 071 274 2379
150 Lowden Road, Herne Hill, LONDON SE24 0BT
Member of: BAC
Quals/training: BSc; Dip Couns (Pellin Inst)
Personal Therapy: Ongoing
Supervision: Ongoing
Counselling offered: General, Eating disorders, Health, Life planning
Service for: Individuals
Specific to: Women only
Theoretical Approach: Integrative
Fees: £20 First free, negot'ble unwaged

London - South East

PAUL Sandra   081 674 6937
18 Berwyn Road, Herne Hill, LONDON SE24 9BD
Member of: BAC
Quals/training: BA(Hons); PGCE; Dip Couns (SW London College) 1984; Adv Dip Gestalt Therapy & Contribution Training (Pellin Inst) 1991
Personal Therapy: Yes
Supervision: Ongoing
Counselling offered: **General, Relationship, Crisis**
Service for: Individuals, Couples, Groups
Theoretical Approach: Person-centred, Gestalt, Humanistic
Fees: £20 - £25

DE BERTODANO Joanna   071 733 5799
37 Red Post Hill, Dulwich, LONDON SE24 9JJ
Member of: BAC, IPC
Quals/training: Dip Advanced Psychodynamic Couns WPF
Personal Therapy: Yes
Supervision: Ongoing
Counselling offered: **General, Bereavement**
Service for: Individuals
Theoretical Approach: Psychodynamic
Fees: £12 - £25 sliding scale

TUNE David   081 653 1465
40 Love Lane, South Norwood, LONDON SE25 4NG
Member of: BAC, AHPP
Quals/training: BSc Psychol; MA Couns State University of NY 1981; Training Bioenergetics NY USA; CQSW; Dip PSW UK 1983; Training Holistic Therapy ongoing; AHPP Acc
Personal Therapy: Ongoing
Supervision: Yes
Counselling offered: **Psychotherapy**
Service for: Individuals, Couples, Groups
Theoretical Approach: Holistic
Fees: £24

CHANDLER Diana   081 656 9209
22 St Lukes Close, South Norwood, LONDON SE25 4SX
Member of: BAC
Quals/training: Cert Couns ICIP'84; Dip Humanistic Psychol IDHP'87; Dip Couns IP '90; trained nurse & teacher
Personal Therapy: Ongoing
Supervision: Ongoing
Counselling offered: **General, Short-term, Long-term, Addiction, Relationship, Terminal illness, Bereavement**
Service for: Individuals
Theoretical Approach: Psychosynthesis, Humanistic
Fees: £25 negotiable

London - South East

LOOMS Suzanne   071 258 0077, 081 655 2284
Flat 2, 195 Woodside Green, South Norwood, LONDON SE25 5EN
Member of:	**BAC, ANLP (PCS)**
Quals/training:	BA(Hons); MA; Cert Couns; Cert Hypnotherapy; Master Practitioner NLP; Massage (ITEC)
Personal Therapy:	Ongoing
Supervision:	Ongoing
Counselling offered:	**Hypnotherapy, Problem solving, Relationship, Stress**
Service for:	Individuals, Couples, Families, Groups, Organisations
Specific to:	Elderly
Theoretical Approach:	Ericksonian, NLP
Other languages:	Danish, Spanish
Fees:	£25

GORDON Sheila   081 771 7074
West Side Row, 222 South Norwood Hill, LONDON SE25 6AS
Member of:	**BAC, LCP**
Quals/training:	Trained AGIP 1978-82
Personal Therapy:	Yes
Supervision:	Ongoing
Counselling offered:	**Psychotherapy**
Service for:	Individuals, Couples, Groups
Theoretical Approach:	Analytical, Object relations
Fees:	£28 - £32

PETERS Sheila   081 653 4242
102a Holmesdale Road, South Norwood, LONDON SE25 6JF
Member of:	**NRHP**
Quals/training:	Dip Hypnosis & Psychotherapy (NCHP) 1984
Personal Therapy:	Yes
Supervision:	Ongoing
Counselling offered:	**General, Relationship, Bereavement**
Service for:	Individuals, Couples
Theoretical Approach:	Rogerian, Gestalt
Fees:	£20

MONYPENNY Helen   081 653 1646
Garden Flat, 7 Upper Grove, South Norwood, LONDON SE25 6JX
Member of:	**BAC, PET**
Quals/training:	BA(Hons) Soc Sci; Foundation Programme in Couns & Personal Development (City Univ); in training (PET)
Personal Therapy:	Ongoing
Supervision:	Ongoing
Counselling offered:	**General, Bereavement, Crisis, Chronic illness**
Service for:	Individuals
Theoretical Approach:	Psychosynthesis, Humanistic
Fees:	£15 - £25

London - South East

ROBERTS Sheila   081 659 0518
65 Tannsfeld Road, Sydenham, LONDON SE26 5DL
Member of: BAC
Quals/training: Dip Couns (SW London Coll) 1986; Cert in Rational Emotive Therapy 1992
Personal Therapy: Yes
Supervision: Ongoing
Counselling offered: **General**
Service for: Individuals, Groups
Specific to: Young people, Women
Theoretical Approach: Eclectic
Fees: £20

RIMMER Annie   081 778 8821
47 Knighton Park Road, Sydenham, LONDON SE26 5RN
Member of: BAC, ITA
Quals/training: MA Education; BEd; Dip Couns; in advanced TA training (metanoia)
Personal Therapy: Ongoing
Supervision: Ongoing
Counselling offered: **General, Psychotherapy**
Service for: Individuals, Groups
Theoretical Approach: TA, Client-centred
Fees: £25 negotiable (£15 groups)

BATTERSBY Elaine   081 659 9498
Flat 5 D, 108 Westwood Hill, Sydenham, LONDON SE26 6PE
Member of: BAC
Quals/training: Dip Couns (CSCT); Cert HIV/AIDS Couns Skills (AIDS Training Associates)
Personal Therapy: Ongoing
Supervision: Ongoing
Counselling offered: **Sexuality, HIV, Relationship, Self-esteem, Sexual abuse**
Service for: Individuals, Couples
Specific to: Gays, Lesbians
Theoretical Approach: Rogerian
Fees: According to income

BRAY Michael   081 778 8601
The Grove Centre, 2 Jews Walk, Sydenham, LONDON SE26 6PL
Member of: BAC Acc, WMIP
Quals/training: BAC Acc; Assoc Memb of W Midlands Institute of Psychotherapy
Personal Therapy: Ongoing
Supervision: Ongoing
Counselling offered: **General, Psychotherapy, Supervision**
Service for: Individuals, Couples
Theoretical Approach: Eclectic
Fees: £20 - £25

London - South East

WARD Roy **081 659 4994**
85 Longton Grove, Sydenham, LONDON SE26 6QQ
Member of: BAC Acc
Quals/training: BAC(Acc); CTA trained '68-'71; Group process Accred
Personal Therapy: Yes
Supervision: Ongoing
Counselling offered: **General, Psychotherapy, Supervision**
Service for: Individuals, Couples, Groups
Theoretical Approach: Psychodynamic, Person-centred
Fees: £27 negotiable

BRUCE Ann **081 670 3783**
54 Uffington Road, West Norwood, LONDON SE27 0ND
Member of: BAC, SAP
Quals/training: 1972 BSc Psychol (London Univ); '73 MBBS; '80 Dip Humanistic
                                    Psychology (IDHP); 1990 Associate Professional Member SAP
Personal Therapy: Ongoing
Supervision: Ongoing
Counselling offered: **Psychotherapy, Analysis, Short-term**
Service for: Individuals
Theoretical Approach: Jungian, Humanistic
Fees: £25 - £35

WILLIAMS Diana **081 670 1035**
17 Chestnut Road, West Norwood, LONDON SE27 9EZ
Member of: BAC
Quals/training: CQSW '67; NMGC training '76 (HK); Cert CTP '84; Dip CTP '92
Personal Therapy: Ongoing
Supervision: Ongoing
Counselling offered: **General, Psychotherapy**
Service for: Individuals
Theoretical Approach: Transpersonal, Jungian
Fees: £20 - £30

London - South East

London - South West

Organisations

CLAPHAM COMMON CLINIC 071 627 8890
151-153 Clapham High Street, LONDON SW4 7SS
Service: Offers a whole range of counselling, psychotherapy and sexual therapy for individuals, couples and relationships
Area served: South London
Other languages: Spanish, French
Referral: Self, Health Practitioner
Training of workers: 4 fully trained therapists who have had personal therapy and receive regular supervision
Code of Ethics: BAC, GMC
Management by: Dr Asun de Marquiequi and Mr Knight
Fees: £25 - £35 dep on therapist; concs

RED ADMIRAL PROJECT 071 835 1495
51a Philbeach Gardens, Earls Court, LONDON SW5 9EB
Service: One-to-one, couple & family counselling for anyone affected by HIV/AIDS, including people living w HIV/AIDS, their partners, friends & family. Specialises in bereavement
Area served: No restriction
Referral: Self, Agencies
Training of workers: In-house & external; all counsellors receive weekly supervision & personal therapy
Code of Ethics: BAC
Management by: Management Committee with Project Director
Fees: Free - donations accepted

PELLIN CENTRE 071 622 0148
43 Killyon Road, LONDON SW8 2XS
Service: Provides training for women in Gestalt therapy with Contribution Training; individual therapy & ongoing therapeutic grp. Low cost therapy with advanced trainees in supervision
Area served: London & other cities
Referral: Self
Training of workers: Runs own training courses and workshops
Code of Ethics: BAC
Management by: Directors, Anna Farrow & Carole Van Artsdalen
Fees: £20 - £35 concessions

MYATTS COMMUNITY COUNSELLING PROJECT 071 735 9794
46 Foxley Square, LONDON SW9 2PJ
Service: General counselling for individuals and groups specialising with ethnic minorities, women and those with mental health problems
Area served: Myatts Field Estate, Brixton and London SW9
Referral: Self, Agencies
Training of workers: Social work training, groupwork training and counselling courses with peer group supervision
Code of Ethics: BAC
Management by: Management Committee
Fees: None

• CPRD 1994 •

London - South West

WANDSWORTH HA FAMILY PLANNING PSYCHOSEXUAL CLINIC
071 223 4211
Bridge Lane Health Centre, 20 Bridge Lane, Battersea, LONDON SW11 3AD
Service: Psychosexual, reproductive health and contraceptive couns for individuals and couples
Area served: Wandsworth and S Lambeth HAs
Referral: Self, Health Practitioner, Health/Soc Work Professional
Training of workers: Instiute of Psychosexual Medicine
Code of Ethics: GMC, Institute of Psychosexual Medicine
Management by: Wandsworth Health Authority
Fees: None

RICHMOND TWICKENHAM & ROEHAMPTON HEALTH CARE NHS TRUST
081 789 6611
Roehampton Rehabilitation Cent, Queen Mary's University Hosp, Roehampton Lane, LONDON SW15 5PN
Service: Wide variety of long and short term work; behavioural, cognitive & psychodynamic for individuals, couples, groups & families
Area served: Richmond, Twickenham and Roehampton DHA
Other languages: Polish, Greek, Spanish, German, Iranian
Referral: GP
Training of workers: Postgraduate clinical psychology with additional training at Tavistock Clinic and Institute of Family Therapy
Code of Ethics: BPS
Management by: Clinical Psychology Service Manager
Fees: None

ELM THERAPISTS, The
081 675 7848
55 Cloudesdale Road, LONDON SW17 8ET
Service: Counselling for marital, sexual, family and personal problems
Area served: London & home counties
Referral: Self or others
Training of workers: Therapists are fully trained in individual, marital/sexual therapy; regular suprvision
Code of Ethics: BAC, Member of UKCP Register
Management by: Groupa
Fees: £25 minimum

SOUTHSIDE COUNSELLORS
081 874 2780
Wandsworth Common, LONDON SW18 3RH
Service: Individual counselling & psychotherapy. Specialises in women
Area served: SW London
Referral: Self or others
Training of workers: All have Masters degrees in Couns Psychol/Psychotherapy, personal therapy and ongoing supervision
Code of Ethics: BAC, BPS
Management by: Counsellors
Fees: £20 - £30

London - South West

EQUILIBRIUM CENTRE 081 870 8761
117 Granville Road, Wandsworth, LONDON SW18 5SF
Service: Counselling service offered in areas of panic attacks, marital problems, gender dysphoria, eating disorders. Assessment of self referrals for suitability
Area served: SW London
Other languages: Polish, French, German
Referral: Self or others
Training of workers: Each counsellor is trained to a professional level & responsible for therapy and supervision. Counsellors meet monthly
Code of Ethics: BAC
Management by: Director - V Mathews
Fees: £5 - £31 negotiable

MERTON FAMILY LINKS 081 543 9691
c/o Merton Wel-Care Assoc, 181 Haydons Road, South Wimbledon, LONDON SW19 8TB
Service: Mediation, contact centre, counselling, information & support to individuals & families, inc children where there is relationship breakdown, divorce; stepfamilies
Area served: South/SW London, Sutton
Other languages: French, Italian
Referral: Self
Training of workers: Minimum 2 years, usually more, or ongoing training
Code of Ethics: BAC, BPS, AFT, CPCP
Management by: Co-ordinator & Executive Committee & Southwark Diocese
Fees: Negotiable; free to low/unwaged

THAMES PSYCHOLOGY & COUNSELLING CENTRE 081 944 8738
38 Ernie Road, Wimbledon, LONDON SW20 0HL
Service: Adult psychotherapy; Cognitive & Behaviour therapy; sex or marital therapy and counselling for a wide range of problems
Area served: South & West London & Surrey
Referral: Self or others
Training of workers: Post graduate degree courses or equivalent including personal therapy. Ongoing supervision
Code of Ethics: BPS
Management by: The directors of the company
Fees: By arrangement

SOUTH LONDON PSYCHOTHERAPY GROUP 081 332 7131
South London Psychotherapy Group, PO BOX111, RICHMOND TW9 2TY
Service: Analytic psychotherapy, some marital therapy and supervision
Area served: S London & Surrey
Referral: Self or others
Training of workers: 4 yr part time training including personal therapy and supervision
Code of Ethics: LCP
Management by: Democratic Team Management
Fees: By arrangement

London - South West

Individual Practitioners

Every individual is a **member of** one or more organisations eligible for entry into this directory. BAC Accredited Counsellors and Recognised Supervisors are shaded.

CAHN Albert   081 942 6956
10 Edgecoombe Close, Warren Road, KINGSTON UPON THAMES KT2 7HP
Member of: BASMT
Quals/training: RELATE trained'76; Marital/Sexual Therapy trainer RELATE '80 trainer in Hypnotherapy
Personal Therapy: No
Supervision: Ongoing
Counselling offered: General, Hypnotherapy, Sexual, Marital
Service for: Individuals, Couples
Fees: £25 - £30

CAHN Malka   081 942 6956
10 Edgecoombe Close, Warren Road, KINGSTON UPON THAMES KT2 7HP
Member of: LCP, BASMT
Quals/training: RELATE trained 1976; trainer in Marital and Sexual Therapy RELATE 1980; 4 year training in Psychotherapy(LCP)
Personal Therapy: Yes
Supervision: Ongoing
Counselling offered: General, Psychotherapy, Marital, Sexual
Service for: Individuals, Couples
Theoretical Approach: Eclectic
Fees: £25 sliding scale

CARRINGTON Norah   ansaphone 081 974 5436
17 Haygreen Close, KINGSTON UPON THAMES KT2 7TS
Member of: BAC
Quals/training: Cert Couns(KCFE); ongoing training in Integrative Psychotherapy(metanoia)
Personal Therapy: Ongoing
Supervision: Yes
Counselling offered: General, Bereavement, Loss, Work, Short-term, Long-term
Service for: Individuals
Theoretical Approach: Psychodynamic, Integrative
Fees: £20 - £25

CULLISS Andrew   071 652 0509, 071 326 4773
55 Trelawn Road, Brixton, LONDON SW2 1DH
Member of: IPSS
Quals/training: Youth & Community Dip 1982; training Psychotherapist IPSS 1989
Personal Therapy: Ongoing
Supervision: Ongoing
Counselling offered: Relationship, Sexual, Psychotherapy, Men's issues
Service for: Individuals
Theoretical Approach: Existential, Psychodynamic
Fees: £18 - £24 sliding scale

London - South West

PARKER Mary **071 274 6531**
66 Brixton Water Lane, LONDON SW2 1QB
Member of: BAC RSup, AHPP
Quals/training: BAC Recognised Supervisor; MSc Psychol Couns
Personal Therapy: Ongoing
Supervision: Ongoing
Counselling offered: General, Bereavement, Relationship, Psychotherapy, Depression
Service for: Individuals, Couples, Groups
Theoretical Approach: Integrative
Fees: £30 negotiable

JANE Melanie **081 671 0102**
4 Elm Park, Brixton, LONDON SW2 2UB
Member of: BAC
Quals/training: CQSW 1979; Adv Dip Gestalt Therapy & Contribution Training (Pellin) 1990
Personal Therapy: Ongoing
Supervision: Ongoing
Counselling offered: General, Relationship, Bereavement, Psychotherapy
Service for: Individuals, Couples, Groups, Families
Theoretical Approach: Integrative
Fees: £18 - £25 sliding scale

SCHOFIELD Caroline **081 674 6318**
48 Kingswood Road, Clapham Park, LONDON SW2 4JH
Member of: BAC Acc
Quals/training: BAC Acc; BSc Psychol;
Personal Therapy: Yes
Supervision: Ongoing
Counselling offered: General, Psychotherapy
Service for: Individuals
Theoretical Approach: Jungian
Fees: £25 sliding scale

REDMAN Christopher **081 674 7460**
14 Blenheim Gardens, Brixton, LONDON SW2 5TE
Member of: BAC
Quals/training: BSc; Dip Social Work 1974; Pellin Advanced Diploma 1989
Personal Therapy: Yes
Supervision: Ongoing
Counselling offered: General, Relationship, Short-term, Long-term
Service for: Individuals, Couples
Theoretical Approach: Eclectic
Fees: £18 Sliding Scale

London - South West

SCHMUCKER Rosemarie 071 5895445
38A Ovington Square, Knightsbridge, LONDON SW3 1HR
Member of: BAC
Quals/training: Adv Dip Integrative Couns (CSCT) 1992; training for Dip Psychotherapy 1994
Personal Therapy: Ongoing
Supervision: Ongoing
Counselling offered: General, Psychotherapy, Eating disorders, Substance abuse
Service for: Individuals, Families, Groups
Specific to: Families of alcoholics, Substance abusers
Theoretical Approach: Client-centred, Psychodynamic, Humanistic
Fees: £30 negotiable

GATTI-DOYLE Fiorella 071 584 9589
Flat A2, Sloane Avenue Mansions, Sloane Avenue, LONDON SW3 3JF
Member of: BAC, CPCP
Quals/training: MA; Dip Therapeutic Hypnosis; Dip NLP; trained in Personal Construct Psychology; trainer in Self-analysis
Personal Therapy: Yes
Supervision: Ongoing
Counselling offered: General, Psychotherapy, Phobias, Crisis, Educational
Service for: Individuals
Theoretical Approach: NLP
Other languages: Italian
Fees: On application

LEWINSOHN Joan 071 352 5315
29 Glebe Place, Chelsea, LONDON SW3 5LD
Member of: BAC Acc, BPS
Quals/training: BAC Acc; MA; MSc Psychol; PhD Psychol; Dip Psychotherapy; Memb Brit Inst Social Psychiatry, CPsychol
Personal Therapy: Yes
Supervision: Ongoing
Counselling offered: General, Psychotherapy
Service for: Individuals
Specific to: Adolescents
Fees: £35

BUTTERFIELD Janet 081-877 9393; 24 h 0941 100 200, Pager no 159004
Argyll House, Suite 24, 1a All Saints Passage, Wandsworth Hgh Street, LONDON SW18 1EP
Member of: BAC
Quals/training: Combined Cert Couns(CSCT); Physiology & Holistic Therapy (ITEC); Dip EHP & NLP; Cognitive Psychotherapy(BHR)
Personal Therapy: Ongoing
Supervision: Ongoing
Counselling offered: General, Health, Stress, Phobias, Weight, Stop smoking, Anxiety, Confidence, Regression therapy
Service for: Individuals, Couples, Groups, Organisations
Specific to: Women, Adolescents, Managers
Theoretical Approach: Cognitive, NLP, Ericksonian, Holistic
Fees: £25 - £50 sliding scale

London - South West

BUCKLEY Miranda　　　　　　　　　　　　　　　　　　071 589 9799
47 Bury Walk, Chelsea, LONDON SW3 6QE
Member of: BAC
Quals/training: BA (Hons); MTh; Inst of Medical Social Workers; Dip in Mental Health Social Work; Dip Couns & Adv Couns (London Univ)
Personal Therapy: No
Supervision: Ongoing
Counselling offered: General
Service for: Individuals
Theoretical Approach: Psychodynamic, CAT
Fees: £25

EDGELL Marjory　　　　　　　　　　　　　　　　　　071 622 4755
23 Crescent Grove, Clapham, LONDON SW4 7AF
Member of: BAC, NRHP
Quals/training: SRN; Dip Psychotherapy & Hypnotherapy 1983; trained PAS
Personal Therapy: Yes
Supervision: Ongoing
Counselling offered: Hypnotherapy, Psychotherapy, Relationship, Alcohol
Service for: Individuals, Couples
Theoretical Approach: Eclectic
Fees: £25 sliding scale

FARMER Eddie　　　　　　　　　　　　　　　　　　081 673 2044
Clapham Park, LONDON SW4
Member of: IPC
Quals/training: BSc; Full Member IPC/WPF in Individual Psychotherapy & Groupwork '81
Personal Therapy: Yes
Supervision: Ongoing
Counselling offered: Spiritual, Psychotherapy, Supervision, Consultation
Service for: Individuals, Couples, Groups, Organisations
Theoretical Approach: Psychodynamic, Existential
Fees: £35 negotiable

KIRBY Babs　　　　　　　　　　　　　　　　　　　071 733 2748
65c Bedford Road, Clapham, LONDON SW4 7RH
Member of: BAC, AHPP
Quals/training: Dip in Transpersonal Perspectives & Skills in Couns & Psychotherapy; AHPP Acc
Personal Therapy: Ongoing
Supervision: Ongoing
Counselling offered: General, Psychotherapy
Service for: Individuals
Theoretical Approach: Eclectic, Transpersonal
Fees: Negotiable

London - South West

MARQUIEGUI Asun de　　　　　　　　　　　　　　071 627 8890
Clapham Common Clinic, 151-153 Clapham High St, LONDON SW4 7SS
Member of:　　　　　　　　BASMT
Quals/training:　　　　　　Licence 'Medicine & Surgery' 1975; Joint Committee on Contraception (London) 1987; Dip Human Sexuality (St Georges Hosp) 1988; Instructing Doctor in Family Planning 1993
Personal Therapy:　　　　Yes
Supervision:　　　　　　　Ongoing
Counselling offered:　　　Short-term, Sexual, Marital, Relationship, Family planning, Abortion
Service for:　　　　　　　Individuals, Couples
Specific to:　　　　　　　Gays, Lesbians
Theoretical Approach:　　Person-centred
Other languages:　　　　Spanish
Fees:　　　　　　　　　　£35

O'NEILL James　　　　　　　　　　　　　　　　071 622 0607
20 Elms Crescent, Clapham, LONDON SW4 8RA
Member of:　　　　　　　　BAC, PA
Quals/training:　　　　　　BA; MA; PGCE; MSc Psychol Couns (Roehampton) 1988; Memb of Philadelphia Assoc
Personal Therapy:　　　　Ongoing
Supervision:　　　　　　　Ongoing
Counselling offered:　　　Psychotherapy
Service for:　　　　　　　Individuals, Groups
Specific to:　　　　　　　Gays
Theoretical Approach:　　Psychoanalytic, Person-centred
Fees:　　　　　　　　　　£25 negotiable

CUSSINS Anne　　　　　　　　　　　　　　　　071 373 3652
178 Coleherne Court, Redcliffe Gardens, LONDON SW5 0DU
Member of:　　　　　　　　IPSS
Quals/training:　　　　　　Dip Psychotherapy (IPSS); MA Couns & Psychotherapy
Personal Therapy:　　　　No
Supervision:　　　　　　　Ongoing
Counselling offered:　　　General
Service for:　　　　　　　Individuals
Theoretical Approach:　　Psychoanalytic
Fees:　　　　　　　　　　£15 - £25 sliding scale

MORRISON Philippa　　　　　　　　　　　　　071 624 8758
21 Bramham Gardens, LONDON SW5 0JE
Member of:　　　　　　　　BAC Acc
Quals/training:　　　　　　BAC Acc; MA in Psychology of Therapy & Couns; Adv Dip Existential Psychotherapy (Regents College); Memb SEA
Personal Therapy:　　　　Yes
Supervision:　　　　　　　Ongoing
Counselling offered:　　　Psychotherapy
Service for:　　　　　　　Individuals, Couples
Theoretical Approach:　　Existential
Fees:　　　　　　　　　　£30

London - South West

WILTON Angela   071 373 7520
27F Bramham Gardens, Earls Court, LONDON SW5 0JE
Member of: IPC/WPF
Quals/training: Behavioural Sciences degree (USA); Dip Adv Psychodynamic Couns (WPF)'88; Assoc Cognitive & Analytic Therapists
Personal Therapy: Yes
Supervision: Ongoing
Counselling offered: Addiction, Co-dependency
Service for: Individuals, Couples
Specific to: Adult children of alcoholics
Theoretical Approach: Psychodynamic, Systemic, Cognitive, Analytic
Fees: £24 - £28 negotiable

BLACK Margaret   071 373 3677
Flat 6, 107 Warwick Road, Earls Court, LONDON SW5 9EZ
Member of: NSHAP, CRAH
Quals/training: NSHAP Dip EHP & NLP; RMN; Cert Health Services Management; Cert in Cognitive Analtical Therapy
Personal Therapy: No
Supervision: No
Counselling offered: General, Bereavement, Hypnotherapy, Psychotherapy, Relationship
Service for: Individuals, Organisations
Specific to: Women
Theoretical Approach: Ericksonian
Fees: £35 - £55 Negotiable

PALLENBERG Susan   071 373 0901
10 Warwick Road, Earls Court, LONDON SW5 9UH
Member of: BAC, BASMT
Quals/training: Dip (London Inst for Study of Human Sexuality)'86; Dip in Couple Therapy (Inst of Psychiatry)
Personal Therapy: Yes
Supervision: Ongoing
Counselling offered: General, Marital, Relationship, Sexual
Service for: Individuals, Couples, Groups
Theoretical Approach: Eclectic
Fees: Negotiable

SILVER-LEIGH Vivienne   071 736 8917
63 Campana Road, Fulham, LONDON SW6 4AT
Member of: BAC
Quals/training: BA; Cert Couns (Roehampton) 1984; Dip Couns 1987 (Roehampton); TA (metanoia) 1990; Qualified Speech Therapist; Parent Link Co-ordinator
Personal Therapy: Yes
Supervision: Ongoing
Counselling offered: General, Educational, Eating disorders, Bereavement
Service for: Individuals
Specific to: Parents, Young adults
Theoretical Approach: Client-centred, Humanistic, TA
Fees: £20 - £30 negotiable

London - South West

CONDER Sue 071 736 0567
11A Rostrevor Road, Fulham, LONDON SW6 5AL
Member of:	BAC, NRHP
Quals/training:	BSc Psychol; CHP NRHP(Assoc)
Personal Therapy:	Ongoing
Supervision:	Ongoing
Counselling offered:	General, Psychotherapy, Hypnotherapy, Stress management
Service for:	Individuals, Groups, Organisations
Theoretical Approach:	Eclectic
Fees:	£30 negotiable

LETO Daphne Anne 071 736 4405, 071 723 6456
50 Burnfoot Avenue, Fulham, LONDON SW6 5EA
Member of:	IPC
Quals/training:	Dip (IPC/WPF) 1983
Personal Therapy:	Yes
Supervision:	Ongoing
Counselling offered:	General, Psychotherapy, Addiction, Identity crisis, Bereavement
Service for:	Individuals, Couples
Theoretical Approach:	Jungian, Transpersonal
Other languages:	Italian, French
Fees:	£25 negotiable

ZINOVIEFF Victoria 071 736 4751
50 Stevenage Road, Fulham, LONDON SW6 6HA
Member of:	BAC
Quals/training:	Dip IPC/WPF '84; General Course IGA '77
Personal Therapy:	Ongoing
Supervision:	Ongoing
Counselling offered:	Psychotherapy
Service for:	Individuals, Couples, Groups
Theoretical Approach:	Jungian, Eclectic
Fees:	£8 - £30 negotiable

MOLNOS Angela 071 381 2796
15 Elm Lodge, River Gardens, Fulham, LONDON SW6 6NZ
Member of:	IGA
Quals/training:	PhD, 1957 Dip Psychol; 1981 Qualified Group Analyst.
Personal Therapy:	Yes
Supervision:	Ongoing
Counselling offered:	General, Brief, Psychotherapy
Service for:	Individuals, Groups
Theoretical Approach:	Psychodynamic
Other languages:	Spanish, Italian, German, Hungarian
Fees:	£40 Some reductions

London - South West

BUTLER John   071 385 1166
37 Orbain Road, Fulham, LONDON SW6 7JZ
Member of: NRHP
Quals/training: BA (Hons) Psychol & Science; Dip Hypnosis & Psychotherapy (National College) 1982; Dip Hypnotherapy (Brit Soc Hypnotherapists) 1983
Personal Therapy: Yes
Supervision: Ongoing
Counselling offered: **General, Psychotherapy**
Service for: Individuals, Couples
Theoretical Approach: Eclectic
Fees: £30 except in financial difficulty

CLIFTON Elaine   071 581 0387
Flat 3, 55 Onslow Square, South Kensington, LONDON SW7
Member of: BAC, MPTI
Quals/training: BA Psychol; training in Integrative Psychotherapy (Metanoia) 1990; group psychotherapy
Personal Therapy: Ongoing
Supervision: Ongoing
Counselling offered: **General, Psychotherapy**
Service for: Individuals, Groups, Organisations
Specific to: Managers
Theoretical Approach: Integrative
Other languages: French
Fees: £25 - £30 sliding scale

HENRIQUES Marika   071 584 9793
54 Campbell Court, Gloucester Road, South Kensington, LONDON SW7 4PD
Member of: BAC, IPC, AHPP
Quals/training: BA; Dip Adv Psychodynamic Couns (WPF) 1988
Personal Therapy: Yes
Supervision: Ongoing
Counselling offered: **General, Psychotherapy**
Service for: Individuals
Theoretical Approach: Psychodynamic
Fees: £25 - £30

BRADY Kate   071 737 5188
33 Lorn Road, Stockwell, LONDON SW9 0AB
Member of: BAC, IPS
Quals/training: Diploma in Psychosynthesis Counselling; BA; PGCE
Personal Therapy: Ongoing
Supervision: Ongoing
Counselling offered: **General, Relationship, Bereavement, Addiction**
Service for: Individuals, Groups
Specific to: Recovering addicts/alcoholics
Theoretical Approach: Psychosynthesis, Psychodynamic
Fees: £25 negotiable

London - South West

WILLSON Sheila   071 352 7935
Flat 14, 93 Elm Park Gardens, West Brompton, LONDON SW10 9QW
Member of: BAC
Quals/training: Cert Competence(WPF)'77; Jungian Psychotherapist
Personal Therapy: Yes
Supervision: Ongoing
Counselling offered: Psychotherapy
Service for: Individuals
Theoretical Approach: Jungian
Fees: Negotiable

BAWS Helen   071 350 1715, 081 949 3206
42 Chivalry Road, Wandsworth Common, LONDON SW11 1HX
Member of: BAC, BASMT
Quals/training: BA; MSc (London) in Life Course Development; RELATE Trained; short courses on Bereavement, divorce; Workplace Counsellor
Personal Therapy: Yes
Supervision: Ongoing
Counselling offered: **Relationship, Work, Stress management, Midlife, Bereavement**
Service for: Individuals, Couples
Theoretical Approach: Psychodynamic, Behavioural
Fees: £25 daytime, £30 evenings

DENING Sarah   071 350 1001
29 Sunbury Lane, Battersea, LONDON SW11 3NP
Member of: BAC
Quals/training: BA (Hons) Psychol 1965 Univ of London; training Analysis with Jungian Analyst
Personal Therapy: Ongoing
Supervision: Ongoing
Counselling offered: General, Psychotherapy, Eating disorders
Service for: Individuals, Couples
Theoretical Approach: Jungian, Gestalt
Other languages: French
Fees: £25 sliding scale

GANDY Rus   071 223 4269
5 Avenue Mansions, Battersea, LONDON SW11 5SL
Member of: BAC Acc, BPS, Member of UKCP Register
Quals/training: BAC(Acc); BA(Hons) Psychol (Liverpool) '69; C Psychol; Certified Psychotherapist (Gerda Boyeson Inst)
Personal Therapy: Yes
Supervision: Ongoing
Counselling offered: **General, Career, Marital, Sexual, Bereavement, Psychotherapy**
Service for: Individuals, Couples, Groups
Theoretical Approach: Rogerian, Person-centred
Other languages: French, German
Fees: £25 - £40 negotiable

London - South West

REUVID Jennie 071 223 9236
26 Birley Street, Battersea, LONDON SW11 5XF
Member of: BAC, BASMT
Quals/training: Dip Couns; Dip in Human Sexuality (London Univ); Qualified Teacher of Autogenic Training
Personal Therapy: Ongoing
Supervision: Ongoing
Counselling offered: General, Marital, Relationship, Stress management, Bereavement, Cancer
Service for: Individuals, Couples
Theoretical Approach: Eclectic
Fees: £30 - £35 negotiable

DONINGTON Laura 071 228 1107
39 Blenkarne Road, Battersea, LONDON SW11 6HZ
Member of: BAC, Member of UKCP Register
Quals/training: BA(Hons); MSc Soc Psychol 1968; Rog Couns (WPF) & Core Process Psychotherapy (Karuna); additioanl Training in object relations & Jungian approach bodywork & birth process
Personal Therapy: Ongoing
Supervision: Ongoing
Counselling offered: General, Relationship, Psychotherapy, Personal growth
Service for: Individuals, Couples
Theoretical Approach: Integrative, Holistic, Transpersonal
Fees: £20 - £35

JONES David 071 223 7020
39 Blenkarne Road, Battersea, LONDON SW11 6HZ
Member of: BAC, AHPP
Quals/training: MA (Oxon); BA Pscyhology & Philosophy; Dip Humanistic Psychology (IDHP) 1982-4; Graduate of Karuna Inst 1993
Personal Therapy: Yes
Supervision: Ongoing
Counselling offered: General, Stress, Relationship
Service for: Individuals, Groups
Specific to: Executives, Business people, Islamic
Theoretical Approach: Humanistic, Psychospiritual
Fees: £25 means tested

ELVIN Gillian 071 585 3025
69 Muncaster Road, Battersea, LONDON SW11 6NX
Member of: BAC Acc
Quals/training: BAC Acc; ASC Acc; Adv Study in Couns; Dip Group Therapy
Personal Therapy: Yes
Supervision: Ongoing
Counselling offered: General
Service for: Individuals, Groups
Theoretical Approach: Psychodynamic, Group analysis
Fees: £22 - £30 Sliding scale

London - South West

LOVE Jacqui 081 671 6303
2 Rosethorn Close, Thornton Road, Balham, LONDON SW12 0JP
Member of:	BAC
Quals/training:	Dip Couns (SW London Coll); Sexual, Bereavement; Cert THT HIV/AIDS Trainer; CSCT/AEB Reg Trainer
Personal Therapy:	Ongoing
Supervision:	Ongoing
Counselling offered:	**General, Sexual, Abuse, Bereavement, HIV, AIDS, Relationship, Psychotherapy, Assertiveness, Self-esteem**
Service for:	Individuals, Couples, Groups
Theoretical Approach:	Person-centred, Gestalt, Holistic, Eclectic
Fees:	Negotiable

WALSH Aine 081 767 8997
56c Sarsfeld Road, Balham, LONDON SW12 8HN
Member of:	BAC, IPC
Quals/training:	Dip Couns (SW London Coll) '79; Graduate Memb IPC/WPF '80
Personal Therapy:	Yes
Supervision:	Ongoing
Counselling offered:	**General, Psychotherapy**
Service for:	Individuals
Theoretical Approach:	Jungian
Fees:	£22 - £28 negotiable

O'HALLORAN Mike 081 675 9218
Flat 5, 92 Nightingale Lane, Clapham, LONDON SW12 8NP
Member of:	BAC
Quals/training:	MA Couns (Durham); Adv Cert Couns, ACCEPT (Dublin); Fundamentals of Gestalt Psychotherapy Programme (metanoia); Various training workshops (metanoia, Spectrum)
Personal Therapy:	Ongoing
Supervision:	Ongoing
Counselling offered:	**General, Relationship, Bereavement, Psychotherapy**
Service for:	Individuals
Theoretical Approach:	Rogerian, Gestalt
Fees:	£25

REEVE Gill ansa 081 675 9218
Flat 5, 92 Nightingale Lane, Balham, LONDON SW12 8NP
Member of:	BAC
Quals/training:	CQSW; training in co-dependency; cert in adv group dynamics (Inst Grp Dyn); training in race & psychotherapy (Freud Mus & NAFSIYAT)
Personal Therapy:	Yes
Supervision:	Ongoing
Counselling offered:	**General, Co-dependency, Relationship, Bereavement, Self-esteem**
Service for:	Individuals, Groups
Specific to:	Women
Theoretical Approach:	Rogerian, Gestalt
Other languages:	French
Fees:	£25 Enquire for groups

London - South West

COUMONT Val   081 673 6122
24 Lynn Road, Balham, LONDON SW12 9LA
Member of: ITHP
Quals/training: BA; Dip Psychotherapy(Minster Centre)'86; Cognitive- Analytic Therapy Project, Guy's Hospital; CTP
Personal Therapy: Yes
Supervision: Ongoing
Counselling offered: General, Psychotherapy, Short-term
Service for: Individuals
Theoretical Approach: Winnicottian, Humanistic, CAT
Other languages: French
Fees: £30 concessions negotiable

COURTAULT Susie   081 673 1457
5 Culverden Road, Balham, LONDON SW12 9LR
Member of: IPSS
Quals/training: 1976 Dip in Social Work; 1981-84 training in Psychotherapy IPSS; Dip Dramatherapy
Personal Therapy: Yes
Supervision: Ongoing
Counselling offered: Psychotherapy, Drama therapy, Relationship
Service for: Individuals, Couples, Groups
Specific to: Women
Theoretical Approach: Eclectic, Feminist, Existential
Other languages: French
Fees: £22 - £25 sliding scale; £30 groups

THOMPSON Sholto   081 878 1720
26 Elm Grove Road, Barnes, LONDON SW13 0BT
Member of: BAC
Quals/training: BEd (Hons) Sussex 1971; Dip Art Therapy (St Albans) 1975; Dip Person Centred Therapy 1991
Personal Therapy: Yes
Supervision: Ongoing
Counselling offered: General, Relationship
Theoretical Approach: Rogerian, Person-centred
Fees: £20 - £25 sliding scale

JACOB Emily   081 878 5835
8 Beverley Road, Barnes, LONDON SW13 0LX
Member of: BASMT
Quals/training: RELATE Trained; Dip Couns; BASMT Acc; Acc Cognitive Analytic Therapist
Personal Therapy: Yes
Supervision: Ongoing
Counselling offered: General, Marital, Fear of flying
Service for: Individuals, Couples
Theoretical Approach: Integrative
Fees: £25 - £35

London - South West

BUTLER Catherine   081 748 1348
12 Cumberland Road, Barnes, LONDON SW13 9LY
Member of: BAC
Quals/training: LRAM; 1981 Cert Couns (Middx Poly); '87 Dip CPCP; '86 Cert Student Couns (London Univ); ASC Acc; '91 IGA general course in Group Work; '93 MPhil Research Psychology
Personal Therapy: Yes
Supervision: Ongoing
Counselling offered: General, Crisis, Sexual, Psychotherapy
Service for: Individuals, Couples, Groups
Specific to: Creative people, Gays, Adolescents
Theoretical Approach: Eclectic
Fees: £25 - £30

PRYOR Tim   081 563 0237
30 Castelnau Mansions, Castelnau, Barnes, LONDON SW13 9QX
Member of: BAC Acc
Quals/training: BAC and ASC Acc; Diploma in Guidance & Counselling '79 (Reading Univ); MA in Counselling (Reading Univ) '88; in training for Dip Couns/pyschotherapy supervision (WPF)
Personal Therapy: Yes
Supervision: Ongoing
Counselling offered: General
Service for: Individuals
Specific to: Gays
Theoretical Approach: Jungian, Psychodynamic
Fees: £30

ISAACS Joy   081 876 5223
105 Christchurch Road, East Sheen, LONDON SW14 7AT
Member of: LCP, OPTI
Quals/training: CQSW 1972; 4 yr training in Psychotherapy (LCP 1977-80; currently in Adv Gestalt training (metanoia)
Personal Therapy: Yes
Supervision: Ongoing
Counselling offered: Psychotherapy, Bereavement, Art therapy, Imaging
Service for: Individuals, Groups
Specific to: Helping professions
Theoretical Approach: Eclectic, Gestalt
Fees: £15 - £30 sliding scale

WILLETT Eleanor   081 876 6328
8 Langdale Close, Clifford Avenue, Mortlake, LONDON SW14 7BW
Member of: BAC
Quals/training: Ongoing Dip Couns using Client-centred Approach (metanoia)
Personal Therapy: Ongoing
Supervision: Ongoing
Counselling offered: General, Unknown
Service for: Individuals, Couples, Groups
Specific to: Women only
Theoretical Approach: Rogerian
Fees: £15 - £20

London - South West

CHANCER Anne 081 876 1523
35 Temple Sheen Road, East Sheen, LONDON SW14 7QF
Member of:	Guild of Psychotherapists
Quals/training:	BEd 1979; member of Guild of Psychotherapists
Personal Therapy:	Ongoing
Supervision:	Ongoing
Counselling offered:	General, Psychotherapy
Service for:	Individuals, Couples, Groups
Theoretical Approach:	Kleinian, Object relations
Fees:	£25 - £30 sliding scale

SOMERVILLE Jenny 081 878 3058
5 Carlton Road, East Sheen, LONDON SW14 7RJ
Member of:	BAC
Quals/training:	Dip Couns (Kingston Coll); bereavement training
Personal Therapy:	Ongoing
Supervision:	Ongoing
Counselling offered:	General, Relationship, Bereavement
Service for:	Individuals
Theoretical Approach:	Psychodynamic, Jungian
Fees:	£25 negotiable

MUNT Stephen 081 876 9023
279 Sheen Lane, Mortlake, LONDON SW14 8RN
Member of:	BAC, BPS, AHPP, UKCP
Quals/training:	BSc Psychol '72; CQSW '75, Dip Psychotherapy '80; Msc Psychol Couns (Surrey Univ), CPsychol; Mermb AHP & PPA
Personal Therapy:	Yes
Supervision:	Ongoing
Counselling offered:	General, Psychotherapy
Service for:	Individuals, Groups, Organisations
Theoretical Approach:	Psychodynamic, Humanistic
Fees:	£30

COLEBY Nik 0202 490065
14 Ashlone Road, Putney, LONDON SW15 1LR
Member of:	BAC
Quals/training:	BSc Communications Science & Linguistics; Couns training (metanoia); TA Therapy - 1 yr (metanoia)
Personal Therapy:	Yes
Supervision:	Ongoing
Counselling offered:	General, Relationship, Abuse, Crisis
Service for:	Individuals, Couples
Specific to:	Women
Theoretical Approach:	Rogerian, TA
Other languages:	German
Fees:	£15 - £25

London - South West

GULLIVER Pamela 081 785 7149
6 Cardinal Place, Putney, LONDON SW15 1NX
Member of:	BAC, IPC
Quals/training:	Registered Art Therapist 1971; Trained Psychotherapist (WPF) 1980; Trained supervisor (Maudesley Hospital)
Personal Therapy:	Yes
Supervision:	Ongoing
Counselling offered:	General, Psychotherapy
Service for:	Individuals, Couples
Theoretical Approach:	Psychodynamic
Fees:	£20 - £25

BURNETT Mrs Joan 081 789 9934
91 Chelverton Road, Putney, LONDON SW15 1RW
Member of:	BAC, BAP
Quals/training:	NMGC trained 1966; qualified BAP 1980; BAP Training therapist and supervisor 1989
Personal Therapy:	Yes
Supervision:	Ongoing
Counselling offered:	Psychotherapy
Service for:	Individuals
Theoretical Approach:	Psychoanalytic
Fees:	£23 - £30

SMITH Lionel 081 789 8258
2 White Court, 200 West Hill, Putney, LONDON SW15 3JB
Member of:	BAC
Quals/training:	Dip Couns
Personal Therapy:	Yes
Supervision:	Ongoing
Counselling offered:	General, Alcohol
Service for:	Individuals, Couples
Theoretical Approach:	Psychodynamic
Fees:	£12 - £25 sliding scale

WIDLAKE Bernard 081 876 0868
1 Redenham House, Tangley Grove, Roehampton, LONDON SW15 4DW
Member of:	BAC, BPA, BPS
Quals/training:	MSc Psychol Couns (Surrey) '88; Adv Cert Couns (WPF)'85; Pastoral Care & Couns (RF) '79-'80
Personal Therapy:	Yes
Supervision:	Yes
Counselling offered:	General, Stress, Bereavement
Service for:	Individuals, Groups
Theoretical Approach:	Integrative, Gestalt, Rogerian, Psychodrama, Analytic
Fees:	£28

London - South West

COLLIS June   0483 67753
1 Redenham House, Tangley Grove, Roehampton, LONDON SW15 4DW
Member of:	BAC, BPS
Quals/training:	BA Psychol; MSc Psychol Counselling
Personal Therapy:	Ongoing
Supervision:	Ongoing
Counselling offered:	**General, Bereavement, Relationship, Psychotherapy**
Service for:	Individuals, Couples, Groups
Theoretical Approach:	Humanistic
Fees:	£30

THOLSTRUP Margaret   081 392 3636
Student Counselling Service, Roehampton Institute, LONDON SW15 5PJ
Member of:	BAC Acc, BPS
Quals/training:	BAC(Acc); Couns Skills (WPF) '86; MSc Couns Psychol (Surrey) '88; Integrative Psychotherapy training (metanoia) ongoing; CPsychol
Personal Therapy:	Ongoing
Supervision:	Ongoing
Counselling offered:	**General, Psychotherapy, Eating disorders**
Service for:	Individuals, Groups
Theoretical Approach:	Integrative
Fees:	£15 - £35

CURTIS Jill   081 788 6226
39 Chartfield Avenue, Putney, LONDON SW15 6HP
Member of:	BAC, BAP
Quals/training:	Trained & qualified BAP 1979; BAP training Therapist/ Supervisor 1987
Personal Therapy:	Yes
Supervision:	Ongoing
Counselling offered:	**Psychotherapy**
Service for:	Individuals
Theoretical Approach:	Psychoanalytic
Fees:	£30 - £35

NEY Judy   081 788 2808
56 Luttrell Avenue, Putney, LONDON SW15 6PE
Member of:	BAC, BPS, AFT
Quals/training:	Chartered Couns Psychol; Cert & Acc in Family & Marital Therapy (IFT); Cert Cognitive Analytic Therapy
Personal Therapy:	Ongoing
Supervision:	Ongoing
Counselling offered:	**General, Relationship, Short-term**
Service for:	Individuals, Couples, Families
Specific to:	Women, Adolescents
Theoretical Approach:	Developmental, Systemic
Fees:	£25 ind;£35 cpls;£45 families

London - South West

HIPPS Hilary 081 672 1255 x 57158
21 Malbrook Road, Putney, LONDON SW15 6UH
Member of:	BAC, MPTI
Quals/training:	CQSW; Intro Psychotherapy couses(Tavistock); IFT Course; Principles of theory & practice of supervision (metanoia); Integrative Psychotherapy Training (metanoia) comm.1992
Personal Therapy:	Yes
Supervision:	Ongoing
Counselling offered:	**General, Relationship, Health, Disability, Bereavement**
Service for:	Individuals
Theoretical Approach:	Psychoanalytic, Psychodynamic, Integrative, Family therapy
Fees:	£20 - £28 negotiable

GAIRDNER Wendy 081 788 7953
17 Larpent Avenue, Putney, LONDON SW15 6UP
Member of:	BAC
Quals/training:	BA Psychol; Dip Psychol Couns (Roehampton Inst)
Personal Therapy:	Ongoing
Supervision:	Ongoing
Counselling offered:	**General, Bereavement, Addiction, Relationship**
Service for:	Individuals, Couples
Specific to:	Young people
Theoretical Approach:	Integrative
Fees:	£20 - £30 negotiable

MUIR Margaret 081 769 3896
53 Sunnyhill Road, Streatham, LONDON SW16 2UG
Member of:	BAC Acc
Quals/training:	BAC Acc; Course at Tavistock Inst 1975; 1980 Dip Couns SW London College
Personal Therapy:	Ongoing
Supervision:	Ongoing
Counselling offered:	**General**
Service for:	Individuals, Couples
Theoretical Approach:	Rogerian, Gestalt, TA, Psychosynthesis
Fees:	£20 Negotiable

BLACKLOCK Neil 081 664 6916
8 Harborough Road, Streatham, LONDON SW16 2XW
Member of:	BAC
Quals/training:	BA Soc Psychol; Adv Dip (Pellin) & 3 years training in Gestalt & Contribution training; Pellin Acc
Personal Therapy:	Yes
Supervision:	Ongoing
Counselling offered:	**General, Psychotherapy**
Service for:	Individuals, Couples, Groups
Theoretical Approach:	Gestalt
Fees:	£25 Negotiable

SCHAPIRA Sylvie 081 764 7292
44 Beatrice Avenue, Norbury, LONDON SW16 4UN
Member of: BAC Acc
Quals/training: BAC Acc; 1987 Dip Couns & Supervision (Roehampton)
Personal Therapy: Ongoing
Supervision: Ongoing
Counselling offered: General, Bereavement, Personal growth
Service for: Individuals, Groups
Theoretical Approach: Integrative
Other languages: French
Fees: £25

LEVY Sipora 081 677 7503
79 Pathfield Road, Streatham, LONDON SW16 5PA
Member of: BAC
Quals/training: BSc Social Sciences; Cert Gestalt Therapy & Contribution Training (Pellin)
Personal Therapy: Ongoing
Supervision: Ongoing
Counselling offered: General, Relationship
Service for: Individuals, Couples, Groups
Specific to: Women, Lesbians, Gays
Theoretical Approach: Feminist, Gestalt
Fees: £20 - £30 sliding scale

ROSE-NEIL Wendy fax 081 664 6897
40 Barrow Road, Streatham, LONDON SW16 5PF
Member of: BAC, BPS, AHPP, ANLP (PCS)
Quals/training: Chartered Psychologist; BA (Hons) Psychology; MSc Counselling Psychology; Diploma in NLP; training in Humanistic Psychotherapy
Personal Therapy: Yes
Supervision: Ongoing
Counselling offered: General, Assertiveness, Crisis, Loss, Relationship, Psychotherapy, Supervision
Service for: Individuals, Couples, Groups
Theoretical Approach: Humanistic, Integrative
Fees: £30 negotiable

PARRITT Simon 081 677 6375
10 Eastwood Street, Streatham, LONDON SW16 6PX
Member of: BAC
Quals/training: BA Psychol; Cert Couns (London Inst Human Sexuality) 1985; Cert Psychosexual Couns 1987; Memb SPOD
Personal Therapy: Yes
Supervision: Ongoing
Counselling offered: General, Relationship, Sexual, Marital
Service for: Individuals, Couples
Specific to: People with disabilities
Theoretical Approach: Cognitive, Rogerian
Fees: £18 - £25 sliding scale

London - South West

TIMMERMAN Robert   081 769 4426
48 Pendel Road, Streatham, LONDON SW16 6RU
Member of: BAC
Quals/training: BSc; PCGE; MA Psychol/Couns, USA; Cert in Couns (Roehampton Inst); courses in Couns, TA, Gestalt, Stress Management, Assessment & Statementing
Personal Therapy: Yes
Supervision: Ongoing
Counselling offered: **General, Assertiveness, Bereavement, Career, Educational, Marital, Parenting problems, Personal growth, Relationship**
Service for: Individuals, Couples, Families, Groups
Theoretical Approach: Rogerian, Eclectic
Fees: £25 (cpls £30; fam, grp £40)

CAMPBELL Julia   081 677 7552
76 Ribblesdale Road, Streatham, LONDON SW16 6SE
Member of: BAC
Quals/training: Couns training Sutton Pastoral Foundation 1984-87; Cert of competence (WPF)
Personal Therapy: Yes
Supervision: Ongoing
Counselling offered: **General, Psychotherapy, Sexual abuse**
Service for: Individuals, Couples, Families, Groups
Specific to: Survivors of sex abuse
Theoretical Approach: Psychodynamic, Eclectic
Fees: Negotiable

HILL Joanne   081 674 1722
Flat E, 82 Elmbourne Road, Tooting, LONDON SW17
Member of: IPC
Personal Therapy: Ongoing
Supervision: Ongoing
Counselling offered: **Psychotherapy**
Service for: Individuals, Couples, Groups
Specific to: Adolescents
Theoretical Approach: Eclectic
Fees: Sliding scale

RODGERS Susan   081 946 3933
Flat E, 82 Elmbourne Road, Tooting Bec, LONDON SW17
Member of: BAC, IPC
Quals/training: Dip Institute of Psychotherapy & Counselling (WPF)
Personal Therapy: Yes
Supervision: Ongoing
Counselling offered: **General, Psychotherapy**
Service for: Individuals
Theoretical Approach: Analytical
Fees: £15 - £25 sliding scale

London - South West

THROWER Gillian   081 783 0686
82 Elmbourne Road, Tooting Bec, LONDON SW17
Member of:	BAC, IPC
Quals/training:	Memb of IPC/WPF; Dip Adv Psychodynamic Couns; CQSW
Personal Therapy:	Yes
Supervision:	Ongoing
Counselling offered:	General, Long-term, Short-term, Bereavement
Service for:	Individuals
Theoretical Approach:	Eclectic, Psychodynamic
Fees:	£15 - £25 sliding scale

MARKHAM Sonia   081 672 9698, ansaphone 081 767 9857
28 Wandle Road, Tooting, LONDON SW17 1DT
Member of:	BAC Acc
Quals/training:	BAC Acc; Dip Couns Skills SW London College 1984; Pellin Dip & Advanced Dip Gestalt Therapy & Contribution Training 1986
Personal Therapy:	Yes
Supervision:	Ongoing
Counselling offered:	General, Relationship, Psychotherapy, Supervision
Service for:	Individuals, Couples, Groups
Theoretical Approach:	Rogerian, Gestalt, Contribution training
Fees:	£20 - £25 negotiable

LAW Susan   ansaphone 081 767 0938
4c Trinity Crescent, Tooting, LONDON SW17 7AE
Member of:	BAC
Quals/training:	BSc Soc Sci; CQSW 1973; Dip AT; BAAT Registered Art Therapist 1981
Personal Therapy:	Yes
Supervision:	Ongoing
Counselling offered:	General, Art therapy, Eating disorders
Service for:	Individuals
Specific to:	Survivors of child abuse
Theoretical Approach:	Eclectic
Fees:	£25 - £30

MUMFORD Susan   081 672 9911
Department of Psychology, Springfield Hospital, LONDON SW17 7DJ
Member of:	BPS, BABCP
Quals/training:	BA(Hons) Psychol; CPsychol; Clinical Psychol; BPS(Assoc); Cognitive therapy course (Inst Psychiatry)
Personal Therapy:	No
Supervision:	No
Counselling offered:	General, Relationship, Bereavement, Obsessions, Stress
Service for:	Individuals
Theoretical Approach:	Cognitive
Other languages:	French
Fees:	£25 - £55

London - South West

DAVIS Janet 081 767 2935
7 Hereward Road, Tooting, LONDON SW17 7EY
Member of: BAC
Quals/training: Dip Couns SW London College 1981-4; Pellin Centre psychotherapy training 1985-6
Personal Therapy: Yes
Supervision: Ongoing
Counselling offered: **General, Sexuality, Relationship, Loss, Bereavement**
Service for: Individuals, Couples, Groups
Theoretical Approach: Psychodynamic, Gestalt, TA, Humanistic
Fees: £20 - £25

WYNN PARRY Charlotte 081 672 9258
11a Moring Road, Tooting, LONDON SW17 8DN
Member of: ITHP
Quals/training: Trained in psychotherapy(Minster Centre)'80-'83; Analytical Psychotherapy course(Queen Mary's Hosp, Roehampton)'89-'91
Personal Therapy: Yes
Supervision: Ongoing
Counselling offered: **General, Relationship, Psychotherapy**
Service for: Individuals, Couples
Theoretical Approach: Integrative, Analytic, Jungian
Fees: £18 - £26

MURRAY Cecil Dr 081 767 9006
131 Franciscan Road, Tooting Bec, LONDON SW17 8DZ
Member of: BAC, BPS
Quals/training: PhD Psychol; 1986 Couns Cert LCIP; Cert Couns Skills CAC '87 Dip Hypnotherapy & Psychotherapy; Biofeedback Trainer; Memb IAH
Personal Therapy: Yes
Supervision: Ongoing
Counselling offered: **General, Sexual, Marital, Bereavement, Hypnotherapy**
Service for: Individuals, Couples
Theoretical Approach: Cognitive/Behavioural, Eclectic
Fees:£25 - £50

RIDDELL Caroline 081 673 2139
70 Childebert Road, Tooting Bec, LONDON SW17 8EX
Member of: BAC Acc, NRHP
Quals/training: BAC Acc; Cert Hypnotherapy & Psychotherapy (NCHP): Group courses with WPF; Adlerian Society; Women's Therapy Centre
Personal Therapy: Ongoing
Supervision: Ongoing
Counselling offered: **General, Eating disorders, Hypnotherapy, Phobias, Psychotherapy, Bulimia, Weight**
Service for: Individuals, Couples, Groups
Theoretical Approach: Eclectic, Cognitive, Ericksonian, Jungian, Rogerian
Other languages: French
Fees: £25 - £40 sliding scale

London - South West

MARSDEN Patricia   081 672 4277, ansaphone 081 682 3094
Flat E, 82 Elmbourne Road, LONDON SW17 8JH
Member of: BAC, IPC/WPF
Quals/training: MA; Full Member in Psychotherapy (IPC/WPF)
Personal Therapy: Yes
Supervision: Ongoing
Counselling offered: General, Psychotherapy
Service for: Individuals
Theoretical Approach: Psychodynamic
Fees: £25 - £35

WHISTLER Jennifer Mrs   081 870 6083
5 Fullerton Road, Wandsworth, LONDON SW18
Member of: BAC Acc
Quals/training: BAC(Acc); BA; Cert Couns (LCIP)'83
Personal Therapy: Yes
Supervision: Ongoing
Counselling offered: General, Psychotherapy
Service for: Individuals
Theoretical Approach: Analytical
Fees: £18 - £27

STOKES Jean   081 874 6631
Putney/Southfields, LONDON SW18
Member of: BAC, IPC
Quals/training: MA; Full Memb IPC/WPF; Training with AJA
Personal Therapy: Ongoing
Supervision: Ongoing
Counselling offered: General, Psychotherapy
Service for: Individuals
Theoretical Approach: Analytical, Psychodynamic
Fees: Negotiable

MEADEN Rosaleen   081 870 0743
78 Ringford Road, Wandsworth, LONDON SW18 1RR
Member of: BAC, IPC, Member of UKCP Register
Quals/training: WPF Counsellor, Psychotherapist & Supervisor
Personal Therapy: Yes
Supervision: Ongoing
Counselling offered: General, Psychotherapy
Service for: Individuals
Theoretical Approach: Psychoanalytic
Fees: £20 - £27 sliding scale

London - South West

MEIGS Melinda 081 870 4422
24 Knoll Road, Wandsworth, LONDON SW18 2DF
Member of:	BAC Acc
Quals/training:	BAC (Acc) 92; BA (Hons) 75; Jungian Training in Analysis 76- 84; Seminars in Couns (WPF) 85-6; Dip Couns (London Univ) 91
Personal Therapy:	Ongoing
Supervision:	Ongoing
Counselling offered:	**General, Marital, Career, Voice work**
Service for:	Individuals, Couples, Groups
Theoretical Approach:	Eclectic
Other languages:	French, German
Fees:	£30 sliding scale

FISHER Suze 081 874 7132
7 Herndon Road, Wandsworth, LONDON SW18 2DQ
Member of:	BAC
Quals/training:	BA; Dip Couns 1990 (CSCT)
Personal Therapy:	Ongoing
Supervision:	Ongoing
Counselling offered:	**General, Stress, Abortion, Relationship, Obsessions**
Service for:	Individuals
Theoretical Approach:	Psychodynamic, Person-centred
Fees:	£25 negotiable

COLCLOUGH Pam 081 870 0028
LONDON SW18
Member of:	BAC, BPS
Quals/training:	MSc Psychol; Cert Applied Couns (Thames Poly)'86; Bereavement training '87; Postgrad Dip Couns (Univ E London) '99; RSA Post Traumatic Stress Couns Cert '93
Personal Therapy:	Yes
Supervision:	Ongoing
Counselling offered:	**General, Bereavement, Loss, PTSD, Trauma**
Service for:	Individuals, Couples, Groups
Theoretical Approach:	Person-centred, Eclectic
Fees:	£20 - £30 sliding scale

BERGER Jocelyn 081 874 0763
15 Sandgate Lane, (formerly Lyford Road), Wandsworth, LONDON SW18 3JP
Member of:	BAC Acc
Quals/training:	BAC Acc; Dip Couns Skills (SW London) 1986; foundation year in groupwork (IGA) 1986-88; on MA programme (Psych & Couns) Antioch
Personal Therapy:	Ongoing
Supervision:	Ongoing
Counselling offered:	**General, Psychotherapy**
Service for:	Individuals
Theoretical Approach:	Client-centred
Fees:	£25

London - South West

RIPPON Lynda   081 540 2049
4 Stratton Road, Merton Park, Wimbledon, LONDON SW19 3JG
Member of:	BAC
Quals/training:	BA (Hons) Psychology/English; Dip Psychological Counselling
Personal Therapy:	Ongoing
Supervision:	Ongoing
Counselling offered:	**General**
Service for:	Individuals
Theoretical Approach:	Psychodynamic
Fees:	£20 - £30

EGGELING Celia   081 542 3234
Torridon, 19 Langley Road, Wimbledon, LONDON SW19 3NZ
Member of:	BAC
Quals/training:	Marriage Guidance training; CQSW; Dip Psychological Couns, Roehampton Inst
Personal Therapy:	Yes
Supervision:	Ongoing
Counselling offered:	**General, Marital, Crisis, Loss, Bereavement**
Service for:	Individuals, Couples
Theoretical Approach:	Rogerian, Psychodynamic
Fees:	Negotiable

SMALLACOMBE Ruth
LONDON SW19
Member of:	BAC
Quals/training:	Dip Couns; CQSW; trained as Mental Health Social Worker; HIV couns
Personal Therapy:	Yes
Supervision:	Ongoing
Counselling offered:	**General, Crisis, HIV, Sexual abuse, Occupational, Personal growth, Work, Violence, Infertility**
Service for:	Individuals, Couples, Organisations
Theoretical Approach:	Person-centred, Eclectic
Fees:	Negotiable

SMITH Phyllis   081 946 7076
3 Worple Court, Worple Road, Wimbledon, LONDON SW19 4EG
Member of:	BAC, IPC
Quals/training:	Dip Couns (IPC/WPF); SRN; Cert Social Work; Dip Sociology (London)
Personal Therapy:	Yes
Supervision:	Ongoing
Counselling offered:	**General, Bereavement**
Service for:	Individuals
Theoretical Approach:	Jungian, Psychodynamic, Person-centred
Fees:	£16 negotiable in some circs

London - South West

ELLIOT Patricia 081 947 6059
4 Denmark Avenue, Wimbledon, LONDON SW19 4HF
Member of:	BAC, PET
Quals/training:	BEd Psychol; Cert Couns; Training in Psychosynthesis; Parent Network Co-ordinator
Personal Therapy:	Yes
Supervision:	Ongoing
Counselling offered:	**General, Family, Bereavement, Educational**
Service for:	Individuals, Couples, Families, Groups
Theoretical Approach:	Rogerian, Psychosynthesis
Fees:	£15 - £30

RAYMOND Caroline 081 947 0962
4 Clare Court, Grosvenor Hill, Wimbledon Village, LONDON SW19 4RZ
Member of:	BAC, NRHP
Quals/training:	Dip Hypnotherapy & Psychotherapy (NC); MNRHP; MISMA
Personal Therapy:	No
Supervision:	Ongoing
Counselling offered:	**Midlife, Relationship, Stress management**
Service for:	Individuals, Organisations
Theoretical Approach:	Eclectic
Fees:	£35

ANDREW Elizabeth 081 947 2732
3 Camp View, Wimbledon, LONDON SW19 4UL
Member of:	IPC/WPF
Quals/training:	MA; Member Assoc of Family Therapists; Full Member IPC/WPF IPC/WPF
Personal Therapy:	Yes
Supervision:	Ongoing
Counselling offered:	**Psychotherapy, Marital**
Service for:	Individuals, Couples
Theoretical Approach:	Psychodynamic, Systemic
Fees:	£30 - £65 sliding scale

ALLEN Mrs Regina 081 947 5541
23 Leeward Gardens, Wimbledon, LONDON SW19 7QR
Member of:	BAC, GAPPSW, Guild of Psychotherapists
Quals/training:	BA Sociology (LSE) & Cert Youthwork; Tavistock adv casework course; Staff Tavistock Inst Marital Studies; Snr Psychiatric Social Worker Family Clinic
Personal Therapy:	Yes
Supervision:	Ongoing
Counselling offered:	**General, Marital, Bereavement, Psychotherapy, Supervision**
Service for:	Individuals, Couples, Families
Specific to:	Clergy/priests, Social workers, Counsellors
Theoretical Approach:	Analytical, Dynamic
Fees:	£30 negotiable in special circs

London - South West

KNIGHT-EVANS Alison　　　　　　　　　　　　　　　　081 944 8738
Thames Psychology & Couns Cent, 38 Ernie Road, Wimbledon, LONDON SW20 0HL
Member of:	BAC, BPS
Quals/training:	BSc Psychol; MSc Psychol Couns; Cert Couns(KCFE); Cert Transpersonal Psychol
Personal Therapy:	Yes
Supervision:	Ongoing
Counselling offered:	General, Psychotherapy, Eating disorders
Service for:	Individuals, Groups
Theoretical Approach:	Psychodynamic, Transpersonal
Fees:	£30 sliding scale

STEWART Lisa　　　　　　　　　　　　　　ansaphone 081 944 8738
Thames Psychology/Counselling, 38 Ernie Road, Wimbledon, LONDON SW19
Member of:	BAC
Quals/training:	RMN; RGN; CPN Dip; Cert Couns (South London College); Cert CBT (ENB A12)
Personal Therapy:	Yes
Supervision:	Ongoing
Counselling offered:	General, Bereavement, Trauma, Child abuse
Service for:	Individuals
Specific to:	Women
Theoretical Approach:	Eclectic, Integrative
Fees:	£35 - £45 also in Woking

WESTLAKE Robert　　　　　　　　　　　　　　　　　081 879 0135
108 Coombe Lane, West Wimbledon, LONDON SW20 0AY
Member of:	BAC, BPS
Quals/training:	BSc(Hons) Psychol; CPsychol; AFBPsS; Masters Cert NLP
Personal Therapy:	No
Supervision:	Ongoing
Counselling offered:	General, Relationship, Addiction, Psychotherapy
Service for:	Individuals, Couples, Families, Groups
Theoretical Approach:	NLP, Eclectic
Other languages:	Norwegian
Fees:	£35 - £45

SPY Terri　　　　　　　　　　　　　　　　　　　　　081 330 4045
12 Derwent Road, West Wimbledon, LONDON SW20 9NH
Member of:	BAC Acc RSup
Quals/training:	BAC(Acc); BAC Recognised Supervisor & Trainer; RMN '66; Dip Couns Skills(SW London Coll)'79; PG Cert Ed(Adults)
Personal Therapy:	Ongoing
Supervision:	Ongoing
Counselling offered:	General, Relationship, Sexual, Bereavement, Pastoral
Service for:	ndividuals, Couples, Families, Groups
Specific to:	People with disabilities, Gays, Ethnic minorities
Theoretical Approach:	Rogerian, Gestalt, TA, Integrative
Fees:	£30 negotiable

London - West

Organisations

CHIRON CENTRE FOR HOLISTIC PSYCHOTHERAPY 081 997 5219
26 Eaton Rise, Ealing, LONDON W5 2ER
Service:	Individual & group psychotherapy, massage therapy. Holistic approach with particular emphasis on the body/mind relation ship. Also offers training in holistic psychotherapy
Area served:	London
Other languages:	German
Referral:	Self
Training of workers:	3 years basic training and 2 years post-graduate training, weekly in-service supervision
Code of Ethics:	CCHP
Management by:	Bernd Eiden & Jochen Lude
Fees:	£20 - £27

HOBBS-GORDON COUNSELLING 081 569 8031
183a South Ealing Road, South Ealing, LONDON W5 4RH
Service:	Individual and couple counselling and sex therapy
Area served:	West London and Middlesex
Referral:	Self or others
Training of workers:	RELATE trained, 10 years experience with agency, psychotherapy training
Code of Ethics:	BAC, BASMT
Management by:Partners:	Anita Hobbs, Norman Gordon
Fees:	£30

WESTMINSTER BEREAVEMENT SERVICE 071 289 6597
24 Formosa Street, LONDON W9 2QA
Service:	Trained volunteers offer emotional support to the bereaved, make regular home visits & enable peopel to rebuild their links in the community
Area served:	London Borough of Westminster residents only
Referral:	Self or others
Training of workers:	Training over two months; monthly supervision
Code of Ethics:	Agency's own code
Management by:	Voluntary Management Committee
Fees:	None, donations welcome

WEST LONDON FAMILY SERVICE UNIT 071 229 9941
289 Westbourne Park Road, Notting Hill, LONDON W11 1EE
Service:	Family social work service providing general counselling, groupwork, family therapy to families with children
Area served:	North Kensington
Other languages:	Punjabi, Hindi
Referral:	Self or others
Training of workers:	CQSW; regular supervision
Code of Ethics:	BASW
Management by:	Local Management Committee
Fees:	None

London - West

POST ABORTION COUNSELLING SERVICE 071 221 9631
340 Westbourne Park Road, Notting Hill, LONDON W11 1EQ
Service:	Post Abortion counselling
Area served:	London, Home Counties
Referral:	Self
Training of workers:	All fully trained & supervised
Code of Ethics:	Agency's own code
Management by:	Trustees - Registered Charity
Fees:	£17 assessment, £15-£35 negotiable

CENTRE FOR COUNSELLING & PSYCHOTHERAPY EDUCATION (CCPE)
071 221 3215
21 Lancaster Road, Notting Hill, LONDON W11 1QL
Service:	Individual, couple & family counselling & psychotherapy. Spiritual perspective on psychotherapy also provided. Member of UK Council for Psychotherapy
Area served:	No restrictions
Other languages:	French, German, Portuguese, Greek, Spanish
Referral:	Self or others
Training of workers:	4 years, weekly ongoing supervision
Code of Ethics:	BAC
Management by:	Management Committee
Fees:	£8 - £35 depending on income

ENTERPRISE COUNSELLING SERVICES   071 243 8576, Fax 071 792 2612
145 Elgin Crescent, Holland Park, LONDON W11 2JH
Service:	Career, crisis, redundancy, retirement counselling, taking stock, goals, options, CV, interviews & job search for individuals. Counselling skills packages for organisations
Area served:	UK working in Manchester, Wolverhampton, London, Bristol
Referral:	Self, Organisations
Training of workers:	Relevant professional training and ongoing supervision
Code of Ethics:	BAC
Management by:	Director
Fees:	By arrangement

NOTTING HILL CENTRE FOR COUNSELLING & CONSULTATION
071 727 9551
59 Ladbroke Grove, Notting Hill, LONDON W11 3AT
Service:	Individuals, couples, groups, families, groupwork with adolescent sex offenders; team development; counselling and groupwork training
Other languages:	French
Referral:	Self or others
Training of workers:	Dip Couns Individual & Group psychotherapy; family therapy; social work; personal therapy; individual/peer supervision
Code of Ethics:	BAC
Management by:	Therapists, Clinical Director
Fees:	Sliding scale, dep on income

London - West

HELP ADVISORY CENTRE 071 221 9974, 071 221 7914
57 Portobello Road, Notting Hill Gate, LONDON W11 3EB
Service:	General counselling and information on pregnancy, post-abortion, contraception. Emotional and relationship cllng. Evening groups in assertiveness, communication skills, etc
Area served:	No restriction
Referral:	Self
Training of workers:	Relevant counselling and psychotherapy training
Code of Ethics:	BAC
Management by:	Director
Fees:	None

ASIAN FAMILY COUNSELLING SERVICE 081 997 5749
74 The Avenue, West Ealing, LONDON W13 8LB
Service:	Marital counselling and family & relationship problems. Counselling to the Asian community
Area served:	London
Other languages:	Punjabi, Urdu, Hindi, Gujerati
Referral:	Self or others
Training of workers:	1 year part-time basic training. Regular supervision
Code of Ethics:	-
Management by:	Management & advisory board
Fees:	None

CORNERSTONE
30 Amherst Road, Ealing, LONDON W13 8LT
Service:	A network of Christians offering professional psychotherapy & counselling for individuals, couples, families & groups
Area served:	London & surrounding area
Referral:	Self
Training of workers:	Relevant professional training in counselling or psychotherapy
Code of Ethics:	BAC
Management by:	Steering group
Fees:	£20 - £30

WEST LONDON COUNSELLING & PSYCHOTHERAPY GROUP
081 740 8336, 081 446 4854, 081 579 6582
LONDON W3
Service:	Analytical counselling and psychotherapy for individuals
Area served:	Clinical practices based in Acton, Ealing & Shepherds Bush
Other languages:	French
Referral:	GP, Health/Soc Work Professional, Companies, Self
Training of workers:	BAC(Acc) counsellors and or analytically trained psychotherapists
Code of Ethics:	BAC
Management by:	Directors
Fees:	£20 - £35

London - West

COUNSELLING PARTNERSHIP (LONDON)   071 487 3766
5 Albert Mansions, Luxborough Street, LONDON W1M 3LN
Service:	A confidential, prompt, personal, marital and sexual counselling and therapy service
Area served:	Central & Greater London
Other languages:	French, Spanish
Referral:	Self or others
Training of workers:	NMGC trained including sex therapy & group counselling. Personal psychotherapy and supervision
Code of Ethics:	BAC
Management by:	Management Committee
Fees:	£25 - £40 negotiable

WELBECK COUNSELLING SERVICE   071 935 3073
22 Upper Wimpole Street, LONDON W1M 7TA
Service:	Counselling for career & professional development, retirement, redundancy, job change, work relationships, job performance and stress management
Area served:	Clients seen in Central London
Referral:	Companies
Training of workers:	Qualified psychologists
Code of Ethics:	BPS
Management by:	Patricia Wright
Fees:	By arrangement with employers

ALBANY ASSOCIATES   071 637 5505
12 Harley Street, LONDON W1N 1ED
Service:	Psychosexual couns practice offering once-weekly therapy on a long term basis following a psychodynamic approach which can also incorporate sex therapy techniques where suitable
Area served:	Central London
Referral:	Self
Training of workers:	BAC(Acc); Cert Couns(LCIP); Cert Psychosexual Couns(Albany Trust); Dip Human Sexuality(St George's Hosp)
Code of Ethics:	BAC
Management by:	Dr C Headon
Fees:	£35 (£45 couples)

CENTRE FOR HEALTH AND HEALING   071 437 7118
Ann Silverleaf, St James' Church, 197 Piccadilly, LONDON W1V 9LF
Service:	A holistic approach to helping people deal with physical, emotional & spiritual pain & illness & to search for their potential. Intake system for new clients. Healing clinic
Referral:	Self
Training of workers:	16 fully qualified practitioners in on-going therapy and peer supervision: counsellors, therapists, body workers and healers
Code of Ethics:	BAC, Therapists' Professional body
Management by:	Staff group and Administrator
Fees:	£20 negotiable for low/unwaged

London - West

PINK PRACTICE, THE   081 809 7218
BCM Pink Pactice, LONDON WC1N 3XX
Service:	Face to Face counselling for lesbians, gay men;those struggling with issues about their sexuality. Individuals, couples, families. Training, supervision. Consultation also.
Area served:	London
Referral:	Self
Training of workers:	Psychodynamic & systemic psychotherapy & counselling, CQSW, BAC Acc
Code of Ethics:	BAC
Management by:	Partners
Fees:	£18 - £28 inds, £25-£50 couples/families

CAMDEN BEREAVEMENT SERVICE   071 833 4138
First Floor, Instrument House, 207 Kings Cross Road, LONDON WC1X 9DB
Service:	Bereavement counselling
Area served:	Camden
Other languages:	Italian, German
Referral:	Self or others
Training of workers:	In house and ongoing training, fortnightly supervision
Code of Ethics:	BAC
Management by:	Voluntary Action Camden
Fees:	None

CAMDEN PSYCHOTHERAPY UNIT   071 837 5628
Instrument House, 207/215 Kings Cross Road, LONDON WC1X 9DB
Service:	Information, referrals, consultations and once weekly psychoanalytic psychotherapy, mainly for adults, individuals and occasionally couples
Area served:	London Borough of Camden
Other languages:	Polish, Hebrew, Spanish
Referral:	Self or others
Training of workers:	Must be fully trained psychoanalytic psychotherapists, each adheres to own prof code of ethics
Code of Ethics:	Therapists' Professional body
Management by:	Voluntary Action Camden
Fees:	Dependent on income

SIGNPOST   0923 239495
206 Lower High Street, WATFORD WD1 2EL
Service:	Face to face counselling for young people and/or their families, by appointment. Sat Drop-in 10am-1pm
Area served:	SW Herts
Referral:	Self or others
Training of workers:	Variously trained; all have had personal therapy and are in supervision
Code of Ethics:	BAC
Management by:	Voluntary Management Committee & Herts Youth & CommunityService
Fees:	None

London - West

UNIVERSITY COLLEGE HOSPITAL PSYCHOSEXUAL CLINIC
071 380 9759

Obstetric Hospital, Huntley Street, LONDON
Service: Psychosexual & relationship counselling for individuals & couples, brief psychotherapy
Area served: London
Referral: GP, Self or others
Training of workers: Institute of Psychosexual Medicine
Code of Ethics: IPM, BAC
Management by: NHS

Individual Practitioners
*Every individual is a **member of** one or more organisations eligible for entry into this directory. BAC Accredited Counsellors and Recognised Supervisors are shaded.*

FREEMAN Martin   071 262 3693
2 Clarendon Place, LONDON W2 2NP
Member of: BAC, BAP, LCP
Quals/training: 1980 Couns Dip (CTP); 1981 MA Humanistic Psychology; 1986 Assoc Member BAP; Member Int Assoc for Analytical Psychology
Personal Therapy: Yes
Supervision: Ongoing
Counselling offered: Psychotherapy
Service for: Individuals
Theoretical Approach: Analytical
Fees: £26 - £32

ROBERT Leslie   071 402 9567
74 Devonport, Southwick Street, Hyde Park, LONDON W2 2QH
Member of: BAC
Quals/training: Trained as a Samaritan '81-'83; Course at London Institute for Study of Sexuality
Personal Therapy: Yes
Supervision: Ongoing
Counselling offered: General, Psychosexual, Psychotherapy, Relationship
Service for: Individuals, Couples
Theoretical Approach: TA
Fees: £20 - £25

SAUNDERS Christina   071 221 5344
16 Artesian Road, Paddington, LONDON W2 5AR
Member of: BAC, MPTI
Quals/training: Dip Couns(metanoia); short courses(WPF); intro to Gestalt; workshops in Sexual Abuse
Personal Therapy: Yes
Supervision: Ongoing
Counselling offered: General, Relationship
Service for: Individuals
Specific to: Women, Managers
Theoretical Approach: Rogerian
Fees: £12 - £20 sliding scale

London - West

CAMERON Mary
Ansaphone 081 922 4851
3 Birkbeck Road, Acton, LONDON W3 6BG
Member of: BAC Acc
Quals/training: BAC(Acc); Cert in Student Couns(Univ of London)'84; Memb Brit Assoc for Psychological Type
Personal Therapy: Yes
Supervision: Ongoing
Counselling offered: General, Career, Marital, Psychotherapy
Service for: Individuals, Couples, Groups, Organisations
Theoretical Approach: Psychodynamic
Fees: £20 - £30 (£25-£40 couples)

DUCKWORTH Moira
081 743 1990
17 Perryn Road, Acton, LONDON W3 7LR
Member of: BAC, IPC
Quals/training: BA Cert ED; Prof Memb AJA & IPC/WPF
Personal Therapy: Yes
Supervision: Ongoing
Counselling offered: General, Marital, Psychotherapy, Analysis
Service for: Individuals, Couples
Theoretical Approach: Jungian, Eclectic
Fees: £25 - £35 sliding scale

HEUER Birgit
081 749 4388
13 Mansell Road, Acton, LONDON W3 7QH
Member of: AHPP
Quals/training: Cert Biodynamic Psychotherapy 1981; Dip (Int Therapy Examination Council) 1979; Jungian Analyst in Training
Personal Therapy: Ongoing
Supervision: Ongoing
Counselling offered: Psychotherapy, Analysis, Psychosomatic, Supervision
Service for: Individuals, Groups
Specific to: Women
Theoretical Approach: Analytical, Jungian
Other languages: German
Fees: £31 reductions possible

HEUER Gottfried
081 749 4388
13 Mansell Road, Acton, LONDON W3 7QH
Member of: AJA, AHPP
Quals/training: Jungian Analyst; BA, BE (German); Cert Biodynamic Psychotherapy 1977; Dip Int Therapy Examination Council
Personal Therapy: Ongoing
Supervision: Ongoing
Counselling offered: Analysis, Psychotherapy, Relationship, Addiction, Psychosomatic
Service for: Individuals
Theoretical Approach: Jungian, Neo-Reichian
Other languages: German, French, Spanish
Fees: £40 reductions possible

London - West

GRACE Carole 081 743 8096
170 Valetta Road, Acton, LONDON W3 7TP
Member of: BAC
Quals/training: BA; BSc; Adv Dip Psychotherapy (Pellin)
Personal Therapy: Ongoing
Supervision: Ongoing
Counselling offered: General, Supervision, Drama therapy
Service for: Individuals, Groups
Specific to: Women, Ethnic minorities
Theoretical Approach: Gestalt
Fees: £15 - £25

HARRINGTON Elizabeth 081 993 4050
28 Gunnersbury Court, Bollo Lane, Acton, LONDON W3 8JN
Member of: BAC, IPC
Quals/training: Cert Ed; Dip IPC/WPF 1984; Groupwork (IGA) 1987-8
Personal Therapy: Yes
Supervision: Ongoing
Counselling offered: General, Psychotherapy
Service for: Individuals
Theoretical Approach: Psychodynamic
Fees: £25 Reduced fees for some

HITCHINGS Paul 081 992 3736
132 Princes Avenue, Gunnersbury Park, Acton, LONDON W3 8LT
Member of: BAC Acc, BPS, ITA
Quals/training: BAC Acc; Psychotherapy Training(metanoia)'84-'87; Sex Therapy training (London Institute for Study of Human Sexuality)'85-'88; MSc Psychological Couns '89
Personal Therapy: Yes
Supervision: Ongoing
Counselling offered: General, Relationship, Sexual, Psychotherapy
Service for: Individuals, Couples, Groups
Specific to: Gays
Theoretical Approach: TA, Integrative
Fees: £28 individuals; £18 per 2hr group; £40 couples

McDERMOTT Olive 081 993 3286
Flat 2, 17 Twyford Avenue, Acton, LONDON W3 9PY
Member of: IPC
Quals/training: Full Member IPC/WPF 1986
Personal Therapy: Ongoing
Supervision: Ongoing
Counselling offered: General, Psychotherapy
Service for: Individuals
Theoretical Approach: Psychodynamic
Fees: £28 negotiable

London - West

ENCKE Jochen 081 992 9514
23 Whitehall Gardens, LONDON W3 9RD
Member of:	AHPP
Quals/training:	MA in Psychology & Sociology; Dip Biodynamic Psychotherapy; Dip Transpersonal Perspectives & Skills in Couns & Psychotherapy
Personal Therapy:	Ongoing
Supervision:	Ongoing
Counselling offered:	Depression, Relationship, Crisis, Bereavement, Spiritual, Men's issues
Service for:	Individuals, Couples, Groups, Organisations
Theoretical Approach:	Humanistic, Jungian
Other languages:	German
Fees:	£30

ENCKE Ulrike 081 992 9514
23 Whitehall Gdns, LONDON W3 9RD
Member of:	AHPP
Quals/training:	MA Pedagogics (Germany); Boyesen/Chiron training; Astrology; various short courses - Laing, Gordon-Brown, Boadella, H. Davies, Jungian
Personal Therapy:	Ongoing
Supervision:	Ongoing
Counselling offered:	Long-term, Psychotherapy, Astrological, AIDS
Service for:	Individuals, Couples, Groups, Organisations
Specific to:	Jewish, Refugees
Theoretical Approach:	Reichian, Jungian, Humanistic
Other languages:	German
Fees:	£30 individuals; Astrological £50; £40 organisations

THACKRAY Ms Dayle 081 995 8607
52 Elliot Road, Chiswick, LONDON W4 1PE
Member of:	BAC
Quals/training:	Dip Social Studies 1969; Dip Applied Soc Studies/CQSW; IPSW Tavistock Clinic; advanced training/supervision IMS; Family/Marital Work IGA; BAP trainee
Personal Therapy:	Ongoing
Supervision:	Ongoing
Counselling offered:	Psychotherapy
Service for:	Individuals
Theoretical Approach:	Analytical, Jungian
Fees:	£22.50

DALTON Peggy 081 994 7959
20 Cleveland Avenue, Chiswick, LONDON W4 1SN
Member of:	BAC, Member of UKCP Register
Quals/training:	MA; Dip PCP (Therapy & Couns); trained Speech Therapist
Personal Therapy:	Yes
Supervision:	Ongoing
Counselling offered:	General, Relationship, Psychotherapy, Educational
Service for:	Individuals, Couples
Specific to:	People with language problems
Theoretical Approach:	PCP, Eclectic
Fees:	£15 - £25 negotiable

London - West

WENHAM Jane   081 995 8426
1 Dale Street, Chiswick, LONDON W4 2BJ
Member of: BAC, IPC
Quals/training: Cert Couns (LCIP) '83; Dip Adv Psychodynamic Couns (IPC/WPF) '88
Personal Therapy: Ongoing
Supervision: Ongoing
Counselling offered: **General, Psychotherapy**
Service for: Individuals
Theoretical Approach: Psychodynamic, Analytical
Fees: £15 - £30

WINKWORTH Maggie   081 994 6546
46 Quick Road, Chiswick, LONDON W4 2BU
Member of: BPS, BASMT
Quals/training: C Psychol; BSc Psychol; Dip Couns & Psychotherapy (CTP) Dip Human Sexuality & Cert Brief Psychotherapy (London Uni); qualified teacher of Autogenic Training
Personal Therapy: Yes
Supervision: Ongoing
Counselling offered: **General, Marital, Bereavement, Cancer, HIV, Stress**
Service for: Individuals, Couples
Theoretical Approach: Cognitive, Analytic
Fees: £35

EDWARDS Mary   081 747 3087
44 Duke Road, Chiswick, LONDON W4 2DD
Member of: BAC
Quals/training: 1985-87 Westminster Pastoral Foundation; Couns Skills; 1987-89 metanoia; 2 year Couns Dip Course; brief psychotherapy; Workshops assc; sexual abuse
Personal Therapy: Ongoing
Supervision: Ongoing
Counselling offered: **General, Sexual abuse, Bereavement, Depression, Relationship**
Service for: Individuals
Theoretical Approach: Rogerian
Other languages: French
Fees: £25 sliding scale

WALSH Eileen   081 995 1934
2 Campden Terrace, Linden Gardens, Chiswick, LONDON W4 2EP
Member of: BAC, ANLP (CPS)
Quals/training: MA; CQSW; Group Dynamics '77-'81; NLP Dip/Master '88; Cert Ericksonian Hypnosis '89; Acc Mediator(Family Mediators Assoc)
Personal Therapy: Yes
Supervision: Ongoing
Counselling offered: **Psychotherapy, General, Marital, Crisis, Personal growth, Change, Mediation**
Service for: Individuals, Couples, Families, Groups
Specific to: Trauma victims
Theoretical Approach: Jungian, NLP
Fees: On request

London - West

WEAVER Martin 081 994 5700
13 Chiswick Village, LONDON W4 3BY
Member of: BAC, ANLP (CPS)
Quals/training: NLP Practitioner
Personal Therapy: Ongoing
Supervision: Ongoing
Counselling offered: HIV, AIDS, Psychotherapy, Health, Bereavement, Sexuality
Service for: Individuals, Groups, Organisations
Specific to: Gays, Managers
Theoretical Approach: NLP, Humanistic, Holistic
Fees: £40 negotiable

SICHEL David 081 995 7175
194 Sutton Court Road, Chiswick, LONDON W4 3HR
Member of: BAC, ITHP
Quals/training: MA Humanistic Psychol; Dip Psychotherapy (Minster Centre); AHP
Personal Therapy: Yes
Supervision: Ongoing
Counselling offered: General, Crisis, Relationship, Psychotherapy, Supervision
Service for: Individuals, Couples, Groups
Theoretical Approach: Integrative
Fees: £30 negotiable

CLARE John 081 747 3213
15 Waldeck Road, Strand-on-the-Green, Chiswick, LONDON W4 3NL
Member of: BAC, IPSS
Quals/training: BSc Sociology; Dip Psychotherapy
Personal Therapy: Yes
Supervision: Ongoing
Counselling offered: Psychotherapy
Service for: Individuals
Specific to: Ethnic minorities
Theoretical Approach: Psychodynamic, Winnicottian
Fees: £15 - £25 sliding scale

LITTLE Ray 081 994 2905
6 Cambridge Road North, Chiswick, LONDON W4 4AA
Member of: BAC, ITA
Quals/training: Cert Yout & Community Work 1980; Dip Couns (SW London College) 1984; Clinical Transactional Analyst (ITAA)
Personal Therapy: Yes
Supervision: Ongoing
Counselling offered: General, Psychotherapy
Service for: Individuals, Couples, Groups
Specific to: Adolescents
Theoretical Approach: TA
Fees: £30 (£40 couples, £14 group)

London - West

READ Jane   081 994 2905
6 Cambridge Road North, Chiswick, LONDON W4 4AA
Member of: BAC, BASMT
Quals/training: Dip Couns(S W London College)'84; Dip Human Sexuality (St
                         George's Hospital)'87; Sex Therapy Training; BASMT Acc
Personal Therapy: Yes
Supervision: Ongoing
Counselling offered: **General, Marital, Relationship, Sexual, Crisis, Infertility**
Service for: Individuals, Couples
Fees: £30 - £40 £30 individuals £40 couples

WINTERSTEIN Mani   081 742 0089
56 Wavendon Avenue, Chiswick, LONDON W4 4NS
Member of: BAC Acc
Quals/training: BAC(Acc);RELATE trained marital counsellor & group therapist
Personal Therapy: Unknown
Supervision: Ongoing
Counselling offered: **General, Relationship**
Service for: Individuals, Couples
Theoretical Approach: Psychodynamic
Fees: £35 negotiable

O'BRIEN Jane   081 994 3631
10 Rothschild Road, Chiswick, LONDON W4 5HS
Member of: BAC Acc
Quals/training: BAC Acc; Dip Couns (IP) 1988; Memb NCPHR, ICM Register & Nat
                         Federation of Spiritual Healers
Personal Therapy: Ongoing
Supervision: Ongoing
Counselling offered: **General, Personal growth, Spiritual, Transformation, Sexual-
                         ity, Self-understanding**
Service for: Individuals, Groups
Specific to: Musicians, Executives
Theoretical Approach: Psychosynthesis, Eclectic
Fees: According to work required

FELL Angela   081 994 6206
87 Rothschild Road, Chiswick, LONDON W4 5NT
Member of: BAC, ITHP
Quals/training: Psychotherapist 3 year training (Minster Centre); ITHP Acc;
                         Homeopath
Personal Therapy: Ongoing
Supervision: Ongoing
Counselling offered: **Psychotherapy, Health, Mental health**
Service for: Individuals, Couples, Groups
Theoretical Approach: Integrative
Fees: £35 sliding scale

London - West

FURNEAUX Anne   081 567 9759
New Life Potential, Ealing Common, LONDON W5
Member of: ANLP (PCS), Member of UKCP Register
Quals/training: NLP Masters (PACE); BHR Adv
Personal Therapy: Ongoing
Supervision: Ongoing
Counselling offered: Personal growth, Hypnotherapy
Service for: Individuals, Couples, Families, Groups, Organisations
Theoretical Approach: NLP, Ericksonian
Fees: £30 some concessions

KINDER Diana   081 997 1207
23 Woodville Gardens, Ealing, LONDON W5 2LL
Member of: BAC Acc, IGA
Quals/training: BAC Acc; Former RELATE Counsellor 1978-87; Dip Couns Skills
                        (SW London College) 1983; Group analyst (IGA) 1991
Personal Therapy: Ongoing
Supervision: Ongoing
Counselling offered: General, Relationship, Sexual, Psychotherapy
Service for: Individuals, Couples, Groups
Theoretical Approach: Analytic, Psychodynamic
Fees: £18 - £25

BUTLER Todd   081 998 9390
37 Madeley Road, Ealing, LONDON W5 2LS
Member of: BAC, MPTI, GPTI
Quals/training: Dip Couns (metanoia) ; Dip Psychotherapy (GPTI)
Personal Therapy: Ongoing
Supervision: Ongoing
Counselling offered: General, AIDS, Relationship, Bereavement
Service for: Individuals, Couples, Groups
Specific to: Gays
Theoretical Approach: Rogerian, Gestalt
Fees: £25, £15/2 hr group

LEITMAN Norman   081 998 9390
37 Madeley Road, Ealing, LONDON W5 2LS
Member of: BAC, ITA
Quals/training: MA Psychol of Couns & Psychotherapy (Antioch Univ); Dip (Level
                        2) Systemic Integrative Psychotherapy (metanoia)
Personal Therapy: Ongoing
Supervision: Ongoing
Counselling offered: General
Service for: Individuals, Couples, Groups
Specific to: Gays
Theoretical Approach: Systemic, Integrative
Fees: £35 negotiable

London - West

BORSIG Su
081 579 2505
c/o metanoia, 13 North Common Road, Ealing, LONDON W5 2QB
Member of: BAC, ITA
Quals/training: Dip Hum Psy (IDHP); Psycho-sexual Couns 1984-86; 4 years TA (metanoia) 1986-90 & also Gestalt 1986-91; Couple Work 1987-88 & 1993; Adv Integrative Psychotherapy 1989-91
Personal Therapy: Ongoing
Supervision: Ongoing
Counselling offered: General, Psychotherapy
Service for: Individuals, Couples, Groups
Theoretical Approach: Integrative
Fees: £28 - £40

GILBERT Maria
081 998 9866
P O Box 2512, LONDON W5 2QG
Member of: BAC RSup, ITA, GPTI, BPS
Quals/training: MA; Clinical Teaching Memb ITAA; Teaching Memb GPTI; C Psychol
Personal Therapy: Yes
Supervision: Ongoing
Counselling offered: Psychotherapy
Service for: Individuals, Couples
Theoretical Approach: Integrative, TA, Gestalt
Fees: £35 - £45

SAMARI Samandar Mr
081 904 8239, 081 997 2489, Fax 081 998 8236
14 Haven Green, Ealing, LONDON W5 2UZ
Member of: BAC
Quals/training: Adlerian, Rogerian & Psychodynamic courses have been undertaken
Personal Therapy: Yes
Supervision: Ongoing
Counselling offered: General, Stress, Relationship, Short-term, Relaxation, Imaging
Service for: Individuals, Couples, Families
Specific to: Young people
Theoretical Approach: Adlerian
Other languages: Farsee
Fees: £15 - £30 negotiable for unwaged

WEXLER Jean
081 567 9045
16 Warwick Road, Ealing, LONDON W5 3XJ
Member of: BAC
Quals/training: Trained with Person Centered Approach Institute
Personal Therapy: Yes
Supervision: Ongoing
Counselling offered: General
Service for: Individuals, Groups
Theoretical Approach: Rogerian
Fees: £25 negotiable

London - West

SMITH Patsy   081 568 3811
4 Ealing Park Gardens, Ealing, LONDON W5 4EU
Member of: BAC, IPC
Quals/training: BEd (Hons); Dip Adv Psychodynamic Couns (IPC/WPF)
Personal Therapy: Ongoing
Supervision: Ongoing
Counselling offered: General, Psychotherapy, Relationship, Bereavement
Service for: Individual
Theoretical Approach: Analytic, Psychodynamic
Fees: £15 - £25 sliding scale

WOOD Christine   081 840 4385
1 Sunderland Road, Ealing, LONDON W5 4JY
Member of: BAC
Quals/training: GAUK; Dip Gestalt Therapy; Adv Dip Gestalt Therapy (Pellin); BSc Soc/Psych; MPhil Mental Health
Personal Therapy: Ongoing
Supervision: Ongoing
Counselling offered: General, Psychotherapy, Supervision
Service for: Individuals, Groups, Organisations
Theoretical Approach: Gestalt, Integrative
Fees: £15 - £25

PLOTEL Angela   081 579 4323
Broadway Natural Therapy Ctre, 52 The Broadway, Ealing, LONDON W5 5JN
Member of: NRHP
Quals/training: Dip Hypnotherapy & Psychotherapy (NCHP); Dip FA (London); Hypnotherapy for Bulimia (Lond Coll Clin Hypnosis); Stress Management (LCCH)
Personal Therapy: Yes
Supervision: Ongoing
Counselling offered: Hypnotherapy, Psychotherapy
Service for: Individuals
Theoretical Approach: Eclectic
Fees: £30

SANDERS Cheryl   081 579 7487
112 Windermere Road, Ealing, LONDON W5 4TH
Member of: NRHP
Quals/training: Cert Hypnotherapy & Psychotherapy (NCHP) 1992; ongoing training for DHP; CRUSE trained
Personal Therapy: Ongoing
Supervision: Ongoing
Counselling offered: General, Bereavement, Stress, Psychotherapy, Hypnotherapy, Assertiveness
Service for: Individuals, Groups, Organisations
Theoretical Approach: Eclectic, Cognitive/Behavioural
Fees: £25 Hypnotherapy £30

London - West

BAKER Jan　　　　　　　　　　　　　　　　　　　　　　081 840 3849
30 Beaconsfield Road, Ealing, LONDON W5 5JE
Member of:　　　　　　BAC Acc
Quals/training:　　　　　　BAC & ASC Acc; BA 1970; Dip Couns Skills (SW London College) 1987;Humanistic and Traditional Psychotherapy (Minister Centre)
Personal Therapy:　　　　Ongoing
Supervision:　　　　　　　Ongoing
Counselling offered:　　**General, Psychotherapy**
Service for:　　　　　　　Individuals, Groups
Theoretical Approach:　　Person-centred, Integrative
Fees:　　　　　　　　　　£18 - £30 sliding scale

MAHABIR Joel　　　　　　　　　　　　　　　　　　　　　081 567 0398
6A The Park, Ealing, LONDON W5 5NE
Member of:　　　　　　BAC
Quals/training:　　　　　　BSc (Warwick); Couns & Communication; Relationship Couns (Rayid International); Cert Colour Couns (Living Colour); MIACT
Personal Therapy:　　　　Yes
Supervision:　　　　　　　Ongoing
Counselling offered:　　**General, Relationship, Stress, Psychotherapy, Anxiety**
Service for:　　　　　　　Individuals
Specific to:　　　　　　　Managers
Theoretical Approach:　　Holistic, Person-centred, Gestalt
Other languages:　　　　　German
Fees:　　　　　　　　　　£30

MATTHEWS Carol　　　　　　　　　　　　　　　　　　　081 840 0621
12 Park Place, Ealing, LONDON W5 5NQ
Member of:　　　　　　BAC
Quals/training:　　　　　　Dip Advanced Psychodynamic Couns (WPF)
Personal Therapy:　　　　Yes
Supervision:　　　　　　　Ongoing
Counselling offered:　　**Short-term**
Service for:　　　　　　　Individuals
Theoretical Approach:　　Psychodynamic
Fees:　　　　　　　　　　On request

SILLS Charlotte　　　　　　　　　　　　　　　　　　　　081 567 9217
Rectory Lawn, 2 Richmond Road, Ealing, LONDON W5 5NS
Member of:　　　　　　BAC Acc
Quals/training:　　　　　　MA; Teaching & Supervising Transactional Analysis (ITAA); Dip Integrative Psychotherapy
Personal Therapy:　　　　Yes
Supervision:　　　　　　　Ongoing
Counselling offered:　　**General, Psychotherapy, Bereavement**
Service for:　　　　　　　Individuals, Couples, Groups
Theoretical Approach:　　Integrative
Other languages:　　　　　French
Fees:　　　　　　　　　　£30 negotiable

London - West

RUTLEDGE Joan   081 871 3162
17 Bute Gardens, Hammersmith, LONDON W6 7DR
Member of:	BAC Acc
Quals/training:	BAC Acc; MSc Couns Psychol (Surrey Univ)
Personal Therapy:	Ongoing
Supervision:	Ongoing
Counselling offered:	General
Service for:	Individuals
Theoretical Approach:	Psychodynamic
Fees:	£20 negotiable

BRICKMAN Louisette   071 221 3817 (24 hr), 081 748 6414
165a Hammersmith Grove, LONDON W6 0NJ
Member of:	BAC
Quals/training:	Dip Couns
Personal Therapy:	Yes
Supervision:	Ongoing
Counselling offered:	General, Relationship, Stress management, Bereavement, ME, Crisis
Service for:	Individuals, Groups, Organisations
Specific to:	Incest survivors, Women
Theoretical Approach:	Eclectic, Psychodynamic
Other languages:	French, Dutch
Fees:	£16 - £30 Sliding scale. Home visits

STOTT Ken   081 748 0192
77 Kings Court, King Street, Hammersmith, LONDON W6 0RW
Member of:	BAC
Quals/training:	Qualified teacher; LGSM (Speech & Drama); Course in Couns & Psychotherapy (Poly of Central London); Cert Couns LCIP; Dip ITEC
Personal Therapy:	Yes
Supervision:	Ongoing
Counselling offered:	General, Relationship, Communication skills, Relaxation, Personal growth, Massage
Service for:	Individuals, Couples
Theoretical Approach:	Person-centred, Eclectic, Psychodynamic
Fees:	£15 - £25

NEEDS-GARDINI Liliana   081 748 8065
17 Ravenscourt Square, Hammersmith, LONDON W6 0TW
Member of:	BAC
Quals/training:	Dip Couns Skills (SW London College); Dip Pract NLP; Co- counselling teachers training; Cognitive-Behavioural therapy training; currently training at Tavistock Clinic
Personal Therapy:	Yes
Supervision:	Ongoing
Counselling offered:	General, Short-term, Long-term, Relationship
Service for:	Individuals, Couples
Theoretical Approach:	Psychodynamic
Other languages:	Spanish, Italian
Fees:	£30 negotiable

London - West

BURTT Lucy 081 968 4894
5 Ravenscourt Place, Hammersmith, LONDON W6 0UN
Member of: ANLP (PCS)
Quals/training: Master Practitioner NLP (NLP Proficiency Asscs); Integrated Therapy Diploma (British Hypnosis Research)
Personal Therapy: Ongoing
Supervision: Ongoing
Counselling offered: Hypnotherapy, Eating disorders
Service for: Individuals
Theoretical Approach: NLP, Cognitive
Fees: £20 - £30 Sliding scale

FAIZ Nasim 071 385 0180
48 Cox House, Field Road, Hammersmith, LONDON W6 8HN
Member of: BAC
Quals/training: 1970 RGN; 1972 RMN; 1984 Diploma in Counselling Skills (South West London College)
Personal Therapy: Yes
Supervision: Ongoing
Counselling offered: General, Bereavement, Crisis, Psychotherapy, Drinking problems
Service for: Individuals, Groups
Specific to: Ethnic minorities, Young people, Women, Families of alcoholics
Theoretical Approach: Rogerian, Analytical
Other languages: Urdu, Punjabi, Hindi
Fees: £15 - £35 sliding scale

CHAPMAN Maureen 081 748 0718
27 Beryl Road, Hammersmith, LONDON W6 8JS
Member of: IPC/WPF
Quals/training: Full Member of IPC/WPF 1989
Personal Therapy: Ongoing
Supervision: Ongoing
Counselling offered: General, Psychotherapy
Service for: Individuals, Couples
Theoretical Approach: Jungian
Fees: £20 - £30 sliding scale

PHILLIPS Dot 081 578 7761
239 Greenford Avenue, Hanwell, LONDON W7 1AD
Member of: BAC, IPC
Quals/training: RELATE Trained 1985; Dip (IPC/WPF) 1992
Personal Therapy: Ongoing
Supervision: Ongoing
Counselling offered: Marital, Relationship, Sexual, Sexual abuse
Service for: Individuals, Couples
Theoretical Approach: Psychodynamic
Fees: £17 - £25

London - West

SCHMID Doria 081 579 3196
71 Clitherow Avenue, Boston Manor, Hanwell, LONDON W7 2BJ
Member of: BAC Acc, BASMT, BPS
Quals/training: BAC Acc; MA Psychol of Therapy & Couns 1989; BA Psychol; Couns Cert 1987; Dip Human Sexuality (London Univ) 1990
Personal Therapy: Ongoing
Supervision: Ongoing
Counselling offered: General, Marital, Sexual, Psychotherapy
Service for: Individuals, Couples
Theoretical Approach: Integrative
Other languages: French, Portuguese
Fees: £30

MOORE Joan 081 840 3087
90 Cumberland Road, Hanwell, LONDON W7 2EB
Member of: BAC, BPS, ITA, MPTI
Quals/training: BA(Hons) Humanities - major Psychol '87 CNAA; Dip Couns '90 & yr 1 TA '88-9 (metanoia); Gestalt Introduction '89; Cert in Principles of the theory & practice of Supervision
Personal Therapy: Ongoing
Supervision: Ongoing
Counselling offered: General, Psychotherapy, Supervision
Service for: Individuals, Groups
Specific to: People with learning difficulties
Theoretical Approach: Rogerian, TA, Gestalt
Fees: £25 - £35 negotiable (£15 groups)

HARPER Suzanne
The Life Centre, 15 Edge Street, LONDON W8
Member of: ANLP (PCS)
Quals/training: Master Practitioner NLP; Hypnosis trainig with Richard Bandler
Personal Therapy: Ongoing
Supervision: Ongoing
Counselling offered: Personal growth, Hypnotherapy, Relationship
Service for: Individuals, Couples
Theoretical Approach: NLP
Fees: £40

GIBSON Melanie 071 937 6280
99 Vicarage Court, Vicarage Gate, Kensington, LONDON W8 4HQ
Member of: BAC, IPC
Quals/training: BEd(Hons); IPC/WPF (Full memb) 1982
Personal Therapy: Yes
Supervision: Ongoing
Counselling offered: General, Psychotherapy
Service for: Individuals
Theoretical Approach: Psychodynamic, Jungian, Analytical
Fees: £30 a few reduced fee places

London - West

LITMAN Gloria Dr 071 937 9267
22 Stafford Terrace, Kensington, LONDON W8 7BH
Member of: BPS
Quals/training: BA; MSc; PhD; C Psychol
Personal Therapy: Yes
Supervision: Ongoing
Counselling offered: General, Psychotherapy, Marital, Sexual, Stress management, Alcohol
Service for: Individuals, Couples
Theoretical Approach: Eclectic
Fees: £40 - £50

CRADDOCK Jenny 071 286 2812
13 Randolph Road, Maida Hill, LONDON W9 1AN
Member of: BAC, LCP
Quals/training: Trained Psychotherapist (LCP)
Personal Therapy: Yes
Supervision: Ongoing
Counselling offered: General, Addiction, Marital, Sexual, Bereavement, Psychotherapy
Service for: Individuals, Couples
Theoretical Approach: Jungian, Eclectic
Other languages: French
Fees: £20 - £30 negotiable for low incomes

LAWLEY James 071 289 8626
75A Castellain Road, Maida Vale, LONDON W9 1EU
Member of: ANLP (PCS), Member of UKCP Register
Quals/training: NLP Master Practitioner; Adv NLP Applications; Time Line Therapy Practitioner
Personal Therapy: Ongoing
Supervision: Ongoing
Counselling offered: Psychotherapy, Phobias, Time Line Therapy, Brief
Service for: Individuals, Couples, Groups, Organisations
Theoretical Approach: NLP
Fees: £30 - £60 sliding scale for individuals

TOMPKINS Penny 071 289 8626
75A Castellain Road, Maida Vale, LONDON W9 1EU
Member of: ANLP (PCS)
Quals/training: Validated ANLP (PCS); Master Practitioner NLP; Adv NLP Applications; TimeLine Therapy Practitioner
Personal Therapy: Ongoing
Supervision: Ongoing
Counselling offered: General, Brief, Co-dependency, Phobias, Weight, Time Line Therapy
Service for: Individuals, Couples, Groups, Organisations
Theoretical Approach: NLP
Fees: £30 - £60 Sliding scale

London - West

ARZOUMANIDES Yiannis   **071 238 8955**
218 Randolph Avenue, Maida Hill, LONDON W9 1PF
Member of:	BAC
Quals/training:	BSc Psychology; Group Analytic Psychotherapy (LCP); MA Psychology of Therapy & Counselling
Personal Therapy:	Ongoing
Supervision:	Ongoing
Counselling offered:	**General, Psychotherapy**
Service for:	Individuals, Couples, Groups
Theoretical Approach:	Analytic, Psychodynamic, Existential, Humanistic
Other languages:	Greek
Fees:	£20 - £30 Group £7-£10

TUCKER Alison   **081 968 6728**
141 Fernhead Road, Queen Park, Maida Hill, LONDON W9 3ED
Member of:	BAC
Quals/training:	BSc Psychol & Social (City Univ); Dip Couns (Reading Univ)
Personal Therapy:	Ongoing
Supervision:	Ongoing
Counselling offered:	**General, Addiction, Bereavement, Relationship, Depression, Self-esteem, Psychotherapy**
Service for:	Individuals, Couples
Specific to:	Gays, Ethnic minorities
Theoretical Approach:	Rogerian, Eclectic
Fees:	£12 - £25 sliding scale

KIRTON Myrtle   **081 969 7258**
5 Trinity Court, 1a Croxley Road, Maida Vale, LONDON W9 3HD
Member of:	BAC
Quals/training:	BA(Hons) Soc Sci; MA Social Work; CQSW; NMGC trained; Memb of Assoc of Black Counsellors
Personal Therapy:	Ongoing
Supervision:	Ongoing
Counselling offered:	**General, Relationship, Cross/multi-cultural**
Service for:	Individuals, Couples
Theoretical Approach:	Rogerian
Fees:	£18 - £25 sliding scale

SCHULTZ Evelyn   **ansaphone 081 968 7165**
46 Saltram Crescent, LONDON W9 3HR
Member of:	MIN, ITHP
Quals/training:	BA Soc Sci; training in Traditional & Humanistic Psychotherapy (Minster Centre) 1987
Personal Therapy:	Ongoing
Supervision:	Ongoing
Counselling offered:	**General, Bereavement, Relationship, Trauma, Psychotherapy**
Service for:I	ndividuals
Theoretical Approach:	Psychodynamic, Analytic
Other languages:	German
Fees:	£20 - £30 sliding scale

London - West

HICKMAN Barbara 081 969 6336
56 Dalgarno Gardens, LONDON W10 6AB
Member of: BAC, IPC
Quals/training: Dip Adv Psychodynamic Couns (WPF) 1992
Personal Therapy: Ongoing
Supervision: Ongoing
Counselling offered: General, Addiction, Bereavement, Depression, Relationship
Service for: Individuals
Theoretical Approach: Psychodynamic
Fees: £20 negotiable

RODGER Hilary 081 960 8537
Flat D, 199 Ladbroke Grove, North Kensington, LONDON W10 6HQ
Member of: BAC Acc, IPC
Quals/training: BAC(Acc)
Personal Therapy: Yes
Supervision: Ongoing
Counselling offered: General, Bereavement, AIDS, Psychotherapy
Service for: Individuals
Specific to: Clergy/priests, Religious
Theoretical Approach: Psychodynamic
Fees: £15 - £25 sliding scale

WILLIAMS Tony 081 969 3057
51d Bassett Road, Kensington, LONDON W10 6JR
Member of: BAC
Quals/training: Memb of Inst for Individual Psychol; Cert in Theory of Individual Psychol & Adlerian Couns; Dip in Adlerian Psychol; Accredited Adlerian Counsellor
Personal Therapy: Ongoing
Supervision: Ongoing
Counselling offered: General, Alcohol, Bereavement, Depression
Service for: Individuals, Couples, Groups
Theoretical Approach: Adlerian, Humanistic
Fees: Negotiable

DOUGLAS Carolyn 081 969 7718, 081 960 1678
7 St Quintin Avenue, LONDON W10 6NX
Member of: AFT
Quals/training: BA(Hons) Psychol & Social Admin; Dip Mental Health (LSE); courses in Family Therapy (IFT, Tavistock Inst)
Personal Therapy: Yes
Supervision: Ongoing
Counselling offered: Short-term, Family, Consultation
Service for: Individuals, Couples, Families, Groups, Organisations
Theoretical Approach: Psychodynamic
Other languages: French
Fees: £25

London - West

ARNOLD Lynn   071 727 0688
296 Westbourne Park Road, Notting Hill, LONDON W11 1EH
Member of:	BAC
Quals/training:	Trained at Inst of Traditional & Humanistic Psychotherapy; Postgrad Dip Art; Ongoing at Tavistock Centre
Personal Therapy:	Ongoing
Supervision:	Ongoing
Counselling offered:	**General, Sexual, Bereavement, Creative potential**
Service for:	Individuals, Couples
Theoretical Approach:	Holistic
Fees:	£25 negotiable

GARRARD Patricia   071 727 2780, ansaphone 071 221 9361
340 Westbourne, Park Road, Notting Hill, LONDON W11 1EQ
Member of:	BAC
Quals/training:	Dip Couns Skills (SW London College)1985; Adv Couns Dip 1988
Personal Therapy:	Yes
Supervision:	Ongoing
Counselling offered:	**Abortion, Marital, Sexual, Relationship**
Service for:	Individuals, Couples
Specific to:	Women
Theoretical Approach:	Rogerian, Gestalt, TA
Fees:	£20 concessions for unwaged

ROSS Vicky   071 727 0167
Flat 43, Leamington Road Villas, Notting Hill, LONDON W11 1HT
Member of:	BAC
Quals/training:	CQSW 1978; Dip Adult Couns (London Univ) 1987; Adv Course in Couns Practice (London Univ) 1991
Personal Therapy:	Ongoing
Supervision:	Ongoing
Counselling offered:	**General, Bereavement, Tranquillisers**
Service for:	Individuals
Theoretical Approach:	Psychodynamic
Other languages:	French
Fees:	£20 negotiable

HAMILTON Nigel   071 221 3215
Centre for Counselling &, Psychotherapy Education, 21 Lancaster Road, LONDON W11 1QL
Member of:	CCPE
Quals/training:	MA Couns Psychol; Dip Clinical Psychotherapy & Social Psychiatry
Personal Therapy:	Unknown
Supervision:	Ongoing
Counselling offered:	**General, Psychotherapy, Spiritual**
Service for:	Individuals, Couples, Families, Groups, Organisations
Theoretical Approach:	Transpersonal
Fees:	£30 - £35

London - West

PIMENTEL Allan 071 221 3215
CCPE, 21 Lancaster Road, LONDON W11 1QL
Member of: CCPE
Quals/training: Dip Couns & Psychotherapy (CCPE) 1989; training in Psychodrama & TA
Personal Therapy: Ongoing
Supervision: Ongoing
Counselling offered: General, Relationship, Psychotherapy
Service for: Individuals, Couples, Families, Groups, Organisations
Theoretical Approach: Transpersonal
Fees: £25 for 50 minutes

SANDERS Susie 071 221 3215
CCPE, 21 Lancaster Road, LONDON W11 1QL
Member of: CCPE
Quals/training: BA; Dip Psych; training (CCPE) 1989
Personal Therapy: Ongoing
Supervision: Ongoing
Counselling offered: General, Psychotherapy, Eating disorders
Service for: Individuals, Couples, Families, Groups, Organisations
Theoretical Approach: Transpersonal
Fees: £25

POOLE Robert 071 727 9551
59a Ladbroke Grove, Notting Hill, LONDON W11 3AT
Member of: BAC, LCP
Quals/training: Dip Advanced Couns; Group Psychotherapist; Dip Applied Social Studies; CQSW; Memb GAS
Personal Therapy: Yes
Supervision: Ongoing
Counselling offered: General, Bereavement, Relationship, Psychotherapy
Service for: Individuals, Couples, Families, Groups
Specific to: Access for disabled people
Theoretical Approach: Psychodynamic
Fees: £20 - £30 - £8 for group

ASSITER Shelley 017 727 2515
87 St. Annes Road, Notting Hill, LONDON W11 4BT
Member of: BAC
Quals/training: 3 years Social Science study, 3 year training for Couns/Facilitators - FACETS
Personal Therapy: Ongoing
Supervision: Ongoing
Counselling offered: General, Relationship, Addiction, Crisis
Service for: Individuals, Groups
Specific to: Women, Adolescents
Theoretical Approach: Client-centred, Humanistic
Other languages: French, Hebrew
Fees: £30

London - West

BRUNO Virginia　　　　　　　　　　　　　　　　　　081 740 8336
34 Galloway Road, Shepherds Bush, LONDON W12 0PJ
Member of:	BAC Acc, FAE
Quals/training:	BAC Acc; BA; BAC Assessor; Memb: FAETT, APPNHS, "Young Minds" - the Nat Assoc for Child & Family Mental Health
Personal Therapy:	Yes
Supervision:	Ongoing
Counselling offered:	General, Relationship, Psychotherapy
Service for:	Individuals
Specific to:	Women
Theoretical Approach:	Psychodynamic
Fees:	£20 - £35

PLOTEL Angela　　　　　　　　　　　　　　　　　　081 740 4674
Shepherds Bush, LONDON W12
Member of:	NRHP
Quals/training:	Dip Hypnotherapy & Psychotherapy (Nat Coll); Dip FA (London); Hypnotherapy for Bulimia (Lond Coll Clin Hypnosis) Stress Management (LCCH)
Personal Therapy:	Yes
Supervision:	Ongoing
Counselling offered:	Hypnotherapy, Psychotherapy
Service for:	Individuals
Theoretical Approach:	Eclectic
Fees:	£30

POPE Alan　　　　　　　　　　　　　　　　　　　　081 749 2085
38 Greenside Road, Shepherds Bush, LONDON W12 9JG
Member of:	BAC
Quals/training:	Combined Cert Couns (CSCT) 1990-91; currently training with Philadelphia Assoc
Personal Therapy:	Ongoing
Supervision:	Ongoing
Counselling offered:	Psychotherapy, HIV
Service for:	Individuals, Couples
Specific to:	Gays, Creative people
Theoretical Approach:	Analytic, Phenomenological
Fees:	£20 sliding scale

RAWSON Penny　　　　　　　　　　　　　　　　　081 749 7970
194 Emlyn Road, Shepherds Bush, LONDON W12 9TB
Member of:	BAC Acc
Quals/training:	BA;Cert Ed; Cert Couns WPF;RF & Dympna Ctre training; BAC Acc; BAC Rec Supervisor; Pract Memb Human Social Functioning Soc; Acc Pract Memb ASSP
Personal Therapy:	Yes
Supervision:	Ongoing
Counselling offered:	General, Psychotherapy, Short-term, Supervision
Service for:	Individuals, Groups
Theoretical Approach:	Psychodynamic
Fees:	£35 (groups negotiable)

London - West

FRY Caroline   081 579 6582
56 Elers Road, West Ealing, LONDON W13 9QD
Member of:	BAC Acc
Quals/training:	BAC Acc; BA; Cert Couns LCIP; Dip Student Couns and Advanced Course in Couns Practice (London Univ); Guild of Psychotherapists (training member)
Personal Therapy:	Yes
Supervision:	Ongoing
Counselling offered:	General, Psychotherapy
Service for:	Individuals
Theoretical Approach:	Analytical
Fees:	£20 - £30 sliding scale

JONES Monica   081 579 9785
Roseleigh, 80 Elers Road, West Ealing, LONDON W13 9QD
Member of:	BAC, CRA
Quals/training:	BA; BSc Psychol; Cert Couns (Regent's College); Dip EHP & NLP (NSHAP); CRAH (Assoc); Memb BCMA
Personal Therapy:	Ongoing
Supervision:	Ongoing
Counselling offered:	Hypnotherapy
Service for:	Individuals
Specific to:	Women
Theoretical Approach:	Ericksonian, NLP
Other languages:	Swedish
Fees:	£25

JARVIS Cecilia   081 567 1331
11 Walmer Gardens, Ealing, LONDON W13 9TS
Member of:	BAC Acc, PET
Quals/training:	BAC Acc; BA; PGCE; Dip Psychosynthesis Psychotherapy; Memb of AAPP
Personal Therapy:	Ongoing
Supervision:	Ongoing
Counselling offered:	General, Phobias, Psychotherapy, Supervision
Service for:	Individuals
Theoretical Approach:	Psychosynthesis, Transpersonal
Fees:	£25 - £30

REES Susan   071 603 3685
32 Sterndale Road, LONDON W14 0HS
Member of:	BAC Acc, ACP
Quals/training:	BAC Acc; CQWSW; AMACP
Personal Therapy:	Ongoing
Supervision:	Ongoing
Counselling offered:	General, Marital, Psychotherapy
Service for:	Individuals, Couples
Specific to:	Children
Theoretical Approach:	Analytical
Other languages:	German
Fees:	£26 - £35 Negotiable for children

London - West

ASSEILY Alexandra
13 Addison Road, LONDON W14 8DJ
Member of: ANLP (PCS)
Quals/training: NLP Master
Personal Therapy: Ongoing
Supervision: Ongoing
Counselling offered: Kinesiology
Service for: Individuals, Couples, Families
Theoretical Approach: NLP
Other languages: French, Arabic
Fees: £30 Half to charity

BOMMER Herman   071 603 6373 x 248
Richmond Fellowship College, 8 Addison Road, West Kensington, LONDON W14 8DL
Member of: BAC
Quals/training: Training at Richmond Fellowship 1980-82; Memb APCC
Personal Therapy: Ongoing
Supervision: Ongoing
Counselling offered: General
Service for: Individuals
Theoretical Approach: Rogerian, Psychodynamic
Other languages: Dutch
Fees: Negotiable

HORROCKS Roger   071 385 4091
5 West Kensington Mansions, North End Road, LONDON W14 9PE
Member of: AHPP
Quals/training: BA; PhD; Dip Humanistic Psychology (IDHP) 1979
Personal Therapy: Yes
Supervision: Ongoing
Counselling offered: Psychotherapy
Service for: Individuals, Couples
Theoretical Approach: Humanistic, Analytical
Fees: £27 - £35

London - West

Avon

Organisations

OPENINGS 0225 445013
Bluecoat House, Sawclose, BATH BA1 1EY
Service: Individual therapy, group (mixed or single sex) therapy for particular problems or for those wishing to pursue personal developments in depth. Training in groupwork
Area served: Bath, Bristol & the South West
Referral: Self
Training of workers: Appropriate training for services offered, supervision checked by management committee, ongoing supervision
Code of Ethics: Varies with professional seen
Management by: Management Committee
Fees: Negotiable with practitioner

BATH CENTRE FOR PSYCHOTHERAPY & COUNSELLING 0225 429720
1 Walcot Terrace, London Road, BATH BA1 6AB
Service: General counselling and psychotherapy
Area served: South West England
Referral: Self
Training of workers: Own training course. All must have personal therapy. Regular supervision
Code of Ethics: BCPC
Management by: Directors of Charity through a management group. Reg Charity number 1010547
Fees: £10 - £20

ALED RICHARDS TRUST 0272 551000, Helpline 0272 553355
Queen Anne House, 8-10 West Street, Old Market, BRISTOL BS2 0BH
Service: Ind & couple couns for people concerned about and/or with HIV/AIDS, their partners, carers, family and friends on all HIV related issues. External training in HIV couns skills
Area served: Avon, W Wilts and E Somerset
Referral: Self
Training of workers: Various. Centre provides supervision
Code of Ethics: BAC
Management by: Management Committee
Fees: None; training negotiable

SEVERNSIDE INSTITUTE FOR PSYCHOTHERAPY (SIP) 0272 562049
PO Box 75, BRISTOL BS16 6EW
Service: Provides a consultation service and can offer a limited number of treatment vacancies for those wishing to undertake individual psychotherapy
Area served: South West
Referral: Self or others
Training of workers: All are fully qualified psychotherapists; personal therapy; ongoing supervision
Code of Ethics: SIP
Management by: Executive Committee
Fees: £20 approx

Avon

BROADWAY LODGE 0934 815515
Oldmixon Road, WESTON-SUPER-MARE BS24 9NN
Service: Individual & group counselling for drug & alchohol addicts to reduce 'at risk' behaviour, pre & post HIV test & for the worried well. Training in counselling skills
Area served: UK & abroad
Referral: Self
Training of workers: 1 year in house trainig
Code of Ethics: -
Management by: Charitable Trust
Fees: On application

Individual Practitioners
*Each individual is a **member of** one or more organisations eligible for entry into this directory. BAC Accredited Counsellors and Recognised Supervisors are shaded.*

SHEPHERD Jane 0225 314694
21 Newbridge Road, BATH BA1 3HE
Member of: BAC, BCPC
Quals/training: BSc (St Andrews); RELATE trained; 3yrs Counselling Training (BCPC); work with Cruse & Aled Richards Trust(HIV/AIDS)
Personal Therapy: Ongoing
Supervision: Ongoing
Counselling offered: General, Bereavement, AIDS
Service for: Individuals, Couples
Theoretical Approach: Humanistic, Integrative
Fees: £15

JAMES Ken ansaphone 0225 337 640
8 Evelyn Road, Weston, BATH BA1 3QF
Member of: BAC Acc
Quals/training: BAC(Acc); BA(Bristol); PhD(London); PG Dip Couns(Bristol)
Personal Therapy: Unknown
Supervision: Ongoing
Counselling offered: General, Alcohol, Bereavement, Crisis, Relationship, Occupational, Stress
Service for: Individuals, Couples, Families, Groups, Organisations
Specific to: Managers, Students, Parents
Theoretical Approach: Eclectic, Egan, Person-centred
Fees: £18 - £25 sliding scale

DAVIES Elizabeth 0225 331904, Ansaphone 0225 826826 x 5416
5 Camden Terrace, Camden Road, BATH BA1 5HZ
Member of: BAC Acc
Quals/training: BAC Acc; ASC Acc; MA in Social Science; Cert in Student Couns
Personal Therapy: Yes
Supervision: Ongoing
Counselling offered: General, Short-term, Long-term
Service for: Individuals
Specific to: Young people
Theoretical Approach: Psychodynamic
Fees: £20 negotiable

Avon

HALL June 0225 421033
The Firs, 7 Belgrave Road, BATH BA1 6LU
Member of:	**BCPC**
Quals/training:	BA (Hons); completed 3rd yr of training for Dip Humanistic & Integrative Couns (BCPC); short training in Psychosynthesis, Gestalt, etc; Approved Glos Prob Service Staff Counsellor
Personal Therapy:	Yes
Supervision:	Ongoing
Counselling offered:	**General, Loss, Change, Stress, Crisis, Work**
Service for:	Individuals, Groups, Organisations
Theoretical Approach:	Integrative, Humanistic
Fees:	£15 - £18

RYDE Judith 0225 833657
285 Bloomfield Road, BATH BA2 2NU
Member of:	**AHPP, BCPC**
Quals/training:	Trained Psychotherapist; Teacher BCPC
Personal Therapy:	Ongoing
Supervision:	Ongoing
Counselling offered:	**Psychotherapy**
Service for:	Individuals
Theoretical Approach:	Humanistic, Integrative
Fees:	£25 sliding scale

VALENTINE Christine 0225 337372
74 Lower Bristol Road, BATH BA2 3BG
Member of:	**BAC, BCPC**
Quals/training:	BA(Hons); Dip Humanistic Psychol(IDHP)'85; Dip Humanistic & Integrative Psychotherapy '91
Personal Therapy:	Yes
Supervision:	Ongoing
Counselling offered:	**General, Psychotherapy**
Service for:	Individuals
Theoretical Approach:	Psychodynamic, Analytical, Humanistic
Fees:	£24

SELBY Anne 0225 428826
4 Prospect Place, Beechen Cliff Road, BATH BA2 4QP
Member of:	**BCPC**
Quals/training:	BSc Hons; MA Occupational Psychol; 3 years training Psychosynthesis Couns PET; Post 5th yr BCPC
Personal Therapy:	Yes
Supervision:	Ongoing
Counselling offered:	**General, Psychotherapy**
Service for:	Individuals
Theoretical Approach:	Psychodynamic, Integrative
Fees:	£22 negotiable

Avon

WOODBRIDGE Gill　　　　　　　　　　　　　　　0225 466506
3 Darlington Place, BATH BA2 6BX
Member of:	BAC
Quals/training:	BICA; CQSW; RELATE trained; Family Mediators Assoc
Personal Therapy:	Yes
Supervision:	Ongoing
Counselling offered:	General, Abortion, Bereavement, Divorce, Infertility, Marital, Relationship, Sexual abuse
Service for:	Individuals, Couples
Specific to:	Women
Theoretical Approach:	Eclectic
Fees:	£20 - £25

WOODLEY Jan　　　　　　　　　　　　　　　　0225 462303
94 Sydney Place, BATH BA2 6NE
Member of:	BAC
Quals/training:	PG Dip Couns(CNAA)'83; MSc in Health Education(London Univ) '87
Personal Therapy:	Yes
Supervision:	Ongoing
Counselling offered:	General, Crisis, Bereavement, Marital, Redundancy
Service for:	Individuals, Couples
Theoretical Approach:	Rogerian, Gestalt
Fees:	£22 - £35 sliding scale

BORSIG Su　　　　　　　　　　　　　　　　　0225 461563
The Squirrels, Bathampton Lane, BATH BA2 6SW
Member of:	BAC, ITA
Quals/training:	Dip Hum Psy (IDHP); Psycho-sexual Couns 1984-86; 4 years TA (metanoia) 1986-90 & also Gestalt 1986-93; Couple Work 1987-88 & 1993; Adv Integrative Psychotherapy 1989-91
Personal Therapy:	Ongoing
Supervision:	Ongoing
Counselling offered:	General, Psychotherapy
Service for:	Individuals, Couples, Groups
Theoretical Approach:	Integrative
Fees:	£28 - £40

LAPWORTH Phil　　　　　　　　　　　　　　　0225 722348
Lilac Cottage, 65 Murhill, Limpley Stoke, BATH BA3 6HQ
Member of:	BAC Acc, ITA
Quals/training:	BAC Acc; Dip Couns Skills (SW London College); Clinical Transactional Analyst (ITAA); Dip Integrative Psychotherapy (metanoia); Memb BIIP
Personal Therapy:	Ongoing
Supervision:	Ongoing
Counselling offered:	Psychotherapy
Service for:	Individuals, Groups
Theoretical Approach:	Integrative
Fees:	£35 Negotiable, £22 groups

Avon

MARSTON-WYLD Joanna   ansaphone 0272 427207
4 Somerset Street, Kingsdown, BRISTOL BS2 8NB
Member of:	BAC, BPS
Quals/training:	MSc Applied Psychol (Occupational); Dip Couns
Personal Therapy:	Yes
Supervision:	Ongoing
Counselling offered:	General, Crisis, Change, Transition
Service for:	Individuals, Organisations
Specific to:	Young adults, Students, Parents
Theoretical Approach:	Humanistic, Person-centred
Fees:	Negotiable

HASTINGS Jon   0272 542230
32 Saxon Road, St Werburghs, BRISTOL BS2 9UG
Member of:	BCPC, AHPP
Quals/training:	BSc Psychol; Cert Couns (SW London College); stage 5 of BCPC Psychotherapy Training; Reichian Therapy; Cert Applied Studies CQSW (Bristol Univ); Gen Groupwork (IGA)
Personal Therapy:	Ongoing
Supervision:	Ongoing
Counselling offered:	General, Psychotherapy
Service for:	Individuals, Groups, Organisations
Specific to:	Men
Theoretical Approach:	Integrative, Humanistic, Analytic
Fees:	£22 negotiable

DEMETER Katherine   0272 631509
53 Langton Park, Southville, BRISTOL BS3 1EQ
Member of:	BAC
Quals/training:	Extensive training in Humanistic Psychology with eclectic base over 11 yrs
Personal Therapy:	Ongoing
Supervision:	Ongoing
Counselling offered:	General, Sexual abuse, Psychotherapy
Service for:	Individuals, Groups
Theoretical Approach:	Rogerian, Humanistic, Gestalt, Transpersonal
Fees:	£22 negotiable for low or un-waged

PURKISS Jane   0272 665462
63 Stackpool Road, Southville, BRISTOL BS3 1NL
Member of:	BCPC
Quals/training:	BA(Hons); PGCE; 3 yrs Psychotherapy Training (BCPC) 1986-9; 3 yrs training (CTP) 1989-92
Personal Therapy:	Ongoing
Supervision:	Ongoing
Counselling offered:	General, Bereavement, Psychotherapy
Service for:	Individuals
Theoretical Approach:	Rogerian, Jungian
Other languages:	French
Fees:	£15 - £22

Avon

GALANT Irene 0272 771940
12 Goolden Street, Totterdown, BRISTOL BS4 3BB
Member of: BCPC
Quals/training: Dip Humanistic Psychol 1986; RSA Cert Couns 1988; currently training with BCPC
Personal Therapy: Yes
Supervision: Ongoing
Counselling offered: General, Psychotherapy
Service for: Individuals
Theoretical Approach: Humanistic, Integrative
Other languages: German
Fees: £18 some concessions

HUMPHREYS Jacky 0272 510060
24 Walton Street, Easton, BRISTOL BS5 0JG
Member of: BAC
Quals/training: BSc (Hons) Psychol '87; Cert in Couns Skills '90; Dip Couns (Bristol Univ) '92
Personal Therapy: Ongoing
Supervision: Ongoing
Counselling offered: General, Sexuality, Loss
Service for: Individuals, Couples
Theoretical Approach: Integrative
Fees: Sliding scale

NOBLE Katina 0272 232 108
110 St Andrew's Road, BRISTOL BS6 5EJ
Member of: BCPC
Quals/training: BA(Hons); Game-method, groupwork & drama (Inter-Action Trust, London); Workshop Leader WTC 1978-90; currently Dip Humanistic & Integrative Counselling
Personal Therapy: Yes
Supervision: Ongoing
Counselling offered: General, Eating disorders
Service for: Individuals, Groups
Specific to: Women, Students
Theoretical Approach: Humanistic, Integrative, Feminist
Fees: £12 - £15 concessions

COLLIS Elizabeth 0272 559600
74 York Road, Montpelier, BRISTOL BS6 5QF
Member of: AHPP, BCPC, BPA
Quals/training: In training with BCPC; advanced training completed
Personal Therapy: Ongoing
Supervision: Ongoing
Counselling offered: General, Psychotherapy
Service for: Individuals, Couples, Groups
Theoretical Approach: Humanistic, Integrative
Fees: £22 negotiable

Avon

CLEMENTS Pip 0272 732962
21 Rokeby Avenue, Cotham, BRISTOL BS6 6EJ
Member of: **BAC, IPS**
Quals/training: CQSW; Dip in Psychosynthesis IP
Personal Therapy: Ongoing
Supervision: Ongoing
Counselling offered: **General, Addiction**
Service for: Individuals
Specific to: Recovering addicts/alcoholics
Theoretical Approach: Psychosynthesis
Fees: £25

PARLETT Malcolm 0272 240126
51 Fernbank Road, Redland, BRISTOL BS6 6PX
Member of: **BPS, GPTI**
Quals/training: BA; PhD; C Psychol; Trained at Gestalt Inst of Cleveland, USA; Founding teaching memb GPTI
Personal Therapy: Ongoing
Supervision: Ongoing
Counselling offered: **Psychotherapy**
Service for: Individuals, Couples, Groups, Families
Theoretical Approach: Gestalt
Fees: £20 - £50 sliding scale

MILTON Thelma 0272 427518
Redland, BRISTOL BS6 7AP
Member of: **BCPC**
Quals/training: Psychotherapist in training with BCPC; RSA Couns Skills in Development of Learning
Personal Therapy: Yes
Supervision: Ongoing
Counselling offered: **General, Psychotherapy**
Service for: Individuals
Theoretical Approach: Integrative
Fees: £20 (2 reduced places)

BOWES Ann Ansaphone 0272 735844
St Alban's Vicarage, 21 Canowie Road, Westbury Park, BRISTOL BS6 7HR
Member of: **BAC**
Quals/training: BSc (Hons); Qualified Medical '67 & Psychiatric '68 Social Worker; counselling training '69-; training in Psychoanalytic Psychotherapy, ASC Acc
Personal Therapy: Ongoing
Supervision: Ongoing
Counselling offered: **Psychotherapy, Supervision**
Service for: Individuals, Groups
Theoretical Approach: Psychoanalytic
Fees: Negotiable

Avon

STEVEN Hilary　　　　　　　　　　　　　　　　　0272 428649
14 Wolseley Road, Bishopston, BRISTOL BS7 8EN
Member of:	BAC, BCPC
Quals/training:	Basic & in service training at Off the Record(Bristol);BCPC Stages 2,3 & 4
Personal Therapy:	Yes
Supervision:	Ongoing
Counselling offered:	General, Psychotherapy
Service for:	Individuals
Theoretical Approach:	Humanistic, Integrative
Fees:	£18

LANE Judy　　　　　　　　　　　　　　　　　　0272 240732
28 Melbourne Road, Bishopston, BRISTOL BS7 8LB
Member of:	BCPC
Quals/training:	BA; Qualified Medical Social Worker (Edinburgh Univ) 1959; Dip Ed; BCPC Acc
Personal Therapy:	Ongoing
Supervision:	Ongoing
Counselling offered:	Psychotherapy
Service for:	Individuals
Theoretical Approach:	Humanistic, Integrative
Fees:	£22

WARING Judith　　　　　　　　　　　　ansaphone 0272 429956
11 Falmouth Road, Bishopston, BRISTOL BS7 9DU
Member of:	BAC Acc
Quals/training:	BAC(Acc); Dip Couns; RMN
Personal Therapy:	Yes
Supervision:	Ongoing
Counselling offered:	General, Bereavement, Psychotherapy
Service for:	Individuals
Specific to:	Women
Theoretical Approach:	Person-centred, Gestalt
Fees:	£20

VINE Francis　　　　　　　0272 466035, Home 0272 273205
The Natural Therapy Centre, Neal's Yard, 126 Whiteladies Road, BRISTOL BS8
Member of:	ANLP (PCS)
Quals/training:	Dip Ericksonian Psychotherapy, Hypnosis & NLP; Practitioner of NLP; trained in Client-centred counselling
Personal Therapy:	Yes
Supervision:	Ongoing
Counselling offered:	General, Short-term, Psychotherapy, Hypnotherapy, Stress
Service for:	Individuals, Couples
Theoretical Approach:	NLP, Ericksonian, Client-centred
Fees:	£25 - £40 sliding scale

Avon

SINCLAIR Ilse 0272 733384
19 Whatley Court, Whatley Road, BRISTOL BS8 2PS
Member of: BAC, BASMT
Quals/training: NMGC Acc
Personal Therapy: Yes
Supervision: Ongoing
Counselling offered: General, Marital, Sexual
Service for: Individuals, Couples
Other languages: German
Fees: £20 - £25

ISON Mary 0272 297730
Clifton Counselling Clinic, 21 Clifton Wood Road, Clifton Wood, BRISTOL BS8 4TN
Member of: BAC
Quals/training: BA; Cert Ed; CQSW; Dip & Cert Hypnotherapy & Psychology; Healer Memb National Federation of Spiritual Healter; over 30 years experience
Personal Therapy: Ongoing
Supervision: Ongoing
Counselling offered: General, Sexual, Psychotherapy, Hypnotherapy, Relationship, Stress management, Homeopathy
Service for: Individuals, Couples, Families
Specific to: People with disabilities
Theoretical Approach: Eclectic, Holistic
Other languages: French
Fees: £22 - £38

HAMNETT Jennifer 0272 683218
23 Rockleaze Road, Sneyd Park, BRISTOL BS9 1NF
Member of: BAC, IPC
Quals/training: Dip Couns (WPF) 1983; Cert CTP 1986
Personal Therapy: Ongoing
Supervision: Ongoing
Counselling offered: General, Personal growth, Psychotherapy
Service for: Individuals
Theoretical Approach: Analytical, Jungian
Fees: £20 - £25

SAWERS Martin 0272 629746
71a Westbury Hill, Westbury on Trym, BRISTOL BS9 3AD
Member of: BCPC
Quals/training: MA; BA; Stage 4 BCPC Training; Cert Postural Integration
Personal Therapy: Ongoing
Supervision: Ongoing
Counselling offered: Psychotherapy
Service for: Individuals
Theoretical Approach: Humanistic, Object relations
Other languages: German, Swiss-German
Fees: £20 (60mins) £27 (90mins)

Avon

CARR Jean　　　　　　　　　　　　　　　　　　　　　0272 623110
Autumn, 32 Wanscow Walk, Henleaze, BRISTOL BS9 4LE
Member of:	BAC
Quals/training:	Gloucester Counselling Service; Junian/Senoi dreamwork (Journey Centre-Stroud)
Personal Therapy:	Yes
Supervision:	Ongoing
Counselling offered:	**General, Rape, Phobias**
Service for:	Individuals
Specific to:	Victims of crime, Unknown
Theoretical Approach:	Eclectic
Fees:	£5 - £18

HORTON David　　　　　　　　　　　　　　　　　　　0272 505517
21a Blethwin Close, Henbury, BRISTOL BS10 7BH
Member of:	BAC Acc
Quals/training:	BAC Acc; Cert Couns (WPF) 1975; Cert Groupwork (WPF) 1978; Cert in Psychodynamic Counselling Supervision (WPF) 1993
Personal Therapy:	Yes
Supervision:	Ongoing
Counselling offered:	**Psychotherapy**
Service for:	Individuals, Groups
Theoretical Approach:	Psychodynamic, Analytic
Fees:	£30

ROBINS Jane　　　　　　　　　　　　　　　　　　　　0454 412643
29 Severn Drive, Thornbury, BRISTOL BS12 1EU
Member of:	BAC
Quals/training:	BA(Hons) Sociology; Dip Couns (Bristol Univ); Dip Yoga (FRYOG)
Personal Therapy:	Ongoing
Supervision:	Ongoing
Counselling offered:	**General, Bereavement, Crisis, Long-term, Personal growth**
Service for:	Individuals, Couples
Specific to:	Women
Theoretical Approach:	Eclectic, Alice Miller
Fees:	£20 - £25 sliding scale

HOBBS Sandra　　　　　　　　　　　　　　　　　　　0272 719106
16 Whitwell Road, Hengrove, BRISTOL BS14 9DP
Member of:	BAC Acc
Quals/training:	BAC Acc; Dip Couns
Personal Therapy:	Ongoing
Supervision:	Ongoing
Counselling offered:	**General, Addiction, Relationship, Sexual abuse**
Service for:	Individuals
Specific to:	Women
Theoretical Approach:	Humanistic, Integrative
Fees:	£20 some concessions

Avon

ROBBINS Peter   **0272 679576**
13 Wood Road, Kingswood, BRISTOL BS15 2DT
Member of: BPS
Quals/training: BEd; BA Psychol; Cert Couns Skills (RSA) 1989; Cert Groupwork (RSA) 1990 (Bristol Poly)
Personal Therapy: Ongoing
Supervision: Ongoing
Counselling offered: **General, Career**
Service for: Individuals, Groups
Theoretical Approach: Person-centred, Cognitive
Fees: £15 - £27 sliding scale

LESTER Anne   **0272 655163**
19 Wickham View, Stapleton, BRISTOL BS16 1TH
Member of: BAC
Quals/training: BA; Cert Ed; Dip Couns 1973; training in Gestalt & Psychosynthesis
Personal Therapy: Yes
Supervision: Ongoing
Counselling offered: **General, Bereavement, Crisis, Marital**
Service for: Individuals, Couples, Groups
Theoretical Approach: Rogerian, Integrative
Fees: £20 - £25

OPENSHAW Pamela Diana   **0272 565776**
24 Millward Grove, Fishponds, BRISTOL BS16 5AJ
Member of: BAC
Quals/training: Cert Psychotherapy & Counselling (Regent's College)
Personal Therapy: Ongoing
Supervision: Ongoing
Counselling offered: **General, Bereavement, Transition**
Service for: Individuals
Theoretical Approach: Eclectic
Fees: £10

DIX Francoise   **0272 864679**
63 Dunster Road, Keynsham, BRISTOL BS18 2QB
Member of: BCPC
Quals/training: Licence es Lettres; Stage 4 of BCPC; Cert Couns (Centre for Transpersonal Psychology)
Personal Therapy: Ongoing
Supervision: Ongoing
Counselling offered: **General, Bereavement, Psychotherapy**
Service for: Individuals
Theoretical Approach: Transpersonal, Humanistic
Other languages: French
Fees: £18 sliding scale

Avon

CRAIGEN Jenny 0275 851078
The Observatory, 4 Archfield Road, BRISTOL BS6 6BE
Member of:	BAC
Quals/training:	Cert Ed; Dip Music; Gestalt Therapy & Contribution Training (Pellin) 1988
Personal Therapy:	Ongoing
Supervision:	Ongoing
Counselling offered:	**General, Assertiveness, Bereavement, Relationship, Sexual**
Service for:	Individuals, Couples, Families, Groups
Specific to:	Women, Gays, Lesbians
Theoretical Approach:	Humanistic
Fees:	£20 individuals, £30 couples,groups by negotiation

HOPKINS Ian 0934 834814
Fern Cottage, 105 Claverham Road, Yatton, BRISTOL BS19 4LE
Member of:	BAC
Quals/training:	Dip Soc Admin; Cert Applied Social Studies; MSc Social Science
Personal Therapy:	No
Supervision:	Ongoing
Counselling offered:	**General, Marital, Sexual**
Service for:	Individuals, Couples
Theoretical Approach:	TA, Behavioural
Fees:	£25

EDEN Glenis 0275 843872
Bay Cottage, 12 Springfield Road, Portishead, BRISTOL BS20 9LH
Member of:	BAC
Quals/training:	Dip Hypnotherapy, Psychotherapy & Couns (UK Training Coll); Adv Cert Hypnotherapy (City & Guilds): Dip (Massage Training Inst); APT; MCHC
Personal Therapy:	Ongoing
Supervision:	Ongoing
Counselling offered:	**General, Psychotherapy, Bereavement, Crisis, Stress management, Abuse, Depression, Relationship, Unwanted habits**
Service for:	Individuals, Couples
Theoretical Approach:	Psychodrama, Rogerian, Gestalt, TA
Fees:	£23 - £28 sliding scale

HENLEY Philippa 0934 628730
11 Hatfield Road, WESTON-SUPER-MARE BS23 2UT
Member of:	BAC, BCPC
Quals/training:	BSc (Hons); PGCE; final year of Dip Integrative & Humanistic Counselling (BCPC)
Personal Therapy:	Ongoing
Supervision:	Ongoing
Counselling offered:	**General, Bereavement**
Service for:	Individuals
Specific to:	Parents
Theoretical Approach:	Humanistic, Integrative
Fees:	£15

Avon

ALDER Judith 0934 815283
4 Beechmount Close, Oldmixon, WESTON-SUPER-MARE BS24 9EX
Member of: BAC
Quals/training: Dip Couns; CQSW; BASW
Personal Therapy: No
Supervision: Ongoing
Counselling offered: General, Bereavement, Depression, Stress management
Service for: Individuals, Groups, Organisations
Theoretical Approach: Humanistic, TA
Fees: £15

RUSSELL Hazel appt 0934 842231
Winterhead Hill Farm, Shipham, WINSCOMBE BS25 1RS
Member of: BAC Acc
Quals/training: BAC Acc; BA; IDHP; RELATE; training in Psychodrama; Gestalt
Personal Therapy: Ongoing
Supervision: Ongoing
Counselling offered: General, Personal growth, Crisis
Service for: Individuals, Couples
Specific to: Women
Theoretical Approach: Humanistic, Gestalt, Psychodrama
Fees: £20 - £30 sliding scale

QUINLAN Jennifer 0934 844247
Cedarfield, 1b Sandford Road, WINSCOMBE BS25 1HD
Member of: BAC
Quals/training: Dip Psychol; Dip Hypnotherapy; City & Guilds Cert Couns & Hypnotherapy; Cert Couns Psychotherapy; Memb IAH & ICM
Personal Therapy: Yes
Supervision: Ongoing
Counselling offered: General, Crisis, Trauma, Depression, Anxiety, Unwanted habits
Service for: Individuals
Theoretical Approach: Psychodynamic, Client-centred, Analytical, Hypnotherapy
Fees: £30 - £40

Avon

Bedfordshire

Organisations

SURVIVORS (BEDFORDSHIRE) ansaphone 0582 410688
PO Box 398, Caddington, LUTON LU1 4HR
Service:	Helpline. Individual counselling and groupwork for any male victim or survivor of sexual abuse or rape. Also work with abusers or partners
Area served:	Bedfordshire and local counties
Referral:	Self or others
Training of workers:	Relevant professional training/qualifications plus 1 year part-time counselling course minimum; personal therapy; regular supervision
Code of Ethics:	BAC
Management by:	Management Committee
Fees:	£0-15 dependent on income

HERTS & BEDS PASTORAL FOUNDATION 0234 346077
Counselling Centre, Elmstone Lodge, 116 Bromham Road, BEDFORD MK40 2QR
Service:	General counselling (weekly) at Bedford (inds & groups) 0234 346077(9.30-12.30) & Dunstable/Luton (inds) 0582 668461
Area served:	Bedfordshire (see also Herts)
Referral:	Self
Training of workers:	WPF Accreditation; weekly supervision
Code of Ethics:	BAC
Management by:	Director, Council of Management, Trustees. Affiliated to WPF
Fees:	£2 - £25 registration fee, no-one turned away

BEDFORD PSYCHOSEXUAL COUNSELLING CLINIC 0234 267697
Union Street Clinic, BEDFORD MK40 2SF
Service:	Psychosexual counselling for individuals and couples
Area served:	N bedfordshire and surrounding areas
Referral:	Health Practitioner
Training of workers:	Dr Perl is an Associate Fellow BPS, Dr Harrison is a member of Inst of Psychosex Med.
Code of Ethics:	BPS, IPM
Management by:	Bedford and Shires Health and Care NHS Trust
Fees:	None

NORTH BEDS DISTRICT PSYCHOLOGY SERVICE 0234 55122 x 2723
Weller Wing, Bedford General Hospital, Kempston Road, BEDFORD MK42 9DJ
Service:	Psychological service for individuals and couples offering cognitive, behavioural & psychodynamic approaches
Area served:	North Bedfordshire & surrounding area
Other languages:	French, Punjabi
Referral:	Health Practitioner, Health/Soc Work Professional
Training of workers:	Postgraduate clinical psychology with additional training in psychotherapy
Code of Ethics:	BPS
Management by:	Bedford & Shires Health & Care NHS Trust
Fees:	None

Bedfordshire

Individual Practitioners

Every individual is a **member of** one or more organisations eligible for entry into this directory.
BAC Accredited Counsellors and Recognised Supervisors are shaded.

ROGERS Anne 0234 212618
36 St Michael's Road, BEDFORD MK40 2LU
Member of:	AGIP
Quals/training:	Dip in Couns (London Univ); BA(Hons) Psychology
Personal Therapy:	Yes
Supervision:	Ongoing
Counselling offered:	**Psychotherapy, Supervision**
Service for:	Individuals
Theoretical Approach:	Freudian, Kleinian, Psychoanalytic
Fees:	Negotiable

BUTLER Ruth Non given
4 The Crescent, BEDFORD MK40 2RU
Member of:	BAC
Quals/training:	Dip Couns; BA Psychol (OU); RN; National Dip District Nursing; HV Dip; Cert Ed
Personal Therapy:	Yes
Supervision:	Ongoing
Counselling offered:	**General, Stress, Stress management, Loss, Addiction, Assertiveness, Stop smoking**
Service for:	Individuals, Couples
Theoretical Approach:	Client-centred
Fees:	£20 - £30

BENNETT Valerie 0234 47342
6 St Minver Road, BEDFORD MK40 3DQ
Member of:	BAC RSup
Quals/training:	Group Dynamics training 1967; NMGC trained; Gestalt Practitioner training 1986-89; BAC Rec Supervisor 1988; Memb GAUK & AHP
Personal Therapy:	Ongoing
Supervision:	Ongoing
Counselling offered:	**General, Work**
Service for:	Individuals, Couples, Groups
Theoretical Approach:	Integrative, Gestalt
Fees:	£25 - £30

BREWER Caroline 0234 357471
68 The Grove, BEDFORD MK40 3JN
Member of:	BAC
Quals/training:	RELATE trained; training in Gestalt (Gestalt Centre, London); Group Therapy training
Personal Therapy:	Yes
Supervision:	Ongoing
Counselling offered:	**General, Crisis, Marital**
Service for:	Individuals, Couples
Theoretical Approach:	Psychodynamic, Gestalt
Fees:	£20 - £25

Bedfordshire

PARAMOUR Anabelle   0234 345553
30 Bushmead Avenue, BEDFORD MK40 3QN
Member of: CSP
Quals/training: RELATE trained; training in Psychoanalytic Psychotherapy (Camb Soc Psychotherapy)
Personal Therapy: Yes
Supervision: Ongoing
Counselling offered: **General, Psychotherapy**
Service for: Individuals, Couples
Theoretical Approach: Psychoanalytic
Fees: £20

CLARE Louise   0234 267405
11 Warden Abbey, BEDFORD MK41 0SW
Member of: Guild of Psychotherapists
Quals/training: BA; Cert in Couns, WPF; Member Guild of Psychotherapists
Personal Therapy: Yes
Supervision: Ongoing
Counselling offered: **Psychotherapy**
Service for: Individuals
Theoretical Approach: Analytical, Eclectic
Fees: £20 sliding scale

WALKER Jane   0234 365954
18 Falcon Avenue, Brickhill, BEDFORD MK41 7DT
Member of: BAC
Quals/training: SRN; Dip Couns; Dip RET(Acc); training in TA(metanoia)
Personal Therapy: Yes
Supervision: Ongoing
Counselling offered: **General, Bereavement, Crisis, Sexual abuse**
Service for: Individuals, Couples, Groups, Organisations
Specific to: Christians
Theoretical Approach: RET, Cognitive
Fees: £25 negotiable

SIMMONS Peg   0234 268212
68 Falcon Avenue, BEDFORD MK41 7DX
Member of: BAC
Quals/training: RELATE trained 1958; City & Guilds Cert in AIDS Care 1989
Personal Therapy: Yes
Supervision: Ongoing
Counselling offered: **General, Marital, Sexual, Bereavement, Crisis, AIDS, Assertiveness, Stress, Disability**
Service for: Individuals, Couples
Theoretical Approach: Person-centred, TA, Gestalt, Psychodynamic
Fees: £18 - £20 negotiable

PAPE Maureen   0234 349223, 0234 261162
296 Kimbolton Road, BEDFORD MK41 8AG
Member of: BAC Acc
Quals/training: BAC Acc; MA Couns; PG Dip Couns; trained in Psychodynamic Couns; trained in Gestalt Psychotherapy; Psychosexual training; tutor/trainer
Personal Therapy: Yes
Supervision: Ongoing
Counselling offered: **General, Relationship, Marital, Supervision**
Service for: Individuals, Couples, Groups
Theoretical Approach: Eclectic
Fees: £25

Bedfordshire

JOHNSON Duncan B　　　　　　　　　　　　　　　　0234 212155
12 Aldwyck Court, Riverside Close, BEDFORD MK42 9QQ
Member of:　　　　　　　NRHP
Quals/training:　　　　　Dip Hypnotherapy and Psychotherapy (National College)
Personal Therapy:　　　No
Supervision:　　　　　　Ongoing
Counselling offered:　　General, Hypnotherapy, Psychotherapy
Service for:　　　　　　Individuals, Couples, Families, Groups
Theoretical Approach:　Eclectic
Fees:　　　　　　　　　£25 Reduced for unemployed

CODD Anne Marie　　　　　　　　　　　　　　　　　0525 406300
The Old School House, High Street, Lidlington, BEDFORD MK43 0RN
Member of:　　　　　　　AGIP
Quals/training:　　　　　CQSW 1982; training member of AGIP (Psychoanalytical Psychotherapy)
Personal Therapy:　　　Ongoing
Supervision:　　　　　　Ongoing
Counselling offered:　　General, Depression, Crisis, Psychotherapy
Service for:　　　　　　Individuals, Couples, Groups
Specific to:　　　　　　Survivors of sex abuse
Theoretical Approach:　Psychoanalytic, Systemic
Fees:　　　　　　　　　£20 - £25 negotiable

TRUSTAM Gillian　　　　　　　　　　ansaphone 0234 822985
86 High Street, Oakley, BEDFORD MK43 7RH
Member of:　　　　　　　BAC, AGIP
Quals/training:　　　　　NMGC; AGIP
Personal Therapy:　　　Yes
Supervision:　　　　　　Ongoing
Counselling offered:　　General, Psychotherapy
Service for:　　　　　　Individuals, Couples
Theoretical Approach:　Eclectic, Integrative
Fees:　　　　　　　　　Sliding scale

STOCK Pauline　　　　　　　　　　　　　　　　　　0234 781533
1 Mill Cottage, 101 Mill Road, Sharnbrook, BEDFORD MK44 1NP
Member of:　　　　　　　BAC, NRHP
Quals/training:　　　　　BA Psychol/Phil; training in Psychotherapy & Hypnotherapy (NCHP)
Personal Therapy:　　　Yes
Supervision:　　　　　　Ongoing
Counselling offered:　　General
Service for:　　　　　　Individuals, Couples, Families, Groups, Organisations
Specific to:　　　　　　Children, Adolescents, Women, Managers
Theoretical Approach:　Eclectic
Other languages:　　　　French
Fees:　　　　　　　　　£15 - £25

Bedfordshire

BRICKELL John   0525 851588
Centre for Reality Therapy, Green House, 43 George Street, LEIGHTON BUZZARD LU7 8JX
Member of: **BAC**
Quals/training: BEd; Institute for Reality Therapy Certification (USA)
Personal Therapy: Ongoing
Supervision: Ongoing
Counselling offered: **General, Career, Marital, Occupational, Redundancy, Relationship, Stress management**
Service for: Individuals, Couples, Groups, Organisations
Specific to: Young people, Students
Theoretical Approach: Reality therapy, Cognitive/Behavioural
Fees: £20 - £40 Sliding scale

MULLINS Daphne   0525 373538
46 Albany Road, LEIGHTON BUZZARD LU7 8NS
Member of: **BAC**
Quals/training: Training in Couns & Groupwork (Cambridge Univ); Cert Couns, Clinical psychol (Frank Lake); Homoeopath & Remedial Masseuse
Personal Therapy: Ongoing
Supervision: Ongoing
Counselling offered: **General, Stress management**
Service for: Individuals, Couples, Groups, Organisations
Theoretical Approach: Person-centred, Eclectic, Holistic
Fees: £20 - £25

ADLER Eve   0582 22555
The Surgery, 26 Ashcroft Road, Stopsley, LUTON
Member of: **BAC, BASMT**
Quals/training: SRN; Dip Human Sexuality; BASMT Acc
Personal Therapy: Yes
Supervision: Ongoing
Counselling offered: **Sexual, Relationship**
Service for: Individuals, Couples
Specific to: People with disabilities
Theoretical Approach: Eclectic
Fees: £30

HAMILTON-WILSON Dr Adrian   0582 415494
14 West Hill Road, LUTON LU1 3DT
Member of: **BAC**
Quals/training: Dip Psychol 1990; Cert Couns 1989; NCH Couns 1988
Personal Therapy: Yes
Supervision: Ongoing
Counselling offered: **General, Relationship, Sexual, Bereavement**
Service for: Individuals, Couples, Families
Specific to: Gays
Theoretical Approach: Rogerian
Fees: £10 - £30 no-one turned away

Bedfordshire

LIGHTOWLER Peter 0582 458457
8 Milton Road, LUTON LU1 5HZ
Member of: BAC
Quals/training: SEN(M); Cert Couns; Cert Hypnotherapy
Personal Therapy: Ongoing
Supervision: Ongoing
Counselling offered: General, Sexual abuse
Service for: Individuals
Specific to: Men, Abusers, Gays
Theoretical Approach: Psychodynamic, Person-centred
Fees: £15 - £25 Sliding Scale

PEARCE Gerald 0582 26744
152 Turners Road North, LUTON LU1 9AH
Member of: BAC Acc
Quals/training: BAC Acc; Dip Couns; MA Couns (Univ of Hertfordshsire)
Personal Therapy: Yes
Supervision: Ongoing
Counselling offered: General, Relationship, PTSD, Personal growth
Service for: Individuals, Couples, Groups
Theoretical Approach: Integrative
Fees: £18 - £25 sliding scale

BUDGELL Rosemary 0582 488808
7 Blaydon Road, LUTON LU2 0RP
Member of: BAC Acc
Quals/training: BAC Acc; BD (hons); NMGC trained in Marital & Relationship Therapy 1982; CTA trained
Personal Therapy: Yes
Supervision: Ongoing
Counselling offered: General, Bereavement, Relationship, Sexual, Eating disorders, Sexual abuse, Supervision
Service for: Individuals, Couples
Theoretical Approach: Psychodynamic
Fees: £23 - £25

PEART Mary 0582 455272
15 Dorrington Close, LUTON LU3 1XL
Member of: BAC, IPS
Quals/training: Dip Psychosynthesis Couns; Psychotherapy (IP); SRN; Further Ed Teacher's Cert
Personal Therapy: Ongoing
Supervision: Ongoing
Counselling offered: General, Bereavement, Relationship, Psychotherapy
Service for: Individuals, Couples, Groups
Theoretical Approach: Psychosynthesis, Transpersonal
Fees: £25 some concessions

Berkshire

Organisations

NO 5 YOUNG PEOPLE'S COUNS ADVICE & INFO CENTRE
Couns 0734 585858, Admin 0734 585304, Info 0734 586702
2/4 Sackville Street, READING RG1 1NT
Service: A generic counselling & information service for young people & adults (Ring-loop for deaf people)
Area served: Not restricted
Other languages: Welsh, Punjabi, Bengali, Please enquire
Referral: Self
Training of workers: Own in-service training; supervision & professional support
Code of Ethics: BAC
Management by: Management Committee (Reg Charity)
Fees: None

EAST BERKSHIRE PSYCHOLOGICAL SERVICES   0753 821789
Oak House, Upton Hospital, Albert Street, SLOUGH SL1 2BJ
Service: A range of therapies, counselling & support for people with all kinds of emotional & psychological problems, people with learning difficulties, elderly, drug & alcohol misusers
Area served: Slough, Windsor, Maidenhead, Bracknell, Ascot
Other languages: Interpreters available
Referral: GP
Training of workers: Mostly postgraduate clinical psychology & counsellors
Code of Ethics: BPS
Management by: East Berkshire Community Health Trust
Fees: None

WOKINGHAM & DISTRICT COUNSELLING SERVICE   0734 787879
50 Reading Road, WOKINGHAM RG11 1EH
Service: General counselling
Area served: Wokingham & District
Referral: Self
Training of workers: WPF Affiliated Centre; counsellors in training; regular supervision
Code of Ethics: WPF
Management by: Committee
Fees: Donations welcomed

Individual Practitioners

*Every individual is a **member of** one or more organisations eligible for entry into this directory. BAC Accredited Counsellors and Recognised Supervisors are shaded.*

NEVILLE-SMITH Graeme   0344 885902
Drumindoora, 24 Nursery Lane, ASCOT SL5 8PY
Member of: BAC
Quals/training: Dip Couns & Guidance (Middx Poly) 1079
Personal Therapy: Yes
Supervision: Ongoing
Counselling offered: General, Marital, Addiction, Alcohol, Drugs
Service for: Individuals, Couples, Organisations
Theoretical Approach: Rogerian, Reality therapy
Fees: £25 - £40 dependent on income(Ind/cples)

Berkshire

ANDERSON Jackie   0344 778931, 0734 328529
Woden, 84 Wokingham Road, CROWTHORNE RG11 7QA
Member of:	BAC
Quals/training:	RELATE trained; Bereavement training; Cert in Stress Management; Cert in RET, PCP, Multimodal
Personal Therapy:	Yes
Supervision:	Ongoing
Counselling offered:	**General, Bereavement, Marital, Stress**
Service for:	Individuals, Couples, Groups
Fees:	£25

RIDGEWAY Christopher   Appts 0628 770011
Weir Bank, Bray on Thames, MAIDENHEAD SL6 2ED
Member of:	BPS
Quals/training:	BSc; MPhil; PhD; C Psychol; AFBPsS; FIPM; experience equivalent to Dip Couns Psychol
Personal Therapy:	Ongoing
Supervision:	Ongoing
Counselling offered:	**Psychotherapy, Career, Redundancy**
Service for:	Individuals, Groups, Organisations
Specific to:	Employees
Theoretical Approach:	Eclectic, Analytic
Fees:	Negotiable

MABERLEY Diana   0628 34777
Endellion, Money Row Green, Holyport, MAIDENHEAD SL6 2NA
Member of:	BAC
Quals/training:	Adlerian Society for Individual Psychology; Person Centred Art Therapy; Memb PCATA
Personal Therapy:	Ongoing
Supervision:	Ongoing
Counselling offered:	**General, Imaging, Relaxation, Art therapy, Crisis, Stress management**
Service for:	Individuals, Couples, Families, Groups
Specific to:	People with language problems, Children
Theoretical Approach:	Adlerian, Rogerian, Person-centred, Art therapy, Holistic
Fees:	£30 per 90 mins, negotiable

SWINBANK Doris   0628 36469
35A Pinkeys Road, MAIDENHEAD SL6 5DX
Member of:	BAC
Quals/training:	NMGC trained; Introductory Course(IGA); Family Therapy(WPF) Supervision/Consultation(Maudsley Hospital); General Synod Board od Ed Acc Trainer
Personal Therapy:	No
Supervision:	Ongoing
Counselling offered:	**General, Marital, Sexual, Bereavement, Supervision**
Service for:	Individuals, Couples, Families, Groups
Theoretical Approach:	Rogerian, Gestalt, Behavioural, Psychodynamic
Fees:	Negotiable

Berkshire

McGREGOR Tony 0635 34231
127 Kingsley Close, Shaw, NEWBURY RG13 2EB
Member of: NRHP
Quals/training: BSc (Hons) Psychol; Dip Hypno & Psychotherapy (Nat Register)
Personal Therapy: Yes
Supervision: Ongoing
Counselling offered: General, Psychotherapy, Hypnotherapy
Service for: Individuals
Theoretical Approach: Analytical
Fees: £30

LANE Corinne 0734 576864
11 The Grove, READING RG1 4RB
Member of: BAC, NRHP, BPS
Quals/training: BA (Hons) Psychol; Cert Couns; CHP
Personal Therapy: Ongoing
Supervision: Ongoing
Counselling offered: General, Crisis, Psychotherapy, Hypnotherapy, Regression therapy
Service for: Individuals, Couples
Theoretical Approach: Eclectic, Holistic
Fees: £30 negotiable

WAGSTAFF Sheila 0734 666094
36 Carnarvon Road, READING RG1 5SD
Member of: BAC
Quals/training: RELATE trained; Dip Humanistic Psychol
Personal Therapy: Ongoing
Supervision: Ongoing
Counselling offered: General, Marital, Relationship, Stress
Service for: Individuals, Couples, Groups
Theoretical Approach: Eclectic
Fees: £30 negotiable Assessment free

BURL Emma 0734 393154
11 The Grove, READING RG1 4RB
Member of: BAC, BPS
Quals/training: BSc (Hons) Psychol; Cert Couns; Cert Training
Personal Therapy: Ongoing
Supervision: Ongoing
Counselling offered: General, Bereavement, Relationship
Service for: Individuals, Couples
Theoretical Approach: Eclectic
Fees: £30 Negotiable

Berkshire

PARR John   0734 598198
42 Water Road, READING RG3 2NN
Member of: BAC
Quals/training: CQSW; Trained at Heimler Inst; currently training in TA; memb of ITAA
Personal Therapy: Ongoing
Supervision: Ongoing
Counselling offered: **General, Marital, Addiction, Psychotherapy**
Service for: Individuals, Couples, Groups
Theoretical Approach: TA
Fees: £25 - £35 couples; £50/month groups

FERRARA Linda   ansaphone 0734 462356
57 Star Road, Caversham, READING RG4 0BE
Member of: BAC
Quals/training: BA Psychol; Dip Couns; Foundation Course in Group Analysis
Personal Therapy: Ongoing
Supervision: Ongoing
Counselling offered: **General, Bereavement, Sexual abuse, Tranquillisers**
Service for: Individuals
Theoretical Approach: Psychodynamic
Fees: £30

TREVIS Geoffrey   0734 476529
40 All Hallows Road, Caversham, READING RG4 0LP
Member of: BAC, NRHP
Quals/training: Seminars in Gestalt (Surrey Univ); Couns & Co-couns (Reading Univ); Assoc Memb NRHP
Personal Therapy: Yes
Supervision: Ongoing
Counselling offered: **General, Hypnotherapy, Stress management**
Service for: Individuals
Theoretical Approach: Gestalt, Reichian
Fees: £16 - £20 Sliding scale

CHEVALLIER Thelma Ann   0734 470081
22 Highmoor Road, Caversham, READING RG4 7BJ
Member of: BAC
Quals/training: BEd; Cert Couns; on 3rd year Diploma (metanoia)
Personal Therapy: Ongoing
Supervision: Ongoing
Counselling offered: **General, Cancer**
Service for: Individuals, Families
Theoretical Approach: Person-centred
Fees: Negotiable

Berkshire

BANKS Liz 0734 473686
38a Priest Hill, Caversham, READING RG4 7RY
Member of: BAC Acc
Quals/training: BAC Acc; 1974 Dip Couns and Career Work
Personal Therapy: Ongoing
Supervision: Ongoing
Counselling offered: General
Service for: Individuals, Couples, Groups
Specific to: Young people
Theoretical Approach: Rogerian, TA
Other languages: Dutch
Fees: £20 sliding scale

ALLEN Caroline 0734 463564
60 Queens Road, Caversham, READING RG4 8DL
Member of: BAC
Quals/training: BA Hons, Dip Couns (Reading Univ 1989); MA Couns (Reading Univ) 1993
Personal Therapy: Ongoing
Supervision: Ongoing
Counselling offered: General, Sexual abuse, Personal growth
Service for: Individuals
Theoretical Approach: Eclectic
Fees: £15 - £30 sliding scale

DELLER William 0734 476946
42 Surley Row, Caversham, READING RG4 8NA
Member of: BAC
Quals/training: Dip Psychosynthesis Couns (PET) 1987-1991
Personal Therapy: Yes
Supervision: Ongoing
Counselling offered: General, Psychotherapy, Relationship, Work
Service for: Individuals, Couples, Families, Groups
Theoretical Approach: Transpersonal, Existential
Fees: £15 - £25

GRIFFITHS Thelma 0734 668092, mornings 0734 318620
Wessex Hall, Whiteknights Road, READING RG6 2BQ
Member of: BAC, CCPE
Quals/training: CCPE: Dip Couns & Psychotherapy; Co-Counselling & Teacher Training (Univ of Surrey); PDCP Cert(Univ of Surrey)
Personal Therapy: Ongoing
Supervision: Ongoing
Counselling offered: General, Bereavement, Confidence, Relationship, Psychotherapy
Service for: Individuals, Couples
Specific to: Incest survivors
Theoretical Approach: Jungian, Gestalt
Fees: £20 negotiable

Berkshire

POLLOCK Josephine Seton   0734 332231
The Haven, King Street, Mortimer, READING RG7 3RS
Member of: BAC
Quals/training: Youth Couns Course (Berks Training Agency) 1975; CQSW 1979; ongoing workshops & training:
Personal Therapy: Yes
Supervision: Ongoing
Counselling offered: General, Marital, Stress management, Relaxation
Service for: Individuals, Couples, Groups
Theoretical Approach: Eclectic
Fees: £20

SUTCLIFFE Patricia   0734 842904
9 Hartslock Court, Pangbourne, READING RG8 7BJ
Member of: BAC
Quals/training: Cert Biodynamic Psychotherapy(BTC)'79-'81
Personal Therapy: Ongoing
Supervision: Ongoing
Counselling offered: General, Bodywork, Short-term, Spiritual, Psychotherapy
Service for: Individuals, Couples
Theoretical Approach: Analytical, Transpersonal
Fees: £27 some reduced fee places

THORNE Heather   0734 843803
23 Horseshoe Road, Pangbourne, READING RG8 7JQ
Member of: BAC
Quals/training: BA (Hons) Social Studies 1975; Dip Applied Social Studies 1976 (Hull); CQSW 1976
Personal Therapy: Yes
Supervision: Ongoing
Counselling offered: General, Relationship, Alcohol, Stress
Service for: Individuals, Couples, Groups
Specific to: GP referrals
Theoretical Approach: Rogerian
Fees: £20 negotiable

EDWARDS John   0734 422955
Ridgedale, 7 Allison Gardens, Purley on Thames, READING RG8 8DF
Member of: BAC Acc
Quals/training: BAC Acc; APT Acc; Brit Register of Complementary Practitioners (Hypnotherapy); Fellow Chartered Inst of Marketing
Personal Therapy: Yes
Supervision: Ongoing
Counselling offered: General, Psychotherapy, Hypnotherapy
Service for: Individuals
Theoretical Approach: Eclectic
Fees: By arrangement

Berkshire

ROSE Suzanna   0734 341 046
Mulberry Mead, Waltham Road, Twyford, READING RG10 0AD
Member of:	BAC
Quals/training:	MA (Counselling); RGN; RHV; UKCC
Personal Therapy:	Ongoing
Supervision:	Ongoing
Counselling offered:	**General, Crisis, Crit. incident debriefing**
Service for:	Individuals, Groups, Organisations
Specific to:	Trauma victims, Victims of crime, Victims of violence
Theoretical Approach:	Psychodynamic, Cognitive/Behavioural
Other languages:	Dutch
Fees:	£20 - £40 sliding scale

CLARKE Catherine   0734 404052
Thames Cottage, 63 High Street, Wargrave, READING RG10 8BU
Member of:	BAC
Quals/training:	RELATE trained
Personal Therapy:	No
Supervision:	Ongoing
Counselling offered:	**General, Marital, Sexual**
Service for:	Individuals, Couples
Theoretical Approach:	Client-centred, Psychodynamic, Behavioural
Fees:	£30

DAVIES Jennifer   0734 404052
63 High Street, READING RG10 8BU
Member of:	BAC
Quals/training:	BA; RELATE Counsellor and Supervisor training
Personal Therapy:	No
Supervision:	Ongoing
Counselling offered:	**General, Marital, Sexual**
Service for:	Individuals, Couples
Theoretical Approach:	Client-centred, Psychodynamic, Behavioural
Fees:	£30

ROBINSON Fran   0753 820303
74 Ledgers Road, SLOUGH SL1 2RL
Member of:	BAC
Quals/training:	Dip in Couns(metanoia); RSA in Development of Learning Couns
Personal Therapy:	Ongoing
Supervision:	Ongoing
Counselling offered:	**General, Personal growth, Women's issues**
Service for:	Individuals
Specific to:	Women
Theoretical Approach:	Person-centred
Fees:	£15 - £20 negotiable

Berkshire

WARNER Kerri   0753 820303
74 Ledgers Road, Chalvey, SLOUGH SL1 2RL
Member of: BAC
Quals/training: Dip Couns; training in TA Psychotherapy (metanoia); Memb ITAA
Personal Therapy: Yes
Supervision: Ongoing
Counselling offered: General, Psychotherapy
Service for: Individuals, Groups
Specific to: Women, Adolescents
Theoretical Approach: Person-centred, Rogerian, TA
Fees: £15 - £20 flexible

MACKINNON Sylvia   0628 665467
27 Harkness Road, Burnham, SLOUGH SL1 7BL
Member of: ANLP (PCS), CRAH
Quals/training: Dip Therapeutic Hypnosis & Psychotherapy (SHAP) 1988; Dip NLP (UKTC) 1989; Dip Adv Hypnotherapy & Hypnohealing (ABC) 1991; CAHyp. ICM Register
Personal Therapy: Yes
Supervision: Ongoing
Counselling offered: General, Hypnotherapy, Psychotherapy, Hypnohealing
Service for: Individuals
Theoretical Approach: Eclectic
Fees: £40

DICKSON Carole   0753 655 556
Love Hill House, Love Hill Lane, Langley, SLOUGH SL3 6DE
Member of: BAC
Quals/training: Certs Counselling Theory & Skills (CAC); Dip Counselling (AEB); Cert Rational Emotive Therapy; Cert Critical Incident Stress Debriefing, Psychotherapy training
Personal Therapy: Ongoing
Supervision: Ongoing
Counselling offered: General, Bereavement, Relationship, Stress, Crit. incident debriefing
Service for: Individuals, Couples, Organisations
Specific to: Employees
Theoretical Approach: Psychodynamic, Integrative, Person-centred
Fees: £15 - £35 sliding scale, 1st appt free

WILLINGSON Tom   0753 862819
37 Bell Lane, Eton Wick, WINDSOR SL4 6LQ
Member of: BAC, CRAH
Quals/training: Dip Therapeutic Hypnosis & Psychotherapy(SHAP)'84; Assoc Memb Inst of Training & Development
Personal Therapy: Yes
Supervision: Ongoing
Counselling offered: General, Hypnotherapy, Career, Relationship
Service for: Individuals, Couples, Families
Other languages: French, Swedish, Danish, Norwegian
Fees: £30

Berkshire

ANDERSON Jackie 0344 778931, 0734 328529
Cedar House Surgery, 269a Nine Mile Ride, WOKINGHAM RG11 3NS
Member of: BAC
Quals/training: RELATE trained; Bereavement training; Cert in Stress Management; Cert in RET, PCP, Multimodal
Personal Therapy: Yes
Supervision: Ongoing
Counselling offered: **General, Bereavement, Relationship, Stress**
Service for: Individuals, Couples, Groups
Fees: £25

JACKSON Gerry 0734 731 546
4 Dodsells Well, WOKINGHAM RG11 4YE
Member of: BAC
Quals/training: Dip Counselling; RELATE trained; Various courses; Post Trauma Training
Personal Therapy: Ongoing
Supervision: Ongoing
Counselling offered: **General, Crit. incident debriefing, PTSD, Relationship, Stress**
Service for: Individuals, Couples, Groups, Organisations
Specific to: Helping professions
Theoretical Approach: Psychodynamic, Cognitive/Behavioural
Fees: Negotiable

Berkshire

Buckinghamshire

Organisations

AYLESBURY VALE NHS TRUST   0296 393363 x 545
Clinical Psychology Services, Tindale Centre Bierton Road, AYLESBURY HP20 1EG
Service: Individual therapy for adults & children, marital therapy. Advice & teaching to care workers & voluntary groups
Area served: Buckinghamshire
Referral: GP, Health/Soc Work Professional
Training of workers: Postgraduate Clinical Psychology
Code of Ethics: BPS
Management by: Psychology Services Manager
Fees: None

YOUTH INFORMATION SERVICE   0908 604700
Barnhouse, 402 North Row, MILTON KEYNES MK9 2NL
Service: General counselling for 14-25 year olds
Area served: Milton Keynes and area
Referral: Self or others
Training of workers: 100 hrs initial training; regular in-service training; ongoing individual and group supervision
Code of Ethics: BAC
Management by: Sub Committee of VIS Executive Committee
Fees: None

MILTON KEYNES PASTORAL FOUNDATION   0908 230644
c/o Church of Christ, The Cornerstone, 300 Saxon Gate West, MILTON KEYNES MK19 5ES
Service: Counselling for individuals in a centre associated with the WPF
Area served: Milton Keynes area
Referral: Self or others
Training of workers: Group experience, theoretical base with personal therapy and regular supervision group
Code of Ethics: BAC
Management by: Management Committee with Advisory Council to fulfil WPF conditions
Fees: Sliding scale

Individual Practitioners
*Every individual is a **member of** one or more organisations eligible for entry into this directory. BAC Accredited Counsellors and Recognised Supervisors are shaded.*

SPOOR Lin   ansaphone 0494 433896
Greenways, 2 Amersham Road, Chesham Bois, AMERSHAM HP6 5PE
Member of: BAC
Quals/training: AEB Cert & Dip Couns; RGN; RM; Cruse training; Youth Couns training
Personal Therapy: Ongoing
Supervision: Ongoing
Counselling offered: General, Bereavement, Stress management, Art therapy
Service for: Individuals
Specific to: Young people
Theoretical Approach: Psychodynamic
Fees: £21 - £25 sliding scale

Buckinghamshire

WAUMSLEY Elizabeth 0494 727062
89 Station Road, AMERSHAM HP7 0AT
Member of:	BAC
Quals/training:	BA; Dip Couns
Personal Therapy:	Yes
Supervision:	Ongoing
Counselling offered:	**General, Peri-natal, Depression**
Service for:	Individuals, Couples
Specific to:	Parents
Theoretical Approach:	Psychodynamic
Fees:	£20

WENHAM Peter 0844 291932
1 Great Stone Cottages, Cuddington, AYLESBURY HP18 0AZ
Member of:	BAC
Quals/training:	BA; Cert Couns; Dip Marriage & Family Couns (Inst of Counselling); Cruse Bereavement counsellor
Personal Therapy:	No
Supervision:	Ongoing
Counselling offered:	**General, Bereavement**
Service for:	Individuals, Groups
Specific to:	Teachers
Theoretical Approach:	Eclectic
Fees:	£20

BEATTIE Lilian 0296 622153
Coniston House, 36 Dobbins Lane, Wendover, AYLESBURY HP22 6DH
Member of:	BAC
Quals/training:	1959 (MB,BS); 1982 Dip Adlerian Counselling; DHP; Memb Adlerian Soc of GB
Personal Therapy:	Yes
Supervision:	Ongoing
Counselling offered:	**General, Bereavement, Crisis, Psychotherapy**
Service for:	Individuals, Couples, Families
Specific to:	Children, Young people, Parents
Theoretical Approach:	Adlerian
Fees:	£35 - £45

CHANDLER David 0525 240420, Fax 0525 240003
DJ Chandler & Associates, Brooke House Business Centre, Brooke House, Market Square, AYLESBURY HP20 1SN
Member of:	BAC Acc, BPS
Quals/training:	BAC Acc; BSc Psychol; Practitioner Memb BPS Special Group in Couns Psychol; C Psychol
Personal Therapy:	Yes
Supervision:	Ongoing
Counselling offered:	**General, Drugs, Alcohol, Substance abuse, Work**
Service for:	Individuals, Couples, Unknown
Specific to:	Employers
Theoretical Approach:	Client-centred, Eclectic
Fees:	£20 - £40 + VAT, sliding scale

Buckinghamshire

BUTCHER Barbara   0494 674224
31 Ledborough Lane, BEACONSFIELD HP9 2DB
Member of:	**NSHAP, CRAH**
Quals/training:	Dip Therapeutic Psychotherapy & Hypnotherapy (SHAP) 1983; Cert NLP; Memb ICM Hypnotherapy Register
Personal Therapy:	Yes
Supervision:	Ongoing
Counselling offered:	**General, Tranquillisers, Dependency, Stress, Pain**
Service for:	Individuals, Couples, Groups, Families
Fees:	£25 negotiable

REDPATH Robert   02407 4102
Woodland Cottage, Wilton Lane, Jordans, BEACONSFIELD HP9 2UW
Member of:	**BAC**
Quals/training:	Dip Couns CAC
Personal Therapy:	Yes
Supervision:	Ongoing
Counselling offered:	**General**
Service for:	Individuals
Theoretical Approach:	Eclectic
Fees:	£25

YOUNG Delia   0494 671361
35 Barrards Way, Seer Green, BEACONSFIELD HP9 2YZ
Member of:	**BPS**
Quals/training:	NAHP; BSECH; BA Psychol; Dip Hypnotherapy & Psychotherapy; training in Gestalt Psychotherapy; Cert in Couns Psychol; Adv Cert in Stress Management
Personal Therapy:	Yes
Supervision:	Ongoing
Counselling offered:	**General, Sexual, Children's problems, Stress, Bereavement, Depression, Eating disorders**
Service for:	Individuals, Couples, Families, Groups
Theoretical Approach:	Cognitive/Behavioural, Gestalt, Rogerian, Ericksonian
Fees:	£30 reductions for children & OAPs

BAILEY Dr Roy   0280 816157
Independent Counselling Svce, Firs House, 64 Overn Avenue, BUCKINGHAM MK18 1LT
Member of:	**BAC, BPS, ANLP (PCS)**
Quals/training:	1974 MA Psychology; 1985 PhD Psychology; various counselling courses; Chartered Clinical Psychologist; AFBPsS
Personal Therapy:	Yes
Supervision:	Ongoing
Counselling offered:	**General, Career, Stress management, Addiction, Bereavement, Crisis, Divorce, Redundancy, PTSD**
Service for:	Individuals, Couples, Families, Groups, Organisations
Specific to:	Children, Employees
Theoretical Approach:	Eclectic, Integrative, Cognitive/Behavioural, NLP, Ericksonian
Fees:	£40 negotiable fee for companies

Buckinghamshire

BOLLINGHAUS Elaine   0494 765947
Loudhams, Burton Lane, Little Chalfont, CHALFONT ST. GILES HP8 4BS
Member of: BAC
Quals/training: MA; NMGC/RELATE trained; Dip in Marital Psychotherapy; TIMS (Assoc)
Personal Therapy: Yes
Supervision: Ongoing
Counselling offered: Marital, Psychotherapy
Service for: Individuals, Couples
Specific to: Couples with co-therapist
Theoretical Approach: Psychoanalytic
Fees: Negotiable

CLARKE Wendela   0753 885618
Advisory C for Stress Mgment, The Village House Nicol Road, Chalfont St Peter, GERRARDS CROSS SL9 9ND
Member of: NRHP
Quals/training: BSc; Dip Psychol & Psychotherapy; Master Practitioner NLP; Chartered Biologist
Personal Therapy: Yes
Supervision: Ongoing
Counselling offered: **General, Eating disorders, Hypnotherapy, Psychotherapy, Stress management**
Service for: Individuals, Couples, Groups
Specific to: Children
Theoretical Approach: NLP, Eclectic
Fees: £50

PARKINSON Diana   0438 832408
Dunedin, Windsor Road, GERRARDS CROSS SL9 7NA
Member of: BAC
Quals/training: Trained at the Hypnotherapy Centre, Bournemouth & Hert Social Services; Accredited Drugcare, St Albans
Personal Therapy: Yes
Supervision: Ongoing
Counselling offered: **General, Relationship, Eating disorders, Substance abuse, Alcohol, Psychotherapy**
Service for: Individuals, Couples, Families
Theoretical Approach: Eclectic
Fees: £30 negotiable, 1st session free

BRIDGMAN Michelle   0494 815083
7 Taplin Way, Penn, HIGH WYCOMBE HP10 8DW
Member of: BAC
Quals/training: Dip Couns; training in Crisis Counselling
Personal Therapy: Yes
Supervision: Ongoing
Counselling offered: **General, Gender dysphoria, Crisis, Stress**
Service for: Individuals, Couples, Families
Specific to: Women, Managers
Theoretical Approach: Humanistic, Gestalt
Fees: £15 - £35 sliding scale

Buckinghamshire

SELBY-BOOTHROYD Judith   0628 529970
Flackwell Lodge, Oakland Way, Flackwell Heath, HIGH WYCOMBE HP10 9ED
Member of:	BAC
Quals/training:	RELATE trained
Personal Therapy:	No
Supervision:	Ongoing
Counselling offered:	Relationship
Service for:	Individuals, Couples, Organisations
Specific to:	Survivors of child abuse
Theoretical Approach:	Client-centred
Fees:	£25

LEVITSKY Patricia   0494 81229, 071 435 0816
Sportsman's Cottage, Beacon Hill, Penn, HIGH WYCOMBE HP10 8NJ
Member of:	BAC, GPTI, Member of UKCP Register
Quals/training:	MA Couns Psychol (Antioch Univ, USA) 1986; 4 yr Gestalt Psychotherapy Training (USA)
Personal Therapy:	Yes
Supervision:	Ongoing
Counselling offered:	General, Crisis, Psychotherapy
Service for:	Individuals, Couples
Theoretical Approach:	Humanistic, Integrative
Other languages:	Hebrew, Spanish, German, French
Fees:	£25 negotiable, also NW London

PORTSMOUTH Francziska   0753 630757
Paddock Barn, Hollow Hill Lane, IVER SL0 0JJ
Member of:	BAC, BPS
Quals/training:	BSc Psychol; MSc Research Methods; MSc Psychological Couns (ongoing); Post Grad Dip Management Studies
Personal Therapy:	Yes
Supervision:	Ongoing
Counselling offered:	General, Eating disorders, Relationship, Employment
Service for:	Individuals, Organisations
Theoretical Approach:	Psychodynamic
Fees:	£25 negotiable

GALLOWAY Jan   0628 482738
1 Henley Road, MARLOW SL7 2BZ
Member of:	BAC, BASMT
Quals/training:	NMGC training including sexual therapy
Personal Therapy:	Yes
Supervision:	Ongoing
Counselling offered:	General, Marital, Sexual
Service for:	Individuals, Couples
Theoretical Approach:	Eclectic
Fees:	£25

Buckinghamshire

CORDER Francisca 0628 478095
10 Portland Gardens, MARLOW SL7 2LR
Member of: BAC
Quals/training: CQSW; Dip Couns
Personal Therapy: Ongoing
Supervision: Ongoing
Counselling offered: General, Bereavement, Crisis, Abuse
Service for: Individuals
Specific to: Gays, Women
Theoretical Approach: Rogerian
Fees: £20

BLAKE Christy 0628 47 2220, 071 636 6504, 0753 869755
Valley Cottage, 200 Marlow Bottom, MARLOW SL7 3PR
Member of: BAC Acc
Quals/training: BAC Acc; Dip Couns (CTA); RGN; Trained in TA(Hons), Gestalt, Family therapy, Hypnosis, NLP, Art therapy, Redecision therapy (UK USA Canada) 1978-83; Memb ITAA, CTA, ISMA, MHA
Personal Therapy: Ongoing
Supervision: Ongoing
Counselling offered: General, Psychotherapy, Anorexia, Stress, Relationship
Service for: Individuals, Couples, Groups, Families
Theoretical Approach: TA, Gestalt, Hypnotherapy, Art therapy, Redecision therapy
Fees: £30 (£60 London, £38 Windsor)

DESSAUER Helga 0908 643 320
2 Elmers Park, Church Green, Bletchley, MILTON KEYNES MK3 6DJ
Member of: BAC, NRHP, NCHP, BPS
Quals/training: BA (Hons); Cert Hypnotherapy (National College); NRHP Ass.; Dip NLP; Rogerian; Gestalt; Cognitve therapy/Hypnotherapy; Autogenic Therapy; Imagery; Personal Construct; Erickson
Personal Therapy: Yes
Supervision: Ongoing
Counselling offered: General, Bereavement, Cancer, Marital, Psychotherapy
Service for: Individuals, Couples, Groups, Organisations
Theoretical Approach: Rogerian, Gestalt, NLP, Cognitive, Ericksonian
Other languages: German
Fees: £15 - £40 sliding scale

JOHNSON Joan 0908 667660
10 Olde Bell Lane, Loughton, MILTON KEYNES MK5 8EN
Member of: BAC Acc
Quals/training: BAC Acc; Teaching Cert 1971; WPF Acc Affiliate; Dip Multi Media Art Therapy
Personal Therapy: Ongoing
Supervision: Ongoing
Counselling offered: General, Art therapy, Bereavement, Spiritual
Service for: Individuals, Groups
Specific to: Teachers, Clergy/priests, Women
Theoretical Approach: Eclectic, Art therapy, Gestalt, Psychodynamic
Fees: £10 - £20

Buckinghamshire

FRIEDMAN Elizabeth　　　　　　　　　　　　　　　　0908 562269
St Athelstane, 1 Calverton Road, Stoney Stratford, MILTON KEYNES MK11 1LE
Member of: BAC
Quals/training: BA; MEd; Dip Couns (CAC); PG Cert in Group Psychotherapy
Personal Therapy: Ongoing
Supervision: Ongoing
Counselling offered: **General, Relationship, Bereavement, Crisis, Anxiety, Stress management, Brief, Psychotherapy**
Service for: Individuals
Theoretical Approach: Psychodynamic, Person-centred
Fees: £20 negotiable

FAITH Patricia　　　　　　　　　　　　　　　　　　0908 616317
1 Huntsman Grove, Blakelands, MILTON KEYNES MK14 5HS
Member of: BAC, ITA, NCHP
Quals/training: MA; Cert Ed; Dip Professional Studies in Education; NRHP (Affil); Insight Diploma (personal development); Trainer, The Oxsem Divorced & Separated Recovery Programme
Personal Therapy: Yes
Supervision: Ongoing
Counselling offered: **General, Psychotherapy, Hypnotherapy**
Service for: Individuals, Groups
Specific to: Teachers, Lecturers
Theoretical Approach: Person-centred
Fees: £30 - £40 - unwaged negotiable

FREESTONE Eileen　　　　　　　　　ansaphone 0908 661455
MILTON KEYNES MK14
Member of: BAC
Quals/training: Combined Cert Couns(CSCT/CAC)'92; Dip NLP; Memb Coll of Radiographers - DCR(R)
Personal Therapy: Ongoing
Supervision: Ongoing
Counselling offered: **General, Bereavement, Cancer**
Service for: Individuals, Groups, Organisations
Theoretical Approach: Eclectic
Fees: £40

BRAZIER John　　　　　　　　　　　　　　　　　　0908 582239
Rose Cottage, Broughton Road, Salford, MILTON KEYNES MK17 8BQ
Member of: BAC
Quals/training: FIPM; Currently studying for MA in Counselling & Guidance; RELATE Counsellor
Personal Therapy: Yes
Supervision: Ongoing
Counselling offered: **General, Bereavement, Crisis, Redundancy, Employment, Relationship, Marital, Stress**
Service for: Individuals, Couples, Groups, Organisations
Specific to: Employees, Managers
Theoretical Approach: Person-centred, Eclectic
Fees: Negotiable

Buckinghamshire

ROSSETER Bill
14 Lower Way, Great Brickhill, MILTON KEYNES MK17 9AG
Member of: BAC Acc, IPC
Quals/training: BAC Acc; Dip Adv Psychodynamic Couns (WPF); Currently undertaking Psychotherapy training (WPF)
Personal Therapy: Ongoing
Supervision: Ongoing
Counselling offered: General
Service for: Individuals
Theoretical Approach: Psychodynamic
Fees: £20 - £25

ERICKSON Margaret 0908 510259
Ancient Lights, 2 Gold St, Hanslope, MILTON KEYNES MK19 2LU
Member of: BAC, BPS
Quals/training: BA; MA; EdD; C Psychol; Memb of New York Academy of Sciences
Personal Therapy: Yes
Supervision: Ongoing
Counselling offered: General, Stress, Sexual, Relationship, Learning difficulties
Service for: Individuals, Couples, Families
Fees: £30 some free places

WOMPHREY Jenny 0908 564736
17 London Road, Old Stratford, MILTON KEYNES MK19 6AE
Member of: BAC Acc
Quals/training: BAC(Acc); CQSW; training in Psychodynamic Couns with FWA; BSc Soc; BA(Hons)
Personal Therapy: Ongoing
Supervision: Ongoing
Counselling offered: General, Bereavement, PTSD, Sexual abuse
Service for: Individuals, Groups
Specific to: Lesbians, Survivors of sex abuse, Caring professions
Theoretical Approach: Psychodynamic
Fees: £22 - £25 sliding scale

JOHNSTON Candice 0908 582069
Asplands Medical Centre, Asplands Close, Woburn Sands, MILTON KEYNES MK17
Member of: BAC
Quals/training: BA(Hons); Post Grad training in Couns Psychol (Minnesota, USA) 1979
Personal Therapy: Yes
Supervision: Ongoing
Counselling offered: General, Relationship, Psychotherapy, Alcohol, Co-dependency, Women's issues
Service for: Individuals, Couples, Families
Theoretical Approach: Psychodynamic, Minnesota model
Fees: £30

Buckinghamshire

LESLIE Jenny 0908 612333
49 Broad Street, NEWPORT PAGNELL MK16 0AW
Member of: BAC Acc
Quals/training: BAC Acc; WPF Affiliated Course 1984-87; Post grad Dip Couns (Hatfield Poly) 1991; Student memb AGIP
Personal Therapy: Yes
Supervision: Ongoing
Counselling offered: General, Short-term, Long-term
Service for: Individuals
Theoretical Approach: Eclectic, Psychodynamic
Fees: £17 - £22

DIMMOCK Cherryll 0908 612717
18 Wodehouse Walk, NEWPORT PAGNELL MK16 8PX
Member of: BAC
Quals/training: Dip in Couns; training in psychodynamic couns; alchohol/ drug abuse, HIV counselling
Personal Therapy: Yes
Supervision: Ongoing
Counselling offered: General, Addiction, Crisis
Service for: Individuals, Couples, Families, Groups
Specific to: Women, Substance abusers
Theoretical Approach: Cognitive, Behavioural, Client-centred, Psychodynamic
Fees: £20 - £25 sliding scale

HARE Lesley 0442 827284
63 Mill View Road, TRING HP23 4EW
Member of: BAC
Quals/training: Post Grad Dip Couns(Herts Univ)
Personal Therapy: Yes
Supervision: Ongoing
Counselling offered: General
Service for: Individuals
Theoretical Approach: Psychodynamic
Fees: £15 - £25 sliding scale

Buckinghamshire

Cambridgeshire

Organisations

CAMBRIDGE SOCIETY FOR PSYCHOTHERAPY   0223 248959
c/o 70 Cavendish Avenue, CAMBRIDGE CB1 4UT
Service: Psychoanalytic & psychodynamic psychotherapy, mostly for individuals but some offer couple & group therapy & mother / infant psychotherapy.
Area served: Cambridge & district
Other languages: Spanish, Finnish
Referral: Self
Training of workers: All trained with institutions approved by UKCP and includes personal therapy and ongoing supervision.
Code of Ethics: Cam SP
Management by: Co-operative
Fees: £15 - £30 according to therapist

CAMBRIDGE BODY PSYCHOTHERAPY PRACTICE   0223 302303
26A Russell Court, Panton Street, CAMBRIDGE CB2 1HW
Service: Body psychotherapy, body-centred counselling, biodynamic massage, relaxation and stress management. Appointments only
Area served: Cambridge and surrounding area
Referral: GP, Self or others
Training of workers: Staff have trained with organisational members of UKCP. Some are also nurses or occupational therapists
Code of Ethics: BAC, AHPP, KI, ACP
Management by: Director
Fees: £15 - £25 initial consultation £25

CAMBRIDGE GROUP WORK   0223 64543
4 George Street, CAMBRIDGE CB4 1AJ
Service: Group-Analytic psychotherapy in small groups designed to meet a range of needs. Also training in groupwork
Area served: Anywhere, but mostly East Anglia
Referral: Self, GP, Psychiatrist
Training of workers: All are fully trained and members of professional bodies, regular peer supervision
Code of Ethics: Guild of Psychotherapists, IGA
Management by: Council of management
Fees: £8 per session

CAMBRIDGE PASTORAL GROUP   0954 781180
The Rectory, 2 High Street, Longstanton, CAMBRIDGE CB4 5BP
Service: Pastoral Counselling for individuals, couples, groups and families
Area served: East & Mid Anglia
Referral: Self or others
Training of workers: Cert in Human Relationships, Pastoral Care & Counselling; CTA supervision
Code of Ethics: CTA
Management by: CTA local tutor group
Fees: Free or by arrangement

Cambridgeshire

CAMBRIDGESHIRE CONSULTANCY IN COUNSELLING
0480 461524, 0223 312597
6 Fairfields Crescent, St Ives, HUNTINGDON PE17 4QH
Service: General counselling for individuals & couples (over 16) at a variety of venues - St Ives 461524, Cambridge 312597, Peterborough 390607 & 69808, Grantham 700062
Area served: Cambridgeshire and nearby
Referral: Self or others
Training of workers: Three yr part-time course, personal therapy and regular supervision
Code of Ethics: BAC
Management by: Executive committee (WPF Associated Centre)
Fees: Negotiable according to income

PERSONAL DEVELOPMENT CENTRE
0733 349656
Thorpedene, 70 Thorpe Park Road, PETERBOROUGH PE3 6LJ
Service: Individual, marital & sexual therapy; drug dependency couns; TA couns(social & organisational skills); Counselling & assertiveness training
Area served: Cambridgeshire and Norfolk
Referral: Self or others
Training of workers: Psychology degree; Dip Humanistic Psychology
Code of Ethics: BAC
Management by: Director - Leonard Phillips
Fees: £25 £40 couples, £10 Group Workshops

Individual Practitioners

*Each individual is a **member of** one or more organisations eligible for entry into this directory. BAC Accredited Counsellors and Recognised Supervisors are shaded.*

HARDY Liz
0223 67850
90 Tenison Road, CAMBRIDGE CB1 2DW
Member of: BAC, PA
Quals/training: BA; Cert Couns; currently training in Psychotherapy (PA)
Personal Therapy: Ongoing
Supervision: Ongoing
Counselling offered: General, Bereavement, Relationship, Psychotherapy, Work
Service for: Individuals
Theoretical Approach: Psychodynamic
Fees: £20 negotiable

RANDALL Rosemary
0223 313 539
113 Gwydir Street, CAMBRIDGE CB1 2LG
Member of: Camb SP
Quals/training: Training in Psychoanalytic Psychotherapy (Cambridge Soc. for Psychotherapy) 1989
Personal Therapy: Yes
Supervision: Ongoing
Counselling offered: General, Psychotherapy
Service for: Individuals
Specific to: Women
Theoretical Approach: Psychodynamic, Feminist
Fees: £20 - £25 negotiable

Cambridgeshire

TINSLEY Maureen 0223 214488
72 Coleridge Road, CAMBRIDGE CB1 2PJ
Member of: BAC Acc, WMI
Quals/training: BAC Acc 1986; BA; LCIP 1985; IGA 1983
Personal Therapy: Yes
Supervision: Ongoing
Counselling offered: General, Relationship, Bereavement, Eating disorders, Psychotherapy, Supervision
Service for: Individuals, Groups
Theoretical Approach: Psychodynamic, Object relations
Fees: £35 negotiable

PEGLAR Graham 0223 355233
Parkside Counselling Group, Community Education Office, Parkside Community College, CAMBRIDGE CB1 1EH
Member of: BAC
Quals/training: Various courses in counselling, psychotherapy & supervision
Personal Therapy: Yes
Supervision: Ongoing
Counselling offered: General
Service for: Individuals, Couples
Theoretical Approach: Psychodynamic, Person-centred
Fees: £18

WHITTLE Lorna ansaphone 0223 213969
7 Missleton Court, CAMBRIDGE CB1 4BL
Member of: BAC Acc, ARBAS
Quals/training: BAC Acc; RMN; ITEC; Fond Course in Groupwork (IGA); training in Psychotherapy (Arbours Assoc)
Personal Therapy: Ongoing
Supervision: Ongoing
Counselling offered: General, Bereavement, Crisis, Relationship, Abuse, Eating disorders, Psychotherapy
Service for: Individuals, Groups
Specific to: Women
Theoretical Approach: Psychodynamic, Psychoanalytic
Other languages: French
Fees: £20 - £25

WALLACE Anthea 0223 248897
9 Wort's Causeway, CAMBRIDGE CB1 4RJ
Member of: BAC Acc
Quals/training: BAC(Acc)'85; BA; MA; Acc Cambs Consultancy in Couns '81
Personal Therapy: Yes
Supervision: Ongoing
Counselling offered: General, Marital, Bereavement, Crisis
Service for: Individuals, Couples
Theoretical Approach: Person-centred, Psychodynamic
Fees: Negotiable

Cambridgeshire

GULIAN-MINSHULL Edith　　　　　　　　　　　　0223 240088
14 Alwyne Road, CAMBRIDGE CB1 4RR
Member of:	BAC, BPS
Quals/training:	MA Psychol; PhD Psychol (Bucharest) 1966; C Psychol; FBPsS
Personal Therapy:	Yes
Supervision:	Ongoing
Counselling offered:	General, Psychotherapy, Stress management
Service for:	Individuals
Theoretical Approach:	Rogerian, Cognitive
Other languages:	French, Romanian
Fees:	£25 - £30 negotiable

HINDMARSH Roland　　　　　　　　　　　　0223 245441
19 Topcliffe Way, CAMBRIDGE CB1 4SJ
Member of:	BAC
Quals/training:	BA Philosophy & Psychol; Cert Couns & Groupwork (Cambridge Univ) 1986; training in Psychodynamic Couns, Gestalt Psychotherapy
Personal Therapy:	Yes
Supervision:	Ongoing
Counselling offered:	General, Relationship, Bereavement
Specific to:	Asian, African
Theoretical Approach:	Rogerian, Gestalt, Jungian
Other languages:	French, German, Swedish, Dutch, Italian
Fees:	£25

HEAL Christianne　　　　　　　　　　　　0223 314620
1 Saxon Street, CAMBRIDGE CB2 1HN
Member of:	BAC
Quals/training:	1977 Diploma from the Lincoln Centre for Psychotherapy; 1979 Diploma in Counselling (Middlesex Poly)
Personal Therapy:	Ongoing
Supervision:	Ongoing
Counselling offered:	General, Crisis, Eating disorders, Bereavement, Spiritual, Psychotherapy
Service for:	Individuals, Couples
Theoretical Approach:	Eclectic
Other languages:	Italian
Fees:	£25 negotiable

GRILLET Kate　　　　　　　　　　　　0223 64185
1 St Eligius Place, CAMBRIDGE CB2 1HY
Member of:	BAC
Quals/training:	Cert Couns & Groupwork (Norwich Centre)'83; Cert Biodynamic Massage; Memb of Person Centre Cambridge
Personal Therapy:	Yes
Supervision:	Ongoing
Counselling offered:	General, Career, Bodywork, Art therapy
Service for:	Individuals, Couples, Groups
Theoretical Approach:	Person-centred
Fees:	£25 negotiable

Cambridgeshire

CAMERON Angela 0223 61043
35 Newton Road, CAMBRIDGE CB2 2AL
Member of: BAC Acc
Quals/training: BAC Acc; NMGC trained; '87 Cert Couns (Albany Trust); '85-'88 Dip PCT Britain
Personal Therapy: Yes
Supervision: Ongoing
Counselling offered: General, Relationship, Sexual, Gender dysphoria, Health
Service for: Individuals, Couples
Theoretical Approach: Person-centred
Fees: £28 (£35 couples)

WARWICK Heather 0223 245380
31 Sedley Taylor Road, CAMBRIDGE CB2 2PN
Member of: BASMT
Quals/training: RELATE training '76; sex therapy '82; supervisor '86; BASMT Accred
Personal Therapy: Yes
Supervision: Ongoing
Counselling offered: General, Divorce, Marital, Sexual, Psychotherapy, Supervision
Service for: Individuals, Couples, Groups
Specific to: Students
Theoretical Approach: Psychodynamic
Fees: £25 negotiable

TAUSSIG Hanna 0223 246643
296 Hills Road, CAMBRIDGE CB2 2QG
Member of: Guild of Psychotherapists
Quals/training: BA; MA (Cantab); CQSW; Dip Social Work (London); Full memb Guild of Psychotherapists
Personal Therapy: -
Supervision: -
Counselling offered: Psychotherapy
Service for: Individuals, Couples
Theoretical Approach: Psychoanalytic
Fees: Negotiable

SERPELL Vivienne 0223 833218
Scotts, High Street, Whittlesford, CAMBRIDGE CB2 4LT
Member of: BAC
Quals/training: RELATE trained; BASMT
Personal Therapy: No
Supervision: Ongoing
Counselling offered: Relationship, Sexual
Service for: Individuals, Couples
Theoretical Approach: Behavioural, Psychodynamic
Fees: £25 negotiable

Cambridgeshire

RIES Paul　　　　　　　　　　　　　　　　　　　　0223 328745
2 Eltisley Avenue, CAMBRIDGE CB3 9JG
Member of:　　　　　BAC
Quals/training:　　　　Training in Individual Psychodynamic Therapy & Marital Therapy(Dept of Psychotherapy, Addenbrooke's, Cambridge) Cambridge
Personal Therapy:　　Yes
Supervision:　　　　　Ongoing
Counselling offered:　**Psychotherapy**
Service for:　　　　　Individuals, Couples
Theoretical Approach:　Psychodynamic, Psychoanalytic, Object relations
Other languages:　　　German, Danish, Norwegian, Swedish
Fees:　　　　　　　　£20 - £30 sliding scale

GORDON Leila　　　　　　　　　　　　　　　　　0223 67912
20 Herbert Street, CAMBRIDGE CB4 1AQ
Member of:　　　　　Cam SP
Quals/training:　　　　MSc Soc Sci; training in Ananlytic Psychotherapy
Personal Therapy:　　Yes
Supervision:　　　　　Ongoing
Counselling offered:　**General, Crisis, Long-term, Short-term, Psychotherapy**
Service for:　　　　　Individuals, Organisations
Theoretical Approach:　Analytical, Psychodynamic
Other languages:　　　Finnish
Fees:　　　　　　　　£18 - £25 sliding scale

MACKAY Mel, Mrs　　　　　　　　　　　　　　　　0223 62668
53 Hamilton Road, CAMBRIDGE CB4 1BP
Member of:　　　　　BAC
Quals/training:　　　　Dip Couns (Parkside Community College) 1982-7; RELATE Trained 1984-6; Marital Psychotherapy Cours (TIMS) 1990
Personal Therapy:　　Yes
Supervision:　　　　　Ongoing
Counselling offered:　**General**
Service for:　　　　　Individuals, Couples
Specific to:　　　　　Women
Theoretical Approach:　Rogerian, Psychodynamic
Fees:　　　　　　　　£20 - £25

DELL Jacqueline　　　　　　　　　　　　　　　　0223 262281
The Practise, 19 Hamilton Road, CAMBRIDGE CB4 1BP
Member of:　　　　　BAC
Quals/training:　　　　Dip in Couns, Midsummer Centre, Cambridge; trained psychotherapist
Personal Therapy:　　Ongoing
Supervision:　　　　　Ongoing
Counselling offered:　**General, Crisis, Psychotherapy**
Service for:　　　　　Individuals
Specific to:　　　　　Managers
Theoretical Approach:　Client-centred, Integrative
Fees:　　　　　　　　£22

Cambridgeshire

MILLAR Anthea 0223 314827
51 De Freville Avenue, CAMBRIDGE CB4 1HW
Member of: BAC Acc
Quals/training: BAC (Acc); Memb IIP; BA; Dip Adlerian Couns 1983; Licentiate of College of Speech and Language Therapists 1973
Personal Therapy: Ongoing
Supervision: Ongoing
Counselling offered: General, Stress, Crisis, Relationship, Bereavement
Service for: Individuals, Couples, Groups, Families
Theoretical Approach: Adlerian, Humanistic
Fees: £25 Negotiable

ROBINSON Lisa 0223 353268
27 De Freville Avenue, CAMBRIDGE CB4 1HW
Member of: BAC
Quals/training: Cert Couns (WPF Affiliate) 1987; CQSW 1984; + Numerous additional short courses 1985-1993:
Personal Therapy: Yes
Supervision: Ongoing
Counselling offered: General, Relationship, Crisis, Health, Loss, Midlife, Self-esteem
Service for: Individuals, Couples, Families
Theoretical Approach: Psychodynamic, Integrative
Other languages: French
Fees: £18 - £22 Individuals/Couples Negotiable

BULL Martin 0954 50791
22 Cow Lane, Rampton, CAMBRIDGE CB4 4QG
Member of: BAC
Quals/training: Dip SHAP; Practitioners (Hypnotherapy)
Personal Therapy: -
Supervision: Ongoing
Counselling offered: General, Hypnotherapy
Service for: Individuals, Couples
Theoretical Approach: Ericksonian
Fees: £25 - £35 sliding scale

MILLER Bonnie 0954 52527
327C High Street, Cottenham, CAMBRIDGE CB4 4TX
Member of: BAC
Quals/training: Dip Couns; training in TA and Drug, Alchohol & Relationship Dependence
Personal Therapy: Ongoing
Supervision: Ongoing
Counselling offered: General, Assertiveness, Bereavement, Phobias, Obsessions, Dependency, Eating disorders, Relationship, Self-esteem
Service for: Individuals, Couples, Groups, Organisations
Specific to: Women, People with disabilities
Theoretical Approach: Integrative, RET
Fees: £5 upwards, negotiable

Cambridgeshire

BATY Ted 0954 781180
The Rectory, 2 High Street, Longstanton, CAMBRIDGE CB4 5BP
Member of: BAC
Quals/training: 1961 Ordained; CTA authorized tutor; training in Bioenergetic Psychotherapy, Primal Intergration and Relaxation/Stress Management
Personal Therapy: Yes
Supervision: Ongoing
Counselling offered: **General, Psychotherapy, Primal therapy, Spiritual, Stress management**
Service for: Individuals, Couples, Families, Groups
Specific to: Religious
Theoretical Approach: Psychodynamic, Object relations, Bioenergetic, Gestalt
Fees: 25 individuals/couples(negotiable in cases of hardship)

GUEST Hazel 0223 69148
44 Beaufort Place, Thompsons Lane, CAMBRIDGE CB5 8AG
Member of: BAC Acc, AHPP
Quals/training: BAC Acc; AHPP Acc; Trained in Sequential Analysis by its originator Dr I N Marshall 1968-9; Dip Couns (CTP) 1980
Personal Therapy: Yes
Supervision: Ongoing
Counselling offered: **General, Psychotherapy, Relaxation**
Service for: Individuals, Groups
Theoretical Approach: Transpersonal
Fees: £26

HASLOP Rosemary 0223 64371
69 Stanley Road, CAMBRIDGE CB5 8LF
Member of: BAC
Quals/training: 4 year part-time course in Psychotherapy and Couns (Cambridge); OQOW
Personal Therapy: Yes
Supervision: Ongoing
Counselling offered: **General, Bereavement, Crisis, Short-term, Long-term**
Service for: Individuals
Theoretical Approach: Person-centred
Fees: £20

WEST John 0223 248018
6a Whitehill Close, CAMBRIDGE CB5 8NE
Member of: BAC
Quals/training: Hypnotherapy training 1981; Cert Couns (CSCT); Cert Ed; Dip FE
Personal Therapy: Yes
Supervision: Ongoing
Counselling offered: **General, Sport, Stop smoking, Stress, Hypnotherapy, Occupational, Problem solving**
Service for: Individuals
Fees: £32 (£16 initial consultation)

Cambridgeshire

LANGRAN Michael   0223 811007
35 High Street, Lode, CAMBRIDGE CB5 9EW
Member of: BAC Acc
Quals/training: BAC Acc; RMN; Cert Ed; trained Cambridgeshire Consultancy in Counselling 1980-82; Dip Couns
Personal Therapy: Yes
Supervision: Ongoing
Counselling offered: General
Service for: Individuals
Theoretical Approach: Rogerian, Psychodynamic
Fees: £10 - £15

PAIN Jean   0223 860356
7 Way Lane, Water Beach, CAMBRIDGE CB5 9NQ
Member of: NRHP
Quals/training: BA (Hons) Hispanic Studies; DHP (NC); Master Practitioner NLP, Reiki & Seichim therapist; NRHP(Assoc)
Personal Therapy: Yes
Supervision: No
Counselling offered: General, Psychotherapy, Depression, Anxiety, Creative potential, Learning difficulties
Service for: Individuals, Couples, Groups
Specific to: Actors, Artists, Writers
Theoretical Approach: NLP, Ericksonian, Reiki & Seichim healing
Other languages: Spanish, French
Fees: £30

NELSON Margaret   0353 662 659
37 Annesdale, ELY
Member of: BAC Acc, RCSPC, Member of UKCP Register
Quals/training: BAC Acc; Cert Couns; Adv Dip Existential Psychotherapy
Personal Therapy: Ongoing
Supervision: Ongoing
Counselling offered: General, Depression, Dependency, Trauma
Service for: Individuals, Couples, Groups
Specific to: Survivors of child abuse
Theoretical Approach: Existential
Fees: £25

NEWMAN Margaret   0480 461524
6 Fairfields Crescent, St Ives, HUNTINGDON PE17 4QH
Member of: BAC Acc
Quals/training: BAC Acc; Trained with Cambridge Consultancy in Counselling
Personal Therapy: Yes
Supervision: Ongoing
Counselling offered: General
Service for: Individuals, Couples
Theoretical Approach: Jungian
Fees: £10 - £18 dependent on income

Cambridgeshire

HOPKINS John 08323 388
Mill House, Old Weston, HUNTINGDON PE17 5LW
Member of: **BPS**
Quals/training: MA (Cambridge); PhD (London); Clinical Psychol; qualified Psychotherapist (LCP)
Personal Therapy: Ongoing
Supervision: No
Counselling offered: **General, Relationship, Work, Career**
Service for: Individuals
Other languages: French
Fees: £25 - £50 sliding scale

SCOTT Ann 0480 462589
3 Langley Way, Hemingford Grey, HUNTINGDON PE18 9DB
Member of: **BAC Acc, IPC**
Quals/training: BAC Acc; Dip Advanced Psychodynamic Couns (IPC/WPF)
Personal Therapy: Ongoing
Supervision: Ongoing
Counselling offered: **General, Bereavement, Relationship, Psychotherapy**
Service for: Individuals
Theoretical Approach: Jungian, Psychodynamic
Fees: £12 - £18 negotiable

SCHAVERIEN Joy 0780 720117
1 The Square, South Luffenham, OAKHAM LE15 8NS
Member of: **BAC, WMI**
Quals/training: PhD; MA; DFA (Lond); Reg Art Therapist, Psychotherapist
Personal Therapy: Yes
Supervision: Ongoing
Counselling offered: **Art therapy, Educational, Psychotherapy, Short-term, Long-term**
Service for: Individuals, Groups
Theoretical Approach: Analytical
Fees: £25

KILGOUR Mimi 0733 312900
332 Eastfield Road, PETERBOROUGH PE1 4RA
Member of: **ANLP (PCS)**
Quals/training: NLP/PCS Master Practitioner (PPD); Adv Dip Ericksonian Hypnotherapy (BHR); training in Gestalt Psychotherapy
Personal Therapy: Ongoing
Supervision: Ongoing
Counselling offered: **General, Psychotherapy**
Service for: Individuals, Couples, Organisations
Theoretical Approach: NLP, Ericksonian
Other languages: Farsee
Fees: £25 - £30

Cambridgeshire

BRADSHAW Norma　　　　　　　　　　　　　　0733 390607
92 Winyates, Orton Goldhay, PETERBOROUGH PE2 5RG
Member of: BAC Acc
Quals/training: BAC Acc; counsellor member of Cambridgeshire Consultancy in Counselling 1990
Personal Therapy: Yes
Supervision: Ongoing
Counselling offered: General, Marital, Bereavement, Pastoral
Service for: Individuals, Couples
Theoretical Approach: Psychodynamic
Fees: Negotiable

EVAN Rod　　　　　　　　　　　　　　　　　　0733 341539
11 Belle Vue, Stanground, PETERBOROUGH PE2 8RA
Member of: BAC
Quals/training: BEd (Hons); Cert Youth & Community Work; ITAA member
Personal Therapy: Ongoing
Supervision: Ongoing
Counselling offered: General
Service for: Individuals, Couples
Theoretical Approach: Eclectic
Fees: £8 - £15 sliding scale

PHILLIPS Leonard　　　　　　　　　　　　　　0733 349656
Thorpedene, 70 Thorpe Park Road, PETERBOROUGH PE3 6LJ
Member of: BAC, AHPP
Quals/training: BA Psychol 1982; Dip Humanistic Psychol 1983; Memb EATA, ITAA & AHPP(Assoc)
Personal Therapy: Ongoing
Supervision: Ongoing
Counselling offered: Marital, Sexual, Family, Drugs, Assertiveness
Service for: Individuals, Couples, Groups, Families
Theoretical Approach: Eclectic
Fees: £25 - £40 couples (VAT inc)

METCALF Pamela　　　　　　　　　　　　　　08326 302
The Old Black Horse, Tansor, Oundle, PETERBOROUGH PE8 5HS
Member of: BAC
Quals/training: Fully trained RELATE counsellor 1984; Gestalt Foundation 1991
Personal Therapy: Yes
Supervision: Ongoing
Counselling offered: General, Relationship, Sexual, Bereavement, Marital
Service for: Individuals, Couples
Theoretical Approach: Psychodynamic, Gestalt
Other languages: French
Fees: £20 negotiable

Cambridgeshire

Cheshire

Organisations

PSYCHOTHERAPY & COUNSELLING SERVICE　　061 428 9511 x 289
Counselling Service, 100 Wimslow Road, CHEADLE SK8 3DG
Service:	General Psychotherapy & Counselling Service for individuals, couples, groups. Also offer creative therapies - art and psychodrama
Area served:	North West England
Referral:	GP, Psychiatrist, Health/Soc Work Professional
Training of workers:	Diploma in Counselling, Psychotherapy and Psychodrama. Art therapy. BAC Acc, personal therapy
Code of Ethics:	BAC, BPA
Management by:	Consultant Psychotherapist (Cheadle Royal Hospital)
Fees:	£30; £15-20 group; £45 assessment

Individual Practitioners

*Each individual is a **member of** one or more organisations eligible for entry into this directory. BAC Accredited Counsellors and Recognised Supervisors are shaded.*

DAINTREE Jean　　061 928 9777
66 Ellesmere Road, ALTRINCHAM WA14 1JD
Member of:	BAC
Quals/training:	MA(Oxon) Modern Languages; Trained in Hypnotherapy & Psychotherapy (Blythe College) 1977; Memb NAHP & NCP
Personal Therapy:	Ongoing
Supervision:	Ongoing
Counselling offered:	General, Psychotherapy, Hypnotherapy
Service for:	Individuals, Couples
Theoretical Approach:	Rogerian, Gestalt
Other languages:	French
Fees:	£30 negotiable

MACKRODT Kathleen　　061 980 7589
49 Arthog Road, Hale, ALTRINCHAM WA15 0LU
Member of:	BASMT
Quals/training:	BSc; MB; Ch B; Cert Couns (Univ of S Manchester)
Personal Therapy:	Yes
Supervision:	Ongoing
Counselling offered:	General, Bereavement, Addiction, Stress management, Sexual, Marital, Rape
Service for:	Individuals, Couples, Families, Children
Specific to:	Women, Gays, Lesbians
Theoretical Approach:	Eclectic, Behavioural
Fees:	£40

Cheshire

BERMAN Linda　　　　　　　　　　　　　　　　　　　　061 904 0050
Altincham Priory Hospital, Rappax Road, Hale, ALTRINCHAM WA15 0NX
Member of:	ULDP, Member of UKCP Register
Quals/training:	BA(Hons) English; PG Dip Psychotherapy (Liverpool); RELATE Counsellor & Tutor; Cert in Art Therapy
Personal Therapy:	Yes
Supervision:	Ongoing
Counselling offered:	General, Psychotherapy, Marital, Art therapy, Phototherapy
Service for:	Individuals, Couples
Theoretical Approach:	Psychoanalytic
Fees:	£30 - £40 cpls, £40 assessment

KIRKLAND Jean-Pierre　　　　　　　　　　　　　　　　061 941 1162
Positive Attitudes, 43 Ashfield Road, ALTRINCHAM WA15 9QJ
Member of:	BAC
Quals/training:	BA (Hons) (London) 1965; PGCE (London) 1966; MEd Human Relations (Nottingham) 1988; Memb Inst of Training & Development
Personal Therapy:	Yes
Supervision:	Ongoing
Counselling offered:	General, Addiction, Crisis, Relationship, Stress, Psychotherapy
Service for:	Individuals, Families, Groups, Organisations
Specific to:	Men, Managers, Teachers, Lecturers
Theoretical Approach:	Rogerian, Gestalt, Ellis, Egan, Psychosynthesis
Other languages:	French, Italian
Fees:	£30

CLEMENTS Judith　　　　　　　　　　　　　　　　　　061 428 8529
11 Beech Avenue, Gatley, CHEADLE SK8 4LS
Member of:	BAC
Quals/training:	MA Psychol 1969; NMGC trained; Group Psychotherapy (IGA); Memb Psychology & Psychotherapy Assoc; hypnotherapy trained; Cert Psychodynamic Couns Supervision (WPF)
Personal Therapy:	Yes
Supervision:	Ongoing
Counselling offered:	General, Marital, Psychotherapy
Service for:	Individuals
Theoretical Approach:	Rogerian, Psychodynamic
Fees:	£25 sliding scale

PANTALL Marlis Mrs　　　　　　　　　　　　　　　　　061 485 5274
7 Balmoral Avenue, Cheadle Hulme, CHEADLE SK8 5EQ
Member of:	BAC
Quals/training:	Dip Couns; Cert Integrative Psychotherapy; CQSW; MA (Power in relationships and the mentally ill)
Personal Therapy:	Yes
Supervision:	Ongoing
Counselling offered:	General, Psychotherapy
Service for:	Individuals, Couples, Families
Theoretical Approach:	Psychodynamic
Other languages:	German
Fees:	£17.50 negotiable

Cheshire

KEOGH Kate   GPpractice 0244 390396, home 0244 376776
11a Lorne Street, CHESTER CH1 4AE
Member of: BAC, NRHP
Quals/training: Cert Ed; BA Soc Sci; Cert Couns; NRHP (Assoc); MA Couns
Personal Therapy: Yes
Supervision: Ongoing
Counselling offered: **General, Anxiety, Bereavement, Relationship**
Service for: Individuals, Couples, Families, Organisations, Groups
Theoretical Approach: Eclectic
Fees: £25 negotiable

BECK Carol   0244 881224
40 Timberfields Road, Saughall, CHESTER CH1 6AP
Member of: BAC
Quals/training: Adv Dip Coun (Wigan)
Personal Therapy: Yes
Supervision: Ongoing
Counselling offered: **General**
Service for: Individuals, Groups
Theoretical Approach: Person-centred
Fees: £20

FITTON Freda   0244 390411/348843
Upton Natural Health Clinic, 68 Heath Road, CHESTER CH2
Member of: BAC Acc, GPTI
Quals/training: BAC Acc; RELATE Trained; Cert Adv Clinical Psychodrama Therapy 1985; Dip (GPTI) 1990; Cert Psychodynamic Supervision (WPF); Assoc teaching memb GPTI
Personal Therapy: Ongoing
Supervision: Ongoing
Counselling offered: **General, Relationship, Sexual, Bereavement, Cancer, Adoption, Psychotherapy**
Service for: Individuals, Couples, Groups, Families, Organisations
Theoretical Approach: Rogerian, Gestalt
Fees: £22 negotiable

WHITTAM Enid   0244 380737
1 Dorfold Way, Upton-By-Chester, CHESTER CH2 1QS
Member of: BAC
Quals/training: MA Couns (Keele); Cert in Intermediate Couns Skills; ongoing Dip Psychotherapy
Personal Therapy: Yes
Supervision: Ongoing
Counselling offered: **General, Bereavement, Psychotherapy**
Service for: Individuals
Theoretical Approach: Eclectic, Integrative
Fees: £10 - £20 sliding scale

Cheshire

LEWIS Kenneth   0244 336744
7 Brown Heath Road, Waverton, CHESTER CH3 7PN
Member of: BAC, BPS, BABCP
Quals/training: BA Psychol 1983; Dip Youth Work 1968; Dip Guidance & Couns (Keele) 1976; MSc Occupational Psychol (London) 1992
Personal Therapy: No
Supervision: Ongoing
Counselling offered: General, Career, Life planning, Brief
Service for: Individuals, Organisations
Theoretical Approach: Cognitive, Behavioural
Fees: £30 (£20 first session), Orgs POA

RANDLE Rosalind   0244 620212
The Thatched Cottage, School Lane, Aldford, CHESTER CH3 6HY
Member of: BAC, BPS
Quals/training: BA; MSc; C Psychol
Personal Therapy: Ongoing
Supervision: Ongoing
Counselling offered: Brief, Occupational, Stress
Service for: Individuals, Couples, Families, Groups
Specific to: Disturbed children
Theoretical Approach: Humanistic
Fees: £20

FARRELL William   0244 679748
16 Salmon Leap, Handbridge, CHESTER CH4 7JJ
Member of: BAC Acc, BPS, ULDP
Quals/training: BAC Acc; BSc Psychology; CQSW; MSc Psychotherapy; C Psychol; Statement of Equivalence to BPS Diploma in Couns Psychol
Personal Therapy: Yes
Supervision: Ongoing
Counselling offered: Psychotherapy, Supervision, Consultation
Service for: Individuals, Families, Groups, Organisations
Theoretical Approach: Integrative
Fees: £27.50 inds; Orgs negotiable

KETCHELL Helen   0260 279146
5 Newcastle Road, CONGLETON CW12 4HN
Member of: BAC
Quals/training: BA(Hons); PGCE; Adv Dip Couns
Personal Therapy: Ongoing
Supervision: Ongoing
Counselling offered: General
Service for: Individuals
Theoretical Approach: Person-centred
Fees: £18

McCORMCK Helen   0270 256397
13 Lyceum Way, Coppenhall, CREWE CW1 3YF
Member of: WMIP,   Member of UKCP Register
Quals/training: SRN; RMN; adv training in Psychotherapy WMIP; Memb APP(NHS)
Personal Therapy: Yes
Supervision: Ongoing
Counselling offered: Psychotherapy
Service for: Individuals
Theoretical Approach: Analytical
Fees: Negotiable

Cheshire

HORROCKS Pam 0270 872479
The Rectory, Barthomley, CREWE CW2 5PE
Member of: BAC
Quals/training: CQSW (Manchester); MA Couns Studies (Keele); Adv Cert Psychodynamic Couns (Leicester) 1991-3
Personal Therapy: Ongoing
Supervision: Ongoing
Counselling offered: General, Bereavement, Crisis, Relationship, Psychotherapy, Supervision
Service for: Individuals, Couples, Families, Groups
Specific to: Students, Adolescents, Managers
Theoretical Approach: Person-centred, Psychodynamic
Fees: £20

BLAMPIED Annette 0782 751509
30 Wharf Terrace, Madeley Heath, CREWE CW3 9LP
Member of: BAC Acc
Quals/training: MA; B Phil (Couns)
Personal Therapy: Yes
Supervision: Ongoing
Counselling offered: General, Bereavement, Educational
Service for: Individuals
Specific to: Women, Young people
Theoretical Approach: Person-centred
Fees: £15 - £25 Sliding scale

BAKER Yvonne 0925 754118
2 Mayfield View, LYMM WA13 0LB
Member of: BAC
Quals/training: 1985 RELATE Trained
Personal Therapy: Yes
Supervision: Ongoing
Counselling offered: General, Marital, Bereavement, Sexual abuse
Service for: Individuals, Couples
Theoretical Approach: Psychodynamic, Eclectic
Fees: £22 negotiable

COPELAND Sue 0625 425969
1/2 Tower Hill Cottages, Rainow, MACCLESFIELD SK10 5TX
Member of: BAC
Quals/training: Dip Couns (Manchester Poly)'84; Primary Cert in RET'93
Personal Therapy: Yes
Supervision: Ongoing
Counselling offered: General
Service for: Individuals
Specific to: Young people
Theoretical Approach: Rogerian, Integrative
Fees: £15 - £20 according to income

Cheshire

MURRAY Chris　　　　　　　　　　　　　　　　　　　　0625 576181
4 Washpool Cottages, Washpool, Rainow, MACCLESFIELD SK10 5XG
Member of:	BAC Acc
Quals/training:	BAC Acc; 1979 CQSW; Training with ITA & IGA
Personal Therapy:	Ongoing
Supervision:	Ongoing
Counselling offered:	**General, Marital, Relationship, Bereavement, Psychotherapy**
Service for:	Individuals, Couples, Groups, Families
Specific to:	Men
Theoretical Approach:	Eclectic
Fees:	£25 negotiable (£35 families)

BROOKS Louise　　　　　　　　　　　　　　　　　　　0625 433620
10 Hallefield Crescent, MACCLESFIELD SK11 7BL
Member of:	TNS
Quals/training:	BSc(Hons) with Psychology Major; experience of crisis couns; LB Hammersmith & Fulham Experiential Group training; Dip Integrative Psychotherapy (Therapy North Staffs)
Personal Therapy:	Ongoing
Supervision:	Ongoing
Counselling offered:	**Psychotherapy**
Service for:	Individuals
Theoretical Approach:	Analytical, Integrative
Fees:	£6 - £25 sliding scale

LOMAX Carol　　　　　　　　　　　　　　　　　　　　0625 615690
105 High Street, MACCLESFIELD SK11 7QQ
Member of:	BAC Acc, BPS
Quals/training:	BAC (Acc); PhD, C Psychol
Personal Therapy:	Yes
Supervision:	Ongoing
Counselling offered:	**General**
Service for:	Individuals, Couples
Theoretical Approach:	CAT, Behavioural
Fees:	£25

BARKHAM (STURT) Alison　　　　　　　　　　　　　　0625 612720
66 Grasmere, MACCLESFIELD SK11 8PL
Member of:	BAC
Quals/training:	Dip Couns
Personal Therapy:	Yes
Supervision:	Ongoing
Counselling offered:	**General, Supervision**
Service for:	Individuals
Theoretical Approach:	Person-centred
Fees:	£20

Cheshire

REDGRAVE Kenneth 0606 74874
11 Parker Avenue, Hartford, NORTHWICH CW8 3AH
Member of: NRHP
Quals/training: BA Psychol (Durham)'50; Cert Couns & Casework (Liverpool)'56 Dip(Hons) Child Health (Royal Inst Public Health & Hygiene); DHP(NCHP)'89; Reg ICM; BRCP(Inst Compl Medicine)
Personal Therapy: Yes
Supervision: Ongoing
Counselling offered: General, Psychotherapy, Bulimia, Infertility, Anorexia
Service for: Individuals, Couples
Specific to: Survivors of child abuse
Theoretical Approach: Eclectic
Fees: £25

COPPENHALL Kate 0606 854035
1 Dutton Locks, Weaverham, NORTHWICH CW8 3QQ
Member of: BAC
Quals/training: RGN; RM; RHV; RELATE trained; training for Dip in Psychodrama(Holwell Centre); MA in Counselling Studies
Personal Therapy: Yes
Supervision: Ongoing
Counselling offered: General, Bereavement, Marital
Service for: Individuals, Couples, Groups
Specific to: Survivors of sex abuse, Bereavement
Theoretical Approach: Rogerian, Existential, Psychodynamic
Fees: £15 - £30 sliding scale

WRIGHT Marsha 061 973 9913
58 Grosvenor Road, SALE M33 1NW
Member of: BAC
Quals/training: Dip Couns(Manchester Poly); RELATE training completed 1991 RGN 1967
Personal Therapy: Yes
Supervision: Ongoing
Counselling offered: General, Depression, Bereavement, Relationship, Stress management, Sexual abuse
Service for: Individuals, Couples
Theoretical Approach: Person-centred, Psychodynamic
Fees: £25

BURNES David Ansafone 061 432 3792 (24 h)
373 Wellington Road North, Heaton Chapel, STOCKPORT SK4 5AQ
Member of: NRHP
Quals/training: CHP(NCHP); Dip SM (Inst of Stress Management)
Personal Therapy: No
Supervision: No
Counselling offered: General, Bereavement, Stress, Psychotherapy, Hypnotherapy, Phobias
Service for: Individuals, Couples, Families, Groups, Organisations
Theoretical Approach: Humanistic
Fees: £20 - £30 Sliding scale

Cheshire

ACKROYD Rosemary　　　　　　　　　　　　　　　　　　061 427 1568
Marple Bridge, STOCKPORT SK6
Member of:　　　　　　　BAC
Quals/training:　　　　　RELATE trained; TIMS course of Marital Interaction; a Psychodynamic view; AGSM/Teaching; Cert in Orientation & Mobility for the Blind
Personal Therapy:　　　Yes
Supervision:　　　　　　Ongoing
Counselling offered:　　**General, Relationship**
Service for:　　　　　　Individuals, Couples
Specific to:　　　　　　Visually impaired
Theoretical Approach:　Eclectic
Fees:　　　　　　　　　£20

LEWIS Jean　　　　　　　　　　　　　　　　　　　　　061 440 0580
Bramhall, STOCKPORT SK7
Member of:　　　　　　　BAC
Quals/training:　　　　　Teaching Dip; RELATE Trained; Memb IRTAC
Personal Therapy:　　　Yes
Supervision:　　　　　　Ongoing
Counselling offered:　　**General, Disability, Relationship**
Service for:　　　　　　Individuals, Couples, Groups
Specific to:　　　　　　Families of, People with disabilities
Theoretical Approach:　Eclectic
Fees:　　　　　　　　　Negotiable

DAVIES Vera　　　　　　　　　　　　　ansaphone 061 440 0634
10 Warton Close, Bramhall, STOCKPORT SK7 2NA
Member of:　　　　　　　BAC
Quals/training:　　　　　RELATE trained & accredited
Personal Therapy:　　　No
Supervision:　　　　　　Ongoing
Counselling offered:　　**General, Marital**
Service for:　　　　　　Individuals, Couples
Theoretical Approach:　Psychodynamic
Fees:　　　　　　　　　£18 negotiable

GAVIN Lorraine　　　　　　　　　　　　　　　　　　　0663 735354
12 Bingswood Avenue, Whaley Bridge, STOCKPORT SK12 7LX
Member of:　　　　　　　BAC Acc
Quals/training:　　　　　BAC(Acc); BA(Hons); PGCE; Dip Couns; Dip Gestalt Psychotherapy
Personal Therapy:　　　Ongoing
Supervision:　　　　　　Ongoing
Counselling offered:　　**Personal growth, Relationship, Self-esteem, Stress, Grief**
Service for:　　　　　　Individuals, Groups, Organisations
Theoretical Approach:　Person-centred, Gestalt
Fees:　　　　　　　　　£15 - £25 sliding scale

Cheshire

PIERCE Graham   0270 873159
65 Pikemere Road, Alsagar, STOKE-ON-TRENT ST7 2SN
Member of: BAC
Quals/training: Cert Ed; Cert Hypnotherapy & Couns (UK Training College)
Personal Therapy: Yes
Supervision: Ongoing
Counselling offered: **General, Bereavement, Hypnotherapy, Stress management**
Service for: Individuals
Theoretical Approach: Eclectic
Fees: £20

HORROCKS Mary   0270 877589
3 Bibby Street, Rode Heath, STOKE-ON-TRENT ST7 3RR
Member of: BAC
Quals/training: Cert Couns (Manchester Univ)
Personal Therapy: Yes
Supervision: Ongoing
Counselling offered: **General, Relationship, Bereavement**
Service for:I ndividuals, Couples
Theoretical Approach: Psychodynamic, Eclectic
Fees: £10 initial sess, then negotiable

WOOD Judith   0829 760211
Springwood, Fishpool Road, Cotebrook, TARPORLEY CW6 0JN
Member of: BAC
Quals/training: Cert Ed; BA(Hons) Psychol; MSc Couns & couple & family therapy
Personal Therapy: Ongoing
Supervision: Ongoing
Counselling offered: **General, Relationship, Bereavement, Addiction, Abuse, Psychotherapy**
Service for: Individuals, Couples, Families, Groups
Theoretical Approach: Rogerian, TA, Cognitive, Systemic, Family therapy
Fees: £25 - £30

MATTHEWS Frances   0829 52359
Treborth, 43 Old Coach Road, Kelsall, TARPORLEY CW6 0QX
Member of: NRHP, ANLP (PCS)
Quals/training: Dip Hypnosis & Psychotherapy NCHP; NLP Practitioner; SRN; RGN: Health Advisor in STDs; Cert of Teaching in FE
Personal Therapy: Yes
Supervision: Ongoing
Counselling offered: **General, Bereavement, AIDS, Rape, Relationship**
Service for: Individuals, Couples
Theoretical Approach: NLP, Cognitive, Hypnotherapy
Fees: £18 per hour

Cheshire

JAMES-GARDINER Christina   0829 261273
6 The Cottages, Calveley, TARPORLEY CW6 9JT
Member of:	BAC
Quals/training:	BA(Hons) Philosophy (Liverpool University); Psychotherapy/ Hypnotherapy (Blythe College) 1977 Currently: Cert in Counselling (Manchester University); MNACHP
Personal Therapy:	Yes
Supervision:	Ongoing
Counselling offered:	**General**
Service for:	Individuals, Couples
Theoretical Approach:	Integrative
Fees:	£15 - £30 negotiable

HOWE Kenneth   0625 523155
Springfield House, Newgate, WILMSLOW SK9 5LL
Member of:	BAC
Quals/training:	BSc; MSc; PhD; Tavistock Clinic (FDB); Dip Hypnotherapy & Psychotherapy 1983-4; College of Healing, Malvern 1984-6
Personal Therapy:	Yes
Supervision:	Ongoing
Counselling offered:	**General, Psychotherapy**
Service for:	Individuals, Couples
Theoretical Approach:	Eclectic
Fees:	£20 sliding scale

MCNAB Stewart   0925 601622, mobile 0850 676112
58 Parkland Close, Appleton Thorn, WARRINGTON WA4 4RH
Member of:	BAC, BPS
Quals/training:	BA; BA(Hons)(OU); Dip Social Work; Dip Psychotherapy; Cert Ed; currently undertaking PhD in Couns Studies (Keele)
Personal Therapy:	No
Supervision:	Ongoing
Counselling offered:	**General, Psychotherapy, Supervision**
Service for:	Individuals, Couples, Families, Groups
Theoretical Approach:	Integrative
Fees:	£30, £40 couples, £50 families, orgs POA

NORMIE Shirley   0625 525 916
10 Cumber Drive, WILMSLOW SK9 6DZ
Member of:	BAC
Quals/training:	CSW (Leeds Poly)'70; RELATE trained; currently training in sex therapy
Personal Therapy:	Yes
Supervision:	Ongoing
Counselling offered:	**General, Marital, Relationship, Sexual**
Service for:	Individuals, Couples
Theoretical Approach:	Eclectic, Psychodynamic
Fees:	£20

Cleveland

Organisations

STOCKTON PSYCHOTHERAPY TRAINING INSTITUTE   0642 611292
77 Acklam Road, STOCKTON-ON-TEES TS17 7BD

Service:	Psychotherapy service offered by qualified & experienced counsellors & psychotherapists. Group, individual & couple therapy
Area served:	Northern England
Other languages:	French, German
Referral:	Self
Training of workers:	Minimum 4 year training on ITAA recognised course
Code of Ethics:	BAC, ITA, UKCP
Management by:	C Lister-Ford & J McNamara
Fees:#16 - #35	

SOUTH WEST DURHAM HA, DISTRICT PSYCHOLOGY SERVICE
0740 20521 x 2707
Winterton Hospital, Sedgefield, STOCKTON-ON-TEES TS21 3EJ

Service:	Cognitive/behavioural therapy, counselling, psychodynamic therapy for individuals, couples, groups and families
Area served:	SW Durham Health Authority
Referral:	Health Practitioner
Training of workers:	Post graduate clinical psycholoogists and clinical nurse specialists
Code of Ethics:	BPS, UKCC
Management by:	SW Durham DHA
Fees:	None

Individual Practitioners

Each individual is a **member of** one or more organisations eligible for entry into this directory. BAC Accredited Counsellors and Recognised Supervisors are shaded.

COOPER Margaret   091 386 5818
2 The Manor Close, Shincliffe Village, DURHAM DH1 2NS

Member of:	NAAP
Quals/training:	MB; ChB; MRC Psychiatry; Dip Psychotherapy (Leeds)
Personal Therapy:	Yes
Supervision:	Ongoing
Counselling offered:	**Psychotherapy**
Service for:	Individuals, Couples
Theoretical Approach:	Dynamic, Analytical, Kleinian, Freudian
Fees:	£10 - £30

ARUNDALE Rita   0287 610232
52 Church Square, GUISBOROUGH TS14 6BX

Member of:	**BAC, ITA, STPTI**
Quals/training:	Dip Couns (Stockton PTI); RSA Cert Couns & Dip Groupwork Skills; in training as Transactional Analyst with clinical speciality
Personal Therapy:	Ongoing
Supervision:	Ongoing
Counselling offered:	**General**
Service for:	Individuals, Couples, Families
Theoretical Approach:	Rogerian, Humanistic
Fees:	£15 - £20

Cleveland

SHARP Linda 0287 633976
10 Glendale, GUISBOROUGH TS14 8JF
Member of: BAC
Quals/training: NMGC trained 1980
Personal Therapy: No
Supervision: Ongoing
Counselling offered: General, Marital
Service for: Individuals, Couples
Theoretical Approach: Client-centred, Developmental
Fees: £20

LEES Gordon 0429 232876
36 Ashgrove Avenue, HARTLEPOOL TS25 5BU
Member of: BAC
Quals/training: RGN; RMN; CPN; Cert Couns Skills (Durham); Adv Cert Couns Pract & Pers Dev (Durham)
Personal Therapy: Ongoing
Supervision: Ongoing
Counselling offered: General, Bereavement, Loss, Stress, Crisis, Anxiety, Depression
Service for: Individuals, Couples
Theoretical Approach: Egan, Rogerian
Other languages: Sign Language
Fees: Negotiable

MIDGLEY David 0642 821254
New Directions, 13 Barker Road, Linthorpe, MIDDLESBROUGH TS5 5EW
Member of: BAC Acc
Quals/training: BAC Acc; Certified Transactional Analyst 1987; Memb ITAA
Personal Therapy: Yes
Supervision: Ongoing
Counselling offered: General, Marital, Family, Psychotherapy, Stress, Depression, Personality disorders
Service for: Individuals, Couples, Groups
Theoretical Approach: TA, Gestalt
Fees: £25 (Initial £10; Gps £12)

MARSH Carol 0642 312676
Beechcroft, 87 The Grove, Marton, MIDDLESBROUGH TS7 8AN
Member of: BAC, ITA
Quals/training: Dip Humanistic Couns (Stockton PTI); 10 yrs in alcohol couns; currently in clinical training in TA and couples
Personal Therapy: Yes
Supervision: Ongoing
Counselling offered: General, Addiction, Psychotherapy
Service for: Individuals, Couples, Groups
Theoretical Approach: Humanistic, TA
Fees: £20 negotiable

Cleveland

CLARKE Christine   **0642 318740**
9 Larkspur Road, Marton Manor, Marton, MIDDLESBROUGH TS7 8RL
Member of: BAC Acc
Quals/training: BAC Acc; Adv Dip Prac Couns, Cert in Couns Supoervision, Cert Ed
Personal Therapy: Yes
Supervision: Ongoing
Counselling offered: **General, Sexual abuse, Relationship, Grief, Loss, Personal growth**
Service for: Individuals, Groups
Specific to: Women, People w learning difficulties
Theoretical Approach: Person-centred, Gestalt
Fees: £15 - £25 £3-10/hr groupwork

THACKER Rose   **0287 622947**
17 Leven Street, SALTBURN-BY-THE-SEA TS12 1JY
Member of: BAC, ITA
Quals/training: Dip Human Couns (Stockton PTI)
Personal Therapy: Yes
Supervision: Ongoing
Counselling offered: **General, Infertility**
Service for: Individuals, Couples, Groups
Specific to: Adoptees, Children
Theoretical Approach: Person-centred, TA
Fees: £20 - £25

McNAMARA Jennifer   **0642 611292**
Stockton PTI, 77 Acklam Road, Thornaby on Tees, STOCKTON-ON-TEES TS17 7BD
Member of: BAC, BPS
Quals/training: Provisional Teaching Memb Clinical Speciality ITAA 1988; BA Psychol; 8yrs Psychotherapy Training; Memb GAUK
Personal Therapy: Ongoing
Supervision: Ongoing
Counselling offered: General, Psychotherapy
Service for: Individuals, Couples, Families, Groups
Theoretical Approach: TA, Gestalt
Fees: £25 - £35 a few places at lower fee

ANDREWS Robert   **0642 781639**
6 Forest Lane, Kirklevington, YARM TS15 9LY
Member of: BAC
Quals/training: Dip Couns (Univ of Teeside)
Personal Therapy: Ongoing
Supervision: Ongoing
Counselling offered: **General**
Service for: Individuals, Couples
Theoretical Approach: Rogerian, Egan
Fees: £10 - £30 sliding scale

Cornwall

Individual Practitioners

Each individual is a **member of** one or more organisations eligible for entry into this directory. BAC Accredited Counsellors and Recognised Supervisors are shaded.

DAVY Antonia Sybil   028 883 363
Littermouth, Morwenstow, BUDE EX23 9ST
Member of:	BAC
Quals/training:	CQSW '74; Dip in Professional Studies in Couns
Personal Therapy:	Ongoing
Supervision:	Ongoing
Counselling offered:	General, Marital, Bereavement
Service for:	Individuals, Couples, Groups
Theoretical Approach:	Person-centred
Fees:	£20 - £25 negotiable

FRANSELLA Fay, Dr   0326 314871
The Sail Loft, Mulberry Quay, Market Strand, FALMOUTH TR11 3HD
Member of:	CPCP
Quals/training:	FBPsS; BA; PhD; Dip Psychol; Dip PCP Therapy & Counselling; C Psychol
Personal Therapy:	No
Supervision:	Ongoing
Counselling offered:	General, Psychotherapy, Weight
Service for:	Individuals, Organisations
Specific to:	Managers, People with language problems
Theoretical Approach:	PCP
Fees:	£35 minimum, negotiable

TREWHELLA John   0736 711548
Castle Gayer, Leys Lane, MARAZION TR17 0AQ
Member of:	BAC, BPS, NRHP
Quals/training:	MSc Ed Psychol; C Psychol; Dip (NCHP); Cert Psychodynamic Couns (LCIP); ICM Reg (Hypno); Dip Cognitive Psychotherapy; Cert Behavioural Therapy
Personal Therapy:	Yes
Supervision:	Ongoing
Counselling offered:	General, Vocational, Psychotherapy, Hypnotherapy
Service for:	Individuals, Couples, Families
Theoretical Approach:	Integrative, Cognitive
Fees:	£25

FRENCH Jeannie   0637 860435
The 12 Steps, Trenance, Mawgan Porth, NEWQUAY TR8 4BX
Member of:	ITA
Quals/training:	Training in Gestalt, TA, Psychodrama (metanoia) 1981-5; ongoing TA training
Personal Therapy:	Yes
Supervision:	Ongoing
Counselling offered:	General, Psychotherapy
Service for:	Individuals, Groups
Theoretical Approach:	Gestalt, TA, NLP
Fees:	£10 - £20 sliding scale

Cornwall

Cumbria

Individual Practitioners

*Each individual is a **member of** one or more organisations eligible for entry into this directory.*
BAC Accredited Counsellors and Recognised Supervisors are shaded.

CAMPBELL Colin　　　　　　　　　　　　　　　　　　　046 16 288
Carlisle Enterprise Centre, James Street, CARLISLE CA2 5BB
Member of:	**BAC Acc, ITA, NRHP**
Quals/training:	BAC(Acc); Cert Hypnotherapy & Psychotherapy; NRHP(Assoc); Transactional Analyst in clinical training; Cert Anatomy & Physiology; ITEC
Personal Therapy:	Ongoing
Supervision:	Ongoing
Counselling offered:	**General, Relationship, Psychotherapy, Massage**
Service for:	Individuals, Couples, Groups
Theoretical Approach:	TA, Gestalt, Rogerian, Ericksonian, Hypnotherapy
Fees:	£15 - £30 sliding scale

TYLLSEN Ken　　　　　　　　　　　　　　　　　　　05396 20952
Underknotts, Firbank, SEDBERGH LA10
Member of:	**BAC**
Quals/training:	Dip Adlerian Couns; Counsellor group facilitator
Personal Therapy:	Yes
Supervision:	Ongoing
Counselling offered:	**General, Bereavement, Relationship, Sexual**
Service for:	Individuals, Couples, Families, Groups
Theoretical Approach:	Adlerian
Fees:	£20 negotiable

ROE Peter　　　　　　　　　　　　　　　　　　　　05394 88833
2 Meadowcroft, Storrs Park, WINDERMERE LA23 3JG
Member of:	**BAC**
Quals/training:	Trained by Compass counsellors 1985-6
Personal Therapy:	Yes
Supervision:	Ongoing
Counselling offered:	**General**
Service for:	Individuals
Theoretical Approach:	Rogerian
Fees:	None(contributions to charity)

Cumbria

Derbyshire

Organisations

DERWENT RURAL COUNSELLING SERVICE 0629 812710
Newholme Hospital, Baslow Road, BAKEWELL DE4 1AD
Service:	Marital, relationship, bereavement & loss, personal difficulties, stress, anxiety & depression. Individuals, couples, groups and families
Area served:	NW Derbyshire (especially rural areas)
Referral:	Self, GP, Health/Soc Work Professional
Training of workers:	Dip in Guidance; RELATE trained. Regular supervision
Code of Ethics:	BAC
Management by:	Steering Committee of the DRCS
Fees:	None, but donations welcomed

DERBY AIDSLINE 0800 622738
c/o AIDS Liaison Unit, 27 Normanton Road, DERBY DE1 2GJ
Service:	Free, confidential information service about HIV/AIDS and related issues eg reducing at risk behaviour & details about testing. Phone helpline & Buddy service available
Area served:	Derby, Southern Derbyshire & SE Staffordshire
Referral:	Self or others
Training of workers:	Weekend or day sessions. Ongoing support/supervision
Code of Ethics:	BAC
Management by:	Southern Derbyshire HA
Fees:	None

DAPAS 0332 45537
1a College Place, DERBY DE1 3DY
Service:	General & addiction counselling for anyone with an alchohol problem, their families, friends and carers
Area served:	South Derbyshire DHA
Referral:	Self or others
Training of workers:	Various branches of counselling, psychology and psychotherapy
Code of Ethics:	BAC, ITA
Management by:	Counselling Services Manager & Director
Fees:	None

Individual Practitioners

*Each individual is a **member of** one or more organisations eligible for entry into this directory. BAC Accredited Counsellors and Recognised Supervisors are shaded.*

REDFERN Neil 0733 827 632
8 Birch Vale, Pinglewick Hamlet, BELPER DE5 1BR
Member of:	BAC
Quals/training:	Community & Youth Work; Dip Couns
Personal Therapy:	Yes
Supervision:	Ongoing
Counselling offered:	General, Depression, Phobias
Service for:	Individuals, Groups
Specific to:	Adolescents, Men, Teachers
Theoretical Approach:	Rogerian
Fees:	£15 - £25 sliding scale

Derbyshire

PURDY Meg 0773 827601
14 Field Lane, BELPER DE5 1DE
Member of: BAC
Quals/training: Cert Teaching; Dip Education Couns (Notts Univ); Derbs County Council Tutor Couns
Personal Therapy: Yes
Supervision: Ongoing
Counselling offered: General, Relationship, Bereavement, Depression
Service for: Individuals, Couples, Children
Theoretical Approach: Person-centred, Eclectic
Fees: £20 - £25 Sliding Scale

HIGHLEY John 0283 702054
Vine Cottage, Trent Lane, Newton Solney, BURTON-ON-TRENT DE15 0SF
Member of: BAC, SHPTI
Quals/training: In training for Dip Humanistic Couns; BSc Engineering 1966; MBA 1992
Personal Therapy: Ongoing
Supervision: Ongoing
Counselling offered: General, Consultation
Service for: Individuals
Specific to: Senior managers, Managers
Theoretical Approach: Rogerian
Fees: £10 - £30 negotiable

PRATT John 0246 569585
Edge O'Moor, Harewood Road, Holymoorside, CHESTERFIELD S42 7HT
Member of: BAC, BPS
Quals/training: BA(Hons) Psychol; MA Occupational Psychol; NMGC trained; Cert in supervision (WPF)
Personal Therapy: Yes
Supervision: Ongoing
Counselling offered: General, Relationship, Crisis, Bereavement
Service for: Individuals, Couples, Groups
Theoretical Approach: Rogerian, Eclectic
Fees: £20

ATKINSON Laura 0629 823760
32 St John St, Wirksworth, DERBY DE4 4DS
Member of: BAC
Quals/training: Cert Ed; Dip Drama Therapy; Gestalt Training Group, 6 years
Personal Therapy: Yes
Supervision: Ongoing
Counselling offered: Psychotherapy, Addiction, Abuse, Crisis, Depression, Loss, Relationship, Personal growth
Service for: Individuals, Couples, Groups
Theoretical Approach: Gestalt, Humanistic
Fees: £25

Derbyshire

PEARCE Mel 0602 303837
8 Burnham Close, West Hallam, Ilkeston, DERBY DE7 6LT
Member of: BAC
Quals/training: BPhil Couns & Hum Rel; Cert Ed
Personal Therapy: Yes
Supervision: Ongoing
Counselling offered: General, Career, Crisis, Relationship
Service for: Individuals, Couples, Organisations
Theoretical Approach: Person-centred, Eclectic
Fees: £20 - £30 sliding scale

HIGGINBOTHAM Maggie 0332 558704
392 Duffield Road, Darley Abbey, DERBY DE22 1ER
Member of: BASMT
Quals/training: RELATE trained
Personal Therapy: Yes
Supervision: Ongoing
Counselling offered: General, Relationship, Sexual, Bereavement
Service for: Individuals, Couples
Theoretical Approach: Psychodynamic, Behavioural
Fees: Negotiable

THORNHILL Daphne 0332 369385
Victoria Cottage, 61 Wheeldon Avenue, DERBY DE22 1HP
Member of: BAC
Quals/training: CQSW 1970
Personal Therapy: No
Supervision: Ongoing
Counselling offered: General, Relationship, Bereavement, Employment
Service for: Individuals, Couples
Fees: £25 negotiable

ALLISON Jo 0332 551343
JMA Counselling & Therapy Ser., 61 Cavendish Ave, Allestree, DERBY DE22 2AS
Member of: BASMT
Quals/training: Trained counsellor and sex therapist (RELATE)
Personal Therapy: Unknown
Supervision: Ongoing
Counselling offered: General, Marital, Sexual
Service for: Individuals, Couples
Theoretical Approach: Eclectic, Behavioural
Fees: £15 - £25 negotiable

GRAHAM Hilary ansaphone 0602 726151
25 George Road, West Bridgford, NOTTINGHAM NG2 7PT
Member of: NRHP
Quals/training: DHP(NCHP); Cert Past Life Therapy
Personal Therapy: Ongoing
Supervision: Ongoing
Counselling offered: General, Hypnotherapy, Psychotherapy, Regression therapy, Sexual abuse, Anxiety
Service for: Individuals, Couples, Organisations
Specific to: Women, Survivors of child abuse
Theoretical Approach: Eclectic
Fees: £22 negotiable

Derbyshire

WAITE Barbara ansaphone 0246 419868
Dronfield Healing & Therapy, 36 Westbank Close, Coal Aston, SHEFFIELD S18 6DE

Member of:	**BAC, NRHP**
Quals/training:	Cert Hypnotherapy & Psychotherapy (NCHP)
Personal Therapy:	Yes
Supervision:	Ongoing
Counselling offered:	**General, Crisis, ME, Hypnotherapy, Psychotherapy**
Service for:	Individuals, Couples, Groups, Organisations
Specific to:	Women, Students, Carers
Theoretical Approach:	Rogerian, Eclectic
Fees:	£10 - £25 sliding scale

Devon

Organisations

DEPT OF CLINICAL & COMMUNITY PSYCHOLOGY 0392 403171
Church Lane, Heavitree, EXETER EX2 5SH
Service:	Individual psychotherapy, group, family & behaviour therapy. Trauma counselling. For adults and children
Area served:	Exeter, East Devon
Referral:	Self, Health Practitioner
Training of workers:	MSc or Dip Clinical Psychology
Code of Ethics:	BPS, BABCP, AFT, PPA
Management by:	Director of Psychology Services - Dr C Williams. Exeter &District Community Health Service Trust
Fees:	None (NHS)

SEVEN TREES PSYCHOSEXUAL CLINIC 0752 260071/2
Baring Street, PLYMOUTH PL1
Service:	Psychosexual counselling
Area served:	Plymouth, East Cornwall, Mid Devon
Referral:	GP, Health Practitioner, Self
Training of workers:	Institute of Psychosexual Medicine
Code of Ethics	:IPM
Management by:	Plymouth Community Services NHS Trust
Fees:	None

DEVON PASTORAL COUNSELLORS
P O Box 5, TOTNES TQ9 6YB
Service:	General pastoral counselling offered by a network of counsellors based in South Devon. Associate member of WPF
Area served:	South Devon
Other languages:	German
Referral:	Self
Training of workers:	3 year training, regular supervision
Code of Ethics:	BAC
Management by:	Association of Devon Pastoral Counsellors & its committee
Fees:	According to means

Individual Practitioners

Each individual is a **member of** one or more organisations eligible for entry into this directory. BAC Accredited Counsellors and Recognised Supervisors are shaded.

TUNNICLIFFE Michael 0271 42565
11 Park Avenue, BARNSTAPLE EX31 2ET
Member of:	NRHP
Quals/training:	BSc(Econ) Sociology; PGCE (London Univ); CHP; NRHP(Assoc) (National College); Fellow Inst Chartered Secretaries; F Inst Mgt
Personal Therapy:	Yes
Supervision:	Ongoing
Counselling offered:	General, Bereavement, Crisis, Depression, Hypnotherapy, Phobias, Stress, Psychotherapy, Sexual
Service for:	Individuals, Couples, Groups, Organisations
Specific to:	Women, Managers
Theoretical Approach:	Behavioural, Freudian, Gestalt, Eclectic
Fees:	£20 - £30 Sliding scale

Devon

CARTER Ursula 0271 45910
Greenclose, 2 South Park, BARNSTAPLE EX32 9DX
Member of: BAC
Quals/training: BA Psychol '65; Dip Professional Couns Studies (Poly SW)'89
Personal Therapy: Ongoing
Supervision: Ongoing
Counselling offered: General, Psychotherapy
Service for: Individuals, Couples, Groups
Theoretical Approach: Gestalt, Psychodynamic, Person-centred
Fees: £10 - £20 negotiable

COWPER JOHNSON Dinah 0395 45309
2 Stoneborough Lane, BUDLEIGH SALTERTON EX9 6HL
Member of: BAC Acc
Quals/training: BAC Acc; BA(Open Univ); Dip Personnel Management (Aston Univ); Dip (CTP); Dip Hypnosis & Psychotherapy; Cert Reflexology
Personal Therapy: Ongoing
Supervision: Ongoing
Counselling offered: Personal growth, Relationship, Crisis, Bereavement, Mediation, Relaxation, Regression therapy
Service for: Individuals, Couples, Groups
Theoretical Approach: Transpersonal
Fees: £20 1 hr 30 min, reduced rates

KALISCH David 0395 68684
Kelmscot, 23 Fore Steet, Otterton, BUDLEIGH SALTERTON EX9 7HB
Member of: BAC, AHPP, Member of UKCP Register
Quals/training: AHP; Trained in Gestalt and Bioenergetics by Richard Dror; Dip CP (Karuna) 1992; AHPP Assoc; Memb AHP & AAPP
Personal Therapy: Ongoing
Supervision: Ongoing
Counselling offered: General, Relationship, Bereavement, Psychotherapy
Service for: Individuals, Couples, Groups
Theoretical Approach: Gestalt, Core Process Psychotherapy
Fees: £25 negotiable, £30 couples

CONYNGHAM Laura 0363 773000
26 Old Tiverton Road, CREDITON EX17 1EG
Member of: BAC
Quals/training: BA'72; Cert Ed'73; Dip Couns Skills(SW London College)'83-'6
Personal Therapy: Yes
Supervision: Ongoing
Counselling offered: General, Bereavement
Service for: Individuals, Groups
Theoretical Approach: Gestalt
Fees: £20 individuals; £30 groups

Devon

HUNT Ruth 0392 437417
7 Franklin Street, EXETER EX2 4HF
Member of:	BAC
Quals/training:	BSc (Hons); Cert in Couns; therapist in training, EATA
Personal Therapy:	Ongoing
Supervision:	Ongoing
Counselling offered:	General, Psychotherapy, Sexual, PTSD, Mental health, Violence, Abuse
Service for:	Individuals, Couples
Theoretical Approach:	Psychodynamic, TA, Gestalt
Fees:	£20 free half-hour assessment

KNOWLES Gwen 0392 215430
The Chalet, Trood Stables, Trood Lane, Matford, EXETER EX2 8XX
Member of:	BAC, GPTI
Quals/training:	Cert Couns (Exeter Univ); Dip Hypnotherapy & Psychotherapy; Adv Student Gestalt Psychotherapy (Bristol)
Personal Therapy:	Ongoing
Supervision:	Ongoing
Counselling offered:	General, Bereavement, Psychotherapy
Service for:	Individuals, Couples, Groups
Theoretical Approach:	Gestalt, Psychodynamic
Fees:	£24

WILLIAMS Christopher 0392 873579
The Old Vicarage, Holman Way, Topsham, EXETER EX3 0EN
Member of:	BPS, BABCP
Quals/training:	MSc Clinical Psychol; PhD; C Psychol; BPS (Fellow)
Personal Therapy:	No
Supervision:	Ongoing
Counselling offered:	PTSD, HIV, AIDS, Sexual, Disability
Service for:	Individuals, Couples
Specific to:	People with disabilities
Theoretical Approach:	Cognitive/Behavioural
Fees:	£30 - £40

LORD Anne 0392 438768
22 Plassey Close, Pennsylvania, EXETER EX4 5HE
Member of:	BAC
Quals/training:	BA; DipEd; Adv Dip Couns (Exeter); training in Family Therapy (Tavistock)
Personal Therapy:	No
Supervision:	Ongoing
Counselling offered:	General
Service for:	Individuals, Couples, Families
Theoretical Approach:	Rogerian, Psychodynamic
Fees:	£5 - £15 Sliding Scale

Devon

BOWDEN Mandy 0392 874151
45 Winslade Park Avenue, Clyst St Mary, EXETER EX5 1DB
Member of: BAC
Quals/training: Dip Therapeutic Couns
Personal Therapy: Yes
Supervision: Ongoing
Counselling offered: General
Service for: ndividuals
Theoretical Approach: Rogerian, Gestalt, Jungian
Fees: £15

GREEN Fiona 0803 866298
14c Fore Street, TOTNES TQ9 5DX
Member of: BAC, GPTI
Quals/training: Dip Couns(SW London College)'81; MSc(Cranfield)'81; Fellow College of Preceptors '87; Training in Gestalt(metanoia); training with London Marriage Guidance '91
Personal Therapy: Ongoing
Supervision: Ongoing
Counselling offered: General, Sexual, Relationship, Bereavement
Service for: Individuals, Couples, Groups
Theoretical Approach: Gestalt
Other languages: French
Fees: £25 - £45 sliding scale

KYRKE-SMITH Susan 0364 653362
3 Stapledon Lane, Ashburton, NEWTON ABBOT TQ13 7AE
Member of: BAC
Quals/training: Dip Couns (Keele) 1972
Personal Therapy: Yes
Supervision: Ongoing
Counselling offered: General, Relationship, Stress management
Service for: Individuals, Couples
Specific to: Young adults, Women
Theoretical Approach: Person-centred, Developmental
Other languages: French
Fees: £20 - £25

NICHOLLS Sylvie 0364 654149
37 East Street, Ashburton, NEWTON ABBOT
Member of: BAC
Quals/training: Dip A.Th; registered Art Therapist with BAAT
Personal Therapy: Ongoing
Supervision: Ongoing
Counselling offered: General, Eating disorders, Art therapy
Service for: Individuals, Groups
Specific to: Women, Children
Theoretical Approach: Eclectic
Fees: Negotiable

Devon

NEWTON Don 0837 53972
Holistic Therapy Centre, 1 Station Road, OKEHAMPTON EX20 1DY
Member of: BAC Acc
Quals/training: BAC Acc; Dip Hypnosis & Psychotherapy; Cert Couns (LCIP) 1982; Cert Couns (Exeter) 1987
Personal Therapy: Ongoing
Supervision: Ongoing
Counselling offered: General, Psychotherapy
Service for: Individuals, Couples
Specific to: Children
Theoretical Approach: Eclectic, Analytical
Fees: £18 reduced rate possible

TEMPLE Susannah 0404 812691
Finches, Lower Broad Oak, OTTERY ST. MARY EX11 1XH
Member of: BAC, ITA, MPTI
Quals/training: Advanced TA Psychotherapy trainee (Metanoia); PG Dip Couns & Guidance; PG Dip Adult & Community Education
Personal Therapy: Ongoing
Supervision: Ongoing
Counselling offered: General, Crisis, Conflict, Loss, Personal growth
Service for: Individuals, Couples, Families, Groups, Organisations
Specific to: Parents, Teachers, Children
Theoretical Approach: Humanistic, Integrative, TA
Other languages: French, German
Fees: £20 negotiable

LAURET Marti 0752 567048, 0752 661749
The Tower Room, Plymouth Clinic, 152 Mannamead Road, PLYMOUTH
Member of: BAC
Quals/training: BA (Social Work); CQSW; Dip Couns; training in Cognitive Analytical Therapy (Ryle)
Personal Therapy: Yes
Supervision: Ongoing
Counselling offered: General, Bereavement, Crisis, Eating disorders, Relationship, Supervision
Service for: Individuals, Couples, Families
Theoretical Approach: Rogerian, CAT
Fees: £15 - £22 sliding scale

LAWTON Margaret 0752 362504
355 Crownhill Road, West Park, PLYMOUTH PL5 2LL
Member of: BAC Acc
Quals/training: BAC Acc; NMGC Trained 1983; HV 1974; Cert Couns (Plymouth Poly) 1980; Memb Family Mediator Assoc 1991
Personal Therapy: Yes
Supervision: Ongoing
Counselling offered: Marital, Sexual, Personal growth
Service for: Individuals, Couples, Families
Theoretical Approach: Rogerian
Fees: £20

Devon

HUNT Kathleen 0395 516091
Fir Trees, Trow Hill, Sidford, SIDMOUTH EX10 0PW
Member of: BAC
Quals/training: BSc Social Science(London); Cert Couns(Middx Poly)'79; Cert Couns(LCIP)'80
Personal Therapy: Yes
Supervision: Ongoing
Counselling offered: General, Bereavement, Psychotherapy
Service for: Individuals, Couples, Families
Theoretical Approach: Analytical
Fees: £10 - £15 negotiable

DUNKLEY Gillian 0395 579 332
4 Barrington Mead, SIDMOUTH EX10 8QW
Member of: BAC, BPS
Quals/training: BSc; MSc Clinical Psychol; Training Family and Group Therapy; Dip Couns (Univ of London)1991
Personal Therapy: Yes
Supervision: Ongoing
Counselling offered: General, Marital, Psychosomatic, Sexual, Stress
Service for: Individuals, Couples, Families, Groups, Organisations
Specific to: Doctors, Nurses, Carers
Theoretical Approach: Analytical
Other languages: French
Fees: From £10, negotiable

KEENE Margy 0822 612957
Lower Walreddon Farm, TAVISTOCK PL19 9EQ
Member of: BAC
Quals/training: Cert Couns (Exeter Univ); Dip Couns (Plymouth Univ)
Personal Therapy: -
Supervision: Ongoing
Counselling offered: General, Bereavement, Crisis, Medical
Service for: Individuals, Couples
Theoretical Approach: Eclectic
Fees: £20 negotiable

TOUT William 0884 253820
13 The Walronds, TIVERTON EX16 5EA
Member of: BAC
Quals/training: RMN 1957; NHS Psychotherapy Training 1959; Hypnotherapy Training 1986
Personal Therapy: Ongoing
Supervision: Ongoing
Counselling offered: General, Marital, Bereavement, Addiction, Psychotherapy, Eating disorders, Mental health
Service for: Individuals, Couples, Families, Groups
Theoretical Approach: Rogerian
Fees: £12 negotiable dependent on income

Devon

HEWSON Julie 03985 379
Iron Mill, Oakford, TIVERTON EX16 9EN
Member of: BAC RSup, Member of UKCP Register
Quals/training: BAC Recognised Supervisor; BA(Hons); Cert Ed; Dip Social Work; CQSW; Certified Clinical Transactional Analyst; Provisional Trainer & Supervising member of EATA
Personal Therapy: Ongoing
Supervision: Ongoing
Counselling offered: General, Psychotherapy
Service for: Individuals, Groups
Theoretical Approach: Integrative, TA, Gestalt
Fees: £35 + VAT, negotiable

WARREN Steven 0803 329504
The Poplars, 88 Reddenhill Road, Babbacombe, TORQUAY TQ1 3RR
Member of: BAC Acc
Quals/training: BAC(Acc); BA(Hons); Cert Couns
Personal Therapy: Yes
Supervision: Ongoing
Counselling offered: General, Bereavement, Loss, Transition, Change, Divorce, Separation, Health, Stress management
Service for: Individuals, Couples, Groups, Organisations
Theoretical Approach: Analytical, Eclectic
Fees: £35 negotiable, groups on application

MOORE Jill 0803 614664
3 Marlowe Close, Shipway, TORQUAY
Member of: BASMT
Quals/training: Sex Therapy trained, NHS; Person-centred counselling training; RELATE trained; Astrological counselling training
Personal Therapy: Ongoing
Supervision: Ongoing
Counselling offered: General, Marital, Relationship, Sexual, Astrological
Service for: Individuals, Couples, Groups
Theoretical Approach: Eclectic, Integrative
Fees: £15 - £30

COOK Rose 0803 863015
4 Devon Place, Bridgetown, TOTNES TQ9 5AE
Member of: BAC
Quals/training: BA(Hons); PGCE; Dip Couns
Personal Therapy: Ongoing
Supervision: Ongoing
Counselling offered: General
Service for: Individuals, Couples, Families, Groups
Theoretical Approach: Rogerian, Psychodynamic
Fees: £15

Devon

LEVIEN Myra 0803 862584
Midway House, South Street, TOTNES TQ9 5DZ
Member of: BAC
Quals/training: RELATE(NMGC) Trained 1981; Cert Couns (Plymouth Poly) 1983; Sex Therapy Training (Exeter District Psychol Dept) 1984
Personal Therapy: Yes
Supervision: Ongoing
Counselling offered: Marital, Relationship, Bereavement, Psychotherapy
Service for: Individuals, Couples
Theoretical Approach: Psychodynamic, Systems
Fees: £25

OWEN Dave 0364 73343
Diptford Green Cottage, Diptford, TOTNES TQ9 7PA
Member of: BAC
Quals/training: BA; Dip Couns
Personal Therapy: Ongoing
Supervision: Ongoing
Counselling offered: General
Service for: Individuals, Couples
Theoretical Approach: Rogerian, Integrative
Fees: £18 - £24 sliding scale

SEYMOUR CLARK Vivienne 0364 73343
Diptford Green Cottage, Diptford, TOTNES TQ9 7PA
Member of: BAC, Camb SP
Quals/training: Dip Couns (Hatfield Poly) 1986; Memb Cambridge Society for Psychotherapy 1989
Personal Therapy: Yes
Supervision: Ongoing
Counselling offered: General, Marital, Psychotherapy, Supervision
Service for: Individuals, Couples
Theoretical Approach: Psychodynamic, Integrative
Fees: £20

Dorset

Organisations

EAST DORSET CLINICAL PSYCHOLOGY SERVICE 0202 735300
Branksome Clinic, Layton Road, Parkstone, POOLE BH12 2BJ
Service: Comprehensive psychological service for adults with wide range of developmental, emotional and behavioural problems
Area served: East Dorset Health Authority
Other languages: Cantonese, Dutch
Referral: Health Practitioner, Self
Training of workers: Post graduate clinical psychology training
Code of Ethics: BPS
Management by: Dorset Healthcare Trust
Fees: None

POST GREEN PASTORAL CENTRE 0202 622510
56 Dorchester Road, Lytchett Minster, POOLE BH16 6JE
Service: Individual & relationship counselling, short term resident ial breaks, spiritual counselling & direction
Area served: No restriction
Referral: Self or others
Training of workers: CTA trained including personal therapy. Regular supervision
Code of Ethics: Agency's own code
Management by: By the Directors
Fees: £17, Residential £35

SWANAGE COUNSELLING SERVICE 0929 424077
c/o Health Centre, Station Approach, SWANAGE BH19 1HB
Service: General & bereavement counselling and stress management
Area served: Swanage & Isle Purbeck
Referral: Self or others
Code of Ethics: BAC
Management by: Sponsored by Swanage Christian Centre
Fees: Donations

Individual Practitioners

*Each individual is a **member of** one or more organisations eligible for entry into this directory. BAC Accredited Counsellors and Recognised Supervisors are shaded.*

ROBINSON Martin 0258 817301, 081 459 5442
White Hill Farmhouse, Stoke Wake, BLANDFORD FORUM DT11 0HF
Member of: AJA
Quals/training: Qualified Analytical Psychologist
Personal Therapy: Yes
Supervision: Ongoing
Counselling offered: General, Bereavement, Crisis, Psychotherapy, Mental health
Service for: Individuals, Couples
Theoretical Approach: Eclectic, Jungian
Fees: £20 - £30 sliding scale

Dorset

QUINN Asher   **0258 459977**
Crown Cottage, 43 Lower Bryanston, BLANDFORD FORUM DT11 0LR
Member of: BAC, CCPE
Quals/training: BA(Hons) '77; Dip Couns & Psychotherapy '89, Dip Couns '92 & Advanced training in Psychotherapy (CCPE) ongoing
Personal Therapy: Ongoing
Supervision: Ongoing
Counselling offered: **Crisis, Relationship, Eating disorders, Incest, Abuse, Dream**
Service for: Individuals
Theoretical Approach: Transpersonal, Humanistic, Spiritual, Analytical
Fees: £23 - £30

ADAM Madeleine   **0258 480778**
BLANDFORD FORUM
Member of: LCP
Quals/training: MA, Oxon; Assoc Member, London Centre for Psychotherapy
Personal Therapy: Yes
Supervision: Ongoing
Counselling offered: **General, Psychotherapy**
Service for: Individuals
Theoretical Approach: Analytical
Fees: Negotiable

LOWSON Helen   **0202 396282**
Alberta House, Kings Park Drive, BOURNEMOUTH BH7 7AG
Member of: BAC
Quals/training: Dip Psychosynthesis Couns (IP); Art Teaching Degree 1961
Personal Therapy: Yes
Supervision: Ongoing
Counselling offered: **General, Relationship, Art therapy**
Service for: Individuals, Groups
Specific to: Women
Theoretical Approach: Psychosynthesis, Gestalt
Fees: £25 negotiable

HOLMES Elizabeth   **0202 515414, Fax 0202 518100**
Resurgence Counselling, Richmond Court Business Centre, Capstone Road Charminster, BOURNEMOUTH BH8 8AX
Member of: BAC
Quals/training: ENB Cert Couns Skills & Theory for Nurses(Birmingham); RGN
Personal Therapy: Yes
Supervision: Ongoing
Counselling offered: **General, Bereavement, Pet bereavement, Abuse, Medical, AIDS, HIV, Chronic illness, Terminal illness**
Service for: Individuals, Organisations
Specific to: Health care professionals, Gays
Theoretical Approach: Client-centred
Fees: £15 - £25 sliding scale

Dorset

SHELDRICK Linda 0202 516053
13 Stanfield Road, Winton, BOURNEMOUTH BH9 2NJ
Member of: BAC Acc
Quals/training: BAC Acc; RELATE trained; Memb Inst of Stress Management; MISMA
Personal Therapy: No
Supervision: Ongoing
Counselling offered: General, Relationship, Stress management, Conciliation, Redundancy, Bereavement
Service for: Individuals, Couples, Families, Groups, Organisations
Specific to: Business people
Theoretical Approach: Eclectic, Psychodynamic, Client-centred, Behavioural
Fees: £20 - £25 sliding scale

BERG Richard 0202 518968
108 Norton Road, Talbot Park, BOURNEMOUTH BH9 2QA
Member of: BAC
Quals/training: Cert in Couns WESBAC; Co-Counselling International teacher; Training in stress management; Memb ISMA; Fellow Inst of Chartered Accountants
Personal Therapy: Ongoing
Supervision: Ongoing
Counselling offered: General, Stress management
Service for: Individuals, Organisations
Theoretical Approach: Humanistic, Person-centred
Fees: £15 - £50 Sliding scale

JONES Mel Mrs 0308 24770
111 Victoria Grove, BRIDPORT DT6 3AE
Member of: BAC Acc
Quals/training: BAC Acc; BSc; PGCE; Ses DMP; WPF Cert; Training with LCIP 1985-7; IGA 1990; Assoc memb APP
Personal Therapy: Yes
Supervision: Ongoing
Counselling offered: General, Bereavement, Psychotherapy, Short-term, Long-term
Service for: Individuals
Theoretical Approach: Analytic, Jungian
Fees: £20 - £25

DEARDEN Padmini, Ms 0308 421 373
6 Sunnybank, BRIDPORT DT6 5EJ
Member of: BAC
Quals/training: Dip Psychological Counselling; Dip Humanistic Psychology
Personal Therapy: Yes
Supervision: Ongoing
Counselling offered: General, Relationship, Sexual abuse, Self-esteem
Service for: Individuals, Couples, Families, Groups
Theoretical Approach: Eclectic, Humanistic, Psychodynamic
Fees: £20 - £30

Dorset

PHILLIPS Laurie　　　　　　　　　　　　　　　　　　　0425 276417
11 Viking Way, Mudeford, CHRISTCHURCH BH23 4AQ
Member of: AGIP
Quals/training: AGIP trained '85-7
Personal Therapy: Ongoing
Supervision: Ongoing
Counselling offered: **Psychotherapy**
Service for: Individuals, Couples
Theoretical Approach: Analytic, Jungian
Fees: £20 - £30

COLEBY Nik　　　　　　　　　　　　　　　　　　　　0202 490065
10 Pauntley Road, Mudeford, CHRISTCHURCH BH23 3JY
Member of: BAC
Quals/training: BSc Communications Science & Linguistics; Couns training (metanoia); TA Therapy - 1 yr(metanoia)
Personal Therapy: Yes
Supervision: Ongoing
Counselling offered: **General, Relationship, Abuse, Crisis**
Service for: Individuals, Couples
Specific to: Women
Theoretical Approach: Rogerian, TA
Other languages: German
Fees: £15 - £25

HICKLING Sally　　　　　　　　　　　　　　　　　　0202 476939
Brinsons Farmhouse, Burton Green, Burton, CHRISTCHURCH BH23 7HJ
Member of: BAC
Quals/training: NMGC training
Personal Therapy: No
Supervision: Ongoing
Counselling offered: **General, Marital, Sexual, Bereavement, Crisis**
Service for: Individuals, Couples
Theoretical Approach: Eclectic
Fees: £20 lower fee negotiable

MARCH SMITH Rosie　　　　　　　　　　　　　　　　03005 385
Manor Cottage, Buckland Newton, DORCHESTER DT2 7BX
Member of: BCPC, AHPP
Quals/training: Dip Psychotherapy BCPC; Dip Humanistic Psychology IDHP
Personal Therapy: Ongoing
Supervision: Ongoing
Counselling offered: **General, Crisis, Bereavement, Psychotherapy**
Service for: Individuals
Theoretical Approach: Humanistic, Jungian, Gestalt, Transpersonal
Fees: £25 negotiable

Dorset

GARNER Janet 03004 460
The Old Malthouse, Smiths Lane, Piddletrenthide, DORCHESTER DT2 7RA
Member of: BAC Acc
Quals/training: BAC Acc; MA (Oxon); Dip Psychol Couns (Roehampton Inst) 1988 General Course in Groupwork (IGA) 1990
Personal Therapy: Yes
Supervision: Ongoing
Counselling offered: General, Psychotherapy
Service for: Individuals, Couples, Groups
Theoretical Approach: Psychodynamic
Fees: £25 Negotiable (Also Bournemouth)

BARNS Michael 0202 737600
7 Kingsbridge Road, Lower Parktone, POOLE BH14 8TL
Member of: BAC Acc, IPC
Quals/training: BAC Acc; RMN '67; CPN '87; 3yr Couns Course (WPF Affiliate) '84-87; Dip Advanced Psychodynamic Couns (WPF) 1989; Dip Supervision (WPF) '92; Human Sexuality Course '81
Personal Therapy: Yes
Supervision: Ongoing
Counselling offered: General, Psychotherapy, Supervision
Service for: Individuals
Theoretical Approach: Psychodynamic
Fees: £25 negotiable

ESKENAZI Irene 0202 723675
45 Caledon Road, Parkstone, POOLE BH14 9NL
Member of: BAC
Quals/training: BSc Sociology; CQSW; RELATE Trained; Cert Couns (CSCT)
Personal Therapy: Yes
Supervision: Ongoing
Counselling offered: General, Bereavement, Marital, Crisis
Service for: Individuals, Couples
Theoretical Approach: Eclectic, Client-centred
Other languages: French
Fees: £15 - £20 Sliding scale

SKINNER Alan 0202 604727
50 Honeysuckle Lane, Creekmoor, POOLE BH17 7YZ
Member of: BAC
Quals/training: BSc; MA Applied Social Studies 1977; PhD; NMGC trained
Personal Therapy: Yes
Supervision: Ongoing
Counselling offered: General, Relationship, Sexual, Intellectual cramp, Bulimia
Service for: Individuals, Couples
Theoretical Approach: Eclectic
Fees: None

Dorset

CLEAL Robin 0747 811315
Watchfield, Hartgrove, SHAFTESBURY SP7 0LB
Member of: BAC
Quals/training: Cert Personal Couns (Surrey Univ); Cruse; trained in Minnesota Model for treatment of addiction
Personal Therapy: No
Supervision: Ongoing
Counselling offered: **General, Bereavement**
Service for: Individuals
Theoretical Approach: Rogerian
Fees: £12 - £25

WILDASH Sheila 0929 553097
10 Fairway Drive, Northmoor Park, WAREHAM BH20 4SG
Member of: AGIP
Quals/training: Training with AGIP '87
Personal Therapy: Yes
Supervision: Ongoing
Counselling offered: **General, Psychotherapy**
Service for: Individuals
Theoretical Approach: Jungian, Eclectic
Fees: £20 negotiable

SPENCER Susan 0305 834744
1 Allen Cottages, Church Lane, Osmington, WEYMOUTH DT3 6EW
Member of: BAC
Quals/training: BA(Hons)Lit; Dip Couns; PCGE; training in TA
Personal Therapy: Yes
Supervision: Ongoing
Counselling offered: **General, Bereavement, Crisis**
Service for: Individuals
Specific to: Women
Theoretical Approach: Person-centred
Fees: £20 negotiable

NEWBERY Christopher 0305 786 172
12 St George's Ave, WEYMOUTH DT4 7TU
Member of: AHPP, BCPC, NRHP
Quals/training: BA Psychol; Dip in Humanistic & Integrative Psychotherapy; Dip Hypnotherapy & Psychotherapy; training in Primal Integration
Personal Therapy: Ongoing
Supervision: Ongoing
Counselling offered: **General, Primal therapy, Psychotherapy**
Service for: Individuals
Theoretical Approach: Eclectic, Client-centred, Integrative
Fees: £22

Durham

Organisations

DARLINGTON CLINICAL PSYCHOLOGY DEPT　　0325 743566
Memorial Hospital, Hollyhurst Road, DARLINGTON DL3 6HX
Service: All Clinical Psychology Services inc behavioural & cognitive therapy, psychotherapy & psychometrics
Area served: Darlington & Teesdale
Other languages: Dutch, French, German, Danish, Swedish, Norwegian
Referral: GP, Health/Soc Work Professional, Self
Training of workers: Postgraduate Clinical Psychology; some counsellors have RELATE training; supervision
Code of Ethics: BPS, BAC
Management by: Health Service Trust
Fees: None

Individual Practitioners

Each individual is a **member of** one or more organisations eligible for entry into this directory. BAC Accredited Counsellors and Recognised Supervisors are shaded.

BESTFORD Jan　　0833 690580
Jigsaw Counselling, 52 Galgate, BARNARD CASTLE DL12 8BH
Member of: BAC
Quals/training: MA Couns (Durham Univ) 1988; Memb BAPCA & Eating Disorders Assoc
Personal Therapy: Yes
Supervision: Ongoing
Counselling offered: General, Bereavement, Marital, Eating disorders, Sexuality
Service for: Individuals, Couples, Families, Groups
Specific to: Offenders
Theoretical Approach: Rogerian
Fees: £25 Sliding scale

RICKABY Susan　　0325 364115
23 Greenwell Street, DARLINGTON DL1 5DL
Member of: BAC
Quals/training: Dip Psychotherapy; 11 years counselling experience
Personal Therapy: Ongoing
Supervision: Ongoing
Counselling offered: General, Psychotherapy, Stress
Theoretical Approach: Eclectic
Fees: £20

Durham

ERRINGTON Richard 0325 380638
Andar House, 36A Blackwell Gate, DARLINGTON DL1 5HW
Member of: BAC, ANLP (PCS)
Quals/training: CMH; C Hyp; Master Practitioner NLP
Personal Therapy: No
Supervision: Ongoing
Counselling offered: **General, Bereavement, Psychotherapy, Hypnotherapy**
Service for: Individuals, Couples
Theoretical Approach: Eclectic, Integrative
Fees: £30

LOUDON Julia 0325 380100 x 3578
Dept of Clinical Psychology, Darlington Memorial Hospital, Hollyhurst Road, DARLINGTON DL3 6HX
Member of: BAC, BASMT
Quals/training: RELATE Trained; trained sex therapist, conciliator & in working with sexual offenders
Personal Therapy: No
Supervision: Ongoing
Counselling offered: **General, Sexual**
Service for: Individuals, Couples, Groups
Specific to: Survivors of sex abuse, Offenders
Theoretical Approach: Eclectic, Integrative
Fees: Negotiable

KNOWLES Christine 091 384 5772
26 Dindale Drive, Belmont, DURHAM DH1 2TS
Member of: BAC
Quals/training: MA Couns; BA; CQSW
Personal Therapy: No
Supervision: Ongoing
Counselling offered: **Crisis**
Service for: Individuals
Theoretical Approach: Client-centred
Fees: £15

JOHNSON Jannette 091 386 2540
18 Church Street, DURHAM DH1 3DQ
Member of: BAC, ITA
Quals/training: Dip Couns; BEd; Ongoing advanced TA training as a Transactional Analyst with Clinical Speciality
Personal Therapy: Ongoing
Supervision: Ongoing
Counselling offered: **General, Self-esteem, Relationship, Grief, Loss, Occupational, Stress**
Service for: Individuals, Groups
Theoretical Approach: Client-centred, TA
Fees: £15 Groups £8

Essex

Organisations

BENFLEET OPEN DOOR SERVICE   **0268 793025**
6 Mill Hill, BENFLEET SS7 1NJ
Service: Counselling service for personal and family problems
Area served: Mainly Essex & NE London
Referral: Self
Training of workers: One year part-time course plus in-service training. Regular supervision
Code of Ethics: BAC
Management by: Management committee
Fees: Donations

WRITTLE PASTORAL FOUNDATION   **0245 284890**
42 Cedar Avenue, CHELMSFORD CM1 2QH
Service: Counselling service for individuals and couples; a therapy group is also available. Affiliate of WPF
Area served: Chelmsford & surrounding district (30 mile radius)
Referral: NHS, Self or others
Training of workers: 2 year part-time introduction course in couns followed by 2 clinical training years, in-service training, WPF Cert of Competence
Code of Ethics: BAC
Management by: Executive Committee of Departmental Managers & Co-ordinators
Fees: Negotiable

ASHBROOK COUNSELLING SERVICE   **0245 462377**
56 Bouchers Mead, CHELMSFORD CM1 5PJ
Service: Individual, couple and family counselling for a wide range of problems including anxiety, phobias, depression, relationship and work-related difficulties
Area served: Essex, East London. Home visits can be arranged
Referral: Self, GP, Organisations
Training of workers: All are graduate or chartered members of BPS. Some have Couns qualifications, others occupational psychol
Code of Ethics: BPS
Management by: Members of consortium
Fees: £15 - £30 sliding scale

CHELMSFORD RAPE & SEXUAL ABUSE COUNSELLING CENTRE 0245 492123
PO Box 566, CHELMSFORD CM2 8YP
Service: 24 hour answerphone. Face to face service by appointment. Telephone counselling Tues & Fri 7.30-9.30pm
Area served: Mid Essex
Referral: Self
Training of workers: Volunteers have basic training and ongoing training. Face to face counsellors have professional supervision
Management by: Committee
Fees: None

Essex

COUNSELLING & PSYCHOTHERAPY SERVICES 0245 227010
8 Augustine Way, Bicknacre, CHELMSFORD CM3 4ET
Service: Personal, marital and family problems
Area served: Mainly Essex and N London
Referral: Self or others
Training of workers: Post graduate training in various areas of therapy
Code of Ethics: BAC, BPS
Management by: Director
Fees: £21 - £36

LAPIS FELLOWSHIP 0206 572205, Fax 0206 577132
The Trinity Centre, 12 Trinity Street, COLCHESTER CO1 1JN
Service: Individual and group therapy, self help groups, workshops.
Area served: Essex and East Anglia
Other languages: French
Referral: Self
Training of workers: All have relevant professional training
Code of Ethics: BAC
Management by: Board of Directors (Registered Charity)
Fees: £17 - £30 (£8 groups) reduced rates available.

STOCKWELL CENTRE PRACTICE (REG CHARITY) 0206 768211
44 East Stockwell Street, COLCHESTER CO1 1SR
Service: Individual, couple, family and group therapy by 12 therapists in a private practice, offering therapy for a wide range of problems
Area served: East Anglia
Referral: Self or others
Training of workers: Psychodynamic training with various national training institutions; ongoing supervision
Code of Ethics: BAC, Therapists' Professional body
Management by: Practice Committee
Fees: £17 - £25 (£35-£45 assessment)

BARKING, HAVERING & BRENTWOOD H.A. 0277 213241
CLINICAL PSYCHOLOGY SERVICES, Warley Hospital, BRENTWOOD CM14 5HQ
Service: For psychological problems - emotional, behavioural and relationship difficulties
Area served: Barking Havering and Brentwood
Referral: GP, Health Practitioner
Training of workers: Postgraduate Clinical Psychology
Code of Ethics: BPS
Management by: DHA
Fees: None

CARELINE Careline 081 514 1177
Cardinal Heenan Centre, 326-328 High Road, ILFORD IG1 1QP
Service: General & HIV/AIDS counselling for individuals of any age by telephone 10am-4pm & 7pm-9pm. Face to face counselling by appointment at the centre
Area served: The whole of Essex
Referral: Self
Training of workers: Counsellors undertake 10 session course; ongoing training sessions
Code of Ethics: Agency's own code
Management by: Careline Executive Committee
Fees: None

Essex

ROMFORD COUNSELLING SERVICE 0708 766211
The YMCA Roneo Corner, Rush Green Road, ROMFORD RM7 0PT
Service:	General counselling including bereavement, sexual abuse, problem drinking, for people experiencing difficulties in their relationships at home or at work
Area served:	Romford & District
Referral:	Self or others
Training of workers:	Qualifications in counselling; IPC/WPF personal therapy; regular supervision
Code of Ethics:	IPC
Management by:	Romford YMCA
Fees:	According to means

S.A.M.S. (SEXUAL ABUSE MUMS SUPPORT)
0702 435181/339673, 0268 729666
58 Queens Road, SOUTHEND-ON-SEA SS1 1PZ
Service:	Telephone support lines, one to one, groups. Drop in centres. Support for Mums of Sexually Abused Children
Area served:	S E Essex
Referral:	Self or others
Training of workers:	Training days, seminars and courses
Code of Ethics:	Agency's own code
Management by:	Full Executive Committee
Fees:	None

LEAS CENTRE FOR COUNSELLING & COMPLEMENTARY THERAPIES
0992 651171
33 Sun Street, WALTHAM ABBEY
Service:	Holistic counselling & psychotherapy (Gestalt, Psychosynthesis, Integrative). For personal, emotional & relationship difficulties - individuals, couples, groups
Area served:	W Essex, E Herts
Referral:	Self or others
Training of workers:	All have relevant professional training. Counsellors have personal therapy and ongoing supervision
Code of Ethics:	BAC, Varies with professional seen
Management by:	Partners
Fees:	£15 - £35 Sliding scale

Individual Practitioners
*Each individual is a **member of** one or more organisations eligible for entry into this directory. BAC Accredited Counsellors and Recognised Supervisors are shaded.*

MIDDLETON Suzanne 0268 754150
5 Granville Close, BENFLEET SS7 1HR
Member of:	BAC Acc
Quals/training:	BAC Acc; BA(Hons); HE Dip Couns; Memb BAPCA
Personal Therapy:	Ongoing
Supervision:	Ongoing
Counselling offered:	General, Abuse, Bereavement, Crisis, Depression, Marital, Psychotherapy
Service for:	Individuals, Couples, Groups
Theoretical Approach:	Client-centred
Fees:	£15 - £25

Essex

BRANKIN Irene 0702 555420
14 Lynton Road, Hadleigh, BENFLEET SS7 2QQ
Member of: BAC, BPS
Quals/training: BSc(Hons) Psychol; MSc Couns Psychol; Dip Psychosynthesis Psychosynthesis Counselling (PET)
Personal Therapy: Yes
Supervision: Ongoing
Counselling offered: General, Personal growth
Service for: Individuals, Groups
Theoretical Approach: Psychosynthesis
Fees: £30

ROBSON Ian 0702 555185
58 Arcadian Gardens, Hadleigh, BENFLEET SS7 2RP
Member of: NRHP
Quals/training: RELATE; Ass Mem NRHP; BA Sociology (Liverpool Univ); Dip Ed (London Univ); PGCE (Sussex Univ)
Personal Therapy: No
Supervision: Ongoing
Counselling offered: General, Depression, Eating disorders, Hypnotherapy, Psychotherapy, Relationship
Service for: Individuals, Couples
Theoretical Approach: Eclectic
Fees: £25

ANDERSON Julie 0371 810983
Blackbirds, Little Bardfield, BRAINTREE CM7 4TU
Member of: BAC, AFT
Quals/training: BSc; Dip Social Work; Dip in Hypnotherapy & Counselling; Training in Family Therapy
Personal Therapy: Ongoing
Supervision: Ongoing
Counselling offered: General, Psychotherapy, Hypnotherapy, Relationship, Sexual abuse
Service for: Individuals, Couples, Groups, Families
Specific to: Helping professions, Survivors of sex abuse, Gays, Lesbians
Theoretical Approach: Humanistic
Fees: £18 - £25

CONYERS Maria 0277 232585
Crushes Manor House, 247 Rayleigh Road, Hutton, BRENTWOOD CM13 1PJ
Member of: BAC Acc
Quals/training: BAC Acc; BSc; CQSW; Jungian Psychoanalytic Psychotherapist (LCP)
Personal Therapy: Ongoing
Supervision: Ongoing
Counselling offered: General, Bereavement, Marital, AIDS
Service for: Individuals, Couples, Families
Specific to: People with disabilities, Gays
Fees: £15 - £30

Essex

GOUGH Cathy 0227 264518
99 Weald Road, BRENTWOOD CM14 4TP
Member of: BAC Acc, BPS
Quals/training: BAC Acc; C Psychol; MSc Couns Psychol
Personal Therapy: Ongoing
Supervision: Ongoing
Counselling offered: General, Sexual abuse, Rape
Service for: Individuals
Specific to: Women, Adolescents
Theoretical Approach: Eclectic, Psychodynamic
Fees: Negotiable

PAVEY Rosemary 0277 822377
Rowan, Hook End Road, Hook End, BRENTWOOD CM15 0HB
Member of: BAC, BPS
Quals/training: BSC Psych; Cert Couns (WPF)
Personal Therapy: Yes
Supervision: Ongoing
Counselling offered: General
Service for: ndividuals, Couples, Families
Fees: £25

KWEI Daniel 0277 226834
6 Brentwood Place, Sawyers Hall Lane, BRENTWOOD CM15 9DH
Member of: BAC Acc, GPTI, MPTI
Quals/training: BAC Acc; Dip (GPTI); Cert (BHR)
Personal Therapy: Ongoing
Supervision: Ongoing
Counselling offered: General, Psychotherapy
Service for: Individuals, Couples, Families, Groups
Specific to: Adolescents, Asian, Black people
Theoretical Approach: Gestalt
Fees: £35

CLOWES Brenda 081 505 8328
176 Princes Road, BUCKHURST HILL IG9 5DJ
Member of: BAC RSup
Quals/training: RELATE trained; counsellor and tutor
Personal Therapy: Yes
Supervision: Yes
Counselling offered: General, Relationship
Service for: Individuals, Couples
Theoretical Approach: Psychodynamic, Person-centred
Fees: £25 - £35

Essex

CLARK Margaret 081 504 6128
64d Russell Road, BUCKHURST HILL IG9 5QE
Member of: LCP
Quals/training: Dip Couns (Middx Poly); Psychoanalytic Psychotherapist LCP
Personal Therapy: Yes
Supervision: Ongoing
Counselling offered: Psychotherapy, Marital
Service for: Individuals, Couples
Fees: £20 sliding scale

HOLLOWAY Roberta 0268 680826
CANVEY ISLAND SS8
Member of: BAC Acc
Quals/training: BAC(Acc); RMN; Dip Couns Skills '84
Personal Therapy: Yes
Supervision: Ongoing
Counselling offered: General, Rape, Marital, Identity crisis, Bereavement, Alcohol
Service for: Individuals, Couples, Groups
Theoretical Approach: TA, Humanistic, Egan
Fees: £20 negotiable

HUGGINS Alan 0268 682664
3 Juliers Close, CANVEY ISLAND SS8 7EP
Member of: BAC
Quals/training: Cert Skills & Theory; Cert Self Awareness & Theory; training in Gestalt/Rogerian
Personal Therapy: Ongoing
Supervision: Ongoing
Counselling offered: General, Family, Marital, Sexual
Service for: Individuals, Couples, Families
Theoretical Approach: Rogerian
Fees: None

PRABATANI Kala 0245 494730
15 Darrell Close, CHELMSFORD CM1 4EL
Member of: BAC
Quals/training: CQSW; Trained Counsellor (Writtle Pastoral Foundation); Cert in Parks Inner Child Therapy
Personal Therapy: Yes
Supervision: Ongoing
Counselling offered: General, Bereavement, Sexual abuse, Eating disorders, Stress, Depression
Service for: Individuals
Specific to: Women, Young adults
Theoretical Approach: Psychodynamic, Cognitive, Analytic
Fees: £25 - £30

Essex

BROOKS Gill
56 Bouchers Mead, CHELMSFORD CM1 5PJ   **0245 450075**
Member of: BAC, BPS
Quals/training: BSc(Hons) Psychol; Combined Cert Couns (CSCT)
Personal Therapy: Yes
Supervision: Ongoing
Counselling offered: General, Relationship, Bereavement, Psychotherapy
Service for: Individuals
Theoretical Approach: Psychodynamic
Fees: £20 Negotiable

BROOKS Bernard
56 Bouchers Mead, CHELMSFORD CM1 5PJ   **0245 450075**
Member of: BAC, BPS
Quals/training: BSc(Hons) Psychol; Dip Psych (London Univ); C Psychol; Practitioner Memb BPS Counselling Section
Personal Therapy: Yes
Supervision: Ongoing
Counselling offered: Relationship, Short-term, Psychotherapy, Career, Educational
Service for: Individuals, Couples
Theoretical Approach: Psychodynamic, Cognitive
Other languages: French
Fees: £18 - £25 negotiable

JONES Veronica
83 Hillside Grove, CHELMSFORD CM2 9DB   **0245 355476**
Member of: BAC, BPS
Quals/training: BA Psychol; MSc Couns & Guidance (Indiana Univ, USA); Dip Cog Psych (Goldsmiths')
Personal Therapy: Ongoing
Supervision: Ongoing
Counselling offered: General, Relationship, Addiction, Eating disorders, Supervision
Service for: Individuals, Couples, Families
Specific to: Women
Theoretical Approach: Eclectic, Cognitive
Fees: Negotiable

SCOTCHMAN Susan
Brickfields Surgery, Brickfields Road, SOUTH WOODHAM FERRERS CM3 5JX   **0245 328855**
Member of: BAC, BPS
Quals/training: C Psychol; BSc(Hons) Psychol (London) 1981; Cert Adv Marriage & Family Therapy (USA)
Personal Therapy: Yes
Supervision: Ongoing
Counselling offered: Relationship, Family, Health, Disability
Service for: Individuals, Couples, Groups, Families
Theoretical Approach: Systemic, Cognitive
Fees: £20 - £35 sliding scale

Essex

MELBOURNE Benita   081 500 7271
CHIGWELL IG7
Member of: BAC
Quals/training: Post Grad Dip Guidance & Couns CNAA 1987; RELATE (NMGC); Adv Group Therapy (IGA/RELATE); on-going training; GAS Assoc
Personal Therapy: Yes
Supervision: Ongoing
Counselling offered: **General, Assertiveness, Short-term, Relationship**
Service for: Individuals, Couples, Groups
Specific to: Staff, Senior managers, Work teams
Theoretical Approach: Integrative
Fees: £30

WILLCOCK Pamela   081 500 9885
7 Dickens Rise, CHIGWELL IG7 6PA
Member of: BAC
Quals/training: CQSW; Dip Couns (CAC); Cert in Transpersonal skills in Couns
Personal Therapy: Yes
Supervision: Ongoing
Counselling offered: **General, Bereavement, Relationship, AIDS**
Service for: Individuals, Couples, Families, Groups
Theoretical Approach: Humanistic, Transpersonal
Fees: £18 - £30

MANSFIELD Jacqui   0255 436059
6 St John's Road, Great Clacton, CLACTON-ON-SEA CO15 4BP
Member of: BAC
Quals/training: Dip Professional Studies in Couns (Colchester Inst)
Personal Therapy: Yes
Supervision: Ongoing
Counselling offered: **General, Personal growth, Graphological**
Service for: Individuals, Couples, Families, Groups, Organisations
Theoretical Approach: Humanistic
Fees: £18 Minimum

BRIND William   0621 783664, 0206 863843
Oyster House, 9 East Hill, COLCHESTER CO1 2QZ
Member of: BAC, BASMT
Quals/training: Dip Human Sexuality; RMN; SEN(G)
Personal Therapy: Ongoing
Supervision: Ongoing
Counselling offered: **Relationship, Sexual dysfunction, Identity crisis, Sexual deviation, Phobias**
Service for: Individuals, Couples
Theoretical Approach: Psychodynamic, Behavioural
Fees: Negotiable

Essex

RANDALL Sebastian 0206 765303
42 Castle Road, COLCHESTER CO1 1UN
Member of: BAC
Quals/training: BA Psychol; Dip Couns; Memb BAPCA
Personal Therapy: Yes
Supervision: Ongoing
Counselling offered: **General, Short-term, Long-term, Psychotherapy**
Service for: Individuals, Couples, Families, Groups
Theoretical Approach: Integrative
Fees: £15 - £30

SALMON Cindy 0206 573721
Friars Cottages, 68/69 Castle Road, COLCHESTER CO1 1UN
Member of: BAC Acc
Quals/training: BAC Acc; BA (Hons) Sociology; Dip in Person Centred Couns; Cert in Transpersonal Couns
Personal Therapy: Yes
Supervision: Ongoing
Counselling offered: **General, Bereavement, Sexual abuse, Stress, Cancer**
Service for: Individuals, Families
Theoretical Approach: Person-centred, Transpersonal
Fees: £18

TIMS Patricia 0206 348134
29 Greenacrs Road, Layer-De-La-Haye, COLCHESTER CO2 0JP
Member of: BAC
Quals/training: Dip Professional Studies (Person-centred couns)
Personal Therapy: Ongoing
Supervision: Ongoing
Counselling offered: **General, Bereavement, Crisis, HIV**
Service for: Individuals
Specific to: People with disabilities, Carers
Theoretical Approach: Rogerian
Fees: Negotiable

GREGORY Heather
76 Keeler's Way, Great Horkesley, COLCHESTER CO6 4EF
Member of: BAC
Quals/training: Dip Prof Studies (Couns)
Personal Therapy: Ongoing
Supervision: Ongoing
Counselling offered: **General, Bereavement, Sexual abuse**
Service for: Individuals, Couples
Theoretical Approach: Rogerian
Fees: £20

Essex

FABIAN Carole   0206 761660 x 27110, 0206 41499
21 St Albans Road, COLCHESTER
Member of: BAC Acc
Quals/training: BAC Acc; Cert Student Couns (London Univ) '84-86; advanced course in Couns Practice (London Univ) '86-87; intro course (IGA) '91-92; Psychotherapy train'g from Sep 1993
Personal Therapy: Ongoing
Supervision: Ongoing
Counselling offered: **General, Psychotherapy, Relationship**
Service for: Individuals
Theoretical Approach: Psychodynamic, Eclectic
Fees: £20 - £25

ROBERTSON L Hattie   0992 574881
30 Hartland Road, EPPING CM16 4PE
Member of: BAC Acc, BPS
Quals/training: BA; BSc Psychol; Dip COT; Dip Couns 1983; 3 yrs PCP and short courses in TA, NLP, Hypnosis, Sexual Problems, Disabled
Personal Therapy: Yes
Supervision: Ongoing
Counselling offered: **General, Bereavement, Migraine, Disability**
Service for: Individuals
Theoretical Approach: TA, PCP
Fees: £25

BULLER Jemima   0992 573937
43 Thornwood Road, EPPING CM16 6SY
Member of: BAC
Quals/training: Currently engaged in 3 year Dip Course (Inst for Person-Centred Learning); also studying for Dip Psychol; Memb BAPCA
Personal Therapy: Yes
Supervision: Ongoing
Counselling offered: **Mental health, Eating disorders, Stress, Occupational, Relationship, Work**
Service for: Individuals, Couples, Organisations
Theoretical Approach: Client-centred
Fees: £15 Negotiable. 1st session free

CHAPMAN Maureen   09925 78723
The Rectory, Theydon Mount, EPPING CM16 7PW
Member of: IPC
Quals/training: Full Member of IPC/WPF '89
Personal Therapy: Ongoing
Supervision: Ongoing
Counselling offered: **General, Psychotherapy**
Service for: Individuals, Couples
Theoretical Approach: Jungian
Fees: £20 - £30 sliding scale

Essex

SHRIMPTON David   0787 269594
Oakleigh, Church Road, Wickham St Paul, HALSTEAD CO9 2PN
Member of: BAC, WMIP
Quals/training: Psychodynamic Psychotherapy '77-'78 & Clinical Psychodrama '78-'82(Uffculme Clinic, Birmingham Univ)
Personal Therapy: Yes
Supervision: Ongoing
Counselling offered: General, Crisis, Marital, Sexual abuse, Psychotherapy
Service for: Individuals, Couples, Families, Groups
Theoretical Approach: Rogerian, Eclectic
Fees: £20 negotiable

MILLS David   0787 60662
6 St James Street, Castle Hedingham, HALSTEAD CO9 3EL
Member of: BAC Acc, BPS
Quals/training: BAC Acc; MA Oxon 1965; BSc Psychol (NE London Ploy) '88; Dip Couns & Guidance (Poly of E London)
Personal Therapy: Yes
Supervision: Ongoing
Counselling offered: General, Marital, Divorce, Bereavement, Depression, Anxiety, Brief
Service for: Individuals
Theoretical Approach: Cognitive, Analytical
Fees: £15 - £25

UPCHURCH Ms Terry   0787 237184
Tolladine House, Bridge Street, Great Yeldham, HALSTEAD CO9 4HU
Member of: BAC
Quals/training: Dip Prof Studies; Humanistic Person-Centred Couns Course;
Personal Therapy: Ongoing
Supervision: Ongoing
Counselling offered: General, ME, Retirement
Service for: Individuals, Couples
Theoretical Approach: Rogerian
Fees: Negotiable

NEWBOLD Linda M   0787 237 612
4 Little Hyde Close, Great Yeldham, HALSTEAD CO9 4JE
Member of: BAC
Quals/training: BA; Co-counselling teacher training; Mind clearing training
Personal Therapy: Ongoing
Supervision: Ongoing
Counselling offered: General, Weight, Parenting problems
Service for: Individuals, Couples, Groups
Theoretical Approach: Mind clearing, Humanistic, Holistic
Fees: £25 groups by arrangement

Essex

GRANT Yvonne Shirley 0279 424725
13 Westfield, HARLOW CM18 6AB
Member of: BAC
Quals/training: RGN; RMN; Dip Couns
Personal Therapy: No
Supervision: Ongoing
Counselling offered: General, Abuse
Service for: Individuals, Couples
Theoretical Approach: Psychodynamic
Fees: £15 - £25 sliding scale

MAYHEW David 0279 437335
273 Fold Croft, HARLOW CM20 1SR
Member of: BAC
Quals/training: BA (Oxon); Dip in Social Science; Dip in Psychosynthesis Couns, IP 1988
Personal Therapy: Ongoing
Supervision: Ongoing
Counselling offered: General, Abuse, Bereavement, Relationship, Personal growth
Service for: Individuals, Groups
Theoretical Approach: Psychosynthesis, Psychodynamic, Gestalt
Fees: £25 - £40 sliding scale

LOMOND Marsha 0279 413716
97 Ladyshot, HARLOW CM20 3EW
Member of: BAC, ITA, MPTI
Quals/training: Dip Person-centred Couns (metanoia); RSA Cert Couns Skills; currently training in TA (metanoia)
Personal Therapy: Ongoing
Supervision: Ongoing
Counselling offered: General
Service for: Individuals
Specific to: Women
Theoretical Approach: Person-centred, TA
Fees: £10 - £20 sliding scale Dialysis support

BRIGGS Margarete 0279 423093
11 Home Close, HARLOW CM20 3PD
Member of: BAC
Quals/training: Dip Student Couns; ASC Acc; Working with Couples 1 year course (Tavistock Inst); Psychotherapy Training (Camb Soc Psychotherapy)
Personal Therapy: Ongoing
Supervision: Ongoing
Counselling offered: General, Psychotherapy
Service for: Individuals
Specific to: Refugees, People with language problems
Theoretical Approach: Psychodynamic
Other languages: German
Fees: £18 - £22

Essex

HENDRY Devam Mrs 0279 414464
14 Home Close, HARLOW CM20 3PD
Member of:	**BAC, PET**
Quals/training:	BA; RGAN; RHV; Cert Ed; Dip (PET) 1983
Personal Therapy:	Yes
Supervision:	Ongoing
Counselling offered:	**Bereavement, Personal growth**
Service for:	Individuals
Specific to:	Women, Professional carers
Theoretical Approach:	Transpersonal, Feminist
Fees:	£20 - £30

COPLESTON Nora 0708 701250
73 Westmoreland Avenue, HORNCHURCH RM11 2EF
Member of:	**BAC**
Quals/training:	BA; Associate of Inst Medical Social Work; training in Couns (CTA and Writtle Pastoral Foundation)
Personal Therapy:	Ongoing
Supervision:	Ongoing
Counselling offered:	**General, Bereavement, Relationship, Crisis, Occupational, Medical**
Service for:	Individuals
Specific to:	People with disabilities
Theoretical Approach:	Eclectic
Fees:	£17 - £20

SAUNDERSON Adrienne 0708 472420
43 Wakerfield Close, HORNCHURCH RM11 2TH
Member of:	**BAC Acc**
Quals/training:	BAC Acc; RELATE trained as marital & groupwork therapist
Personal Therapy:	Ongoing
Supervision:	Ongoing
Counselling offered:	**General, Bereavement, Relationship, Sexual**
Service for:	Individuals, Couples, Groups
Theoretical Approach:	Psychodynamic, Integrative
Fees:	£25 negotiable

DAVIS Patricia 0708 472 573
56 Burnway, HORNCHURCH RM11 3SG
Member of:	**NCHP, Member of UKCP Register**
Quals/training:	Dip Hypnotherapy & Psychotherapy (National College); Dip Hypnotherapy & Hypnohealing (CAH); Stress Management (Inst Stress Management); Psychol (OU)
Personal Therapy:	–
Supervision:	Ongoing
Counselling offered:	**General, Anxiety, Stress, Hypnotherapy, Psychotherapy**
Service for:	Individuals, Couples
Theoretical Approach:	Ericksonian, Hypnotherapy, NLP
Fees:	£25 consultation, £20 session

Essex

MARCHANT Paul   081 518 1697
19 Mayfair Avenue, ILFORD IG1 3DJ
Member of: BAC Acc
Quals/training: BAC Acc; BSc; Cert Couns Skills (WPF) 1985; Dip Client- Centred Psychotherapy (PersonCentred Approach Inst Int) 1987
Personal Therapy: Ongoing
Supervision: Ongoing
Counselling offered: General, Relationship, Bereavement, Disability, Psychotherapy, Supervision
Service for: Individuals, Couples, Groups
Specific to: Counsellor has disability
Theoretical Approach: Client-centred
Fees: Sliding scales

SONN Gillian   081 518 1732
ILFORD IG1 3ST
Member of: BAC
Quals/training: Cert Couns Skills & Theory 1990; Dip HE in Bereavement Couns 1991; BA (Hons) in Trauma, Disaster & HIV/AIDS Couns (UEL) 1993
Personal Therapy: Yes
Supervision: Ongoing
Counselling offered: Bereavement, AIDS, Disaster
Service for: Individuals
Theoretical Approach: Eclectic
Fees: £15 - £25

BRIGGS Dr Andrew   081 478 3393
62 Courtland Avenue, ILFORD IG1 3DP
Member of: BAC Acc, ACP
Quals/training: DAO & AOO Acc, PhD, MA, DA(Hons); Dip Couns in Educational Settings; ongoing training Tavistock Clinic
Personal Therapy: –
Supervision: Ongoing
Counselling offered: Short-term, Long-term
Service for: Individuals, Couples, Groups, Children
Theoretical Approach: Kleinian, Psychodynamic
Fees: £30

GILBERT Sharon   081 554 0710
128 Meads Lane, Seven Kings, ILFORD IG3 8PE
Member of: BAC
Quals/training: Dip Psychosynthesis Couns & Dip Adv Psychosynthesis Therapy (PET); Accredited by Assoc for Acc Psychospiritual Psychotherapists
Personal Therapy: Ongoing
Supervision: Ongoing
Counselling offered: General, Relationship, Psychotherapy
Service for: Individuals, Groups
Specific to: Survivors of sex abuse
Theoretical Approach: Transpersonal
Fees: £30

Essex

BERNSTEIN Samuel 081 550 5542
83 Abbotswood Gardens, Clayhall, ILFORD IG5 0BH
Member of:	BAC
Quals/training:	Training in Hypnotherapy & Psychotherapy 1986-88; ICM Dip Hypnotherapy & Adv Psychotherapy; Memb SAPP, APT, ICM, MCAHyp & NACHP
Personal Therapy:	No
Supervision:	Ongoing
Counselling offered:	General, Psychotherapy, Hypnotherapy, Educational, Addiction, Stop smoking, Confidence, Depression, Eating disorders
Service for:	Individuals, Couples, Families
Theoretical Approach:	Psychodynamic, Analytical
Other languages:	German
Fees:	On application

FISHMAN Paul 081 551 5980
46 Herent Drive, ILFORD IG5 0HE
Member of:	BAC
Quals/training:	Dip Hypnotherapy & Psychology National College 1984; training in Co-couns, Gestalt and abnormal psychology; Memb APT, MCHC(UK)
Personal Therapy:	No
Supervision:	Ongoing
Counselling offered:	General, Phobias, Hypnotherapy, Psychotherapy
Service for:	Individuals, Couples, Groups
Theoretical Approach:	Eclectic
Fees:	£15 - £20

FAIRHURST Irene 081 550 5761
PCAI (GB), 220 Ashurst Drive, Barkingside, ILFORD IG6 1EW
Member of:	BAC Acc
Quals/training:	BAC(Acc); Dip Client-centred Psychotherapy & Counselling & applications of the Person-Centred Approach(PCAI)
Personal Therapy:	No
Supervision:	Ongoing
Counselling offered:	General, Psychotherapy, Eating disorders, Phobias
Service for:	Individuals
Specific to:	Women only, Survivors of child abuse
Theoretical Approach:	Client-centred
Fees:	£30

WATERFIELD Ruth 081 550 0524
55 Beattyville Gardens, Barkingside, ILFORD IG6 1JY
Member of:	BAC
Quals/training:	BSC Soc Sci; CQSW; Writtle Pastoral Foundation
Personal Therapy:	Ongoing
Supervision:	Ongoing
Counselling offered:	General, Bereavement
Service for:	Individuals
Specific to:	Women
Theoretical Approach:	Psychodynamic
Fees:	£12 - £15 negotiable

Essex

RODKOFF Lesley   **081 551 0816**
6 Horace Road, Barkingside, ILFORD IG6 2BG
Member of: BAC
Quals/training: Initial training as a counsellor; Psychotherapy Foundation Course (IPSS); Dip Couns Client-centred Therapy (PCAI)
Personal Therapy: Yes
Supervision: Ongoing
Counselling offered: General, Anxiety, Depression, Psychotherapy, Relationship, Substance abuse
Service for: Individuals, Couples
Specific to: Women
Theoretical Approach: Client-centred
Fees: £20

HUNTER Lynne   **0702 713715**
103 Woodfield Park Drive, LEIGH-ON-SEA SS9 1LN
Member of: BAC Acc, IPS
Quals/training: BAC Acc; Dip Couns 1987 IP
Personal Therapy: No
Supervision: Ongoing
Counselling offered: General, Eating disorders
Service for: Individuals, Groups
Specific to: Women
Theoretical Approach: Psychosynthesis
Fees: £20

GALE Derek   **081 508 9344, Fax 081 508 1240**
Gale Centre, Whitakers Way, LOUGHTON IG10 1SQ
Member of: BAC, AHPP
Quals/training: BA(Hons); PGCE; Dip Dramatherapy; training in Voicework as therapy; Couns skills; Group Dynamics; Psychodrama; BADTh
Personal Therapy: Ongoing
Supervision: Ongoing
Counselling offered: Drama therapy, Voice work, Eating disorders, Confidence, Sexual abuse, Physical abuse
Service for: Individuals, Couples, Families, Groups, Organisations
Specific to: Actors, Musicians
Theoretical Approach: Humanistic
Fees: £40 negotiable

KYTE Elizabeth   **081 502 5245**
74 Swanshope, Burney Drive, LOUGHTON IG10 2NB
Member of: BAC
Quals/training: RGN, RM; RHV; Currently in training for Dip Couns (metanoia)
Personal Therapy: Yes
Supervision: Ongoing
Counselling offered: General, Bereavement
Service for: Individuals
Theoretical Approach: Person-centred, Rogerian
Fees: £15 - £25 sliding scale

Essex

LEE Terry 0255 870311
Jacques Hall Foundation, Harwich Road, Bradfield, MANNINGTREE CO11 2XW
Member of: BAC
Quals/training: RMN 1975; Cert Couns (LCIP) 1981
Personal Therapy: –
Supervision: Ongoing
Counselling offered: **General, PTSD**
Service for: Individuals, Groups, Families
Specific to: Adolescents, Professional carers, Incest survivors
Theoretical Approach: Client-centred, Psychodynamic, Gestalt
Fees: £15 - £30 dependent on income

MILLER Geraldine 0268 745796
14 South View Close, RAYLEIGH SS6 7LX
Member of: BAC, BPS
Quals/training: BA(Hons) Psychol; Trained in RET and with AHP, Cruse, Nat Assoc of Bereavement Services and Standing Conf on Sexual Abused Children
Personal Therapy: Ongoing
Supervision: Ongoing
Counselling offered: **Sexual abuse, Rape, Bereavement**
Service for: Individuals, Couples
Specific to: Women
Theoretical Approach: Integrative, Rogerian, Gestalt, RET
Fees: £15 - £30 Sliding Scale

GRANGE Jean 0702 540892
244 Ashingdon Road, ROCHFORD SS4 1TQ
Member of: BAC
Quals/training: RCN member; RGN; SCM; RMN; Dip Couns (CSCT)
Personal Therapy: Yes
Supervision: Ongoing
Counselling offered: **General, Bereavement, PTSD, Anxiety, ME**
Service for: Individuals
Theoretical Approach: Person-centred, Cognitive
Fees: £25

SMITH Ann 0708 744569
306 Main Road, Gidea Park, ROMFORD RM2 6PA
Member of: BAC
Quals/training: Trained at Writtle Pastoral Foundation
Personal Therapy: Ongoing
Supervision: Ongoing
Counselling offered: **General**
Theoretical Approach: Psychodynamic
Fees: From £20 negotiable

Essex

HOWTONE Christina 0708 373175
139 Sevenoaks Close, Harold Hill, ROMFORD RM3 7EF
Member of: **NSHAP, CRAH**
Quals/training: Dip Therapeutic Hypnosis SHAP; Dip Hypnotherapist & Hypnohealer MABCH, MCAHyp
Personal Therapy: Yes
Supervision: Ongoing
Counselling offered: **General, Panic attacks, Phobias, Depression, Psychotherapy, Hypnohealing, Sexual abuse, Food allergies**
Service for: Individuals, Couples, Families
Specific to: Children
Theoretical Approach: Jungian
Fees: £30 - £35 negotiable

McKENZIE Jemma 081 590 9989
46 Geneva Gardens, Chadwell Heath, ROMFORD RM6 6SL
Member of: **BAC, ITA**
Quals/training: Dip Couns; training in Psychotherapy (metanoia)
Personal Therapy: Yes
Supervision: Ongoing
Counselling offered: **General, Psychotherapy**
Service for: Individuals, Couples, Groups
Theoretical Approach: Eclectic, TA
Fees: £25 negotiable

BULL Graham 0708 753037
64 Braithwaite Avenue, ROMFORD RM7 0DS
Member of: **BAC**
Quals/training: BA(Hons); MA; CQSW; Dip Psychiatric Social Work; Cert in Brief Psychotherapy; Dip in Inter-Cultural Therapy; currently in psycho-analytical training with CFAR
Personal Therapy: Yes
Supervision: Ongoing
Counselling offered: **General, Analysis**
Service for: Individuals, Couples
Specific to: Minorities
Theoretical Approach: Psychoanalytic, Lacanian
Fees: Negotiable

COUSSENS Kay 0708 755384
42 Glenwood Drive, Gidea Park, ROMFORD
Member of: **BAC, ITHP**
Quals/training: Minster Centre Acc
Personal Therapy: Yes
Supervision: Ongoing
Counselling offered: **Psychotherapy**
Service for: Individuals
Theoretical Approach: Analytical, Humanistic
Fees: £20

Essex

CAMERON Katherine 0799 527449
57 Castle Street, SAFFRON WALDEN CB10 1BD
Member of: BAC, IPSS
Quals/training: BA(Oxon); training in analytic psychotherapy (IPSS)
Personal Therapy: Ongoing
Supervision: Ongoing
Counselling offered: General, Psychotherapy
Service for: Individuals
Theoretical Approach: Analytic
Fees: Negotiable

JOHNSTONE Janice 0799 524123
10 De Bohun Court, SAFFRON WALDEN CB10 2BA
Member of: BAC, NRHP
Quals/training: BA Psychol; Dip Hypnotherapy & Psychotherapy
Personal Therapy: Yes
Supervision: Ongoing
Counselling offered: General
Service for: Individuals, Couples, Groups, Families
Theoretical Approach: Rogerian
Fees: £35

MOUCHET Francoise 0799 528323
134 Thaxted Road, SAFFRON WALDEN CB11 3BJ
Member of: BAC
Quals/training: Dip Applied Psychol; Dip Couns (IP); training in Gestalt Therapy (Gestalt Centre)
Personal Therapy: Ongoing
Supervision: Ongoing
Counselling offered: General, Relationship, Crisis, Psychotherapy
Service for: Individuals, Couples, Groups
Theoretical Approach: Psychosynthesis, Gestalt
Other languages: French
Fees: £15 - £30 Sliding Scale

PENN Joyce 0702 462191
213 York Road, SOUTHEND-ON-SEA SS1 2RU
Member of: NRHP
Quals/training: Dip Therapeutic Hypnosis & Psychotherapy 1980; DHP 1981;
Personal Therapy: Ongoing
Supervision: No
Counselling offered: General, Psychotherapy, Bereavement, Psychosomatic
Service for: Individuals, Couples, Families
Theoretical Approach: Psychodynamic, Eclectic, Imagery
Fees: £20 - £25 - Consultation £30

Essex

BAILEY Lyn   0702 354118
Victoria Counselling Service, 133 Victoria Avenue, SOUTHEND-ON-SEA SS2 6EL
Member of:	BAC
Quals/training:	BA; RELATE trained; MIAH
Personal Therapy:	Yes
Supervision:	Ongoing
Counselling offered:	General, Bereavement, Relationship, Psychotherapy, Hypnotherapy
Service for:	Individuals, Couples
Fees:	£25

SHEPHERD David   0702 354118
Victoria Counselling Service, 137 Victoria Avenue, SOUTHEND ON SEA
Member of:	BAC, BPS
Quals/training:	BA(Hons) Psychol 1986; MSc Psychol Couns (Surrey Univ) 1987; training in TA Psychotherapy (metanoia) 1989; C Psychol
Personal Therapy:	Yes
Supervision:	Ongoing
Counselling offered:	General, Crisis, Marital
Service for:	Individuals, Couples, Groups
Theoretical Approach:	TA, Gestalt, Cognitive/Behavioural
Fees:	£30 (£10 groups)

THOMPSON Joan   0702 613828
31 Priory Crescent, Prittlewell, SOUTHEND-ON-SEA SS2 6JY
Member of:	BPS, BABCP, ANLP (PCS)
Quals/training:	BA Sociology of Ed; BSc Psychol; CPsychol; training in TA, Personal Construct Psychol, Family Therapy, Hypnosis, NLP Trainer's Cert; ANLP PCS Validated Psychotherapist
Personal Therapy:	Yes
Supervision:	Ongoing
Counselling offered:	General, Addiction, Bereavement, Marital, Psychotherapy
Service for:	Individuals, Couples, Families, Groups, Organisations
Theoretical Approach:	Integrative
Fees:	Negotiable

CROMWELL Sheila   099289 3405
Monkhams Cottage, Aimes Green, Galleyhill, WALTHAM ABBEY EN9 2AU
Member of:	BAC, ANLP (PCS)
Quals/training:	MB ChB; DCH; Master NLP (PACE); Adv Dip EH.P.NLP (Brit Hypnosis Research); Master NLP (Adv Master: Sensory Systems)
Personal Therapy:	Yes
Supervision:	Ongoing
Counselling offered:	General
Specific to:	People w learning difficulties
Theoretical Approach:	NLP, Ericksonian, Hypnotherapy, Adlerian
Fees:	£30

Essex

LOMAC Gina 0702 353652
79 Avenue Road, WESTCLIFF-ON-SEA SS0 7PJ
Member of: BAC
Quals/training: MA Psychol Couns & Therapy (Antioch); Dip Psychosynthesis Psychotherapy (IP) 1987
Personal Therapy: Yes
Supervision: Ongoing
Counselling offered: General, Crisis, Play therapy, Psychotherapy
Service for: Individuals, Groups
Theoretical Approach: Psychosynthesis, Jungian
Fees: £28 negotiable in hardship cases

WARDE Janet 0702 334915
79 Avenue Road, WESTCLIFF-ON-SEA SS0 7PJ
Member of: BAC
Quals/training: BA(Hons); Dip Ed; Dip Couns
Personal Therapy: Ongoing
Supervision: Ongoing
Counselling offered: General, Anxiety, Bereavement, Crisis, Depression, Relationship, Assertiveness
Service for: Individuals, Couples
Specific to: Survivors of child abuse
Theoretical Approach: Psychosynthesis
Other languages: French
Fees: £15 - £25 sliding scale

McNEILL Rab 081 504 3973
32 St Albans Crescent, WOODFORD GREEN IG8 9EH
Member of: BAC
Quals/training: BSc (Soc Sc); DSW; Tavistock Clinic; Inst Marital Studies
Personal Therapy: Yes
Supervision: Ongoing
Counselling offered: General, Psychotherapy
Service for: Individuals
Theoretical Approach: Psychoanalytic, CAT
Fees: £25

Gloucestershire

Organisations

GLOUCESTERSHIRE COUNSELLING SERVICE   0453 766310
50 Lansdown, STROUD GL5 1BN
Service:	General counselling and psychotherapy for individuals, couples and families
Area served:	Gloucestershire
Referral:	Self or others
Training of workers:	All have completed a substantial counselling/psychotherapy training, have had personal therapy and are in supervision
Code of Ethics:	BAC, WPF
Management by:	Trustees. Service is associated with WPF
Fees:	£10 - £25

HIGHLIGHT TRUST   0453 844441
108 Bearlands, WOTTON-UNDER-EDGE GL12 7SB
Service:	Individual & group couns in rural areas only. The service is peripatetic. The Trust will invite counsellors to work for it on a freelance basis. Educative & research element
Area served:	Gloucestershire
Referral:	Self, Agencies
Training of workers:	Cert Couns (minimum)
Code of Ethics:	BAC
Management by:	The Partners/Founders: Humphrey Agard-Evans and CatherineAgard-Evans
Fees:	Fees for workshops & training

Individual Practitioners

Each individual is a **member of** one or more organisations eligible for entry into this directory. BAC Accredited Counsellors and Recognised Supervisors are shaded.

ELLIOTT Lea K   0242 518642
18 Eldorado Road, CHELTENHAM GL50 2PT
Member of:	**SIP, WMIP**
Quals/training:	B Ed; Dip in Child Psychol; Psychoanalytical Psychotherapist (SIP)
Personal Therapy:	Yes
Supervision:	Ongoing
Counselling offered:	**Psychotherapy**
Service for:	Individuals
Specific to:	Young people, Mothers
Theoretical Approach:	Winnicottian
Other languages:	Portuguese, Spanish
Fees:	£20 negotiable

SWEENEY Margaret   0242 239096, ansaphone 0242 222027
CHELTENHAM
Member of:	**BAC**
Quals/training:	BA; Dip Ed; Cert Couns; Dip Couns (ongoing to Jan '94)
Personal Therapy:	Ongoing
Supervision:	Ongoing
Counselling offered:	**General, Brief, Stress management**
Service for:	Individuals, Organisations
Theoretical Approach:	Humanistic, Integrative
Fees:	£20 negotiable

Gloucestershire

SIMPSON Rosie   **0242 238559**
The Basement, 33 Pittville Lawn, CHELTENHAM GL52 2BU
Member of: BAC
Quals/training: BA Dip Couns
Personal Therapy: Yes
Supervision: Ongoing
Counselling offered: **General**
Service for: Individuals
Theoretical Approach: Integrative
Fees: £25

ALLEN, Kay   **0242 224779**
Consulting Rooms, Alcoholism, 11 Imperial Square, CHELTENHAM GL50 1QU
Member of: **BAC, IPC**
Quals/training: Member IPC Psychotherapy
Personal Therapy: Yes
Supervision: Yes
Counselling offered: **Psychotherapy**
Service for: Individuals
Theoretical Approach: Psychoanalytic
Fees: £26

THOMAS Clive   **0242 517801**
Los Pepones, Copt Elm Road, Charlton Kings, CHELTENHAM GL53 8AG
Member of: **BAC Acc**
Quals/training: BAC Acc; BSc; Dip Ed; Acc Shiatsu Practitioner; Acc Craniosacral Therapist; Memb AHP, Shiatsu Soc & Craniosacral Therapy Assoc
Personal Therapy: Ongoing
Supervision: Ongoing
Counselling offered: **General, Bodywork, Psychotherapy**
Service for: Individuals, Couples, Groups
Other languages: Spanish, French
Fees: £14 - £28 sliding scale

CARTER Paula   **Sex therap 0451 820757**
Clutters, Great Rissington, CHELTENHAM GL54 2LR
Member of: **BAC, BASMT**
Quals/training: SRN; Registered Sick Children's Nurse; RELATE trained '83- '85; Sex Therapy training '86-'87
Personal Therapy: Ongoing
Supervision: Ongoing
Counselling offered: **General, Marital, Sexual, Sexual abuse**
Service for: Individuals, Couples
Specific to: People with disabilities, Gays
Theoretical Approach: Psychodynamic, Behavioural, Eclectic
Fees: £15 - £25 sliding scale

Gloucestershire

CARTER Paula 0242 523215
RELATE, 24 Cambray Place, CHELTENHAM GL50 1JN
Member of: BAC, BASMT
Quals/training: SRN; Registered Sick Children's Nurse; RELATE training '83- '85; Sex Therapy training '86-'87
Personal Therapy: Ongoing
Supervision: Ongoing
Counselling offered: General, Sexual, Marital
Service for: Individuals, Couples
Specific to: People with disabilities, Gays
Theoretical Approach: Psychodynamic, Behavioural, Eclectic
Fees: £15 - £25 sliding scale

MARTINO Barbara A 0386 438010
Twelfhouse, Cedar Road, Mickleton, CHIPPING CAMPDEN GL55 6SY
Member of: BAC
Quals/training: Cert Master Clin Soc Work; training with Inst for Mental Health Pract, Adv Inst Analytical Psychotherapy & Centre for Appl Metapsychol; Fellow NYS Soc Clin SW Psychoth'p'sts
Personal Therapy: Yes
Supervision: Ongoing
Counselling offered: General, Anxiety, Bereavement, Career, Educational, Depression, Trauma, Crisis, Sexual abuse, PTSD
Service for: Individuals, Couples, Groups
Specific to: Professionals, Young adults, Trauma victims, Women
Theoretical Approach: Integrative, Holistic
Fees: £25 - £40 Offices Oxford & C. Norton

PRITCHETT Ruth 0285 740 280
Sunset House, Bibury, CIRENCESTER GL7 5ND
Member of: BAC
Quals/training: RSA Cert Couns Skills; ongoing training for Dip Couns (BCPC)
Personal Therapy: Ongoing
Supervision: Ongoing
Counselling offered: General, Bereavement, Sexual abuse, Marital, Divorce
Service for: Individuals, Couples, Groups
Theoretical Approach: Humanistic, Integrative
Fees: £20

TUCKER Frances 0453 860492
East Cottage, The Green, Uley, DURSLEY GL11 5SN
Member of: BAC
Quals/training: RELATE trained; Sex Therapy Training
Personal Therapy: No
Supervision: Ongoing
Counselling offered: General, Marital, Sexual
Service for: Individuals, Couples
Fees: £20 negotiable in hardship

Gloucestershire

LLEWELYN Billie   0452 524497
St Catharine's Vicarage, 29 Denmark Road, GLOUCESTER GL1 3JQ
Member of:	BAC
Quals/training:	Cert Ed; Dip Theol; Cert Couns (Glos Counselling Service) 1989
Personal Therapy:	Ongoing
Supervision:	Ongoing
Counselling offered:	General, Psychotherapy
Service for:	Individuals, Couples
Theoretical Approach:	Psychodynamic
Fees:	£18 - £25 sliding scale

GREENSLADE Josephine   0452 780437
The Pink Cottage, The Green, Apperley, GLOUCESTER GL19 4DQ
Member of:	BAC
Quals/training:	Pastoral Care & Couns (RF); Cert Couns Skills (CAC); Cert Cancer Couns (Brit Psycho Oncology Group/CAC); WPF Affiliate GCS Forum; ongoing workshops
Personal Therapy:	Yes
Supervision:	Ongoing
Counselling offered:	General
Service for:	Individuals
Theoretical Approach:	Psychodynamic
Fees:	£20

BRAITHWAITE Dana   0242 620548
Tewkesbury, GLOUCESTER GL2
Member of:	NCHP, NRHP
Quals/training:	NRHP (Assoc); training in Hypnotherapy & Psychotherapy
Personal Therapy:	Ongoing
Supervision:	Ongoing
Counselling offered:	Stress management, Hypnotherapy, Psychotherapy
Service for:	Individuals, Couples, Groups, Organisations
Specific to:	Infertile couples
Theoretical Approach:	Eclectic
Fees:	£15 - £30

MOGGRIDGE Cass   0367 253334
Priory Mill, LECHLADE GL7 3HB
Member of:	BAC Acc
Quals/training:	BAC (Acc); BA Psychol; BADTh; Dip Dramatherapy; NMGC trained
Personal Therapy:	Yes
Supervision:	Ongoing
Counselling offered:	General, Relationship, Addiction, Rape, Bereavement, Midlife
Service for:	Individuals, Couples, Groups
Theoretical Approach:	Humanistic
Fees:	£25 Negotiable

MANN Elizabeth   ansaphone 0451 83166
The Rectory, Broadwell, MORETON-IN-MARSH GL56 0TU
Member of:	BAC
Quals/training:	BA; MSc Psychol of Couns (Surrey Univ); Dip Ed; Pastoral Care & Counselling (RF); Cert LCIP
Personal Therapy:	Ongoing
Supervision:	Ongoing
Counselling offered:	General, Stress, Work, Sexual abuse, Bereavement, Depression, Terminal illness, Psychotherapy
Service for:	Individuals
Specific to:	Managers, Students, Clergy/priests, Ethnic minorities
Theoretical Approach:	Client-centred, Integrative
Fees:	Negotiable, according to means

Gloucestershire

LUTHY Barbara   0452 720 934
College Farm, Beacon Lane, STONEHOUSE GL10 3EF
Member of: BAC, BCPC
Quals/training: Five yrs training with BCPC; Adv Dip Postural Integration
Personal Therapy: Yes
Supervision: Ongoing
Counselling offered: **General, Psychotherapy, Bodywork**
Service for: Individuals, Groups
Theoretical Approach: Humanistic, Integrative
Fees: £24; £50/2 hr session

GRANT Karen   0453 823061
28 Orchard Road, Ebley, STROUD GL5 4UA
Member of: BAC
Quals/training: Dip Therapeutic Hypnosis & Advanced Psychotherapy (NSHAP)
Personal Therapy: Yes
Supervision: Yes
Counselling offered: **General, Relationship, Hypnotherapy, Psychotherapy, Child abuse**
Service for: Individuals, Couples
Specific to: Women
Fees: £25

WALKLEY Stuart   0453 757784
The Old School, Bowl Hill, STROUD GL5 5DS
Member of: BAC
Quals/training: BA; Dip Ed; M Ed(Psych); MA(Psych); MITD; AIPM, Cert Competence & Occupational Testing (BPS), MIMgt
Personal Therapy: Yes
Supervision: Ongoing
Counselling offered: **Bereavement, Family, Occupational**
Service for: Individuals, Families, Groups, Organisations
Theoretical Approach: Eclectic, Myers Briggs, Cognitive
Fees: £25 - £40

HALL June   0453 834803, 0225 421033
Wood Cottage, Chapel Lane, Minchinhampton, STROUD GL6 9DL
Member of: BCPC
Quals/training: BA (Hons); completed 3rd yr of training for Dip Humanistic & Integrative Couns (BCPC); short training in Psychosynthesis, Gestalt etc; Approved Glos Prob Service Staff Counsellor
Personal Therapy: Yes
Supervision: Ongoing
Counselling offered: **General, Loss, Change, Stress, Crisis, Work**
Service for: Individuals, Groups, Organisations
Specific to: Students
Theoretical Approach: Integrative, Humanistic
Fees: £15 - £18 individuals

Gloucestershire

LACEY Frances 0453 836277
Farne House, Star Hill, Nailsworth, STROUD GL6 0NJ
Member of: BAC, ITA, MPTI
Quals/training: BSc; CQSW; Cert Transactional Analyst; Provisional Teaching & Supervising Transactional Analyst; training in Person-centred Couns
Personal Therapy: Yes
Supervision: Ongoing
Counselling offered: General, Bereavement, Crisis, Trauma
Service for: Individuals, Couples, Organisations
Specific to: Adolescents
Theoretical Approach: Person-centred, TA
Fees: £25

GREATOREX Christopher 0435 836077
Leaways, Downend, Horsley, STROUD GL6 0PQ
Member of: IPS
Quals/training: Dip Psychotherapy (IP)
Personal Therapy: Yes
Supervision: Ongoing
Counselling offered: General, Crisis, Cancer, Psychotherapy
Service for: Individuals, Couples, Groups
Theoretical Approach: Psychosynthesis, Humanistic, Winnicottian
Fees: £25 - £35 (75 min sessions)

HALL Kelvin 0453 833861
Cherry Tree Cottage, Shortwood, Nailsworth, STROUD GL6 0SB
Member of: BCPC
Quals/training: BA(Hons); Dip Social Studies; Cert Ed; Cert Transpersonal Skills in Couns; Dip Humanistic & Integrative Psychotherapy
Personal Therapy: Yes
Supervision: Ongoing
Counselling offered: General, Bereavement, Relationship, Crisis, Psychotherapy
Service for: Individuals
Theoretical Approach: Transpersonal, Humanistic, Integrative
Fees: £23

PENN-TAPLIN Pam ansaphone 0666 503043
45 New Church Street, TETBURY GL8 8DS
Member of: BAC
Quals/training: Combined Cert Couns (CSCT)
Personal Therapy: Yes
Supervision: Ongoing
Counselling offered: General, Bereavement, Relationship
Service for: Individuals, Couples
Specific to: Women
Theoretical Approach: Person-centred
Fees: £12 - £20 sliding scale

Greater Manchester

Organisations

MIND TAMESIDE & GLOSSOP 061 330 9223
18 Chester Square, ASHTON UNDER LYNE OL6 7NS
Service: General counselling, groupwork & relaxation courses
Area served: Tameside & Glossop
Referral: Self or others
Training of workers: Fully trained counsellor, in-service training for volunteers; regular supervision
Code of Ethics: BAC
Management by: Executive Committee
Fees: None

CHURCH ARMY COUNSELLING SERVICE NORTH 061 236 1081
Central Hall, Oldham Street, MANCHESTER M1 1JT
Service: Individual counselling for emotional & spiritual problems, depression and marital difficulties, in strict confidence for those of any creed or none
Area served: Manchester & Sheffield
Referral: Self or others
Training of workers: Professional Counsellors; BAC Accredited
Code of Ethics: BAC
Management by: Church Army
Fees: £3 - £18 negotiable

42ND STREET COMMUNITY MENTAL HEALTH RESOURCE/YOUNG PEOPLE 061 832 0170
Ground Floor, Lloyd's House, 22 Lloyd Street, MANCHESTER M2 5WA
Service: Individual counselling & psychotherapy for young people (15-25) experiencing stress and mental health problems. Also provide groups & work in community settings
Area served: City of Manchester boundaries
Referral: Self or others
Training of workers: Dip Couns; Dip Psychotherapy; regular supervision
Code of Ethics: BAC
Management by: Voluntary Management Committee
Fees: None

ST MARY'S CENTRE(SEXUAL ASSAULT REFERRAL CENTRE)
061 276 6515
St Mary's Hospital, Hathersage Road, Whitworth Park, MANCHESTER M13 0JH
Service: Crisis intervention & follow-up counselling for men & women who have been raped or sexually assaulted. NB Not for childhood sexual abuse
Area served: Greater Manchester only
Other languages: Please enquire
Referral: Self or others
Training of workers: Counselling experience & diploma in couns
Code of Ethics: BAC
Management by: Multidisciplinary Management Committee
Fees: None

Greater Manchester

MANCHESTER CENTRE FOR COUNSELLING 061 256 2616/3209
Brow House, 1 Mabfield Road, Fallowfield, MANCHESTER M14
Service: Individuals and groups on a wide range of personal issues
Area served: Manchester
Referral: Self or others
Training of workers: Depends upon therapists seen; regular supervision; personal therapy
Code of Ethics: BAC
Management by: Co-operative
Fees: Negotiable

COMMUNITY COUNSELLING SERVICE 061 434 9804
30 Longton Avenue, Withington, MANCHESTER M20 9JN
Service: General, relationshp, sexual, loss/bereavement counselling for individuals, couples (co-therapy available), groups and families; also supervision
Training of workers: RELATE (NMGC) training 1977; Psychosexual training 1980; WPF training in Supervision 1990-91
Code of Ethics: BAC, BASMT
Fees: £25 - 35 couples; £35-45 Concessions

MANCHESTER INSTITUTE FOR INTEGRATIVE PSYCHOTHERAPY
061 862 9456
Lifestream House, 454 Barlow Moor Road, Chorlton, MANCHESTER M21 1BQ
Service: Brief and extended therapy and counselling with the major modalities being in TA and Gestalt
Area served: North-West
Referral:S elf, Health Practitioner
Training of workers: All the therapists are trained or in training in TA, Gestalt or Psychosynthesis
Code of Ethics: BAC
Management by: A therapist
Fees: £15 - 35 sliding scale

Individual Practitioners
Each individual is a **member of** one or more organisations eligible for entry into this directory. BAC Accredited Counsellors and Recognised Supervisors are shaded.

HAWORTH Ann 061 928 7101
Gifford Mount, East Downs Road, Bowdon, ALTRINCHAM WA14 2LG
Member of: BAC Acc
Quals/training: BAC Acc; RELATE trained; Cert Couns Manchester Univ 1983; Cert Group Psychotherapy IGA; Dip Psychotherapy LIV; currently couns in General Practice
Personal Therapy: Yes
Supervision: Ongoing
Counselling offered: General, Bereavement, Marital, Psychotherapy
Service for: Individuals, Couples
Theoretical Approach: Psychodynamic
Fees: £32

Greater Manchester

HOBBES Robin 061 928 9997
Elan Psychotherapy Train Inst, Hilltop Centre, 217 Ashley Road   Hale, ALTRINCHAM WA15 9SZ
Member of: ITA
Quals/training: BA; CQSW; Certified Transactional Analyst 1985
Personal Therapy: Ongoing
Supervision: Ongoing
Counselling offered: Psychotherapy, Bereavement, Marital
Service for: Individuals, Couples, Groups, Families
Theoretical Approach: TA
Fees: £32 negotiable, £18 group

HARDY Jennifer 061 330 9598
21 Holland Grove, ASHTON UNDER LYNE OL6 8TN
Member of: BAC
Quals/training: Dip Couns (ACP); Acc Trainer (Co-Counselling International)
Personal Therapy: Ongoing
Supervision: Ongoing
Counselling offered: General
Service for: Individuals
Theoretical Approach: Person-centred, Eclectic, Integrative
Other languages: Spanish
Fees: £18 - £28 sliding scale

MAKIN Anne 0204 594000
27 Beeston Close, BOLTON BL1 7RT
Member of: BAC, GPTI
Quals/training: BEd (Hons); Cert Couns (Manchester Univ); currently in advanced clinical training in Gestalt Psychotherapy (4th yr)
Personal Therapy: Ongoing
Supervision: Ongoing
Counselling offered: General, Relationship, Childhood trauma, Grief, Loss, Personal growth
Service for: Individuals, Couples, Groups
Theoretical Approach: Gestalt
Fees: £20 - £30 sliding scale

VORA Valerie 0942 813647
196 Manchester Road, Westhoughton, BOLTON BL5 3LA
Member of: BAC Acc, BASMT
Quals/training: BAC(Acc); Cert Ed; RGN; RELATE trained including sexual therapy; Adv Dip Couns (Wigan)
Personal Therapy: Ongoing
Supervision: Ongoing
Counselling offered: General, Marital, Relationship, Psychosexual, Psychotherapy
Service for: Individuals, Couples, Families, Groups
Theoretical Approach: Eclectic
Other languages: Italian, French
Fees: £20 - £25 negotiable

Greater Manchester

ASHWORTH Freda   **0706 68193**
Mulsanne, Harefield Drive, HEYWOOD OL10 1RN
Member of:	NRHP
Quals/training:	Dip Psychotherapy & Hypnotherapy (National College) 1985; Analytic Psychotherapy & NLP, Sex Therapy 1986; HIV/AIDS counselling (Burnley AIDSLine)
Personal Therapy:	Yes
Supervision:	Yes
Counselling offered:	**General, Relationship, Sexual, Bereavement, Crisis, HIV, AIDS, Hypnotherapy, Psychotherapy**
Service for:	Individuals, Couples
Fees:	£25

MOUNTAIN Sylvia   **0706 373034**
Prospect House, 40 Smithy Bridge Road, LITTLEBOROUGH OL15 0DX
Member of:	BAC, NRHP, Member of UKCP Register
Quals/training:	Manchester Cert in Couns; Dip Hypnotherapy & Psychotherapy (NAT College); Dip Stress Management; Memb ISMA & IFH (International Fellowship of Healing)
Personal Therapy:	Yes
Supervision:	Ongoing
Counselling offered:	**Personal growth, Relationship, Anxiety, Depression, Bereavement, Eating disorders, Psychotherapy, Hypnotherapy, Supervision**
Service for:	Individuals, Couples
Theoretical Approach:	NLP, Psychodynamic, Humanistic, Integrative
Fees:	£22

FLATMAN Brian   **061 224 6561**
1 Moon Grove, Rusholme, MANCHESTER M14 5HE
Member of:	BAC, BPS
Quals/training:	AFPBsS; C Psychol; BA(Hons) Psychol; PGCE; Post Grad training in Ed Psychol (Tavistock); Dip Humanistic Psychol (IDHP); Cert Couns; AEP member
Personal Therapy:	Yes
Supervision:	Ongoing
Counselling offered:	**General, Bereavement, Crisis, Self-esteem, Assertiveness, Relationship**
Service for:	Individuals, Couples, Families, Groups, Organisations
Specific to:	Managers
Theoretical Approach:	Client-centred, Gestalt, Psychodynamic
Fees:	£40 some negotiable

McDONNELL Frances   **061 224 5341**
22 Victoria Road, Fallowfield, MANCHESTER M14 6AP
Member of:	BAC
Quals/training:	1989 Dip Couns (NMGC)
Personal Therapy:	Ongoing
Supervision:	Ongoing
Counselling offered:	**General**
Service for:	Individuals, Groups
Theoretical Approach:	Person-centred
Fees:	£15 - £25 sliding scale

Greater Manchester

DAVIS James 061 225 2556
7 Talbot Road, MANCHESTER M14 6TA
Member of: BAC, ITA
Quals/training: BA Oxon; MSc; RELATE trained; training in TA & Gestalt
Personal Therapy: Ongoing
Supervision: Ongoing
Counselling offered: General, Relationship, Stress, Anxiety, Bereavement, Psychotherapy
Service for: Individuals, Couples, Groups
Theoretical Approach: TA, Gestalt
Fees: £25

PORTER Danny 061 226 9413
27 Whalley Road, Whalley Range, MANCHESTER M16 8AD
Member of: BAC
Quals/training: BA Sociology; Dip Couns
Personal Therapy: Ongoing
Supervision: Ongoing
Counselling offered: General, Depression, Relationship
Service for: Individuals, Groups
Theoretical Approach: Rogerian, Eclectic
Fees: £15 - £25 sliding scale

CROUAN Michele 061 432 1430
Levenshulme, MANCHESTER M19 2RN
Member of: BAC
Quals/training: Dip Couns; MA Couns Studies
Personal Therapy: Yes
Supervision: Ongoing
Counselling offered: General, Bereavement, Psychotherapy
Service for: Individuals, Groups
Specific to: Women, Lesbians, Gays
Theoretical Approach: Person-centred, Gestalt
Fees: £6 - £25 sliding scale

GOULDING Barbara 061 236 1081
Church Army Couns Service Nth, Central Hall, Oldham Street, MANCHESTER M1 1JT
Member of: BAC Acc
Quals/training: BAC Acc; Trained (CTA) 1973-5; various courses & workshops 1976-80; Group Psychotherapy Course (IGA) 1983-4
Personal Therapy: Yes
Supervision: Ongoing
Counselling offered: General
Service for: Individuals, Couples
Theoretical Approach: Eclectic, Person-centred
Fees: £18 negotiable, £3 unwaged

Greater Manchester

BLATCH Chrissi 061 248 8439
31 Cromwell Grove, Levenshulme, MANCHESTER M19 3QD
Member of: NRHP
Quals/training: Trained with NCHP resulting in CHP(NC) & NRHP(Assoc); BEd(Hons); Dip Youth & Community Work
Personal Therapy: Ongoing
Supervision: Ongoing
Counselling offered: **Hypnotherapy, Psychotherapy, Bereavement**
Service for: Individuals
Specific to: Survivors of child abuse, Adult children of alcoholics
Theoretical Approach: Person-centred, Humanistic, Rogerian, Gestalt
Fees: £15 - £25

SCOTT Mary 061 445 1018
Crossway Clinic, 39 Crossway, Didsbury Village, MANCHESTER M20 0TU
Member of: BAC
Quals/training: Dip Couns; RGN; RM; ongoing Gestalt training
Personal Therapy: Ongoing
Supervision: Ongoing
Counselling offered: **General**
Service for: Individuals
Specific to: Parents
Theoretical Approach: Person-centred
Fees: Sliding scale

LENDRUM Susan ansaphone 061 434 9709
2 Kingston Avenue, Didsbury, MANCHESTER M20 8SB
Member of: BAC Acc
Quals/training: BAC Acc; Dip Psychotherapy (Univ of Sheffield) 1985; Supervision Training Course (WPF)
Personal Therapy: Yes
Supervision: Ongoing
Counselling offered: **General, Psychotherapy, Supervision**
Service for: Individuals, Groups
Theoretical Approach: Psychodynamic
Other languages: German, French
Fees: £30 dependent on income

BROWN Dee 061 434 5932
20 Everett Road, Withington, MANCHESTER M20 9DT
Member of: BAC, BPS
Quals/training: BSc(Hons) Psychol; Dip Couns; training in Dynamic Psychotherapy
Personal Therapy: Ongoing
Supervision: Ongoing
Counselling offered: **General, Bereavement, Crisis, Addiction, Psychotherapy**
Service for: Individuals
Theoretical Approach: Rogerian, Psychodynamic
Fees: £15 - £30 Sliding scale

Greater Manchester

LOBEL Sandra 061 434 9804
30 Longton Avenue, Withington, MANCHESTER M20 9JN
Member of: BAC, BASMT
Quals/training: BASMT Acc; RELATE/NMGC Trained; Psychosexual training 1980; trained in Supervision 9WPF) 1990-1
Personal Therapy: Yes
Supervision: Ongoing
Counselling offered: General, Relationship, Sexual, Loss, Bereavement, Supervision, Co-therapy
Service for: Individuals, Couples, Groups, Families
Theoretical Approach: Psychodynamic
Fees: £25 - £35 Couples £35-45, some concessions

LOBEL Sydney 061 434 9804
30 Longton Avenue, Withington, MANCHESTER M20 9JN
Member of: BAC, BASMT
Quals/training: BASMT Acc; RELATE/NMGC training 1958; Tutor training 1968; Psychosexual training 1976
Personal Therapy: Yes
Supervision: Ongoing
Counselling offered: General, Sexual, Relationship, Separation, Co-therapy
Service for: Individuals, Couples, Groups, Families
Theoretical Approach: Psychodynamic
Fees: £25 - £35 couples £35-45, some concessions

MUIR Liz 061 434 1260
27 Sandileigh Avenue, Withington, MANCHESTER M20 9LN
Member of: BAC
Quals/training: MA(Hons); PGCE; Dip Couns; Dip Assertiveness (RWTA)
Personal Therapy: Yes
Supervision: Ongoing
Counselling offered: General, Bereavement, Eating disorders, Body image
Service for: Individuals, Couples
Specific to: Women
Theoretical Approach: Person-centred
Fees: £20 - £28

BURKE Terry Ansaphone 061 881 6818
2 Devonshire Road, Chorlton Cum Hardy, MANCHESTER M21 2XB
Member of: BAC
Quals/training: Dip Couns; CQSW
Personal Therapy: Ongoing
Supervision: Ongoing
Counselling offered: General, Loss, Anxiety, Self-esteem, Relationship, Men's issues, Personal growth, Health
Service for: Individuals, Couples, Groups
Specific to: Health care professionals
Theoretical Approach: Person-centred, Psychodynamic
Fees: £15 - £25 Sliding scale

Greater Manchester

BACHA Claire 061 773 0409
20 Kersal Road, Prestwich, MANCHESTER M25 8SJ
Member of: ULDP, IGA
Quals/training: PhD Sociology; training in Individual Analytical Psychotherapy; Dip Group Analysis (IGA); Memb GAS & Group Analysis North
Personal Therapy: Yes
Supervision: Ongoing
Counselling offered: General, Assessment, Relationship, Psychotherapy, Consultation, Supervision
Service for: Individuals, Couples, Groups, Organisations
Specific to: Young adults, Women, Ethnic minorities
Theoretical Approach: Rogerian, Analytical, Integrative
Other languages: Portuguese, Spanish
Fees: £30

HARDEN Bev 061 736 0556
36 Park Lane West, Pendlebury, Swinton, MANCHESTER M27 2TR
Member of: BAC
Quals/training: In training for Dip Couns (yr2)
Personal Therapy: Ongoing
Supervision: Ongoing
Counselling offered: General
Service for: Individuals
Specific to: Lesbians, Women
Theoretical Approach: Integrative
Fees: Negotiable

THORP Cherry 061 799 9333
50 Glendale Road, Worsley, MANCHESTER M28 4AZ
Member of: BAC
Quals/training: RELATE trained; BA(Hons) ongoing (OU)
Personal Therapy: Ongoing
Supervision: Ongoing
Counselling offered: General, Bereavement, Marital
Service for: Individuals, Couples
Theoretical Approach: Eclectic, Rogerian
Fees: £20 negotiable

SHARPLES Geraldine 061 775 7498
85 Baines Avenue, Irlam, MANCHESTER M30 6AS
Member of: BAC
Quals/training: Dip Psychotherapy; also training in creative therapies, psychodrama, group therapy
Personal Therapy: Yes
Supervision: Ongoing
Counselling offered: General, Psychotherapy, Bereavement, Retirement, Substance abuse, Chronic illness
Service for: Individuals, Couples, Groups
Specific to: Women, People with disabilities
Theoretical Approach: Psychodynamic, Integrative
Fees: £15 - £30 sliding scale

Greater Manchester

HARVEY Anna 061 707 2406
31 Pine Grove, Monton, Eccles, MANCHESTER M30 9JP
Member of: BAC
Quals/training: RELATE trained 1984; Cruse bereavement couns course; Inst Marital Studies Course on Marital Interaction: A Psychodynamic View
Personal Therapy: Ongoing
Supervision: Ongoing
Counselling offered: Marital, Personal growth, Eating disorders, Body image, Long-term
Service for: Individuals, Couples
Theoretical Approach: Person-centred
Fees: £20

YATES Ann ansaphone 061 747 7174
5 Lichfield Road, Urmston, MANCHESTER M31 1RU
Member of: BAC
Quals/training: Dip Careers Guidance; Cert Couns(Univ Manchester)
Personal Therapy: Yes
Supervision: Ongoing
Counselling offered: General, Bereavement, Crisis, Occupational, Stress, Midlife
Service for: Individuals, Couples
Theoretical Approach: Integrative
Fees: £15 - £25 sliding scale

McDONNELL Fokkina 061 865 3193
65 Norwood Road, Stretford, MANCHESTER M32 8PN
Member of: BAC, BPS, ANLP (PCS)
Quals/training: BSc Psychol; MA Occup Psychol; Intermediate & Advanced Skills training in TA 1988; Practitioner Cert in NLP 1991; Master Practitioner Cert in NLP 1993
Personal Therapy: Yes
Supervision: Ongoing
Counselling offered: General, Bereavement, Career, Change, Crisis
Service for: Individuals
Theoretical Approach: TA, NLP
Other languages: Dutch
Fees: £40 - £45

WINTER Pamela 0457 871597
7 West View, Delph, OLDHAM OL3 5TR
Member of: BAC
Quals/training: BSc; Dip Couns; Assoc Memb NWIDP
Personal Therapy: Yes
Supervision: Ongoing
Counselling offered: General, Psychotherapy
Service for: Individuals
Specific to: Women
Fees: £15 - £25 negotiable

Greater Manchester

MACALISTER Eileen   **0706 45883**
14 Oulder Hill Drive, Bamford, ROCHDALE OL11 5LB
Member of: BAC
Quals/training: Dip Human Relations in Professional Settings (Nottingham Univ); Full Memb Inst of Training & Development; Cert in Supervision (WPF); in training with IGA
Personal Therapy: Ongoing
Supervision: Ongoing
Counselling offered: **General, Bereavement, Psychotherapy, Rape**
Service for: Individuals, Groups
Specific to: Survivors of sex abuse
Theoretical Approach: Psychodynamic
Fees: £22 negotiable

WILLIAMS Jane   **0706 860083**
Personal Counselling Centre, Enterprise Generation C, Dane Street, ROCHDALE OL12 6XB
Member of: BAC
Quals/training: RELATE Trained; Family Mediator; Dip Student in Group Psychotherapy (IGA); NAFMACS (Acc); GAN; FMA
Personal Therapy: Yes
Supervision: Ongoing
Counselling offered: **General, Bereavement, Marital, Divorce, Mediation, Psychotherapy**
Service for: Individuals, Couples
Specific to: Stepfamilies
Theoretical Approach: Psychodynamic
Fees: £25 first session, then negotiable

KABERRY Sue   **0706 860083**
Personal Counselling Centre, Dane Street, ROCHDALE OL12 6XB
Member of: BAC RSup
Quals/training: BAC Recog Supervisor; RGN; RNT; RELATE Trained; Dip Humanistic Psychol; Cert Supervision
Personal Therapy: Yes
Supervision: Ongoing
Counselling offered: **General, Bereavement, Psychotherapy**
Service for: Individuals, Couples
Theoretical Approach: Psychodynamic
Fees: £15 - £25 sliding scale

ELSWORTH Gillian   **0706 712150**
4 Woodstock Street, Meanwood, ROCHDALE OL12 7DG
Member of: BAC
Quals/training: Adv Dip Couns (Wigan) 1988
Personal Therapy: Ongoing
Supervision: Ongoing
Counselling offered: **General**
Service for: Individuals, Groups
Theoretical Approach: Person-centred
Fees: Negotiable

Greater Manchester

TWEEDALE Beryl ansaphone 0706 47928
6 Healey Hall Farm, Shawclough Road, Lowerfold, ROCHDALE OL12 7HA
Member of: BAC
Quals/training: RELATE trained
Personal Therapy: Yes
Supervision: Ongoing
Counselling offered: General, Bereavement, Relationship, Sexual abuse
Service for: Individuals, Couples
Theoretical Approach: Psychodynamic, Eclectic
Fees: £20 sliding scale

COURTNEY Joy 0706 842965
5 Brook Terrace, Milnrow, ROCHDALE OL16 3QA
Member of: BAC
Quals/training: RGN & HV; Cert Couns (Manchester Univ) 1983-84
Personal Therapy: Ongoing
Supervision: Ongoing
Counselling offered: General, Bereavement, PTSD, Depression, Relationship
Service for: Individuals, Groups
Specific to: Helping professions
Theoretical Approach: Client-centred, Eclectic
Fees: £15 - £30 sliding scale

DENSHAM Deborah 061 973 9221, 061 929 1725
1 Forest Drive, SALE M33 4SR
Member of: BAC
Quals/training: BA(Hons); Adv Dip Couns
Personal Therapy: Yes
Supervision: Ongoing
Counselling offered: General, Bereavement, Relationship
Service for: Individuals, Couples
Theoretical Approach: Rogerian, Client-centred
Fees: £20 negotiable, also in Altrlncham

HARDEN Bev 061 737 3467
c/o Face-To-Face, CRACA, 5 Churchill Court, SALFORD M6 5HB
Member of: BAC
Quals/training: In training for Dip Couns (Yr 2)
Personal Therapy: Ongoing
Supervision: Ongoing
Counselling offered: General
Service for: Individuals
Specific to: Lesbians, Women
Theoretical Approach: Integrative
Fees: None

Greater Manchester

GODDARD Moira　　　　　　　　　　　　　　　　　　　　　　　　**061 440 0673**
18 Patch Lane, Bramhall, STOCKPORT SK7 1JB
Member of:　　　　　　BAC Acc
Quals/training:　　　　BAC Acc; NMGC/RELATE Trained; Cert Supervision of Couns (WPF)
Personal Therapy:　　Yes
Supervision:　　　　　Ongoing
Counselling offered:　General, Bereavement, Relationship, Psychotherapy, Supervision
Service for:　　　　　Individuals, Couples
Theoretical Approach:　Rogerian, Psychodynamic
Fees:　　　　　　　　£15 - £30 Sliding scale

TAYLOR Sylvia　　　　　　　　　　　　　　　　　　　　　　　　**061 483 3470**
53 Haddon Road, Hazel Grove, STOCKPORT SK7 6LD
Member of:　　　　　　BAC, BASMT
Quals/training:　　　　NMGC & GAS trained
Personal Therapy:　　Yes
Supervision:　　　　　Ongoing
Counselling offered:　General, Stress, Relationship, Sexual, Psychotherapy, Bereavement
Service for:　　　　　Individuals, Couples
Theoretical Approach:　Person-centred, Psychodynamic
Fees:　　　　　　　　£15 - £30 sliding scale

BUCKERIDGE Shane　　　　　　　　　　　　　　　　　　　　　　**0942 494749**
WIGAN WN1
Member of:　　　　　　BAC
Quals/training:　　　　BA Psychol; Adv Dip Couns
Personal Therapy:　　Yes
Supervision:　　　　　Ongoing
Counselling offered:　General, Anxiety, Bereavement, Depression, Relationship, Stress
Service for:　　　　　Individuals
Theoretical Approach:　Rogerian
Fees:　　　　　　　　£15 - £25 Negotiable

CAVENDISH Jean　　　　　　　　　　　　　　　　　　　　　　　**0257 464 475**
Stanley House, Ash Brow, Newburgh, WIGAN WN8 7NG
Member of:　　　　　　BAC
Quals/training:　　　　Adv Dip Couns; trained in couple counselling
Personal Therapy:　　Yes
Supervision:　　　　　Ongoing
Counselling offered:　General, Bereavement, Crisis, Abuse
Service for:　　　　　Individuals, Couples
Theoretical Approach:　Person-centred
Fees:　　　　　　　　£10 - £25 sliding scale

Hampshire

Organisations

ALTON COUNSELLING SERVICE 0420 89207
Friend's Meeting House, Church Street, ALTON GU34 2DA
Service: Individual counselling for AIDS, bereavement, depression, addiction, marital & family problems. Affiliate of WPF
Area served: North East Hampshire
Referral: Self or others
Training of workers: Three year part-time WPF course. Regular supervision
Code of Ethics: WPF
Management by: Management committee, clinical committee & WPF advisors
Fees: Donation

LODDON NHS TRUST, PSYCHOLOGY SERVICES 0256 473202 x 4400
The Hollies, Park Prewett, BASINGSTOKE RG24 9LZ
Service: Psychodynamic psychotherapy and counselling for anxiety depression & emotional difficulties; marital, sexual & behavioural therapy; for adults, children & families.
Area served: Basingstoke & Nth Hants
Referral: GP, Self or others
Training of workers: Postgraduate Clinical Psychology & additional training in psychotherapy, marital/sexual counselling
Code of Ethics: BPS
Management by: Psychology Services Management Team
Fees: None

FAREHAM & GOSPORT PSYCHOSEXUAL CLINIC, OSBORN CLINIC
0329 288331
Osborn Road, FAREHAM PO16 7ES
Service: Psychosexual counselling/therapy for individuals, couples, male and female sexual dysfunction, incest and rape victims
Area served: Fareham & Gosport
Referral: Health/Soc Work Professional
Training of workers: Appropriate qualifications with additional training, regular supervision
Code of Ethics: Varies with professional seen
Management by: NHS
Fees: -

ISLE OF WIGHT YOUTH TRUST 0983 529569
1 St John's Place, NEWPORT PO30 1LH
Service: Wide range of support, counselling & therapy for young people up to 25 years. Individual, group & family therapy. Family planning clinic & psychosexual counselling.
Area served: Isle of Wight
Referral: Self or others
Training of workers: Diploma Level, 3 year part-time. External supervision mandatory
Code of Ethics: BAC
Management by: Board of Trustees via Directors
Fees: None

Hampshire

PETERSFIELD COUNSELLING SERVICE 0730 267788
PO Box 43, PETERSFIELD GU32 3RB
Service: General & marital counselling
Area served: Petersfield & district
Referral: Self or others
Training of workers: Two year part time counselling course, ongoing supervision
Code of Ethics: BAC
Management by: Management Committee
Fees: Donations

SOUTHAMPTON PASTORAL COUNSELLING SERVICE 0703 639966
Union Road, Northam, SOUTHAMPTON SO2 0PT
Service: General counselling
Area served: Hampshire, Dorset, Wiltshire & W Sussex
Referral: Self or others
Training of workers: 3 year part time training; personal therapy & supervision
Code of Ethics: BAC
Management by: Executive Committee
Fees: Contributions negotiated

GROVE NATURAL THERAPY CENTRE 0703 582245
22 Grosvenor Road, SOUTHAMPTON SO2 1RT
Service: Individuals, couples & group psychotherapy & couns. Related holistic therapies practised in aromatherapy, colonic hydrotherapy, homeopathy, reflexology, massage, etc
Area served: West Sussex, Hampshire, Isle of Wight, Dorset
Other languages: Danish, Norwegian, French, German
Referral: Health Practitioner, Self or others
Training of workers: Accreditation by relevant Therapeutic Training Establishment or Institute; ongoing supervision is essential
Code of Ethics: BAC
Management by: Partners: J Dahle, B Deacon, J Franks
Fees: £18 - £38 some negotiable

WINCHESTER DISTRICT PSYCHOLOGY SERVICES 0962 825139
Connaught House, 63b Romsey Road, WINCHESTER SO22 5DE
Service: Mainly short-term problem oriented therapy for individuals, couples and groups
Area served: Winchester, Andover, Eastleigh
Referral: GP, Health/Soc Work Professional
Training of workers: Postgraduate clinical psychology with further training in specific therapies
Code of Ethics: BPS
Management by: Winchester & Eastleigh Health Care Unit
Fees: None

Hampshire

Individual Practitioners

*Each individual is a **member of** one or more organisations eligible for entry into this directory. BAC Accredited Counsellors and Recognised Supervisors are shaded.*

BRINTON Patricia 0252 622488
Grove Cottages, 18 Grove Road, Church Crookham, Fleet, ALDERSHOT
Member of: BAC
Quals/training: BA (Hons); Cert Couns Univ of Surrey 1982; Accredited member & supervisor Family Mediators Assoc
Personal Therapy: Ongoing
Supervision: Ongoing
Counselling offered: General, Marital, Bereavement, Sexual, Abuse
Service for: Individuals, Couples, Families, Groups
Theoretical Approach: Rogerian, TA, Psychodynamic
Fees: £20

KERLOGUE Margaret ansaphone 0420 84219
ALTON GU34
Member of: BAC, IPC
Quals/training: Cert Groupwork IGA; IPC/WPF Diploma '87
Personal Therapy: Yes
Supervision: Ongoing
Counselling offered: General, Bereavement
Service for: Individuals, Organisations
Theoretical Approach: Psychodynamic, Eclectic, Analytic
Fees: £25 Negotiable

HATSWELL Valerie 0420 82385
Stillions, Windmill Hill, ALTON GU34 2RY
Member of: BAC Acc, GCSP
Quals/training: BAC Acc 1984; Dip Couns 1972; TA & Gestalt Course 1973; GAS, Family Therapy 1974-8
Personal Therapy: Yes
Supervision: Ongoing
Counselling offered: General, Marital, Family, Supervision
Service for: Individuals, Couples, Families, Groups
Theoretical Approach: Psychodynamic
Fees: £17.50 - £20

SCHEMBRI Veronica 0256 465853
5 Solent Drive, Hatch Warren, BASINGSTOKE RG22 4XS
Member of: BAC Acc, BPS, GPTI
Quals/training: BAC Acc; BA Psychol 1989; Advanced Gestalt Psychotherapy Training 1987-91; currently - Masters Degree in Couns & Psychotherapy (Regents College)
Personal Therapy: Ongoing
Supervision: Ongoing
Counselling offered: General, Bereavement, Psychotherapy, Crisis, Supervision, Occupational
Service for: Individuals, Groups
Specific to: Helping professions
Theoretical Approach: Existential, Gestalt
Fees: £22 - £35 sliding scale

Hampshire

BROCK Sue 0256 26176
4 Paddockfields, Old Basing, BASINGSTOKE RG24 0DB
Member of: ITA
Quals/training: Childcare Cert (Home Office); AIMSW; in clinical training TA psychotherapy (Metanoia); advanced training in Supervision
Personal Therapy: Ongoing
Supervision: Ongoing
Counselling offered: General, Bereavement, Disability, Relationship, Psychotherapy, Change
Service for: Individuals
Theoretical Approach: TA, Rogerian, Egan
Fees: £20 initial interview no charge

GOOD Patricia 0256 58814
10 Clover Field, Lychpit, BASINGSTOKE RG24 8SR
Member of: BAC Acc, Guild of Psychotherapists
Quals/training: BAC(Acc); RGN; SCM; 3yrs Counsellor Trainer (WPF affiliated centre); 1 yr (Surrey Univ)
Personal Therapy: Yes
Supervision: Ongoing
Counselling offered: General, Bereavement
Service for: Individuals
Fees: £20 negotiable

STOKES Anne 0256 397223
Rainich, North Waltham, BASINGSTOKE RG25 2BL
Member of: BAC
Quals/training: Dip Couns (Reading Univ); MSc Couns (Bristol Univ)
Personal Therapy: Yes
Supervision: Ongoing
Counselling offered: General, Relationship, Crisis
Service for: Individuals, Groups, Organisations
Theoretical Approach: Person-centred
Fees: £20 - £25

RITCHIE Ann 0256 850436
Compton House, Monk Sherbourne, BASINGSTOKE RG26 5HH
Member of: BAC
Quals/training: Trained in psychodynamic couns (Albany Trust)
Personal Therapy: Ongoing
Supervision: Ongoing
Counselling offered: General, Marital, Relationship, Bereavement
Service for: Individuals
Theoretical Approach: Psychodynamic, Person-centred
Fees: £20 negotiable

Hampshire

WYNNE-JONES Christa
Eversley House, 21 Reading Road, Eversley, BASINGSTOKE RG27 0RP
Member of: BAC
Quals/training: Bereavement Couns 1986; Wokingham & District Couns Service (WPF Affiliated Centre); WPF Acc 1991
Personal Therapy: Ongoing
Supervision: Ongoing
Counselling offered: **General, Bereavement, Marital, Personal growth, Relationship, Eating disorders**
Service for: Individuals
Theoretical Approach: Psychodynamic
Fees: £18

CLIFFORD Andrea   0420 82415
Osborne House, Kingsley, BORDON GU35 9LW
Member of: BAC
Quals/training: MEd; Couns Aspects of Education course, Tavistock Inst; basic & advanced courses in child/young people counselling; course in family therapy with a handicapped/sick member(IFT)
Personal Therapy: Yes
Supervision: Ongoing
Counselling offered: **General, Supervision**
Service for: Individuals, Couples, Families
Specific to: Children, Parents, People with disabilities
Theoretical Approach: Eclectic, Psychodynamic
Fees: £30 negotiable

TOWERS Anne   0252 873843
53 Coleridge Avenue, Yateley, CAMBERLEY GU17 7BJ
Member of: BAC
Quals/training: BA Soc Sci; CQSW; Dip Couns(SACE)'93
Personal Therapy: Yes
Supervision: Ongoing
Counselling offered: **General, Bereavement, Relationship**
Service for: Individuals
Specific to: Carers
Theoretical Approach: Person-centred, Humanistic
Fees: £15 - £20

BETTS Toni   Ansaphone 0703 322134
Eastleigh College, Chestnut Avenue, EASTLEIGH SO5 5HT
Member of: BAC
Quals/training: Dip Couns (Southampton Pastoral Couns Service); City & Guilds Teacher Training Cert; Ongoing Dip Couns
Personal Therapy: Yes
Supervision: Ongoing
Counselling offered: **General, Short-term**
Service for: Individuals
Specific to: Students, Teachers
Theoretical Approach: Egan, Rogerian
Fees: £15 - £25

Hampshire

BETTS Toni Ansaphone 0703 254579
4 Marlborough Road, Chandler's Ford, EASTLEIGH SO5 1DH
Member of:	BAC
Quals/training:	Dip Couns (Southampton Pastoral Couns Service); City & Guilds Teacher Training Cert; Ongoing Dip Couns (Portsmouth Univ)
Personal Therapy:	Yes
Supervision:	Ongoing
Counselling offered:	General, Short-term
Service for:	Individuals
Specific to:	Students, Teachers
Theoretical Approach:	Egan, Rogerian
Fees:	£15 - £25

GLASSPOOL Patricia 0703 255678
12 Hocombe Drive, Chandlesford, EASTLEIGH SO5 1QE
Member of:	BAC, NRHP
Quals/training:	Dip Hypnotherapy & Psychotherapy; Cert Couns; training in Groupwork
Personal Therapy:	Yes
Supervision:	Ongoing
Counselling offered:	General, Abuse, Bereavement, Marital, Relationship, Hypnotherapy, Regression therapy, Psychotherapy
Service for:	Individuals, Couples, Families, Groups
Theoretical Approach:	Eclectic
Fees:	£26.50

COX George 0703 644094
222 Twyford Road, EASTLEIGH SO5 4LF
Member of:	BAC
Quals/training:	Adv Dip Couns
Personal Therapy:	Yes
Supervision:	Ongoing
Counselling offered:	General, Personal growth, Relationship, Medical, Psychotherapy, Stress management
Service for:I	ndividuals, Groups, Organisations
Theoretical Approach:	Humanistic, Psychodynamic
Fees:	£25

STIMPSON Quentin 0329 826621
3 Grove Cottages, Gordon Road, FAREHAM PO16 7TD
Member of:	BAC
Quals/training:	Dip in Psychotherapy
Personal Therapy:	Yes
Supervision:	Ongoing
Counselling offered:	General, Bereavement, Psychotherapy, Substance abuse
Service for:	Individuals, Groups
Theoretical Approach:	Psychodynamic
Fees:	£20; initial session £30

Hampshire

VON BUHLER Jose   **0252 543973**
33 High Street, FARNBOROUGH GU14 6ES
Member of:	BASMT
Quals/training:	Lic Psi Edu (Spain); RMN; CPN; BASMT Accred; Dip Human Sexuality
Personal Therapy:	Ongoing
Supervision:	Ongoing
Counselling offered:	**Marital, Sexual abuse, HIV, AIDS, Psychosexual, Long-term**
Service for:	Individuals, Couples
Specific to:	Abusers, Survivors of sex abuse
Theoretical Approach:	Eclectic
Other languages:	Spanish
Fees:	£30; Assessment £50

RUSSELL Dorothy   **0252 549224**
14 Highgate Lane, FARNBOROUGH GU14 8AF
Member of:	BAC
Quals/training:	Dip Couns
Personal Therapy:	Yes
Supervision:	Ongoing
Counselling offered:	**General, Bereavement**
Service for:	Individuals
Fees:	Negotiable

ASHLEY Owen   **0252 617 673**
1 Cygnet Court, Old Cove Road, FLEET GU13 8RL
Member of:	BAC Acc
Quals/training:	BAC(Acc); BSc Sociology; Dip Couns '89 & MA Couns (Reading Univ); IGA course
Personal Therapy:	Unknown
Supervision:	Ongoing
Counselling offered:	**General, Bereavement, Relationship, Psychotherapy, Stress**
Service for:	Individuals, Couples, Groups
Theoretical Approach:	Eclectic, Christian
Fees:	£20 - £25 sliding scale

BUSS Heather   **0252 622691**
5 Howard Close, FLEET GU13 9ER
Member of:	BAC
Quals/training:	BA (Hons); Dip Ed (Bristol Univ); 1982 Cert Couns (Surrey Univ)
Personal Therapy:	Ongoing
Supervision:	Ongoing
Counselling offered:	**General, Relationship, Bereavement, Anxiety, Depression, Stress, Redundancy**
Service for:	Individuals, Couples, Families, Groups
Theoretical Approach:	Rogerian, Gestalt, Psychodynamic
Fees:	£15 - £25

Hampshire

LOWINGER Leah   0425 474737
12 Ashford Road, FORDINGBRIDGE SP6 1BZ
Member of:	BAC, BPS
Quals/training:	MSc 1971; AFBPsS; C Psychol
Personal Therapy:	Yes
Supervision:	Ongoing
Counselling offered:	**General, Stress management, Psychotherapy**
Service for:	Individuals, Couples, Groups, Families
Theoretical Approach:	Eclectic
Fees:	Negotiable

DUPONT-JOSHUA Aisha   0428 727 694
32 Lark Rise, LIPHOOK GU30 7QT
Member of:	BAC
Quals/training:	Dip Inter-cultural Therapy 1991; Youthwork 1990; Art Therapy training (Geneva) 1987; member of NAFSIYAT
Personal Therapy:	Yes
Supervision:	Ongoing
Counselling offered:	**General, Cross/multi-cultural, Art therapy**
Service for:	Individuals, Couples, Families, Groups
Specific to:	Adolescents, Ethnic minorities, Women
Theoretical Approach:	Eclectic
Other languages:	French
Fees:	£15 - £20

BODDINGTON Daphne   0428 722007
Coopers Bridge Farm, Bramshott, LIPHOOK GU30 7RF
Member of:	BAC Acc, BASMT
Quals/training:	BAC Acc; BASMT Acc; MA Psychol (Cambridge); Dip Social Admin (LSE); Cert Couns (Univ of Surrey) 1984
Personal Therapy:	Yes
Supervision:	Ongoing
Counselling offered:	**General, Family, Marital, Sexual, Bereavement, Crisis, Supervision**
Service for:	Individuals, Couples, Families
Theoretical Approach:	Eclectic
Fees:	£20 - £30

LEWIS Gretl   0983 522014
1 Cedar Hill, Carisbrooke, NEWPORT PO30 1DN
Member of:	BAC Acc, BASMT
Quals/training:	BAC Acc; BASMT Acc; RELATE Trained
Personal Therapy:	Yes
Supervision:	Ongoing
Counselling offered:	**General, Psychotherapy, Bereavement, Sexual, Supervision**
Service for:	Individuals, Couples, Families, Groups
Theoretical Approach:	Psychodynamic, Behavioural
Fees:	£25

Hampshire

LETHBRIDGE CLEGG Sue   0730 264056
16 Bannerman Road, PETERSFIELD GU32 2HQ
Member of:	**AGIP**
Quals/training:	Completed AGIP training
Personal Therapy:	Yes
Supervision:	Ongoing
Counselling offered:	**Psychotherapy, Relationship, Self-esteem, Personal growth**
Service for:	Individuals
Theoretical Approach:	Psychodynamic, Eclectic
Fees:	£18 - £25 Also practises in Portsmouth

HEAL Felicity   0730 260410
40 Rushes Road, PETERSFIELD GU32 3BW
Member of:	**BAC Acc**
Quals/training:	BAC(Acc); Dip Pastoral Couns(St John's College Nottingham) '83; Dip Couns(Brighton Poly)'88
Personal Therapy:	Ongoing
Supervision:	Ongoing
Counselling offered:	**General**
Service for:	Individuals, Couples
Theoretical Approach:	Rogerian, Gestalt, TA
Fees:	£20 sliding scale

WILSON Mick   0705 876543
Univ of Portsmouth, School of Social Studies, Milldam, Burnaby Road, PORTSMOUTH PO1 3AS
Member of:	**BAC**
Quals/training:	BA; MA (Ed); PGCE; Dip Ed; Couns Skills training (ILEA) 1984 Dip Student Couns (London Univ) 1988; Introductory Course (IGA) 1989; Supervision Course (Maudsley Hosp) 1992
Personal Therapy:	Ongoing
Supervision:	Ongoing
Counselling offered:	**General, Relationship, Marital, Career**
Service for:	Individuals, Couples, Groups
Specific to:	GP referrals
Theoretical Approach:	Psychodynamic
Fees:	£20

WATKINS Jean   0425 33224
25 Copse Road, Burley, RINGWOOD BH24 4EG
Member of:	**BAC Acc**
Quals/training:	BAC(Acc); MBBS; MRCGP '55
Personal Therapy:	No
Supervision:	Ongoing
Counselling offered:	**General, Psychosexual, Bereavement**
Service for:	Individuals
Specific to:	Women, Survivors of sex abuse
Fees:	£15 - £30 negotiable

Hampshire

BENNETT Ross Ms   0794 68012
Kwanti, Jermyn's Lane, Ampfield, ROMSEY SO51 0QA
Member of:	BAC
Quals/training:	BSc(Hons) Psychol; BA; PGCE; 1 year course in Psychotherapy 1987 & PG course in Psychotherapy (Spectrum) 1991
Personal Therapy:	Yes
Supervision:	Ongoing
Counselling offered:	**General, Psychotherapy**
Service for:	Individuals, Couples, Groups, Organisations
Specific to:	Women
Theoretical Approach:	Client-centred, Eclectic
Fees:	£25 inds £30 couples

SUTTON Janet   0794 22127
Greenacres, Whinwhistle Road, East Wellow, ROMSEY SO51 6BH
Member of:	BAC
Quals/training:	Training in Psychdynamic Couns (Southampton Past Couns Serv); Group Analytic Psychotherapy(SGCGW); Human Sexuality (Southampton Univ); CAES
Personal Therapy:	Yes
Supervision:	Ongoing
Counselling offered:	**General, Addiction, Sexual abuse, Assertiveness, Personal growth, Stress management**
Service for:	Individuals, Groups, Organisations
Specific to:	Women
Theoretical Approach:	Psychodynamic, Behavioural
Fees:	£20 - £30 sliding scale

ELDRIDGE Rodney   0794 22062
Little Acorns, The Drove, West Wellow, ROMSEY SO51 6DT
Member of:	NRHP
Quals/training:	Trained by NCHP and Inst of Stress Management
Personal Therapy:	Yes
Supervision:	No
Counselling offered:	**General, Sexual, Psychotherapy**
Service for:	Individuals, Couples, Families
Fees:	£20 - £30 negotiable

HALL Cherrie   8-9pm 0703 730589
47 The Hundred, ROMSEY SO51 8GE
Member of:	BAC
Quals/training:	Dip Couns (Aston); Adv Dip PE (Leeds); Cert Ed (Nottingham)
Personal Therapy:	Ongoing
Supervision:	Ongoing
Counselling offered:	**Psychotherapy**
Service for:	Individuals
Theoretical Approach:	Analytical
Fees:	£20 - £25 sliding scale

Hampshire

CLEGG Adrienne ansaphone 0705 412230
119 Finchdean Road, ROWLANDS CASTLE PO9 6EN
Member of: BAC
Quals/training: MA; Adv Dip Couns '91; ongoing training in Gestalt Therapy (Chester - affil GPTI)
Personal Therapy: Yes
Supervision: Ongoing
Counselling offered: Loss, General, Redundancy, Transition
Service for: Individuals
Theoretical Approach: Eclectic, Gestalt
Fees: £18 - £20

EASTON Simon 0703 334752
Centre for the Study of, Complementary Medicine, 51 Bedford Place, SOUTHAMPTON SO1 2DG
Member of: BPS
Quals/training: BSc Psychol; MA Clinical Psychol; Chartered Clinical Psychologist
Personal Therapy: No
Supervision: Yes
Counselling offered: General, Psychotherapy
Service for: Individuals, Couples
Theoretical Approach: Cognitive/Behavioural
Fees: £40

LOMAX Maggie 0703 788110
77 Jessamine Road, Shirley, Warren, SOUTHAMPTON SO1 6AJ
Member of: BAC
Quals/training: BA; MSc Applied Soc Studies; Cert Couns; CQSW; Trining in Re-evaluation Co-counselling, Groupwork; Anger management, assertiveness
Personal Therapy: Ongoing
Supervision: Ongoing
Counselling offered: General, Bereavement, Crisis, Personal growth, Relationship
Service for: Individuals, Couples, Families, Groups
Specific to: Oppressed groups
Theoretical Approach: Humanistic, Rogerian, Gestalt
Fees: £16 - £32 unwaged £12

CASTLE Steve 0703 220 393
25 Hartington Road, St. Marys, SOUTHAMPTON SO2 0EW
Member of: BAC
Quals/training: BTh; MSc (Soc Sc); Dip Couns
Personal Therapy: Ongoing
Supervision: Ongoing
Counselling offered: General, Psychotherapy
Service for: Individuals, Couples, Groups, Organisations
Theoretical Approach: Rogerian, Eclectic
Fees: Negotiable

Hampshire

DAHLE Josephine 0703 324046, 0703 582245
Grove Natural Therapy Centre, 22 Grosvenor Road, Highfield, SOUTHAMPTON SO2 1RT
Member of:	**BAC**
Quals/training:	MA Ed (Southampton); training in Re-evaluation Counselling Psychotherapy and Family therapy
Personal Therapy:	Ongoing
Supervision:	Ongoing
Counselling offered:	**General, Psychotherapy, Eating disorders, Marital, Crisis, Work**
Service for:	Individuals, Couples, Groups, Families
Specific to:	Women
Theoretical Approach:	Humanistic
Other languages:	Danish, Norwegian, French
Fees:	£32 negotiable

BYFORD Annette 0703 582238
14 Westbourne Crescent, SOUTHAMPTON SO2 1EE
Member of:	**BPS**
Quals/training:	MA Literature; BSc Psychol; trained in Psychotherapy Tavistock Clinic & Dept Psychotherapy Southampton
Personal Therapy:	Yes
Supervision:	Yes
Counselling offered:	**Psychotherapy**
Service for:	Individuals
Theoretical Approach:	Analytic
Other languages:	German
Fees:	£25 negotiable

RYVES Meg 0703 672202
14 Belmont Road, Portswood, SOUTHAMPTON SO2 1GE
Member of:	**BAC**
Quals/training:	Adv Dip Couns(West Sussex Inst H E)'88; RELATE trained; Cert Ed; MITD; Dip Adv Ed Studies (Southampton Univ)
Personal Therapy:	Ongoing
Supervision:	Ongoing
Counselling offered:	**General, Career, Marital, Stress**
Service for:	Individuals, Couples, Groups, Organisations
Theoretical Approach:	Eclectic
Fees:	£25

TAYLOR Donald 0703 671558
Grove House, 2 University Road, Highfield, SOUTHAMPTON SO2 1TJ
Member of:	**BAC, BPS**
Quals/training:	Chartered Occupational Psychologist; Psychotherapy training (Royal South Hants Hospital)
Personal Therapy:	Yes
Supervision:	Ongoing
Counselling offered:	**Occupational, Psychotherapy**
Service for:	Individuals, Organisations
Theoretical Approach:	Psychodynamic
Fees:	£30 (companies negotiable)

Hampshire

MARTIN Peter   0703 322332
25 Langhorn Road, Swaythling, SOUTHAMPTON SO2 3TP
Member of: BAC Acc
Quals/training: BAC Acc; BA Soc Sci; BEd (Couns Component); MA (Thesis on Psychotherapy): Dip Couns (Chichester Couns Services) '84; Human Sexuality Course; MSc (Roehampton) Psych Couns '92-4
Personal Therapy: Ongoing
Supervision: Ongoing
Counselling offered: General, Psychotherapy
Service for: Individuals
Theoretical Approach: Analytic
Fees: £27 (£45 initial session)

MUGRIDGE Helle   0489 894240
15 Basingwell Street, Bishops Waltham, SOUTHAMPTON SO3 1AJ
Member of: BAC Acc, AFT
Quals/training: BAC Acc; trained in psychodynamic counselling (WPF) and family therapy; NMGC (Relate) trained; a counsellor in General Practice.
Personal Therapy: Yes
Supervision: Ongoing
Counselling offered: General, Bereavement, Relationship
Service for: Individuals, Couples, Families
Theoretical Approach: Psychodynamic, Eclectic
Other languages: Danish
Fees: £20 Negotiable

TOLEMAN Olive   Ansaphone 0489 893788
5 Langton Road, Bishops Waltham, SOUTHAMPTON SO3 1GF
Member of: BAC Acc
Quals/training: BAC Acc; Dip Couns (Reading 1984); Human Sexuality course 1986
Personal Therapy: Ongoing
Supervision: Ongoing
Counselling offered: General, Bereavement, Relationship, Retirement, Stress management
Service for: Individuals, Couples, Groups, Organisations
Specific to: Women, Adolescents
Theoretical Approach: Humanistic, Gestalt
Other languages: French
Fees: £20

SALTER Gill   0703 582245
The Grove Centre, SOUTHAMPTON & IOW
Member of: BAC
Quals/training: Dip Couns (Spectrum); Memb AHP
Personal Therapy: Ongoing
Supervision: Ongoing
Counselling offered: Psychotherapy
Service for: Individuals, Couples, Groups
Theoretical Approach: Humanistic
Fees: £30 negotiable

Hampshire

CLARK Jackie　　　　　　　　　　　　　　　　　　　　0703 476579
Coltwood House, 151 Albert Road South, SOUTHAMPTON SO1 1FR
Member of:	BAC
Quals/training:	RELATE Trained
Personal Therapy:	Yes
Supervision:	Ongoing
Counselling offered:	**General, Marital, Relationship**
Service for:	Individuals, Couples
Theoretical Approach:	Eclectic
Fees:	£25

GOSS Diana　　　　　　　　　　　　　　　　　　　　0703 582245
The Grove Natural Therapy Cent, 22 Grosvenor Road, Highfield, SOUTHAMPTON SO2 1RT
Member of:	BAC, BASMT
Quals/training:	Dip Couns; Cert in Psychosexual & Relationship Therapy(Lond Inst Human Sexuality)
Personal Therapy:	Ongoing
Supervision:	Ongoing
Counselling offered:	**General, Marital, Psychosexual, Relationship, Stress**
Service for:	Individuals, Couples
Theoretical Approach:	Eclectic
Fees:	£22 special rates for low earners

PERRY Pamela　　　　　　　　　　　　　　　　　　　0489 575693
SOUTHAMPTON SO3
Member of:	BAC
Quals/training:	PG Dip AT; RATh '83; BAAT; Cert in Psychodynamic Counselling Supervision (WPF)'93; Cruse training; Cruse Supervisor
Personal Therapy:	Yes
Supervision:	Ongoing
Counselling offered:	**General, Psychotherapy, Art therapy, Bereavement, Supervision**
Service for:	Individuals, Groups
Theoretical Approach:	Jungian, Kleinian
Fees:	£15 - £30 dependent on income

BENNETT Ross　　　　　　　　　　　　　　　　　　　0705 830558
Portsmouth Natural Health Ctre, 35 Osborne Road, SOUTHSEA PO5 3LR
Member of:	BAC
Quals/training:	BSc(Hons) Psychol; BA; PGCE; 1yr course in Psychotherapy '87 & PG course in Psychotherapy (Spectrum) 1991
Personal Therapy:	Yes
Supervision:	Ongoing
Counselling offered:	**General, Psychotherapy**
Service for:	Individuals, Couples, Groups, Organisations
Specific to:	Women
Theoretical Approach:	Client-centred, Eclectic
Fees:	£25 - £30 couples

Hampshire

FORD Mandy 0705 829469
9 Herbert Road, SOUTHSEA PO4 0QA
Member of: BAC
Quals/training: NMGC/RELATE trained including sex therapy
Personal Therapy: Yes
Supervision: Ongoing
Counselling offered: **Marital, Sexual**
Service for: Individuals, Couples
Theoretical Approach: Eclectic
Fees: £20

GOSS Diana 0705 830671, 0705 818080
The Clinic, 149A Eastney Road, Eastney, SOUTHSEA PO4 8DZ
Member of: BAC, BASMT
Quals/training: Dip Couns; Cert in Psychosexual & Relationship Therapy(Lond Inst Human Sexuality)
Personal Therapy: Ongoing
Supervision: Ongoing
Counselling offered: **General, Marital, Psychosexual, Relationship, Stress**
Service for: Individuals, Couples
Theoretical Approach: Eclectic
Fees: £22 special rates for low earners

WILLIAMS Ann 0926 714621
The Mill, Shawford, WINCHESTER SO21 2BP
Member of: NRHP
Quals/training: Diploma in Hypnotherapy & Psychotherapy; Couns training with Southampton Pastoral Service; NLP
Personal Therapy: Yes
Supervision: Ongoing
Counselling offered: **General, Anxiety, Phobias, Depression, Confidence, Career, Redundancy, Psychotherapy**
Service for: Individuals, Groups
Theoretical Approach: Eclectic
Fees: £25 - £40

PITT Rosemary 0962 841515 x 246, ansaphone 0962 868005
King Alfred's College, Sparkford Rd, WINCHESTER SO22 4NR
Member of: BAC
Quals/training: BA; MA; Dip Couns Skills 1986; ASC Student Counsellor:
Personal Therapy: Ongoing
Supervision: Ongoing
Counselling offered: **General, Body image, Eating disorders, Sexuality, Loss, Bereavement, Relationship, Stress management**
Service for: Individuals, Couples
Theoretical Approach: Psychodynamic, Rogerian
Fees: £15 - £30 Sliding Scale

Hampshire

FIRTH David **0962 852028**
24 West End Terrace, WINCHESTER SO22 5EN
Member of: **BAC Acc**
Quals/training: BAC Acc; BA(Hons) (Cantab); PGCE (London); MPhil (Southampton); WPF Affiliate Cert; Cert in Psychodynamic Couns (WPF) 1989
Personal Therapy: Yes
Supervision: Ongoing
Counselling offered: **General**
Service for: Individuals, Couples
Theoretical Approach: Psychodynamic
Fees: £23 negotiable

VERNEY Juliet **0962 851563**
Flat 1A, 58 Chilbolton Avenue, WINCHESTER SO22 5HQ
Member of: **BAC**
Quals/training: RELATE & WPF trained
Personal Therapy: Ongoing
Supervision: Ongoing
Counselling offered: **General, Bereavement, Relationship, Sexual**
Service for: Individuals, Couples, Groups
Fees: £15 - £25 negotiable

HULME Kendall **0962 869604**
25 Owens Road, WINCHESTER SO22 6RU
Member of: **BAC**
Quals/training: CQSW; MSc Mental Health; 3 yr training in Psychodynamic Counselling (Albany Trust)
Personal Therapy: Ongoing
Supervision: Ongoing
Counselling offered: **General, Relationship, Bereavement, Marital, AIDS**
Service for: Individuals, Couples
Theoretical Approach: Psychodynamic
Other languages: French
Fees: £25 sliding scale

TITMAN Ann **0962 853026**
Eldon Lodge, Edington Road, WINCHESTER SO23 7AF
Member of: **BAC, AFT**
Quals/training: Assoc Memb Inst of Almoners; Cert post qualifying studies - Visual Handicap; Approved Social Work
Personal Therapy: Yes
Supervision: Ongoing
Counselling offered: **General, Relationship, Conciliation, Abuse**
Service for: Individuals, Couples, Families, Groups, Organisations
Specific to: Women, Parents
Theoretical Approach: Psychodynamic, Eclectic
Fees: £20

Hampshire

LEWIN Elisabeth   0962 883680
31 Wesley Road, Kingsworthy, WINCHESTER SO23 7PX
Member of:	BAC Acc
Quals/training:	BAC Acc; BA(Hons); Cert Ed; CQSW; RELATE Trained; Dip CTP; Autogenic Trainers Acc (BAFATT); Memb Human Social Functioning Soc
Personal Therapy:	Ongoing
Supervision:	Ongoing
Counselling offered:	General, Cancer, Personal growth, Relaxation, Stress management
Service for:	Individuals, Couples, Groups, Families
Theoretical Approach:	Humanistic, Jungian, Transpersonal, Integrative
Other languages:	German
Fees:	£20 negotiable

GLASSPOOL, Patricia   0962 867196
The Square Centre, 18 The Square, WINCHESTER SO23 9EX
Member of:	BAC, NRHP
Quals/training:	Dip Hypnotherapy & Psychotherapy; Cert Couns; training in Groupwork
Personal Therapy:	Yes
Supervision:	Ongoing
Counselling offered:	General, Abuse, Bereavement, Marital, Relationship, Hypnotherapy, Psychotherapy, Regression therapy
Service for:	Individuals, Couples, Families, Groups
Theoretical Approach:	Eclectic
Fees:	£26.50

PROSSER Susan   ansaphone 0926 867031
20A St Faiths Road, St Cross, WINCHESTER SO23 9QD
Member of:	BAC
Quals/training:	MA Psychol Therapy & Couns (Regents Coll)
Personal Therapy:	Ongoing
Supervision:	Ongoing
Counselling offered:	General, Eating disorders, Psychotherapy, Crisis, Trauma, Disaster, Transition
Service for:	Individuals, Couples, Groups
Specific to:	Young people
Theoretical Approach:	Kleinian, Integrative, TA, Gestalt, Ericksonian
Fees:	£15 - £25

BUCHANAN Gill   0962 866416
Clovercombe, Kingsgate Road, WINCHESTER SO23 9QQ
Member of:	BAC
Quals/training:	Dip in Counselling (Surrey Adult & Continuing Ed)
Personal Therapy:	Yes
Supervision:	Ongoing
Counselling offered:	General
Service for:	Individuals
Theoretical Approach:	Humanistic
Fees:	£15 - £20 Negotiable

Hampshire

GASKELL Judy Ms 0962 842853
Spring Cottage, 18 Back Street, St Cross, WINCHESTER SO23 9SB
Member of: **BAC**
Quals/training: Cert Couns(Surrey Univ)'90; Dip Couns(Surrey Adult & Cont Ed Service)'92
Personal Therapy: Ongoing
Supervision: Ongoing
Counselling offered: **General, Loss, Spiritual, Personal growth**
Service for: Individuals, Groups
Specific to: Bereavement, Survivors of child abuse
Theoretical Approach: Psychodynamic, Humanistic
Fees: £20 - £25 sliding scale

Hereford & Worcester

Organisations

SAINT ANNE'S 0568 708632
The Leys, Aston, Kingsland, LEOMINSTER HR6 9PU
Service:	Psychotherapy & counselling for individuals, couples, groups
Area served:	Hereford & Worcester, Glos & Shropshire
Referral:	Self, GP, Church
Training of workers:	All are professionally qualified viz: IPC, WPF, BPS, RELATE Ongoing supervision; personal therapy
Code of Ethics:	BAC, IPC, WPF
Management by:	The Director
Fees:	£30 Initial consultation, then negotiable

BROMSGROVE & REDDITCH DEPT OF CLINICAL PSYCHOLOGY
0527 596059
Smallwood House, Church Green West, REDDITCH B97 4BD
Service:	Comprehensive psychology service for individuals, couples, groups and families
Area served:	Bromsgrove and Redditch
Referral:	GP, Health/Soc Work Professional
Training of workers:	Postgraduate clinical psychology
Code of Ethics:	BPS
Management by:	North East Worcestershire Community Healthcare Trust
Fees:	None

SOUTH WORCESTERSHIRE HYPNOTHERAPY CENTRE
ansaphone 0905 612846
16 Sansome Walk, WORCESTER WR1 1LN
Service:	Curative Hypnotherapy, individual counselling and training
Area served:	West Midlands
Referral:	Self or others
Training of workers:	Practical hypnotherapy training to the standard required by the Guild of Curative Hypnotherapists & Assoc of Natural Medicines
Code of Ethics:	Therapists' Professional body
Management by:	The Partners
Fees:	£17 - £20 (£45 anti-smoking)

Individual Practitioners
*Each individual is a **member of** one or more organisations eligible for entry into this directory. BAC Accredited Counsellors and Recognised Supervisors are shaded.*

O'NEILL Teresa 021 445 1566
The Cottage, 15 Station Road, Blackwell, BROMSGROVE B60 1QB
Member of:	BAC
Quals/training:	CQSW 1977; Dip Couns (IP); Memb BASW
Personal Therapy:	Ongoing
Supervision:	Ongoing
Counselling offered:	General, Relationship, Addiction, Abuse, Cancer
Service for:	Individuals, Couples
Theoretical Approach:	Eclectic
Fees:	£20 - £25 negotiable

Hereford & Worcester

BEELEY Linda   0905 796691
3 Newland Road, DROITWICH WR9 7AF
Member of:	BAC, BPS, WMIP
Quals/training:	Dip Couns (PCT); MA; BM; BCh
Personal Therapy:	Yes
Supervision:	Ongoing
Counselling offered:	General, Psychotherapy
Service for:	Individuals, Couples
Theoretical Approach:	Person-centred
Fees:	£25 - £35

HAMMERSLEY Diane   0905 776197
52 Hanbury Road, DROITWICH WR9 8PR
Member of:	BAC, BPS
Quals/training:	BSc; MEd; C Psychol; trained in TA, Cognitive & Behavioural Therapy; Cruse counsellor
Personal Therapy:	Yes
Supervision:	Ongoing
Counselling offered:	General, Addiction, Tranquillisers, Bereavement, Psychotherapy, Eating disorders, Work
Service for:	Individuals, Couples, Groups
Fees:	£30

OLIVER Jenny   0531 670477
The Willows, Yarkhill, HEREFORD HR1 3TE
Member of:	BAC
Quals/training:	BA(Hons) Psychol & Sociology; Memb CTA; in training (IP)
Personal Therapy:	Ongoing
Supervision:	Ongoing
Counselling offered:	General, Relationship, Bereavement, Psychotherapy, Primal therapy, Crisis, Spiritual
Service for:	Individuals, Couples, Groups
Specific to:	Women
Theoretical Approach:	Gestalt, Psychosynthesis
Other languages:	French
Fees:	£15 - £30 sliding scale

PAYNE Jean   0432 870 339
Bethesda, Dinedor, Holme Lacy, HEREFORD HR2 6LQ
Member of:	BAC
Quals/training:	SRN; SCM; HV; Dip Couns (Manchester Poly)
Personal Therapy:	Yes
Supervision:	Ongoing
Counselling offered:	General, Marital, Bereavement, Stress management, Pregnancy, Abortion
Service for:	Individuals, Couples
Theoretical Approach:	Eclectic
Fees:	Negotiable

Hereford & Worcester

FULLER Dianne 0992 583525
Silver Maples, Warren Park Road, Bengeo, HERTFORD SG14 3JA
Member of:	BAC
Quals/training:	RSA Couns Skills Cert; Adlerian Cert (Individual Psychology)
Personal Therapy:	Yes
Supervision:	Ongoing
Counselling offered:	**General, Bereavement**
Service for:	Individuals
Theoretical Approach:	Rogerian, TA, Adlerian
Fees:	£15 - £25 sliding scale

RICHARDSON Naomi 0562 829297
2 Farfield, KIDDERMINSTER DY10 1UG
Member of:	BAC
Quals/training:	Dip Hypnosis & Psychotherapy;
Personal Therapy:	Ongoing
Supervision:	Ongoing
Counselling offered:	**General, Crisis, Psychotherapy**
Service for:	Individuals, Couples, Groups
Specific to:	People with learning difficulties
Theoretical Approach:	Psychodynamic, Eclectic
Fees:	£25 Negotiable

BURSTON Helen 0684 40788
The Lodge, Old Colwell, MALVERN WR13 6HF
Member of:	BAC, BCPC
Quals/training:	B Soc Sci; Dip Couns; Psychotherapist in training (BCPC)
Personal Therapy:	Yes
Supervision:	Ongoing
Counselling offered:	**General, Short-term, Psychotherapy, Long-term**
Service for:	Individuals
Theoretical Approach:	Integrative, Humanistic
Fees:	£15 - £20

FORD Eileen 0684 893430
Fairseat, 34 Avenue Road, MALVERN WR14 3BJ
Member of:	BAC, BASMT
Quals/training:	Cert Ed (Lond Univ); RELATE trained in counselling and sexual therapy
Personal Therapy:	Yes
Supervision:	Ongoing
Counselling offered:	**General, Relationship, Marital, Sexual**
Service for:	Individuals, Couples
Theoretical Approach:	Psychodynamic, Behavioural
Fees:	£25

Hereford & Worcester

TURNER Mary   0684 563336
MALVERN WR14
Member of:	BAC, AFT, ANLP PCS)
Quals/training:	BA; CQSW; MSc; Dip Couns
Personal Therapy:	Ongoing
Supervision:	Ongoing
Counselling offered:	**General, Bereavement**
Service for:	Individuals, Couples, Families, Groups, Organisations
Specific to:	Children, Adolescents
Theoretical Approach:	Psychodynamic, Humanistic, Integrative
Fees:	£20 Negotiable, initial cons free

MILLETT Hugh Rev   0684 567056
151 Upper Welland Road, MALVERN WR14 4LB
Member of:	BAC
Quals/training:	BAC, Counsellor and Group Facilitator, CTA
Personal Therapy:	Yes
Supervision:	Ongoing
Counselling offered:	**General, Relationship, Bereavement, Cancer, Psychotherapy, Primal therapy**
Service for:	Individuals, Couples, Families, Groups, Organisations
Theoretical Approach:	Rogerian, Gestalt, TA
Fees:	£20 Negotiable

HILL Jenny   054 421 698
Harpton Gardens, New Radnor, PRESTEIGNE LD8 2RE
Member of:	WMIP, SIP
Quals/training:	Dip Social Studies(London)1974; Cert Individual Therapeutic Work(Birmingham)1983; IGA Oxford Intro Course 1988; Currently training in Psychotherapy SIP
Personal Therapy:	Ongoing
Supervision:	Ongoing
Counselling offered:	**General, Psychotherapy**
Service for:	Individuals, Couples
Theoretical Approach:	Psychoanalytic, Psychodynamic
Fees:	£18 concessions negotiable

GEE Ann   0527 62530
340 Birmingham Road, Bordesley, REDDITCH B97 6RJ
Member of:	BAC
Quals/training:	BSc Human Psychol '83; Dip Soc Work '85; Cert Couns '84; Psychotherapy '86-7; Dip Hypnotherapy & NLP '88; Cert sexual Couns (RELATE) '88; Dip Couns '90; MSc Occ Psychol '92
Personal Therapy:	Ongoing
Supervision:	Ongoing
Counselling offered:	**General, Marital, Sexual, Psychotherapy, Stress management, Career, Occupational**
Service for:	Individuals, Couples, Groups, Families
Theoretical Approach:	Eclectic, Rogerian, Cognitive/Behavioural, Hypnotherapy
Fees:	£20 negotiable

Hereford & Worcester

TOWNSEND Angela 0684 299371
Bow Cottage, Bow Lane, Ripple, TEWKESBURY GL20 6EW
Member of: BAC, BPS
Quals/training: RSA Couns Skills; Cert Couns (Glos Couns Serv)
Personal Therapy: Ongoing
Supervision: Ongoing
Counselling offered: General, Crisis, Bereavement
Service for: Individuals, Couples, Organisations
Specific to: Employees
Theoretical Approach: Psychodynamic
Fees: £12 - £25 sliding scale

FREEMAN CARTWRIGHT John ansaphone 0905 612846
South Worcs Hypnotherapy Ctre, 16 Sansome Walk, WORCESTER WR1 1LN
Member of: BAC
Quals/training: Training in Curative Hypnotherapy, Erickson & NLP; Reg Memb Guild of Curative Hypnotherapists; Reg Memb Assoc of Natural Medicines
Personal Therapy: No
Supervision: Ongoing
Counselling offered: General, Hypnotherapy, Psychotherapy, Stop smoking
Service for: Individuals
Theoretical Approach: Hypnotherapy, Ericksonian, NLP
Fees: £17 - £20 concessions, £45 anti-smoking

FREEMAN CARTWRIGHT Josephine ansaphone 0905 612846
Sth Worcs Hypnotherapy Centre, 16 Sansome Walk, WORCESTER WR1 1LN
Member of: BAC
Quals/training: Training in Curative Hypnoptherapy, Erickson & NLP; Reg memb of Guild of Curative Hypnotherapists; Reg memb Assoc of Natural Medicines
Personal Therapy: No
Supervision: Ongoing
Counselling offered: General, Hypnotherapy, Psychotherapy, Stop smoking
Service for: Individuals
Theoretical Approach: Hypnotherapy, Ericksonian, NLP
Fees: £17 - £20 concessions, £45 anti-smoking

HARRIS Cynthia 0905 420746
Southwick Lodge, Lower Wick, WORCESTER WR2 4BU
Member of: BAC
Quals/training: RELATE trained
Personal Therapy: No
Supervision: Ongoing
Counselling offered: General, Marital, Sexual, Bereavement, Stress, Crisis, Career
Service for: Individuals, Couples, Families, Groups
Specific to: Clergy/priests
Theoretical Approach: Psychodynamic, Behavioural, Systemic
Other languages: French
Fees: £25 per hour, negotiable

Hereford & Worcester

ASHWELL Veronica 0905 428764
40 Canada Way, Lower Wick, WORCESTER WR2 4ED
Member of: NRHP
Quals/training: DHP. NRHP; Assoc member 1989, full member 1990 Nat Col Hypnosis and Psychotherapy
Personal Therapy: No
Supervision: Ongoing
Counselling offered: Hypnotherapy, Psychotherapy
Service for: Individuals, Couples
Fees: £15 negotiable

WILLIAMS Royston 0905 830316
St Pirans House, 31 Upton Road, Callow End, WORCESTER WR2 4TY
Member of: WMIP
Quals/training: AFBPsS; BSc Psychol; MSc Psychotherapy; C Psychol
Personal Therapy: Yes
Supervision: Ongoing
Counselling offered: General, Bereavement, Sexual, Psychotherapy
Service for: Individuals
Specific to: Religious, Clergy/priests
Theoretical Approach: Psychodynamic, Humanistic
Fees: £20 - £35 negotiable

WOOD Anne 0905 723383 x 277, 0905 350591
Worcester Coll of Technology, Deansway, WORCESTER WR1 2JF
Member of: BAC
Quals/training: RGN; SCM; BTA; RSA Couns Skills in a Work Setting
Personal Therapy: Ongoing
Supervision: Ongoing
Counselling offered: General, Crisis
Service for: Individuals, Couples, Families, Groups
Specific to: Students, People with disabilities
Theoretical Approach: Rogerian, Gestalt
Fees: Negotiable

Hertfordshire

Organisations

BARNET HEALTHCARE NHS TRUST SEXUAL/RELATIONSHIP THERAPY CLINIC   **081 440 5111 x 4603**
Psychiatric Unit, Barnet General Hospital, Wellhouse Lane, BARNET EN5 3DT
Service: Individual and couple counselling for a wide range of sexual dysfunctions and difficulties, paraphilias and relationship difficulties and issues around HIV
Area served: Barnet Healthcare NHS Trust area and others by negotiation
Referral: GP
Training of workers: BASMT Accredited therapist
Code of Ethics: BAC, BASMT
Management by: Barnet Healthcare NHS Trust
Fees: None

RICKMANSWORTH COUNSELLING SERVICE   **0923 775065**
Skidmore Way Clinic, Skidmore Way, RICKMANSWORTH WD3 1SZ
Service: Client-centred, Psychodynamic, eclectic, psychosexual, groupwork, PTSD, marital, relationship, crisis
Area served: South West Hertfordshire, Middlesex
Referral: Self, Health/Soc Work Professional
Training of workers: RELATE & Institute of Group Analysis trained Personal therapy. Regular supervision
Code of Ethics: BAC
Management by: Counsellors
Fees: £23

HOLISTIC PSYCHOTHERAPY   **0923 672880**
16 Brackendene, Bricket Wood, ST. ALBANS AL2 3SX
Service: Specialists in Career/Stress/Outplacement counselling for organisations. Couns & psychotherapy for depression/stress/phobias/eating disorders/confidence/sports/exams/stammering
Area served: Hertfordshire & London
Referral: Self
Training of workers: Chartered Occupational Psychologist; BA(Hons) Psych; MSc; DHP; NAHP; Personal therapy & supervision
Code of Ethics: BPS
Management by: Therapist
Fees: £35 - £50

HERTS & BEDS PASTORAL FOUNDATION   **0727 868585**
1 College Yard, Lower Dagnall Street, ST. ALBANS AL3 4PA
Service: General cllg (weekly sessions): St Albans (ind & group) or Stevenage & N Herts (ind) 0438 871259 & Broxbourne District (ind & marital) 0992 447863
Area served: Hertfordshire; see also under Bedfordshire
Referral: Self
Training of workers: Dip in Advanced Psychodynamic Counselling (validated by WPF) or WPF accreditation. Ongoing weekly supervision
Code of Ethics: BAC
Management by: Trustees, Council of Management, Director. Affiliate of WPF
Fees: £2 - £25 reg'n fee, no-one turned away

Hertfordshire

MAGDALEN CENTRE TRUST FOR GROUP PSYCHOTHERAPY
0707 390980
c/o 26 Bridge Road East, WELWYN GARDEN CITY AL7 1HL
Service: Group psychotherapy for large & small groups for people with mental health, social & emotional problems. Once a week attendance
Area served: Herts and within reach of WG City
Referral: GP, Health/Soc Work Professional, Self
Training of workers: Appropriate professional training, experience and personal therapy. All attend weekly supervision with group analyst
Code of Ethics: Agency's own code
Management by: Trustees and advisory group
Fees: According to means

Individual Practitioners
Each individual is a **member of** one or more organisations eligible for entry into this directory. BAC Accredited Counsellors and Recognised Supervisors are shaded.

MORRIS Elizabeth   0462 895531
12 Bell Row, High Street, BALDOCK SG7 6AS
Member of: BAC, ITA
Quals/training: BA(Psych); Dip Couns; training in Gestalt & TA
Personal Therapy: Ongoing
Supervision: Ongoing
Counselling offered: General, Bereavement, Relationship, Psychotherapy
Service for: Individuals, Couples, Groups
Theoretical Approach: Rogerian, TA
Fees: £17 - £25 Sliding Scale

SHATTOCK Avril   081 449 4810
87 Westpole Avenue, Cockfosters, BARNET EN4 0BA
Member of: BAC
Quals/training: RELATE Trained 1980; Course (Tavistock Inst) 1986-7; Introductory Groupwork course (IGA) 1990
Personal Therapy: Ongoing
Supervision: Ongoing
Counselling offered: General, Marital, Relationship, Bereavement
Service for: Individuals, Couples
Theoretical Approach: Psychodynamic, Rogerian
Fees: £25 negotiable

WHITESON Riva   081 449 2489
93 Westpole Avenue, Cockfosters, BARNET EN4 0BA
Member of: BAC
Quals/training: RELATE/NMGC Trained 1980
Personal Therapy: Ongoing
Supervision: Ongoing
Counselling offered: General, Bereavement, Relationship, Marital, Sexual
Service for: Individuals, Couples
Theoretical Approach: Client-centred, Psychodynamic, Object relations
Fees: £25

Hertfordshire

BERGER Iris   081 449 5973
BARNET EN4
Member of: BASMT
Quals/training: 1982-5 NMGC training including sex therapy; '86 group therapy training London MG and IGA; Full Member BASMT
Personal Therapy: Yes
Supervision: Ongoing
Counselling offered: General, Relationship, Psychosexual
Service for: Individuals, Couples
Theoretical Approach: Psychodynamic
Fees: £30 - £35

OVERTON David   081 368 2144
BARNET
Member of: BAC, AHPP
Quals/training: NMGC/RELATE Trained; Dip Couns(SW London Coll)'83
Personal Therapy: Yes
Supervision: Ongoing
Counselling offered: General, Marital, Relationship, Alcohol
Service for: Individuals, Couples, Groups
Specific to: Young people
Theoretical Approach: Psychodynamic, Person-centred
Fees: £25 - £30 reduced in cases of need

GRAFF Avril   081 441 6905
12 Evelyn Road, Cockfosters, BARNET EN4 9JT
Member of: BAC
Quals/training: Dip Couns; Outreach training course 1988-92
Personal Therapy: Ongoing
Supervision: Ongoing
Counselling offered: General, Addiction, Crisis, Eating disorders, AIDS, Tranquillisers
Service for: Individuals
Specific to: Gays, Students, Adolescents
Theoretical Approach: Psychodynamic
Fees: £20 - £30 sliding scale

GOODMAN Helen   081 441 6212
2 St Wilfrids Close, New Barnet, BARNET EN4 9SE
Member of: BAC
Quals/training: Dip Couns (CSCT) 1990; Barnet Bereavement Project 1989
Personal Therapy: Ongoing
Supervision: Ongoing
Counselling offered: General, Bereavement
Service for: Individuals, Groups
Specific to: Women only
Theoretical Approach: Client-centred, Psychodynamic
Fees: £20 negotiable

Hertfordshire

FITZSIMMONS Janet   081 449 3868
10 Salisbury Road, High Barnet, BARNET EN5 4JP
Member of: BAC, LCP
Quals/training: 1960 Dip in Social Science; '86 Full Member LCP
Personal Therapy: Yes
Supervision: Ongoing
Counselling offered: **Psychotherapy, Anorexia, Bulimia**
Service for: Individuals, Couples, Families
Specific to: Adolescents
Theoretical Approach: Psychodynamic
Fees: £15 - £25 sliding scale

STEDMAN John   081 440 8487
13 Duncan Close, Plantagenet Road, BARNET EN5 5JJ
Member of: BAC
Quals/training: Dip Theology (London); trained Psychotherapists (LCIP)
Personal Therapy: Yes
Supervision: Yes
Counselling offered: **General, Marital, Sexual, Bereavement, Psychotherapy, Supervision**
Service for: Individuals
Specific to: Social workers, Clergy/priests
Theoretical Approach: Psychoanalytic, Eclectic
Fees: £18 - £25 dependent on income

LESTER Frances   081 449 3665
Monkenmead, Hadley Common, BARNET EN5 5QE
Member of: BAC Acc
Quals/training: BAC Acc; Couns Courses (Harrow CHE) 1981/2; Dip Couns (Stevenage College) 1987
Personal Therapy: Yes
Supervision: Ongoing
Counselling offered: **General**
Service for: Individuals, Couples, Groups
Theoretical Approach: Psychodynamic, Humanistic
Fees: £25 negotiable

HEWSON Jean   0442 873352
16 Fieldway, BERKHAMSTED HP4 2NX
Member of: BAC, BPS
Quals/training: BA (Hons) Psychol; MSc Couns Psychol
Personal Therapy: Yes
Supervision: Ongoing
Counselling offered: **General, Bereavement, Crisis, Psychotherapy**
Service for: Individuals, Couples
Theoretical Approach: Person-centred, Psychodynamic
Fees: £22

Hertfordshire

### WOLF-PHILLIPS Lisa	0442 864876
33 Tresco Road, BERKHAMSTED HP4 3LA
Member of:	BAC
Quals/training:	BA; BEd; Dip Couns(SW London Coll)'81
Personal Therapy:	Ongoing
Supervision:	Ongoing
Counselling offered:	**General, Crisis, Relationship, Educational, Stress**
Service for:	Individuals, Families, Groups
Specific to:	Young people, Adolescents, Teachers
Theoretical Approach:	Person-centred, Humanistic
Other languages:	German
Fees:	£20 - £25 negotiable

### WALKER Jillian	0442 256738
Boxwell Road Surgery, BERKHAMSTED HP4 3EU
Member of:	BAC Acc
Quals/training:	BAC Acc; NMGC Trained; Cert Ed Couns; AEB/CSCT Reg Trainer
Personal Therapy:	Yes
Supervision:	Ongoing
Counselling offered:	**Marital, Sexual, Bereavement, Psychotherapy, Sexual abuse**
Service for:	Individuals, Couples
Specific to:	Incest survivors
Theoretical Approach:	Integrative, Psychodynamic, Person-centred, TA
Fees:	£20 - £30

### SMITH Kathleen	0279 730489
Claremont, Sheering Road, Hatfield Heath, BISHOPS STORTFORD CM22 7LJ
Member of:	BAC
Quals/training:	Post Grad Dip in Couns (University of Hertfordshire) 1991-93
Personal Therapy:	Ongoing
Supervision:	Ongoing
Counselling offered:	**General, Bereavement, Crisis, Relationship, Work**
Service for:	Individuals, Couples
Theoretical Approach:	Psychodynamic, Rogerian
Fees:	£20 negotiable

### BURNETT-STUART Sarah	0279 777 269
The Old Vicarage, Berden, BISHOPS STORTFORD CM23
Member of:	BAC
Quals/training:	RELATE (NMGC) trained counsellor
Personal Therapy:	No
Supervision:	Ongoing
Counselling offered:	**General, Marital, Bereavement, Eating disorders**
Service for:	Individuals, Couples
Specific to:	Mentally ill
Fees:	£12 - £15

Hertfordshire

STACEY Linda   0279 504048
218 Stansted Road, BISHOPS STORTFORD CM23 2AR
Member of: BAC Acc, Member of UKCP Register
Quals/training: BAC(Acc); MA; Dip Psychosynthesis(PET, Counselling Staff Member); Family Guidance work
Personal Therapy: Ongoing
Supervision: Ongoing
Counselling offered: **General, Psychotherapy, Personal growth, Sexual abuse, Substance abuse**
Service for: Individuals, Families, Groups
Specific to: Survivors of sex abuse, Adult children of alcoholics
Theoretical Approach: Transpersonal, Integrative
Fees: On application

ERSKINE Angela   081 207 3454
Manaton House, High Street, Elstree, BOREHAMWOOD WD6 3BY
Member of: BAC Acc
Quals/training: BAC Acc; SRN; RMN; CQSW; CAP Course 1983
Personal Therapy: Yes
Supervision: Ongoing
Counselling offered: **General, Marital, Bereavement, Addiction, Crisis, Panic attacks, Phobias, Relaxation**
Service for: Individuals, Couples, Families
Theoretical Approach: Eclectic
Fees: £24 Negotiable

GERRARD Jackie, Mrs   081 207 5019
39 Lodge Avenue, Elstree, BOREHAMWOOD WD6 3NA
Member of: LCP
Quals/training: 1992 qualified in Psychoanalytic Psychotherapy
Personal Therapy: Yes
Supervision: Ongoing
Counselling offered: **General, Marital, Psychotherapy**
Service for: Individuals, Couples
Theoretical Approach: Object relations, Psychoanalytic
Other languages: Hebrew
Fees: £25 - £32 Negotiable

LEWIN Ann   081 953 1940
21 Red Road, BOREHAMWOOD WD6 4SR
Member of: BAC
Quals/training: BA; Cert of Competence (WPF); Memb Guild of Pastoral Psychology
Personal Therapy: Yes
Supervision: Ongoing
Counselling offered: **General**
Service for: Individuals
Theoretical Approach: Analytical
Fees: £22 - £25

Hertfordshire

WOODER Bernie   081 207 3457
17 Farrant Way, BOREHAMWOOD WD6 4TE
Member of: KI
Quals/training: Cert Couns (Herts & Beds Past Found); In Core Process Psychotherapy (Karuna Inst)
Personal Therapy: Ongoing
Supervision: Ongoing
Counselling offered: General, Bereavement, Crisis, Self-esteem, Psychotherapy
Service for: Individuals, Organisations
Specific to: Trade Union members, Managers
Theoretical Approach: Humanistic, Transpersonal
Fees: £19 - £30 sliding scale

BUTTERWICK Marcia   0763 87312
Danyells, Sandon, BUNTINGFORD SG9 0RF
Member of: BAC
Quals/training: BA; NMGC/RELATE Trained; Cert CTP
Personal Therapy: Yes
Supervision: Ongoing
Counselling offered: General, Marital
Service for: Individuals, Couples
Theoretical Approach: Psychodynamic, Gestalt, Transpersonal
Fees: £25

SPENCER Mary   0582 766024
14 Roundwood Lane, HARPENDEN AL5 3BZ
Member of: BAC Acc
Quals/training: BAC Acc; 1987 Dip & 1991 MA in Counselling (Univ of Herts)
Personal Therapy: Yes
Supervision: Ongoing
Counselling offered: General
Service for: Individuals, Couples
Theoretical Approach: Psychodynamic
Fees: £22 negotiable, acc. to income

THORMAN Chris   0582 712454
115 Pickford Hill, HARPENDEN AL5 5HJ
Member of: CPCP, BPS
Quals/training: BA, Dip PCP
Personal Therapy: Yes
Supervision: Ongoing
Counselling offered: General
Service for: Individuals, Couples, Groups, Organisations
Theoretical Approach: PCP
Fees: £25

Hertfordshire

YOUNG Louise 0707 273344
10 White Lion House, Town Centre, HATFIELD AL10 0JN
Member of:	BAC
Quals/training:	OPUS; Probation; Drug & Alcohol Abuse; Foundation Course in Couns; Post Grad Dip Couns (Univ of Herts) - BAC Recog; other courses inc Psychosynthesis
Personal Therapy:	Ongoing
Supervision:	Ongoing
Counselling offered:	**General, Child abuse, Rape, Incest, Bereavement, Relationship, Supervision**
Service for:	Individuals, Couples, Families, Groups
Theoretical Approach:	Client-centred, Psychodynamic, Psychosynthesis
Fees:	£25 negotiable

REDMILL-SORENSEN Bernice 0707 273457
9 Selwyn Avenue, HATFIELD AL10 9NR
Member of:	BAC Acc
Quals/training:	BAC Acc; MA Psychotherapy & Couns (Regents College); Dip Couns; Dip Person-centred Art Therapy; Cert HIV/AIDS Couns
Personal Therapy:	Ongoing
Supervision:	Ongoing
Counselling offered:	**General, Crisis, Psychotherapy, Supervision, Cross/multi-cultural**
Service for:	Individuals, Couples
Specific to:	Women, Young people
Theoretical Approach:	Integrative, Phenomenological, Existential
Fees: £	28 individuals; £32 couples

GOUGH Anna 0442 245443
00 River Park, Boxmoor, HEMEL HEMPSTEAD HP1 1QZ
Member of:	BAC
Quals/training:	Cert Couns (LCIP) 1982; Dip CTP 1984; Family Therapy Course (Tavistock)
Personal Therapy:	Yes
Supervision:	Ongoing
Counselling offered:	**General, Bereavement**
Service for:	Individuals
Theoretical Approach:	Psychodynamic
Fees:	By arrangement

NAYLOR-SMITH Alan 0442 247230
2 Fishery Passage, Horsecroft Road, HEMEL HEMPSTEAD HP1 1RF
Member of:	BAC, Guild of Psychotherapists
Quals/training:	Trained Psychotherapist (Guild of Psychotherapists) 1987
Personal Therapy:	Ongoing
Supervision:	Ongoing
Counselling offered:	**General, Psychotherapy**
Service for:	Individuals, Couples
Theoretical Approach:	Analytical, Psychodynamic
Fees:	£20 - £24 limited sliding scale

Hertfordshire

BLOCH Sue 0442 68586
HEMEL HEMPSTEAD HP1
Member of: BAC
Quals/training: Dip Couns & Community Skills (Manorhouse Centre for Psychodynamic Couns) '90; Imagework Practitioners Course (Skyros Inst)
Personal Therapy: Ongoing
Supervision: Ongoing
Counselling offered: General, Bereavement
Service for: Individuals
Theoretical Approach: Humanistic, Rogerian
Fees: £20

RICKETT Marion 0442 61712, 0442 250294
40 High Street, Old Town, HEMEL HEMPSTEAD HP1 3AE
Member of: BAC Acc
Quals/training: BAC & ASC Acc; Dip Couns (Hatfield Poly) '85; Postgraduate Dip Couns (CNAA) '87; currently training with Guild of Psychotherapists;
Personal Therapy: Ongoing
Supervision: Ongoing
Counselling offered: General
Service for: Individuals, Groups
Theoretical Approach: Psychodynamic, Analytical
Fees: £25

HUMPHREYS Lorraine 0442 230179
40 High Street, HEMEL HEMPSTEAD
Member of: BAC Acc
Quals/training: BAC(Acc); Post-Grad Dip Couns (Hatfield Poly) 1987; WPF
Personal Therapy: Yes
Supervision: Ongoing
Counselling offered: General, Bereavement
Service for: Individuals
Theoretical Approach: Psychodynamic
Fees: £22

JACKSON Barbara 0992 586084
7 Purkiss Road, HERTFORD SG13 8JA
Member of: BAC Acc
Quals/training: BAC Acc; MA (Counselling)
Personal Therapy: Ongoing
Supervision: Ongoing
Counselling offered: General, Marital, Bereavement, Depression, Oppression
Service for: Individuals, Couples
Theoretical Approach: Rogerian, Psychodynamic
Fees: £10 - £25 sliding scale

DEACON David Ansaphone 0992 554427
103 North Road, HERTFORD SG14 2BU
Member of: BAC
Quals/training: WPF/IPC Acc (Affiliate Cert) 1988; CNAA Postgraduate Dip Couns 1992
Personal Therapy: Yes
Supervision: Ongoing
Counselling offered: General, Psychotherapy
Service for: Individuals
Theoretical Approach: Psychodynamic
Fees: £25 negotiable

Hertfordshire

MANN Angela
0438 832733
50 Parkfield Crescent, Kimpton, HITCHIN SG4 8EQ
Member of:	BAC Acc
Quals/training:	BAC Acc; 1979-81 NMGC (RELATE) training; 1990-91 course in Marital Psychotherapy at TIMS; Currently training in Short-term/ Focal Psychotherapy
Personal Therapy:	Yes
Supervision:	Ongoing
Counselling offered:	**General, Marital, Bereavement, Psychotherapy, Short-term**
Service for:	Individuals, Couples
Theoretical Approach:	Psychodynamic
Fees:	£25

PARKINSON Diana
0438 832 408
43 High Street, Kimpton, HITCHIN SG4 8RA
Member of:	BAC
Quals/training:	Trained at the Hypnotherapy Centre, Bournemouth & Herts Social Services. Accredited by Drugcare St Albans
Personal Therapy:	Yes
Supervision:	Ongoing
Counselling offered:	**General, Relationship, Eating disorders, Substance abuse, Alcohol, Psychotherapy**
Service for:	Individuals, Couples, Families
Theoretical Approach:	Eclectic
Fees:	£30 negotiable, 1st session free

HARE Lesley
0442 827284
40 High Street, HEMEL HEMPSTEAD HP1 3AE
Member of:	BAC
Quals/training:	Post Grad Dip Couns (Herts Univ)
Personal Therapy:	Yes
Supervision:	Ongoing
Counselling offered:	**General**
Service for:	Individuals
Theoretical Approach:	Psychodynamic
Fees:	£15 - £25

EDWARDS Lyn
0462 459931
Birchwood, 22 The Chilterns, HITCHIN SG4 9PP
Member of:	BAC, ANLP (PCS)
Quals/training:	BEd (Hons); Dip Couns; NLP practitioner; training in Gestalt Psychotherapy, Transactional Analysis, assertiveness & stress management
Personal Therapy:	Yes
Supervision:	Ongoing
Counselling offered:	**General, Bereavement, Relationship, Sexual**
Service for:	Individuals, Couples, Groups
Theoretical Approach:	Rogerian, Gestalt, NLP, TA
Fees:	£20 - £30 negotiable

Hertfordshire

PITCAIRN Richard 0462 453929
Flat 2, 43 Benslow Lane, HITCHIN SG4 9RE
Member of: BAC
Quals/training: Dip Couns (Herts Univ); CQSW
Personal Therapy: Ongoing
Supervision: Ongoing
Counselling offered: General, Bereavement, Sexuality, Short-term, Long-term
Service for: Individuals, Couples
Specific to: Survivors of child abuse, Men
Theoretical Approach: Client-centred, Psychodynamic
Fees: £15 - £20

KELL Christine 0462 432802
19 Tilehouse Street, HITCHIN SG5 2DY
Member of: BAC Acc, WMIP
Quals/training: BAC(Acc); BA Applied Soc Studies; CQSW; Dip Couns
Personal Therapy: Yes
Supervision: Ongoing
Counselling offered: General, Crisis, Marital, Psychotherapy
Service for: Individuals, Couples
Theoretical Approach: Integrative
Fees: £25 - £30

MABEY Judith 0462 458063
7 Balliol Road, HITCHIN SG5 1TT
Member of: BAC Acc
Quals/training: BAC (Acc); BA; Cert Ed; Dip Couns; MA (Psychology of Couns & Therapy)
Personal Therapy: Yes
Supervision: Ongoing
Counselling offered: General, Bereavement, Crisis, Personal growth, Redundancy, Relationship
Service for: Individuals, Couples, Families, Groups, Organisations
Theoretical Approach: Existential, Person-centred
Fees: £28 individuals, £35 couples

McCLEMENT Shirley
HODDESDON EN11
Member of: BAC
Quals/training: RGN; RMN; Combined Cert in Couns (CAC); Memb ISMA
Personal Therapy: Yes
Supervision: Ongoing
Counselling offered: General, Anxiety, Stress management, Relaxation
Service for: Individuals
Theoretical Approach: Person-centred
Fees: Negotiable

Hertfordshire

STANTON Andrew   0562 755338
157 Hoo Road, KIDDERMINSTER DY10 1LP
Member of:	**BAC**
Quals/training:	Cert Couns 1983; CQSW; MITD
Personal Therapy:	Yes
Supervision:	Ongoing
Counselling offered:	**General, Relationship**
Service for:	Individuals, Couples, Groups
Theoretical Approach:	Rogerian, Eclectic
Fees:	From £10 negotiable

YOUNG Louise   0438 812149
110 London Road, KNEBWORTH SG3 6NB
Member of:	**BAC**
Quals/training:	OPUS; Cruse; SCS; Probation; Drug & Alcohol Abuse; PG Dip Couns(Herts Univ) - BAC Recog; other courses inc Psychosynthesis
Personal Therapy:	Ongoing
Supervision:	Ongoing
Counselling offered:	**General, Child abuse, Rape, Incest, Bereavement, Relationship, Supervision**
Service for:	Individuals, Couples, Families, Groups
Theoretical Approach:	Client-centred, Psychodynamic, Psychosynthesis
Fees:	£25 negotiable

LEVENE Tricia   0707 873677
17 Homewood Avenue, Cuffley, POTTERS BAR EN6 4QG
Member of:	**BAC**
Quals/training:	RELATE (NMGC) Trained; Group Therapy (RELATE & IGA); Adv Cert Couns (CAC)
Personal Therapy:	Yes
Supervision:	Ongoing
Counselling offered:	**General, Relationship, Eating disorders, Anorexia, Bulimia, Imaging, Personal growth**
Service for:	Individuals, Couples, Groups
Theoretical Approach:	Psychodynamic
Fees:	£25

MONJACK Carol   0923 6380
Whytes Cottage, 14 The Warren, RADLETT WD7 7BX
Member of:	**BAC**
Quals/training:	Outreach Training Programme; Dip Couns & Community Skills
Personal Therapy:	Ongoing
Supervision:	Ongoing
Counselling offered:	**Psychotherapy**
Service for:	Individuals, Organisations
Theoretical Approach:	Humanistic, Psychodynamic
Fees:	£20

Hertfordshire

SALFIELD Angela 0923 854470
Shenley, RADLETT WD7
Member of: BAC
Quals/training: BA Psychol; MA Linguistics; CNAA PG Dip Couns
Personal Therapy: Yes
Supervision: Ongoing
Counselling offered: General, Bereavement, Crisis, Marital, Peri-natal
Service for: Individuals
Specific to: Women
Theoretical Approach: Psychodynamic
Fees: £15 - £20 sliding scale

MILLER Morris 0923 776258
62 Townfield, RICKMANSWORTH WD3 2DD
Member of: BAC, NRHP
Quals/training: 1988 Cert Hypnotherpy & Psychotherapy; Memb Assoc for Complementary Medicine
Personal Therapy: Yes
Supervision: Ongoing
Counselling offered: Psychotherapy, Hypnotherapy, Anxiety, Depression, Stress
Service for: Individuals, Couples
Theoretical Approach: Eclectic
Fees: £20 Negotiable in cases of need

YOUNG Anne
St Oswald's Vicarage, 159 Baldwin's Lane, Croxley Green, RICKMANSWORTH WD3 3LL
Member of: IPC/WPF
Quals/training: Dip Adv Psychodynamic Couns(WPF); Dip in Transpersonal Perspectives & Skills in Counselling & Psychotherapy
Personal Therapy: Ongoing
Supervision: Ongoing
Counselling offered: General, Addiction, Relationship, Sexual abuse
Service for: Individuals
Theoretical Approach: Jungian, Developmental, Eclectic
Fees: £20 - £30

WELLER Alan 0923 255354
62 Durrants Drive, Croxley Green, RICKMANSWORTH WD3 3NS
Member of: NRHP
Quals/training: BA Psych; PGCE; Dip Psychotherapy; training in NLP & Couns; training in bereavement couns
Personal Therapy: Yes
Supervision: Ongoing
Counselling offered: General, Psychotherapy
Service for: Individuals, Couples
Fees: £20 free initial consultation

Hertfordshire

DIETZ Doreen 0923 264 256
Toby House, Belsize Farm, Plough Lane, Belsize, Sarratt, RICKMANSWORTH WD3 4NP
Member of:	BAC
Quals/training:	Dip Counselling & Community Skills; Training in Psychodynamic Counselling (Outreach) 1991
Personal Therapy:	Yes
Supervision:	Ongoing
Counselling offered:	**General, Addiction, Bereavement, Marital, Stress**
Service for:	Individuals, Couples, Organisations
Theoretical Approach:	Psychodynamic
Fees:	£20

DOREY Mary 0763 242 157
6 Victoria Crescent, ROYSTON SG8 7AX
Member of:	BAC
Quals/training:	BA English; FE Teacher's Cert; PG Dip in Pastoral Theology; Training with CCPE & BAP; Cert in Psychodynamic Counselling Supervision (WPF)
Personal Therapy:	Yes
Supervision:	Ongoing
Counselling offered:	**General, Bereavement, Pastoral, Supervision**
Service for:	Individuals, Groups, Organisations
Theoretical Approach:	Jungian, Psychodynamic
Other languages:	French
Fees:	£10 - £20 sliding scale

LEGG Christopher 0279 726490
73 Sheering Mill Lane, SAWBRIDGEWORTH CM21 9LW
Member of:	BAC
Quals/training:	Dip Social Studies 1950, Dip Couns 1000 (CAC)
Personal Therapy:	Yes
Supervision:	Ongoing
Counselling offered:	**General**
Service for:	Individuals
Theoretical Approach:	Eclectic
Fees:	£20 negotiable

STEEL Sandra 0727 830378
10 Abbots Park, London Road, ST. ALBANS AL1 1TN
Member of:	BAC, ITHP
Quals/training:	Dip Integrative Psychotherapy(Minster Centre)
Personal Therapy:	Yes
Supervision:	Ongoing
Counselling offered:	**General, Psychotherapy, Eating disorders, Anorexia, Bulimia**
Service for:	Individuals
Theoretical Approach:	Psychodynamic
Fees:	£27 negotiable

Hertfordshire

PAYNE Helen   0438 833440
Inst for Arts in Psychotherapy, 1 Beaconfield Road, ST. ALBANS AL1 3RD
Member of:	**BAC, AHPP**
Quals/training:	Cert Ed; Adv Dip Special Education (Couns); MPhil; Group Analysis; Memb of ADMT; AHPP Acc
Personal Therapy:	Ongoing
Supervision:	Ongoing
Counselling offered:	**Psychotherapy, Movement therapy, Eating disorders**
Service for:	Individuals, Groups
Specific to:	Adolescents, Children, Survivors of child abuse, People with disabilities
Theoretical Approach:	Integrative
Fees:	£30 concessions available

ADKINS Dee   0272 862026
36 The Dell, ST. ALBANS AL1 4HF
Member of:	**BAC**
Quals/training:	1946 Dip Occupational Therapy
Personal Therapy:	Ongoing
Supervision:	Ongoing
Counselling offered:	**Psychotherapy, Bereavement, Eating disorders**
Service for:	Individuals, Couples, Groups
Theoretical Approach:	TA
Fees:	£20 Negotiable

NEWTON Angela   0727 839719
5 Laurel Road, ST. ALBANS AL1 4JH
Member of:	**BAC**
Quals/training:	Dip Ed (Northern Counties College) 1971; Dip Couns (SW London College) 1981
Personal Therapy:	Yes
Supervision:	Ongoing
Counselling offered:	**General, Relationship, Crisis**
Service for:	Individuals, Couples, Groups
Theoretical Approach:	Existential, Psychodynamic
Fees:	Up to £20 negotiable

WAKELING Linda   0727 839686
3 Sandfield Road, ST. ALBANS AL1 4JZ
Member of:	**BAC**
Quals/training:	PG Dip Couns (Hatfield Poly); PG Dip Art Therapy; BA(Hons)
Personal Therapy:	Yes
Supervision:	Ongoing
Counselling offered:	**General, Bereavement, Depression, Trauma**
Service for:	Individuals
Specific to:	Women
Theoretical Approach:	Psychodynamic
Fees:	£18 - £22

Hertfordshire

GORTON Elisabeth   0727 863571
37 Clarence Road, ST. ALBANS AL1 4NP
Member of:	BAC
Quals/training:	WPF Accred; trained at Herts & Beds Pastoral Foundation
Personal Therapy:	Yes
Supervision:	Ongoing
Counselling offered:	**General**
Service for:	Individuals
Theoretical Approach:	Psychodynamic
Fees:	£15 - £20

PERMAN KERR Lesley   0727 868754
ST. ALBANS AL1 4RY
Member of:	BPS
Quals/training:	PhD; BSc(Hons); CPsychol; Dip (Psychotherapy & Hypnotherapy Training Assoc); Dip EHP NLP(BHR)
Personal Therapy:	Yes
Supervision:	Ongoing
Counselling offered:	**General, Psychotherapy, Hypnotherapy**
Service for:	Individuals, Couples, Groups, Organisations
Theoretical Approach:	Eclectic
Fees:	£35

CHITTY Kenneth   0727 861288
15 Ashley Road, ST. ALBANS AL1 5DA
Member of:	BAC, BASMT
Quals/training:	1972 Diploma in vocational Guidance (Hatfield Poly); '73-81 Jungian Ananlysis training; '73-85 trainings in contemporary therapies ie Gestalt, TA, Art/Dramatherapy
Personal Therapy:	Ongoing
Supervision:	Ongoing
Counselling offered:	**General, Relationship, Sexual, Psychosomatic**
Service for:	Individuals, Couples, Groups
Theoretical Approach:	Jungian, Eclectic
Fees:	£25 - £35 concessions negotiated

CHEW Alex   0923 858 232, fax 0729 826 371
'On Course', 3 Seaton Road, London Colney, ST. ALBANS AL2 1RL
Member of:	BAC
Quals/training:	Dip Couns; Dip Dramatherapy; member of BADTh; Cert Stress Management Trainer (HPRG); ITEC Holistic Massage Tutor; PGCEA; RNT; RMN
Personal Therapy:	No
Supervision:	Ongoing
Counselling offered:	**General, Crisis, Drama therapy, Loss, Massage, Supervision**
Service for:	Individuals, Couples, Groups, Organisations
Specific to:	Health care professionals, Teachers, Managers
Theoretical Approach:	Humanistic
Fees:	Negotiable

Hertfordshire

CLAYTON Maureen   0727 863599
13 Hawthorn Way, ST. ALBANS AL2 3BG
Member of:	BAC, BPS
Quals/training:	C Psychol; BSc(Hons) Psychol; MSc Occ Psy; Cert Couns & Dip Couns (CSCT)
Personal Therapy:	Yes
Supervision:	Ongoing
Counselling offered:	General, Bereavement, Relationship
Service for:	Individuals
Theoretical Approach:	Rogerian, Eclectic
Fees:	£30

BURTON Mary   0727 855214
5 Offa Road, ST. ALBANS AL3 4QR
Member of:	BPS, WMIP
Quals/training:	PhD in Clinical Psychol; Chartered Clinical Psychologist; training in Psycho-analytic Psychotherapy; Doctor of Ministry
Personal Therapy:	Yes
Supervision:	Ongoing
Counselling offered:	General, Psychotherapy
Service for:	Individuals, Couples
Specific to:	Religious
Theoretical Approach:	Psychoanalytic
Fees:	£35

DUNSTAN Gina   0727 838952
15 Old Garden Court, ST. ALBANS AL3 4RQ
Member of:	BAC
Quals/training:	BA; trained Pastoral Coun WPF; trained with RF & Herts & Beds Pastoral Foundation; WPF Acc 1988; RF Course in Human Relations 1984
Personal Therapy:	Ongoing
Supervision:	Ongoing
Counselling offered:	General
Service for:	Individuals
Theoretical Approach:	Psychodynamic
Fees:	£22 - £25 negotiable

CROUCHMAN Tinky (Ms)   0727 863488
130 Beech Road, ST. ALBANS AL3 5AX
Member of:	BAC
Quals/training:	BA Soc Sci (Wits Univ); MA Mental Health (Univ of S Africa); Cert Mental Health (LSE); BASW
Personal Therapy:	Yes
Supervision:	Ongoing
Counselling offered:	General, Crisis, Bereavement, Relationship, Family
Service for:	Individuals, Couples
Specific to:	Women
Theoretical Approach:	Eclectic
Fees:	£15

Hertfordshire

JACOBS Marion 0727 58454
23 Worley Road, ST. ALBANS AL3 5NR
Member of: BAC
Quals/training: BSc(Hons); trained with Herts & Beds Pastoral Foundation (WPF Affiliate); WPF Acc
Personal Therapy: Yes
Supervision: Ongoing
Counselling offered: General
Service for: Individuals, Couples
Theoretical Approach: Psychodynamic
Fees: £22 - £30 sliding scale

HURFORD Patricia 0727 862492
Broom House, St Bernards Road, ST. ALBANS AL3 5RA
Member of: BAC Acc, BASMT
Quals/training: BAC Acc; MA; RELATE (NMGC) trained; Registrar Tavistock Inst Marital Studies 1978-9
Personal Therapy: Yes
Supervision: Ongoing
Counselling offered: General, Marital, Relationship
Service for: Individuals, Couples
Theoretical Approach: Psychodynamic
Fees: £20 - £30 sliding scale

SNYDER Maggie 0727 867931
17 Pinewood Close, ST. ALBANS AL4 0DS
Member of: BAC
Quals/training: Dip Couns (Stevenage College) '85
Personal Therapy: Yes
Supervision: Ongoing
Counselling offered: General, Addiction, Bereavement, Crisis
Service for: Individuals, Couples
Theoretical Approach: Eclectic
Fees: £12 - £22 sliding scale

PALLENBERG Susan 0727 32403
110 High Street, Sandridge, ST. ALBANS AL4 9BY
Member of: BAC, BASMT
Quals/training: Dip (London Inst for Study of Human Sexuality) 1986; Dip Couple Therapy (Inst Psychiatry)
Personal Therapy: Ongoing
Supervision: Ongoing
Counselling offered: General, Marital, Relationship, Sexual
Service for: Individuals, Couples, Groups
Theoretical Approach: Eclectic
Fees: By negotiation

Hertfordshire

MUSKETT Florence   0707 873712
19 Beehive Road, Goffs Oak, WALTHAM CROSS EN7 5NL
Member of: BAC
Quals/training: Dip Guidance & Couns (Middx Poly) 1978; Teachers Cert (Goldsmiths); BA (OU)
Personal Therapy: Yes
Supervision: Ongoing
Counselling offered: **General, Bereavement, Sexual**
Service for: Individuals, Groups
Theoretical Approach: Eclectic
Fees: £18 Reduced in hardship cases

STOTT Joan   0920 870287
3 Hoddesdon Road, St Margarets, WARE SG12 8EG
Member of: BAC Acc
Quals/training: BAC Acc; Dip Couns (Hatfield Poly) 1985; Post Grad Dip Couns (CNAA) 1987; MA Couns 1991 (Research: Couns & Spirituality)
Personal Therapy: Yes
Supervision: Ongoing
Counselling offered: **General**
Service for: Individuals
Theoretical Approach: Psychodynamic
Fees: £20 - £25

FREEMAN Ruth   0920 464679
4 Coronation Road, WARE SG12 9DX
Member of: BAC
Quals/training: Dip Art Therapy 1978; WPF trained 1984
Personal Therapy: Ongoing
Supervision: Ongoing
Counselling offered: **General, Art therapy, Brief**
Service for: Individuals
Theoretical Approach: Psychodynamic
Fees: £20 negotiable

WISEMAN Anna   0920 870048
The Flint House, Hillside Lane, Great Amwell, WARE SG12 9SE
Member of: BAC
Quals/training: BA(Hons); in 5th year of training in Traditional & Humanistic Psychotherapy & Couns (Minster Centre)
Personal Therapy: Ongoing
Supervision: Ongoing
Counselling offered: **General, Psychotherapy**
Service for: Individuals, Couples
Theoretical Approach: Integrative
Fees: £6 - £25 sliding scale

Hertfordshire

DE LA COUR Gill 0923 244 628
66 Sutton Road, WATFORD WD1 2QQ
Member of:	BAC
Quals/training:	BA Literature; Dip Adult Counselling (Univ London, Birbeck) 1992
Personal Therapy:	Yes
Supervision:	Ongoing
Counselling offered:	**General, Anxiety, Bereavement, Crisis, Depression, Relationship**
Service for:	Individuals
Specific to:	Women, Survivors of child abuse
Theoretical Approach:	Psychodynamic
Fees:	£20 - £30 negotiable

MAYHEW Richard 0923 230080
73 Gladstone Road, WATFORD WD1 2RA
Member of:	BAC
Quals/training:	Cert Adlerian Couns; ongoing training in Adlerian Group Couns & Couples; Memb ASIP
Personal Therapy:	Yes
Supervision:	Ongoing
Counselling offered:	**General, Relationship**
Service for:	Individuals, Couples, Groups
Theoretical Approach:	Adlerian, Integrative
Fees:	£25 Negotiable

CHIVERTON-HUNT Ann 0923 234862
16 Anthony Close, WATFORD WD1 4NA
Member of:	BAC, BPS
Quals/training:	Cert Ed; BA (Hons)Psychol; Couns Cert (Lincoln Institute); Dietary Course; 10 years experience
Personal Therapy:	Yes
Supervision:	Ongoing
Counselling offered:	**General, Relationship, Educational, Crisis, Trauma, Eating disorders**
Service for:	Individuals, Couples
Specific to:	Women, People with disabilities, Carers, Students, Counsellor has disability
Theoretical Approach:	Rogerian
Fees:	- £35 £0-£35, sliding scale

KILICH-WALPOLE Suna 0923 247744
52 Kingsfield Road, Oxhey, WATFORD WD1 4PS
Member of:	BAC, LCP
Quals/training:	BA(Hons) Psychol 1980; training in Psychoanalytic Psychotherapy (LCP)
Personal Therapy:	Ongoing
Supervision:	Ongoing
Counselling offered:	**General, Psychotherapy**
Service for:	Individuals
Theoretical Approach:	Analytic, Eclectic
Fees:	£15 - £30

Hertfordshire

LAW Heather 0923 231174
344 Whippendell Road, WATFORD WD1 7PD
Member of: BAC, AHPP, IPSS
Quals/training: BA(Hons); Dip RSA; Cert Ed; Cert Couns (CAC); Psychotherapy training IPSS
Personal Therapy: Ongoing
Supervision: Ongoing
Counselling offered: General, Psychotherapy
Service for: Individuals, Couples, Groups
Theoretical Approach: Integrative
Other languages: German
Fees: Negotiable

HAMILTON Mr Kim 0923 212230
222 Hagden Lane, WATFORD WD1 8LS
Member of: AGIP
Quals/training: Trained in Analytical Psychotherapy; Cert Ed
Personal Therapy: Ongoing
Supervision: Ongoing
Counselling offered: General, Psychotherapy, Crisis
Service for: Individuals, Couples
Specific to: Sexual minorities
Theoretical Approach: Eclectic
Fees: £12 - £30

HERMAN Yvette 081 950 1006
Barbary House, California Lane, Bushey Heath, WATFORD WD2 1EX
Member of: BAC
Quals/training: Certificate in Counselling Theory (Middx Poly)'85; Bereavement Couns Course (CRUSE)'87; Marital/Sexual Couns Course (Marriage Research Centre); Cert Couns Skills '89
Personal Therapy: Yes
Supervision: Ongoing
Counselling offered: General, Marital, Bereavement, Eating disorders
Service for: Individuals, Couples, Families
Theoretical Approach: Psychodynamic
Fees: £25

ALLEN Joanne 043 879 749
Hunters Chase, 47 Bishops Road, Tewin Wood, WELWYN AL6 0NP
Member of: BAC Acc
Quals/training: MA Applied Social Studies; BA Psychol; CQSW
Personal Therapy: Yes
Supervision: Ongoing
Counselling offered: General, Psychotherapy
Service for: Individuals, Couples, Families
Theoretical Approach: Analytical, Psychodynamic
Fees: £23 - £25

Hertfordshire

PERREN Mary   0707 327289
WELWYN GARDEN CITY AL7
Member of: BAC Acc
Quals/training: BAC Acc; APCC Acc Supervisor; Hum Relations (RF) 1975; Family & Marital therapy (IGA) 1976; Bereavement 1980; Full Memb GAS
Personal Therapy: Yes
Supervision: Ongoing
Counselling offered: General, Psychotherapy, Supervision
Service for: Individuals
Theoretical Approach: Psychodynamic
Fees: £22 - £32 according to means

HARRISON MAYOR Susan   0707 320782
86 Handside Lane, WELWYN GARDEN CITY AL8 6SJ
Member of: BAC Acc, ITHP
Quals/training: BAC Acc; BA; CQSW; Dip (Minster Centre)'82
Personal Therapy: Yes
Supervision: Ongoing
Counselling offered: General, Psychotherapy
Service for: Individuals
Theoretical Approach: Integrative
Fees: £25

BAGENAL Beauchamp   0707 331 391
15 Springfields, WELWYN GARDEN CITY AL8 6XS
Member of: BAC, ANLP (PCS)
Quals/training: Alexander Technique Teacher; Master Practitioner of NLP
Personal Therapy: Ongoing
Supervision: Ongoing
Counselling offered: Time Line Therapy, Brief, Change
Service for: Individuals, Organisations
Theoretical Approach: NLP
Fees: £25

RICHARDSON Elizabeth   0707 336696
35 Marsden Green, WELWYN GARDEN CITY AL8 6YD
Member of: BAC Acc, BAP, Member of UKCP Register
Quals/training: BAC Acc; Post-grad Dip Couns (Hatfield Poly); Jungian Analytical Psychologist trained with BAP; MA Analytical Psychotherapy(University of Hertfordshire)
Personal Therapy: Yes
Supervision: Yes
Counselling offered: General, Bereavement, Psychotherapy, Crisis, Bulimia, Supervision, Sexual abuse
Service for: Individuals
Specific to: Incest survivors
Theoretical Approach: Analytical, Psychodynamic
Fees: £20 - £28

HULL HA, DEPARTMENT OF CLINCAL PSYCHOLOGY   0482 676243
Kingston General Hospital, Beverley Road, HULL HU3 7UR
Service:	Individual, group and family therapy
Area served:	Hull and Holderness
Referral:	GP, Health/Soc Work Professional
Training of workers:	Postgraduate clinical psychology
Code of Ethics:	BPS
Management by:	District Psychologist on behalf of Hull HA
Fees:	None

SOUTH HUMBERSIDE H A, DEPT CLINICAL PSYCHOLOGY
                                           0724 282282 x 2652
Butterwick House, Scunthorpe General Hospital, Cliff Gardens, SCUNTHORPE DN15 7BH
Service:	Cognitive-behavioural therapy and psychotherapy for adults & children; hypnosis
Area served:	Scunthorpe H A Boundaries
Referral:	GP, Health/Soc Work Professional, Consultant
Training of workers:	Postgraduate clinical psychology; peer supervision
Code of Ethics:	BPS
Management by:	District Psychologist
Fees:	None

DRUG ADVICE & TREATMENT PROJECT   0274 856948
30A Doncaster Road, SCUNTHORPE DN15 7RQ
Service:	HIV testing. Counselling on all aspects, for those worried or involved with HIV/AIDS, drug problems, volatile substance sniffing. Tailor made training in couns skills and HIV/AIDS
Area served:	Scunthorpre Health District
Other languages:	Others arranged
Referral:	Self, Health/Soc Work Professional
Training of workers:	Doctors, Social workers, nurses & counsellors all with HIV/AIDS counselling training. Supervision
Code of Ethics:	BAC
Management by:	Executive Committee
Fees:	None

Individual Practitioners
*Each individual is a **member of** one or more organisations eligible for entry into this directory. BAC Accredited Counsellors and Recognised Supervisors are shaded.*

DAVIES Pam   0482 862 706
3 Melrose Park, BEVERLEY HU17 8JL
Member of:	BAC Acc
Quals/training:	BAC Acc; BA; PhD; CQSW; Dip Advanced Counselling & Therapy Skills
Personal Therapy:	Unknown
Supervision:	Ongoing
Counselling offered:	General, Abuse, Bereavement, Change, Relationship
Service for:	Individuals, Groups, Organisations
Specific to:	Women
Theoretical Approach:	Person-centrec
Fees:	£10 - £25 sliding scale

Humberside

DALTON Frances   0482 667354, 0482 668512
West Croft, 7 Sands Lane, Elloughton, BROUGH HU15 1JH

Member of:	**BAC Acc, BPS, AFT**
Quals/training:	BAC Acc; MA Hons, St Andrews; BSc Hons Hull Univ; Dip Ed; Dip Assertiveness Training, Redwood; Dip in Couns BPS Chartered Psychologist
Personal Therapy:	Yes
Supervision:	Ongoing
Counselling offered:	**General, Assertiveness, Bereavement, Midlife, Psychotherapy, Family, Eating disorders, Trauma**
Service for:	Individuals, Couples, Families, Groups
Theoretical Approach:	Integrative, Systems
Other languages:	French, German
Fees:	£20 - £35 negotiable

MOLE Elizabeth   0262 488138
The Lodge, Mill Lane, Foston-on-the-Wolds, DRIFFIELD YO25 8BP

Member of:	**BAC**
Quals/training:	BEd; Dip Psychol and Couns (Newcastle) 1974
Personal Therapy:	Ongoing
Supervision:	Ongoing
Counselling offered:	**General, Marital, Bereavement**
Service for:	Individuals, Couples, Families
Specific to:	Children, Young people
Theoretical Approach:	Client-centred
Fees:	£15 - £25 Sliding Scale

HARRIS Richard   0405 839688
31 The Green, Rawcliffe, GOOLE DN14 8QF

Member of:	**BAC**
Quals/training:	MSc Couns Psychology; Dip Cot
Personal Therapy:	Ongoing
Supervision:	Ongoing
Counselling offered:	**General, Psychotherapy, Relationship, Sexual, Sexuality**
Service for:	Individuals, Couples, Groups
Theoretical Approach:	Egan, Eclectic, Integrative
Fees:	£15 - £30 sliding scale

BOLSOVER Dr G N   0482 641579
Ravensthorpe, 22 Station Road, HESSLE HU13 0BB

Member of:	**BPS, IFT, YAPP**
Quals/training:	BA; MSc Clinical Psychology; Cert in Psychodynamic Psychotherapy; PhD; Dip Psychotherapy; C Psychol; AFBPsS; adv clinical training in family therapy
Personal Therapy:	Yes
Supervision:	Ongoing
Counselling offered:	**Psychotherapy, Marital, Family**
Service for:	Individuals, Couples, Families
Theoretical Approach:	Psychoanalytic, Systems
Fees:	On request

Humberside

MIDDLETON Alice   0482 565387
82 Arcon Drive, Anlaby Road, HULL HU4 6AD
Member of:	BAC
Quals/training:	Training in Egan; MSc Couns
Personal Therapy:	Yes
Supervision:	Ongoing
Counselling offered:	**General, Bereavement**
Service for:	Individuals, Couples, Groups
Specific to:	People with disabilities, Counsellor has disability, Suicide survivors
Theoretical Approach:	Egan, Rogerian, Gestalt
Fees:	£10 - £20 Sliding Scale

STRAWBRIDGE Sheelagh   0482 446324
28 Victoria Avenue, HULL HU5 3DR
Member of:	BAC, BPS
Quals/training:	BSc (Hons) Psychol; C Psychol training including RELATE; Tutor for Dip Course (Univ of Humberside) since 1988
Personal Therapy:	Ongoing
Supervision:	Ongoing
Counselling offered:	**General, Relationship, Personal growth**
Service for:	Individuals, Couples
Theoretical Approach:	Humanistic
Fees:	Negotiable

BLAKE Nancy   0482 447765
102 Park Avenue, HULL HU5 3ET
Member of:	BAC Acc
Quals/training:	BAC Acc; BA Hons; Dip Teaching Adults; Postgraduate Dip Social Administration; Dip Applied Social Studies; CQSW; NLP Practitioner Cert
Personal Therapy:	Yes
Supervision:	Ongoing
Counselling offered:	**General, Psychotherapy, Bereavement, Eating disorders**
Service for:	Individuals, Couples, Families, Groups
Theoretical Approach:	Eclectic, TA, NLP, Systems
Other languages:	French
Fees:	£25 Negotiable

GARRY Lesley   0482 43301
55 Park Avenue, HULL HU5 3EW
Member of:	BAC Acc
Quals/training:	BAC Acc; BA(Hons)(Hull); Dip Adv Couns & Therapy
Personal Therapy:	Ongoing
Supervision:	Ongoing
Counselling offered:	**General, Assertiveness, Relationship, Abuse, Bereavement**
Service for:	Individuals, Couples, Groups
Theoretical Approach:	Person-centred
Fees:	£15 - £20 negotiable

Humberside

DRUMMOND Mary 0482 449823
135 Park Avenue, HULL HU5 3EX
Member of:	BAC, BPS
Quals/training:	BSc Psychol; Advanced Dip Couns; Training in Supervision (Ripon & York St John 1993)
Personal Therapy:	Ongoing
Supervision:	Ongoing
Counselling offered:	**General**
Service for:	Individuals, Couples, Groups
Specific to:	Young people, Helping professions
Theoretical Approach:	Existential
Fees:	£15 dependant on income

HORNBY Garry Dr 0482 632 245
55 Dale Road, Swanland, NORTH FERRIBY HU14 3QH
Member of:	BPS
Quals/training:	Dip Educ Psychol 1981; Scholarship to study Couns Psychol at Univ of British Columbia 1984-5; C Psychol; BSc 1970; MA 1981; PhD 1992
Personal Therapy:	Yes
Supervision:	Ongoing
Counselling offered:	**General**
Service for:	Individuals, Couples, Groups, Families
Specific to:	Families of, People with disabilities
Theoretical Approach:	Humanistic, Developmental
Fees:	Donation to charity

ANDERSON James 0430 860106
Brackley House, High Street, Holme on Spalding, YORK YO4 4AA
Member of:	BAC Acc, YAPP
Quals/training:	BAC(Acc); RELATE trained; Cert Couns(Lincoln Centre); Dip Psychotherapy(Sheffield Univ)
Personal Therapy:	Yes
Supervision:	Ongoing
Counselling offered:	**General, Relationship**
Service for:	Individuals, Couples
Theoretical Approach:	Psychodynamic
Fees:	£15 - £20 negotiable

Kent

Organisations

ASHFORD COUNSELLING SERVICE 0233 610083
Albert Villas, 1 Chart Road, Kingsnorth, ASHFORD TN23 3HT
Service:	General counselling and psychotherapy
Area served:	Ashford & district
Referral:	Self, GP
Training of workers:	Minimum 3 yr part-time training. Regular supervision
Code of Ethics:	BAC
Management by:	Trustees (Reg charity)
Fees:	Donations accepted

COUNSELLING CONSULTANCY 0732 840070, 0732 843739
19 Brook Road, Larkfield, AYLESFORD ME20 6JD
Service:	Individual and couples counselling for stress, anxiety, depression, relationship difficulties and bereavement
Area served:	South East of England
Referral:	Self or others
Training of workers:	Dip in Psych Couns & Hypnotherapy. Ongoing therapy and ongoing supervision
Code of Ethics:	BAC
Management by:	The Partnership
Fees:	£20

MARGATE HOSPITAL - AIDS/ HAEMOPHILIA CENTRE
0483 225544 x2308
St Peter's Road, BROADSTAIRS CT10 4AW
Service:	Individual, face to face counselling for all aspects of HIV/AIDS for those with HIV/AIDS, their carers, relations & friends. Drop-in centre Thurs 12-1, other by appt/at home
Area served:	Canterbury & Thanet (E Kent)
Referral:	Self or others
Training of workers:	Tailor-made training in counselling skills & HIV/AIDS familiarisation. Supervision
Code of Ethics:	-
Fees:	None

WAYMARK TRUST 0227 781891
35B Broad Street, CANTERBURY CT1 2LR
Service:	Psychodynamic counselling service mainly to local churches
Area served:	East Kent
Referral:	Self, Church, GP, Agencies
Training of workers:	Counselling skills courses, ongoing Dip Couns
Code of Ethics:	BAC
Management by:	Trustees
Fees:	£5 - £25 negotiable (£10 assessment)

Kent

MEDWAY DISTRICT CLINICAL PSYCHOLOGY SERVICE
0634 407311 x 5335
All Saints Hospital, CHATHAM ME4 5NG
Service: Psychological assessment & treatment of adults, children, couples, groups, families for anxiety, depression, HIV/AIDS, emotional & relationship problems, behavioural difficulties
Area served: Medway DHA
Other languages: Dutch, Urdu
Referral: GP, Agencies, Self
Training of workers: Postgraduate clinical psychology
Code of Ethics: BPS
Management by: District Psychologist for DHA
Fees: None

DOVER COUNSELLING CENTRE   0304 204123
9 St James's Street, DOVER CT16 1QD
Service: Centre offers a multi-disciplinary team of RELATE, Cruse, Kent Council on Addiction & Support Line employee counselling counsellors. Also non-specific counselling
Area served: Dover, Deal, Sandwich
Referral: Self or others
Training of workers: All are trained in specific areas of counselling. Regular supervision and ongoing multi-disciplinary training
Code of Ethics: BAC
Management by: Board of Directors
Fees: Contributions are requested

MAIDSTONE COUNSELLING SERVICE   0622 672806
Maidstone Counselling Centre, 60 Marsham Street, MAIDSTONE ME14 1EW
Service: General counselling
Area served: Kent
Referral: Self, Health/Soc Work Professional
Training of workers: All are trained and have ongoing supervision. WPF associated Centre
Code of Ethics: BAC, WPF
Management by: Committee
Fees: £7 - £20 (assessment £20)

KENT COUNSELLING SERVICE   0622 406820, 0622 762538, 0622 754853
Rm 1, The Community Centre, Marsham Street, MAIDSTONE ME14 1HH
Service: Marital, relationship, sexual difficulties, sex therapy. Specialises in disabled, incest/sexual abuse survival for individuals, couples, groups, families
Other languages: French
Referral: Self, Health/Soc Work Professional
Training of workers: HMHO Cert in Childcare & Family Therapy; RELATE trained; Education Acc (Women's Therapy Centre)
Code of Ethics: BAC
Management by: Carol Hassall & Alison Nixon
Fees: Initial assessment fee

Kent

OFF THE RECORD, THANET   0843 223363
38 Foreland Avenue, Cliftonville, MARGATE CT9 3NQ
Service:	General, medical, sexual & career counselling especially for young people, married couples and families
Area served:	Margate, Ramsgate, Broadstairs & Isle of Wight
Referral:	Self, Agencies
Code of Ethics:	BAC
Management by:	Committee
Fees:	None

ROTHER COUNSELLING SERVICE (S E Kent Division)   0797 270335
Barry Wright, RYE TN31
Service:	General counselling
Area served:	Rye, Lydd, New Romney, Hythe
Referral:	Self or others, GP
Training of workers:	Minimum 3 yrs part-time training. Fortnightly supervision
Code of Ethics:	BAC
Management by:	Committee of counsellors (Reg as charity applied for)
Fees: Donations accepted	

SWALE COUNSELLING PRACTICE   0795 431105
Greenhurst, Hearts Delight Road, SITTINGBOURNE ME9 8JA
Service:	General, bereavement, crisis, abuse survivors, life stages, relationships, infertility counselling for individuals and couples - psychodynamic, behavioural, remedial
Area served:	Swale (Sittingbourne, Faversham, Isle of Sheppey) Kent
Referral:	Self
Training of workers:	RELATE trained; 6 years experience
Code of Ethics:	BAC
Management by:	Barbara Miller & Pamela Margrie
Fees:	£20

TUNBRIDGE WELLS COUNSELLING CENTRE   0892 548750
St Georges Centre, 7 Chilston Road, TUNBRIDGE WELLS TN4 9LP
Service:	General, bereavement & loss counselling by appointment only for individuals. Centre also runs training courses in counselling skills. Associate member of WPF
Area served:	West Kent & East Sussex
Referral:S	elf, Health Practitioner
Training of workers:	Weekly supervision & ongoing training
Code of Ethics:	BAC, WPF
Management by:	Management Committee
Fees:	According to means

Kent

Individual Practitioners

*Each individual is a **member of** one or more organisations eligible for entry into this directory. BAC Accredited Counsellors and Recognised Supervisors are shaded.*

PICKETT Alan 0233 820053
Jasmine Cottage, The Street, Bethersden, ASHFORD TN26 3AE
Member of:	BAC Acc
Quals/training:	BAC Acc; Cert Couns (WPF Associate) 1986; Cert Transpersonal Couns (CTP); 1987; Dip Psychol Couns (Roehampton) 1989
Personal Therapy:	Ongoing
Supervision:	Ongoing
Counselling offered:	**General, Bereavement, Relationship, Crisis, Supervision**
Service for:	Individuals, Couples, Groups
Theoretical Approach:	Jungian, Transpersonal
Other languages:	Dutch, German
Fees:	£10 - £25

WILSON Veronica 0233 860593
Park Farmhouse, Kirkwood Avenue, Woodchurch, ASHFORD TN26 3SE
Member of:	BAC, AHPP
Quals/training:	Integrative Arts Therapist; Dip IATE; RELATE trained both as counsellor and trainer 1988-89
Personal Therapy:	Ongoing
Supervision:	Ongoing
Counselling offered:	**General, Relationship, Sexual abuse, Psychotherapy**
Service for:	Individuals, Couples, Organisations
Specific to:	Children
Theoretical Approach:	Humanistic, Integrative
Fees:	£20 negotiable

EVANS Jane 0233 712294, Fax 0233 713651
Archdeacons House, The Hill, Charing, ASHFORD TN27 0LU
Member of:	BAC
Quals/training:	Couns Course (WPF); Dynamic Psychotherapy Course (Kent); Supervision Course; currently training for Adv Dip Couns; Memb NCPHR
Personal Therapy:	Ongoing
Supervision:	Ongoing
Counselling offered:	**General, Personal growth, Relationship, Stress, Career, Work, Supervision**
Service for:	Individuals, Couples
Theoretical Approach:	Client-centred, Humanistic, Egan, TA, Gestalt
Fees:	£20 negotiable

RANDOLPH Jenefer 0233 77 216
Little Smarden House, The Street, Smarden, ASHFORD TN27 8NB
Member of:	BAC
Quals/training:	RELATE trained (Accredited counsellor, supervisor & trainer)
Personal Therapy:	Unknown
Supervision:	Ongoing
Counselling offered:	**General, Marital, Bereavement, Supervision**
Service for:	Individuals, Couples
Theoretical Approach:	Psychodynamic
Fees:	Negotiable

Kent

DEAN Harry 081 650 1581
36 Embassy Gardens, Blakeney Road, BECKENHAM BR3 1HF
Member of: BAC
Quals/training: 1966-68 training with CTA; '72 Cert in Human Relations (RF); Consultant to APCC
Personal Therapy: Yes
Supervision: Ongoing
Counselling offered: General, Marital, Psychotherapy
Service for: Individuals, Couples
Theoretical Approach: Rogerian, Gestalt, TA, Analytical
Fees: Sliding scale up to £15

CARSLEY Carol 081 650 7264
Boulders, Beckenham Place Park, BECKENHAM BR3 2BP
Member of: BAC
Quals/training: RELATE trained (1990); State Registered Occupational Therapist
Personal Therapy: Yes
Supervision: Ongoing
Counselling offered: General, Bereavement, Marital, Sexual
Service for: Individuals, Couples
Theoretical Approach: Psychodynamic
Fees: £20 - £30 sliding scale

TELLING Susan 081 650 4679
7 Barnfield Wood Road, BECKENHAM BR3 2SR
Member of: BAC, BPS
Quals/training: BA (Hons) Psychol; CQSW; Adv Dip Couns; Stress Management
Personal Therapy: Yes
Supervision: Ongoing
Counselling offered: General, Relationship, Loss, Stress, Crisis
Service for: Individuals, Couples
Specific to: Young people
Theoretical Approach: Psychodynamic, Cognitive
Fees: £20 - £25

FRENCH Jean 081 658 4046
Park Langley, BECKENHAM BR3
Member of: BAC, ITA
Quals/training: In training (3rd yr) Transactional Analysis & Psychotherapy; Cognitive Behavioural Therapy & RET; Elementary Couns Skills
Personal Therapy: Ongoing
Supervision: Ongoing
Counselling offered: General, Alcohol, Personal growth
Service for: Individuals
Theoretical Approach: TA, Object relations, Cognitive/Behavioural
Fees: £20

Kent

SANDERSON Adelheid   081 650 2162
10 Forest Ridge, BECKENHAM BR3 3NH
Member of:	BAC
Quals/training:	NMGC trained 1982
Personal Therapy:	Ongoing
Supervision:	Ongoing
Counselling offered:	**General, Marital, Sexual, Bereavement**
Service for:	Individuals, Couples
Theoretical Approach:	Psychodynamic
Other languages:	German
Fees:	Negotiable

THOMPSON Jean   081 659 4960
80 Birkbeck Road, BECKENHAM BR3 4SP
Member of:	BAC
Quals/training:	BEd; Dip Vocational Guidance, Dip Couns (SW London College); Supervision & Consultation Course (Tavistock)
Personal Therapy:	Yes
Supervision:	Ongoing
Counselling offered:	**Short-term**
Service for:	Individuals, Couples, Groups, Organisations
Specific to:	People with disabilities, Counsellor has disability
Theoretical Approach:	Eclectic, Multimodal
Fees:	£25

ROBERTS Pauline   0322 553807
Basildon, 2 Knoll Road, BEXLEY DA5 1AZ
Member of:	**BAC RSup, IPC, BPS**
Quals/training:	BA Hons Psychol; Memb IPC/WPF
Personal Therapy:	Yes
Supervision:	Ongoing
Counselling offered:	**General**
Service for:	Individuals
Theoretical Approach:	Analytical
Fees:	£30

HOLMES Phyllis   081 304 1840
53 St. Audrey Avenue, BEXLEYHEATH DA7 5DA
Member of:	BAC
Quals/training:	Cert Ed; Dip Hypnotherapy; Cert RET; Training in Rogerian/ Egan & Ellis approaches; Gestalt
Personal Therapy:	Yes
Supervision:	Ongoing
Counselling offered:	**General, Crisis, Hypnotherapy, Psychotherapy, Eating disorders, Phobias**
Service for:	Individuals, Couples
Specific to:	Children, Young people
Theoretical Approach:	Person-centred, Gestalt
Fees:	£15 - £20 sliding scale

Kent

MEISE Linda 0843 860895
Gull Cottage, 2 Howard Road, BROADSTAIRS CT10 1QX
Member of: NRHP
Quals/training: Stages 1-3 Hypnotherapy & Psychotherapy training (NCHP)
Personal Therapy: Ongoing
Supervision: Ongoing
Counselling offered: General, Hypnotherapy, Psychotherapy
Service for: Individuals
Theoretical Approach: Eclectic, Cognitive/Behavioural
Fees: On application

ROGERS Brenda 0843 63361
Harbour Rise, Pier Approach, BROADSTAIRS CT10 1TY
Member of: BAC, AHPP
Quals/training: Registered Practitioner AHPP; NMGC training; Gestalt Therapist trained with London Growth Centre; Couns Supervisor(metanoia)
Personal Therapy: Yes
Supervision: Ongoing
Counselling offered: General, Creative potential, Personal growth, Supervision, Creative therapies
Service for: Individuals, Couples, Groups
Theoretical Approach: Rogerian, Gestalt
Fees: £25 inds, negotiable(£35 groups)

RUSSELL Valerie 081 467 6826
The Roses, Woodside Road, Bickley, BROMLEY BR1 2ES
Member of: BAC
Quals/training: Cert Couns (LCIP) 1981; Dip Hypnosis & Psychotherapy (National College) 1982
Personal Therapy: Ongoing
Supervision: Ongoing
Counselling offered: General
Service for: Individuals
Theoretical Approach: Psychodynamic
Fees: £18

BANKS Mary 081 467 1405
Fernside Lodge, 6 Rosemount Drive, Bickley, BROMLEY BR1 2LQ
Member of: BAC Acc RSup, BAP
Quals/training: BAC Acc; BAC Recognised Supervisor; 1984 Dip Couns (Univ of London); BAP (Assoc) 1993
Personal Therapy: Yes
Supervision: Ongoing
Counselling offered: Psychotherapy
Service for: Individuals, Couples, Groups
Theoretical Approach: Analytic, Psychoanalytic
Fees: £35

Kent

LUSTY Robert   ansaphone 081 402 0763
54 London Lane, BROMLEY BR1 4HE
Member of: BAC Acc
Quals/training: BAC (Acc); BSc; MSc; Dip Couns & Psychotherapy (PCAI) Memb BAPCA
Personal Therapy: Yes
Supervision: Ongoing
Counselling offered: General, Psychotherapy, Relationship
Service for: Individuals, Couples, Grous
Theoretical Approach: Person-centred
Fees: £15 - £30 sliding scale

BELL Linda   081 464 2418
31 Durham Road, BROMLEY BR2 0SN
Member of: BAC
Quals/training: Cert in Pastoral Care & Couns; Dip in Theory of Pastoral Care & Couns; RELATE Couns training & trainer
Personal Therapy: Yes
Supervision: Ongoing
Counselling offered: General, Relationship, Sexual
Service for: Individuals, Couples, Groups, Organisations
Theoretical Approach: Psychodynamic
Fees: £20 - £25 Sliding scale

EDWARDS Jennifer Jane   081 462 9656
64 Bourne Way, Hayes, BROMLEY BR2 7EY
Member of: BAC, BASMT
Quals/training: RELATE Trained; Dip Human Sexuality (St George's Medical School); BASMT (Assoc)
Personal Therapy: Yes
Supervision: Yes
Counselling offered: General, Relationship, Marital, Psychosexual
Service for: Individuals, Couples, Groups
Theoretical Approach: Eclectic
Fees: £20 Negotiable

PEARSON Althea   0227 459781
20 Pilgrims Way, CANTERBURY CT1 1XU
Member of BAC Acc, BPS
Quals/training: BAC Acc; BA(Hons) Psychol 1978; Dip Couns (Brighton Poly) 1984; PhD Psychol (London Univ) 1985; CPsychol 1988; AFBPsS
Personal Therapy: Yes
Supervision: Ongoing
Counselling offered: General, Pastoral, Stress, Bereavement, Loss, Sexual abuse
Service for: Individuals, Groups
Specific to: Survivors of sex abuse
Theoretical Approach: Eclectic
Fees: £30 less in hardship

Kent

AMBROSE Sheila 0227 831 847
11 The Close, Union Road, Bridge, CANTERBURY CT4 5NJ
Member of: BAC
Quals/training: Private psychotherapy practice 30 years; 2 years RF; 3 years counsellor in General Practice; training analysis with the late Dr J A Hadfield; Cert LCIP; Memb BAAT
Personal Therapy: Yes
Supervision: Ongoing
Counselling offered: General, Relationship, Sexual, Psychotherapy, Supervision
Service for: Individuals, Groups
Specific to: Counsellors
Theoretical Approach: Eclectic
Other languages: French
Fees: £15 - £30 negotiable

KLINEFELTER Polly 0227 731 648
43 Shalmsford Street, Chartham, CANTERBURY CT4 7RS
Member of: BAC
Quals/training: BA; Humanistic psychology 1971; MSW 1979; Memb IIP
Personal Therapy: Yes
Supervision: Ongoing
Counselling offered: General, Marital, Family, Bereavement, Addiction, Eating disorders, Drugs
Service for: Individuals, Couples, Groups, Families
Specific to: Adolescents
Theoretical Approach: Client-centred
Fees: £20 negotiable

BLEASDALE Roz 0634 864406
6 Greenacre Close, Princes Park, Walderslade, CHATHAM ME5 7JS
Member of: BAC Acc
Quals/training: BAC Acc; NMGC trained; IGA course; trainer & supervisor
Personal Therapy: Ongoing
Supervision: Ongoing
Counselling offered: General, Marital, Bereavement, Supervision
Service for: Individuals, Couples, Families, Groups
Theoretical Approach: Psychodynamic, Eclectic
Fees: £25 - £30 Some lower cost places

DAVIES Peggy
11 Oakhurst Close, Walderslade, CHATHAM ME5 9AN
Member of: BAC, ITA
Quals/training: CQSW '72; Dip Management Studies; Clinical Transactional Analysis
Personal Therapy: Yes
Supervision: Ongoing
Counselling offered: General, Bereavement, Career, Personal growth, Psychotherapy
Service for: Individuals, Couples, Groups
Specific to: Young people
Theoretical Approach: TA, Developmental
Fees: £25 - £40

Kent

COLE Rosemary 081 467 3931
11 Laneside, CHISLEHURST BR7 6BP
Member of:	**BAC, IPC**
Quals/training:	Dip (IPC/WPF) 1987
Personal Therapy:	Yes
Supervision:	Ongoing
Counselling offered:	**General, Bereavement**
Service for:	Individuals
Theoretical Approach:	Psychodynamic
Fees:	£10 - £20 sliding scale

HOLLIDAY Rebecca 0698 826087
Lucan, Orpington Road, CHISLEHURST BR7 6RA
Member of:	**BAC, BASMT, MPTI**
Quals/training:	BA Psychol/Biology'84; Certs Couns(London Univ)'83-'85 & (metanoia)'85; Marital Therapy(Tavistock Inst) & Sexual Therapy(St George's Hospital)'89-'90
Personal Therapy:	Ongoing
Supervision:	Ongoing
Counselling offered:	**General, Marital, Sexual, Psychotherapy**
Service for:	Individuals, Couples
Theoretical Approach:	Humanistic, Analytical, Eclectic
Fees:	£30 upwards

THOMASON June 0474 703704
5 Ashwood Place, Bean, DARTFORD DA2 8BD
Member of:	**BAC**
Quals/training:	CQSW; Analytical Psychotherapist LCIP 1988
Personal Therapy:	Yes
Supervision:	Ongoing
Counselling offered:	**General, Psychotherapy**
Service for:	Individuals
Theoretical Approach:	Analytical
Fees:	£25 - £30 negotiable

WEAVER Daphne 047470 5287
21 Drudgeon Way, Bean, DARTFORD DA2 8BJ
Member of:	**BAC**
Quals/training:	CQSW; Attendance Cert Couns Skills (LCIP)'64
Personal Therapy:	Ongoing
Supervision:	Ongoing
Counselling offered:	**General, Bereavement, Relationship**
Service for:	Individuals
Theoretical Approach:	Freudian
Fees:	£20

Kent

GARLINGE Margaret 0304 820843
7 Witley Walk, Whitfield, DOVER CT16 3NR
Member of:	BAC
Quals/training:	Experienced residential social worker; completed 2 yrs training for Adv Dip Couns (metanoia)
Personal Therapy:	Yes
Supervision:	Ongoing
Counselling offered:	**General, Personal growth, Relationship**
Service for:	Individuals
Specific to:	Adolescents, People with disabilities, Women
Theoretical Approach:	Rogerian
Fees:	£20 negotiable

WRIGHT Regina 0732 865565
Three Gables, Swan Lane, EDENBRIDGE TN8 6AJ
Member of:	BAC, BPS
Quals/training:	BA Hons(Psych); Dip Psychol Couns(Roehampton Inst); Memb Soc Existential Analysis; Certified AE & FE College Couns Skills Tutor; Ongoing PG Dip in Couns Psychol(BPS)
Personal Therapy:	Yes
Supervision:	Ongoing
Counselling offered:	**General, Bereavement, Relationship, Crisis, Psychotherapy, Supervision**
Service for:	Individuals
Theoretical Approach:	Phenomenological, Existential, Transpersonal
Other languages:	German
Fees:	£15 - £25 sliding scale

EXALL Jean 03224 41905
Denton Counselling, 187 West Street, ERITH DA8 1AN
Member of:	BAC
Quals/training:	BA Psychol; RELATE Trained 1983
Personal Therapy:	Yes
Supervision:	Ongoing
Counselling offered:	**General, Relationship**
Service for:	Individuals, Couples
Theoretical Approach:	Eclectic
Fees:	£25

TWELVETREES Heidy 03224 49239
27 Nurstead Road, ERITH DA8 1LS
Member of:	BAC, AHPP
Quals/training:	Lic Phil (Zurich); Dip Gestalt Psychotherapy (Gestalt Centre)
Personal Therapy:	Ongoing
Supervision:	Yes
Counselling offered:	**General, Bereavement, Relationship, Crisis, Psychotherapy**
Service for:	Individuals, Groups
Theoretical Approach:	Gestalt, Humanistic
Other languages:	German, Swiss-German
Fees:	£18 - £25 negotiable

Kent

LOBB Brian 0322 337812
6 Arran Close, ERITH DA8 3SL
Member of: NRHP
Quals/training: Cert Hypnotherapy (NCHP); NRHP (Assoc)
Personal Therapy: No
Supervision: Ongoing
Counselling offered: **General, Hypnotherapy, Psychotherapy**
Service for: Individuals, Couples, Families, Groups, Organisations
Theoretical Approach: Eclectic
Fees: £15 - £30 Sliding Scale

MERRICKS Belinda 0303 230126
143 Church road, Cheriton, FOLKESTONE CT20 3ER
Member of: BAC
Quals/training: Dip Adlerian Couns - Acc (IIP) 1992; TA & Person-centred training 1993
Personal Therapy: Ongoing
Supervision: Ongoing
Counselling offered: **General, Sexual abuse, Addiction, Eating disorders, Brief, Crisis**
Service for: Individuals, Couples, Families, Groups, Organisations
Specific to: Survivors of sex abuse
Theoretical Approach: Integrative, Humanistic, Adlerian, TA, Person-centred
Fees: £18 - £30 Sliding Scale

HUDSON Rosmy 0227 361969
3 Pigeon Lane, HERNE BAY CT6 7EH
Member of: BAC
Quals/training: BSc; PGCE; Cert Couns(KCC)
Personal Therapy: Yes
Supervision: Ongoing
Counselling offered: **Relationship, Redundancy, Retirement, Stress management, Career**
Service for: Individuals
Theoretical Approach: Person-centred, Jungian
Fees: Negotiable

SCOTT-MCCARTHY Brian 0689 852153
Pocket Gate House, West Common Road, KESTON BR2 6AJ
Member of: AGIP
Quals/training: MA Cantab; extensive clinical experience in NHS and private psychiatric hospitals; Supervisor of Psychotherapy (University College Cork, Applied Psychology Dept)
Personal Therapy: Ongoing
Supervision: Yes
Counselling offered: **Psychotherapy**
Service for: Individuals, Couples, Families
Theoretical Approach: Analytical, Imagery
Fees: £30 - £40

Kent

BUNN Jeanne 0474 705468
Longfield House, Longfield Hill, LONGFIELD DA3 7AS
Member of:	BAC
Quals/training:	SRN; Health Visitor; Dip Couns (IP); Memb APP
Personal Therapy:	Ongoing
Supervision:	Ongoing
Counselling offered:	**General, Relationship, Crisis, Bereavement, Health, Peri-natal, Loss**
Service for:	Individuals
Specific to:	Mothers, Adult survivors of abuse
Theoretical Approach:	Psychosynthesis, Existential
Fees:	£20 - £25 sliding scale

THORNE Angela 0474 873570
Kaleidoscope, 36 Knights Croft, New Ash Green, LONGFIELD DA3 8HT
Member of:	BAC
Quals/training:	Dip Couns; Redwood Dip; training in Integrative Child Therapy
Personal Therapy:	Ongoing
Supervision:	Ongoing
Counselling offered:	**General, Relationship, Assertiveness, Child psychotherapy, Work**
Service for:	Individuals, Couples
Theoretical Approach:	Client-centred, Rogerian, TA, Gestalt
Fees:	£25 - £35

BLOOMFIELD Robert 0622 754858
64 Bower Mount Road, MAIDSTONE ME16 8AT
Member of:	BAC
Quals/training:	Fellow of British Inst of Management; Memb Institute of Public Relations; Attendance Cert Couns (Mid Kent College) 1987
Personal Therapy:	Yes
Supervision:	Ongoing
Counselling offered:	**General, Psychotherapy**
Service for:	Individuals
Theoretical Approach:	Analytical
Fees:	£15 less in hardship cases

BROOKS Carole 0622 842979
Wheelspin, The Street, Ulcombe, MAIDSTONE ME17 1DR
Member of:	BAC Acc
Quals/training:	BAC Acc; BA Psychol; Dip Couns & Interpersonal Skills (SW London College); Cert Indiv Psychosynthesis therapy (Re Vision); training in Gestalt Psychotherapy (metanoia)
Personal Therapy:	Yes
Supervision:	Ongoing
Counselling offered:	**General, Bereavement, Cancer, Crisis, Supervision**
Service for:	Individuals, Couples
Theoretical Approach:	Rogerian, Gestalt, Psychosynthesis
Fees:	£22 - £25 negotiable, also in Maidstone

Kent

COOKSON Diana 0622 843102
Heaven Cottage, Sutton Valence, MAIDSTONE ME17 3HR
Member of: BAC
Quals/training: Dip in Counselling Skills(SW London College)'86; Advanced Counselling course '87-'88
Personal Therapy: Ongoing
Supervision: Ongoing
Counselling offered: General, Educational
Service for: Individuals, Groups
Specific to: Students
Theoretical Approach: Rogerian, Gestalt, Eclectic
Fees: £20 - £25 negotiable

YOUNG Mary 0843 223363
38 Foreland Avenue, Cliftonville, MARGATE CT9 3NQ
Member of: BAC
Quals/training: Catholic Marriage Advisory Council training '68; Dip in Couns & Guidance(Exeter Univ)'70; B Ed(Hons) Health Educ
Personal Therapy: Yes
Supervision: Ongoing
Counselling offered: General, Occupational, Career, Crisis, Marital
Service for: Individuals, Couples, Families, Groups
Theoretical Approach: Eclectic
Fees: Variable

GODDEN Mary 0843 223453
Ty Mawr, 17 Barnes Avenue, Westbrook, MARGATE CT9 5EQ
Member of: BAC Acc
Quals/training: BAC Acc 1984; NMGC/RELATE Cert 1979; CTA Training
Personal Therapy: Yes
Supervision: Ongoing
Counselling offered: General, Bereavement, Supervision
Service for: Individuals, Couples
Theoretical Approach: Rogerian, Psychodynamic
Fees: £15 - £20 negotiable

MICHAELIS Rae 0689 831897
Lynfield, 2d Lynwood Grove, ORPINGTON BR6 0BG
Member of: BAC, IPC
Quals/training: 1986 IPC/WPF Dip; '87 Cert Person-centred Art Therapy; '89 Cert Training in Supervision (WPF)
Personal Therapy: Ongoing
Supervision: Ongoing
Counselling offered: General, Psychotherapy, Crisis, Bereavement, Supervision
Service for: Individuals, Groups
Theoretical Approach: Analytical, Jungian, Psychodynamic
Fees: £15 - £30 Sliding Scale

Kent

WEIGHT Dawn   0689 72702
59 Blenheim Road, ORPINGTON BR6 9BQ
Member of:	**BAC**
Quals/training:	SRN; SCM pt 1; HV FWT; FP Cert; Dip Couns (CAC) '89; Intermediate groupwork course (GCT) '91
Personal Therapy:	Yes
Supervision:	Ongoing
Counselling offered:	**General, Bereavement, Disability**
Service for:	Individuals
Specific to:	People with disabilities
Theoretical Approach:	Jungian
Fees:	£20 - £25

AUSTIN Adela   0634 402167
Chertsey's Gate, College Yard, QUEENBOROUGH ME11 1LB
Member of:	**BAC**
Quals/training:	CQSW; Psychotherapy training (Los Angeles, USA) '76-'79; Hypnotherapy & Transpersonal Therapy training (Calif, USA) '79-'81; Dip Couns; currently Cruse supervisor & trainer
Personal Therapy:	Ongoing
Supervision:	Ongoing
Counselling offered:	**General, Bereavement, Life threatening illnesses, Stress management, Psychotherapy**
Service for:	Individuals, Groups
Theoretical Approach:	Eclectic, Transpersonal
Fees:	£20 - £30 sliding scale

MURTON Jean   0843 587929
46 Belmont Road, RAMSGATE CT11 7QG
Member of:	**BAC**
Quals/training:	Fellow World Federation of Hypnotherapy 1986; Memb Brit Assoc Therapeutic Hypnotists; Master Practitioner NLP PACE.
Personal Therapy:	No
Supervision:	Ongoing
Counselling offered:	**General, Psychotherapy, Hypnohealing, Stress**
Service for:	Individuals, Groups
Theoretical Approach:	TA, NLP
Fees:	£25 per 1hr 30 mins

WEBSTER Annie   0843 592407
Villa Marina, 18 Albion Hill, RAMSGATE CT11 8HG
Member of:	**BAC**
Quals/training:	Dip Therapeutic & Educ Applic of the Arts; Combined Cert Couns; Cert Couns Skills in Dev of Learning; Dip Welfare Studies; Adv Dip Integrative Couns; MIWO & AHP(B)
Personal Therapy:	Ongoing
Supervision:	Ongoing
Counselling offered:	**General, Abuse, Depression, Relationship, Redundancy, Bereavement, Loss, Creative therapies**
Service for:	Individuals, Couples, Families, Groups, Organisations
Specific to:	Children, Adolescents, Survivors of child abuse, Professional carers
Theoretical Approach:	Humanistic, Integrative
Other languages:	German
Fees:	£5 - £15 sliding scale

Kent

WILKINSON Margaret   0732 451114
Spinneys, 122 Kippington Road, SEVENOAKS TN13 2LN
Member of:	BAC Acc
Quals/training:	BAC(Acc); trained and accredited with RELATE; Cert in Psychodynamic Couns(WPF)
Personal Therapy:	Yes
Supervision:	Ongoing
Counselling offered:	**General**
Service for:	Individuals, Couples
Theoretical Approach:	Psychodynamic
Fees:	£22 negotiable

TONGE Dr Anne   0732 452046
8 Dartford Road, SEVENOAKS TN13 3TQ
Member of:	BAC, IPC
Quals/training:	Qualified Doctor 1959; IPC (WPF) Membership
Personal Therapy:	Yes
Supervision:	Ongoing
Counselling offered:	**General, Psychotherapy**
Service for:	Individuals
Theoretical Approach:	Analytical
Fees:	£25 negotiable; assess. £30

MURPHY Pam   0959 524309
Herons, Church Street, Shoreham, SEVENOAKS TN14 7RY
Member of:	NRHP
Quals/training:	CQSW '981; RELATE trained '83; BA(Hons) Psychol '89; Cert Hypnosis & Psychotherapy '87; Memb International Federation of Aromatherapists & BHMA
Personal Therapy:	Yes
Supervision:	Yes
Counselling offered:	**General, Psychotherapy, Hypnotherapy, Aromatherapy**
Service for:	Individuals, Couples
Theoretical Approach:	Eclectic
Other languages:	French
Fees:	£35

GORTON Patricia   0732 61914, 0732 761914
Little Waterden, Seal Chart, SEVENOAKS TN15 0EL
Member of:	BAC Acc
Quals/training:	BAC Acc; Post Grad Dip Couns (CNAA)
Personal Therapy:	Ongoing
Supervision:	Ongoing
Counselling offered:	**General**
Service for:	Individuals
Specific to:	Adolescents, Parents
Theoretical Approach:	Psychodynamic
Fees:	£20 negotiable

Kent

LONG Audrey 0732 61778
Bridleway Cottage, Heverham Road, Kemsing, SEVENOAKS TN15 6NE
Member of:	BAC Acc
Quals/training:	BAC Acc; Dip Adult Couns (London Univ); Introductory Course (IFT); Victim Support
Personal Therapy:	Yes
Supervision:	Ongoing
Counselling offered:	**General, Sexual abuse**
Service for:	Individuals, Couples, Families
Theoretical Approach:	Psychodynamic
Fees:	£25 Negotiable

DENNIS JONES Kathleen 0959 523196
80 Dynes Road, Kemsing, SEVENOAKS TN15 6RF
Member of:	BAC Acc, IPC
Quals/training:	BAC Acc; 1988 IPC/WPF Dip
Personal Therapy:	Yes
Supervision:	Ongoing
Counselling offered:	**General, Psychosomatic**
Service for:	Individuals
Theoretical Approach:	Psychodynamic
Fees:	£25 or by arrangement

BLAKE Adrian 081 300 5465
93 Birkbeck Road, SIDCUP DA14 4DJ
Member of:	BAC, NRHP
Quals/training:	BA (Hons); Dip Psyc (London Univ); Dip (National College of Hypnotherapy & Psychotherapy)
Personal Therapy:	Yes
Supervision:	Ongoing
Counselling offered:	**General, Sexual abuse, Hypnotherapy, Psychotherapy**
Service for:	Individuals
Specific to:	Survivors of child abuse
Theoretical Approach:	Humanistic, Analytical
Fees:	£30

MOTH Lenise 081 302 3289
267 Days Lane, SIDCUP DA15 8JX
Member of:	BAC
Quals/training:	MA (Social Work)/CQSW Univ of Kent; Cert Couns (metanoia); Cert Hypnotherapy; Dip NLP, NLP Practitioner; Phobic Action NRAH.
Personal Therapy:	Ongoing
Supervision:	Ongoing
Counselling offered:	**General, Relationship, Hypnotherapy, Psychotherapy**
Service for:	Individuals, Couples
Specific to:	Survivors of child abuse, Lesbians, Gays
Theoretical Approach:	Eclectic
Fees:	Negotiable in hardship cases

Kent

SMITH Thomas   081 302 3289
267 Days Lane, SIDCUP DA15 8JX
Member of: NRHP
Quals/training: Dip Hypnosis & Psychotherapy (Nat College) 1985; Dip NLP 1987; Cert Psycho-muscular Release therapy; Cert Radical Hypnotherapy
Personal Therapy: Yes
Supervision: Ongoing
Counselling offered: **General, Addiction, Sexual, Hypnotherapy, Psychotherapy**
Service for: Individuals, Couples
Specific to: Adult survivors of abuse, Lesbians, Gays
Theoretical Approach: Eclectic
Fees: Negotiable according to means

SEMPLE Beryl   0732 364805
Conifers, Old Hadlow Road, TONBRIDGE TN10 4EY
Member of: BAC Acc
Quals/training: BAC Acc; Cert Advanced Couns(WPF)1987; Trainer & Supervisor (Cruse Bereavement Care)
Personal Therapy: Yes
Supervision: Ongoing
Counselling offered: **Anxiety, Depression, Relationship, Bereavement**
Service for: Individuals
Theoretical Approach: Psychodynamic
Fees: £25 negotiable

HARDAKER Susan   0732 810556
Church House, Stumble Hill, Shipbourne, TONBRIDGE TN11 9PE
Member of: BAC
Quals/training: RELATE Counsellor, tutor & group leader
Personal Therapy: No
Supervision: Ongoing
Counselling offered: **Marital, Relationship, Bereavement, Loss, Change, Personal growth**
Service for: Individuals, Couples, Families, Groups, Organisations
Theoretical Approach: Psychodynamic
Fees: £21

TOYNE Joy K   0892 723799
Oast Meadow, Burrs Hill, Brenchley, TONBRIDGE TN12 7AT
Member of: BAC, NRHP
Quals/training: Cert Hypnotherapy & Psychotherapy 1987; Dip Hypnotherapy & Psychotherapy 1988; BRCM; WKAPCC
Personal Therapy: Ongoing
Supervision: Ongoing
Counselling offered: **General, Psychotherapy, Hypnotherapy**
Service for: Individuals, Couples, Families, Groups
Theoretical Approach: Eclectic
Fees: £25

Kent

NIGHTINGALE Eileen   0892 518999
65 Grosvenor Road, TUNBRIDGE WELLS TN1 2AY
Member of:	**BAC, PET**
Quals/training:	Dip Psychosynthesis Counselling & Therapy; training in Gestalt & Bio-energetics
Personal Therapy:	Yes
Supervision:	Ongoing
Counselling offered:	**General, Abuse, Bereavement, Inner child, Substance abuse, Co-dependency**
Service for:	Individuals
Theoretical Approach:	Psychosynthesis, Gestalt, Bioenergetic
Fees:	£15 - £25 sliding scale

CUNNINGHAM Valerie   0892 529903
19 Birling Road, TUNBRIDGE WELLS TN2 5LX
Member of:	**BAC, Member of UKCP Register, ITA**
Quals/training:	Art Therapy (St Albans) '85; Qualified & endorsed TA Psychotherapist '90; trainer & supervisor in TA'91
Personal Therapy:	Ongoing
Supervision:	Ongoing
Counselling offered:	**Crisis, Bereavement, Career, Marital, Personal growth, Psychotherapy, Disaster, Supervision**
Service for:	Individuals, Groups
Specific to:	Trauma victims
Theoretical Approach:	Art therapy, TA, Humanistic, Integrative
Fees:	£30 indiv; £16 group

ECCLES Susan Mrs   0892 862417
17 Holmewood Ridge, Langton Green, TUNBRIDGE WELLS TN3 0ED
Member of:	**BAC, MPTI**
Quals/training:	Dip Couns (metanoia)'93; training in supervision
Personal Therapy:	Yes
Supervision:	Ongoing
Counselling offered:	**General, Bereavement, Personal growth, Relationship**
Service for:	Individuals, Couples
Theoretical Approach:	Rogerian
Fees:	£10 - £25 negotiable

GOODCHILD Angela   0892 512798
43 Bounds Oak Way, TUNBRIDGE WELLS TN4 0TW
Member of:	**BAC**
Quals/training:	Dip Sociology; Dip Couns; Dip Hypnotherapy & Psychotherapy; some Gestalt Psychotherapy training
Personal Therapy:	Yes
Supervision:	Ongoing
Counselling offered:	**General, Hypnotherapy**
Service for:	Individuals, Couples
Specific to:	Women
Theoretical Approach:	Rogerian, Eclectic
Other languages:	British Sign Language
Fees:	£25

Kent

RAE Frances   0892 543 025
21 Court Road, TUNBRIDGE WELLS TN4 8EB
Member of:	BAC, KCC, Member of UKCP Register
Quals/training:	BA Psychol; Dip Systemic Therapy (KCC) 1992
Personal Therapy:	No
Supervision:	Ongoing
Counselling offered:	**General, Bereavement, Relationship**
Service for:	Individuals, Couples, Families, Groups
Theoretical Approach:	Systemic, Family therapy
Other languages:	Spanish
Fees:	£25

MARINER Gail   0892 528935
Botley, 7 Nevill Park, TUNBRIDGE WELLS TN4 8NW
Member of:	ANLP (PCS)
Quals/training:	Master Practitioner of the art of NLP, Practitoner in Time Line Therapy(TM)
Personal Therapy:	Yes
Supervision:	Ongoing
Counselling offered:	**General, Trauma, Phobias, Grief, Relationship, Educational**
Service for:	Individuals, Couples, Groups, Organisations
Specific to:	Children, Victims of violence
Theoretical Approach:	NLP
Fees:	None stated

ADDIE Georgia   0732 847533
2 + 4 The Rocks Road, East Malling, WEST MALLING ME19 6AN
Member of:	BAC
Quals/training:	RELATE (NMGC) trained
Personal Therapy:	No
Supervision:	Ongoing
Counselling offered:	**General, Crisis, Marital, Psychosexual**
Service for:	Individuals, Groups
Theoretical Approach:	Psychodynamic, Behavioural
Other languages:	Greek
Fees:	£25 Negotiable

HEADON Christopher   ansaphone 081 777 6422
79 Goodhart Way, WEST WICKHAM BR4 0ET
Member of:	BAC Acc, BASMT
Quals/training:	BAC(Acc); MA(Oxford); PhD(McGill)'74; Cert Couns(LCIP)'83; Cert in Psychosexual Couns(Albany Trust)'84; Dip in Human Sexuality(St George's Hosp Med Sch)'89
Personal Therapy:	Yes
Supervision:	Ongoing
Counselling offered:	**General, Relationship, Sexual**
Service for:	Individuals, Couples
Theoretical Approach:	Psychodynamic, Humanistic
Fees:	£30 individuals, £40 couples

Kent

RAYMOND Liz   0959 561 610
Groombridge House, 52A Madan Road, WESTERHAM TN16 1DX
Member of:	BAC
Quals/training:	Counselling & Adolescence course; Adv Dip Couns(ongoing training); OXSEM training for divorced & separated recovery programme
Personal Therapy:	Ongoing
Supervision:	Ongoing
Counselling offered:	**General, Assertiveness, Bereavement, Marital, Sexual**
Service for:	Individuals, Couples, Families, Groups
Theoretical Approach:	Person-centred
Fees:	£20 (£25 cpls/fams) negotiable

KUYPERS Birgit   0959 561351
1 Lockyer Place, Vicarage Hill, WESTERHAM TN16 1TG
Member of:	BAC, MPTI
Quals/training:	MSc; MPhil; Cert Couns & Guidance (King Alfred's Coll, Winchester) 1988; Dip couns (metanoia) 1992; currently in supervision training
Personal Therapy:	Ongoing
Supervision:	Ongoing
Counselling offered:	**General, Bereavement, Relationship, Supervision**
Service for:	Individuals, Groups
Specific to:	Adolescents, Young adults, Teachers
Theoretical Approach:	Client-centred
Other languages:	German
Fees:	£25

HAYFIELD Elaine   0959 574747
44 Main Road, WESTERHAM TN16 3EB
Member of:	BAC
Quals/training:	Assertion(RWTA)'90; RET '90; Cruse Bereavement training; Adolescent '91; Drug & Alcohol(SADAS)'93
Personal Therapy:	Ongoing
Supervision:	Ongoing
Counselling offered:	**Addiction, Anxiety, Substance abuse, Alcohol, Eating disorders, Grief, Relationship**
Service for:	Individuals, Organisations
Theoretical Approach:	Eclectic, Behavioural
Fees:	£25 negotiable

GAUSDEN Chris   0959 571109
Alsirat, Biggin Hill, WESTERHAM TN16 3NB
Member of:	NRHP, Member of UKCP Register
Quals/training:	BA Psychol; Dip Hypnotherapy & Psychotherapy (NCHP); training in TA
Personal Therapy:	Yes
Supervision:	Ongoing
Counselling offered:	**General, Abuse, Crisis, Psychotherapy, Loss**
Service for:	Individuals, Couples, Families, Organisations
Specific to:	Victims of violence, Managers
Theoretical Approach:	Psychoanalytic, TA, Cognitive/Behavioural
Fees:	£20 - £25

Lancashire

Organisations

BLACKPOOL AND FYLDE COUNSELLING CENTRE   0253 56624
Beaufort Avenue Methodist Church, Bispham, BLACKPOOL
Service:	Client-centred listening and support
Area served:	Blackpool and districts
Referral:	Self or others
Training of workers:	Own training course. Regular supervision and ongoing training
Code of Ethics:	BAC
Management by:	Management committee
Fees:	Voluntary donations

LANCASTER HD, DEPT OF CLINICAL PSYCHOLOGY   0524 586400
Lancaster Moor Hospital, LANCASTER LA1 3JR
Service:	Marital, sexual, individual and group psychotherapy
Area served:	Lancaster & adjacent health districts
Referral:	GP
Training of workers:	All therapists have appropriate postgraduate clinical psycho logy training. Weekly supervision & discussion
Code of Ethics:	BPS
Management by:	Head of District Psychology Service
Fees:	None

WELL WOMAN CENTRE   0772 555813
18-20 New Hall Lane, PRESTON PR1 1TQ
Service:	General couns & specialist couns by clinical psychologist, doctors, health visitors etc
Area served:	Preston Mainly
Other languages:	Main Asian
Referral:	Self
Training of workers:	All trained in listening skills; regular group meetings for supervision
Code of Ethics:	Varies with professional seen
Management by:	Well Woman Centre
Fees:	None

PRESTON PSYCHOTHERAPY CENTRE   Not yet available
1 Albert Road, Fulwood, PRESTON PR2 4PJ
Service:	Range of psycho-analytically oriented psychotherapy for individuals & groups
Area served:	North West
Referral:	Health/Soc Work Professional
Training of workers:	Core professional with additional psycho-analytic training in individual & group psychotherapy
Code of Ethics:	Varies with professional seen
Management by:	Preston DHA
Fees:	None

Lancashire

PERSONAL COUNSELLING CENTRE 0706 860083
Unit 7 Rochdale Enterprise, Generation Centre, Dane Street, ROCHDALE OL12 6XE

Service:	Personal, relationship counselling and stress management for individuals, couples and families in the process of change. Supervision offered for counselling work
Area served:	Rochdale & area
Referral:	Self or others
Training of workers:	RELATE trained with a variety of additional training; ongoing supervision
Code of Ethics:	BAC
Management by:	Partners
Fees:	£25 1st session, then negotiable

Individual Practitioners

*Each individual is a **member of** one or more organisations eligible for entry into this directory. BAC Accredited Counsellors and Recognised Supervisors are shaded.*

LYONS Gill 0254 812443
Park Gate, Osbaldeston, BLACKBURN BB2 7LZ

Member of:	BAC
Quals/training:	Cert Couns (Manchester Univ); MA Health Care Ethics; RGN; training in Pastoral Couns; Medical Student
Personal Therapy:	Ongoing
Supervision:	Ongoing
Counselling offered:	**General, Bereavement, Crisis, Psychotherapy, Eating disorders, Abuse**
Service for:	Individuals, Couples, Families, Children
Specific to:	Women, People with disabilities
Theoretical Approach:	Eclectic, Psychodynamic, Christian
Fees:	£15 - £30 income to charity

HARRISON Eileen 0282 424535
Redcote, 264 Manchester Road, BURNLEY BB11 4HF

Member of:	BAC
Quals/training:	BA (Hons); PGCE; CRUSE Acc; Adv Dip Couns (Manchester Univ)
Personal Therapy:	Ongoing
Supervision:	Ongoing
Counselling offered:	**General, Bereavement, Stress, Terminal illness**
Service for:	Individuals
Specific to:	Bereavement
Theoretical Approach:	Person-centred, Eclectic
Other languages:	French
Fees:	Negotiable

DALE John 0282 776821
176 Victoria Road, Padiham, BURNLEY BB12 8TA

Member of:	BAC
Quals/training:	Trained Psychotherapist & Hypnotherapist; PhD Psychol & Health Sciences; memb NAHP & ICM Reg (Hypnotherapy)
Personal Therapy:	Ongoing
Supervision:	Ongoing
Counselling offered:	**General, Psychotherapy, Hypnotherapy**
Service for:	Individuals, Couples
Theoretical Approach:	Rogerian, Gestalt
Fees:	£15

Lancashire

WESSON Peter 0706 213615, 061 763 1660
The Bury Clinic, 8 Bank Street, off Silver Street, BURY BL9 0DL
Member of:	BAC, NRHP
Quals/training:	Dip Hypnotherapy & Psychotherapy (National Coll) '85; Sexual-Emotional couns; Analytic Psychotherapy; NLP; HIV / AIDS couns (Burnley Aidsline); Memb BRCP(Hyp)
Personal Therapy:	Yes
Supervision:	Ongoing
Counselling offered:	**General, Relationship, Sexual, Bereavement, Crisis, HIV, AIDS, Hypnotherapy, Psychotherapy**
Service for:	Individuals, Couples
Theoretical Approach:	NLP
Other languages:	French
Fees:	£25

LOGIE Robin 0257 272451
Willow House, 21 Weldbank Lane, CHORLEY PR7 3NG
Member of:	BPS
Quals/training:	BSc Psychol 1978; MSc Clinical Psychol (Birmingham); Chartered Clinical Psychologist
Personal Therapy:	Yes
Supervision:	No
Counselling offered:	**General, Anxiety, Marital, Family, Psychotherapy**
Service for:	Individuals, Couples, Families
Theoretical Approach:	Behavioural, Cognitive, Family therapy
Fees:	£35 - £45

BROOKS-CARLISLE Allan 0850 210781, 0257 231041
63 Draperfield, CHORLEY PR7 3PL
Member of:	BAC
Quals/training:	Dip CPC (Inst of Couns, Glasgow); Dip Psy (Open Inst of Psychotherapy, Southport)
Personal Therapy:	Ongoing
Supervision:	Ongoing
Counselling offered:	**Marital, Family, Psychotherapy, Psychosexual**
Service for:	Individuals, Couples, Families, Groups, Organisations
Theoretical Approach:	Gestalt
Fees:	Initial session £20, then £30 per session

AARON WALKER Jean 0257 793414
Lindisfarne, 285 Chapel Lane, Coppull Moor, CHORLEY PR7 4NA
Member of:	BAC
Quals/training:	1977 Dip Advanced Studies in Education (Couns); Creative Therapy (Red House Psychotherapy Centre Salford); MA Thesis on Mental Health Issues
Personal Therapy:	Yes
Supervision:	Ongoing
Counselling offered:	**General, Career, Stress management**
Service for:	Individuals
Specific to:	Adolescents, Social workers
Theoretical Approach:	Person-centred
Fees:	£5 - £15 Negotiable, lower rate unwaged

Lancashire

MICKELBOROUGH Peter   0254 873356
55 Railway Road, DARWEN BB3 2RJ
Member of:	BAC
Quals/training:	Adv Dip Counselling (Wigan); training in Couple and Bereavement Counselling; working with survivors of abuse
Personal Therapy:	Yes
Supervision:	Ongoing
Counselling offered:	**General, Relationship, Bereavement, Abuse**
Service for:	Individuals, Couples, Families
Theoretical Approach:	Rogerian, Client-centred
Other languages:	French
Fees:	£18

CRAN Ros   0524 34906
1 Brook Street, LANCASTER LA1 1SL
Member of:	BAC
Quals/training:	Adv Dip Couns; Cert Ed; training in Expressive Arts Therapy
Personal Therapy:	Yes
Supervision:	Ongoing
Counselling offered:	**General, Bereavement, Crisis, Art therapy, Stop smoking**
Service for:	Individuals, Groups
Specific to:	Women, Gays
Theoretical Approach:	Person-centred
Fees:	£12 - £16 sliding scale

GILES Gail   0524 841406
6 Hartington Street, LANCASTER LA1 3EW
Member of:	BAC
Quals/training:	Dip Couns (Wigan); BA(Hons); Cert Ed
Personal Therapy:	Ongoing
Supervision:	Ongoing
Counselling offered:	**General, Psychotherapy, Assertiveness**
Service for:	Individuals, Couples, Groups
Theoretical Approach:	Integrative, Client-centred, Gestalt, TA, RET
Fees:	£20 negotiable

GROVE-WHITE Helen   0524 382501
LANCASTER LA2
Member of:	BAC
Quals/training:	PhD; Dip Couns (CAC)
Personal Therapy:	Yes
Supervision:	Ongoing
Counselling offered:	**General, Crisis, Eating disorders, Sexual abuse**
Service for:	Individuals, Couples
Specific to:	Parents, Women
Theoretical Approach:	Psychodynamic, Eclectic
Fees:	£20 negotiable

Lancashire

SCOTT Catherine 041 632 7843
1 Deep Cutting Farm, Ashton Road, LANCASTER LA2 0AA
Member of: **NRHP, BPS**
Quals/training: MEd(Hons) Psych; Dip Couns & Educ; Dip Spec Ed; Dip Hypnotherapy & Psychotherapy (NC)
Personal Therapy: Yes
Supervision: Ongoing
Counselling offered: **General, Psychotherapy, Hypnotherapy**
Service for: Individuals
Theoretical Approach: Integrative
Fees: £20

HOLLANDERS Henry 0282 697211
5 Barnoldswick Road, Barrowford, NELSON BB9 6BH
Member of: **BAC Acc**
Quals/training: BAC Acc; BD London; 1985 Cert Couns (Manchester Univ)
Personal Therapy: Yes
Supervision: Ongoing
Counselling offered: **General, Relationship, Bereavement, Psychotherapy**
Service for: Individuals, Couples, Families, Groups
Theoretical Approach: Psychodynamic, Eclectic, Integrative
Fees: £15 (1st session), sliding scale

CORBETT Michael 0704 840858
5 Rosemary Lane, Haskayne, Downholland, ORMSKIRK L39 7JP
Member of: **BAC**
Quals/training: PhD; Dip Couns (Sandown College Liverpool)'88; Cert in Hypnotherapy & Psychotherapy (National College of Hypnosis & Psychotherapy); Cert in NLP
Personal Therapy: Yes
Supervision: Ongoing
Counselling offered: **Hypnotherapy, Bereavement, Anxiety, Depression, Crisis, Addiction, Health**
Service for: Individuals, Couples, Groups
Theoretical Approach: NLP
Fees: £25

SIMONS Timothy 0772 703275
150 Watling Street road, Fulwood, PRESTON PR2 4AH
Member of: **BAC**
Quals/training: PGCE, Adv Dip Couns; Member Brit Reg Complementary Practitioners, PPA
Personal Therapy: Yes
Supervision: Ongoing
Counselling offered: **General, Depression, Relationship, Personal growth, Self-esteem, Men's issues**
Service for: Individuals, Couples
Theoretical Approach: Rogerian, Client-centred
Fees: £15 - £25

Lancashire

JOHNSON Elaine
ansaphone 0772 863889
31 Brookfield Drive, Fulwood, PRESTON PR2 4ST
Member of:	BAC
Quals/training:	Cert in Counselling (Manchester University)
Personal Therapy:	Ongoing
Supervision:	Ongoing
Counselling offered:	**General, Bereavement, Child abuse, Marital**
Service for:	Individuals, Couples, Families
Specific to:	Women, Survivors of child abuse
Theoretical Approach:	Rogerian, Jungian
Fees:	£20 per hour; concessions available

POWER Anne
ansaphone 0995 605049
2 Sunny View, Oakenclough, Garstang, PRESTON PR3 1UL
Member of:	BAC
Quals/training:	Dip Couns (Keele) 1977; ASC Acc '86; FDI Workshops:
Personal Therapy:	Ongoing
Supervision:	Ongoing
Counselling offered:	**General, Relationship, Sexual, Bereavement, Personal growth**
Service for:	Individuals, Couples, Groups
Specific to:	Oppressed groups
Theoretical Approach:	Person-centred
Fees:	£15 - £20 Negotiable

DIDSBURY Patricia
0772 314153
6 Little Bank Close, Bamber Bridge, PRESTON PR5 6BU
Member of:	BAC, BPS
Quals/training:	CPsychol (Counselling); BSc (Hons) Psychol '86; Advanced Dip Couns Wigan College '87; Cert Clinical Psychodrama '88
Personal Therapy:	Yes
Supervision:	Ongoing
Counselling offered:	**General, Eating disorders, Personal growth, Women's issues, Abuse**
Service for:	Individuals, Groups
Specific to:	Survivors of sex abuse
Theoretical Approach:	Person-centred, Psychodynamic, Psychodrama
Fees:	£22 negotiable

SCOTT Mary
0706 59287
Earnsdale, 3 Bamford Way, ROCHDALE OL11 5NA
Member of:	BAC
Quals/training:	Dip Couns; RGN; RM; ongoing Gestalt training
Personal Therapy:	Ongoing
Supervision:	Ongoing
Counselling offered:	General
Service for:	Individuals
Specific to:	Parents
Theoretical Approach:	Person-centred
Fees:	Sliding scale

Lancashire

EATOCK John   **0706 222531**
57 Heys Avenue, Haslingden, ROSSENDALE BB4 5DU
Member of: BAC
Quals/training: Anglican theological training; MA (Lancaster); Cert Couns Supervision (Leeds Univ)
Personal Therapy: Ongoing
Supervision: Ongoing
Counselling offered: **General, Supervision**
Service for: Individuals, Couples, Families, Groups, Organisations
Theoretical Approach: Person-centred
Fees: £20 minimum

WILMERS Kath   **0706 220375**
9 Moorland Rise, Haslingden, ROSSENDALE BB4 6UA
Member of: BAC
Quals/training: BA(Hons) Soc Sci; Adv Cert Couns(Wigan Coll)1990; In-service Teacher Training (NWRAC) 1986-88; ongoing Couns Trainer (inc Reg Alcohol Council: Wigan College)
Personal Therapy: Ongoing
Supervision: Ongoing
Counselling offered: **General**
Service for: Individuals, Couples, Groups
Theoretical Approach: Person-centred
Fees: Negotiable

MILLER Margaret   **0706 358559, 0706 222825**
Heightside Mews, Newchurch Road, ROSSENDALE BB4 9HQ
Member of: BAC, BASMT
Quals/training: Dip Welfare Studies; Psychosexual Counselling Cert; Dip Couns; CSS Cert in Social Work
Personal Therapy: Yes
Supervision: Ongoing
Counselling offered: **General, Psychosexual, Mental health**
Service for: Individuals, Couples, Groups
Specific to: Mentally ill
Theoretical Approach: Rogerian, Gestalt, Analytical
Fees: £25 first session, then negotiable

Lancashire

Leicestershire

Organisations

LEICESTER COUNSELLING CENTRE   **0533 558801**
Sovereign House, 17 Princess Road West, LEICESTER LE1 6TR
Service: General counselling service for individuals and groups
Area served: Leicestershire
Referral: Self or others
Training of workers: Most counsellors have undertaken a three year part-time counselling training course and have regular supervision
Code of Ethics: BAC
Management by: Management Committee
Fees: £20 negotiable; no minimum

BAKER-VAUGHAN COUNSELLING SERVICES   **0533 470880**
Victoria House, 172 London Road, LEICESTER LE2 1ND
Service: Working with individuals or couples with personal or marital problems, stress, bereavement, sex therapy
Referral: Self
Training of workers: Audrey Baker BAC Acc, Derek Ball RELATE Acc
Code of Ethics: BAC
Fees: £25, Assessment £20

Individual Practitioners

*Each individual is a **member of** one or more organisations eligible for entry into this directory. BAC Accredited Counsellors and Recognised Supervisors are shaded.*

FISZER Mike   **Mobile 0831 198 448, 0530 835883**
Most Consultants, 20 The Green, Hugglescote, COALVILLE LE67 2GE
Member of: BAC, BPS
Quals/training: BSc Psychol; MBA; Cert Ed; BPS (Statement of Competence in Occupational Testing)
Personal Therapy: Yes
Supervision: Ongoing
Counselling offered: General, Bereavement, Career, Occupational, Redundancy, Stress
Service for: Individuals, Families, Groups, Organisations
Specific to: Managers
Theoretical Approach: Schein, Levin
Fees: £30 - £60 negotiable

DENT Peter   **0455 633 400**
8 Drake Way, HINCKLEY LE10 1UW
Member of: BAC Acc
Quals/training: BAC Acc '90; BA '75; RMN '79; CQSW '81; Couns Training (Vaughan College) '83-'85; NHS Psychotherapy training '83-8; Advanced Cert Psychotherapy (Vaughan College) '91-93
Personal Therapy: Yes
Supervision: Ongoing
Counselling offered: General, Stress management, Marital, Supervision
Service for: Individuals, Couples, Families, Groups, Organisations
Theoretical Approach: Rogerian, Psychodynamic
Fees: £25

Leicestershire

PERRY Janet 0533 739912
78 Holmfield Road, Stoneygate, LEICESTER LE2 1SB
Member of: BAC
Quals/training: BA; MPhil, CQSW; NMGC/RELATE Trained; Sex therapist
Personal Therapy: Yes
Supervision: Ongoing
Counselling offered: **General, Marital, Eating disorders, Sexual dysfunction**
Service for: Individuals, Couples, Groups
Specific to: Women, Survivors of sex abuse
Fees: £25 less in hardship cases

WOOD Richard 0533 739912
Camsgill, 78 Holmfield Road, Stoneygate, LEICESTER LE2 1SB
Member of: BAC
Quals/training: MA;MSc; Dip Couns in Educational Settings(Aston Univ)'81; RELATE trained
Personal Therapy: Yes
Supervision: Ongoing
Counselling offered: **General, Marital, Personal growth**
Service for: Individuals, Couples
Theoretical Approach: Rogerian, Eclectic, Integrative
Fees: £25 maximum

STERN James 0533 709363
37 Landseer Road, Clarendon Park, LEICESTER LE2 3EF
Member of: BAC
Quals/training: BA Psychol/Phil 1982; Found Cert Psychotherapy (CSCT) 1990; currently studying for MA (Therapy)
Personal Therapy: Yes
Supervision: Ongoing
Counselling offered: **General**
Service for: Individuals
Theoretical Approach: Existential
Fees: £18 negotiable

RIDGEWELL Margaret 0533 707197
68 Elms Road, LEICESTER LE2 3JB
Member of: BAC, GPTI, MPTI
Quals/training: BA; MEd Studies; Dip IDHP; Dip Couns; ITEC; Gestalt Psychotherapy (metanoia) 1989-present
Personal Therapy: Yes
Supervision: Ongoing
Counselling offered: **General, Relationship, Self-esteem, Psychotherapy**
Service for: Individuals, Couples, Groups, Organisations
Specific to: Teachers, Managers
Theoretical Approach: Rogerian, Gestalt
Other languages: French
Fees: £22 - £30 sliding scale

Leicestershire

CALLAGHAN Joan   0533 705766
6 Link Road, Knighton, LEICESTER LE2 3RA
Member of:	BAC
Quals/training:	2 yr Counselling Course (Univ of Leicester Adult Centre) '83-'85; training at Centre for Psychotherapy and Counselling Education '86-'89
Personal Therapy:	Yes
Supervision:	Ongoing
Counselling offered:	**General, Psychotherapy**
Service for:	Individuals, Couples
Theoretical Approach:	Jungian
Fees:	£20 negotiable for low income

SUTTON Carole   0533 715772
108 Stoughton Road, Oadby, LEICESTER LE2 4FN
Member of:	**BAC, BPS**
Quals/training:	BA Psychol; MSc; PhD; C Psychol; Counselling Psychologist
Personal Therapy:	Yes
Supervision:	Ongoing
Counselling offered:	**General, Bereavement, Relationship, Children's problems, Problem solving**
Service for:	Individuals, Couples, Families
Specific to:	Children, Young people, Women
Theoretical Approach:	Humanistic, Eclectic
Other languages:	French
Fees:	£15

REEVE Jean   0533 714622
29 Holme Drive, Oadby, LEICESTER LE2 4HF
Member of:	**BAC**
Quals/training:	BA (Hons); MA Social Work; NMGC; BASW
Personal Therapy:	Ongoing
Supervision:	Ongoing
Counselling offered:	**General, Bereavement, Problem solving, Relationship**
Service for:	Individuals, Couples
Theoretical Approach:	Eclectic
Fees:	£20

GOUGH Tony   0533 854284
410 Hinckley Road, Western Park, LEICESTER LE3 0WA
Member of:	**BAC Acc**
Quals/training:	BAC Acc; CTA Acc; D MIN (Chicago); training with Asoc Clinical Pastoral Education (USA)
Personal Therapy:	Yes
Supervision:	Ongoing
Counselling offered:	**General, Marital, Sexual, Bereavement, Crisis, Psychotherapy**
Service for:	Individuals, Couples, Groups, Families
Specific to:	Clergy/priests, Doctors
Theoretical Approach:	Psychodynamic, Gestalt, TA
Fees:	£25 upwards inds, £35 couples

Leicestershire

HOLT Alan 0533 858300
6 Brampton Avenue, Glenfield Road, LEICESTER LE3 6DA
Member of:	BAC
Quals/training:	Ongoing Cert Couns (Leicester Univ); RELATE '87; IAH '88; CAH '89; Gen Psychol (OU) '89
Personal Therapy:	Ongoing
Supervision:	Ongoing
Counselling offered:	General, Relationship, Loss, Co-dependency
Service for:	Individuals, Couples
Theoretical Approach:	Eclectic, Person-centred
Fees:	£20 - £30 sliding scale

BEAK Richard 0533 760550
41 Abbots Road, Humberstone, LEICESTER LE5 1DD
Member of:	BAC
Quals/training:	BA; CQSW; Dip Soc Work; Dip Social Learning Theory in Applied Settings
Personal Therapy:	Ongoing
Supervision:	Ongoing
Counselling offered:	General, Bereavement, Family, Crisis
Service for:	Individuals, Couples, Families
Theoretical Approach:	Cognitive/Behavioural, Client-centred
Fees:	Negotiable

WILLIAMS Sherly 0533 737713
31 Kingsway Road, LEICESTER LE5 5TN
Member of:	IPC/WPF, WMIP
Quals/training:	BA(Hons); MA; Dip Couns(WPF) '87; full psychotherapy training '88
Personal Therapy:	Yes
Supervision:	Ongoing
Counselling offered:	Psychotherapy
Service for:	Individuals
Theoretical Approach:	Analytical
Fees:	£28

DEANS Guy 0533 735450
9 St Philips Road, LEICESTER LE5 5TR
Member of:	BAC, BASMT
Quals/training:	RELATE Trained; Cert AIDS Couns; Psychotherapy BASMT Acc
Personal Therapy:	Yes
Supervision:	Ongoing
Counselling offered:	Marital, Psychosexual, Anxiety, Depression
Service for:	Individuals, Couples
Theoretical Approach:	Eclectic
Fees:	£20

Leicestershire

HAMORY Eva 0533 413765
99 Davenport Road, LEICESTER LE5 6SE
Member of:	**RCP**
Quals/training:	MD; BSc Psychol; T Psych
Personal Therapy:	Yes
Supervision:	No
Counselling offered:	**Psychotherapy, Supervision**
Service for:	Individuals, Groups, Couples
Specific to:	Health care professionals
Theoretical Approach:	Jungian
Other languages:	Hungarian
Fees:	Negotiable

BONSER Wendy 0533 601013
16 Lincoln Drive, LEICESTER LE7 2JW
Member of:	**BAC**
Quals/training:	Couns Studies Cert (Vaughan College) 1990
Personal Therapy:	Ongoing
Supervision:	Ongoing
Counselling offered:	**General, Crisis, Loss, Bereavement, Depression, Relationship**
Service for:	Individuals, Couples
Specific to:	People with disabilities
Theoretical Approach:	Psychodynamic, Eclectic
Fees:	Negotiable

MARSHALL Hazel MEd 0533 364256
52 Station Road, Cropston, LEICESTER LE7 7HD
Member of:	**BAC Acc**
Quals/training:	BAC Acc; Cert CTP 1980; Dip CTP 1992
Personal Therapy:	Ongoing
Supervision:	Ongoing
Counselling offered:	**General, Psychotherapy**
Service for:	Individuals
Theoretical Approach:	Rogerian, Jungian, Transpersonal
Fees:	£23 negotiable

NICHOLLS Stephen 0533 866 709
33 Coltbeck Avenue, Narborough, LEICESTER LE9 5EJ
Member of:	**BAC**
Quals/training:	Dip Psychosynthesis Counselling & Therapy (Psychosynthesis & Education Trust)
Personal Therapy:	Ongoing
Supervision:	Ongoing
Counselling offered:	**Psychotherapy**
Service for:	Individuals, Couples, Families, Groups, Organisations
Theoretical Approach:	Psychosynthesis
Fees:	£25 negotiable

Leicestershire

BLEACH Andrew 0455 822277
4 High Street, Desford, LEICESTER LE9 9JF
Member of:	**BAC, BPS, ITA**
Quals/training:	BSc Behavioural Science 1980; Cert Ed Educational Psychology 1982; MA/CQSW 1986; Grad Member BPS
Personal Therapy:	Yes
Supervision:	Ongoing
Counselling offered:	**General, Bereavement, Change, Mental health**
Service for:	Individuals, Couples, Groups
Theoretical Approach:	TA, NLP
Fees:	£15 - £25 Sliding scale

KIRK Ruth 0509 843961
6 West End, Long Whatton, LOUGHBOROUGH LE12 5DW
Member of:	**BAC**
Quals/training:	Cert Couns Studies (distinction) 1990 & Adv Cert Couns (Leicester Univ) 1992
Personal Therapy:	Yes
Supervision:	Ongoing
Counselling offered:	**General, Relationship, Assertiveness, Anxiety, Loss, Depression, Abuse**
Service for:	Individuals
Specific to:	Women
Theoretical Approach:	Person-centred, Psychodynamic
Fees:	£18

WHITWORTH Patricia 0509 413327
Wisteria Cottage, 93 Melton Road, Barrow on Soar, LOUGHBOROUGH LE12 8NT
Member of:	**BAC**
Quals/training:	Dip Occ Therapy '60; Cert Ed '71; Dip Couns In Educational Settings (Aston Univ) '80; Primary Cert in RET '82; BA '85; Currently training as Supervisor (Sherwood PTI)
Personal Therapy:	Yes
Supervision:	Ongoing
Counselling offered:	**General, Bereavement, Crisis, Occupational, Stress, Redundancy**
Service for:	Individuals
Specific to:	Adolescents, People with disabilities
Theoretical Approach:	Psychodynamic
Fees:	£20 students & unwaged negotiable

GOULD Geraldine 0455 556808
22 High Street, LUTTERWORTH LE17 4AD
Member of:	**BAC, CRAH**
Quals/training:	Psychology/Sociology; IPM; NSHAP Training; Inst of Management
Personal Therapy:	Ongoing
Supervision:	Ongoing
Counselling offered:	**General, Psychotherapy, Hypnotherapy, Anxiety, Stress, Depression, Relationship, Phobias, Addiction, Bereavement**
Service for:	Individuals, Couples, Groups, Families, Organisations
Specific to:	Survivors of child abuse
Theoretical Approach:	Ericksonian, NLP, Psychosynthesis, Eclectic
Fees:	£35

Leicestershire

CHEVERTON Gordon   045 202275
19 The Dell, Ullesthorpe, LUTTERWORTH LE17 5BL
Member of:	**BAC**
Quals/training:	CQSW; Dip Soc Work
Personal Therapy:	Ongoing
Supervision:	Ongoing
Counselling offered:	**General, Marital, Sexual, Bereavement, Depression, Psychotherapy, Hypnotherapy**
Service for:	Individuals, Couples, Families
Theoretical Approach:	Psychoanalytic
Fees:	Negotiable

MADDEN Felicity   0536 770320
Linden House, Great East, MARKET HARBOROUGH LE16 8SJ
Member of:	**BAC Acc**
Quals/training:	BAC Acc; Advanced Cert in Counselling
Personal Therapy:	Ongoing
Supervision:	Ongoing
Counselling offered:	**Short-term, Long-term, General**
Service for:	Individuals, Couples
Theoretical Approach:	Psychodynamic
Fees:	£20 negotiable

SCHAVERIEN Joy   0780 720117
1 The Square, South Luffenham, OAKHAM LE15 8NS
Member of:	**BAC, WMIP**
Quals/training:	PhD; MA; DFA (Lond); Reg Art Therapist, Psychotherapist
Personal Therapy:	Yes
Supervision:	Ongoing
Counselling offered:	**Art therapy, Educational, Psychotherapy, Short-term, Long-term**
Service for:	Individuals, Groups
Theoretical Approach:	Analytical
Fees:	£25

Leicestershire

Lincolnshire

Organisations

NORTH LINCOLNSHIRE HA DISTRICT DEPT OF CLINICAL PSYCHOLOGY 0522 560617
Baverstock House, Sewell Road, LINCOLN

Service:	Broad range of psychological therapies for a variety of personal problems available in speciality services for all ages inc families, people with learning difficulties, etc
Area served:	North Lincolnshire
Other languages	:Norwegian, Swedish, Danish, French, Greek
Referral:	Self, GP
Training of workers:	Postgraduate clinical psychology minimum
Code of Ethics:	BPS
Management by:	District Psychologist
Fees:	None (private - charged)

Individual Practitioners
*Each individual is a **member of** one or more organisations eligible for entry into this directory. BAC Accredited Counsellors and Recognised Supervisors are shaded.*

LARGE Wendy A 0778 33463
Somersby House, Witham On The Hill, BOURNE PE10 0JH

Member of:	**BAC, BPS, ITA**
Quals/training:	BSc Psychol; Cert Couns; Cert(ITA)
Personal Therapy:	Yes
Supervision:	Ongoing
Counselling offered:	**General, Addiction, Tranquillisers, Work**
Service for:	Individuals, Couples, Groups, Families, Organisations
Theoretical Approach:	Integrative, Eclectic
Fees:	£30 maximum, negotiable

OLLEY Margaret 0476 870750
Lilac Cottage, Middle Street, Croxton Kerrial, GRANTHAM NG32 1QP

Member of:	**BAC**
Quals/training:	Cruse'92; Cert Couns & Personal Support & Cert Understanding People with Psychiatric Problems (S Lincs HA)'89; TA 101; Adv Cert Couns (Leicester Univ)'93
Personal Therapy:	Ongoing
Supervision:	Ongoing
Counselling offered:	**General, Mental health, PTSD**
Service for:	Individuals, Groups
Specific to:	People with disabilities
Theoretical Approach:	Psychodynamic, Eclectic
Fees:	£15 - £25 sliding scale

Lincolnshire

HOPKINS Barbara   0522 513359
14 Woburn Avenue, LINCOLN LN1 3HJ
Member of: BAC
Quals/training: BSc; MPhil; Cert Pastoral Couns (St John's College, Nottingham)
Personal Therapy: Ongoing
Supervision: Ongoing
Counselling offered: **General, Bereavement, Crisis**
Service for: Individuals, Groups, Organisations
Theoretical Approach: Eclectic
Fees: £5 sliding scale

WOOD Pam   0522 568288
Walnut Cottage, Springfields, Old Lincoln Road, LINCOLN LN2
Member of: BAC
Quals/training: RGN; Adv Dip in Guidance & Counselling
Personal Therapy: Ongoing
Supervision: Ongoing
Counselling offered: **General, Bereavement, HIV, AIDS**
Service for: Individuals
Theoretical Approach: Eclectic
Fees: Free

WILLIAMSON Derrick   0522 532023
114 Wolsey Way, Nettleham Park, LINCOLN LN2 4TW
Member of: BAC
Quals/training: MA Psychology of Therapy & Couns(Antioch Univ)'90; Basic & Advanced Couns(Goldsmiths Coll)
Personal Therapy: Yes
Supervision: Ongoing
Counselling offered: **General, Marital, Co-dependency, Psychotherapy**
Service for: Individuals, Couples, Groups
Theoretical Approach: Person-centred
Fees: £15 (£10 financial difficulty)

POPPLEWELL Sue   0522 682051
Bowland, Wood Bank, Skellingthorpe, LINCOLN LN6 5UD
Member of: BAC
Quals/training: SRN; RELATE trained Cert Couns Studies (Leics Univ):
Personal Therapy: Yes
Supervision: Ongoing
Counselling offered: **General, Marital, Bereavement, Psychotherapy**
Service for: Individuals, Couples
Theoretical Approach: Psychodynamic
Fees: £20 - £25

Lincolnshire

ELLIS Roger   0522 681510
Frogs Leap, 615 Newark Road, LINCOLN LN6 8SA
Member of:	BAC Acc
Quals/training:	BAC Acc; BSc; MEd; Dip Student Couns (Univ of London); Cert Psychodynamic Couns Supervision (WPF)
Personal Therapy:	Yes
Supervision:	Ongoing
Counselling offered:	**General, Psychotherapy**
Service for:	Individuals
Theoretical Approach:	Psychodynamic
Fees:	£15 - £25 negotiable

JORDAN Pauline   0507 605 924
12 Church Close, LOUTH LN11 9LR
Member of:	BAC
Quals/training:	Dip Counselling for Pastoral Care (Nottingham); Cert Ed
Personal Therapy:	Ongoing
Supervision:	Ongoing
Counselling offered:	**General, Relationship, Loss**
Service for:	Individuals
Specific to:	Women only
Theoretical Approach:	Person-centred
Fees:	£12 - £18 sliding scale

Lincolnshire

Merseyside

Organisations

MERSEYSIDE BROOK ADVISORY CENTRE 051 709 4558
104 Bold Street, LIVERPOOL L1 4HY
Service:	Contraception & pregnancy counselling for under 25's
Area served:	Merseyside
Referral:	Self
Training of workers:	Appropriate training and qualifications
Code of Ethics:	Varies with professional seen
Management by:	Executive Committee
Fees:	None

COMPASS 051 708 6688
25 Hope Street, LIVERPOOL L1 9BQ
Service:	**General counselling service for those suffering from anxiety, depression and other problems, including relationships, bereavement etc.**
Area served:	Merseyside
Referral:	Self
Training of workers:	Two & a half year part-time course (CENTRA diploma) including self growth/personal therapy and supervision
Code of Ethics:	BAC
Management by:	Management Committee
Fees:	Donation negotiated at 1st interview

ALDER CENTRE Day 051 252 5391, eve h/line 051 228 9759
Royal Liverpool Children's Hos, Alder Hey, Eaton Road, LIVERPOOL L12 2AP
Service:	**Bereavement counselling, therapy and consultation for families and professionals affected by the death of a child. Service for individuals, couples, groups and prof. workers**
Area served:	Dependant on service required
Other languages:	French
Referral:	Self or others
Training of workers:	Cert Counselling (Man/Cr Univ); Dip Couns (Sandown Coll); CMAC; RELATE; regular supervision
Code of Ethics:	BAC
Management by:	Hospital Trust
Fees:	None

Individual Practitioners

*Each individual is a **member of** one or more organisations eligible for entry into this directory. BAC Accredited Counsellors and Recognised Supervisors are shaded.*

CAWLEY Tony 051 727 1485
44 Wellesley Road, LIVERPOOL L8 3SU
Member of:	**NRHP**
Quals/training:	Dip Hypnotherapy & Psychotherapy National College; experience in Therapeutic Communities
Personal Therapy:	Ongoing
Supervision:	Ongoing
Counselling offered:	**General, Hypnotherapy, Psychotherapy**
Service for:	Individuals, Groups
Theoretical Approach:	Eclectic
Fees:	£20 - £25

Merseyside

ELMS Gill   051 523 8565
31 Amanda Road, Fazakerley, LIVERPOOL L10 4YE
Member of: BAC
Quals/training: PG Dip Couns & Psychol
Personal Therapy: Yes
Supervision: Ongoing
Counselling offered: General, Psychotherapy, Bereavement, Crisis
Service for: Individuals, Couples, Groups
Specific to: Women, Young people
Theoretical Approach: Rogerian, Psychodynamic
Fees: £15 - £30 sliding scale

CHARNOCK Donald   051 220 1554
The Arbour, Room 4, 87 Lord Street, LIVERPOOL
Member of: BAC
Quals/training: BA (Hons) Soc Psy/Health Studies; 1986 Dip Hyp (member international Assoc of Professional Hypnosis; Cert Couns (Liverpool John Moores University)
Personal Therapy: Yes
Supervision: Ongoing
Counselling offered: General, Psychotherapy, Hypnotherapy, Anxiety, Stress management
Service for: Individuals, Couples, Groups
Theoretical Approach: Person-centred, Integrative
Fees: £18 - £30 sliding scale

SUMMERFIELD Solharra Gene   051 722 0401
'The Rowans', 122 Bowring Park Road, Broadgreen, LIVERPOOL L14 3NP
Member of: BAC Acc
Quals/training: BAC Acc; 1970 Hypnotherapy Dip USA; couns experience in hospital work and at Compass (Liverpool)
Personal Therapy: Yes
Supervision: Ongoing
Counselling offered: Personal growth, Crisis, Stress management, Bereavement, Marital, Psychosexual, Family, Psychotherapy, Inner child
Service for: Individuals, Couples, Families, Groups
Theoretical Approach: Rogerian, Gestalt, TA
Fees: £30

CANTER Anita   051 728 7550
25 Siddeley Street, LIVERPOOL L17 8XU
Member of: BAC Acc
Quals/training: BAC(Acc); Cert in Couns Theory; Cert in Individual Psychotherapy, trained with Compass, Liverpool; Re-evaluation Counselling training
Personal Therapy: Yes
Supervision: Ongoing
Counselling offered: General
Service for: Individuals
Specific to: Holocaust survivors
Theoretical Approach: Eclectic, Adlerian
Other languages: Danish
Fees: Up to £25 sliding scale

Merseyside

ROBERTS Ellis
26 Gorsebank Road, LIVERPOOL L18 1HL
051 733 9117
Member of:	BAC Acc
Quals/training:	PhD'76; trained with Compass '79-'81; Llys Fasi Spirituality Workshop '86; Maudsley Hospital Supervision Course '86-'87; Assoc Psychol Type '90
Personal Therapy:	Ongoing
Supervision:	Ongoing
Counselling offered:	General, Supervision
Service for:	Individuals
Theoretical Approach:	Eclectic
Fees:	£15 - £35 sliding scale

RUDNICK Joan
22 Mather Avenue, LIVERPOOL L18 5HS
051 724 4606
Member of:	BAC
Quals/training:	RELATE trained; BASMT
Personal Therapy:	No
Supervision:	Ongoing
Counselling offered:	General, Marital, Relationship
Service for:	Individuals, Couples, Families
Theoretical Approach:	Psychodynamic
Fees:	£15

WHITTAKER Ann
38 De Villiers Avenue, Grosby, LIVERPOOL L23 2TJ
051 931 2115
Member of:	BAC
Quals/training:	RELATE trained; COMPASS trained
Personal Therapy:	Yes
Supervision:	Ongoing
Counselling offered:	General, Marital
Service for:	Individuals, Couples
Fees:	£12 negotiable

SMITH Margaret
13 St Anthonys Road, Blundellsands, LIVERPOOL L23 8TN
051 931 5194
Member of:	**BAC, Member of UKCP Register**
Quals/training:	Dip Psychotherapy (Liverpool Univ) 1990
Personal Therapy:	Ongoing
Supervision:	Ongoing
Counselling offered:	General, Supervision
Service for:	Individuals, Groups
Theoretical Approach:	Psychodynamic
Fees:	£30 negotiable; £10 group

Merseyside

STELL Peter PhD   051 520 0116
14 Langdale Drive, Maghull, LIVERPOOL L31 9BR
Member of:	BAC
Quals/training:	Cert Psychol & Soc Studies(Leeds Univ)'78; Psychotherapy & Couns(NHS)'88; Cert Couns(Peterborough Reg Coll)'91;training in client-centred couns,TA,RET,stress management,group ther
Personal Therapy:	Yes
Supervision:	Ongoing
Counselling offered:	**General, Crisis, Bereavement, Fertility, Terminal illness, Stress, Marital, Abuse, HIV, AIDS**
Service for:	Individuals, Couples, Families, Groups
Specific to:	Mentally ill, Substance abusers, Survivors of sex abuse
Theoretical Approach:	Rogerian, Client-centred, TA, RET
Fees:	£15 - £20

CHADWICK Kay   051 531 9771
Windhover, 5 Croxteth Close, Maghull, LIVERPOOL L31 9BZ
Member of:	BAC Acc
Quals/training:	BAC Acc; Dip Couns '74; Cert Human Social Functioning; training with IGA and ITA
Personal Therapy:	Yes
Supervision:	Ongoing
Counselling offered:	**General, Bereavement, Supervision**
Service for:	Individuals, Couples, Groups
Specific to:	Clergy/priests, Religious
Theoretical Approach:	Eclectic, TA, Egan
Fees:	£20 negotiable

ENTWISTLE Paul Andrew
The Rodney Fertility Clinic, 37 Rodney Street, LIVERPOOL L1 9EN
Member of:	BAC
Quals/training:	M Phil; Dip Clinical Chemistry; Consultant Reproductive Biologist; Hypnotherapist; Memb BICA, NAHP & BHMA
Personal Therapy:	Ongoing
Supervision:	Ongoing
Counselling offered:	**Infertility, Psychosexual, Hypnotherapy**
Service for:	Individuals, Couples
Theoretical Approach:	Eclectic
Fees:	£25 sometimes free

DAVIES Lisa   051 920 9056
6 Parkholme, Park Road, Waterloo Park, LIVERPOOL L22 3XE
Member of:	BAC
Quals/training:	Dip Welfare'82; Fellow IWO; H Ed Teacher
Personal Therapy:	No
Supervision:	Ongoing
Counselling offered:	**General, Crisis, Career, Bereavement, Redundancy, Outplacement, Retirement**
Service for:	Individuals, Couples, Groups, Organisations
Other languages:	Welsh
Fees:	£25 + travel, negot rates for orgs

Merseyside

SCRIMSHAW George 0704 29438
20 St Annes Road, Marshside, SOUTHPORT PR9 9TQ
Member of: NCHP, NRHP
Quals/training: PhD; Dip Hypnotherapy & Psychotherapy (NCHP); NRHP (assoc)
Personal Therapy: No
Supervision: No
Counselling offered: General, Bereavement, Hypnotherapy, Phobias, Stress
Service for: Individuals
Fees: £18

STEWART June Home 074 488 2968, Office 051 489 6136
Sunnyside, Reeds Brow, Rainford, ST. HELENS WA11 8PD
Member of: BAC, ULDP
Quals/training: CQSW (Liverpool) 1975; Dip Psychotherapy (Liverpool Univ) 1989
Personal Therapy: Yes
Supervision: Ongoing
Counselling offered: General, Bereavement, Loss, Psychotherapy
Service for: Individuals, Couples
Specific to: Adolescents
Theoretical Approach: Psychodynamic, Eclectic
Fees: £25

WELLER Celia 0744 895 645, Fax 0744 895754
Derbyshire House, Crank Road, Kings Moss, ST. HELENS WA11 8RJ
Member of: BAC, GPTI
Quals/training: Dip Couns; training in Gestalt Psychotherapy since 1990
Personal Therapy: Ongoing
Supervision: Ongoing
Counselling offered: General, Stress, Relationship, Health, Psychotherapy
Service for: Individuals, Couples, Groups
Specific to: Women, Executives
Theoretical Approach: Rogerian, Gestalt
Other languages: French
Fees: £20 - £25 sliding scale

MARNELL Rose 051 639 6464
39 Serpentine Road, WALLASEY L44 0AT
Member of: NRHP
Quals/training: Stages 1 & 2 NCHP Cert
Personal Therapy: Yes
Supervision: Ongoing
Counselling offered: Hypnotherapy, Psychotherapy, Anxiety, Confidence, Depression, Panic attacks, Relationship, Stop smoking, Weight
Service for: Individuals, Groups, Organisations
Theoretical Approach: Metaphysical, Rogerian, Gestalt, Jungian
Fees: £35 Sessions up to 2 hrs

Merseyside

McNAB Stuart
051 608 1991, evening 0925 601622
Bridge House Clinic, Fairway House, 73 Village Road, Higher Bebington, WIRRAL L63 8PS
Member of: BAC, BPS
Quals/training: BA; BA(Hons)(OU); Dip Social Work; Dip Psychotherapy; Cert Ed; currently undertaking PhD in Couns Studies(Keele Univ)
Personal Therapy: No
Supervision: Ongoing
Counselling offered: General, Psychotherapy, Supervision
Service for: Individuals, Couples, Families, Groups, Organisations
Theoretical Approach: Integrative
Fees: £30 £40 couples, £50 families, orgs negotiable

KENNEDY Des
051 625 9839
Shalom, 36 Hillside Road, West Kirby, WIRRAL L48 8BB
Member of: BAC, GPTI, MPTI
Quals/training: Dip GPTI; MPhil; Training in Gestalt (metanoia)
Personal Therapy: Ongoing
Supervision: Ongoing
Counselling offered: General, Marital, Psychotherapy
Service for: Individuals, Couples, Groups
Specific to: Religious
Theoretical Approach: Gestalt
Fees: £20 - £30 negotiable

OWEN Angela
051 606 0681
2 Redford Close, Greasby, WIRRAL L49 2QQ
Member of: BAC
Quals/training: Dip Couns; currently training in Neuro-Linguistic Programming
Personal Therapy: Yes
Supervision: Ongoing
Counselling offered: General, Relationship, PTSD, Phobias
Service for: Individuals
Theoretical Approach: Rogerian, Gestalt, Art therapy, NLP
Fees: Sliding scale

WALKER Pat
051 342 2300
The Wirral Float Centre, Quietways, The Mount, Heswall, WIRRAL L60 4RE
Member of: BAC
Quals/training: BA(Hons); Dip Couns(Compass); Memb CTA
Personal Therapy: Ongoing
Supervision: Ongoing
Counselling offered: General, Bereavement, Loss
Service for: Individuals
Specific to: People with disabilities
Theoretical Approach: Eclectic, Person-centred
Fees: £15 - £20

JONES Judith
051 648 1728
Irby Farm, Thingwall Road, Irby, WIRRAL L61 3UA
Member of: BAC Acc, BASMT
Quals/training: BAC Acc; BASMT Acc; RELATE Trained
Personal Therapy: Yes
Supervision: Ongoing
Counselling offered: General, Relationship, Sexual
Service for: Individuals, Couples
Theoretical Approach: Psychodynamic, Behavioural, Eclectic
Fees: £20

Middlesex

Organisations

NORTH LONDON COUNSELLING PRACTICE 081 958 8086
4 Princes Close, EDGWARE HA8 7QB

Service:	Counselling for individuals and couples, general, marital and sexual therapy
Area served:	N & NW London, Herts & Middlesex
Referral:	Self
Training of workers:	Trained by NMGC, IGA, Inst Family Therapy, Tavistock Clinic personal therapy, ongoing supervision
Code of Ethics:	BAC
Management by:	Counselling partnership
Fees:	£30 negotiable

FELTHAM OPEN DOOR PROJECT LTD 081 844 0309
De Brome Building, 77 Boundaries Road, FELTHAM TW13 5DT

Service:	Individual, short term counselling. Various drop-in social groups for lonely and isolated
Area served:	Borough of Hounslow & Surrounding areas
Referral:	Self
Training of workers:	Have attended recognised courses, had personal therapy, supervision provided
Code of Ethics:	BAC
Management by:	Voluntary management committee
Fees:	Donations accepted

HARROW & WEMBLEY COUNSELLING FOUNDATION 081 427 4665
The Lodge, 64 Pinner Road, HARROW HA1 4HZ

Service:	General Counselling for individuals. Affiliated to WPF
Area served:	Harrow, Wembley and surrounding areas
Referral:	Self
Training of workers:	3 year training, personal therapy required, supervision provided
Code of Ethics:	BAC
Management by:	Trustees through Executive Committee
Fees:	Contribution according to means

HOUNSLOW YOUTH COUNSELLING SERVICE 081 568 1818
78 St John's Road, ISLEWORTH TW7 6RU

Service:	Drop-in counselling & information service for young people 14-25 years covering range of problems - anxiety, depression, relationships, homelessness
Area served:	Mainly London Borough of Hounslow
Other languages:	Many
Referral:	Self or others
Training of workers:	Counselling skills course followed by residential selection weekend, supervision ongoing, training ongoing
Code of Ethics:	BAC
Management by:	Management Committee
Fees:	None

Middlesex

EALING HOSPITAL NHS TRUST (PASTEUR SUITE)   081 967 5555/3
General Wing, Uxbridge Road, SOUTHALL UB1 3HW
Service:	Individual face to face & telephone counselling for all aspects of HIV/AIDS. Regular courses & tailor-made training in HIV/AIDS familiarisation. Supervision
Other languages:	French, Others arranged
Referral:	Self or others
Training of workers:	SRN - many years experience as counsellor. Supervision
Code of Ethics:	Society of Health Advisers in STD
Management by:	Consultant in Infectious Diseases NHS
Fees:	None

PERSON TO PERSON   081 422 8045
5 Mountside, STANMORE HA7 2DS
Service:	Personal counselling for individuals, couples covering personal, emotional or relationship problems. Training in self awareness and counselling offered. Also supervision
Area served:	NW London, Hertfordshire & Buckinghamshire
Referral:	Self or others, GP
Training of workers:	WPF training, MSc, personal therapy, regular supervision
Code of Ethics:	BAC
Management by:	By the three co-directors
Fees:	£25 negotiable

FELLOWSHIP CHARITABLE FOUNDATION   081 332 7374
Richmond Counselling Service, 13 Rosslyn Road, TWICKENHAM TW1 2AR
Service:	General counselling for individuals or couples including those with mental health problems or learning difficulties
Area served:	South West London
Referral:	Self
Training of workers:	Training and qualification inclusue CQSW, Cert Couns (CSCT), BSc & Dip Psych, Transpersonal Psych, Dip Couns; personal therapy and regular supervision
Code of Ethics:	BAC
Management by:	The Foundation
Fees:	£10 - £20 (concessions for low income)

WATERS & WINTERSTEIN ASSOCIATES   081 891 0987, Fax 081 994 0597
2 Cornwall Road, TWICKENHAM TW1 3LS
Service:	Provide a counselling & consultancy service, including psychological testing, for individuals and organisations
Area served:	Greater London
Referral:	Self, Organisations
Training of workers:	All have relevant professional training
Code of Ethics:	BAC, BPS, BASMT
Management by:	Dr Sue Waters, C Psychol & Mani Winterstein, BA(Hons)
Fees:	£50

Middlesex

COMMUNICARE COUNSELLING SERVICE 0985 256056
Redford Way, UXBRIDGE UB8 1SZ
Service:	Individual and couple counselling for a wide range of problems from depression, stress and anxiety to marital and relationship difficulties & bereavement. Also groupwork
Area served:	Not restricted
Referral:	Self or others
Training of workers:	All have relevant professional training including personal therapy and on-going support and supervision
Code of Ethics:	BAC
Management by:	Committee of governors
Fees:	- £25 no-one refused help

HILLINGDON HOSPITAL, DEPT OF CLINICAL PSYCHOLOGY
0895 279616
Hillingdon Hospital, Pield Heath Road, UXBRIDGE UB8 3NN
Service:	Offers assessment, consultation and psychotherapy (individual, group, family, marital) to people with a wide range of emotional & psychological problems
Area served:	Hillingdon Borough
Referral:	Health Practitioner
Training of workers:	Postgraduate clinical psychology, with further training in particular therapies
Code of Ethics:	BPS
Management by:	District Clinical Psychologist
Fees:	None

Individual Practitioners

*Each individual is a **member of** one or more organisations eligible for entry into this directory. BAC Accredited Counsellors and Recognised Supervisors are shaded.*

WHITESON Riva 081 449 2489
93 Westpole Avenue, Cockfosters, BARNET EN4 0BA
Member of:	BAC
Quals/training:	RELATE/NMGC Trained 1980
Personal Therapy:	Ongoing
Supervision:	Ongoing
Counselling offered:	**General, Bereavement, Relationship, Marital, Sexual**
Service for:	Individuals, Couples
Theoretical Approach:	Client-centred, Psychodynamic, Object relations
Fees:	£25

JONES Heather 081 568 9600
46 The Butts, BRENTFORD TW8 8BL
Member of:	BAC
Quals/training:	BA(Hons) Sociology; AIMSW; Trained psychotherapist - Memb LCIP
Personal Therapy:	Yes
Supervision:	Ongoing
Counselling offered:	**Psychotherapy, Supervision**
Service for:	Individuals, Couples
Theoretical Approach:	Psychodynamic
Fees:	£20 - £35

Middlesex

CERNER Ruth 081 958 9758
65 Green Lane, EDGWARE HA8 7PZ
Member of:	BAC Acc
Quals/training:	BAC Acc; Cert Couns (Middx Poly) '83; Advanced Cert Psychodynamic Couns (WPF) '88; 3 yr training in Psychotherapy (IP)
Personal Therapy:	Yes
Supervision:	Ongoing
Counselling offered:	**General, Bereavement, Short-term, Crisis**
Service for:	Individuals
Theoretical Approach:	Eclectic
Fees:	£20 - £25

HOWARD David 081 952 6841
46 Cheyneys Avenue, Canons Park, EDGWARE HA8 6SS
Member of:	BAC
Quals/training:	Cert Couns in formal & informal settings 1988; Dip Couns & Supervision 1991; LLB(Hons)
Personal Therapy:	Ongoing
Supervision:	Ongoing
Counselling offered:	**General, Relationship, Family, Personal growth**
Service for:	Individuals, Couples, Families
Theoretical Approach:	Rogerian, RET, Cognitive
Fees:	£12 - £20 sliding scale

MICHAUD-LENNOX Suzanne 081 952 2418
20 Heming Road, EDGWARE HA8 9AE
Member of:	IPSS
Quals/training:	Dip Psycho-Anaytic & Humanistic Psychotherapy 1983 IPSS; Dip HE Humanistic & Transpersonal Psychotherapy NE London Poly 1985
Personal Therapy:	Ongoing
Supervision:	Ongoing
Counselling offered:	**General, Eating disorders, Crisis, Stress, Bereavement, Primal therapy, Psychotherapy**
Service for:	Individuals, Groups
Theoretical Approach:	Humanistic, Psychodynamic, Transpersonal
Fees:	£15 - £25 negotiable

SINGER Sidney 081 952 3931
1 Fairfield Avenue, EDGWARE HA8 9AG
Member of:	BPS
Quals/training:	BSc Psychol; Dip in Ed Psych; Chartered Clinical Psych; AFBPsS
Personal Therapy:	Yes
Supervision:	Ongoing
Counselling offered:	**Psychotherapy, Educational**
Service for:	Individuals, Couples
Theoretical Approach:	Psychodynamic, Feuerstein instrumental enrichent
Other languages:	Hebrew
Fees:	£25 per hour

Middlesex

BRUMWELL Pauline   081 363 6792
23 Dimsdale Drive, Bush Hill Park, ENFIELD EN1 1HE
Member of:	**BAC Acc**
Quals/training:	BAC Acc; BA Social analysis; Dip Couns (metanoia) 1989; 3 yr training in Gestalt psychtherapy; foundation yr integrative psychotherapy; f'nd'n yr supervision training (metanoia)
Personal Therapy:	Yes
Supervision:	Ongoing
Counselling offered:	**General, Psychotherapy, Supervision**
Service for:	Individuals, Groups
Theoretical Approach:	Person-centred, Gestalt
Fees:	£15 - £25 sliding scale

TARJAN Claire   081 367 2805
41 Lincoln Road, Bush Hill Park, ENFIELD EN1 1JS
Member of:	**BAC, IPS**
Quals/training:	BA(Hons); Dip Psychotherapy (IP) 1990; Dip Psychosynthesis Couns (IP) 1988; Couns Course WPF 1984-86; trained in assertiveness, equal opportunities/racial awareness
Personal Therapy:	Yes
Supervision:	Ongoing
Counselling offered:	**General, Crisis, Psychotherapy, Supervision**
Service for:	Individuals
Specific to:	Ethnic minorities, Managers
Theoretical Approach:	Eclectic
Fees:	£10 - £25

SALFIELD Angela   0923 854470
ENFIELD EN2
Member of:	**BAC**
Quals/training:	BA Psychol; MA Linguistics; CNAA PG Dip Couns
Personal Therapy:	Yes
Supervision:	Ongoing
Counselling offered:	**General, Bereavement, Crisis, Marital, Peri-natal**
Service for:	Individuals
Specific to:	Women
Theoretical Approach:	Psychodynamic
Fees:	£15 - £20

TAYLOR Lesley   081 367 7723
9 Sterling Road, ENFIELD EN2 0LN
Member of:	**BAC**
Quals/training:	BSc(Hons) Psychol (London) 1977; CQSW/MA Social Work (York) 1983; Dip Couns Skills (SW London College) 1988; Cert Person-centred Art Therapy 1989
Personal Therapy:	Yes
Supervision:	Ongoing
Counselling offered:	**General, Relationship, Personal growth**
Service for:	Individuals, Groups
Specific to:	Women
Theoretical Approach:	Rogerian, Art therapy
Fees:	£20 negotiable

Middlesex

MORGAN Katina ansaphone 081 804 9511
125 Curlew House, 4 Napier Road, ENFIELD EN3 4QP
Member of:	**BAC**
Quals/training:	BA(Hons) Person-centred Couns/Education; Dip Person-centred Couns/Psychotherapy; Memb BAPCA & AHP
Personal Therapy:	Ongoing
Supervision:	Ongoing
Counselling offered:	**General, Bereavement, Disability, Loss, Sexuality, Relationship, Psychotherapy**
Service for:	Individuals, Couples
Specific to:	People with disabilities, Victims of violence
Theoretical Approach:	Client-centred, Humanistic, Rogerian
Fees:	£15 - £30 Sliding Scale

BOSTOCK Elizabeth 081 998 2883
1 Selborne Gardens, Perivale, GREENFORD UB6 7BD
Member of:	**BAC, BAP**
Quals/training:	NGMC 1972; CQSW 1976; ASW 1983; BAP 1989; CMS 1991
Personal Therapy:	Yes
Supervision:	Ongoing
Counselling offered:	**Psychotherapy, Supervision, Consultation, Eating disorders**
Service for:	Individuals, Couples, Families, Groups
Specific to:	Adult survivors of abuse
Theoretical Approach:	Analytical, Eclectic
Fees:	£25 - £35 Sliding scale

HOUGHTON Christine 081 941 6609
HAMPTON TW12
Member of:	**BAC**
Quals/training:	Adv Dip Gestalt Psychotherapy (Pellin)
Personal Therapy:	Yes
Supervision:	Ongoing
Counselling offered:	**General, Crisis, Eating disorders, Psychotherapy**
Service for:	Individuals, Couples, Organisations
Specific to:	Women
Theoretical Approach:	Gestalt
Fees:	£25 (£15 concessions) £40 couples

SIM Wendy 081 979 3834
60 Percy Road, HAMPTON TW12 2JR
Member of:	**BAC**
Quals/training:	BSc; MSc Psychol Couns(Surrey Univ)'86; ASC Acc; NMGC trained
Personal Therapy:	Yes
Supervision:	Ongoing
Counselling offered:	**General**
Service for:	Individuals, Couples
Specific to:	Students, Young people, Women
Theoretical Approach:	Eclectic, Psychodynamic
Fees:	£15 - £25

Middlesex

ROWLEY Jill 081 979 1135
31 Courtlands Avenue, HAMPTON TW12 3NS
Member of: BAC
Quals/training: CRUSE Acc; Counselling Skills & Attitudes '88-89; 2yr course (WPF, Kingston College of FE) '89-91; 3yr p-t training course in Professional Counselling
Personal Therapy: Yes
Supervision: Ongoing
Counselling offered: **General, Bereavement, Loss, Health, Marital, Redundancy**
Service for: Individuals
Theoretical Approach: Eclectic
Fees: £18 sliding scale for hardship

COOPER Cassie 071 911 5000 ex 4030
Counselling & Advisory Service, University of Westminster, Harrow Campus, Northwick Park, HARROW HA1 3TP
Member of: BAC, BPS, CPCP
Quals/training: BSc Applied Social Studies'50; BSc Special Degree in Psychology'69; trained at Birkbeck College & Tavistock Inst; ASC Acc
Personal Therapy: Yes
Supervision: Ongoing
Counselling offered: **General, Sexual, Bereavement, Psychotherapy**
Service for: Individuals, Groups
Theoretical Approach: Eclectic, Adlerian
Other languages: French, German
Fees: No fees to students

SEAMAN Daphne 081 863 2865
29 Manor Way, HARROW HA2 6BZ
Member of: BAC, BASMT, Member of UKCP Register
Quals/training: RELATE trained (couns & sexual therapy); Adv Cert Psychodynamic Couns (WPF) 1990; BASMT Acc
Personal Therapy: Yes
Supervision: Ongoing
Counselling offered: **General, Marital, Sexual**
Service for: Individuals, Couples
Theoretical Approach: Psychodynamic
Fees: £17 - £25

RIMMER Janet ansaphone 081 863 1913
Northlands, 24 Parkfield Gardens, HARROW HA2 6JR
Member of: BAC, PET
Quals/training: BA; Dip Psychosynthesis; 1yr IGA; GAS; 2yrs Group Training with London Diocese; Myers Briggs Type Indicator Registered Practitioner; 2yrs counselling (N London Univ); 3yrs PET
Personal Therapy: Yes
Supervision: Ongoing
Counselling offered: **General, Personal growth**
Service for: Individuals, Couples, Groups, Organisations
Theoretical Approach: Psychosynthesis
Fees: £25 - £35 (£27 assess; grps negotiable)

Middlesex

MILLER Janet   081 868 3121
6 Imperial Court, Imperial Drive, North Harrow, HARROW HA2 7HU
Member of:	BAC Acc
Quals/training:	BAC Acc; BA(Hons); MSc; Dip Adult Couns (London Univ) 1990; Cruse training 1988
Personal Therapy:	Yes
Supervision:	Ongoing
Counselling offered:	**General, Bereavement, Eating disorders, Relationship**
Service for:	Individuals
Theoretical Approach:	Psychodynamic
Fees:	£25 Negotiable

SKONE Carolyn   081 954 4337
Woodlands, 7 West Drive Gardens, Harrow Weald, HARROW HA3 6TT
Member of:	BAC, PET
Quals/training:	Dip Psychosynthesis (PET)
Personal Therapy:	Ongoing
Supervision:	Ongoing
Counselling offered:	**General, Eating disorders, Alcohol, Dependency**
Service for:	Individuals, Groups, Organisations
Theoretical Approach:	Psychosynthesis
Fees:	£20 - £32 sliding scale

COOPER Dawn   081 560 7229
51 Sidmouth Avenue, ISLEWORTH TW7 4DR
Member of:	BAC Acc
Quals/training:	BAC Acc; BA(Hons) Psychol 1980; Cert Dynamic Psychology of Couns (Lincoln Clinic & Institute for Psychotherapy)1985; Cert Couns in Multi-racial Community 1989
Personal Therapy:	Yes
Supervision:	Ongoing
Counselling offered:	**General, Crisis, Relationship, Transition, Sexual abuse**
Service for:	Individuals, Organisations
Theoretical Approach:	Person-centred, Psychoanalytic
Fees:	£20 - £35 negotiable

EDWARDS Dagmar   081 569 8001
5 The Brooklands, Eversley Crescent, ISLEWORTH TW7 4LP
Member of:	BAC, MPTI, GPTI
Quals/training:	Dip Couns (metanoia)
Personal Therapy:	Ongoing
Supervision:	Ongoing
Counselling offered:	**General**
Service for:	Individuals, Couples, Groups
Theoretical Approach:	Person-centred, Gestalt
Fees:	£20 - £25

Middlesex

RIBET Oonagh 081 568 0110
22 Redesdale Gardens, ISLEWORTH TW7 5JB
Member of: IPC
Quals/training: Dip. IPC/WPF
Personal Therapy: Ongoing
Supervision: Ongoing
Counselling offered: General
Service for: Individuals
Theoretical Approach: Jungian, Analytical
Fees: £25

HOBBS Anita 081 568 4967
89 Syon Park Gardens, Osterley, ISLEWORTH TW7 5NF
Member of: BAC, BASMT
Quals/training: RELATE training; CAC Cert Couns Theory; RELATE Sex Therapy training
Personal Therapy: Ongoing
Supervision: Ongoing
Counselling offered: General, Relationship, Marital, Sexual
Service for: Individuals, Couples
Theoretical Approach: Psychodynamic, Eclectic
Fees: £30

LEWIS Penny 081 891 4867
10 Haweswater House, Summerwood Road, ISLEWORTH TW7 7QL
Member of: BAC, CPPE, AFT, Member of UKCP Register
Quals/training: Dip Systemic Therapy (KCC); Dip Systemic Teaching Training & Supervision (Award pending)
Personal Therapy: Yes
Supervision: Ongoing
Counselling offered: General, Bereavement, Stress, Panic attacks, HIV, AIDS, Terminal illness, Chronic illness, Supervision
Service for: Individuals, Couples, Families
Specific to: Caring professions, People with disabilities
Theoretical Approach: Systemic
Fees: £20 - £25 negotiable

CASSIDY Janis
16 Beech Court, Lilliput Avenue, NORTHOLT UB5
Member of: NRHP, NCHP
Quals/training: Assoc member of NRHP, NCPHR
Personal Therapy: Ongoing
Supervision: Ongoing
Counselling offered: General, Hypnotherapy, Relationship, Eating disorders
Service for: Individuals, Couples
Theoretical Approach: Behavioural, Cognitive/Behavioural, NLP, RET
Fees: £20 - £30 sliding scale

Middlesex

FITZGERALD-BUTLER Albina   081 841 4092
Ivy Cottage, Ealing Road, NORTHOLT UB5 6AA
Member of:	NRHP
Quals/training:	Dip Psychotherapy/Hypnotherapy; training in stress management, NLP & general psychotherapy; Memb ICM
Personal Therapy:	Yes
Supervision:	Ongoing
Counselling offered:	**General, Crisis, Psychotherapy, Hypnotherapy**
Service for:	Individuals
Theoretical Approach:	Adlerian, Psychosynthesis, Analytical
Other languages:	Polish
Fees:	£30

GREEN June   0923 824858
Redholme, 15 Ducks Hill Road, NORTHWOOD HA6 2NW
Member of:	BAC, IPSS
Quals/training:	CQSW; IPSS. ITEC
Personal Therapy:	Ongoing
Supervision:	Ongoing
Counselling offered:	**General, Psychotherapy**
Service for:	Individuals, Couples, Groups
Theoretical Approach:	Humanistic
Fees:	£25 - £30

DUFFELS Catharina   0923 826058
30 Thirlmere Gardens, NORTHWOOD HA6 2RS
Member of:	BAC
Quals/training:	Dip Couns (CAC); Cert AIDS Couns; IGA one year course; RN
Personal Therapy:	Ongoing
Supervision:	Ongoing
Counselling offered:	**General, AIDS, Bereavement, Crisis**
Service for:	Individuals, Couples
Theoretical Approach:	Psychodynamic, Rogerian
Other languages:	Dutch, German
Fees:	£25 negotiable

SHAW Marion   0923 820306
Oriel Lodge, 26 Linksway, NORTHWOOD HA6 2XB
Member of:	BAC
Quals/training:	Cert (Counselling Training Programme); Psychology Dip (Rusland College); VSS
Personal Therapy:	No
Supervision:	Ongoing
Counselling offered:	**Crisis, Relationship, Anxiety, Depression, PTSD, Abuse**
Service for:	Individuals
Theoretical Approach:	Eclectic
Fees:	£15 - £20 negotiable

Middlesex

DEERING Christine   0923 823790
6a Murray Road, NORTHWOOD HA6 2YJ
Member of:	**BAC, LCP**
Quals/training:	BSc; Master of Clinical Social Work; Psychoanalytical Psychotherapist (LCP); Dip Hypnosis (BHR); LICSW (USA)
Personal Therapy:	Yes
Supervision:	Ongoing
Counselling offered:	**General, Bereavement, Psychotherapy, Assertiveness, Personal growth, Stress management, Employment, Consultation, Sexual abuse, Depression**
Service for:	Individuals, Couples, Families, Groups, Organisations
Specific to:	Young adults
Theoretical Approach:	Psychodynamic, Systemic, Family therapy, Eclectic
Fees:	Sliding scale

SHAW Maureen   081 866 5444
17 Malpas Drive, PINNER HA5 1DG
Member of:	**BAC**
Quals/training:	Dip Couns (Hertford Univ); Cert Psychodynamic Couns (London Univ); Bereavement training
Personal Therapy:	Yes
Supervision:	Ongoing
Counselling offered:	**General, Bereavement**
Service for:	Individuals
Theoretical Approach:	Psychodynamic, Client-centred
Fees:	Negotiable

COOPER Suzanne   081 866 1521
5 Lawrence Road, PINNER HA5 1LH
Member of:	**CCHP**
Quals/training:	CQSW 1974; ITEC 1989; training in Holistic Psychotherapy & Biodynamic Massage (Chiron) 1990
Personal Therapy:	Ongoing
Supervision:	Ongoing
Counselling offered:	**General, Psychotherapy, Massage**
Service for:	Individuals
Specific to:	Women, Creative people, Carers
Theoretical Approach:	Gestalt, Neo-Reichian, Integrative, Holistic
Fees:	£25 negotiable

BROWN Eileen   081 868 7684
17 St Ursula Grove, PINNER HA5 1LN
Member of:	**BAC**
Quals/training:	CQSW; Cert Couns (WPF); CRUSE trained counsellor; training in Psycho-analytic Psychotherapy (CPP)
Personal Therapy:	Ongoing
Supervision:	Ongoing
Counselling offered:	**Bereavement, Loss, Stress, Depression**
Service for:	Individuals
Specific to:	Young adults
Theoretical Approach:	Psychoanalytic
Fees:	£10 - £20

Middlesex

CHANDLER Stanley　　　　　　　　　　　　　　　　　　081 86 1372
Shandon, Poplar Close, PINNER HA5 3PZ
Member of:	NRHP
Quals/training:	Qualified in Hypnotherapy NCHP, Memb Brit Register Complementary Practitioners (Hypnotherapy)
Personal Therapy:	Yes
Supervision:	Ongoing
Counselling offered:	**General, Cancer, Phobias**
Service for:	Individuals
Theoretical Approach:	Eclectic
Fees:	£30 sliding scale

GOULD Jean　　　　　　　　　　　　　　　　　　　　081 868 2700
Cervantes, Pinner Hill, PINNER HA5 3XU
Member of:	BAC Acc
Quals/training:	BAC Acc; Counselling for 14 yrs; RELATE trained; substantial training in counselling and therapy skills
Personal Therapy:	Yes
Supervision:	Ongoing
Counselling offered:	**General, Marital, Psychotherapy**
Service for:	Individuals, Couples
Theoretical Approach:	Eclectic
Fees:	£12 - £25 dependent on income

FELLOWS Ruth　　　　　　　　　　　　　　　　　　　081 429 0607
10 Central Avenue, PINNER HA5 5BS
Member of:	BAC
Quals/training:	BSc (Hons) Psychol '89; MSc Couns Psychol '91
Personal Therapy:	Ongoing
Supervision:	Ongoing
Counselling offered:	**General, Bereavement, Relationship**
Service for:	Individuals
Theoretical Approach:	Eclectic
Fees:	£25 sliding scale

SUSSMAN Susan　　　　　　　　　　　　　　　　　　0895 622202
3 Hope Cottages, Breakspear Road, RUISLIP HA4 7SE
Member of:	BAC
Quals/training:	Dip Soc(London Univ); Cert Group Couns(WPF)'75; Family & Marital Course(IGA)'77; CQSW '80; ongoing training Psychotherapy(CCPE)
Personal Therapy:	Yes
Supervision:	Ongoing
Counselling offered:	**General, Relationship, Mental health, Psychotherapy**
Service for:	Individuals, Couples, Families
Theoretical Approach:	Psychodynamic, Humanistic
Fees:	£10 - £25 sliding scale

Middlesex

WADDELL Susie 0932 224512
23 Crescent Road, SHEPPERTON TW17 8BL
Member of:	BAC
Quals/training:	DipCouns (Kingston Coll FE); CRUSE Counsellor
Personal Therapy:	Yes
Supervision:	Ongoing
Counselling offered:	General, Bereavement, Crisis, Relationship
Service for:	Individuals
Theoretical Approach:	Psychodynamic
Fees:	£15 negotiable

HAMMOND Margaret 0932 222712
Fulford Sandhills Meadow, SHEPPERTON TW17 9HY
Member of:	BAC Acc RSup, BASMT
Quals/training:	BAC Acc RSup; BA; Dip Sociology (London); RELATE Trained
Personal Therapy:	Ongoing
Supervision:	Ongoing
Counselling offered:	General, Relationship, Sexual
Service for:	Individuals, Couples
Theoretical Approach:	Psychodynamic, Behavioural
Other languages:	French
Fees:	£25 daytime, £30 evenings

MATTAR Greta 0784 464567
14 Chestnut Manor Close, STAINES TW18 1AQ
Member of:	NRHP
Quals/training:	Dip Hypnotherapy & Psychotherapy, RGN, RHV
Personal Therapy:	Ongoing
Supervision:	Ongoing
Counselling offered:	General, Bereavement, Crisis, Hypnotherapy, Psychotherapy
Service for:	Individuals
Theoretical Approach:	Rogerian, Integrative
Fees:	£25

CURTIS JENKINS Graham 0784 455518
38 Richmond Road, STAINES TW18 2AB
Member of:	BAC, PET
Quals/training:	MA; MB; DRCOG; FRCGP; Non Dip Graduate PET 1987
Personal Therapy:	Yes
Supervision:	Ongoing
Counselling offered:	Psychotherapy
Service for:	Individuals, Couples, Groups, Families
Theoretical Approach:	Psychosynthesis
Fees:	Sliding scale

Middlesex

ELDER Mary   0784 456040
106 Penton Road, STAINES TW18 2LJ
Member of:	BAC
Quals/training:	1949 RGN; '51 IRN (Canada); '83 Dip Couns Skills (SW London College); '83 Supervisors Course; '86 Pastoral Counselling Course (WPF)
Personal Therapy:	Yes
Supervision:	Ongoing
Counselling offered:	**General**
Service for:	Individuals, Couples, Families, Groups, Children
Theoretical Approach:	Person-centred
Fees:	£15 negotiable

GARROD Nigel   0784 458270
STAINES TW18
Member of:	BAC
Quals/training:	TA 101 1988; Dip Person-centred Couns (metanoia) 1992; currently studying for Psychol degree (OU); couples workshop
Personal Therapy:	Ongoing
Supervision:	Ongoing
Counselling offered:	**General**
Service for:	Individuals
Theoretical Approach:	Rogerian
Fees:	£18

FRANKHAM Hans   081 427 7369
5 Mountside, STANMORE HA7 2DS
Member of:	BAC
Quals/training:	CQSW; MSc Counselling Psychol
Personal Therapy:	Yes
Supervision:	Ongoing
Counselling offered:	**General, Relationship, Bereavement, Psychotherapy, Consultation, Supervision**
Service for:	Individuals, Couples, Families
Theoretical Approach:	Psychodynamic, Eclectic
Fees:	£30 negotiable in hardship cases

SPIERS Carole   081 954 1593
Gordon House, 83-85 Gordon Avenue, STANMORE HA7 3QR
Member of:	BAC
Quals/training:	RELATE trained; training in stress management, post trauma stress, psychological debriefing; Memb Inst Health & Educ
Personal Therapy:	–
Supervision:	Ongoing
Counselling offered:	**Crisis, PTSD, Divorce, Bereavement, Stress management, Redundancy, Harassment, Occupational**
Service for:	Individuals, Couples, Groups
Theoretical Approach:	Client-centred
Fees:	On application

Middlesex

SILKE Phillipa **081 954 2665**
22 Temple Mead Close, Gordon Avenue, STANMORE HA7 3RG
Member of: BAC
Quals/training: B Soc Sci(S Africa); Dip Social Work; CQSW (LSE); Dip in Human Sexuality 1990-92 (St George's Medical School)
Personal Therapy: Yes
Supervision: Ongoing
Counselling offered: General, Bereavement, Marital, Sexual, Depression, Psychotherapy
Service for: Individuals, Couples, Families
Theoretical Approach: Psychodynamic
Fees: £25 negotiable

WATERS Sue **0932 781183**
The Old Vicarage, Church Street, SUNBURY-ON-THAMES TW16 6RQ
Member of: BAC, BPS, BASMT
Quals/training: BSc Econ; MA Psychol; PhD Psychol; Dip Couns (London Univ); RELATE Trained marital counsellor & sex therapist; CPsychol
Personal Therapy: Ongoing
Supervision: Ongoing
Counselling offered: General, Relationship, Sexual, Psychotherapy, Hypnotherapy
Service for: Individuals, Couples
Theoretical Approach: Psychodynamic, Jungian
Fees: £35 basic

COLE Laurence **081 614 8027**
35A The Grove, TEDDINGTON TW11 8AT
Member of: BAC
Quals/training: BA(Hons); Cert Ed; Dip Couns Skills(Southwark College); in training as a group psychotherapist
Personal Therapy: Ongoing
Supervision: Ongoing
Counselling offered: General, Bereavement, Social skills, Midlife, Psychotherapy, Relationship, Sexuality
Service for: Individuals, Couples, Families, Groups, Organisations
Specific to: Elderly
Theoretical Approach: Analytical, Existential
Fees: £15 - £35 sliding scale

POWELL Glyn **081 943 9215**
67 Waldegrave Road, TEDDINGTON TW11 8LA
Member of: ANLP (PCS), Member of UKCP Register
Quals/training: BA(Hons) Phil (London) 1979; PGCE Moral Educ 1981; Adv Dip NLP 1988; over 2 yrs experience in Freudian based therapy; Special Dalcroze Teachers' Cert 1992
Personal Therapy: Ongoing
Supervision: Ongoing
Counselling offered: General, Psychotherapy, Relationship, Psychosomatic, Personal growth
Service for: Individuals
Theoretical Approach: Constructivist
Fees: £40 negotiable

Middlesex

KEENES Susan   081 977 6545
66 Langham Road, TEDDINGTON TW11 9HJ
Member of: **BAC, AFT**
Quals/training: BSc Sociology; BASW; Cert Applied Social Studies 1960; Post graduate cert in Education 1971; trained in Family/Marital therapy (IFT) '84; Cert Couns (LCIP) '87
Personal Therapy: Yes
Supervision: Ongoing
Counselling offered: **General, Marital, Psychotherapy**
Service for: Individuals, Couples, Families
Theoretical Approach: Psychodynamic, Behavioural
Fees: £18 - £25

HILL Lorna   081 977 2401
18 Melbourne Road, TEDDINGTON TW11 9QX
Member of: **BAC, IPC**
Quals/training: BSc: Dip Ed; CQSW; Dip Advanced Psychodynamic Couns (IPC)
Personal Therapy: Ongoing
Supervision: Ongoing
Counselling offered: **General, Bereavement, Crisis, Long-term**
Service for: Individuals
Specific to: Adolescents
Theoretical Approach: Psychodynamic
Fees: £25

WATERS Sue   081 891 0987
2 Cornwall Road, TWICKENHAM TW1 3LS
Member of: **BAC, BPS, BASMT**
Quals/training: BSc Econ; MA Psychol; PhD Psychol; Dip Couns (London Univ); RELATE trained marital counsellor & sex therapist; C Psychol
Personal Therapy: Ongoing
Supervision: Ongoing
Counselling offered: **General, Relationship, Sexual, Psychotherapy, Hypnotherapy**
Service for: Individuals, Couples
Theoretical Approach: Psychodynamic, Jungian
Fees: £35 basic

DAVIS Josephine   081 892 0633
Cole Cottage, Cole Park Road, TWICKENHAM TW1 1HP
Member of: **BAC Acc**
Quals/training: BAC Acc; Cert Ed; Dip Ed(Special Needs); Dip Information & Advice Studies; Counselling & Psychotherapy training over 10 years; Counselling Supervision Training
Personal Therapy: Yes
Supervision: Ongoing
Counselling offered: **General, Crisis, Loss, Marital, Psychotherapy, Supervision**
Service for: Individuals, Couples, Families, Groups
Theoretical Approach: Humanistic, Psychodynamic
Fees: £15 - £27

Middlesex

BRISTOW Margot Hogan 081 892 0838
261 St Margarets Road, TWICKENHAM TW1 1NJ
Member of:	BAC
Quals/training:	Dip Couns; Dip Art Therapy; RhAT; SRN; SCM; RMN
Personal Therapy:	Ongoing
Supervision:	Ongoing
Counselling offered:	General, Depression, Divorce, Substance abuse, Bereavement, Trauma, Abortion, Child abuse
Service for:	Individuals, Groups
Theoretical Approach:	Client-centred, Jungian, Art therapy
Fees:	£25 negotiable

DAY Lesley ansaphone 081 892 2076
3 Newry Road, St Margaret's, TWICKENHAM TW1 1PJ
Member of:	MPTI
Quals/training:	BA Hons, Sociology; MSc Econ; Dip in Psychological Counselling (Roehampton Institute); Trainee Integrative Psychotherapist (metatonia)
Personal Therapy:	Yes
Supervision:	Ongoing
Counselling offered:	General, Depression, Eating disorders, Incest, Relationship, Psychotherapy
Service for:	Individuals, Couples
Specific to:	Women
Theoretical Approach:	Psychodynamic, Integrative
Fees:	£18 - £25

LUCAS Tina 081 892 6584
24 Montpelier Row, TWICKENHAM TW1 2NQ
Member of:	IGA, AFT
Quals/training:	Trained in Psychotherapy (IGA); Memb of GAS
Personal Therapy:	Yes
Supervision:	Ongoing
Counselling offered:	General, Psychotherapy, Supervision
Service for:	Individuals, Couples, Groups, Families
Specific to:	Young people
Theoretical Approach:	Psychodynamic
Fees:	£20 - £70 according to type of therapy

WALLBANK Susan 081 892 9607
20 Haggard Road, TWICKENHAM TW1 3AF
Member of:	BAC
Quals/training:	Dip Sociol; In-house training(London Univ Student Health Services); Nat Dip Art & Design; Art Therapy
Personal Therapy:	Yes
Supervision:	Ongoing
Counselling offered:	General, Assessment, Crisis, Bereavement, Loss
Service for:	Individuals, Couples, Groups
Specific to:	Young people
Theoretical Approach:	Eclectic
Fees:	£5 - £25 sliding scale

Middlesex

BLAKE Raymond   Ansaphone 081 892 9494
31 Upper Grotto Road, TWICKENHAM TW1 4NG
Member of:	BAC, IGA
Quals/training:	Trained with IGA
Personal Therapy:	Yes
Supervision:	Ongoing
Counselling offered:	General, Separation, Crisis, Psychotherapy
Service for:	Individuals, Couples, Groups, Organisations
Theoretical Approach:	Psychoanalytic
Fees:	£20 - £30

AGAR James   081 891 0743
Tean, 19 Swan Island, Strawberry Vale, TWICKENHAM TW1 4RU
Member of:	BAC
Quals/training:	BA; Dip Alcohol Couns & Consultation; psychotherapist in training (metanoia)
Personal Therapy:	Yes
Supervision:	Ongoing
Counselling offered:	General
Service for:	Individuals
Theoretical Approach:	Client-centred
Fees:	£22 Negotiable

WARD Shona   081 891 0743
'Tean', 19 Swan Island, Strawberry Vale, TWICKENHAM TW1 4RU
Member of:	BAC, ITA, MPTI
Quals/training:	BSc Psychol (London); Dip Couns Skills (SW London College) Psychotherapist in training (metanoia)
Personal Therapy:	Ongoing
Supervision:	Ongoing
Counselling offered:	General
Service for:	Individuals
Theoretical Approach:	Integrative
Fees:	£25

WESTON Sarah   081 755 0133
19 Belmont Road, TWICKENHAM TW2 5DA
Member of:	BAP
Quals/training:	BAP Assoc '90 (Jungian); BA '65; Dip Careers Education & Guidance (Hatfield Poly) '83; Cert Adlerian Couns '84
Personal Therapy:	Yes
Supervision:	Ongoing
Counselling offered:	Psychotherapy
Service for:	Individuals
Theoretical Approach:	Jungian
Fees:	£25 - £30

Middlesex

DEAN Paul 081 898 2522
74 Lincoln Avenue, TWICKENHAM TW2 6NP
Member of:	**BAC, AHPP, MPTI**
Quals/training:	Dip Art Therapy; Dip Group Psychotherapy; Dip Systemic Integrative Psychotherapy
Personal Therapy:	Yes
Supervision:	Ongoing
Counselling offered:	**General, Psychotherapy, Art therapy, Supervision**
Service for:	Individuals, Couples, Groups
Theoretical Approach:	Integrative
Fees:	Ind £30+VAT; Grp £17+VAT 2.5Hr

DEAN Sally 081 898 2522
74 Lincoln Avenue, TWICKENHAM TW2 6NP
Member of:	**BAC, IPC**
Quals/training:	1978 in-service training (RF); '79 General Course (IGA); 1982 WPF membership training
Personal Therapy:	Ongoing
Supervision:	Ongoing
Counselling offered:	**General, Bereavement, Psychotherapy, Supervision**
Service for:	Individuals
Theoretical Approach:	Analytical
Fees:	£33

BRUNT Clare 081 755 0353
97 Warren Road, Whitton, TWICKENHAM TW2 7DJ
Member of:	**AHPP**
Quals/training:	MSc; Dip ED; Cert Biodynamic Psychotherapy 1984
Personal Therapy:	Ongoing
Supervision:	Ongoing
Counselling offered:	**Psychotherapy, Massage**
Service for:	Individuals, Couples, Groups
Theoretical Approach:	Integrative
Fees:	£28 negotiable

REES-ROBERTS Diane 081 977 7282
12 Cambridge Crescent, TEDDINGTON TW11 8DY
Member of:	**BAC, IPC, BPS**
Quals/training:	BA Hons Psychol; Dip Advanced Psychodynamic Couns
Personal Therapy:	Yes
Supervision:	Ongoing
Counselling offered:	**General**
Service for:	Individuals
Theoretical Approach:	Psychodynamic
Fees:	£25 negotiable

Middlesex

NEWSON Mary 0895 256056
Communicare Couns Service, Christchurch, Redford Way, UXBRIDGE UB8 1SZ
Member of:	**BAC Acc**
Quals/training:	BAC(Acc); Dip Couns; Psychosynthesis Psychotherapy(IP)'92; Dip Psychotherapy'93
Personal Therapy:	Yes
Supervision:	Ongoing
Counselling offered:	**General, Psychotherapy**
Service for:	Individuals
Theoretical Approach:	Psychosynthesis
Fees:	£30

HAMPTON Wendy 0895 633021
24 Austins Lane, Ickenham, UXBRIDGE UB10 8RH
Member of:	**BAC**
Quals/training:	RELATE Trained
Personal Therapy:	No
Supervision:	Ongoing
Counselling offered:	**General, Bereavement, Crisis, Marital**
Service for:	Individuals, Couples
Theoretical Approach:	Rogerian, Behavioural
Fees:	£25

BURKE Dorothy 081 904 3073
86 Blockley Road, WEMBLEY HA0 3LW
Member of:	**BAC, BPS**
Quals/training:	BA (Hons) Psychol; Dip Couns; Training in Transactional Analysis - metanoia (1989)
Personal Therapy:	Ongoing
Supervision:	Ongoing
Counselling offered:	**General, Addiction, Bereavement, Eating disorders**
Service for:	Individuals, Groups
Specific to:	Managers
Theoretical Approach:	Client-centred
Fees:	£25 Individuals; £17 Group

WINDISCH Thelma 081 904 1076
137 Preston Road, WEMBLEY HA9 8NW
Member of:	**BAC**
Quals/training:	Dip Couns (CAC); Seminars & Group (WPF)'85-'87; bereavement course; now in psychotherapy training (CSCT)
Personal Therapy:	Ongoing
Supervision:	Ongoing
Counselling offered:	**General, Bereavement, Addiction, Occupational, Stress, Depression, Anxiety**
Service for:	Individuals
Specific to:	Ethnic minorities
Theoretical Approach:	Person-centred, Psychodynamic
Fees:	£18 - £25

Norfolk

Organisations

ST BARNABAS COUNSELLING CENTRE 0603 625222
Derby Street, NORWICH NR2 4PU
Service:	Counselling service
Area served:	Norfolk & Suffolk
Referral:	Self
Training of workers:	Internal 7 week self awareness/sensitivity training & various external courses; regular supervision
Code of Ethics:	BAC
Management by:	Board of Trustee Directors
Fees:	Donations encouraged

Individual Practitioners

*Each individual is a **member of** one or more organisations eligible for entry into this directory. BAC Accredited Counsellors and Recognised Supervisors are shaded.*

McCLINTOCK Jane 0379 783209
Rectory Farm, Thrandeston, DISS IP21 4BN
Member of:	**BAC Acc**
Quals/training:	BAC Acc; BSc(Hons), RELATE Trained; Cert Supervision (WPF); BAP (External)
Personal Therapy:	Yes
Supervision:	Ongoing
Counselling offered:	**General, Long-term, Psychotherapy, Childhood trauma, Crisis, Depression**
Service for:	Individuals, Couples
Theoretical Approach:	Psychodynamic, Eclectic
Fees:	£25

PAYNE Martin 0379 853809
145 High Road, Needham, HARLESTON IP20 9LG
Member of:	**BAC**
Quals/training:	Dip Couns; BA(Hons) English; Cert Ed
Personal Therapy:	Yes
Supervision:	Ongoing
Counselling offered:	**General, Grief, Relationship, Marital**
Service for:	Individuals, Couples
Other languages:	French
Fees:	£12 - £20 sliding scale

LING Felicity 0553 769437
8 Nelson Street, KING'S LYNN PE30 5DY
Member of:	**BAC Acc**
Quals/training:	BAC Acc; BEd Movement, Teaching; MA Educ, therapy (Goldsmiths'); MA Psychol of Couns & Therapy (Antioch)
Personal Therapy:	Yes
Supervision:	Ongoing
Counselling offered:	**General, Psychotherapy, Movement therapy**
Service for:	Individuals, Groups, Families
Specific to:	Prisons, Military
Theoretical Approach:	Person-centred, Psychodynamic
Fees:	£12 - £25 sliding scale

Norfolk

SALTER E Alan   0553 769437
8 Nelson Street, KING'S LYNN PE30 5DY

Member of:	**BPS**
Quals/training:	BSc; MSc Ergonomics; PhD Aesthetics; PGTC Teaching; Adv Cert Psychol; Dip THP (Therapy); training in Movement (GLG Laban), Drama (ADB) & Speech (ALAM)
Personal Therapy:	Yes
Supervision:	Ongoing
Counselling offered:	**General, Psychotherapy, Hypnotherapy, Work, Educational, Creative therapies**
Service for:	Individuals, Groups
Theoretical Approach:	Person-centred, Cognitive, Behavioural
Fees:	£12 - £25 sliding scale

KERKHAM Pat   0553 773854
Banklands, Clenchwarton, KING'S LYNN PE34 4DB

Member of:	**BAC, IPSS**
Quals/training:	Dip Couns; CQSW; Psychotherapy training (IPSS); Forensic Psychotherapy (Portman Clinic); GAPPSW, IAFP
Personal Therapy:	Yes
Supervision:	Ongoing
Counselling offered:	**General, Relationship, Depression, Psychotherapy**
Service for:	Individuals, Couples
Theoretical Approach:	Analytic
Fees:	Negotiable

PARROTT Heather   0263 860543
Huntsmans Cottage, The Street, Swanton Novers, MELTON CONSTABLE NR24 2QZ

Member of:	**BAC**
Quals/training:	Herts & Beds Pastoral Foundation 3 yr course (WPF) 1985; Relationship Couns (TIMS) 1988; Psychotherapy Training (CCPE)
Personal Therapy:	Ongoing
Supervision:	Ongoing
Counselling offered:	**General**
Service for:	Individuals, Couples
Theoretical Approach:	Eclectic
Fees:	£15 negotiable

MONSON Janet   0603 621001
1 Cathedral House, Cathedral Street, NORWICH NR1 1LU

Member of:	**BAC**
Quals/training:	Cert Hypnosis & Couns
Personal Therapy:	Yes
Supervision:	Ongoing
Counselling offered:	**Anxiety, Phobias, Personal growth, Unwanted habits**
Service for:	Individuals
Theoretical Approach:	Rogerian, Ericksonian
Fees:	£20 - £30 Sliding Scale

Norfolk

ASHBY Jean   0603 764736
3 Southgate Lane, NORWICH NR1 2DB
Member of:	BAC
Quals/training:	One year course WPF 1984-5; FDI Cert Person-centered Approach to Couns and Psychotherapy 1985-88
Personal Therapy:	Ongoing
Supervision:	Ongoing
Counselling offered:	General, Personal growth
Service for:	Individuals
Theoretical Approach:	Person-centred
Fees:	£20

POCKLINGTON Michael   0603 623039
93 Netherwood Green, NORWICH NR1 2JG
Member of:	BAC
Quals/training:	Dip Couns (Person Centred Therapy GB); CSCT/AEB Registered Trainer
Personal Therapy:	Yes
Supervision:	Ongoing
Counselling offered:	General, Alcohol, Marital, Bereavement
Service for:	Individuals, Couples
Theoretical Approach:	Rogerian
Fees:	£15 - £25 Sliding Scale

VARNEY Peter   0603 34855
8 High Green, Thorpe Hamlet, NORWICH NR1 4AP
Member of:	BAC
Quals/training:	Cert Couns(LCIP)'80; Cert Psychol Testing '81; MA (Durham)
Personal Therapy:	Ongoing
Supervision:	Ongoing
Counselling offered:	General, Bereavement, Career, Anxiety, Depression
Service for:	Individuals, Couples
Theoretical Approach:	Person-centred
Fees:	£20 - £25 negotiable

HARRISON Jenny   0603 56508
Pottergate Centre, for Psychotherapy, 11 Pottergate, NORWICH NR2 1DS
Member of:	BAC Acc
Quals/training:	BAC(Acc); Dip Soc Sci(London Univ)'65; Cert Appl Soc Studies (Assoc Inst Medical SW); Introd course in Psychoanalytic Psychotherapy(Tavistock)'89-'91
Personal Therapy:	Yes
Supervision:	Ongoing
Counselling offered:	General, Psychotherapy
Service for:	Individuals
Theoretical Approach:	Psychodynamic
Fees:	£18 - £25 sliding scale

Norfolk

PLATT John 0603 632604
95 Cambridge Street, NORWICH NR2 2BD
Member of: BAC, MPTI
Quals/training: MA; Cert Ed; Dip Couns (metanoia); training in Gestalt Psychotherapy
Personal Therapy: Ongoing
Supervision: Ongoing
Counselling offered: General
Service for: Individuals, Couples
Theoretical Approach: Person-centred, Gestalt
Fees: £20 negotiable

CLARK Jean 0603 617828
109 Rupert Street, NORWICH NR2 2AU
Member of: BAC Acc
Quals/training: BAC(Acc); Dip Psychol & Sociology of Education (Univ of Leicester)'71; Group Psychotherapy Course(IGA)'76; Dip in Psychosynthesis & Communication Skills For Profs (CCF) '93
Personal Therapy: Yes
Supervision: Ongoing
Counselling offered: General, Psychotherapy, Supervision
Service for: Individuals
Theoretical Approach: Psychosynthesis, Jungian, Person-centred
Fees: £26 negotiable

COMBER Philippa 0603 612919
28 Ampthill Street, NORWICH NR2 2RG
Member of: BAC, BPS
Quals/training: BA; Dipl-Psych Berlin '73
Personal Therapy: Yes
Supervision: Ongoing
Counselling offered: General, Psychotherapy
Service for: Individuals, Couples
Theoretical Approach: Psychodynamic, Cognitive/Behavioural
Other languages: German, French
Fees: £25 negotiable

THOMAS Clive 0603 626614
The Retreat House, 20 Unthank Road, NORWICH NR2 2RA
Member of: BAC Acc
Quals/training: BAC(Acc); BSc; Dip Ed; AHP; Acc Shiatsu Practitioner; Acc Craniosacral Therapist
Personal Therapy: Ongoing
Supervision: Ongoing
Counselling offered: General, Bodywork, Psychotherapy
Service for: Individuals, Couples, Groups
Other languages: Spanish, French
Fees: £14 - £28 sliding scale

Norfolk

CONRADI Prue ansaphone 0603 405302, ansaphone 0603 617709
7 Earlham Road, NORWICH NR2 3RA
Member of:	BAC Acc
Quals/training:	BAC Acc; Dip Couns (Aston Univ)
Personal Therapy:	Yes
Supervision:	Ongoing
Counselling offered:	General, Psychotherapy, Dream
Service for:	Individuals, Groups, Organisations
Theoretical Approach:	Person-centred, Jungian
Fees:	£25 negotiable

MANSFIELD Jacqui 0603 616221
Sackville Place, 44-48 Magdalen Street, NORWICH NR3 1JE
Member of:	BAC
Quals/training:	Dip Professional Studies in Couns (Colchester Inst)
Personal Therapy:	Yes
Supervision:	Ongoing
Counselling offered:	General, Personal growth, Graphological
Service for:	Individuals, Couples, Families, Groups, Organisations
Theoretical Approach:	Humanistic
Fees:	£18 minimum

HOPKINS Eric 0603 52541
6 Claremont Road, NORWICH NR4 6SH
Member of:	BPS
Quals/training:	BA Psychol; Post Grad Child Psychol; training in TA, Gestalt; AFBPsS; Member of ITA, EATA
Personal Therapy:	Yes
Supervision:	Ongoing
Counselling offered:	General, Addiction, Bereavement, Crisis, Relationship, Psychotherapy
Service for:	Individuals, Couples, Groups
Theoretical Approach:	TA, Gestalt, Behavioural
Fees:	£20 - £30 sliding scale

RAYMENT Jenny 0603 425 615
1 Parkside Drive, Old Catton, NORWICH NR6 7DP
Member of:	BAC
Quals/training:	Gestalt (Cambridge Gestalt Awareness Training & Experience); Gestalt Assoc UK
Personal Therapy:	Yes
Supervision:	Ongoing
Counselling offered:	General, Psychotherapy
Service for:	Individuals, Couples, Groups, Organisations
Theoretical Approach:	Gestalt
Fees:	£20

Norfolk

RICHARDSON Susan   0603 861 019
25 Cypress Close, Taverham, NORWICH NR8 6AG
Member of:	NRHP
Quals/training:	Dip HP (NCHP); MNAHP
Personal Therapy:	Ongoing
Supervision:	Ongoing
Counselling offered:	General, Hypnotherapy, Psychotherapy
Service for:	Individuals, Groups, Organisations
Theoretical Approach:	Eclectic
Fees:	£15 - £25

BROADBENT Faith   0236 77 661
19 The Street, Matlaske, NORWICH NR11 7AQ
Member of:	BAC Acc
Quals/training:	BAC Acc; Dip Occ Therapy; CQSW; Dip Psychosynthesis & Communication Skills & Attitudes for Professionals
Personal Therapy:	Yes
Supervision:	Ongoing
Counselling offered:	General
Service for:	Individuals, Couples, Groups
Theoretical Approach:	Person-centred
Fees:	£25 negotiable

PURTON Campbell   0603 616872
Ber Street Centre, 103 Ber Street, NORWICH NR1 3EY
Member of:	BAC Acc
Quals/training:	BAC Acc; BSc; MPhil; PhD; Dip Couns/Person-centred Therapy
Personal Therapy:	Yes
Supervision:	Ongoing
Counselling offered:	General, Psychotherapy
Service for:	Individuals, Couples
Theoretical Approach:	Jungian, Rogerian
Fees:	£25 negotiable

KENNEDY Caroline   ansaphone 095 387 333
Pottergate Centre, for Psychotherapy, 11 Pottergate, NORWICH
Member of:	BAC Acc
Quals/training:	BAC Acc; BA; Dip Couns (London Univ) 1980; IGA General Course; RELATE
Personal Therapy:	Yes
Supervision:	Ongoing
Counselling offered:	General, Psychotherapy, Supervision
Service for:	Individuals, Couples
Specific to:	Young adults
Theoretical Approach:	Psychodynamic
Fees:	£18 - £25 Sliding Scale

Norfolk

GABELL Yvonne 0263 822781
51 Beeston Common, SHERINGHAM NR26 8EU
Member of:	**BAC**
Quals/training:	MA (Oxon); Cert Ed; Trained with WPF and ITAA
Personal Therapy:	Yes
Supervision:	Ongoing
Counselling offered:	**General, Spiritual, Crisis, Bereavement, Psychosomatic**
Service for:	Individuals, Couples, Families
Specific to:	Young people, Religious, Retired
Theoretical Approach:	Client-centred, TA
Fees:	£5 - £20 Sliding scale

HART Chris 0728 688134
Hulver Cottage, School Hill, Blaxhall, WOODBRIDGE IP12 2DZ
Member of:	**BAC**
Quals/training:	Dip Psychosynthesis(PET)'93
Personal Therapy:	Ongoing
Supervision:	Ongoing
Counselling offered:	**Psychotherapy**
Service for:	Individuals
Theoretical Approach:	Humanistic, Transpersonal
Fees:	£20

Norfolk

Northamptonshire

Organisations

KATIE MARIE STRESS & CANCER SURVIVAL CHARITY 0604 36838
Holistic Health Centre, 71 Lawrence Court, NORTHAMPTON NN2 3HD
Service: Holistic natural clig & psychotherapy service offering moral support, practical help & stress management. Cancer transformations & diet/vitamin therapy.
Referral: Self, GP
Training of workers: Trained nurses & counsellors, supported by doctors & stress consultant
Code of Ethics: Agency's own code
Management by: Board of Trustees and Management Committee
Fees: £10 gps/families - donations

STRESS AT WORK FOUNDATION (OCCUPATIONAL/MENTAL WELFARE)
Flat 87, 81 Trinity Avenue, NORTHAMPTON NN2 6LD
Service: Non-directive psychotherapeutic counselling for individuals; guidance for managers and organisations in the management of potentially stressful situations; PTSD, bereavement/loss
Area served: Northants and adjacent areas
Referral: Self, Employer
Training of workers: Medical & psychiatric social workers. Personal therapy, ongoing supervision
Code of Ethics: BAC
Management by: Management Group
Fees: Donations sought

NORTHAMPTON PASTORAL COUNSELLING SERVICE 0604 784330
Emmanuel Shared Church, Weston Favell Centre, NORTHAMPTON NN3 4JR
Service: General, bereavement & marital counselling. WPF affiliated
Area served: Northamptonshire
Referral: Self
Training of workers: Trained by Leicester University, regular supervision
Code of Ethics: BAC
Management by: Management Council
Fees: Donations according to income

RUGBY PROFESSIONAL COUNSELLING SERVICE 0604 891436
47 Bedford Road, Brafield on the Green, NORTHAMPTON NN7 1BD
Service: General, bereavement, relationship, anxiety management and psychotherapy for individuals, couples and families; groupwork available
Area served: Warwickshire and adjacent areas
Referral: Self or others
Training of workers: Fully trained counsellors and therapists; regular supervision
Code of Ethics: Varies with professional seen
Management by: 3 partners: L Bunn, F Bishop, S Thorpe
Fees: £25 - £50 negotiable

Northamptonshire

INSIGHT COUNSELLING & CONSULTANCY   0604 890924
45 Bridge Meadow, Denton, NORTHAMPTON NN7 1DA
Service: Setting up of workplace policies on alcohol, drugs & smoking employee occupational health couns support system; career development; smoke stop groups
Area served: Northamptonshire
Referral: Companies, Health/Soc Work Professional
Training of workers: Trained counsellors, consultants
Code of Ethics: BAC
Management by: Mrs H E Warden
Fees: Negotiable

Individual Practitioners
*Each individual is a **member of** one or more organisations eligible for entry into this directory. BAC Accredited Counsellors and Recognised Supervisors are shaded.*

PHILLIPS Richard   0536 514997
6 Paradise Avenue, KETTERING NN15 6LU
Member of: BAC
Quals/training: Bereavement worker since 1973; CSCT Trained; special interest in reality modelling and loss
Personal Therapy: Ongoing
Supervision: Ongoing
Counselling offered: **General, Bereavement, Loss**
Service for: Individuals, Families
Theoretical Approach: Eclectic
Fees: Negotiable, first session free

FLINSPACH Elisabeth   0536 373058
Brigstock, KETTERING NN14
Member of: BAC, ITHP, BPA
Quals/training: Trained in Humanistic & Analytic Psychotherapy(Minster Centre), Assertiveness Trainer(Redwood)
Personal Therapy: Ongoing
Supervision: Ongoing
Counselling offered: **General, Relationship, Crisis, Bereavement, Assertiveness**
Service for: Individuals, Couples, Groups
Specific to: Women
Theoretical Approach: Psychodynamic, Eclectic
Other languages: German
Fees: £18 - £25 negotiable

PASSINGHAM Carol   ansaphone 0604 718327
20 St Georges Place, NORTHAMPTON NN2 6EP
Member of: BAC
Quals/training: CQSW; BA; MEd (Couns) to be completed Jan 94
Personal Therapy: Yes
Supervision: Ongoing
Counselling offered: **General, Loss, Crisis, Relationship, Adoption**
Service for: Individuals, Couples
Theoretical Approach: Eclectic
Fees: £20 first session then negotiable

Northamptonshire

SIMONS William 0604 713767
54 Park Avenue North, NORTHAMPTON NN3 2JE
Member of: BAC
Quals/training: MA; trained with CTA, WPF
Personal Therapy: Yes
Supervision: Ongoing
Counselling offered: General
Service for: Individuals, Couples
Specific to: Religious, Ethnic minorities
Theoretical Approach: Eclectic
Fees: Donations

HARRIS Debra 0604 761882
16 Langford Drive, Wootton, NORTHAMPTON NN4 0JY
Member of: BAC Acc
Quals/training: BAC Acc; BA (Hons) Psychol; 1982-3 Dip Couns (Aston Univ); NMGC training
Personal Therapy: Yes
Supervision: Ongoing
Counselling offered: General, Marital, Bereavement, Psychotherapy
Service for: Individuals, Couples, Groups
Theoretical Approach: Psychodynamic
Fees: £27

BEAUMONT Caroline 0604 765513
Church House, High Street, Hardingstone, NORTHAMPTON NN4 6BZ
Member of: BAC Acc
Quals/training: BAC Acc; BA; B Phil (Couns)
Personal Therapy: Ongoing
Supervision: Ongoing
Counselling offered: General, Psychotherapy
Service for: Individuals
Theoretical Approach: Psychodynamic
Fees: £25

SMITH Gordon 0604 755948
97 Harlestone Road, NORTHAMPTON NN5 7AB
Member of: BAC
Quals/training: MA; Dip Pastoral Studies; Cert Couns (CSCT)
Personal Therapy: Ongoing
Supervision: Ongoing
Counselling offered: General, Crisis, Personal growth, Stress management
Service for: Individuals
Theoretical Approach: Psychodynamic, Person-centred
Fees: £25 - £35

Northamptonshire

WELCH Rosie   0604 755948
Helix Counselling, 97 Harlestone Road, NORTHAMPTON NN5 7AB

Member of:	**BAC, BASMT**
Quals/training:	BSc; BA Psychol; NMGC trained '73; Sex therapist; Fellow ITD
Personal Therapy:	Ongoing
Supervision:	Ongoing
Counselling offered:	**General, Change, Personal growth**
Service for:	Individuals, Couples, Groups
Theoretical Approach:	Person-centred, Transpersonal, TA, Gestalt, Reiki & Seichim healing
Fees:	£25 negotiable

WARDEN Rita   0604 890924
45 Bridge Meadow, Denton, NORTHAMPTON NN7 1DA

Member of:	**BAC**
Quals/training:	Dip Alcohol Couns & Consultation (Kent Univ) '87; Marital & Family Therapy '86; Cert in Training '90
Personal Therapy:	No
Supervision:	Ongoing
Counselling offered:	**General, Addiction, Relationship, Occupational**
Service for:	Individuals, Couples, Families, Groups
Specific to:	Professionals, Women, Ethnic minorities
Theoretical Approach:	Eclectic
Fees:	£25 - £40 negotiable

Northumberland

Individual Practitioners
*Each individual is a **member of** one or more organisations eligible for entry into this directory. BAC Accredited Counsellors and Recognised Supervisors are shaded.*

BRANSON Clare   0434 604784
Causey Grange, Causey Hill, HEXHAM NE46 2DW
Member of: BAC
Quals/training: BEd; training in Person-centred couns, Psychosynthesis, TA, journalling, clay therapy
Personal Therapy: Yes
Supervision: Ongoing
Counselling offered: General, Bereavement, Eating disorders, Psychotherapy
Service for: Individuals, Groups
Theoretical Approach: Person-centred
Fees: £20 inds; £25-30 grp negotiable

BEARMAN Patricia   0670 790261
Lindisfarne, Ulgham, MORPETH NE61 3AR
Member of: BAC, NAAP
Quals/training: RNMS 1971; RMN 1977; Intro yr (IGA) 1982; Phenomenology / Social Studies & 5 yr training (PA) 1985; Assoc NAAP; Assoc AHP
Personal Therapy: Yes
Supervision: Ongoing
Counselling offered: General, Psychotherapy, Relationship, Personality disorders
Service for: Individuals, Couples, Groups
Theoretical Approach: Analytical, Humanistic, Existential
Fees: £15 - £30 sliding scale

IRVINE Barbara   0661 824913
242 Western Way, Ponteland, NEWCASTLE-UPON-TYNE NE20 9ND
Member of: BAC
Quals/training: Ed Cert; Dip Groupwork; Dip Counselling
Personal Therapy: Ongoing
Supervision: Ongoing
Counselling offered: Imaging, Homeopathy, Bach flower remedies, Regression therapy, Menopause
Service for: Individuals, Couples, Families, Groups, Organisations
Specific to: Widowed
Theoretical Approach: Person-centred, Psychosynthesis
Fees: £25

GOODACRE David   0661 832273
St Mary's Vicarage, Ovingham, PRUDHOE NE42 6BS
Member of: BAC
Quals/training: CTA Training '62-'68; Dip Pastoral Studies (Birmingham)'69; C of E Board of Ed Group Dynamics Training
Personal Therapy: Yes
Supervision: Ongoing
Counselling offered: General, Spiritual
Service for: Individuals, Couples
Theoretical Approach: Object relations
Fees: £12.50 voluntary contribution

Organisations

CLINICAL PSYCHOLOGY SERVICES 0623 22515 x 4571
Ransom Hospital, Rainworth, MANSFIELD NG21 0ER
Service:	Comprehensive services for individuals with psychological problems
Area served:	Central Notts inc Mansfield/Ashfield, Newark & Sherwood
Referral:	GP, Health Practitioner
Training of workers:	Post-graduate clinical psychology training, some also have post-graduate psychotherapy training qualifications
Code of Ethics:	BPS
Management by:	HA
Fees:	None

SHERWOOD PSYCHOTHERAPY TRAINING INSTITUTE
Thiskney House, 2 St James Terrace, NOTTINGHAM NG1 6FW
Service:	Psychotherapy & counselling offered by qualified psychotherapists & counsellors. Also sessions at a reduced fee by trainees (supervised)
Area served:	Notts, Leics, Lincs, Derbyshire & Sheffield
Referral:	Self
Training of workers:	Dip Couns or min 4 yr psychotherapy training for qualified staff
Code of Ethics:	BAC, UKCP, Agency's own code
Management by:	Kenneth Evans
Fees:	£10 - £30 Dependent on training

Individual Practitioners

*Each individual is a **member of** one or more organisations eligible for entry into this directory. BAC Accredited Counsellors and Recognised Supervisors are shaded.*

WOODHEAD Chez Ms ansaphone 0623 824537
Ho Barn, Ollerton Road, Edwinstowe, MANSFIELD NG21 9QE
Member of:	BAC
Quals/training:	BA(Hons) Contemp Cultural Studies; Dip Couns
Personal Therapy:	Yes
Supervision:	Ongoing
Counselling offered:	**General, Bereavement, Infertility, Relationship**
Service for:	Individuals, Couples
Specific to:	Women, Adolescents
Theoretical Approach:	Rogerian, Eclectic
Fees:	Sliding scale £20 1st interview

WYATT Gill 0602 243994
Thiskney House, 2 St James Terrace, NOTTINGHAM NG1 6FW
Member of:	BAC Acc
Quals/training:	BAC(Acc); BSc Soc Sci; RGN; Memb EATA & BHMA; Dip Couns; training in TA & Gestalt Psychotherapy(Metanoia)
Personal Therapy:	Ongoing
Supervision:	Ongoing
Counselling offered:	**General, Relationship, Psychotherapy**
Service for:	Individuals, Groups
Theoretical Approach:	Rogerian, TA, Gestalt
Fees:	£30 negotiable

Nottinghamshire

PIGOTT Sheila   0602 233492
St Pauls House, Boundary Road, West Bridgford, NOTTINGHAM NG2 7DB
Member of:	**BAC Acc, GPTI**
Quals/training:	BAC Acc; Dip GPTI:
Personal Therapy:	Ongoing
Supervision:	Ongoing
Counselling offered:	**General, Supervision**
Service for:	Individuals, Groups
Theoretical Approach:	Gestalt
Fees:	£23 - £28 Negotiable

GRAHAM Hilary   0602 455290
25 George Road, West Bridgford, NOTTINGHAM NG2 7PT
Member of:	**NRHP**
Quals/training:	DHP (NCHP); Cert in Past Life Therapy (Dr Roger Wooger)
Personal Therapy:	Ongoing
Supervision:	Ongoing
Counselling offered:	**General, Hypnotherapy, Psychotherapy, Regression therapy, Sexual abuse, Anxiety**
Service for:	Individuals, Couples, Organisations
Specific to:	Women, Survivors of child abuse
Theoretical Approach:	Eclectic
Fees:	£22 negotuable

BROADLEY Richard   0602 693396
16 Villa Road, NOTTINGHAM NG3 4GG
Member of:	**BAC**
Quals/training:	Dip Couns '84; Dip Careers Guidance '68; training in TA, Gestalt, Marital Therapy; Senior Lecturer in Couns (Nottm Trent Univ); ASC Acc; Cert Psychodynamic Couns Sup '01
Personal Therapy:	Yes
Supervision:	Ongoing
Counselling offered:	**General, Vocational, Sexual, Bereavement, Self-understanding, Change, Disability, Relationship, Midlife**
Service for:	Individuals, Couples
Specific to:	People with disabilities
Theoretical Approach:	Humanistic, Person-centred
Fees:	£25 - £35 negotiable

RICHARDSON Maureen   0602 608218
4 Gretton Road, Mapperley Plains, NOTTINGHAM NG3 5JT
Member of:	**BAC**
Quals/training:	Trained & experienced mainly in practice of Rogerian counselling
Personal Therapy:	Yes
Supervision:	Ongoing
Counselling offered:	**General, Bereavement, Psychotherapy, Creative potential**
Service for:	Individuals, Couples, Families, Groups, Organisations
Specific to:	Creative people
Theoretical Approach:	Eclectic
Fees:	£14 - £28 (£20 initial session)

Nottinghamshire

MURPHY Antonia   0602 606810
9 Cannon Street, Sherwood, NOTTINGHAM NG5 2HB
Member of:	BAC, IPC
Quals/training:	BA; Dip Adv Psychodynamic Couns(WPF)
Personal Therapy:	Yes
Supervision:	Ongoing
Counselling offered:	General
Service for:	Individuals
Theoretical Approach:	Psychodynamic
Fees:	£18 - £30 sliding scale

TRAN Van, Mr   0602 268749
13 Marlborough Road, Woodthorpe, NOTTINGHAM NG5 4FG
Member of:	BAC
Quals/training:	BA(Hons) Psychol; trained at Nottingham Couns Centre; Ongoing post grad training in Humanistic Couns
Personal Therapy:	Yes
Supervision:	Ongoing
Counselling offered:	General, Cross/multi-cultural
Service for:	Individuals
Theoretical Approach:	Humanistic, Psychodynamic, Integrative
Fees:	Negotiable

SANDERSON Lesley   0602 532128
51 Grange Road, Woodthorpe, NOTTINGHAM NG5 4FU
Member of:	BAC
Quals/training:	BSc (Econ); CQSW; Cert Couns (Nottingham Couns Service); Cert in Couns Studies (Leicester Univ)
Personal Therapy:	Yes
Supervision:	Ongoing
Counselling offered:	General, Depression, Psychotherapy, Relationship, Self-esteem, Abuse
Service for:	Individuals
Specific to:	Women, Helping professions
Theoretical Approach:	Psychodynamic
Fees:	£20 negotiable

SHORT Deborah   0602 272940
17 Brancaster Close, Cinderhill, NOTTINGHAM NG6 8SL
Member of:	BAC, GPTI, SHPTI
Quals/training:	Adv training Gestalt Psychotherapy; training leading to Dip in Gestalt Psychotherapy (SHPTI)
Personal Therapy:	Ongoing
Supervision:	Ongoing
Counselling offered:	General, Psychotherapy, Bereavement, Loss
Service for:	Individuals, Groups
Specific to:	People with learning difficulties
Theoretical Approach:	Gestalt, Rogerian
Fees:	£17 - £25 (1 reduced fee place @ £12)

Nottinghamshire

REX Imogen 0602 470 220
23a Lenton Avenue, The Park, NOTTINGHAM NG7 1DX
Member of: BAC
Quals/training: BA Psychol; Dip Music; Dip Couns; Gestalt & Group Facilitation (Australia); RELATE trained 1979; Process-Oriented Psychol (Zurich); Adv Cert Psychotherapy (Leicester)
Personal Therapy: Ongoing
Supervision: Ongoing
Counselling offered: Psychotherapy, Brief, Supervision
Service for: Individuals, Couples, Families, Groups
Theoretical Approach: Process-oriented psychology, Psychodynamic
Fees: £18

DEACON Jerry 0860 788964
Fern Lodge, 4 Third Avenue, Sherwood Rise, NOTTINGHAM NG7 6JH
Member of: BAC Acc
Quals/training: BAC Acc; ASC Acc; BA (Hons); Cert Couns Studies & Advanced Couns; training in Psychodynamic Couns & Client Centred Therapy (1987-90)
Personal Therapy: Ongoing
Supervision: Ongoing
Counselling offered: General, Psychotherapy, Relationship, Depression, Anxiety, Crisis, Abuse, Bereavement, Self-esteem, Change
Service for: Individuals, Couples, Groups
Theoretical Approach: Person-centred, Psychodynamic
Fees: £20 - £32

DAVIES Dominic ansaphone 0602 297215, minicom 0602 297215
245 Charlbury Road, Woollaton, NOTTINGHAM NG8 1NF
Member of: BAC Acc
Quals/training: BAC Acc; ASC Acc; Dip Person-Centred Couns & Psychotherapy (FDI/PCT)
Personal Therapy: Yes
Supervision: Ongoing
Counselling offered: General, Psychotherapy, Sexuality, AIDS
Service for: Individuals, Couples, Groups
Specific to: Gays, Lesbians, People with disabilities
Theoretical Approach: Client-centred
Fees: £22 - £32 sliding scale

MACDONALD Marsali 0602 701278
8 Biant Close, Aspley, NOTTINGHAM NG8 5NY
Member of: BAC
Quals/training: MA; Dip Careers Guidance; Cert Couns; Training in Psychodynamic Couns, Nottingham Counselling Centre
Personal Therapy: Yes
Supervision: Ongoing
Counselling offered: General, Midlife
Service for: Individuals
Specific to: Women
Theoretical Approach: Psychodynamic, Eclectic
Fees: £15 - £25 Sliding Scale

Nottinghamshire

BULLEN-SPICER Robert 0602 259083
Ten Hampden Grove, Beeston, NOTTINGHAM NG9 1FG
Member of: BAC, SHPTI
Quals/training: Developmental Groupwork/Group Dynamics; Suicide/Crisis Couns; Alchohol Couns; Cert Couns Skills (Leicester Univ); Dip Gestalt Psych (GPTI); Dip Clinical Supervision
Personal Therapy: Yes
Supervision: Ongoing
Counselling offered: General
Service for: Individuals, Couples, Families, Groups
Theoretical Approach: Rogerian, Gestalt, Psychodynamic
Fees: £25 negotiable

DANIELS Frank 0773 532195]
The Wellbeing Centre, 11 Musters Road, West Bridgford, NOTTINGHAM NG8 6LA
Member of: ANLP (PCS)
Quals/training: NLP Master Practitioner; Dip NLP Trainer; Dip Eriksonian Hypnosis; Cert Hypnotherapy; Foundations in Gestalt & Psychosynthesis
Personal Therapy: No
Supervision: Ongoing
Counselling offered: Psychotherapy
Service for: Individuals
Theoretical Approach: NLP, Ericksonian, Hypnotherapy
Fees: £30

CALVERT Jane 0602 335645
8 Cropwell Road, Radcliffe on Trent, NOTTINGHAM NG12 2FS
Member of: BAC Acc, WMIP, Member of UKCP Register
Quals/training: BAC Acc; MA; MSc Psychol Couns; RELATE trained; Senior lecturer in Counselling (University of Derby); Experience within NHS; Psychotherapy training with WMIP
Personal Therapy: Ongoing
Supervision: Ongoing
Counselling offered: General, Relationship, Psychotherapy
Service for: Individuals, Couples, Groups
Theoretical Approach: Psychodynamic
Fees: £30 sliding scale

BARTYS Anita 0949 42074
Field Cottage, Normanton, Bottesford, NOTTINGHAM NG13 0EP
Member of: BAC, NRHP
Quals/training: Dip Hypnotherapy & Psychotherapy (NCHP) '92; courses undertaken in basic psychodynamic counselling and NLP; BSc(Hons); PGCE;
Personal Therapy: Yes
Supervision: Ongoing
Counselling offered: General, Hypnotherapy, Psychotherapy
Service for: Individuals
Theoretical Approach: Integrative
Fees: £25

Nottinghamshire

ANDERSON Judith 0949 20871
115 Main Street, East Bridgford, NOTTINGHAM NG13 8NH
Member of: WMIP, AUTP
Quals/training: MB; ChB; MRCPsych
Personal Therapy: Ongoing
Supervision: Ongoing
Counselling offered: Psychotherapy
Service for: Individuals
Theoretical Approach: Analytical, Dynamic
Fees: £30

HAYMAN Penny 0602 486487
50 Clarendon Street, NOTTINGHAM
Member of: BAC
Quals/training: BA 1974; MA 1975; Cert Ed 1978; Dip Group Psychotherapy 1981 some hypnotherapy training; currently Clinical Supervision training
Personal Therapy: Ongoing
Supervision: Ongoing
Counselling offered: **General, Bereavement, Crisis, Addiction, Psychotherapy**
Service for: Individuals, Groups
Theoretical Approach: Psychodynamic
Other languages: French, Spanish
Fees: £20

PHILLIPS Sue 0636 813794
1 Orchard Close, SOUTHWELL NG25 0DY
Member of: BAC, MPTI
Quals/training: RGN; CQSW; NMGC/RELATE Trained; HV Cert; Memb ITAA
Personal Therapy: Ongoing
Supervision: Ongoing
Counselling offered: **General, Marital, Bereavement, Psychotherapy**
Service for: Individuals, Couples, Groups
Theoretical Approach: Psychodynamic, TA, Integrative
Fees: £25 - £35

HUNT Bruce 0909 478214
14 Dunstan Crescent, WORKSOP S80 1AF
Member of: BAC
Quals/training: BA; Dip Ed; Advanced Cert Couns Studies
Personal Therapy: Ongoing
Supervision: Ongoing
Counselling offered: **General, Depression, Bereavement, Marital, Relationship, Abuse, Spiritual**
Service for: Individuals, Couples, Families
Specific to: Religious
Theoretical Approach: Psychodynamic
Fees: £15 negotiable

Oxfordshire

Organisations

ISIS CENTRE 0865 56648
Little Clarendon Street, OXFORD OX1 2HS
Service:	**NHS counselling & psychotherapy service for individuals, couples and families & groups, consultation & information. Consultation service for workers in field of mental health.**
Area served:	Oxfordshire
Referral:	Self
Training of workers:	Counsellors all have relevant training and experience
Code of Ethics:	BAC
Management by:	Oxfordshire Health Authority
Fees:	No charge - NHS

OXFORD CHRISTIAN INSTITUTE FOR COUNSELLING 0865 58154
OCIC, 11 Norham Gardens, OXFORD OX2 6PS
Service:	**Counselling in a Christian context; providing support & training in pastoral care, supervision for carers & helpers in local churches**
Area served:	Oxford & adjacent areas
Referral:	Self or others
Training of workers:	Varied. Regular supervision
Code of Ethics:	BAC
Management by:	Council of Management of Institute
Fees:	£16 negotiable; intl assess £18

ARC 0865 247003
37 Marston Street, OXFORD OX4 1JU
Service:	**Personal and all work-related counselling for individuals and workshops for groups covering interpersonal skills. Consultancy to assist change & development in organisations**
Area served:	South of England, Midlands
Referral:	Self or others, Agencies, Organisations
Training of workers:	All trained counsellors, supervision and ongoing training
Code of Ethics:	BAC
Management by:	Associates
Fees:	By arrangement

WANTAGE COUNSELLING SERVICE 0235 769744
9 Church Street, WANTAGE OX12 8BL
Service:	**Individual couns for personal & relationship difficulties (couples counselled at discretion on intake assessor)**
Area served:	Wantage & surrounding areas
Referral:	Self
Training of workers:	3 year part-time training; regular supervision & further training
Code of Ethics:	BAC, WPF
Management by:	Management Committee
Fees:	Contributions

Oxfordshire

MALE SURVIVORS GROUP 0491 833474
9b Thames Street, Wallingford, WATLINGTON OX10 0HD
Service: Counselling for men who have been sexually abused or raped including for all aspects of HIV/AIDS. Telephone counselling for first contact; face to face counselling with abusers.
Area served: Reading and Oxford areas
Referral: Self
Training of workers: Fully trained counsellor; certificates in counselling and trainee in Gestalt therapy (metanoia); ongoing supervision
Code of Ethics: BAC
Management by: Counsellor
Fees: £5 - £20 free to some

BEREAVEMENT COUNSELLING SERVICE FOR GAYS & LESBIANS
0491 833474
9b Thames Street, Wallingford, WATLINGTON OX10 0HD
Service: Bereavement counselling; gay and lesbian support group; 24 hour telephone counselling service; face to face counselling. Referral service, teaching
Area served: Upper Thames Valley
Referral: Self
Training of workers: Trained volunteers
Code of Ethics: Agency's own code
Management by: Volunteers and clients
Fees: None

Individual Practitioners
*Each individual is a **member of** one or more organisations eligible for entry into this directory. BAC Accredited Counsellors and Recognised Supervisors are shaded.*

CATTLE Liese 0235 524307
43 East Saint Helen Street, ABINGDON OX14 5EE
Member of: BAC Acc
Quals/training: BAC(Acc); RELATE trained; registered Art Therapist
Personal Therapy: Yes
Supervision: Ongoing
Counselling offered: **General, Art therapy**
Service for: Individuals
Specific to: Children
Theoretical Approach: Psychodynamic, Client-centred
Fees: £23 - £35 sliding scale

NASH Mallory 0295 730 652
Crown Yard Cottage, Wroxton, BANBURY OX15 6PT
Member of: BAC Acc
Quals/training: BAC(Acc); RELATE trained; Cert in Gestalt Fundamentals(EGI); currently in further training in Gestalt Psychotherapy (EGI)
Personal Therapy: Ongoing
Supervision: Ongoing
Counselling offered: **General, Abuse, Psychotherapy, Relationship**
Service for: Individuals, Couples, Groups
Theoretical Approach: Psychodynamic, Gestalt
Fees: £20 - £30 sliding scale-some fee assist

Oxfordshire

LUNT William 0993 831182
10 High Street, Ascott-u-Wychwood, CHIPPING NORTON OX7 6AW
Member of:	BAC
Quals/training:	AEB Dip Couns (CAC); Memb Inst of Chartered Accountants; Assoc Swindon Counselling Service (WPF)
Personal Therapy:	Yes
Supervision:	Ongoing
Counselling offered:	General, Bereavement, Work, Health
Service for:	Individuals, Couples, Groups
Theoretical Approach:	Integrative
Fees:	£20 negotiable

OCHIENS Samuel 0608 83676
4 Manor Farm Cottages, Sandford St Martin, CHIPPING NORTON OX7 7AG
Member of:	BAC, BPS
Quals/training:	BA; MA (San Diego); CSCT
Personal Therapy:	Ongoing
Supervision:	Ongoing
Counselling offered:	General, Relationship
Service for:	Individuals, Couples, Families
Theoretical Approach:	Jungian
Fees:	£25

GALLOP Margaret 0235 813599
16A New Road, East Hagbourne, DIDCOT OX11 9JU
Member of:	BAC
Quals/training:	BEd (Cantab); Dip Couns (Reading) 1988
Personal Therapy:	Ongoing
Supervision:	Ongoing
Counselling offered:	General
Service for:	Individuals
Theoretical Approach:	Person-centred, Psychodynamic
Fees:	£20

PARKINSON Frank 0793 784406
9 Priory Mead, Longcot, FARINGDON SN7 7TJ
Member of:	BAC
Quals/training:	BA Sociology & Education; Dip Theology; RELATE Trained; teacher of Couns Skills for 12 yrs
Personal Therapy:	No
Supervision:	Ongoing
Counselling offered:	General, Bereavement, PTSD, Crit. incident debriefing
Service for:	Individuals, Couples, Families, Groups
Specific to:	Caring professions
Theoretical Approach:	Eclectic, Psychodynamic, Person-centred
Fees:	To be mutually arranged

Oxfordshire

EMANUEL Kay 0491 572052
Nicholas Hill Cottage, Valley Road, HENLEY-ON-THAMES RG9 1RR
Member of: BAC
Quals/training: Voluntary therapist at Therapeutic Community '88/9; Introductory course (IGA) 88/9; Foundation yr - Dip Psycho drama 89/90; Couns course (metanoia) 89-92
Personal Therapy: Yes
Supervision: Ongoing
Counselling offered: General, Addiction, Bereavement, Crisis, Depression, Relationship, Stress
Service for: Individuals
Theoretical Approach: Rogerian
Fees: £20

HOLBORN Julie 0494 881731
2 West Cottage, Perrin Springs, Frieth, HENLEY-ON-THAMES RG9 6PG
Member of: BAC Acc
Quals/training: BAC Acc; BA; MA; CQSW 1972; courses at Tavistock Inst; RF; Grubb Inst; Cert Supervision of Couns WPF 1989
Personal Therapy: Yes
Supervision: Ongoing
Counselling offered: General, Marital
Service for: Individuals, Couples
Theoretical Approach: Psychodynamic
Fees: £26 negotiable

STEWARD Jill 0491 638250
Cobstone Mill Farmhouse, Turville, HENLEY-ON-THAMES RG9 6QL
Member of: BAC, IPC
Quals/training: BA; IPC/WPF (full member)
Personal Therapy: Yes
Supervision: Ongoing
Counselling offered: General, Psychotherapy
Service for: Individuals
Theoretical Approach: Object relations, Jungian
Fees: £16 - £24 dependent on income

UNWIN Toni 0865 790938
1 Green Place, OXFORD OX1 4RF
Member of: BAC
Quals/training: Dip Couns (Reading Univ) 1989; Tavistock Clinic 1989-90
Personal Therapy: Yes
Supervision: Ongoing
Counselling offered: General, Psychotherapy
Service for: Individuals
Theoretical Approach: Jungian
Fees: £20

Oxfordshire

ROBERTS Ellie   0865 514568
31 Charlbury Road, OXFORD OX2 6QU
Member of: BAC
Quals/training: BEd; Dip Couns
Personal Therapy: Ongoing
Supervision: Ongoing
Counselling offered: General, Bereavement, Relationship, Crisis, Psychotherapy
Service for: Individuals, Couples
Fees: £15 - £30 negotiable

MARLER Sally   0865 515919
38 Stratfield Road, Summertown, OXFORD OX2 7BQ
Member of: BAC
Quals/training: MA (Oxon); Dip Couns (Reading)
Personal Therapy: Ongoing
Supervision: Ongoing
Counselling offered: General, Psychotherapy
Service for: Individuals, Couples
Theoretical Approach: Psychodynamic
Fees: £15 - £30 sliding scale

RIDGEWELL Margaret   0865 54413
2b Carlton Road, OXFORD OX2 7RZ
Member of: **BAC, GPTI, MPTI**
Quals/training: BA; MEd Studies; Dip IDHP; Dip Couns; ITEC; Gestalt Psychotherapy (metanoia) 1989-present
Personal Therapy: Yes
Supervision: Ongoing
Counselling offered: General, Relationship, Self-esteem, Psychotherapy
Service for: Individuals, Couples, Groups, Organisations
Specific to: Teachers, Managers
Theoretical Approach: Rogerian, Gestalt
Other languages: French
Fees: £22 - £30 sliding scale

HUMPHRIES Tamsin   0865 513371
5 Wentworth Road, OXFORD OX2 7TG
Member of: BAC
Quals/training: BA; MA (Oxon); Postgraduate Dip Couns (Reading Univ)'78
Personal Therapy: Yes
Supervision: Ongoing
Counselling offered: General, Identity crisis, Depression, Panic attacks, Bereavement, Relationship, Divorce, Redundancy
Service for: Individuals, Couples, Groups
Theoretical Approach: Psychoanalytic
Fees: £28 - £35

SAUNDERS Dr Chris 0865 62911
36 Malford Road, Headington, OXFORD OX3 8BS
Member of:	BAC
Quals/training:	BA (Hons)1983; PhD Psych/Anthro/Humanities 1989; Massage, Anat & Physiol(ITEC)1989; Comb Cert Couns (CAC)1992; Short courses & workshops on Assertiveness, HIV/AIDS Couns
Personal Therapy:	Ongoing
Supervision:	Ongoing
Counselling offered:	**General, Stress management, Relationship, Self-esteem, Sexual abuse, Spiritual**
Service for:	Individuals, Couples, Groups
Theoretical Approach:	Psychodynamic, Behavioural, Humanistic
Fees:	£15 - £25 sliding scale

BRADLEY Lorne Natalie 0865 246879
29 Boulter Street, St Clements, OXFORD OX4 1AX
Member of:	BAC Acc
Quals/training:	BAC Acc; Dip Psychodynamic Couns (London Univ); training at Centre for Psychoanalytical Psychotherapy
Personal Therapy:	Ongoing
Supervision:	Ongoing
Counselling offered:	**General, Relationship, Eating disorders, Abuse, HIV, AIDS**
Service for:	Individuals, Couples
Specific to:	Performing artists, Students
Theoretical Approach:	Psychodynamic, Analytical
Fees:	£10 - £25 based on income

BREWER Madelyn 0865 725588
38 Rectory Road, St Clements, OXFORD OX4 1BU
Member of:	PA
Quals/training:	BSc; MA Antioch Univ; Dip Couns Skills SW London College, trained Psychotherapist Philadelphia Assoc
Personal Therapy:	Yes
Supervision:	Ongoing
Counselling offered:	**General, Psychotherapy**
Service for:	Individuals
Theoretical Approach:	Psychodynamic
Fees:	£22 - £25 sliding scale

HAMPTON Charles 0865 725798
118 Hurst Street, OXFORD OX4 1HG
Member of:	BAC
Quals/training:	MA (Cantab); Dip Couns (Reading); Foundation in Group Analysis (IGA)
Personal Therapy:	Ongoing
Supervision:	Ongoing
Counselling offered:	**General, Relationship, Bereavement, Transition**
Service for:	Individuals, Couples
Theoretical Approach:	Psychodynamic, Eclectic
Fees:	£20

Oxfordshire

DOUGLAS Hazel 0865 247 003
37 Marston Street, OXFORD OX4 1JU
Member of:	BAC
Quals/training:	CSCT Cert Couns (awaiting Dip); Counselling Consultancy Oxford; Fellow of the Inst of Personnel Management; Dip Mmnt
Personal Therapy:	Ongoing
Supervision:	Ongoing
Counselling offered:	**Personal growth, General, Occupational, Career**
Service for:	Individuals
Theoretical Approach:	Psychodynamic
Fees:	By arrangement

LEWIS Maggie 0865 311704
The Wellbeing Clinic, 6 Kingston Road, OXFORD OX2 6EF
Member of:	BAC
Quals/training:	RMN; ENB Cert Couns; ongoing MA Psychotherapy; Dip Couns; Memb Eating Disorders Association
Personal Therapy:	Yes
Supervision:	Ongoing
Counselling offered:	**General, Child abuse, Eating disorders, Psychosomatic, Bereavement, Depression, Long-term**
Service for:	Individuals
Specific to:	Professionals, Elderly
Theoretical Approach:	Psychodynamic, Integrative
Fees:	£20 - £30

MOXLEY Kurt 0865 778489
121 Crescent Road, Temple Cowley, OXFORD OX4 2NY
Member of:	BAC
Quals/training:	BSc (Hons) Psychol; CQSW; Cert in Psychotherapy, Oxon; RF trained; IGA Midland Course in Group-Analytic Work
Personal Therapy:	Yes
Supervision:	Ongoing
Counselling offered:	**General, Psychotherapy**
Service for:	Individuals, Couples, Groups
Specific to:	Men
Theoretical Approach:	Psychodynamic
Fees:	£20 - £30 Sliding Scale

ALLEN Patricia 0865 872388
33 Butts Road, Horspath, OXFORD OX33 1RJ
Member of:	BAC, BPS, ITA
Quals/training:	BAHons Psychol; Dip Humanstic Psychol; training in TA
Personal Therapy:	Yes
Supervision:	Ongoing
Counselling offered:	**General, Psychotherapy**
Service for:	Individuals, Couples, Groups
Theoretical Approach:	TA, Gestalt, Rogerian, Eclectic
Fees:	£25 negotiable

Oxfordshire

CECIL Yvette   **02357 69417**
5 The Pound, Charlton Village Road, WANTAGE OX12 7HN
Member of: BAC, BCPC
Quals/training: Trained with Wantage Counselling Service (WPF Affiliate); 3rd years training with BCPC
Personal Therapy: Yes
Supervision: Ongoing
Counselling offered: **Long-term, Short-term**
Service for: Individuals, Couples
Theoretical Approach: Psychodynamic
Fees: £15

HARRIS Jonathon   **0235 751573**
Odstone House, Westcot Lane, Sparsholt, WANTAGE OX12 9PZ
Member of: NRHP
Quals/training: BSc (Hons) Psychol (London); Cert Hypnotherapy & Psychotherapy (NCHP); Assoc member NRHP
Personal Therapy: No
Supervision: Ongoing
Counselling offered: **Hypnotherapy, Career, Depression, Phobias, Stress, Eating disorders, PTSD, Psychosexual, Redundancy**
Service for: Individuals, Couples, Organisations
Specific to: Gays
Theoretical Approach: Eclectic
Fees: £20 - £35

DOUGLAS Sue   **0367 820 562**
Fawler Barn, Kingston-Lisle, WANTAGE OX12 9QJ
Member of: BAC Acc, BCPC
Quals/training: BA (Hons) Psychol; Dip Social Work; NMGC & BAC Acc; Dip Humanistic Psychol; Dip Humanistic & Integrative Psychotherapy BCPC
Personal Therapy: Ongoing
Supervision: Ongoing
Counselling offered: **Psychotherapy, Supervision**
Service for: Individuals, Couples, Groups, Organisations
Theoretical Approach: Integrative
Fees: £22 - £25 negotiable

COOPER Sandra
WALLINGFORD
Member of: BAC, MPTI
Quals/training: Basic Youth Cert in Couns & Communications; first year of Dip Couns 1992
Personal Therapy: Ongoing
Supervision: Ongoing
Counselling offered: **General, Substance abuse, Alcohol**
Service for: Individuals
Theoretical Approach: Client-centred
Fees: £12

Oxfordshire

ELDERTON John Mon-Fri 0491 833474
9B Thames Street, Wallingford, WATLINGTON OX10

Member of:	**BAC**
Quals/training:	Trained RF, LCIP, IIP, IGA; trainee in Gestalt Psychotherapy (metanoia)
Personal Therapy:	Ongoing
Supervision:	Ongoing
Counselling offered:	**Relationship, Bereavement, AIDS, Sexual abuse**
Service for:	Individuals, Couples, Families, Groups
Specific to:	Gays, Lesbians, Offenders
Theoretical Approach:	Rogerian, Gestalt
Fees:	£25 negotiable dependant on income

TURNBULL Peter 0491 833814
Talcarra, Brightwell cum Sotwell, Wallingford, WATLINGTON OX10 0QT

Member of:	**BAC**
Quals/training:	Training for Cert Couns Studies (Oxford Univ)
Personal Therapy:	Yes
Supervision:	Ongoing
Counselling offered:	**General, Drugs**
Service for:	Individuals
Specific to:	Young adults
Theoretical Approach:	Person-centred
Fees:	£12 - £20 Sliding scale

Oxfordshire

Shropshire

Organisations

INSIGHT - PROFESSIONAL FAMILY THERAPY　　　0742 861122
18 Lincoln Fields, Billingsley, BRIDGNORTH WV16 6PB
Service:	General counselling, psychotherapy, family and marital therapy
Area served:	Shropshire
Referral:	Agencies, Self
Training of workers:	Both NHS trained, 1 psychologist, 1 family therapist. Ongoing supervision
Code of Ethics:	BAC
Management by:	Private partnership
Fees:	By negotiation

CONFIDE, SHROPSHIRE COUNSELLING SERVICE　　　0743 351319
c/o Friends Meeting House, Corporation Lane, SHREWSBURY SY1 2NU
Service:	General & relationship counselling service for individuals
Area served:	Shropshire
Referral:	Self or others
Training of workers:	3 yr course (WPF syllabus) plus supervised practise and personal growth
Code of Ethics:	BAC
Management by:	Management Committee (WPF Associate)
Fees:	Negotiable

PRINCESS ROYAL HOSPITAL DEPT OF GUM, TELFORD　　　0952 222536
Apley Park, TELFORD TF1
Service:	Individual face to face & telephone counselling for people worried about & those with HIV/AIDS. Open Tues, Wed & Fri pm & Thur am. In-house & tailor-made training.
Area served:	Shropshire
Referral:	Self, GP
Training of workers:	Attendance at national & local counselling courses. Supervision
Code of Ethics:	-
Management by:	Shropshire HA
Fees:	None

Individual Practitioners

*Each individual is a **member of** one or more organisations eligible for entry into this directory. BAC Accredited Counsellors and Recognised Supervisors are shaded.*

LOGAN Faith　　　After 6pm 0584 77510
Garden House, Oakley Park, Bromfield, LUDLOW SY8 2JN
Member of:	BAC
Quals/training:	RGN; Registered Health Visitor; CQSW; Dip Couns; MA Couns Studies (Keele)
Personal Therapy:	Yes
Supervision:	Ongoing
Counselling offered:	General, Crisis, Problem solving, PTSD, Bereavement, Sexual abuse, Eating disorders, Stress, Work
Service for:	Individuals, Couples, Families, Groups, Organisations
Specific to:	Women
Theoretical Approach:	Person-centred, Rogerian
Fees:	£2 - £25 Sliding Scale

Shropshire

DAVIES Lisa　　　　　　　　　　　　　　　　　　　　　　0691 780470
4 Y Gerddi, Llanrhaedr Ym Mochnant, OSWESTRY SY10 0JY
Member of:　　　　　　BAC
Quals/training:　　　　　　Dip Welfare '82; Fellow IWO; H Ed Teacher
Personal Therapy:　　　　No
Supervision:　　　　　　　Ongoing
Counselling offered:　**General, Crisis, Career, Bereavement, Redundancy, Outplacement, Retirement**
Service for:　　　　　　　Individuals, Couples, Groups, Organisations
Other languages:　　　　Welsh
Fees:　　　　　　　　　　£25 + travel, negotiable rates for orgs

ANDERS-RICHARDS Donald　　　　　　　　　　　　　0691 653528
Laburnum Cottage, Gwern-y-Brenin, OSWESTRY SY10 8AS
Member of:　　　　　　BAC
Quals/training:　　　　　　MA Med PhD; 1973-82 training at Rogerian Inst La Jolla California; Former Director of Counsellor Training, Sheffield Hallam University, 1975-88
Personal Therapy:　　　　Ongoing
Supervision:　　　　　　　Ongoing
Counselling offered:　**General, Sexual, Marital, Psychotherapy**
Service for:　　　　　　　Individuals, Couples, Groups
Specific to:　　　　　　　Clergy/priests
Theoretical Approach:　　Rogerian, Jungian
Fees:　　　　　　　　　　£25 negotiable

ANDERS-RICHARDS Judith　　　　　　　　　　　　　　0691 653528
Laburnum Cottage, Gwern-y-Brenin, OSWESTRY SY10 8AS
Member of:　　　　　　BAC
Quals/training:　　　　　　BA; MA; MDiv Theology & Psychol; trained since '77 with Guild for Psychol Studies San Francisco; lecturer - Dip in Guidance(Sheffield Hallam University); ordained '77
Personal Therapy:　　　　Yes
Supervision:　　　　　　　Ongoing
Counselling offered:　**General, Crisis, Relationship, Psychotherapy**
Service for:　　　　　　　Individuals, Couples
Specific to:　　　　　　　Women, Clergy/priests
Theoretical Approach:　　Jungian, Rogerian
Fees:　　　　　　　　　　£20 negotiable

COOPER Jacqueline　　　　　　　　　　　　　　　　　0692 655808
Leahurst, 6 Park Street, OSWESTRY SY11 2HD
Member of:　　　　　　BAC Acc, ITA
Quals/training:　　　　　　BAC Acc; BA Psychol; Cert Ed; RELATE trained; in contractual training in TA
Personal Therapy:　　　　Yes
Supervision:　　　　　　　Ongoing
Counselling offered:　**General, Marital, Relationship**
Service for:　　　　　　　Individuals, Groups, Couples
Theoretical Approach:　　TA
Fees:　　　　　　　　　　£20 (£7 groups) negotiable

Shropshire

ARNOLD Susan 0948 81 697
The Grange, Ellesmere, SHREWSBURY SY2 9DE
Member of: BAC
Quals/training: BA(Hons); Dip Couns (COMPASS); training in Gestalt, Primal Therapy, Bereavement; currently training in Psychosynthesis
Personal Therapy: Ongoing
Supervision: Ongoing
Counselling offered: General, Bereavement, Personal growth, Psychotherapy
Service for: Individuals
Theoretical Approach: Eclectic, Psychodynamic, Gestalt
Fees: £20

BLISS Sonia 0743 232745
31 Port Hill Gardens, SHREWSBURY SY3 8SB
Member of: BAC, WMIP
Quals/training: SRN; Cert Social Work 1971; 12 years experience in Psychodynamically Orientated Child Guidance Work
Personal Therapy: Yes
Supervision: Ongoing
Counselling offered: General, Marital
Service for: Individuals, Couples
Theoretical Approach: Analytical
Fees: £18 Negotiable

BUCHANAN-DUNNE Kevin 0952 094289
1 Lawford Close, Iron Bridge, TELFORD TF4 3RW
Member of: BAC
Quals/training: Cert Couns; Dip Curative Hypnotherapy
Personal Therapy: Ongoing
Supervision: Ongoing
Counselling offered: Stress, Career, Redundancy
Service for: Individuals, Couples, Families, Groups, Organisations
Theoretical Approach: Egan, Gestalt, Hypnotherapy, Jungian
Fees: Non stated

McGRATH Kevin 0952 433986
10 Jockey Bank, Iron Bridge, TELFORD TF8 7PD
Member of: BAC
Quals/training: BSc(Special); RELATE trained 1988; training in TA
Personal Therapy: Yes
Supervision: Ongoing
Counselling offered: General, Relationship, Sexual, Personal growth
Service for: Individuals, Couples
Theoretical Approach: Psychodynamic, Eclectic
Fees: £25

Shropshire

PRINGLE Diana 0952 432168
10 Jockey Bank, Ironbridge, TELFORD TF8 7PD
Member of:	**AHPP**
Quals/training:	RELATE trained; training in TA & Gestalt
Personal Therapy:	Ongoing
Supervision:	Ongoing
Counselling offered:	**General, Relationship, Psychotherapy**
Service for:	Individuals, Couples
Theoretical Approach:	Psychodynamic, TA
Fees:	£25

BAYNES Leila 0948 667881
26 Mill Street, WHITCHURCH SY13 1SE
Member of:	**BAC Acc**
Quals/training:	BAC Acc; BA Social Studies (Durham Univ) 1953; CQSW; CTA Training in Pastoral Couns '80
Personal Therapy:	Yes
Supervision:	Ongoing
Counselling offered:	**General, Relationship**
Service for:	Individuals, Couples
Theoretical Approach:	Gestalt, Person-centred, TA
Fees:	£20 sliding scale

Somerset

Organisations

WESSEX COUNSELLING SERVICE 0373 453044
Fairfield House, King Street, FROME BA11 1BH
Service:	General counselling for individuals including marital, bereavement, long and short term psychodynamic couns. Affiliate of WPF
Area served:	Wiltshire & border areas with Avon, Somerset & Dorset
Referral:	Self or others
Training of workers:	WPF training
Code of Ethics:	BAC, WPF
Management by:	Trustees
Fees:	£18 negotiable after init reg

SHARE (NCH) COUNSELLING SERVICES 0823 277133, 0823 332277
3 Upper High Street, TAUNTON TA1 3PX
Service:	Face to face and telephone counselling for 13-25 yr olds or parents for a variety of problems. Part-time branches at Bridgewater and Minehead. Open 9.30-5.30 in Taunton
Area served:	Taunton, Bridgewater & Minehead
Referral:	Self or others
Training of workers:	In service training plus public courses, ongoing supervision
Code of Ethics:	Agency's own code
Management by:	NCH
Fees:	None

AVALON, SOMERSET NHS TRUST 0823 432375
Clinical Psychology Service, Tone Vale Hospital, TAUNTON TA4 1DB
Service:	Brief & behavioural therapy, counselling & psychotherapy for individuals, couples, groups or families
Area served:	Somerset HA - Taunton, Wells & Yeovil
Referral:	Health Practitioner, Health/Soc Work Professional, Self
Training of workers:	Postgraduate Clinical Psychology
Code of Ethics:	BPS
Management by:	Avalon, Somerset NHS Trust
Fees:	None

Individual Practitioners

*Each individual is a **member of** one or more organisations eligible for entry into this directory. BAC Accredited Counsellors and Recognised Supervisors are shaded.*

THOMAS Madeleine 0278 671595
Ashford Lodge, Cannington, BRIDGWATER TA5 2NL
Member of:	BPS, BABCP
Quals/training:	BA; C Psychol
Personal Therapy:	Yes
Supervision:	Yes
Counselling offered:	General
Service for:	Individuals, Couples
Theoretical Approach:	Cognitive, Gestalt, Family therapy
Fees:	Negotiable

Somerset

SIVYER John 0278 653808
Wayland Farm, Stockland-Bristol, BRIDGWATER TA5 2PY
Member of:	BAC
Quals/training:	BEd; Cert Ed; Dip Couns (Herts Univ, Minster Centre & N Herts Coll); presently training at metanoia
Personal Therapy:	Yes
Supervision:	Ongoing
Counselling offered:	**General, Psychotherapy**
Service for:	Individuals, Groups
Theoretical Approach:	Integrative, Person-centred, Gestalt, Psychodynamic
Fees:	£2 - £30 negotiable

PULLIN Andrew 0373 472170
85 Weymouth Road, FROME BA11 1HJ
Member of:	BAC
Quals/training:	Trained with Herts & Beds Pastoral Foundation 1981-4; IGA 1988-93; Cert Supervision (WPF) 1993
Personal Therapy:	Yes
Supervision:	Ongoing
Counselling offered:	**General, Bereavement, Group analysis, Supervision**
Service for:	Individuals, Groups
Specific to:	Staff
Theoretical Approach:	Analytic
Fees:	£22 Negotiable

HOWE Patti 0458 833864
27 Roman Way, GLASTONBURY BA6 8AB
Member of:	BAC Acc
Quals/training:	BAC Acc; BA; 1975 CQSW; 1985 Dip Psychosynthesis (PET)
Personal Therapy:	Ongoing
Supervision:	Ongoing
Counselling offered:	**General, Psychotherapy**
Service for:	Groups, Individuals, Couples, Families
Specific to:	Women
Theoretical Approach:	Integrative
Other languages:	French
Fees:	£20 negotiable for lower incomes

PARFITT Will 0458 833864
27 Roman Way, GLASTONBURY BA6 8AB
Member of:	BAC
Quals/training:	Dip Psychosynthesis (PET) 1981; Memb AAPP
Personal Therapy:	Ongoing
Supervision:	Ongoing
Counselling offered:	**Psychotherapy, Bodywork**
Service for:	Individuals, Couples, Groups
Theoretical Approach:	Integrative, Transpersonal
Fees:	£15 - £25 sliding scale

Somerset

CROUCH Anthony 0458 835333
3 Meadow View, GLASTONBURY BA6 8DY

Member of:	**BAC, BPS**
Quals/training:	BA (Psychol)'79; PhD (Applied Psychol); Cert Couns Skills; Lecturer in Couns(Counselling South West & Somerset College of Arts & Technology); Supervisor
Personal Therapy:	Yes
Supervision:	Ongoing
Counselling offered:	**General, Supervision**
Service for:	Individuals
Theoretical Approach:	Counselling Psychology
Fees:	£20 - £25

RENTOUL Robert 0458 51051
3 Compton Court, Compton Street, Butleigh, GLASTONBURY BA6 8SE

Member of:	**BAC, WMIP, BPS**
Quals/training:	Training Analysis, Seminars & Supervision; MA; BSc; Cert Theol; C Psychol; AFBPsS
Personal Therapy:	Yes
Supervision:	Ongoing
Counselling offered:	**Psychotherapy**
Service for:	Individuals
Theoretical Approach:	Psychoanalytic, Self-psychology (Kohut)
Fees:	On application

ETHERINGTON Kim 0278 760515
Southlea, Brent Street, Brent Knoll, HIGHBRIDGE TA9 4DT

Member of:	**BAC Acc**
Quals/training:	BAC Acc; MSc (Supervision & Training); Dip Couns (Univ of Bristol) 1988
Personal Therapy:	Ongoing
Supervision:	Ongoing
Counselling offered:	**General, Bereavement, Sexual abuse, Relationship, Supervision**
Service for:	Individuals, Couples
Specific to:	People with disabilities
Theoretical Approach:	Humanistic, Integrative
Fees:	£25 Less for those on low income

MOBSBY Sue 0643 862181
33 Bay Road, Porlock, MINEHEAD TA24 8NJ

Member of:	**BAC, BPS**
Quals/training:	Somerset Coun on Alcohol & Drugs trained '86; Cert Couns (RSA) '88; BA(Hons); ongoing Dip Psych Couns
Personal Therapy:	Yes
Supervision:	Ongoing
Counselling offered:	**General, Relationship, Alcohol**
Service for:	Individuals, Couples
Theoretical Approach:	Rogerian, Gestalt, Psychodynamic
Fees:	£15

Somerset

HASLAM Wendy   0749 880757
Shamba House, Doulting, SHEPTON MALLET BA4 4QE
Member of:	BAC
Quals/training:	NMGC; Dip CPC (Institute of Counselling)
Personal Therapy:	Yes
Supervision:	Ongoing
Counselling offered:	**General, Bereavement, Relationship, Abuse, Pastoral**
Service for:	Individuals, Couples, Families, Groups
Fees:	£15 - £20 sliding scale

SCOTT Judy   0749 880263
2 Manor Cottages, Chesterblade, SHEPTON MALLET BA4 4QX
Member of:	BAC
Quals/training:	1974 BSc; CQSW 1978; 1988 Dip & 1989 Adv Dip Gestalt Therapy (Pellin Inst); Currently training at metanoia for Diploma in Integrative Psychotherapy to finish 1995
Personal Therapy:	Yes
Supervision:	Ongoing
Counselling offered:	**General, Relationship, Bereavement, Loss**
Service for:	Individuals, Couples
Theoretical Approach:	Integrative
Fees:	£25 ind; £30 couples

PROCTER Ann   0458 223215
Coombe Quarry, Coombe Hill, Keinton Mandeville, SOMERTON TA11 6DQ
Member of:	BAC Acc
Quals/training:	BAC Acc; ex Psychiatric Social Worker; Dip CTP 1979
Personal Therapy:	Ongoing
Supervision:	Ongoing
Counselling offered:	**General, Psychotherapy, Cancer**
Service for:	Individuals, Couples, Groups
Theoretical Approach:	Transpersonal, Gestalt, TA
Fees:	£20

ROBINSON Louise   0832 337049
CIPC, 38 Belvedere Road, TAUNTON TA1 1HD
Member of:	**ITHP, AHPP, Member of UKCP Register**
Quals/training:	THP & AHPP (Acc); Trained 2yrs full-time counsellor (George Brown College, Toronto, Canada); 4yrs part-time Psychotherapist (Minster Centre)
Personal Therapy:	Ongoing
Supervision:	Ongoing
Counselling offered:	**General**
Service for:	Individuals, Groups
Theoretical Approach:	Psychodynamic, Integrative, Object relations
Fees:	£25

Somerset

WILLIAMS Nigel   0823 337 049
38 Belvedere Road, TAUNTON TA1 1HD
Member of:	**Minster Centre, ITHP, AHPP**
Quals/training:	Dip Psychotherapy (Minster Centre); Cert Supervision (WPF)
Personal Therapy:	Yes
Supervision:	Ongoing
Counselling offered:	**Psychotherapy, Long-term, Assessment, Supervision**
Service for:	Individuals, Groups
Theoretical Approach:	Humanistic, Analytical
Fees:	£25

WELLS Penny   0823 421319
Nutbeam Farmhouse, Blagdon Hill, TAUNTON TA3 7SL
Member of:	**BAC Acc, BASMT**
Quals/training:	BAC(Acc); RGN; NMGC trained '83 & Sex Therapy trained '86
Personal Therapy:	Ongoing
Supervision:	Ongoing
Counselling offered:	**General, Relationship, Sexual**
Service for:	Individuals, Couples
Theoretical Approach:	Psychodynamic
Fees:	£25 - £32

WELLS Roger   0823 421319
Nutbeam Farmhouse, Blagdon Hill, TAUNTON TA3 7SL
Member of:	**Guild of Psychotherapists**
Quals/training:	BSc(Hons); MBBS; GP Principal 16 years; student at Guild of Psychotherapists
Personal Therapy:	Ongoing
Supervision:	Ongoing
Counselling offered:	**Psychotherapy**
Service for:	Individuals
Theoretical Approach:	Analytic
Fees:	£22 - £25

MALLARD Monica   0984 631169
Birdsmoor Cot, 23 Five Bells, WATCHET TA23 0HZ
Member of:	**BAC**
Quals/training:	RSA Couns Cert; CQSW; Dip App Soc Studies
Personal Therapy:	Yes
Supervision:	Ongoing
Counselling offered:	**Bereavement, Loss, Marital, Stress, Short-term, Brief**
Service for:	Individuals, Couples, Families, Groups, Organisations
Theoretical Approach:	Client-centred
Fees:	£25

Somerset

SPEIRS John 0935 22488/822353
Yeovil Clinic of Comp Medicine, 54 The Avenue, YEOVIL

Member of:	**BAC**
Quals/training:	Dip Couns
Personal Therapy:	Yes
Supervision:	Ongoing
Counselling offered:	**General, Alcohol, Drugs, Relationship, Sexual**
Service for:	Individuals, Couples, Families
Specific to:	Young people
Theoretical Approach:	Rogerian
Fees:	£18 - £30 sliding scale

Staffordshire

Organisations

LICHFIELD COUNSELLING SERVICE 0543 414903
30a Tamworth Street, LICHFIELD WS13 6JJ
Service: Counselling, including marital work and psychotherapy for individuals and couples. Affiliated to WPF
Area served: South Staffs & West Midlands
Referral: Self
Training of workers: 2 year part-time cert (Leicester Univ validated), following WPF model, seminars, regular supervision, some personal therapy
Code of Ethics: BAC
Management by: Quarterly meeting of membership, Executive Committee, Advisory Council
Fees: Negotiable

MIND NORTH STAFFS 0782 46363
44 Church Street, STOKE-ON-TRENT ST4 1BL
Service: General counselling and groupwork
Area served: North Staffs Health Authority
Referral: Self or others
Training of workers: All qualified counsellors including personal growth. Regular supervision
Code of Ethics: BAC
Management by: Voluntary council
Fees: Donations

Individual Practitioners

*Each individual is a **member of** one or more organisations eligible for entry into this directory. BAC Accredited Counsellors and Recognised Supervisors are shaded.*

FERNS Patricia 0538 385245
Four Winds, Hillswood Avenue, LEEK ST13 8EG
Member of: BAC
Quals/training: Cert Couns; Cert Bereavement; Cert Stress Management
Personal Therapy: Yes
Supervision: Ongoing
Counselling offered: General, Bereavement, Career
Service for: Individuals, Couples
Theoretical Approach: Person-centred
Fees: £20

McLEOD John 0782 626814
1 Church Bank, Keele, NEWCASTLE ST5 5AT
Member of: BAC, BPS
Quals/training: MA; PhD Psychol; Dip Person-Centred Couns
Personal Therapy: Yes
Supervision: Ongoing
Counselling offered: General
Service for: Individuals, Couples
Theoretical Approach: Person-centred
Fees: £20 - £30

Staffordshire

CHRISTIAN Janet　　　　　　　　　　　　　　　　0785 284263
Bridge Farm, High Offley, STAFFORD ST20 0NE
Member of:	**BAC Acc**
Quals/training:	BAC(Acc); BA(Oxon); professional qualification in Social Work (Leicester Univ)'66; Cert in Individual & Family Counselling (B'ham Poly)'86; Cert Couns (Keele Univ)'91
Personal Therapy:	Yes
Supervision:	Ongoing
Counselling offered:	**General, Marital, Psychotherapy, Co-counselling**
Service for:	Individuals, Couples, Groups
Theoretical Approach:	Rogerian, Gestalt, Reichian
Fees:	£10 - £20 negotiable

PRATT Stephen　　　　　　　　　　　　　　　　0782 791582
11 Nelson Crescent, Cotes Heath, STAFFORD ST21 6ST
Member of:	**BAC, BPS**
Quals/training:	BA (Psychol); MSc in Psychological Counselling (University Surrey) 1987;
Personal Therapy:	Yes
Supervision:	Ongoing
Counselling offered:	**General, Relationship, Loss, Psychotherapy, Assertiveness**
Service for:	Individuals, Couples, Families, Groups
Theoretical Approach:	Eclectic
Fees:	£5 - £25

CORKER Enid　　　　　　　　　　　　　　　　0782 662655
55 The Avenue, Harpfields, STOKE-ON-TRENT ST4 6BT
Member of:	**AGIP**
Quals/training:	BA; RMN'84
Personal Therapy:	Yes
Supervision:	Ongoing
Counselling offered:	**Psychotherapy**
Service for:	Individuals, Groups
Theoretical Approach:	Jungian
Fees:	Sliding scale

MASON Ann　　　　　　　　　　　　　　　　0782 703581
Prospect Villa, 20 Newton Street, Basford, STOKE-ON-TRENT ST4 6JL
Member of:	**BAC**
Quals/training:	BEd; Couns Cert Keele Univ 1988-1991
Personal Therapy:	Ongoing
Supervision:	Ongoing
Counselling offered:	**General, Eating disorders, Substance abuse, Relationship**
Service for:	Individuals, Couples, Groups
Theoretical Approach:	Person-centred
Fees:	£15 - £25 negotiable

Staffordshire

HAYWOOD Rachel　　　　　　　　　　　　　　　　0782 773293
Hawthorn Gardens, Talke, STOKE-ON-TRENT ST7 1TD
Member of:	BPS
Quals/training:	BA (Hons) Psychol; MA Psychol; C Psychol; AFBPsS
Personal Therapy:	Yes
Supervision:	Ongoing
Counselling offered:	General, Crisis, Phobias, PTSD, Gender dysphoria, Psychotherapy, Supervision
Service for:	Individuals, Organisations
Specific to:	Women
Theoretical Approach:	Cognitive, Jungian, Gestalt, Rogerian
Fees:	£20 - £30

WHITTAKER Lesley　　　　　　　　　　　　　　　0782 392259
The Rectory, 7 Cheadle Road, Blythe Bridge, STOKE-ON-TRENT ST11 9PW
Member of:	BAC
Quals/training:	Cert Couns (Keele); training in Clinical Theology; Qualified user of Myers Briggs Type Indicator
Personal Therapy:	Ongoing
Supervision:	Ongoing
Counselling offered:	General, Personal growth
Service for:	Individuals
Specific to:	Christians
Theoretical Approach:	Person-centred, Eclectic
Fees:	Negotiable

DUNN Elizabeth　　　　　　　　　　　　　　　　　0782 372424
The Mount, Longton Road, Barlaston, STOKE-ON-TRENT ST12 9AA
Member of:	BAC
Quals/training:	Cert of Pastoral Counselling (Writtle Pastoral Foundation) 1983; external training with RELATE 1988; Cert in Counselling (Keele Univ) 1991
Personal Therapy:	Yes
Supervision:	Yes
Counselling offered:	General, Bereavement
Service for:	Individuals, Couples
Specific to:	Children
Other languages:	French, German
Fees:	Negotiable

CLEGG Alison　　　　　　　　　　　　　　　　　　0827 289538
The Dower House, 4 Park Lane, Bonehill, TAMWORTH B78 3HX
Member of:	BASMT, Member of UKCP Register
Quals/training:	RELATE trained; BASMT Accred; 2 yr Pastoral Care Course (Richmond Fellowship Trust); UKCP Registered Sexual & Marital Psychotherapist
Personal Therapy:	No
Supervision:	Ongoing
Counselling offered:	Relationship, Marital, Sexual
Service for:	Individuals, Couples
Theoretical Approach:	Psychodynamic, Behavioural
Other languages:	French
Fees:	£25

Staffordshire

COX Margaret   0827 383 212
The Rectory, Elford, TAMWORTH B79 9DA
Member of: **BAC Acc**
Quals/training: BAC(Acc); RELATE trained; Gestalt training(Irish Gestalt Inst)'84-'88
Personal Therapy: Yes
Supervision: Ongoing
Counselling offered: **General, Marital, Bereavement, Psychotherapy**
Service for: Individuals, Couples, Groups
Theoretical Approach: Psychodynamic, Gestalt
Fees: £20

Suffolk

Organisations

BURY PRACTICE FOR COUNSELLING & PSYCHOTHERAPY
0284 705772
64a Southgate Street, BURY ST. EDMUNDS IP33 2BJ
Service:	Flexible psychodynamic approach. Counselling and psychotherapy for individuals, couples and groups
Area served:	West & North Suffolk, to Cambridge
Referral:	Self or others
Training of workers:	Six year counselling course or equivalent, with clinical experience, personal therapy and ongoing supervision
Code of Ethics:	BAC, WPF
Management by:	Partnership of colleagues
Fees:	£18 - £25; assessment £25

SUDBURY COUNSELLING & THERAPY PRACTICE
0787 211095
Siam Surgery, COLCHESTER CO1
Service:	Individual, couple & group counselling & therapy covering a wide range of problems ie psychosomatic, stress related illness, abuse, anxiety, single parenting, relationship
Area served:	West Suffolk & Essex borders
Referral:	Self or others
Training of workers:	Minimum 3 year couns courses + 3 years personal therapy Ongoing supervision & training
Code of Ethics:	BAC
Fees:	£20 negotiable

HELPFULNESS
0728 832282
Spring Field, Mill Lane, Aldringham, LEISTON IP16 4PZ
Service:	Rogerian, Psychodynamic, Behavioural & TA for individuals. General counselling and for crisis, bereavement, child sexual abuse, personal growth
Area served:	East Suffolk
Referral:	Self or others
Training of workers:	CTA, WPF, CSCT (AEB)
Code of Ethics:	BAC, WPF
Management by:	Director RGN, BAC Acc
Fees:	Negotiable

MID-SUFFOLK MIND
0449 676337
1st Floor, 37-39 Ipswich Street, STOWMARKET IP14 1AH
Service:	General counselling
Area served:	Mid-Suffolk
Referral:	Self
Training of workers:	Trained by FDI Britain & Cambridge University, ongoing supervision - monthly peer group supervision plus monthly one to one supervision
Code of Ethics:	BAC
Management by:	Voluntary management committee
Fees:	Donations

Suffolk

Individual Practitioners
*Each individual is a **member of** one or more organisations eligible for entry into this directory. BAC Accredited Counsellors and Recognised Supervisors are shaded.*

JEFFREY Joy　　　　　　　　　　　　　　　　　　　　　　　0502 715428
40 Puddingmoor, BECCLES NR34 9PL
Member of:	BAC
Quals/training:	RELATE 1983; Dip Psychol Couns (Roehampton Inst) 1989; NFCC Conciliation
Personal Therapy:	Yes
Supervision:	Ongoing
Counselling offered:	**General, Marital, Conciliation**
Service for:	Individuals, Couples
Theoretical Approach:	Psychodynamic
Fees:	£15 - £25

HUGHES Linda　　　　　　　　　　　　　　　　　　　　　　0787 227195
16 Friends Field, Bures St Mary, BURES CO8 5LH
Member of:	BAC
Quals/training:	Dip Client-Centred Psychotherapy (PCAI); member of BAPCA
Personal Therapy:	Yes
Supervision:	Ongoing
Counselling offered:	**General, Anorexia, Bulimia, Sexual abuse, Stress, Adoption, Psychotherapy, Parenting problems, Fostering**
Service for:	Individuals, Couples, Groups
Theoretical Approach:	Client-centred
Fees:	£20

GRIMSEY Alan　　　　　　　　　　　　　　　　　　　　　　0638 715581
6 Mulberry Close, Mildenhall, BURY ST. EDMUNDS IP28 7LL
Member of:	BAC, ANLP (PCS)
Quals/training:	Dip Therapeutic Hypnosis & Psychotherapy (SHAP) 1985; NLP Practitioner 1987; NLP Master Practitioner 1992
Personal Therapy:	Ongoing
Supervision:	Ongoing
Counselling offered:	**General, Psychotherapy, Hypnotherapy**
Service for:	Individuals, Groups
Theoretical Approach:	Eclectic, NLP
Fees:	£25

HART Paul　　　　　　　　　　　　　　　　　　　ansaphone 0284 386 737
Little Gate House, Freewood Street, Bradfield St George, BURY ST. EDMUNDS IP30 0AY
Member of:	BAC, AHPP
Quals/training:	Body-oriented Pstchotherapy (Midsummer Assoc, Cambridge) in 3rd yr of certificated course
Personal Therapy	Yes
Supervision:	Ongoing
Counselling offered:	**General, Psychotherapy**
Service for:	Individuals
Theoretical Approach:	Humanistic, Psychodynamic, Transpersonal
Fees:	£15 - £20 sliding scale

Suffolk

SAGOE Vanessa   24hr ansa 0284 386737
Little Gate House, Freewood Street, Bradfield St George, BURY ST. EDMUNDS IP30 0AY
Member of:	**BAC, AHPP**
Quals/training:	Body Oriented Psychotherapy (3rd yr cert course, Midsummer, Camb); Relationship/cpl couns (RELATE) ongoing; workshops in Psychosynthesis, Massage & Aromatherapy, Meditation
Personal Therapy:	Yes
Supervision:	Ongoing
Counselling offered:	**General, Psychotherapy**
Service for:	Individuals, Couples
Theoretical Approach:	Humanistic, Psychodynamic, Transpersonal
Fees:	£15 - £20 sliding scale

MURPHY Maureen   ansasphone 0359 269419
12 Garden Fields, Troston, BURY ST. EDMUNDS IP31 1HA
Member of:	**BAC**
Quals/training:	BA; Cert Couns & Groupwork
Personal Therapy:	Yes
Supervision:	Ongoing
Counselling offered:	**General, Sexual abuse**
Service for:	Individuals, Groups
Specific to:	Women, Lesbians, Gays
Theoretical Approach:	Rogerian, Person-centred
Fees:	£15 - £25 Sliding Scale

WARRELL Jon   0284 754821
17 Sicklesmere Road, BURY ST. EDMUNDS IP33 2BN
Member of:	**BAC, BPS**
Quals/training:	C Psychol
Personal Therapy:	Yes
Supervision:	Ongoing
Counselling offered:	**General**
Service for:	Individuals, Couples
Theoretical Approach:	Client-centred, Psychodynamic
Fees:	£8 - £25 sliding scale

MOHAN Terry   0284 710505
20 Nelson Road, BURY ST. EDMUNDS IP33 3AG
Member of:	**ANLP (PCS)**
Quals/training:	Master Practitioner NLP; Dip Ericksonian Hypnosis; Training in Person-centred Couns; Practitioner in Psychometric Assessment (BPS); ANLP(PCS) Validated Psychotherapist
Personal Therapy:	Yes
Supervision:	Ongoing
Counselling offered:	**General, Brief, Crisis, Phobias, Work**
Service for:	Individuals, Couples, Families, Groups, Organisations
Theoretical Approach:	Eclectic
Fees:	£35 Concessions for unwaged

Suffolk

VAIZEY Philippa   0787 211095
14 The Street, Assington, COLCHESTER CO6 5LJ
Member of:	BAC
Quals/training:	Cert Couns & Groupwork (Cambridge Univ); WPF Couns course (Ipswich); Creative Groupwork, Transpersonal (London)
Personal Therapy:	Yes
Supervision:	Ongoing
Counselling offered:	**General, Psychotherapy, Short-term, Long-term, Anxiety, Relationship, Stress, Personal growth**
Service for:	Individuals, Couples
Specific to:	Single parents
Theoretical Approach:	Integrative, Transpersonal
Fees:	£20 negotiable

UPTON Sonia   0206 298 420
Friary Centre, Old Hall, East Bergholt, COLCHESTER CO7 6TG
Member of:	BAC Acc
Quals/training:	BAC Acc; Dip Couns Skills (SW London College) 1986
Personal Therapy:	Yes
Supervision:	Ongoing
Counselling offered:	**General, Supervision**
Service for:	Individuals
Theoretical Approach:	Eclectic
Other languages:	French
Fees:	£17 - £24 £22-30 supervision

SIMMONS Diana   0379 871 566
Mill House, Pye Hall Lane, EYE IP23 7NT
Member of:	NRHP
Quals/training:	Cert Hypnotherapy & Psychotherapy (CHP); NRHP (Assoc); Dip Ad
Personal Therapy:	Ongoing
Supervision:	Ongoing
Counselling offered:	**Hypnotherapy, Psychotherapy, Brief, Panic attacks, Anxiety, Confidence**
Service for:	Individuals
Theoretical Approach:	Eclectic
Fees:	£20

WADE Gloria   0394 286876
82 Ranelagh Road, FELIXSTOWE IP11 7HY
Member of:	BAC Acc
Quals/training:	BAC(Acc); CHC; DHC; APT Workshop Assocs; Orwell Couns
Personal Therapy:	Ongoing
Supervision:	Ongoing
Counselling offered:	**General, Sexual abuse, Psychotherapy**
Service for:	Individuals, Couples, Groups
Specific to:	Incest survivors, Minorities
Theoretical Approach:	Eclectic, Psychodynamic
Fees:	£25 some reduced fee clients

Suffolk

POWER Lilian 0473 215080
29 Orford Street, IPSWICH IP1 1NS
Member of: BAC, BPS
Quals/training: MSc Psychol Couns (Surrey Univ) 1988; ASC Acc:
Personal Therapy: Ongoing
Supervision: Ongoing
Counselling offered: **General, Psychotherapy, Loss, Anxiety, Depression, Short-term, Long-term**
Service for: Individuals
Theoretical Approach: Psychodynamic
Fees: £25 - £35 Initial Assessmnt fee £35

SEAL Raymond 0473 226650
IPSWICH
Member of: BPS
Quals/training: BA Psychol; trained in Hypnotherapy & Psychotherapy(SHAP)
Personal Therapy: Yes
Supervision: No
Counselling offered: **General, Relationship, Crisis**
Service for: Individuals, Couples
Fees: £25

NETTE-THOMAS Katy 0473 716 813
8 Humber Doucy Lane, IPSWICH IP4 3NP
Member of: BAC
Quals/training: Post Grad Dip Counselling (University East London) 1992
Personal Therapy: Ongoing
Supervision: Ongoing
Counselling offered: **General, Psychosomatic, Stress, Eating disorders**
Service for: Individuals
Theoretical Approach: Humanistic
Fees: £20

CALDWELL Annee
135 Woodbridge Road, IPSWICH
Member of: ITA
Quals/training: MA; Dip Hum Couns (Stockton PTI); completed 4 yr of Clinical Training in TA
Personal Therapy: Ongoing
Supervision: Ongoing
Counselling offered: **General, Short-term, Long-term, Assertiveness**
Service for: Individuals, Couples, Groups
Theoretical Approach: Rogerian, TA
Fees: £20

Suffolk

SMYTHE Ronald 0502 723413
94 Wangford Road, Reydon, SOUTHWOLD IP18 6NY
Member of: BAC, IPC
Quals/training: MA; Trained with CTA; Dip RF; APCC Acc Supervisor
Personal Therapy: Ongoing
Supervision: Ongoing
Counselling offered: General
Service for: Individuals, Couples, Families
Theoretical Approach: Analytical
Fees: £3 - £15 dependent on income

DONOVAN Louise 0502 723 056
1 Church Farm Barns, Wangford Road, Reydon, SOUTHWOLD IP18 6PB
Member of: BAC
Quals/training: BA Psychol; Cert in Psychodynamic Counselling (WPF)
Personal Therapy: Ongoing
Supervision: Ongoing
Counselling offered: General, Bereavement, Long-term, Short-term, Crisis
Service for: Individuals
Theoretical Approach: Psychodynamic, Jungian
Fees: £20 sliding scale

VAIZEY Phillipa 0787 70444
Siam Surgery, SUDBURY CO10
Member of: BAC
Quals/training: Cert in Couns & Groupwork(Camb Univ); WPF Couns Course (Ipswich); Creative Groupwork; Transpersonal(London)
Personal Therapy: Yes
Supervision: Ongoing
Counselling offered: General, Psychotherapy, Brief, Short-term, Stress, Anxiety, Relationship, Personal growth
Service for: Individuals, Couples, Groups
Specific to: Single parents
Theoretical Approach: Integrative, Transpersonal
Fees: £20 negotiable

CRAIB Ian 0787 310210
Mill House, Bulmer Road, SUDBURY CO10 7EZ
Member of: LCP
Quals/training: PhD Sociology (Univ of Manchester)'73; Associate (Group) LCP '87; Associate Member GAS
Personal Therapy: Yes
Supervision: Ongoing
Counselling offered: Psychotherapy
Service for: Groups
Theoretical Approach: Eclectic, Psychodynamic
Fees: Variable

Suffolk

CLARK Isobel 0787 280648
5-6 School Barn Cottages, Pentlow, SUDBURY CO10 7JN
Member of:	BAC
Quals/training:	WPF affiliated training, Ipswich 1988; WPF Cert of Competence 1991
Personal Therapy:	Yes
Supervision:	Ongoing
Counselling offered:	**General, Bereavement**
Service for:	Individuals, Groups
Theoretical Approach:	Psychodynamic, Jungian
Fees:	£12 - £18 sliding scale

BOATWRIGHT Christine 0787 269694
Little Hickbush, Great Henny, SUDBURY CO10 7LU
Member of:	BAC
Quals/training:	Cert Person-Centred Couns; Dip Person-Centred Couns
Personal Therapy:	Yes
Supervision:	Ongoing
Counselling offered:	**General, Anxiety, Stress, Depression, Bereavement, HIV, AIDS, Phobias**
Service for:	Individuals
Theoretical Approach:	Person-centred, Eclectic
Fees:£	16 Negotiable

FIRTH Gail 0394 380254
Crosstrees, Broom Heath, Sandy Lane, WOODBRIDGE IP12 4DL
Member of:	BAC Acc
Quals/training:	BAC Acc; Dip Person-centred Couns & Psychotherapy; Memb Lapis Fellowship
Personal Therapy:	Yes
Supervision:	Ongoing
Counselling offered:	**Anorexia, Bulimia, Phobias, Self-esteem, Depression, Stress, Relationship**
Service for:	Individuals, Families, Groups
Theoretical Approach:	Person-centred
Fees:	£28 negotiable

COULSON Christopher J ansaphone 0394 388222
12 Moorfield Road, WOODBRIDGE IP12 4JN
Member of:	AHPP
Quals/training:	Cambridge Psychotherapy Institute (Massachusetts) - 14 yrs; AHPP Acc
Personal Therapy:	Yes
Supervision:	Ongoing
Counselling offered:	**General, Psychotherapy, Relationship, Supervision**
Service for:	Individuals, Couples, Families, Groups, Organisations
Theoretical Approach:	Psychodynamic, Humanistic
Fees:	£30 initial interview free

Suffolk

Organisations

WALWOOD FAMILY CONSULTATION SERVICE 0737 352626
Walwood House, Park Road, BANSTEAD SM7 3ER

Service:	A private service offering help to families, couples & individuals, including children & adolescents, for emotional & behavioural problems, marital, divorce, bereavement
Area served:	Surrey & bordering counties
Other languages:	French
Referral:	Self, Health/Soc Work Professional
Training of workers:	All qualified in social work with post grad training in family/individual therapy
Code of Ethics:	BASW, AFT, IFT
Management by:	Management Committee
Fees:	£35. May be recoverable via medical insurance

SUTTON BEREAVEMENT SERVICE 081 641 8682
St Helier Hospital, Wrythe Lane, CARSHALTON SM5 1AA

Service:	Trained volunteer Bereavement Counsellors offer free support/counselling to anyone living in the London Borough of Sutton. Home visits arranged daytime or evening.
Area served:	London Borough of Sutton
Referral:	Self
Training of workers:	Training is ongoing following an initial induction course. Regular supervision
Code of Ethics:	BAC
Management by:	The Management Committee
Fees:	None

CROYDON YOUTH COUNSELLING SERVICE 081 680 0404
132 Church Street, CROYDON CR0 1RF

Service:	Short and long term counselling for young people aged 14-25
Area served:	Croydon and surrounding area
Referral:	Self
Training of workers:	All trained and professionally supervised
Code of Ethics:	BAC
Management by:	Management Committee
Fees:	None

CROYDON PASTORAL FOUNDATION 081 760 0665
Kyle House, 4 Frith Road, CROYDON CR0 1TA

Service:	Psychodynamically orientated individual, group, family and marital counselling
Area served:	Croydon & surrounding areas
Referral:	Self or others
Training of workers:	Minimum of 3 years part-time training plus personal therapy and supervision
Code of Ethics:	BAC
Management by:	Executive Committee
Fees:	Contributions negotiable

Surrey - North East
[CR and SM]

MORDEN PASTORAL COUNSELLING CENTRE   081 646 0192
St Lawrence Church Centre, London Road, MORDEN SM4 5QT

Service:	**Pastoral counselling on a one to one basis for adults.**
Area served:	London Boroughs of Merton, Sutton & nearby areas
Referral:	Self or others
Training of workers:	Trained according to WPF model; ongoing supervision
Code of Ethics:	BAC, WPF
Management by:	Council on management; part of work of local churches to the wider community
Fees:	According to means

SOUTH LONDON NETWORK FOR COUNSELLING & PSYCHOTHERAPY   081 641 1792
3 Bushey Road, SUTTON SM1 1QR

Service:	**Individual, group and workshop counselling & psychotherapy; professional supervision; affiliated to North London Network**
Area served:	London & Surrey
Referral:	Self or others
Training of workers:	Pellin Institute; includes personal therapy and supervision
Code of Ethics:	BAC, Therapists' Professional body
Management by:	Network
Fees:	£20 - £40

SUTTON PASTORAL FOUNDATION   081 661 7869
21A Cheam Road, SUTTON SM1 1SH

Service:	**General counselling for individuals aged over 16**
Area served:	Surrey, South London
Referral:	Self
Training of workers:	WPF Affiliated Centre, counsellors trained at SPF, WPF, a WPF centre or equivalent; regular supervision
Code of Ethics:	BAC, WPF
Management by:	Committee
Fees:	Donations

ST GEORGE'S COUNSELLING CENTRE   081 644 5280
c/o 59 Benfleet Close, SUTTON SM1 3SD

Service:	**General counselling for individuals, couples, groups and families**
Area served:	Sutton and surrounding area
Referral:	Health Practitioner, Self or others
Training of workers:	1 year training offered, followed by on-going training and supervision
Code of Ethics:	BAC
Management by:	St George's Counselling Centre Management Committee
Fees:	None (Donations)

Surrey - North East
[CR and SM]

Individual Practitioners
*Each individual is a **member of** one or more organisations eligible for entry into this directory. BAC Accredited Counsellors and Recognised Supervisors are shaded.*

SWEENEY Catherine 081 770 7387
24A Shorts Road, CARSHALTON SM5 3PS
Member of:	**BAC Acc, BPS**
Quals/training:	BAC Acc; BA(Hons) Psychol; BPS Practitioner; Memb SGCP; PGCE
Personal Therapy:	Yes
Supervision:	Ongoing
Counselling offered:	**General, Bereavement, Crisis, Addiction, Redundancy**
Service for:	Individuals, Couples, Groups
Specific to:	Health care professionals
Theoretical Approach:	Integrative, Existential
Fees:	£25 free for unemplyed/unwaged

THISTLE Roger 081 395 5304
36 Harrow Road, CARSHALTON SM5 3QQ
Member of:	**IPC**
Quals/training:	Dip WPF 1986
Personal Therapy:	Yes
Supervision:	Ongoing
Counselling offered:	**General, Stress, Relationship**
Service for:	Individuals
Theoretical Approach:	Eclectic, Psychodynamic
Fees:	On request

HAYFIELD Elaine 0959 574747
15 Raglan Precinct, Town End, CATERHAM CR3 5UG
Member of:	**BAC**
Quals/training:	Assertion(RWTA)'90; RET '90; Cruse Bereavement training; Adolescent '91; Drug & Alcohol(SADAS)'93
Personal Therapy:	Ongoing
Supervision:	Ongoing
Counselling offered:	**Addiction, Anxiety, Substance abuse, Alcohol, Eating disorders, Grief, Relationship**
Service for:	Individuals, Organisations
Theoretical Approach:	Eclectic, Behavioural
Fees:	£25 negotiable

DOOLEY Patricia 081 683 1041
43 Guildford Road, CROYDON CR0 2HL
Member of:	**BAC, IPC**
Quals/training:	WPF training completed 1980
Personal Therapy:	Yes
Supervision:	Ongoing
Counselling offered:	**General, Psychotherapy, Supervision**
Service for:	Individuals, Couples
Theoretical Approach:	Analytical
Fees:	£30 negotiable

Surrey - North East
[CR and SM]

SUFFOLK Toni 081 681 1802
142 Turnpike Link, Park Hill, CROYDON CR0 5NZ
Member of:	BAC, BPS
Quals/training:	BSc(Hons) Psychol; MSc Couns (London) '93
Personal Therapy:	Ongoing
Supervision:	Ongoing
Counselling offered:	**General, Anxiety, Child abuse, Crisis, Depression, Redundancy, Stress**
Service for:	Individuals, Organisations
Specific to:	Managers
Theoretical Approach:	Rogerian, TA, Gestalt, Egan, Cognitive
Fees:	£20 - £30 sliding scale

KIRSON Paula 081 667 1870
8 Dean's Close, CROYDON CR0 5PU
Member of:	NCHP, BAC
Quals/training:	Cert Hynotherapy & Psychotherapy (Nat Coll); NRHP (Assoc)
Personal Therapy:	Yes
Supervision:	Ongoing
Counselling offered:	**Depression, Stress, Eating disorders, Relationship, Anxiety, Phobias, Pain, Bereavement, Psychotherapy**
Service for:	Individuals
Theoretical Approach:	Eclectic
Other languages:	German
Fees:	£25

DUIGNAN K 081 763 1973
Centre for Mid-career Matters, 429 Brighton Road, SOUTH CROYDON CR2 6UD
Member of:	BAC
Quals/training:	BA(Psychology); BA(Economics); Dip in Career Guidance; Memb IPM & ICG
Personal Therapy:	Ongoing
Supervision:	Ongoing
Counselling offered:	**Career, Stress, Relationship**
Service for:	Individuals, Organisations
Theoretical Approach:	PCP
Other languages:	French, Irish
Fees:	£20 minimum

RABE Marie-Louise 081 656 7954
23 Addiscombe Court Road, CROYDON CR0 6TT
Member of:	BAC, ARBAS
Quals/training:	MA; Psychol/Sociology; trained Psychotherapist (Arbours Association)
Personal Therapy:	Ongoing
Supervision:	Ongoing
Counselling offered:	**Psychotherapy, Supervision**
Service for:	Individuals, Couples, Groups
Theoretical Approach:	Psychoanalytic
Other languages:	German
Fees:	£28 - £35 (£35-50) couples, negotiable

Surrey - North East
[CR and SM]

CHANDLER Diana   081 656 9209
c/o 115 Orchard Avenue, Shirley, CROYDON CR0 7NL
Member of:	BAC
Quals/training:	Cert Couns ICIP '84; Dip Humanistic Psychol IDHP '87; Dip Couns IP '90; trained nurse & teacher
Personal Therapy:	Ongoing
Supervision:	Ongoing
Counselling offered:	**General, Short-term, Long-term, Addiction, Relationship, Terminal illness, Bereavement**
Service for:	Individuals
Theoretical Approach:	Psychosynthesis, Humanistic
Fees:	£25 negotiable

LINTERN Fran   ansaphone 081 657 0429
128 Osward, Courtwood Lane, Forestdale, CROYDON CR0 9HE
Member of:	BAC
Quals/training:	BA Cult & Soc Studies; various courses in general & addiction couns; bereavement, co-dependency & child integration work; ongoing Dip (Albany Trust)
Personal Therapy:	Ongoing
Supervision:	Ongoing
Counselling offered:	**General, Addiction, Co-dependency, Loss**
Service for:	Individuals
Theoretical Approach:	Psychodynamic, Behavioural
Fees:	£25 Negotiable

CUMMINS Eddie   081 646 8239
19 Beecholme Avenue, MITCHAM CR4 2HT
Member of:	BAC
Quals/training:	BA (Open Univ); MSc Psych Couns; Dip Couns (SW London College); RMN; RNT
Personal Therapy:	Yes
Supervision:	Ongoing
Counselling offered:	**General**
Service for	Individuals
Theoretical Approach:	Rogerian, Gestalt, Client-centred
Fees:	£15 - £25 negotiable

WHITTLE Alan   081 540 0201
117 Maycross Avenue, MORDEN SM4 4DF
Member of:	BAC
Quals/training:	Dip Pastoral Studies (Birmingham Univ) '68; 5 years training with Lincoln Clinic
Personal Therapy:	Yes
Supervision:	Ongoing
Counselling offered:	**General, Psychotherapy, Spiritual**
Service for:	Individuals
Specific to:	Religious
Theoretical Approach:	Freudian, Rogerian
Fees:	Sliding scale

Surrey - North East
[CR and SM]

ASHLEY Anne   081 660 3099
Timmynoggy House, 49 Godstone Road, PURLEY CR2 2AN
Member of:	BAC Acc
Quals/training:	BAC(Acc); BA; '84 Pastoral Care & Couns (RF); '85 Arbours Assoc Student; ;86-90 NHS training placement Psychotherapy; '89 Psychol DS262(OU);currently SAP trainee
Personal Therapy:	Ongoing
Supervision:	Ongoing
Counselling offered:	Psychotherapy
Service for:	Individuals
Theoretical Approach:	Person-centred
Fees:	Negotiable

MEPSTED Anne, Mrs   081 660 2918
16 Yew Tree Walk, PURLEY CR8 1HB
Member of:	BAC
Quals/training:	Affiliate Cert (IPC/WPF); Cruse training
Personal Therapy:	Ongoing
Supervision:	Ongoing
Counselling offered:	General, Bereavement
Service for:	Individuals
Theoretical Approach:	Psychodynamic, Rogerian
Fees:	£20 - £25 Sliding Scale

DAGLEISH John   081 660 6060
42 Brancaster Lane, PURLEY CR8 1HF
Member of:	BAC
Quals/training:	Southwark Ordination Course; Dip Religious Studies London; Bishop Southwark Cert Pastoral Care & Couns; Southwark Spiritual Direction Course
Personal Therapy:	Ongoing
Supervision:	Ongoing
Counselling offered:	General, Bereavement, Crisis, Personal growth
Service for:	Individuals, Groups
Theoretical Approach:	Jungian, Psychodynamic
Other languages:	French
Fees:	Negotiable

FRANKEL Joyce   081 668 8441
106A Higher Drive, PURLEY CR8 2HL
Member of:	BAC
Quals/training:	Sociology Dip 1955; Applied Social Studies 1965; IGA 1973; IFT 1981; Maudsley Hosp. Supervision & Consultation 1992; GAS (Assoc)
Personal Therapy:	Ongoing
Supervision:	Ongoing
Counselling offered:	General, Crisis, Relationship, Bereavement
Service for:	Individuals, Groups
Theoretical Approach:	Eclectic
Fees:	£20 - £30 sliding scale

Surrey - North East
[CR and SM]

PITCEATHLY Hamish
081 657 3624
13 Beechwood Road, Sanderstead, SOUTH CROYDON CR2 0AE
Member of:	BAC
Quals/training:	MA (Oxon); Dip Primary Cause Analysis by Hypnosis; President Soc for Primary Cause Analysis by Hypnosis founded 1986:
Personal Therapy:	Yes
Supervision:	Ongoing
Counselling offered:	**General, Psychotherapy, Hypnotherapy**
Service for:	Individuals, Couples
Theoretical Approach:	Analytical
Fees:	£30 Reduced in hardship cases

LANSBERRY Christopher
081 668 2078
35 Kendall Avenue South, Sanderstead, SOUTH CROYDON CR2 0QR
Member of:	BAC
Quals/training:	BA Mod Lang; CQSW; Dip Couns
Personal Therapy:	Ongoing
Supervision:	Ongoing
Counselling offered:	**General, Bereavement, Crisis**
Theoretical Approach:	Psychodynamic
Other languages:	French
Fees:	Negotiable

STEMBRIDGE David
081 688 3947
10 Lismore Road, SOUTH CROYDON CR2 7QA
Member of:	LCP
Quals/training:	CQSW '69; Cert Individual Psychotherapy(LCP)'81
Personal Therapy:	Yes
Supervision:	Yes
Counselling offered:	**Psychotherapy**
Service for:	Individuals
Theoretical Approach:	Psychoanalytic
Fees:	£20 - £30

CLAXTON Brenda
081 686 1694
8 High Beech, SOUTH CROYDON CR2 7QB
Member of:	BAC Acc
Quals/training:	BAC Acc; NMGC trained; bereavement training; currently training in psychotherapy (Minster Centre)
Personal Therapy:	Ongoing
Supervision:	Ongoing
Counselling offered:	**General, Bereavement**
Service for:	Individuals
Theoretical Approach:	Psychodynamic
Fees:	£20 negotiable

Surrey - North East
[CR and SM]

JONES Alan 081 641 1792
3 Bushey Road, SUTTON SM1 1QR
Member of:	BAC, AHPP
Quals/training:	AHPP Acc; BSc Psychol; Assoc Pellin Inst; Founder - S London Network for Counselling & Psychotherapy
Personal Therapy:	Yes
Supervision:	Ongoing
Counselling offered:	General, Psychotherapy, Supervision
Service for:	Individuals, Couples, Groups, Families
Theoretical Approach:	Humanistic, Existential, Integrative
Fees:	£20 - £40 dependent on income

JONATHAN Arthur Dr 081 641 1601
The Jays, 27 Aultone Way, SUTTON SM1 3LD
Member of:	BAC
Quals/training:	MA; MSc; PhD Psychol; MA Psychotherapy & Couns (Antioch Univ); Adv Dip Existential Psychotherapy; Memb SEA
Personal Therapy:	Ongoing
Supervision:	Ongoing
Counselling offered:	General, Psychotherapy
Service for:	Individuals, Couples
Theoretical Approach:	Existential
Fees:	£25 - £35

CARDEW David 081 644 5280
Grasmere, 59 Benfleet Close, SUTTON SM1 3SD
Member of:	BAC Acc
Quals/training:	BAC Acc; BA Theology with pastoral care and couns 1959; many short courses including 1 year psychology
Personal Therapy:	No
Supervision:	Ongoing
Counselling offered:	General, Bereavement, Stress
Service for:	Individuals, Couples, Families, Groups
Theoretical Approach:	Eclectic
Fees:	Free or donations to counselling centre

CARDEW Patricia 081 644 5280
Grasmere, 59 Benfleet Close, SUTTON SM1 3SD
Member of:	BAC Acc
Quals/training:	BAC(Acc); 1951 Dip Ed with Sociology and Psychol; many short courses inc psychol; counsellor in schools, colleges, couns centres since '51
Personal Therapy:	No
Supervision:	Ongoing
Counselling offered:	General, Anorexia, Bulimia, Marital, Bereavement
Service for:	Individuals, Couples, Families, Groups
Theoretical Approach:	Eclectic
Fees:	Free or donations to counselling centre

Surrey - North East
[CR and SM]

COHEN Michael
081 643 4925
12 Fairford Court, Grange Road, SUTTON SM2 6RY
Member of:	BAC
Quals/training:	Dip Hypnotherapy & Psychotherapy '86; Dip Eriksonian Hypnosis & NLP '88; Cert in Adlerian Couns '90
Personal Therapy:	Yes
Supervision:	Ongoing
Counselling offered:	**General, Hypnotherapy, Sexual, Psychotherapy, Stress management**
Service for:	Individuals
Theoretical Approach:	Eclectic
Fees:	£30

CHESSELL Susan Tak Chiu
081 661 1803
76a Grange Road, SUTTON SM2 6SN
Member of:	BAC
Quals/training:	MSc Applied Social Studies; BSc Psychol; RMN; CQSW; Dip Couns(SW London College); training in Family Therapy IFT; KCC
Personal Therapy:	Yes
Supervision:	Ongoing
Counselling offered:	**General, Relationship, Marital, Crisis, Cross/multi-cultural**
Service for:	Individuals, Couples, Families
Specific to:	Women, Chinese
Theoretical Approach:	Rogerian, Family therapy
Other languages:	Cantonese
Fees:	£15 - £20 negotiable

DUDLEY Valerie
081 669 1966
15 Woodcote Avenue, WALLINGTON SM6 0QR
Member of:	BAC
Quals/training:	Dip Ed; Dip Couns; training in TA & in Gestalt ongoing (metanoia)
Personal Therapy:	Ongoing
Supervision:	Ongoing
Counselling offered:	**General, Crisis, Bereavement, Psychotherapy**
Service for:	Individuals, Couples
Theoretical Approach:	Rogerian, Gestalt, TA
Fees:	£18 - £25 sliding scale

NATHAN Lesley
081 669 2439
33 Woodcote Avenue, WALLINGTON SM6 0QU
Member of:	BAC
Quals/training:	CQSW 1985; Dip Applied Social Studies; Dip Couns (Croydon College) 1991
Personal Therapy:	Ongoing
Supervision:	Ongoing
Counselling offered:	**General, Marital**
Service for:	Individuals
Theoretical Approach:	Rogerian
Fees:	£20 negotiable

Surrey - North East
[CR and SM]

TOWNSEND Mrs Clare   **081 669 9250**
2 Park Road, Hackbridge, WALLINGTON SM6 7ER

Member of:	**BAC Acc**
Quals/training:	BAC Acc; Dip Couns; DHA Couple Therapy Training; Hon Psychotherapist at Guy's Hospital 1990-92
Personal Therapy:	Ongoing
Supervision:	Ongoing
Counselling offered:	**Psychotherapy**
Service for:	Individuals, Couples
Specific to:	Couples with co-therapist
Theoretical Approach:	Psychoanalytic
Fees:	£20 - £25, couples on request

Surrey - North West
[KT and TW]

Organisations

CONNEXIONS 081 977 7280
1 Burtons Road, Hampton Hill, HAMPTON TW12 1DB
Service:	Individual, couple and family therapy/counselling, family mediation, eating disorders
Area served:	North, West, South West London, Surrey & Middlesex
Referral:	Self
Training of workers:	All are members of AFT, 4 have KCC Dip in Systemic Therapy, 3 are CQSWs, 1 is a Consultant Psychiatrist; regular supervision
Code of Ethics:	KCC
Management by:	Consortium
Fees:	£50 - £150 £25 individuals

ELM THERAPISTS, THE 081 946 1097
45a High Street, Wimbledon, LONDON SW19
Service:	**Counselling for marital, sexual, family and personal problems**
Area served:	London & Home Counties
Referral:	Self or others
Training of workers:	Therapists are fully trained in individual marital/sexual therapy; regular supervision
Code of Ethics:	BAC
Management by:	Counsellor Group
Fees:	£25 minimum

RICHMOND COUNSELLING CENTRE 081 948 3898
77 Church Road, RICHMOND TW10 6LX
Service:	**Therapy for individuals, couples or families with relationship or sexual difficulties**
Area served:	S W London
Referral:	GP, Self
Training of workers:	Professionally trained with regular supervision. BASMT Acc
Code of Ethics:	BASMT
Management by:	Private centre
Fees:	Subject to contract

ARK THERAPY CENTRE ansaphone 081 399 8838, 081 390 8991
27 Victoria Avenue, SURBITON KT6 5DL
Service:	General; addiction; co-dependency; marital and sexual counselling for individuals and couples; bereavement; eating disorders
Area served:	London and Surrey
Referral:	Self or others
Training of workers:	Trained by Albany Trust and Drug & Alchohol Foundation. Personal therapy and ongoing supervision
Code of Ethics:	BAC
Management by:	The counsellors
Fees:	£10 - £20 sliding scale

Surrey - North West
[KT and TW]

SURREY COUNSELLORS   081 398 1741
25 Effingham Road, Long Ditton, SURBITON KT6 5JZ
Service:	**General counselling for individuals, couples or groups**
Area served:	Surbiton(081 398 1741) Egham(0748 33480)
Referral:	Self or others
Training of workers:	All have relevant training and qualifications
Code of Ethics:	BAC
Management by:	Group
Fees:	£24

THAMESIDE COUNSELLING ASSOCIATES   081 979 9149, 081 398 1133
6 Lime Tree Avenue, THAMES DITTON KT7 0NA
Service:	**Group of counsellors providing personal and relationship counselling based on a psychodynamic/integrative approach**
Area served:	Kingston, Richmond & NW Surrey
Referral:	Self
Training of workers:	WPF or affiliated centre; ongoing supervision; personal therapy
Code of Ethics:	BAC
Management by:	The counsellors
Fees:	£20 Negotiable

CONCERN COUNSELLING SERVICE   081 398 3193, 0483 31472
Westward Ho, Church Lane, THAMES DITTON KT7 0NL
Service:	**General, relationship, bereavement, abortion counselling; relaxation techniques taught; Ante-natal and Post-natal couples; Individuals, couples, groups**
Area served:	Kingston, Esher, Thames Ditton, Guildford
Referral:	Self or others
Training of workers:	Personal & Pastoral Couns Cert, RELATE, Cruse training, & training in relaxation techniques; ongoing supervision
Code of Ethics:	BAC
Management by:	The Group of Counsellors
Fees:	£20 £25 couples, negotiable

NORTH SURREY COUNSELLING   081 391 0784, 081 398 1053, 081 330 2118
The Old Vicarage, Church Road, WORCESTER PARK KT4 7RZ
Service:	**General counselling for individuals and couples. Supervision**
Area served:	North Surrey & SW London
Referral:	Self or others
Training of workers:	All qualified counsellors
Code of Ethics:	BAC
Management by:	Counselling group
Fees:	£15 - £30

Surrey - North West
[KT and TW]

Individual Practitioners
*Each individual is a **member of** one or more organisations eligible for entry into this directory. BAC Accredited Counsellors and Recognised Supervisors are shaded.*

O'DELL Tricia 0932 851897
Lichfield, 161 New Haw Road, ADDLESTONE KT15 2DP
Member of: BAC, IPC
Quals/training: BA(Hons) Sociology; Full Memb IPC/WPF; Training in Supervision (WPF)
Personal Therapy: Yes
Supervision: Ongoing
Counselling offered: General, Psychotherapy, Supervision
Service for: Individuals
Theoretical Approach: Psychoanalytic
Fees: £27

HANSON Anne 0932 346281
13 Faris Barn Drive, Woodham, ADDLESTONE KT15 3DZ
Member of: BAC
Quals/training: -
Personal Therapy: Yes
Supervision: Ongoing
Counselling offered: General, Marital, Sexual, Addiction, Gender dysphoria
Theoretical Approach: Client-centred
Fees: £20 - £35 sliding scale

KENNEDY Tony 0372 272756
51 Ottways Lane, ASHTEAD KT21 2PS
Member of: BAC
Quals/training: MA Oxon; Dip Ed; Dip Psychosynthesis Couns & Psychotherapy
Personal Therapy: Ongoing
Supervision: Ongoing
Counselling offered: General, Psychotherapy
Service for: Individuals, Couples, Families
Specific to: Adolescents
Theoretical Approach: Psychosynthesis
Fees: £20 - £25

MAXWELL Brian 081 397 3971
98 Leatherhead Road, CHESSINGTON KT9 2HY
Member of: BAC, IGA
Quals/training: Dip Couns Skills (SW London College); Memb IGA & Median Group Society (GAS)
Personal Therapy: Yes
Supervision: Ongoing
Counselling offered: General, Bereavement, Crisis, Loss, Trauma, Psychotherapy
Service for: Individuals, Couples, Groups, Organisations
Specific to: People with disabilities
Theoretical Approach: Psychodynamic
Fees: £20 - £40 Couples, groups negotiated

Surrey - North West
[KT and TW]

WEITZ Philippa 081 941 1364, 0273 693275
Flat 3, 10 Matham Road, EAST MOLESEY KT8 0SU
Member of:	BAC
Quals/training:	MSc Psychol Couns (Surrey Univ) '87
Personal Therapy:	Ongoing
Supervision:	Ongoing
Counselling offered:	**General, Psychotherapy, Bereavement, Sexual abuse, Psychosomatic**
Service for:	Individuals, Couples, Groups
Specific to:	Gays
Theoretical Approach:	Eclectic
Other languages:	French
Fees:	£30 negotiable, also in Brighton

THORNTON Susanne 0784 433480
Ivy Cottage, Clockhouse Lane East, EGHAM TW20 8PF
Member of:	BAC
Quals/training:	MA Humanistic Psychol; Cert Couns Surrey Univ 1987; courses since 1973 in Transpersonal Psychol, Bioenergetics, Sexuality; Action Profile Practitioner
Personal Therapy:	Ongoing
Supervision:	Ongoing
Counselling offered:	**General, Movement therapy, Sexual, Assertiveness, Stress management**
Service for:	Individuals, Couples, Groups
Fees:	£20 - £25 sliding scale

EDMONDS Jean 0737 352652
The Laurels, 68 Epsom Lane North, Epsom Downs, EPSOM KT18 5QA
Member of:	BAC
Quals/training:	Cert Couns (East Surrey Coll)
Personal Therapy:	Ongoing
Supervision:	Ongoing
Counselling offered:	**General, Loss, Bereavement, Relationship, Stress management**
Service for:	Individuals, Couples
Theoretical Approach:	Client-centred, Eclectic
Fees:	£20 (£25 initial consultation)

LYNCH Dian 0737 357783
29 Merland Rise, Epsom Downs, EPSOM KT18 5RY
Member of:	BAC
Quals/training:	Adv Dip Psychometric Testing & Couns at Work; AIPM; Couns Skills Course (St George's Couns Centre)
Personal Therapy:	Yes
Supervision:	Ongoing
Counselling offered:	**General, Marital, Bereavement, Employment**
Service for:	Individuals, Couples, Organisations
Theoretical Approach:	Eclectic
Fees:	£25 Negotiable

Surrey - North West
[KT and TW]

HUDSON Marjorie 0737 353211
108 Great Tattenhams, EPSOM KT18 5SE
Member of:	**BAC, IPC, Guild of Psychotherapists**
Quals/training:	Full memb IPC/WPF; Supervisor (WPF); Memb Guild of Psychotherapists; RELATE trained
Personal Therapy:	No
Supervision:	Ongoing
Counselling offered:	**General, Bereavement, Marital, Psychotherapy**
Service for:	Individuals
Theoretical Approach:	Eclectic, Psychodynamic
Fees:	£15 - £30 sliding scale

COFFEY V (Ms) 0372 721155
Emmaus Centre, 2 Dorking Road, EPSOM KT18 7LT
Member of:	**BAC**
Quals/training:	Post Grad Dip Couns & Pastoral Care (CNAA) 1981; Cert Couns Psycho-sexual and Relationships (Albany Trust) 1985-87; Course in Alcohol & Drug Bereavement 1988
Personal Therapy:	Yes
Supervision:	Ongoing
Counselling offered:	**General, Relationship, Bereavement, Alcohol**
Service for:	Individuals, Couples, Families
Theoretical Approach:	Rogerian, Eclectic
Fees:	£20 negotiable

SANSOM Lavender 071 373 0901, ansaphone 0372 727005
63 Hookfield, EPSOM KT19 8JQ
Member of:	**BAC**
Quals/training:	BA(Hons)Psych; Adv Dip Hypnotherapy; NLP; PGCE; CSCT/AEB Reg Trainer
Personal Therapy:	Yes
Supervision:	Ongoing
Counselling offered:	**General, Hypnotherapy, Psychotherapy, Depression**
Service for:	Individuals, Couples, Groups
Specific to:	Transsexuals, Children with special needs
Theoretical Approach:	Eclectic
Fees:	£35 negotiable Also at Merton

TYLEE Susan 0372 722767
18 Lower Hill Road, EPSOM KT19 8LT
Member of:	**BAC Acc, BPS**
Quals/training:	BAC Acc; BSc(Hons) Psychol; MSc Psychol Couns (Surrey Univ) 1988; Practitioner Memb BPS; CPsychol
Personal Therapy:	Yes
Supervision:	Ongoing
Counselling offered:	**General, Relationship, Marital, Bereavement, Personal growth, Supervision**
Service for:	Individuals, Couples
Theoretical Approach:	Humanistic, Integrative, Transpersonal
Fees:	£25 inds; £30 couples

Surrey - North West
[KT and TW]

ANDERMAN Margaret　　　　　　　　　　　　　　　　081 398 1868
39 Ember Lane, ESHER KT10 8EA
Member of:	BAC Acc
Quals/training:	BAC(Acc); SRN '61; SCM; Cert Couns(Surrey Univ) '88; Bereavement training hospice & Cruse; Dip Psychol. Couns.(Roehampton Institute)'92
Personal Therapy:	Ongoing
Supervision:	Ongoing
Counselling offered:	**General, Bereavement**
Service for:	Individuals, Couples
Theoretical Approach:	Integrative
Other languages:	Danish
Fees:	£25 negotiable

PHELPS Margaret　　　　　　　　　　　　　　　　081 398 7623
53 Ember Lane, ESHER KT10 8EF
Member of:	BAC
Quals/training:	CQSW 1974; Cert Couns 1978 & Psychotherapy training 1979-84 (LCIP)
Personal Therapy:	Yes
Supervision:	Ongoing
Counselling offered:	**General, Relationship, Crisis, Psychotherapy, Adoption**
Service for:	Individuals, Couples
Theoretical Approach:	Analytical
Fees:	£25 negotiable

LLOYD-JONES Judy　　　　　　　　　　　　　　　　081 398 4007
13 Lower Green Road, ESHER KT10 8HE
Member of:	BAC Acc
Quals/training:	BAC Acc; Professional Couns Course (Kingston CFE) 1988; Minnesota Model for Addiction (WACA) 1988
Personal Therapy:	Ongoing
Supervision:	Ongoing
Counselling offered:	**General, Relationship, Addiction, Eating disorders**
Service for:	Individuals, Couples, Groups
Theoretical Approach:	Client-centred, Humanistic
Fees:	£25 couples, £35/family, negotiable

AITKENS Judy　　　　　　　　　　　　　Ansaphone 081 398 5013
Mead Cottage, 51 Grove Way, ESHER KT10 8HQ
Member of:	BAC
Quals/training:	Cert Couns(Univ of Surrey); Cruse bereavement counsellor; supervisor; skills trainer; hospice trained; Dip Clinical Hypnosis
Personal Therapy:	Ongoing
Supervision:	Ongoing
Counselling offered:	**General, Bereavement, Crisis, Terminal illness, Supervision**
Service for:	Individuals, Groups
Theoretical Approach:	Eclectic, Hypnotherapy
Fees:	£20 - £35 sliding scale

Surrey - North West
[KT and TW]

BUTTERFIELD Janet 081 976 3119
Hampton Homeopathic Clinic, 87 High Street, HAMPTON TW12 2SX
Member of: BAC
Quals/training: Combined Cert Couns(CSCT); Physiology & Holistic Therapy (ITEC); Dip EHP & NLP; Cognitive Psychotherapy(BHR)
Personal Therapy: Ongoing
Supervision: Ongoing
Counselling offered: **General, Health, Stress, Phobias, Weight, Stop smoking, Anxiety, Confidence, Regression therapy**
Service for: Individuals, Couples, Groups, Organisations
Specific to: Women, Adolescents, Managers
Theoretical Approach: Cognitive, NLP, Ericksonian, Holistic
Fees: £25 - £50 sliding scale

PARKINSON Pamela 081 541 4447
7 Chesham Road, KINGSTON UPON THAMES KT1 3AG
Member of: BAC
Quals/training: Dip Human Sexuality (St George's Hospital) 1983; Dip Couns Skills (SW London College); SRN; Supervisor
Personal Therapy: Yes
Supervision: Ongoing
Counselling offered: **Marital, Sexual, Supervision**
Service for: Individuals, Couples
Theoretical Approach: Client-centred
Fees: £20 - £35

PERRIN Jane 081 546 3640
293 Kings Road, KINGSTON UPON THAMES KT2 5JJ
Member of: BAC
Quals/training: SRN; Cert Couns 1985; Dip Couns & Supervision (Roehampton) 1987; Intro yr in Groupwork (IGA) 1991; Supervision & Consultancy (Maudsley Hospital) 1991
Personal Therapy: Yes
Supervision: Ongoing
Counselling offered: **General, Relationship, Bereavement, Supervision**
Service for: Individuals, Groups
Theoretical Approach: Integrative
Fees: £15 - £20

CRICK Jill 081 546 0449
25 Durlston Road, KINGSTON UPON THAMES KT2 5RR
Member of: BAC
Quals/training: Dip Ed Maladjusted Children (London Univ); Couns & Advanced Couns Courses (Tavistock Inst & Chiswick Poly)'72-'75; Person Centred Art Therapy '86
Personal Therapy: Ongoing
Supervision: Ongoing
Counselling offered: **Psychotherapy, Art therapy**
Service for: Individuals, Groups
Specific to: Young people
Theoretical Approach: Psychodynamic, Rogerian
Fees: £20 sliding scale

Surrey - North West
[KT and TW]

JANI Marian 081 541 3817
93A Richmond Park Road, KINGSTON UPON THAMES KT2 6AF
Member of: BAC
Quals/training: Dip in Counselling & Therapy in Psychosynthesis
Personal Therapy: Ongoing
Supervision: Ongoing
Counselling offered: **General, Abuse, Bereavement, Psychotherapy**
Service for: Individuals
Theoretical Approach: Psychosynthesis, Client-centred
Fees: £15 - £25 Sliding Scale

HENSON Tricia ansaphone 081 541 0855
81 Canbury Avenue, KINGSTON UPON THAMES KT2 6JR
Member of: BAC
Quals/training: Dip Couns Skills (Southwark College)1992; Foundation course in working with couples (TIMS); also Way of Psychosynthesis, Alcohol and Anti-smoking training
Personal Therapy: Yes
Supervision: Ongoing
Counselling offered: **General, Addiction, Abortion, Infertility**
Service for: Individuals, Couples, Groups
Specific to: Women
Theoretical Approach: Rogerian, Psychosynthesis, Behavioural
Fees: £15 - £30 sliding scale

GRAYSON Juliet 081 974 5573
268 Canbury Park Road, KINGSTON UPON THAMES KT2 6LG
Member of: BAC, ANLP (PCS)
Quals/training: Cert Prof Couns; Master Practitioner NLP
Personal Therapy: Ongoing
Supervision: Ongoing
Counselling offered: **General**
Service for: Individuals
Theoretical Approach: Integrative, NLP
Fees: £30 negotiable

WINMILL Martin 081 541 0580
26 Manorgate Road, KINGSTON UPON THAMES KT2 7AL
Member of: BAC Acc
Quals/training: BAC(Acc); Cert in Prof Couns(Kingston Coll)'88; training in Gestalt psychotherapy(metanoia)'91; training in child sexual abuse '91
Personal Therapy: Ongoing
Supervision: Ongoing
Counselling offered: **General, Psychotherapy, Sexual abuse**
Service for: Individuals
Theoretical Approach: Psychodynamic, Gestalt, Integrative
Fees: £25

Surrey - North West
[KT and TW]

CAHN Albert   081 942 6956
10 Edgecoombe Close, Warren Road, KINGSTON UPON THAMES KT2 7HP
Member of:	**BASMT**
Quals/training:	RELATE trained'76; Marital/Sexual Therapy trainer RELATE '80 trainer in Hypnotherapy
Personal Therapy:	No
Supervision:	Ongoing
Counselling offered:	**General, Hypnotherapy, Sexual, Marital**
Service for:	Individuals, Couples
Fees:	£25 - £30

CAHN Malka   081 942 6956
10 Edgecoombe Close, Warren Road, KINGSTON UPON THAMES KT2 7HP
Member of:	**LCP, BASMT**
Quals/training:	RELATE trained 1976; trainer in Marital and Sexual Therapy RELATE 1980; 4 year training in Psychotherapy(LCP)
Personal Therapy:	Yes
Supervision:	Ongoing
Counselling offered:	**General, Psychotherapy, Marital, Sexual**
Service for:	Individuals, Couples
Theoretical Approach:	Eclectic
Fees:	£25 sliding scale

CARRINGTON Norah   ansaphone 081 974 5436
17 Haygreen Close, KINGSTON UPON THAMES KT2 7TS
Member of:	**BAC**
Quals/training:	Cert Couns(KCFE); ongoing training in Integrative Psychotherapy(metanoia)
Personal Therapy:	Ongoing
Supervision:	Yes
Counselling offered:	**General, Bereavement, Loss, Work, Short-term, Long-term**
Service for:	Individuals
Theoretical Approach:	Psychodynamic, Integrative
Fees:	£20 - £25

SHEMIS Kamilia   0372 84 3138
Corner Cottage, Danes Close, Oxshott, LEATHERHEAD KT22 0LL
Member of:	**BAC**
Quals/training:	BA Social Sciences; Dip Client-centred Psychotherapy; currently training as CAT therapist; memb BAPCA
Personal Therapy:	Yes
Supervision:	Ongoing
Counselling offered:	**General, Short-term, Psychotherapy**
Service for:	Individuals, Groups
Theoretical Approach:	Client-centred, Cognitive, Analytic
Fees:	£20 - £25 sliding scale

Surrey - North West
[KT and TW]

DRIVER June　　　　　　　　　　　　　　　　　　　　　　　0372 373045
West Folley, Hilltop Close, Windmill Drive, LEATHERHEAD KT22 8PD
Member of:	BAC
Quals/training:	Dip Couns Skills SW London College 1981; Cert Social Psychiatry & Dynamic Psychotherapy (Assoc of Social Psychiatry) 1983
Personal Therapy:	Yes
Supervision:	Ongoing
Counselling offered:	**General, Marital, Bereavement, Psychotherapy, Personal growth, Confidence**
Service for:	Individuals, Couples, Families
Theoretical Approach:	Rogerian, Egan
Fees:	£10 - £25 less in hardship cases

MACINTYRE Theresa　　　　　　　　　　　　　　　　　　0372 454310
64 Little Bookham Street, Bookham, LEATHERHEAD KT23 3AQ
Member of:	BAC
Quals/training:	BA(Hons) Soc Sc; CQSW; NLP Training 1986-88; currently in training Gestalt Psychotherapy
Personal Therapy:	Yes
Supervision:	Ongoing
Counselling offered:	**General, Bereavement, Crisis, Stress**
Service for:	Individuals, Couples, Organisations
Theoretical Approach:	Person-centred, Gestalt, NLP
Fees:	£15 - £30 Sliding Scale

BUCHANAN Dr Sarah-Jill　　　　　　　　　　　　　　　0483 284497
Hastings, Pennymead Drive, East Horsley, LEATHERHEAD KT24 5AH
Member of:	BAC
Quals/training:	Qualified Medical Doctor '58; Cert Couns (Surrey Univ) '87; Cert Transpersonal Psychol '87; Sexuality & Relationship (Albany Trust) 88
Personal Therapy:	Yes
Supervision:	Ongoing
Counselling offered:	**General, Relationship, Psychosexual**
Service for:	Individuals, Couples
Theoretical Approach:	Psychodynamic, Transpersonal
Fees:	£25 - £35

DANBURY Hazel　　　　　　　　　　　　　　　　　　　　081 942 2374
16 Lynton Road, NEW MALDEN KT3 5EE
Member of:	BAP
Quals/training:	Full Memb BAP & LCP 1978
Personal Therapy:	Yes
Supervision:	Ongoing
Counselling offered:	**General, Bereavement, Psychotherapy**
Service for:	Individuals, Couples
Theoretical Approach:	Psychoanalytic
Fees:	£25 sliding scale

Surrey - North West
[KT and TW]

DEBNEY Jacqueline   081 949 1182
18 Maria Theresa Close, NEW MALDEN KT3 5EF

Member of:	BAC
Quals/training:	Cert Counselling (Surrey Adult Education)1992; bereavement training
Personal Therapy:	Ongoing
Supervision:	Ongoing
Counselling offered:	**General, Bereavement, Relationship**
Service for:	Individuals, Couples
Specific to:	Women
Theoretical Approach:	Person-centred
Fees:	£20 negotiable

BROOKE Penelope   081 940 1098
34 Sheen Road, RICHMOND TW9 1AW

Member of:	BAC
Quals/training:	CQSW 1978; Dip Couns (metanoia); Completed advanced training in TA Psychotherapy & Supervision for Counsellors (metanoia)
Personal Therapy:	Ongoing
Supervision:	Ongoing
Counselling offered:	**General, Bereavement, Psychotherapy, Relationship, Supervision**
Service for:	Individuals, Couples
Specific to:	People with disabilities
Theoretical Approach:	Integrative
Fees:	£25 lower fees neg in hardship

TARSH Helen   081 948 1913
Wentworth House, The Green, RICHMOND TW9 1PB

Member of:	BAC Acc, TIMS
Quals/training:	BAC Acc; LLB; NMGC Trained; Pre-clinical Child Psychotherapy Training (TC); Dip Marital Psychotherapy (TIMS)
Personal Therapy:	Yes
Supervision:	Ongoing
Counselling offered:	**General, Marital, Psychotherapy**
Service for:	Individuals, Couples
Specific to:	Couples with co-therapist
Theoretical Approach:	Psychoanalytic
Fees:	£25 negotiable

CHALK Caroline   081 984 8562
3 The Little Green, RICHMOND TW9 1QH

Member of:	BAC, PET
Quals/training:	Dip in Psychosynthesis; Trainer in Counselling Skills
Personal Therapy:	Yes
Supervision:	Ongoing
Counselling offered:	**General, Bereavement, Abuse, Crisis**
Service for:	Individuals, Groups
Theoretical Approach:	Psychosynthesis, Eclectic
Fees:	£25 some concessions

Surrey - North West
[KT and TW]

SKINNER Vivienne — 081 948 3851
60 Hill Street, RICHMOND TW9 1TW
Member of:	BAC
Quals/training:	BEd; MSc; Dip Inst of Training & Development; Dip & Adv Dip Couns & Ges Therapy (Pellin); qualified trainer in Personal Development & Interpersonal Skills
Personal Therapy:	Ongoing
Supervision:	Ongoing
Counselling offered:	**General, Psychotherapy, Relationship, Career, Assertiveness, Bereavement**
Service for:	Individuals
Theoretical Approach:	Humanistic, Eclectic
Fees:	£25 - £30 sliding scale

CHANNON Michael T — 081 940 1092
2 Fabyc House, Cumberland Road, Kew, RICHMOND TW9 3HH
Member of:	IPC
Quals/training:	1985 Full Professional Member IPC/WPF
Personal Therapy:	Ongoing
Supervision:	Ongoing
Counselling offered:	**Psychotherapy, Marital**
Service for:	Individuals, Couples
Theoretical Approach:	Psychodynamic
Fees:	£22 negotiable

CURRA Jenny — 081 940 2046
1 Spring Grove Road, RICHMOND TW10 6EH
Member of:	BAC, IPC/WPF
Quals/training:	BA; Dip Memb IPC(WPF); currently working for Dip Supervision (WPF); ACAT
Personal Therapy:	Yes
Supervision:	Ongoing
Counselling offered:	**General, Relationship, Bereavement, Short-term, Long-term, Supervision**
Service for:	Individuals
Theoretical Approach:	Eclectic, CAT
Fees:	£18 - £28

WHITE John — 081 940 3586
8 Marlborough Road, RICHMOND TW10 6JR
Member of:	BAC
Quals/training:	Dip Psychosynthesis; training in Sports Psychology & Gestalt
Personal Therapy:	Yes
Supervision:	Ongoing
Counselling offered:	**General**
Service for:	Individuals, Groups
Specific to:	Business people, Sportsmen/women
Fees:	£30 negotiable

Surrey - North West
[KT and TW]

HEWETT Rachael 081 940 8010
Flat 4, 83 Mount Ararat Road, RICHMOND TW10 6PL
Member of:	**BAC**
Quals/training:	CQSW 1972; Dip Couns, 1989 & ongoing TA Psychotherapy training (metanoia); Adv training in supervision (metanoia & Roehampton)
Personal Therapy:	Ongoing
Supervision:	Ongoing
Counselling offered:	**General, Marital, Bereavement, Supervision**
Service for:	Individuals, Couples, Groups
Theoretical Approach:	Rogerian, TA
Fees:	£25 - £30

FELDSCHREIBER Lyn 081 948 2066
21 Montague Road, RICHMOND TW10 6QW
Member of:	**BAC**
Quals/training:	BA (Hons) Psychol; Post Grad Cert Ed; Dip Psychol Couns, Roehampton Inst
Personal Therapy:	Yes
Supervision:	Ongoing
Counselling offered:	**General, Bereavement, Relationship, Stress**
Service for:	Individuals
Theoretical Approach:	Client-centred
Fees:	£25 - £30 negotiable

CHANEY Gerry Alide 081 399 7699
1 Plymouth Court, 14 Cranes Park Avenue, SURBITON KT5 8BZ
Member of:	**BAC, MPTI**
Quals/training:	Couns training(metanoia)
Personal Therapy:	Yes
Supervision:	Ongoing
Counselling offered:	**General**
Service for:	Individuals
Theoretical Approach:	Rogerian, Person-centred
Other languages:	Dutch
Fees:	£10 - £15 sliding scale

ROCKLIFFE Elizabeth 081 390 3579
10 Avenue South, SURBITON KT5 8PJ
Member of:	**BAC Acc**
Quals/training:	BAC Acc; BA Cambridge; CQSW 1977; NMGC trained & Acc; Cruse Bereavement Counselling Course
Personal Therapy:	Yes
Supervision:	Ongoing
Counselling offered:	**General, Relationship, Bereavement, Depression**
Service for:	Individuals, Couples
Theoretical Approach:	Psychodynamic
Fees:	£16 - £26 negotiable according to income

Surrey - North West
[KT and TW]

MALONE Ronald   081 390 7529
27c Elgar Avenue, Tolworth, SURBITON KT5 9JH
Member of:	BAC Acc
Quals/training:	BAC Acc; Trained in Psychodynamic Couns, Relaitonship, marital & sexual problems, Depressive illnesses, Dip Hypnotherapy
Personal Therapy:	Yes
Supervision:	Ongoing
Counselling offered:	General, Marital, Relationship, Sexual, Depression, Hypnotherapy
Service for:	Individuals, Couples, Families
Theoretical Approach:	Rogerian
Fees:	£15 - £25 sliding scale

SCOTT Lena   081 399 7873
8 Maple Road, SURBITON KT6 4AB
Member of:	BAC Acc
Quals/training:	BAC Acc; CNAA Dip Soc Studies '85; Dip Prof Couns (KCFE)'88 WACA Cert Addiction '88
Personal Therapy:	Yes
Supervision:	Ongoing
Counselling offered:	Psychotherapy, Short-term, Long-term
Service for:	Individuals, Couples
Theoretical Approach:	Humanistic, Client-centred
Fees:	£25 (£30 assessment)

WILLIS Sally   081 399 3334
50d Maple Road, SURBITON KT6 4AE
Member of:	IGA
Quals/training:	BA((Hons)German & European Studies; qualified Group Analyst
Personal Therapy:	Yes
Supervision:	Ongoing
Counselling offered:	General, Psychotherapy, Eating disorders
Service for:	Individuals, Families, Groups
Specific to:	Adolescents
Theoretical Approach:	Psychodynamic
Other languages:	German
Fees:	£35 some reductions

KEITH Nina   081 390 2398
4 Exeter Court, Maple Road, SURBITON KT6 4AX
Member of:	BAC
Quals/training:	Prof Cert Couns (KCFE)
Personal Therapy:	Ongoing
Supervision:	Ongoing
Counselling offered:	General, Bereavement, Alcohol, Cancer
Service for:	Individuals
Theoretical Approach:	Rogerian, Psychodynamic
Fees:	£25 negotiable

Surrey - North West
[KT and TW]

DAUBENSPECK Viv   081 390 0504
14 St Leonards Road, SURBITON KT6 4DE
Member of: BAC
Quals/training: Cert Ed; Dip in Vocational Guidance & Counselling (East London Univ) 1977; Counsellor for 17 yrs
Personal Therapy: Yes
Supervision: Ongoing
Counselling offered: Bereavement, Health, Educational, Sexual, General
Service for: Individuals, Couples, Groups
Theoretical Approach: Eclectic, Rogerian
Fees: £30 - £35

THOMAS Diana   081 390 3894
Ground floor flat, 19 St Philips Road, SURBITON KT6 4DU
Member of: BAC
Quals/training: Cert Professional Couns (Kingston College FE)
Personal Therapy: Ongoing
Supervision: Ongoing
Counselling offered: General, Crisis, Addiction, Eating disorders, Problem solving
Service for: Individuals, Couples
Theoretical Approach: Jungian, Eclectic
Fees: £20 sliding scale

JACKSON Jennifer   081 399 8838
27 Victoria Avenue, SURBITON KT6 5DL
Member of: BAC
Quals/training: Training in Couns & Psychodynamic Couns (Albany Trust); training in addictive couns using Minnesota Method & Psychodynamic Approach (Drug & Alcohol Foundation)
Personal Therapy: Ongoing
Supervision: Ongoing
Counselling offered: General, Bereavement, Relationship, Sexual, Eating disorders
Service for: Individuals, Couples, Groups, Families
Specific to: People with language problems
Theoretical Approach: Freudian, Jungian
Fees: £10 - £20

DAVISON Judith   081 398 1741
25 Effingham Road, Long Ditton, SURBITON KT6 5JZ
Member of: BAC, RCSPC
Quals/training: Cert Personal & Pastoral Couns Univ of Surrey 1987; Dip Psychol Couns Roehampton Inst 1989
Personal Therapy: Ongoing
Supervision: Ongoing
Counselling offered: General
Service for: Individuals, Couples
Theoretical Approach: Integrative
Fees: £24

Surrey - North West
[KT and TW]

SAWARD Stephanie   081 390 1798
43 Arlington Road, SURBITON KT6 6BW
Member of:	BAC
Quals/training:	Dip Gestalt Therapy, Cert Supervision & Consultation; Analysis Training
Personal Therapy:	Yes
Supervision:	Ongoing
Counselling offered:	**General, Psychotherapy, Supervision**
Service for:	Individuals, Groups
Specific to:	Offenders
Theoretical Approach:	Kleinian, Freudian
Fees:	£20 negotiable

DUFFY Maria Bento   work 081 390 0545, home 081 399 7731
SURBITON KT6
Member of:	BPS
Quals/training:	BSc & Dip Psych; Trained with RF and in Transpersonal Psychol; Group analysis (Tavistock)
Personal Therapy:	Ongoing
Supervision:	Ongoing
Counselling offered:	**Psychotherapy, Short-term, Long-term**
Service for:	Individuals, Groups
Theoretical Approach:	Integrative, Psychodynamic
Other languages:	Portuguese
Fees:	Depending on circumstances

SPRINGALL Lynn   081 399 8838
27 Victoria Avenue, SURBITON KT6 5DL
Member of:	BAC
Quals/training:	Cert Professional Couns (Albany Trust) 1991; Course on Addictions, Relationships & Sexuality (Emmaus Centre); Samaritan
Personal Therapy:	Yes
Supervision:	Ongoing
Counselling offered:	**General, Addiction, Co-dependency, Crisis, Short-term**
Service for:	Individuals, Groups
Theoretical Approach:	Eclectic
Fees:	£20 negotiable

BENNION Jean   0737 812231
Milestone, 42 Downs Way, TADWORTH KT20 5DZ
Member of:	BAC
Quals/training:	CQSW; Psychiatric Social Worker in Child Guidance Service for 20 years; 3 year course in Psychotherapy for Social Workers (Tavistock); training in Marital & Family Therapy
Personal Therapy:	No
Supervision:	Ongoing
Counselling offered:	**Relationship, Personality disorders, Anxiety, Depression, Phobias**
Service for:	Individuals, Couples, Families
Theoretical Approach:	Psychoanalytic
Fees:	£15 - £20 Sliding scale

Surrey - North West
[KT and TW]

SMITHURST June   0737 351843
1 Oakdene, Copleigh Drive, Kingswood, TADWORTH KT20 6BN

Member of:	**NRHP**
Quals/training:	Hypnotherapy & Psychotherapy training (NCHP); MIMgt member
Personal Therapy:	Yes
Supervision:	Ongoing
Counselling offered:	**General, Stress, Management, Psychotherapy**
Service for:	Individuals
Specific to:	Managers
Theoretical Approach:	Integrative
Fees:	£15 - £30

REES-ROBERTS Diane   081 977 7282
12 Cambridge Crescent, TEDDINGTON TW11 8DY

Member of:	**BAC, IPC, BPS**
Quals/training:	BA Hons Psychol; Dip Advanced Psychodynamic Couns
Personal Therapy:	Yes
Supervision:	Ongoing
Counselling offered:	**General**
Service for:	Individuals
Theoretical Approach:	Psychodynamic
Fees:	£25 negotiable

BATCHELOR Carol   081 398 1053
14 Dene Gardens, THAMES DITTON KT7

Member of:	**BAC Acc**
Quals/training:	BAC Acc; BA Humanities; MSc Psychol Couns & Cert Couns (Surrey Univ); Dip Couns Psychol (Roehampton Institute)
Personal Therapy:	Ongoing
Supervision:	Ongoing
Counselling offered:	**General, Psychotherapy**
Service for:	Individuals, Couples
Theoretical Approach:	Integrative
Fees:	£20 - £25

WARREN Jeanne   081 398 1133
6 Lime Tree Avenue, Weston Green, THAMES DITTON KT7 0NA

Member of:	**BAC**
Quals/training:	Trained with Sutton Pastoral Foundation; workshops at WPF; experience in NHS & Social Services; Member of CTA
Personal Therapy:	Ongoing
Supervision:	Ongoing
Counselling offered:	**General**
Service for:	Individuals
Theoretical Approach:	Psychodynamic, Integrative
Fees:	Negotiable

Surrey - North West
[KT and TW]

DOMLEO Jill 081 398 3193
Westward Ho, Church Lane, THAMES DITTON KT7 0NL
Member of:	**BAC**
Quals/training:	Cert Personal & Pastoral Couns, Surrey Univ 1989; RELATE/ NMGC trained
Personal Therapy:	Ongoing
Supervision:	Ongoing
Counselling offered:	**General, Relationship, Relaxation, Abortion, Peri-natal**
Service for:	Individuals, Couples, Groups
Specific to:	Parents, Mothers
Theoretical Approach:	Rogerian, Eclectic
Fees:	£20 - £25

WILMOT Victoria 081 546 1387
Westward Ho, Church Lane, THAMES DITTON KT7 0NL
Member of:	**BAC**
Quals/training:	SRN 1962; Cert Personal & Pastoral Couns (Surrey Univ) 1988
Personal Therapy:	Ongoing
Supervision:	Ongoing
Counselling offered:	**General, Bereavement**
Service for:	Individuals, Couples
Theoretical Approach:	Eclectic, Holistic
Fees:	£20 negotiable

DENNET Annette 0932 348454
Weybridge, WEST BYFLEET KT14 6QD
Member of:	**BAC**
Quals/training:	MIWO; Cert Personal & Pastoral Counselling (Surrey Univ) 1982-4; Cert Ed
Personal Therapy:	Yes
Supervision:	Ongoing
Counselling offered:	**General, Work, Relationship, Bereavement, Depression**
Service for:	Individuals
Theoretical Approach:	Rogerian, Person-centred
Fees:	£20

HIGHAM Debbrah 0932 820482
1st Floor, 23 Baker Street, WEYBRIDGE KT13 8AE
Member of:	**BAC**
Quals/training:	Dip Corporate Psychol; Dip Hypnotherapy, Psychotherapy & NLP (BHR)'93
Personal Therapy:	Yes
Supervision:	Ongoing
Counselling offered:	**General, Stress, Stop smoking, Weight, Confidence, Phobias, Hypnotherapy, Psychotherapy**
Service for:	Individuals
Theoretical Approach:	Ericksonian, NLP, Elman
Fees:	£30

Surrey - North West
[KT and TW]

YALLOP Melanie　　　　　　　　　　　　　　　　　0932 844688
11 Mount Pleasant, WEYBRIDGE KT13 8EP
Member of:　　　　　　　BAC Acc, BPS, IPC/WPF
Quals/training:　　　　　BAC(Acc); BSc(Hons)Psychol/Sociol '83; Full Member IPC/WPF;
　　　　　　　　　　　　　Dip in Supervision(WPF)'91
Personal Therapy:　　　　Yes
Supervision:　　　　　　 Ongoing
Counselling offered:　　 Psychotherapy, General, Supervision
Service for:　　　　　　 Individuals
Theoretical Approach:　　Psychoanalytic
Other languages:　　　　 German
Fees:　　　　　　　　　　£27

MARSHALL Janet　　　　　　　　　　　　　　　　 0932 821721
12 Churchfields Avenue, WEYBRIDGE KT13 9YA
Member of:　　　　　　　BAC
Quals/training:　　　　　Medical Doctor; MBBS (Lond) 1969; Cert Personal & Pastoral
　　　　　　　　　　　　　Couns (Surrey Univ); Cruse (Acc); Member of BAFATT
Personal Therapy:　　　　Ongoing
Supervision:　　　　　　 Ongoing
Counselling offered:　　 General, Bereavement, Autogenic training, Relaxation
Service for:　　　　　　 Individuals
Theoretical Approach:　　Eclectic
Fees:　　　　　　　　　　£25 negotiable

HAWKES Kim　　　　　　　　　　　　　　　　　　 081 337 0754
49 Edenfield Gardens, WORCESTER PARK KT4 7DU
Member of:　　　　　　　BAC
Quals/training:　　　　　Dip Couns 1992
Personal Therapy:　　　　Ongoing
Supervision:　　　　　　 Ongoing
Counselling offered:　　 General, Crisis, Personal growth
Service for:　　　　　　 Individuals
Theoretical Approach:　　Psychodynamic
Fees:　　　　　　　　　　£16 - £25

SHANNON Betty　　　　　　　　　　　　　　　　　 081 330 5186
72 Church Road, WORCESTER PARK KT4 7RW
Member of:　　　　　　　BAC
Quals/training:　　　　　Cert Couns (WPF); Psychotherapy (Spectrum)
Personal Therapy:　　　　Yes
Supervision:　　　　　　 Ongoing
Counselling offered:　　 General, Crisis, Bereavement, Relationship
Service for:　　　　　　 Individuals, Couples, Groups
Specific to:　　　　　　 Women
Theoretical Approach:　　Psychodynamic, Egan, Gestalt
Fees:　　　　　　　　　　£15 - £30 sliding scale

Surrey - North West
[KT and TW]

CORBETT Marjorie 081 330 2118
The Vicarage, Church Road, WORCESTER PARK KT4 7RZ
Member of: **BAC, BPS**
Quals/training: Cert Couns '79; Cert Personal & Pastoral Couns (Univ of Surrey) '84-'86; Tutor in Couns Skills
Personal Therapy: Ongoing
Supervision: Ongoing
Counselling offered: **General, Personal growth, Supervision**
Service for: Individuals, Couples, Groups
Theoretical Approach: Humanistic, Eclectic
Fees: £15 - £30 according to means

THORNE-JONES Angela 081 391 0784
The Old Vicarage, Church Road, WORCESTER PARK KT4 7RZ
Member of: **BAC**
Quals/training: Cert Couns (Kingston CFE) 1986; CQSW; Trained in stress management, bereavement, child abuse
Personal Therapy: Ongoing
Supervision: Ongoing
Counselling offered: **General, Bereavement, Addiction, Sexual abuse, Physical abuse**
Service for: Individuals
Theoretical Approach: Rogerian, Jungian
Fees: £10 - £30 sliding scale

Surrey - South
[GU and RH]

Organisations

L A S COUNSELLING SERVICE   0276 677065
5 Rawdon Rise, CAMBERLEY GU15 1AN
Service:	General counselling for individuals including relationships, bereavement, depression, stress and employment related issues
Area served:	Surrey, Hampshire, Berkshire
Referral:	Self or others
Training of workers:	Dip Couns; personal therapy; regular supervision
Code of Ethics:	BAC
Management by:	Counsellors
Fees:	£15 - £20 negotiable

HOLMWOOD COUNSELLING SERVICE   0306 888776
16 Spring Cottages, South Holmwood, DORKING RH5 4LJ
Service:	General counselling, personal growth, emotional difficulties
Area served:	East Surrey
Referral:	Self or others
Training of workers:	Personal & Pastoral Cert Couns. Currently studying for MSC in counselling. Personal therapy and ongoing supervision
Code of Ethics:	BAC
Management by:	The Counsellors
Fees:	£15 - £25 sliding scale

FLEET COUNSELLING SERVICE   0252 622488, 0252 622691
18 Grove Road, Church Crookham, Fleet, FLEET GU13 0DX
Service:	Individual & couple counselling covering a wide range of problems - depression, anxiety, mid-life crisis, marital and relationship difficulties. Counsellor supervision available
Area served:	Surrey, Hants, Berks
Referral:	Self or others
Training of workers:	2 year counselling diploma, personal therapy, ongoing supervision
Code of Ethics:	BAC
Management by:	Counsellors
Fees:	£20

GUILDFORD CENTRE & SOCIETY FOR PSYCHOTHERAPY   0483 417443
14 Busbridge Lane, GODALMING GU7 1PU
Service:	Individual and group psychoananalytic psychotherapy. General, marital & sexual counselling
Area served:	Surrey, Sussex & Hants
Referral:	Self or others
Training of workers:	All therapists are qualified, experienced members of recognised training organisations & have undergone at least 3 yrs personal therapy. Regular supervision/consulatation
Code of Ethics:	GCSP, UKCP
Management by:	Business meeting of the membership
Fees:	£15 - £30

Surrey - South
[GU and RH]

GUILDFORD COUNSELLING RESOURCE CENTRE 0483 62142
University of Surrey, Ward Street, GUILDFORD GU1 4LH
Service:	Counselling/therapy for individuals, couples & groups for: General, marital, sexual, bereavement, depression, anxiety, stress. Work counselling: educational, career, redundancy
Area served:	Guildford and surrounding area
Other languages:	French, Italian
Referral:	Self or others
Training of workers:	MSc Couns Psychol/3 or more years of approved courses. All in ongoing training & personal therapy. Regular supervision
Code of Ethics:	BAC
Management by:	Dept of Educational Studies, Univ of Surrey
Fees:	£25 After 5pm £28 negotiable

HASLEMERE COUNSELLING SERVICE 0428 642444
Methodist Church, Lion Green, HASLEMERE GU27 1LD
Service:	General, bereavement & marital counselling to help relieve depression, anxiety and stress. Affiliate of WPF
Area served:	Haslemere and district
Referral:	Self or others
Training of workers:	Must have completed approved course & undergone personal therapy. Regular supervision
Code of Ethics:	BAC
Management by:	Management Committee
Fees:	Donations

HIV/AIDS TESTING & COUNSELLING SERVICE 0444 417417
Health Education Unit, Linwood, Butler's Green Road, HAYWARDS HEATH RH16 4BE
Service:	Counselling, support and advocacy for people both infected and affected by HIV. HIV testing including pre and post-test counselling
Area served:	Mid-Downs HA (West Sussex)
Other languages:	British Sign Language, Others arranged
Referral:	Self or others
Training of workers:	BAC Acc or training leading to this. Broad counselling experience including specialist HIV training courses
Code of Ethics:	BAC
Management by:	Health Authority
Fees:	None

WEST SUSSEX & SURREY COUNSELLORS GROUP 0403 266764
3 Heath Way, HORSHAM RH12 5XB
Service:	Counselling for a range of problems such as depression & anxiety, emotional, marital, relationship for individuals, couples, families and groups
Area served:	25 mile radius of Horsham
Referral:	Self or others
Training of workers:	Professional counselling qualifications, some CSQW; personal therapy; regular supervision
Code of Ethics:	BAC
Management by:	Jointly by monthly meeting
Fees:	£12 - £29

Surrey - South
[GU and RH]

REDHILL COUNSELLING CENTRE   ansaphone 0737 772844
Wealden College, East Surrey Hospital, Three Arch Road, REDHILL RH1 5RH
Service: General counselling for individuals with emphasis on psychodynamic methods
Area served: Redhill, Reigate & surrounding area
Referral: Self
Training of workers: In-house training following preliminary course at FE College Regular supervision
Code of Ethics: WPF
Management by: Management Committee supported by an advisory body
Fees: Donations according to means

WOKING COUNSELLING SERVICE   0483 730310
Gloucester Chambers, Town Square, WOKING GU21 1GA
Service: Short-term general counselling for adults and young people. Appointments made between 10am-4pm weekdays
Area served: Woking & District
Other languages: French, Serbo-Croat, Macedonian
Referral: Self or others
Training of workers: Must have completed approved course and have counselling experience; regular supervision
Code of Ethics: BAC
Management by: Management Group, supported by an Advisory Board represent-ing local caring organisations
Fees: None

BRIDGE COUNSELLING CENTRE   0483 755953
Beechfield, Waldens Road, Horsell, WOKING GU21 4RH
Service: Confidential counselling and therapy service for personal, relationship, sexual & bereavement problems for individuals, couples and groups
Area served: Within travelling distance
Referral: Self or others
Training of workers: All are fully trained, have had personal therapy and have regular supervision and group support
Code of Ethics: BAC
Management by: Proprietor
Fees: £25 £28 after 5pm, negotiable in hardship cases

Individual Practitioners
*Each individual is a **member of** one or more organisations eligible for entry into this directory. BAC Accredited Counsellors and Recognised Supervisors are shaded.*

FADER John   0276 472151
23 Guildford Road, BAGSHOT GU19 5JJ
Member of: BAC
Quals/training: CQSW '73; TIMS '79-81
Personal Therapy: Yes
Supervision: Ongoing
Counselling offered: General, Marital
Service for: Individuals, Couples
Theoretical Approach: Psychodynamic
Fees: £40

• CPRD 1994 •

Surrey - South
[GU and RH]

COWEN Lynne 0737 844099
10 Park Close, Strood Green, BETCHWORTH RH3 7JB
Member of: BAC
Quals/training: Dip Psychosynthesis Couns & Therapy; RGN
Personal Therapy: No
Supervision: Ongoing
Counselling offered: General, Bereavement, Relationship, Stress
Service for: Individuals
Theoretical Approach: Person-centred, Psychosynthesis
Fees: £15 - £30 sliding scale

BANNELL Liz 0276 677065
5 Rawdon Rise, CAMBERLEY GU15 1AN
Member of: BAC
Quals/training: Dip Couns (SACE) 1993; CRUSE bereavement training 1990-1
Personal Therapy: Yes
Supervision: Ongoing
Counselling offered: General, Bereavement
Service for: Individuals
Theoretical Approach: Person-centred, Humanistic
Fees: £15 - £20 Negotiable

PHILLIPS Laurie 0276 63977
53 Lime Avenue, CAMBERLEY GU15 2BH
Member of: AGIP
Quals/training: AGIP trained '85-7
Personal Therapy: Ongoing
Supervision: Ongoing
Counselling offered: Psychotherapy
Service for: Individuals, Couples
Theoretical Approach: Analytic, Jungian
Fees: £20 - £30 sliding scale

PROUD Sylvia 0252 872231
75 Beaulieu Gardens, Blackwater, CAMBERLEY GU17 0LP
Member of: BAC
Quals/training: Cert Couns (Surrey AEI)
Personal Therapy: Yes
Supervision: Ongoing
Counselling offered: General, Relationship
Service for: Individuals
Theoretical Approach: Person-centred
Fees: £20 negotiable

Surrey - South
[GU and RH]

ASHBY Susan   0252 876961
Badgers, Millmere, Yateley, CAMBERLEY GU17 7TN
Member of:	**BAC**
Quals/training:	Cruse; Drug & Alcohol Foundation; Albany Trust; Centre for Stress Management; SRN
Personal Therapy:	Ongoing
Supervision:	Ongoing
Counselling offered:	**General, Addiction, Bereavement, Eating disorders, Marital, Psychotherapy, Stress management**
Service for:	Individuals, Couples, Families, Groups
Specific to:	Children, Widowed, Substance abusers
Theoretical Approach:	Rogerian, Cognitive/Behavioural
Fees:	£15 - £25 sliding scale

DOOLEY Patricia   0276 681 684
7 Woburn Close, CAMBERLEY GU16 5NU
Member of:	**BAC, IPC**
Quals/training:	WPF training completed 1980
Personal Therapy:	Yes
Supervision:	Ongoing
Counselling offered:	**General, Psychotherapy, Supervision**
Service for:	Individuals, Couples
Theoretical Approach:	Analytic
Fees:	£30 negotiable

JESSON Alison   ansaphone 0306 882357
85 Fairfield Drive, DORKING RH4 1JG
Member of:	**BAC, ITA**
Quals/training:	RGN; Dip Counselling Skills (South West London College) 1985; BSc(Hons); Ongoing advanced clinical T A Training (metanoia)
Personal Therapy:	Ongoing
Supervision:	Ongoing
Counselling offered:	**General, Bereavement, Psychotherapy**
Service for:	Individuals
Theoretical Approach:	Humanistic, TA
Fees:	£20 Negotiable

SPENCER Fiona   0306 883159
12 St Pauls Road East, DORKING RH4 2HR
Member of:	**BAC**
Quals/training:	BA 1975; BACUP trained 1990; ongoing MSc Psychol Couns; BICA Member
Personal Therapy:	Ongoing
Supervision:	Ongoing
Counselling offered:	**General, Cancer, Infertility**
Service for:	Individuals
Theoretical Approach:	Person-centred
Fees:	£10

Surrey - South
[GU and RH]

PRICE Wendy 0306 888776
16 Spring Cottages, South Holmwood, DORKING RH5 4LU
Member of: BAC
Quals/training: Cert Personal & Pastoral Couns (Surrey) 1990; Dip Drama therapy (York) 1981; Memb BADT; studying for MSc in Psychol Counselling (Roehampton)
Personal Therapy: Yes
Supervision: Ongoing
Counselling offered: General, Personal growth
Service for: Individuals, Couples, Groups
Theoretical Approach: Humanistic, Eclectic
Fees: £15 - £25 sliding scale

SMALLE Sarah 0306 888776
16 Spring Cottages, South Holmwood, DORKING RH5 4LU
Member of: BAC
Quals/training: Cert Personal & Pastoral Couns (Surrey) 1990; currently training for Adv Dip Couns (Surrey), leading to MSc in counselling
Personal Therapy: Yes
Supervision: Ongoing
Counselling offered: General, Personal growth
Service for: Individuals, Couples, Groups
Theoretical Approach: Humanistic, Eclectic
Fees: £15 - £25 sliding scale

HILLMAN Christine 0342 315097
2 The Old Convent, off Moat Road, EAST GRINSTEAD RH19 3RS
Member of: BAC, PET
Quals/training: Dip Couns & Therapy; Dip Sp. Direction (Ignatian)
Personal Therapy: Yes
Supervision: Ongoing
Counselling offered: Regression therapy, Bereavement, Inner child, Midlife, Spiritual
Service for: Individuals
Specific to: Middle aged, Women, Christians
Theoretical Approach: Transpersonal, Gestalt
Fees: £15 - £30 sliding scale

PHILLIPS Mary 0252 723522
The Tudors, 20a Fernhill Lane, Upper Hale, FARNHAM GU9 0JJ
Member of: BAC
Quals/training: Cert Couns (Surrey Univ) 1988; Cruse Acc
Personal Therapy: Yes
Supervision: Ongoing
Counselling offered: General, Bereavement, Marital
Service for: Individuals, Couples
Theoretical Approach: Eclectic
Fees: £22 less in hardship cases

Surrey - South
[GU and RH]

BOWER Margaret — Ansaphone 0252 722556
5 Old Compton Lane, FARNHAM GU9 8BS
Member of:	**BAC, AFT**
Quals/training:	Dip Social Work 1980; CQSW; Dip Family Therapy (London) 1989
Personal Therapy:	Ongoing
Supervision:	Ongoing
Counselling offered:	**General, Bereavement, Relationship, Family**
Service for:	Individuals, Couples, Families
Theoretical Approach:	Psychodynamic, Systemic
Fees:	£15 - £35 sliding scale

NEWBERY Christine — 0252 723589
16 Lancaster Avenue, FARNHAM GU9 8JY
Member of:	**BAC**
Quals/training:	MSc Psychol Couns 1991 & Cert Couns 1986 (Surrey Univ); Training in Couns/Sexuality (FPA) 1990
Personal Therapy:	Yes
Supervision:	Ongoing
Counselling offered:	**General, Relationship, Sexual**
Service for:	Individuals, Couples
Specific to:	Adolescents
Theoretical Approach:	Eclectic
Other languages:	French
Fees:	£25 negotiable

OSBORNE Lynda — 0252 724403
8 Lancaster Avenue, FARNHAM GU9 8JY
Member of:	**BAC Acc**
Quals/training:	BAC Acc; NMGC Trained 1982; GPTI Advanced Student
Personal Therapy:	Ongoing
Supervision:	Ongoing
Counselling offered:	**General, Marital, Sexual**
Service for:	Individuals, Couples, Groups
Theoretical Approach:	Gestalt, Integrative
Fees:	£25 negotiable

HART Azina — 0252 710427
55 Aveley Lane, FARNHAM GU9 8PS
Member of:	**BAC Acc**
Quals/training:	BAC Acc; NLP trained; creative therapy; ongoing training - Dip Individual Systemic Psychotherapy & Couns (KCC)
Personal Therapy:	Ongoing
Supervision:	Ongoing
Counselling offered:	**General, Sexual abuse, Relationship**
Service for:	Individuals, Couples, Families, Groups
Specific to:	Survivors of child abuse
Theoretical Approach:	Eclectic, Systemic
Fees:	£25 some reduced places

Surrey - South
[GU and RH]

VENEMA Ashen   0252 711723
106 Greenfield Road, FARNHAM GU9 8TQ

Member of:	BAC Acc
Quals/training:	BAC Acc; BA; Dip Couns (IP) '87; Group Facilitator
Personal Therapy:	Yes
Supervision:	Ongoing
Counselling offered:	**Crisis, Transition**
Service for:	Individuals, Couples, Groups
Theoretical Approach:	Psychodynamic, Transpersonal, Psychosynthesis
Other languages:	German
Fees:	£35

MOUNTJOY Lesleen   0264 59598
18 Park Road, FARNHAM GU9 9QN

Member of:	BAC, NRHP
Quals/training:	BSc(Hons) Psychol; CQSW; Dip Hypnosis & Psychotherapy; Master Practitioner NLP; Memb ICM
Personal Therapy:	Ongoing
Supervision:	Ongoing
Counselling offered:	**General, Depression, Bereavement, Loss, Relationship, Divorce, Conciliation**
Service for:	Individuals, Couples, Groups
Theoretical Approach:	Integrative
Fees:	£30 - £40

GRUNDY Mary   0252 782238
Richmond Cottage, School Hill, Seale, FARNHAM GU10 1HY

Member of:	BAC Acc
Quals/training:	BAC Acc; BA; Studied Analytical Psychol & Psychiatric Illness 1980-?; Dip Group Psychotherapy (IQA), memb of Guild of Pastoral Psych
Personal Therapy:	Yes
Supervision:	Ongoing
Counselling offered:	**General, Psychotherapy**
Service for:	Individuals, Couples, Groups
Specific to:	People with language problems
Theoretical Approach:	Analytical, Jungian
Fees:	£35 negotiable

ROBERTSON David   02518 2532
Hunters Lodge, 44 Crooksbury Road, FARNHAM GU10 1QB

Member of:	BAC
Quals/training:	In 3rd year Dip in Person-centred Counselling (metanoia)
Personal Therapy:	Yes
Supervision:	Ongoing
Counselling offered:	**General, Career**
Service for:	Individuals
Theoretical Approach:	Rogerian
Fees:	£15 - £30

Surrey - South
[GU and RH]

SORENSEN Barbara   0252 515511 x295
18 Middle Bourne Lane, FARNHAM GU10 3NH
Member of:	BAC
Quals/training:	BA; Cert Ed; Cert in Couns(Surrey Univ); RELATE trained; Family Mediator
Personal Therapy:	Yes
Supervision:	Ongoing
Counselling offered:	General, Bereavement, Addiction, Educational, Co-dependency, Relationship, Marital
Service for:	Individuals, Couples
Theoretical Approach:	Psychodynamic, Eclectic, Reality therapy
Fees:	Negotiable

STRIBBLING Judith   0252 716674
58A Middle Bourne Lane, FARNHAM GU10 3NJ
Member of:	BAC
Quals/training:	1986 Counselling Cert (Surrey Univ)
Personal Therapy:	Ongoing
Supervision:	Ongoing
Counselling offered:	General, Eating disorders, Marital
Service for:	Individuals, Couples
Specific to:	Young adults
Theoretical Approach:	Eclectic
Fees:	£20 negotiable; cpls £25

CHADWICK Anne   025 125 2094
1 Pear Tree Lane, Rowledge, FARNHAM GU10 4DW
Member of:	BAC Acc
Quals/training:	BAC(Acc); Cert Couns (Surrey Univ) '83; Cert in Sexuality (Southampton Univ); Cert Couns Person-Centred Art Therapy (Crawley College); Cert TA; Cert (Hants AFT)
Personal Therapy:	Yes
Supervision:	Ongoing
Counselling offered:	General, Bereavement, Sexual, Marital
Service for:	Individuals, Couples, Families
Specific to:	Young adults
Theoretical Approach:	Eclectic
Fees:	£10 - £25 negotiable

KNIGHT-EVANS Alison   0483 422122
Binscombe Hanger, Mark Way, GODALMING GU7 2BE
Member of:	BAC, BPS
Quals/training:	BSc Psychol; MSc Psychol Couns; Cert Couns (KCFE); Cert Transpersonal Psychol
Personal Therapy:	Ongoing
Supervision:	Ongoing
Counselling offered:	General, Eating disorders, Psychotherapy
Service for:	Individuals, Groups
Theoretical Approach:	Integrative
Fees:	£30 negotiable

Surrey - South
[GU and RH]

BERG Morris L 0483 416421
6 Oakbraes, Frith Hill Road, GODALMING GU7 2EA
Member of:	BAC
Quals/training:	BSc Psychol; Dip Hypnotherapy/Psychotherapy SHAP; Cert Couns LCIP; Certified Professional Memb of Assoc for Past- Life Research & Therapy (APRT); Reg Occupat'l Tester BPsS
Personal Therapy:	Yes
Supervision:	Ongoing
Counselling offered:	**General, Psychotherapy, Trauma, Abuse, Career**
Service for:	Individuals
Theoretical Approach:	Eclectic, Ericksonian, Transpersonal
Fees:	£25 - £60 Sliding scale for 2 hr session

WALSH Frieda 0483 893585
Westfield, Linersh Wood Close, Bramley, GUILDFORD GU5 0EG
Member of:	BAC
Quals/training:	Training in Personal & Pastoral Couns (Univ of Surrey) '80; Practice of Couns (Univ of Surrey) '83
Personal Therapy:	Ongoing
Supervision:	Ongoing
Counselling offered:	**General, Marital**
Service for:	Individuals, Couples
Theoretical Approach:	Eclectic
Fees:	£12 - £30 sliding scale

HAYWARD Marie-Louise 048 632 282
High Leybourne Lodge, Hascombe, GODALMING GU8 4AD
Member of:	BAC
Quals/training:	1981 MSc Management Science Industrial Psychology; SRN 1971; Dip Psychol Studies (Bradford Univ 1978)
Personal Therapy:	Yes
Supervision:	Ongoing
Counselling offered:	**General, Psychotherapy, Career, Life planning, Work**
Service for:	Individuals, Couples, Groups
Theoretical Approach:	Gestalt, Rogerian, Jungian, Holistic
Fees:	£25 - £45 negotiable

NEWNHAM Elizabeth 048 68 7789
Lawn Cottage, Portsmouth Road, Milford, GODALMING GU8 5HZ
Member of:	BAC
Quals/training:	NMGC Trained 1981; Counselling Course (CTP) 1984
Personal Therapy:	Ongoing
Supervision:	Ongoing
Counselling offered:	**General, Marital, Relationship**
Service for:	Individuals, Couples
Theoretical Approach:	Transpersonal
Fees:	£20 negotiable

Surrey - South
[GU and RH]

COLMAN Greta 0342 892564
Little Haven, Byers Lane, GODSTONE RH9 8JH
Member of:	BAC Acc RSup
Quals/training:	BAC Acc & Recognised Supervisor; NMGC Trained; 1 yr course in Therapy & Supervision (TIMS)
Personal Therapy:	Yes
Supervision:	Ongoing
Counselling offered:	**General, Marital, Psychotherapy, Bereavement**
Service for:	Individuals, Couples
Theoretical Approach:	Eclectic
Fees:	£20 - £30 couples £25-35

JORDAN Ruth 0483 62230
Woodbridge Hill Surgery, 1 Deerbarn Road, GUILDFORD GU2 6AT
Member of:	BAC, BPS
Quals/training:	RMN; MSc Couns Psychol; MIND
Personal Therapy:	Yes
Supervision:	Ongoing
Counselling offered:	**General, Anxiety, Phobias, Retirement**
Service for:	Individuals, Couples
Specific to:	Unknown
Theoretical Approach:	Client-centred
Fees:	£25 negotiable

RINK Jane 0483 755953
The Bridge Counselling Centre, Beechfield Waldens Road, Horsell, WOKING GU21 4RH
Member of:	BAC
Quals/training:	NMGC Trained; trained in Psychodynamics; training in: Psychodrama, Gestalt, Jung
Personal Therapy:	Ongoing
Supervision:	Ongoing
Counselling offered:	**General, Bereavement, Marital, Personal growth**
Service for:	Individuals, Couples, Groups
Specific to:	Students
Theoretical Approach:	Psychodynamic, Jungian
Fees:	£25 negotiable

DAVENPORT Hilary 0483 504882
4 Glebe Court, Cross Lanes, GUILDFORD GU1 1SU
Member of:	BAC, BPA
Quals/training:	CTA course in Human Realtions, Pastoral Care & Couns '79-83; Psychodrama training (Howell Ctre) '86-90; Dip Psychodrama/ group analytic psychotherapy (London Ctre)
Personal Therapy:	Ongoing
Supervision:	Ongoing
Counselling offered:	**General, Eating disorders**
Service for:	Individuals, Groups
Theoretical Approach:	Psychodynamic, Analytical, Psychodrama
Fees:	£24 negotiable

Surrey - South
[GU and RH]

DE BERKER Patricia 0483 504554
Ferndown Cottage, 3 Hillier Road, GUILDFORD GU1 2JG
Member of:	LCP
Quals/training:	BA (Hons) London; LCP qualified 1973; Guildford Centre of Psychotherapy
Personal Therapy:	Yes
Supervision:	Yes
Counselling offered:	General, Marital, Psychotherapy, Bereavement
Service for:	Individuals, Couples
Theoretical Approach:	Eclectic, Analytical, Freudian, Kleinian, Rogerian
Other languages:	French, German
Fees:	£23 - £30 sliding scale

DE BERKER Paul 0483 504554
Ferndown Cottage, 3 Hillier Road, GUILDFORD GU1 2JG
Member of:	LCP, GCSP, BAP, BPS
Quals/training:	DPhil (Oxon); FBPS; FBAP; FLCP; corresponding Assoc Royal College of Psychiatry
Personal Therapy:	Yes
Supervision:	Yes
Counselling offered:	Psychotherapy
Service for:	Individuals, Couples, Groups
Theoretical Approach:	Eclectic, Analytical, Freudian, Jungian
Fees:	£20 - £30 sliding scale

IZOD Karen 0483 68516
5 Parklands Place, Merrow, GUILDFORD GU1 2PS
Member of:	BAC
Quals/training:	CQSW; Adv Programme in Social Work (TC)
Personal Therapy:	Yes
Supervision:	Ongoing
Counselling offered:	General, Child abuse, Pregnancy, Parenting problems, Personal growth
Service for:	Individuals, Couples, Families
Specific to:	Children, Parents, Carers
Theoretical Approach:	Psychoanalytic
Fees:	£25; £30 Couples

KILMARTIN Nuala Sister 0483 570122
6 Semaphore Road, GUILDFORD GU1 3TS
Member of:	BAC Acc
Quals/training:	BAC Acc; SRN; training in Gen Couns & Clin Theol Past Couns; physical therapist (ITEC Holistic Body Massage)
Personal Therapy:	Ongoing
Supervision:	Ongoing
Counselling offered:	General, Bereavement, Addiction, Dependency, Sexual abuse
Service for:	Individuals, Groups, Organisations
Specific to:	Trauma victims
Theoretical Approach:	Person-centred, Jungian
Fees:	£20 - £25 sliding scale

Surrey - South
[GU and RH]

COLLIS June 0483 67753
26 Semaphore Road, GUILDFORD GU1 3PT
Member of: BAC, BPS
Quals/training: BA Psychol; MSc Psychol Counselling
Personal Therapy: Ongoing
Supervision: Ongoing
Counselling offered: General, Bereavement, Relationship, Psychotherapy
Service for: Individuals, Couples, Groups
Theoretical Approach: Humanistic
Fees: £30

DEMPSEY Aileen 0483 67246
64 Pewley Way, GUILDFORD GU1 3QA
Member of: BAC
Quals/training: NMGC trained
Personal Therapy: Yes
Supervision: Ongoing
Counselling offered: General, Marital
Service for: Individuals, Couples
Theoretical Approach: Rogerian, Psychodynamic
Fees: £20 sliding scale

DAINTRY Penelope 0483 576040, 081 995 4531
Mount Pleasant Cottage, One Mount Pleasant, GUILDFORD GU2 5HZ
Member of: BAC, GPTI
Quals/training: Dip GPTI; Cert Couns (Surrey Univ) 1986
Personal Therapy: Ongoing
Supervision: Ongoing
Counselling offered: General, Psychotherapy, Eating disorders
Service for: Individuals, Couples, Families, Groups
Theoretical Approach: Gestalt, Rogerian
Fees: £30

DRABBLE Sarah
64 Wodeland Avenue, GUILDFORD GU2 5LA
Member of: BAC
Quals/training: BA (Hons); Cert Couns Surrey Univ 1988; Cruse Acc; Bereavement Counsellor; Introduction to Analytical Therapy (LCP)
Personal Therapy: Ongoing
Supervision: Ongoing
Counselling offered: General, Bereavement, Depression, Eating disorders
Service for: Individuals, Groups
Theoretical Approach: Psychodynamic
Fees: £20 negotiable

HOWARD Susan 0483 504033
85 Wodeland Avenue, GUILDFORD GU2 5LA
Member of: BPS
Quals/training: BA (Hons); MSc Clinical Psychol; C Psychol
Personal Therapy: Yes
Supervision: Ongoing
Counselling offered: Psychotherapy
Service for: Individuals
Theoretical Approach: Psychoanalytic, Psychodynamic
Fees: £25 - £40 sliding scale

Surrey - South
[GU and RH]

PRATT Sheila 0483 572093
44 East Meads, GUILDFORD GU2 5SP
Member of:	Guild of Psychotherapists, WMIP
Quals/training:	Teaching Dip (Edinburgh); Cert Couns; Psychotherapy training
Personal Therapy:	Yes
Supervision:	Ongoing
Counselling offered:	**General, Bereavement, Crisis, Psychotherapy**
Service for:	Individuals, Couples
Theoretical Approach:	Jungian, Developmental
Fees:	Negotiable

VOLLANS Audrey 0483 234861
11 Fairlands Avenue, Fairlands, GUILDFORD GU3 3LX
Member of:	BAC, GPTI
Quals/training:	Cert Couns (Surrey Univ) '87; ongoing training in Gestalt psychotherapy (metanoia)
Personal Therapy:	Ongoing
Supervision:	Ongoing
Counselling offered:	**General, Bereavement, Personal growth, Psychotherapy**
Service for:	Individuals, Groups
Theoretical Approach:	Gestalt, Rogerian
Fees:	£25 negotiable

EDRIDGE Maren 0483 234425
24 Fairlands Avenue, Worplesdon, GUILDFORD GU3 3NB
Member of:	BAC
Quals/training:	Dip supervision (metanoia) 1991-; Msc Couns Psychol (Surrey) 1990; Cert AIDS Couns (CAC) 1986; 2nd Yr Albany Trust Dip Couns 1987; Cert Couns (Surrey) 1984
Personal Therapy:	Ongoing
Supervision:	Ongoing
Counselling offered:	**General, Bereavement, Crisis, Marital, Stress, Supervision**
Service for:	Individuals, Couples
Theoretical Approach:	Humanistic, Integrative
Other languages:	Italian
Fees:	£25 Negotiable, after 5pm £28

CHARLETON Mary 0483 63863
Rosemary Cottage, 4 Juniper Place, Shalford, GUILDFORD GU4 8DA
Member of:	BAC
Quals/training:	BA; Cert Soc Sci; Dip App Soc Studies (LSE); Psychodynamic Casework Training
Personal Therapy:	Yes
Supervision:	Ongoing
Counselling offered:	**General, Personal growth, Addiction, Oppression**
Service for:	Individuals, Couples, Families, Groups, Organisations
Theoretical Approach:	Psychodynamic, Humanistic
Fees:	£25

Surrey - South
[GU and RH]

### HOPWOOD Jean	0483 68669
Waverley, Somerswey, Shalford, GUILDFORD GU4 8EQ
Member of:	BAC Acc
Quals/training:	BAC Acc; 1982 Dip Humanistic Psychol (Surrey Univ); 1986 Dip Transpersonal Psychology (CTP)
Personal Therapy:	Yes
Supervision:	Ongoing
Counselling offered:	**General, Cancer, Relationship**
Service for:	Individuals, Couples
Theoretical Approach:	Transpersonal
Fees:	£22 negotiable

### MAYBANK Alison	0483 577284
3 Oaklands Close, Shalford, GUILDFORD GU4 8JL
Member of:	BAC
Quals/training:	Cert Personal Couns Surrey Univ: Dip Couns; Dip Supervison; JEB Teachers Dip Management
Personal Therapy:	Ongoing
Supervision:	Ongoing
Counselling offered:	**General, Supervision**
Service for:	Individuals, Couples
Theoretical Approach:	Person-centred
Fees:	£25 - £30 sliding scale

### BULL Sonia	0483 893733
Gosden End, Bramley, GUILDFORD GU5 0AE
Member of:	BAC Acc
Quals/training:	BAC Acc; Dip Humanistic Psychol Surrey Univ 1980; Cert Couns Surrey Univ '84; training at IFT '86; '87 Parent Network co-ordinator
Personal Therapy:	Ongoing
Supervision:	Ongoing
Counselling offered:	**General, Marital, Relationship, Sexual, Short-term, Psychotherapy**
Service for:	Individuals, Couples, Groups
Theoretical Approach:	Eclectic
Fees:	£25 - £30

### FERNIE Ann Mrs	0483 892063
Little Potters, Sweetwater Lane, Sharley Green, GUILDFORD GU5 0UP
Member of:	BAC
Quals/training:	Dip Couns (Surrey AEI)
Personal Therapy:	Ongoing
Supervision:	Ongoing
Counselling offered:	**General, Bereavement**
Service for:	Individuals, Couples
Theoretical Approach:	Rogerian
Fees:	£20 negotiable

Surrey - South
[GU and RH]

WICKER Jane   0428 643221
8 Fir Tree Ave, HASLEMERE GU27 1PL
Member of: BAC
Quals/training: RSA Cert Couns Skills in the Development of Learning '87; Dip Couns (Guildford AEI) '89-'92
Personal Therapy: Ongoing
Supervision: Ongoing
Counselling offered: General, Crisis, Redundancy
Service for: Individuals, Groups
Specific to: Homeless, Unemployed, Substance abusers
Theoretical Approach: Phenomenological, Humanistic
Fees: £18 negotiable

LORIMER Angela   0428 643980
Russex Rill, Bellvale Lane, HASLEMERE GU27 3DJ
Member of: BAC Acc
Quals/training: BAC Acc; ex Medical Social Worker; CTA Seminars 1968-72; Asst CTA Tutor 1973-77; Seminars (WPF & Surrey Univ 1976); Group Facilitator Guildford Diocese
Personal Therapy: Yes
Supervision: Ongoing
Counselling offered: General, Relationship, Bereavement
Service for: Individuals, Couples, Groups
Theoretical Approach: Eclectic
Fees: £12 - £18 sliding scale

COX David   0428 607554
4 Hampton Terrace, Beacon Hill Road, Beacon Hill, HINDHEAD GU26 6NR
Member of: BAC
Quals/training: Cert in Couns (Surrey Univ) 1988; training for Dip in Couns (metanoia)
Personal Therapy: Ongoing
Supervision: Ongoing
Counselling offered: General, Bereavement, Loss, Relationship, Sexual, HIV
Service for: Individuals, Couples, Groups
Theoretical Approach: Rogerian
Fees: £10 - £15 sliding scale

CLOUGH Rosemary   0883 714341
106 Bluehouse Lane, OXTED RH8 0AR
Member of: BAC
Quals/training: NMGC trained; RGN; Diploma in Counselling Skills
Personal Therapy: Yes
Supervision: Ongoing
Counselling offered: General, Marital, Bereavement, Addiction, Alcohol, Eating disorders
Theoretical Approach: Rogerian, Reality therapy
Fees: £30

Surrey - South
[GU and RH]

VAUGHAN Katherine 0883 723432
7 Manor House, High Street, Limpsfield, OXTED RH8 0DR
Member of:	BAC
Quals/training:	Cert Couns (East Surrey Coll & Redhill Couns Centre); Cert Psychodynamic Couns (WPF)
Personal Therapy:	Ongoing
Supervision:	Ongoing
Counselling offered:	General, Bereavement
Service for:	Individuals, Couples
Theoretical Approach:	Psychodynamic
Fees:	£15 - £30 sliding scale

HEYWOOD TAYLOR Beatrice 0737 765730
An Cala, 30 Carlton Road, REDHILL RH1 2BX
Member of:	BAC Acc
Quals/training:	BAC Acc; BA (Hons) Humanities; Cert Ed; MSc Psychological Couns
Personal Therapy:	Ongoing
Supervision:	Ongoing
Counselling offered:	General, Crisis, Relationship, Bereavement, Personal growth, Midlife
Service for:	Individuals, Couples, Groups
Theoretical Approach:	Rogerian, Gestalt, Existential
Fees:	£27 - £35 negotiable

HARTLEY Fiona 0737 247940
60 Deerings Road, REIGATE RH2 0PN
Member of:	BAC
Quals/training:	RGN; Post Grad Dip Couns (Brighton Poly) 1989
Personal Therapy:	Ongoing
Supervision:	Ongoing
Counselling offered:	General
Service for:	Individuals
Theoretical Approach:	Person-centred, Psychodynamic
Fees:	£18

GORDON-GRAHAM Vivienne 0737 222179
50 Cockshot Hill, REIGATE RH2 8AN
Member of:	BAC, MPTI
Quals/training:	Dip Person-centred Couns; training at metanoia; PG Management Studies; Adult & FE Teacher Training; TEFL
Personal Therapy:	Ongoing
Supervision:	Ongoing
Counselling offered:	General, Crisis, Work
Service for:	Individuals, Groups, Organisations
Theoretical Approach:	Rogerian
Other languages:	Italian, French
Fees:	£15 - £25 sliding scale

Surrey - South
[GU and RH]

VALLINS Yvonne   0737 247608
21 Hardwicke Road, REIGATE RH2 9HJ
Member of:	BAC
Quals/training:	Dip (WPF); Trained Psychotherapist (Guild of Psychotherapists) 1993
Personal Therapy:	Yes
Supervision:	Ongoing
Counselling offered:	General, Depression, Stress
Service for:	Individuals
Theoretical Approach:	Object relations, Psychodynamic
Fees:	£25 sliding scale

LEWIS Penny   081 891 4867
5a Pembroke Villas, The Green, RICHMOND
Member of:	BAC, CPPE, AFT
Quals/training:	Dip Systemic Therapy (KCC); Dip Systemic Teaching Training & Supervision (Award pending)
Personal Therapy:	Yes
Supervision:	Ongoing
Counselling offered:	General, Bereavement, Stress, Panic attacks, AIDS, HIV, Chronic illness, Terminal illness, Supervision
Service for:	Individuals, Couples
Specific to:	Caring professions, People with disabilities
Theoretical Approach:	Systemic
Fees:	£20 - £25 negotiable

ELLIOT Beryl   0483 472332
22 Limewood Close, St Johns, WOKING GU21 1XA
Member of:	BAC
Quals/training:	Trained in Pastoral Couns with Psychodynamic & Jungian Orientation WPF London
Personal Therapy:	No
Supervision:	Ongoing
Counselling offered:	General, Bereavement, Relationship, Crisis, Spiritual
Service for:	Individuals
Theoretical Approach:	Psychodynamic, Rogerian
Fees:	£20

WIDDICOMBE Howard   0483 721458
32 Armadale Road, Goldsworth Park, WOKING GU21 3LB
Member of:	BAC
Quals/training:	BSc Behavioural Science; training in Eclectic Psychotherapy (Spectrum) 1989-92; Client-centred & Psychodynamic Couns training 1985-93
Personal Therapy:	Ongoing
Supervision:	Ongoing
Counselling offered:	General, Relationship, Bereavement, Stress, Family, Work, Personal growth
Service for:	Individuals, Couples, Families
Theoretical Approach:	Eclectic, Humanistic, Integrative
Fees:	£35 negotiable

Surrey - South
[GU and RH]

GUTHRIE Claire　　　　　　　　　　　　　　　　　　　　0483 755953
Beechfield, Waldens Road, Horsell, WOKING GU21 4RH
Member of:　　　　　　　BAC Acc
Quals/training:　　　　　　BAC Acc; NMGC/RELATE trained 1984; Cert Person-centred Art Therapy 1988; SRN 1962
Personal Therapy:　　　　Yes
Supervision:　　　　　　　Ongoing
Counselling offered:　**General, Relationship, Bereavement, Supervision**
Service for:　　　　　　　Individuals, Couples, Groups
Theoretical Approach:　　Psychodynamic, Gestalt
Fees:　　　　　　　　　　£25 less in hardship cases

RANDELL Peter　　　　　　　　　　　　　　　　　　　　0483 763 824
Wood Dene, Golf Club Road, Hook Heath, WOKING GU22 0LS
Member of:　　　　　　　BAC
Quals/training:　　　　　　Cert Couns Skills & Attitudes (IPC/WPF); Cert Personal Counselling (Univ Surrey); Cruse trained
Personal Therapy:　　　　Yes
Supervision:　　　　　　　Ongoing
Counselling offered:　**General**
Service for:　　　　　　　Individuals, Couples, Families
Theoretical Approach:　　Person-centred
Fees:　　　　　　　　　　£20

RICKARD Pamela　　　　　　　　　　　　　　　　　　　0483 472034
Woodleigh, Heath House Road, WOKING GU22 0RD
Member of:　　　　　　　BAC
Quals/training:　　　　　　BA; Dip Social Administration '71; Cert Couns (Surrey University)'88; Acc Bereavement Cllr (Cruse)
Personal Therapy:　　　　Ongoing
Supervision:　　　　　　　Ongoing
Counselling offered:　**Bereavement, Marital, Depression**
Service for:　　　　　　　Individuals, Couples, Groups
Theoretical Approach:　　Psychodynamic, Client-centred
Fees:　　　　　　　　　　£18 (reductions in cases of need)

PEARMAN Cathy　　　　　　　　　　　　　　　　　　　0483 232030
Gateways Centre, Tzaneen, Blackhorse Road, WOKING GU22 0RE
Member of:　　　　　　　BAC Acc, Member of UKCP Register
Quals/training:　　　　　　BAC Acc; Couns & Psychotherapy 1976 & '79; Transpersonal Psychol Acc (CTP); Psychosynthesis Acc (IP); Family Therapy (IFT); Memb AAPP
Personal Therapy:　　　　Ongoing
Supervision:　　　　　　　Ongoing
Counselling offered:　**General, Psychotherapy, Family, Marital**
Theoretical Approach:　　Transpersonal, Analytical, Psychosynthesis
Fees:　　　　　　　　　　£27

Surrey - South
[GU and RH]

REID Rosamund 0483 764146
The Cottage, Ivy Lane, WOKING GU22 7BY
- **Member of:** GCSP
- Quals/training: Dip Soc Studies; Dip Social Work; CQSW; LCIP Associate
- Personal Therapy: Yes
- Supervision: Ongoing
- **Counselling offered:** General, Psychotherapy
- Service for: Individuals, Couples, Families
- Theoretical Approach: Eclectic
- Fees: £15 - £30

NEWTON Jeanne 0483 223515
Moorings, Boughton Hall Avenue, Send, WOKING GU23 7DD
- **Member of:** BAC
- Quals/training: BA; Cert Ed; Cert Couns (Surrey) 1988; Cruse Acc; trained in Transpersonal Psychology
- Personal Therapy: Ongoing
- Supervision: Ongoing
- **Counselling offered:** Bereavement, Personal growth, Relationship, Stress
- Service for: Individuals, Groups, Couples
- Theoretical Approach: Eclectic
- Fees: £18 - £28 sliding scale

TOPOLSKI Denise 0276 856818
Albury Farm, Gracious Pond Road, Chobham, WOKING GU24 8HJ
- **Member of:** BAC
- Quals/training: Member of ASIP Dip Couns; Cert in Transactional Analysis
- Personal Therapy: Yes
- Supervision: Ongoing
- **Counselling offered:** General, Bereavement, Relationship, Family
- Service for: Individuals, Couples, Families
- Specific to: Adolescents
- Theoretical Approach: Adlerian, TA, Gestalt
- Other languages: Dutch
- Fees: £25

Sussex - East

Organisations

WOODS PLACE CENTRE FOR COUNSELLING AND THERAPY
0424 775337
Mill Lane, Whatlington, BATTLE TN33 0ND
Service:	Individuals, couples or family counselling; short-term crisis counselling, group therapy, workshops. General, bereavement, marital, AIDS & effects of c/hood abuse in adults
Area served:	East Sussex, Kent
Referral:	Self
Training of workers:	Clinical Consultant (Consultant Psychiatrist); RELATE; Richmond Fellowship; CRUSE Pers Ther & Reg Supervision
Code of Ethics:	BAC, BMA
Management by:	Management Committee
Fees:	£15 - £25 negotiable

LIFELINE PREGNANCY COUNSELLING AND CARE   0273 601293
9a Manchester Street, BRIGHTON BN2 1TF
Service:	Non-directive counselling for women with problems relating to unplanned pregnancy, loss of pregnancy, eg post abortion, miscarriage, still-birth
Area served:	Sussex
Referral:	Self, Health Practitioner
Training of workers:	Fully trained working under supervision. In-house training twice a year
Code of Ethics:	BAC
Management by:	Local Management Committee
Fees:	Donations for pregnancy test

HASTINGS & ROTHER NHS TRUST, DEPT OF CLINICAL PSYCHOLOGY
0424 435066
Furness Mount, 4 Holmedale Gardens, HASTINGS TN34 1LY
Service:	Counselling and psychotherapy for individuals, couples and groups
Area served:	Hastings and Rother area
Referral:	GP, Agencies
Training of workers:	Post graduate clinical psychology training or appropriate counselling/psychotherapy qualifications
Code of Ethics:	BPS, BAC
Management by:	Hastings and Rother NHS Trust
Fees:	None

WARREN BROWNE UNIT   0273 461453, 0273 455622 x 681
Southlands Hospital, Upper Shoreham Road, SHOREHAM-BY-SEA BN4 6TQ
Service:	Couns for all HIV related problems, confidential pre & post test HIV/AIDS couns, follow-up support for those with HIV & their relatives/friends; bereavement, sexual health & rape
Area served:	Worthing District HA
Other languages:	French
Referral:	Self or others
Training of workers:	Clinical psychologist & trained psychotherapist with AIDS couns training, health advisor
Code of Ethics:	BAC, BPS
Management by:	NHS Trust
Fees:	None

Sussex - East

ROTHER COUNSELLING SERVICE (East Sussex Division) 0424 813402
Ann Williams, HASTINGS TN34
Service: General counselling
Area served: Hastings & Battle
Referral: Self, GP
Training of workers: Minimum 3 yr BAC Rec Course. Fortnightly supervision
Code of Ethics: BAC
Management by: Committee of counsellors (Reg as charity applied for)
Fees: Donations accepted

Individual Practitioners
*Each individual is a **member of** one or more organisations eligible for entry into this directory. BAC Accredited Counsellors and Recognised Supervisors are shaded.*

DOHERTY Prue 0424 214605
150 Cooden Drive, BEXHILL-ON-SEA TN39 3AW
Member of: BAC
Quals/training: Member of Inst of Linguistics; Dip Couns (CSCT, London) 1990
Personal Therapy: Yes
Supervision: Yes
Counselling offered: General, Relationship, Eating disorders, Abuse
Service for: Individuals, Couples
Theoretical Approach: Rogerian, Psychodynamic, Cognitive
Fees: £20

POWE Roger 0273 726398
10 Cumberland Court, 150 Kings Road, BRIGHTON BN1 2PJ
Member of: DAO
Quals/training: MA, BEd, Dip Humanities (London); Adv Dip Couns (Northbrook College) 1993
Personal Therapy: Ongoing
Supervision: Ongoing
Counselling offered: General, Bereavement, Crisis, Stress, Sexual, Relationship, Educational, Management
Service for: Individuals
Specific to: Young people
Theoretical Approach: Psychodynamic
Fees: £12 - £25 Sliding Scale

Sussex - East

STEDMAN John   0273 739668
Flat 8, Bedford Square, BRIGHTON BN1 2PN
Member of:	BAC
Quals/training:	Dip Theology (London); trained Psychotherapist (LCIP)
Personal Therapy:	Yes
Supervision:	Yes
Counselling offered:	General, Marital, Sexual, Bereavement, Psychotherapy, Supervision
Service for:	Individuals
Specific to:	Social workers, Clergy/priests
Theoretical Approach:	Psychoanalytic, Eclectic
Fees:	£18 - £25 dependent on income

SIDHU Frankie   0273 603896
4 Gerard Street, BRIGHTON BN1 4NW
Member of:	BAC
Quals/training:	Dip(PET)'90; Dip Ericksonian Hypnosis Psychotherapy & NLP (Stockwell)'90; British Hypnosis Research, Brighton
Personal Therapy:	Yes
Supervision:	Ongoing
Counselling offered:	General, AIDS, Bereavement, Sexual, Relationship, Crisis, Addiction, Drugs
Service for:	Individuals, Couples, Groups
Specific to:	Gays
Theoretical Approach:	Psychosynthesis, Gestalt
Fees:	£20 - £35 negotiable

WENHAM Franklin   0273 500647
44 Barn Rise, Westdene, BRIGHTON BN1 5EE
Member of:	BAC
Quals/training:	BA(Hons); Cert Ed; Dip Ind Admin; PG Dip Couns (Brighton Poly); Orientation at Primal Inst (Los Angeles) & training at Primal Therapy Centre (Brighton)
Personal Therapy:	Yes
Supervision:	Ongoing
Counselling offered:	**Primal therapy, General**
Service for:	Individuals, Groups
Theoretical Approach:	Janov, Rogerian, TA
Other languages:	French, Spanish
Fees:	£25(Brighton), £33(London)

BEALE Diana   0273 558507
15 Parkmore Terrace, BRIGHTON BN1 6AL
Member of:	BAC Acc
Quals/training:	BAC Acc; BA Psychol; CQSW & MA Applied Social Studies (Warwick Univ); Dip Couns (Brighton Poly) '87; Dip Gestalt Therapy
Personal Therapy:	Ongoing
Supervision:	Ongoing
Counselling offered:	**General**
Service for:	Individuals, Couples, Groups
Specific to:	People with learning difficulties
Theoretical Approach:	Client-centred, Gestalt
Fees:	£15 - £22 sliding scale

Sussex - East

ACKET Marijke 0273 554264
13b Beaconsfield Villas, BRIGHTON BN1 6HA
Member of: BAC, IPS
Quals/training: Currently in Psychosynthesis Psychotherapy training IP; Dip in Psychosynthesis Counselling
Personal Therapy: Ongoing
Supervision: Ongoing
Counselling offered: General, Psychotherapy, Abuse
Service for: Individuals, Couples, Groups
Specific to: Women, Lesbians
Theoretical Approach: Psychosynthesis, Psychodynamic
Fees: £20 - £28 negotiable

SUSS Lawrence 0273 502900
135 Preston Drove, BRIGHTON BN1 6LE
Member of: BAC Acc, AGIP
Quals/training: BAC Acc; BSc, DMS, Dip Couns (Brighton Poly) 1984; brief psychotherapy (Guys); training in marital, Gestalt, psychoanalytic psychotherapy
Personal Therapy: Ongoing
Supervision: Ongoing
Counselling offered: General, Relationship, Marital, Short-term, Long-term, Psychotherapy, Crisis, Supervision
Service for: Individuals, Couples, Groups
Theoretical Approach: Psychodynamic, Analytic, Eclectic
Fees: £22 - £25 negotiable

CHISWELL JONES Susan 0273 541985
205 Osborne Road, BRIGHTON BN1 6LT
Member of: BAC Acc
Quals/training: BAC Acc; BA (Hons); PGCE: Dip Couns (Brighton Poly) 1985; Gestalt training
Personal Therapy: Yes
Supervision: Ongoing
Counselling offered: General, Relationship, Bereavement, Sexual abuse
Service for: Individuals, Couples, Groups
Theoretical Approach: Eclectic, Rogerian, Gestalt, TA
Fees: £20 sliding scale for unwaged

MARTIN Deidre 0273 507644
1 Knoyle Road, BRIGHTON BN1 6RB
Member of: BAC
Quals/training: Dip in Couns; Cert, LCIP; Cert Clinical Medicine, Member International Inst of Reflexology; Dip, British Wheel of Yoga; Cruse counsellor
Personal Therapy: No
Supervision: Ongoing
Counselling offered: General, Bereavement, Stress management
Service for: Individuals, Groups
Specific to: People with disabilities
Theoretical Approach: Eclectic
Fees: £20 negotiable

Sussex - East

WITHERS Jane 0273 541149
37 Stanmer Villas, BRIGHTON BN1 7HQ
Member of: BAC Acc
Quals/training: BAC(Acc); Dip Couns'86; Teachers Cert; 101; Gestalt Training Group
Personal Therapy: Yes
Supervision: Ongoing
Counselling offered: **Spiritual, Relationship, Bereavement, Long-term**
Service for: Individuals, Couples, Groups
Theoretical Approach: Gestalt, Rogerian, TA
Fees: £20 onwards

RICHARDSON Madeleine   ansaphone 0273 504385, ansaphone 0273 559739
33 Mandalay Court, London Road, BRIGHTON BN1 8QU
Member of: BAC Acc, BASMT, BABCP
Quals/training: BAC Acc; NMGC (Acc); BASMT Acc; Memb ASSP; Sexual Therapist; Parks Inner-Child Therapist
Personal Therapy: Yes
Supervision: Ongoing
Counselling offered: **General, Marital, Sexual, Conciliation, Abuse, PTSD**
Service for: Individuals, Couples
Theoretical Approach: Integrative, Psychodynamic, Behavioural
Fees: £30 negotiable

SHORT Ruth 0273 672938
18c Marine Square, BRIGHTON BN2 1DN
Member of: BAC, BPS
Quals/training: BA Psychol; Dip Social Administration(Oxford); Cert Personal Construct Psychology (CPCP) 1982
Personal Therapy: Yes
Supervision: Ongoing
Counselling offered: **General, Relationship, Bereavement**
Service for: Individuals, Couples, Groups
Theoretical Approach: Rogerian, PCP
Fees: £15 - £35 sliding scale

LIDSTER Wendy 0273 673544
BRIGHTON BN2
Member of: BAC, BASMT
Quals/training: RELATE Acc; Accred member Family Mediators Assoc; BASMT Acc
Personal Therapy: Yes
Supervision: Ongoing
Counselling offered: **General, Relationship, Marital, Sexual**
Service for: Individuals, Couples
Theoretical Approach: Integrative, Psychodynamic, Behavioural
Fees: £30 negotiable

Sussex - East

HALES Jonathan   **0273 670095**
Flat 1, 27 Egremont Place, BRIGHTON BN2 2GA
Member of: BAC Acc
Quals/training: BAC Acc; Dip Couns (Hatfield Poly) 1984
Personal Therapy: Yes
Supervision: Ongoing
Counselling offered: General, Relationship, HIV, AIDS, Bereavement, Supervision
Service for: Individuals, Groups
Theoretical Approach: Client-centred, Psychodynamic, Gestalt
Fees: By arrangement

HEWITT Eva   **0273 605809**
4 Hanover Crescent, BRIGHTON BN2 2SB
Member of: BAC Acc
Quals/training: BAC Acc; BA (Hons); RELATE Trained 1976; Co-counselling training 1975-6; short courses in Humanistic Therapies; Massage 1980; BPAS courses 1984
Personal Therapy: Ongoing
Supervision: Ongoing
Counselling offered: General, Fertility, Loss, Life planning, Creative potential, Pregnancy, Relationship
Service for: Individuals, Couples
Specific to: Creative people
Theoretical Approach: Eclectic
Other languages: French, German
Fees: Negotiable, possible reduced fee for unwaged people

ARMITAGE Jan   **0273 699228**
36 Southampton Street, BRIGHTON BN2 2UT
Member of: BAC
Quals/training: Dip Couns (Brighton Poly)
Personal Therapy: Ongoing
Supervision: Ongoing
Counselling offered: General, Long-term
Service for: Individuals
Theoretical Approach: Primal therapy
Fees: £25; £1075 for 3 weeks intensive

VENNER Ruth   **0273 684858**
23 Upper Wellington Road, BRIGHTON BN2 3AN
Member of: BAC, IPC
Quals/training: BA(Hons) Psychol (London Univ) '60; Dip (IPC/WPF) '83
Personal Therapy: Yes
Supervision: Ongoing
Counselling offered: General, Crisis, ME, Spiritual, Long-term
Service for: Individuals, Couples, Families
Specific to: Ethnic minorities, Survivors of child abuse, Victims of violence
Theoretical Approach: Psychodynamic
Fees: £20 negotiable

Sussex - East

GAYTON Maria 0273 674793
117 Milner Road, BRIGHTON BN2 4BR
Member of: BAC
Quals/training: BA; PG Dip Couns
Personal Therapy: Yes
Supervision: Ongoing
Counselling offered: General, Abuse, Sexuality, Addiction
Service for: Individuals, Groups
Specific to: Sexual minorities, Survivors of sex abuse
Theoretical Approach: Humanistic
Fees: £15 - £20

FLEWETT Dave 0273 672875
37 Princes Terrace, BRIGHTON BN2 5JS
Member of: BAC Acc
Quals/training: BAC Acc; B Phil Couns 1982 Exeter Univ; '87 advanced groupwork training; Dip Ericksonian Hypnotherapy & NLP
Personal Therapy: Ongoing
Supervision: Ongoing
Counselling offered: General, Relationship
Service for: Individuals, Families
Theoretical Approach: Psychodynamic, Person-centred
Fees: £20 - £25 negotiable

BERNACCA Tony 0273 416914
27 Gardener Street, Portslade, BRIGHTON BN41 1SX
Member of: BAC
Quals/training: BA Social Anthropology; Dip Couns
Personal Therapy: Yes
Supervision: Ongoing
Counselling offered: General
Service for: Individuals, Couples
Theoretical Approach: Person-centred, Gestalt
Fees: £15

BEAZLEY RICHARDS Joanna 0892 655195
2 Quarry View, Whitehill Road, CROWBOROUGH TN6 1JT
Member of: BAC Acc, BPS
Quals/training: BAC Acc; M Litt; PTSTA; CPsychol; DipTMHA; AFBPsS; FRSM; MBIM; Memb EATA
Personal Therapy: Yes
Supervision: Ongoing
Counselling offered: General, Psychotherapy, Crisis
Service for: Individuals, Couples, Families, Groups
Theoretical Approach: Humanistic, Integrative
Fees: According to circumstances

Sussex - East

DIXON-NUTTALL Rosemary   **0892 663192**
1 Coronation Cottages, Western Road, Jarvis Brook, CROWBOROUGH TN6 3EX
Member of:	BAC Acc, AGIP
Quals/training:	BAC Acc; Dip Memb ipc/wpf 1984; Adv Cert Groupwork (WPF) 1986; Training memb AGIP 1992; GAS (Assoc)
Personal Therapy:	Yes
Supervision:	Ongoing
Counselling offered:	**General, Bereavement, Crisis, Long-term, Psychotherapy**
Service for:	Individuals, Groups
Theoretical Approach:	Psychodynamic
Fees:	£25 negotiable

COBBAN Joy   **0323 638440**
Chandlers, 85 Pashley Road, EASTBOURNE BN20 8EA
Member of:	BAC
Quals/training:	Combined Cert Couns (CSCT); Sussex Alcohol Advice Service Training
Personal Therapy:	Ongoing
Supervision:	Ongoing
Counselling offered:	**General, Bereavement, Crisis, Abuse, Addiction, Stress, Sexual**
Service for:	Individuals, Couples, Families, Groups, Organisations
Specific to:	Managers
Theoretical Approach:	Rogerian, Gestalt, Egan, Eclectic
Fees:	£15 - £25

WAIN Mary   **0323 724024**
103 Baldwin Avenue, EASTBOURNE BN21 1UL
Member of:	BAC
Quals/training:	Dip Clinical & Pastoral Couns
Personal Therapy:	Ongoing
Supervision:	Ongoing
Counselling offered:	**General, Bereavement, Crisis, Relationship, Family**
Service for:	Individuals, Couples, Families, Groups
Specific to:	Women, Young people, Children
Theoretical Approach:	Rogerian, Client-centred
Fees:	£10 - £25 sliding scale

CHILTON Barbara   **0323 638558**
4 Ashburnham Road, EASTBOURNE BN21 2HU
Member of:	BAC, WMIP, NRHP
Quals/training:	BSc; Dip Hypnotherapy & Psychotherapy
Personal Therapy:	Yes
Supervision:	Ongoing
Counselling offered:	**General, Psychotherapy, Hypnotherapy**
Service for:	Individuals
Theoretical Approach:	Eclectic
Fees:	£20

Sussex - East

MACALEVEY Mike 0342 824339
The Osteopath Clinic, 76 Hartfield Road, FOREST ROW RH18 5BZ
Member of: BAC
Quals/training: BSc (Hons) Occ Psy; DO; Bioenergetic Psychotherapy training; Memb College of Osteopaths; supervisor training; counselling lecturer
Personal Therapy: Ongoing
Supervision: Ongoing
Counselling offered: General, Psychotherapy, Health, Supervision
Service for: Individuals
Theoretical Approach: Holistic, Humanistic, Bioenergetic, Integrative
Fees: £35 per 60 minutes

CROSBY Simon 0342 82 123
Hindleap Corner, Priory Road, FOREST ROW RH18 5JF
Member of: BAC
Quals/training: BSc (London) 1966; Cert Couns (LCIP) 1989; Cert PCP 1991
Personal Therapy: Ongoing
Supervision: Ongoing
Counselling offered: General, Relationship, Crisis
Service for: Individuals, Couples, Families
Specific to: Parents
Theoretical Approach: Eclectic, Constructivist
Fees: £25

GREGORY Christine 0273 721463
1 Wendover Grange, Westbourne Villas, HOVE BN3 4GF
Member of: BAC, IPC
Quals/training: Dip couns (IPC/WPF) 1982
Personal Therapy: Yes
Supervision: Ongoing
Counselling offered: General
Service for: Individuals
Theoretical Approach: Analytical, Psychodynamic
Fees: £20 - £23

MURDOCH Edna 0273 735732
76 Highdown Road, HOVE BN3 6EB
Member of: BAC Acc
Quals/training: BAC Acc; Adv Dip Psychotherapy (Pellin); Dip Transpersonal Psychology (CTP)
Personal Therapy: Ongoing
Supervision: Ongoing
Counselling offered: General, Psychotherapy
Service for: Individuals
Specific to: Adolescents, Women, Gays
Theoretical Approach: Integrative
Fees: £27

Sussex - East

ASHMORE Anne
251 Dyke Road, HOVE BN3 6PA
Ansaphone 0273 557886

Member of:	BAC
Quals/training:	PG Dip Couns (Univ of Brighton) 1992; currently completing MA in Couns Psychol
Personal Therapy:	Yes
Supervision:	Ongoing
Counselling offered:	**General, Bereavement, Crisis**
Service for:	Individuals, Couples, Families, Groups
Specific to:	Survivors of child abuse
Theoretical Approach:	Humanistic, Systemic, Integrative
Fees:	£20 - £30 sliding scale

GLAISYER Alison
27 The Avenue, LEWES BN7 1QT
fax 0273 476529, 0273 479530

Member of:	BAC
Quals/training:	SRN; Dip Couns
Personal Therapy:	Yes
Supervision:	Ongoing
Counselling offered:	**General, Bereavement, Depression, Loss, Abuse, Terminal illness**
Service for:	Individuals, Couples
Specific to:	Women, People with disabilities, Survivors of child abuse
Theoretical Approach:	Rogerian, Psychodynamic
Fees:	£10 - £20 sliding scale

CROWTHER Ann
Tree Bank Cottage, Castle Lane, LEWES BN7 1YU
ansaphone 0273 478542

Member of:	BAC
Quals/training:	Post Grad Couns (Brighton Univ) 1992; Training in HIV/AIDS with Sussex AIDS Helpline, Terence Higgins Trust
Personal Therapy:	Ongoing
Supervision:	Ongoing
Counselling offered:	**Relationship, Sexual abuse, Bereavement, AIDS, Inner child, Dream**
Service for:	Individuals
Specific to:	People with disabilities, Counsellor has disability
Theoretical Approach:	Person-centred, Gestalt, Alice Miller
Fees:	£18 negotiable

CANNAN Philippa
6 Hillcrest Road, NEWHAVEN BN9 9EA
0273 512925

Member of:	BAC
Quals/training:	BA(Hons); Dip Soc Admin; Dip Couns; training in TA Psychotherapy(2 yrs) '88 & '90
Personal Therapy:	Yes
Supervision:	Ongoing
Counselling offered:	**General, Psychotherapy, PTSD, HIV**
Service for:	Individuals, Couples, Groups, Organisations
Theoretical Approach:	Integrative, TA
Fees:	£30 negotiable

Sussex - East

de Vos Maggie 0323 762 883
9 Gresham, PEVENSEY BN24 5JS
Member of: BAC, BPS
Quals/training: BEd (Hons); Adv Dip Spec Ed; BA (Psychol); Cert Couns; Cert Group Analysis; currently systemic Family Therapy (Tavistock); C Psychol
Personal Therapy: Ongoing
Supervision: Ongoing
Counselling offered: General, Child psychotherapy, Family, Bereavement
Service for: Individuals, Couples, Families, Groups, Organisations
Theoretical Approach: Systems, Rogerian, Analytical, Gestalt
Fees: By arrangement

PETHICK Ursula 0797 222480
Howfield, Udimore, RYE TN31 6AE
Member of: BAC, ANLP (PCS)
Quals/training: Certified Master Practitioner NLP (PACE) 1990; Adv Dip Integral Therapy (BHR) 1991; ANLP/PCS Validated Psychotherapist 1993; Memb BHR & LSEPH
Personal Therapy: Yes
Supervision: Ongoing
Counselling offered: General, Hypnotherapy
Service for: Individuals
Theoretical Approach: Rogerian, Ericksonian
Fees: Sliding scale

BENSON Rosemary 0797 223470
2 West Street, RYE TN31 7ES
Member of: BAC
Quals/training: LCIP 1 year Cert
Personal Therapy: Ongoing
Supervision: Ongoing
Counselling offered: General, Relationship
Service for: Individuals
Theoretical Approach: Person-centred
Fees: £18 Negotiable

DALE Peter 0424 424504
No 4, Kendal House, 10 Chapel Park Road, ST. LEONARDS-ON-SEA TN37 6HU
Member of: BAC Acc
Quals/training: BAC Acc; Post Grad Dip in Couns; Gestalt Psychotherapy training
Personal Therapy: Yes
Supervision: Ongoing
Counselling offered: General, Relationship, Trauma
Service for: Individuals, Couples
Specific to: Survivors of child abuse, Helping professions
Theoretical Approach: Eclectic, Gestalt, Psychodynamic, Humanistic
Fees: £25

Sussex - East

ANDERSON Jette 0424 425478
49 Salisbury Road, ST. LEONARDS-ON-SEA TN37 6RX
Member of: BAC
Quals/training: Training in Humanistic Psychology; Dip in Physiotherapy; AHP
Personal Therapy: Ongoing
Supervision: Ongoing
Counselling offered: General
Service for: Individuals
Theoretical Approach: Rogerian
Other languages: Danish, German
Fees: Negotiable

INSKIPP Francesca 0424 427948
2 Market Terrace, ST. LEONARDS-ON-SEA TN38 0DB
Member of: BAC RSup
Quals/training: BAC RSup; Dip Couns (Keele) 1971; Dip Psychosynthesis Couns & Therapy
Personal Therapy: Ongoing
Supervision: Ongoing
Counselling offered: **General, Marital, Loss, Bereavement, Crisis**
Service for: Individuals, Couples
Theoretical Approach: Humanistic, Person-centred, Psychosynthesis
Fees: £20 negotiable

POPKIN Jennifer 0424 428470
The Springfield Centre, 4 Springfield Road, ST. LEONARDS-ON-SEA TN38 0TU
Member of: BAC
Quals/training: MA in Education '85; Cert & Dip Hypnosis & Psychotherapy '82 & '83; Cert Couns (LCIP); Tutor of Couns (CSCT)
Personal Therapy: Ongoing
Supervision: Ongoing
Counselling offered: General, Relationship, Sexual, Unwanted habits, Children's problems, Eating disorders
Service for: Individuals, Children
Theoretical Approach: Rogerian, Egan, Bioenergetic
Fees: £15 - £18 Negotiable

GEER Carol 0580 200730
Elderwood, Wallcrouch, WADHURST TN5 7JJ
Member of: BAC, IPC
Quals/training: Cert Couns Skills (WPF); Cert Person-centred Art Therapy; Dip Adv Psychodynamic Couns (WPF); Marital Interaction (WPF)
Personal Therapy: Yes
Supervision: Ongoing
Counselling offered: General, Bereavement, Relationship, Life threatening illnesses, Short-term
Service for: Individuals, Couples
Theoretical Approach: Analytical, Psychodynamic
Fees: £16 - £25 negotiable

Sussex - West

Organisations

CHICHESTER COUNSELLING SERVICE 0243 789200
Fernleigh Centre, 40 North Street, CHICHESTER PO19 1LX
Service:	Individuals who want psychodynamic counselling
Area served:	Throughout SW Sussex & SE Hampshire
Referral:	Self, GP, Agencies
Training of workers:	Three year part-time programme during which all counsellors have personal therapy; weekly supervision
Code of Ethics:	BAC
Management by:	By Executive Committee & full time Director
Fees:	None, donations towards costs

MID-SUSSEX COUNSELLING CENTRE 0273 846835
Powell House, 21 Keymer Road, HASSOCKS BN6 8AB
Service:	Individual counselling for personal & relationship problems on a psychodynamic basis, for people aged 18 and above. Affiliated to the WPF
Area served:	Mid-Sussex
Referral:	Self or others
Training of workers:	3 years part-time basic training followed by in-service work with group supervision
Code of Ethics:	BAC
Management by:	Director & Executive Committee
Fees:	- £20 (init interview £25)

HORSHAM CITIZENS ADVICE BUREAU & BEREAVEMENT SERVICE
0403 217257
Lower Tanbridge Way, HORSHAM RH12 1PJ
Service:	Bereavement, general, crisis and relationship counselling
Area served:	Horsham district
Other languages:	German
Referral:	Self or others
Training of workers:	Trained with CAB; some staff have had personal therapy; peer supervision
Code of Ethics:	BAC
Management by:	Management Committee
Fees:	None

OFFINGTON COUNSELLING SERVICE 0903 212275
Offington Pk Methodist Church, South Farm Road, WORTHING BN14 7TN
Service:	Counselling for personal, marital & family problems
Area served:	West Sussex
Referral:	Self or others
Training of workers:	Dip in Couns; most counsellors also have other qualifications; all supervised
Code of Ethics:	BAC
Management by:	Management Committee; Registered charity affiliated to WPF
Fees:	£8 + negotiable

Sussex - West

ACT: PSYCHOLOGY SERVICE FOR SEXUAL HEALTH   0903 215151
Southdown, Swandean, Arundel Road, WORTHING BN13 3EP
Service: Couns for all HIV related problems inc rape; pre & post test HIV/
                            AIDS couns; follow-up support for those w HIV infection, their
                            relatives & friends; bereavement, sexual health couns
Area served: Worthing & District
Referral: Self or others
Training of workers: Clinical psychologist, nurse counsellor, trained psychotherapist, all
                            with specialist AIDS/HIV training
Code of Ethics: BAC, BPS, UKCC
Management by: Worthing Priority Care NHS Trust
Fees: None

Individual Practitioners
*Each individual is a **member of** one or more organisations eligible for entry into this directory.
BAC Accredited Counsellors and Recognised Supervisors are shaded.*

MEABY Katy   ansaphone 0243 553936
Copal House, The Street, Wolberton, ARUNDEL BN18 0PJ
Member of: BAC
Quals/training: Dip in Couns, Chichester Couns Services 1990
Personal Therapy: Yes
Supervision: Ongoing
Counselling offered: General, Loss, Crisis, Stress
Service for: Individuals
Theoretical Approach: Psychodynamic, Eclectic
Fees: £20, less in cases of hardship

DAVIES Ruth   0403 266764/241226
Atlantic House, 08 Station Road, Horsham, BETCHWORTH RH3 5EU
Member of: BAC
Quals/training: CQSW 1985; Dip Applied Social Studies (Croydon College); Couns
                            (W Sussex IHE); PTSD
Personal Therapy: Yes
Supervision: Ongoing
Counselling offered: General, Stress, Crisis, Bereavement, Relationship, Anxiety
Service for: Individuals, Couples, Families, Groups
Theoretical Approach: Analytical, Integrative
Fees: £25

KANE Janine   0243 776489
22 Grove Road, CHICHESTER PO19 2AP
Member of: BAC
Quals/training: Dip Couns (Chichester Couns Services); currently in psychotherapy
                            training (Minster Centre)
Personal Therapy: Yes
Supervision: Ongoing
Counselling offered: General, Psychotherapy
Service for: Individuals
Theoretical Approach: Integrative
Fees: Negotiable

Sussex - West

BELLRINGER Helen   Ansaphone **0243 784893**
129 Cedar Drive, CHICHESTER PO19 3EL
Member of: BAC
Quals/training: Adv Dip Couns; CQSW
Personal Therapy: Yes
Supervision: Ongoing
Counselling offered: General, Bereavement, Bullying, Relationship, Supervision
Service for: Individuals, Couples, Families, Groups, Organisations
Specific to: Young people
Theoretical Approach: Eclectic, Person-centred
Fees: £20 Maximum

GREEN Jennifer   **0243 527800, 0273 733830**
20 Highland Road, CHICHESTER PO19 4QX
Member of: BAC
Quals/training: Dip Hypnosis & Psychol (Blythe College) 1977/8; Dip NLP 1984; Adv Dip Couns (2 yr Post Grad) 1991-3
Personal Therapy: Ongoing
Supervision: Ongoing
Counselling offered: General, Hypnotherapy, Psychotherapy, Stress management, Weight
Service for: Individuals
Specific to: Women
Theoretical Approach: Rogerian, Egan
Fees: £30 - £40 sliding scale

HANNEMAN Janet   **0243 782346**
Gastons, Chestnut Walk, Tangmere, CHICHESTER PO20 6HH
Member of: BAC
Quals/training: Dip Couns (WPF Accred Course)
Personal Therapy: Ongoing
Supervision: Ongoing
Counselling offered: General, Abuse, Bereavement, Eating disorders, Relationship
Service for: Individuals, Couples, Organisations
Specific to: Adolescents
Theoretical Approach: Person-centred, Gestalt
Fees: £10 - £20 sliding scale

MURPHY Val   **0293 525605**
165 Buckswood Drive, Gossops Green, CRAWLEY RH11 8JD
Member of: BAC
Quals/training: Cert Couns Skills (Thomas Bennett College) '87; Dip Couns (Crawley) 1992; Person Centred Art Therapy Certificate 1992; Memb PCATA
Personal Therapy: Ongoing
Supervision: Ongoing
Counselling offered: General
Service for: Individuals
Theoretical Approach: Egan, Rogerian, Gestalt
Fees: £18 Negotiable

Sussex - West

COLMAN Greta   0342 892564
Little Haven, Byers Lane, GODSTONE RH9 8JH
Member of:	BAC Acc RSup
Quals/training:	BAC Acc & Recognised Supervisor; NMGC Trained; 1 yr course in Therapy & Supervision (TIMS)
Personal Therapy:	Yes
Supervision:	Ongoing
Counselling offered:	**General, Marital, Psychotherapy, Bereavement**
Service for:	Individuals, Couples
Theoretical Approach:	Eclectic
Fees:	£20 - £30, couples £25-35

FISHER Maggie   ansaphone 0273 832478, bleep 0293 547333
66 Western Road, Hurstpierpoint, HASSOCKS BN6 9TB
Member of:	BAC Acc
Quals/training:	BAC Acc; Dip couns; Jungian picture interpetation; Gestalt therapy; Psychosynthesis
Personal Therapy:	Ongoing
Supervision:	Ongoing
Counselling offered:	**Personal growth, Dream, Sexual abuse, Life threatening illnesses, Loss, Grief, Stress**
Service for:	Individuals, Couples, Families
Theoretical Approach:	Eclectic, Psychodynamic, Jungian
Fees:	£15 - £30 sliding scale

McMINNIES Patricia   0273 834454
51 Highfield Drive, Hurstpierpoint, HASSOCKS BN6 9AU
Member of:	BAC
Quals/training:	BA; Dip Couns; Trainee Psychotherapist with AGIP
Personal Therapy:	Ongoing
Supervision:	Ongoing
Counselling offered:	**General**
Service for:	Individuals
Theoretical Approach:	Psychodynamic
Fees:	£20 neg unemployed/low wage

TOMAN Ann   0273 843642
24 Wilmington Close, HASSOCKS BN6 8QB
Member of:	BAC
Quals/training:	RELATE trained in Relationship, Marital & Individual Couns & Sex Therapy; Family Mediation (Fam Med Assoc)
Personal Therapy:	Yes
Supervision:	Ongoing
Counselling offered:	**Relationship, Sexual, Divorce, Separation**
Service for:	Individuals, Couples
Theoretical Approach:	Eclectic, Psychodynamic, Behavioural
Fees:	£20 - £30

Sussex - West

WALLIS Simon 0444 401210
Hyde Lodge, Hand Cross, HAYWARDS HEATH RH17 6HD
Member of: BAC
Quals/training: BSc; PhD; Dip Couns
Personal Therapy: Yes
Supervision: Ongoing
Counselling offered: General, Abuse, Crisis, Drugs, Disability, Relationship
Service for: Individuals, Couples
Theoretical Approach: Psychodynamic
Fees: £15 - £35

DOWNER Yvonne 0273 857484
Downers Vineyard, Clappers Lane, Fulking, HENFIELD BN5 9NH
Member of: BAC
Quals/training: CQSW; Dip Applied Social Studies 1973; Eclectic Approach Victims Support
Personal Therapy: Yes
Supervision: Ongoing
Counselling offered: General, Marital, Bereavement, Stress, Trauma, Disability, Supervision
Service for: Individuals, Couples, Families, Groups
Theoretical Approach: Eclectic
Fees: £12 - £15

EVANS Len 0403 263419
88 Farhalls Crescent, HORSHAM RH12 4BY
Member of: BAC
Quals/training: Cert Chichester Counselling Services '87
Personal Therapy: Yes
Supervision: Ongoing
Counselling offered: General, Bereavement, Stress, Crisis, Relationship, Anxiety
Service for: Individuals, Couples
Specific to: Managers
Theoretical Approach: Jungian, Rogerian, Eclectic
Fees: £20

GOODARE Heather 0403 261674
1 Heron Way, HORSHAM RH13 6DF
Member of: BAC
Quals/training: MA (Oxon); PG Dip Couns (Brighton); BPOG
Personal Therapy: Yes
Supervision: Ongoing
Counselling offered: General, Relationship, Loss, Bereavement, Crisis, Life threatening illnesses, Cancer
Service for: Individuals, Groups
Theoretical Approach: Eclectic, Existential
Other languages: French
Fees: £15 negotiable

Sussex - West

ORWIN Judith 0403 251928
3 Heath Way, HORSHAM RH12 5XB
Member of:	BAC
Quals/training:	Cert Ed '61; BA Psychol '82; CQSW; Dip in Applied Social Studies '84; MSc in Stress (Surrey Univ) '88; RSA Couns Cert '89; Dip Couns (Albany Trust) '92
Personal Therapy:	Ongoing
Supervision:	Ongoing
Counselling offered:	**General, Bereavement, Relationship, Crisis, Addiction, PTSD, Depression, Personal growth, Co-dependency**
Service for:	Individuals, Couples, Groups, Families
Specific to:	Women, Young people, Minorities
Theoretical Approach:	Person-centred, TA, Gestalt, Integrative
Fees:	£10 - £25 sliding scale

WILD Sue 0403 254697
78 Farhalls Crescent, HORSHAM RH12 4BZ
Member of:	BAC
Quals/training:	Cert Couns (W Sussex Inst HE) '83; CQSW; Dip Applied Soc Studies '84; LEA Working with Young People Course '82
Personal Therapy:	Ongoing
Supervision:	Ongoing
Counselling offered:	**General, Bereavement, Marital**
Service for:	Individuals, Couples, Families, Groups
Theoretical Approach:	Eclectic, TA
Fees:	£20 ind, £30 couples

ADDENBROOKE Mary 0293 851362
The Vicarage, Colgate, HORSHAM RH12 4SZ
Member of:	Guild of Psychotherapists
Quals/training:	BA Hons; Membership of Guild of Psychotherapists 1986
Personal Therapy:	Ongoing
Supervision:	Ongoing
Counselling offered:	**Psychotherapy, Supervision**
Service for:	Individuals, Groups
Specific to:	Substance abusers
Theoretical Approach:	Jungian
Fees:	Negotiable

FROST Charles 0403 264665
5 Searles View, HORSHAM RH12 4FG
Member of:	BAC
Quals/training:	Dip Hypnosis & Psychotherapy 1984; courses in Ericksonian Therapy 1985; NLP 1988
Personal Therapy:	Yes
Supervision:	Ongoing
Counselling offered:	**General, Hypnotherapy, Psychotherapy, Psychosexual, Analysis**
Service for:	Individuals, Families
Theoretical Approach:	Freudian
Fees:	£30 one and a half hour session

Sussex - West

AUBREY Christine 0903 752152
Little Houghton, Hoe Court, LANCING BN15 0QX
Member of: BAC Acc, AFT
Quals/training: BAC(Acc); PG Dip Couns; PQ training in Family Therapy; 1 yr course in Group Analysis; Practitioner Memb Special Group in Couns Psychol (BPS); MA Couns Psychol
Personal Therapy: Yes
Supervision: Ongoing
Counselling offered: General, Bereavement, Terminal illness, Marital, Family
Service for: Individuals, Couples, Families, Groups
Theoretical Approach: Psychodynamic, Systemic
Fees: £15 - £25 negotiable

COLE Sara 0903 767027
Moidart House, Hoe Court, LANCING BN15 0QX
Member of: BAC Acc
Quals/training: BAC(Acc); BA Hons; Dip Couns (Brighton Poly)'86; Cert TEAA (creative art therapies)'92
Personal Therapy: Ongoing
Supervision: Ongoing
Counselling offered: General, Short-term, Long-term
Service for: Individuals
Specific to: Young people
Theoretical Approach: Integrative, Client-centred, Gestalt, TA, Art therapy
Fees: £20 negotiable

FRANCIS Pippa 0798 42638
Grange House, Grange Centre Car Park, Grange Road, MIDHURST GU29 9LS
Member of: BAC
Quals/training: Adv Dip Couns(W Sussex Inst of HE)
Personal Therapy: Ongoing
Supervision: Ongoing
Counselling offered: General, Relationship, Stress, Loss, Crisis
Service for: Individuals, Couples, Families, Groups
Specific to: Women, Children, Young people, Gays
Theoretical Approach: Person-centred, Eclectic
Fees: £25 negotiable

GLOVER Jan 0428 707477
Yew Tree Cottage, North Chapel, PETWORTH GU28 9HL
Member of: BAC
Quals/training: Dip Couns; Accredited CAT therapist
Personal Therapy: Ongoing
Supervision: Ongoing
Counselling offered: General, Crisis, Marital
Service for: Individuals
Theoretical Approach: CAT, Jungian, Existential
Fees: £15 - £25 negotiable

Sussex - West

KIERNAN Ursula 0903 743289
13 Manor Close, Storrington, PULBOROUGH RH20 4LF
Member of: BAC
Quals/training: BA Psychol 1972 London; Msc Clinical Psychol Surrey '75; Dip Couns WPF '85; Dip Psychotherapy IPSS '87; 2 yrs attachment to the Inst Marital Studies
Personal Therapy: Yes
Supervision: Ongoing
Counselling offered: **Psychotherapy, Relationship, Crisis, Loss, Personal growth**
Service for: Individuals
Specific to: Helping professions
Theoretical Approach: Object relations
Fees: £12 - £25 Negotiable

HOPPE Maggie 0273 464127
110 Old Shoreham Road, SHOREHAM-BY-SEA BN4 5TE
Member of: BAC
Quals/training: 1976 CQSW; '86 Diploma in Counselling (Brighton Poly)
Personal Therapy: Yes
Supervision: Ongoing
Counselling offered: **General, Marital, Sexual, Bereavement, Addiction, Family**
Service for: Individuals, Couples, Families
Specific to: Young people, Children, People with disabilities
Theoretical Approach: Rogerian, Client-centred
Fees: £15 - £20 red. rates for low oncome

CAMPBELL Robbi 0903 208041
49 King Street, WORTHING BN14 7BN
Member of: BAC Acc
Quals/training: BAC (Acc); BA(Hons); Dip RSA; Post Grad Dip Couns, CNAA; RSA Cert Couns Skills; TA training; current training: MA Counselling Psychology until Sept '93
Personal Therapy: Ongoing
Supervision: Ongoing
Counselling offered: **General, Bereavement, Long-term, Supervision**
Service for: Individuals, Couples, Groups
Specific to: Survivors of child abuse, Visually impaired
Theoretical Approach: Psychodynamic, Eclectic
Fees: £15 - £30 sliding scale

DALE Marjorie 0903 501510
12 Falmer Close, Goring by the Sea, WORTHING BN12 4TB
Member of: BAC
Quals/training: Sussex Dip Couns 1986; trained with RELATE
Personal Therapy: Yes
Supervision: Ongoing
Counselling offered: **Marital, Stress, Depression, Personal growth**
Service for: Individuals, Couples
Theoretical Approach: Rogerian, Gestalt, TA
Fees: £18 initial session, then £15 negotiable

Sussex - West

ROBINSON Gerald 0903 266771
64 Burnham Road, WORTHING BN13 2NJ
Member of: BAC
Quals/training: BA Psychol '78; Fellow Inst of Management '81; Couns course (W Sussex Inst of HE) '86; GBR of BPS '93
Personal Therapy: Ongoing
Supervision: Ongoing
Counselling offered: General
Service for: Individuals, Families
Theoretical Approach: Rogerian, Cognitive/Behavioural
Fees: £15 - £20

RUIJTERMAN Caroline 0903 502048
Worthing Clinic of Traditional, Chinese Acupuncture, 2a Goring Road, WORTHING BN12 4AJ
Member of: BAC
Quals/training: BSc; CQSW; Dip Couns
Personal Therapy: Yes
Supervision: Ongoing
Counselling offered: General, Bereavement, Crisis, Sexual abuse
Service for: Individuals
Specific to: Adoptees
Theoretical Approach: Psychodynamic
Fees: £14 - £18

PULLEN Denise, Dr 0903 505626
11 Arlington Close, Goring by Sea, WORTHING BN12 4ST
Member of: Institute of Psychosexual Medicine
Quals/training: MB BS LRCP; MRCS trained in Marital and Sexual Therapy:
Personal Therapy: Ongoing
Supervision: Ongoing
Counselling offered: Psychosexual, Marital
Service for: Individuals, Couples
Theoretical Approach: Balint
Fees: £40

Sussex - West

Tyne & Wear

Organisations

NEWCASTLE PSYCHOSEXUAL CLINIC 091 232 5131
Dept Obstetrics & Gynaecology, Royal Victoria Infirmary, NEWCASTLE-UPON-TYNE NE1 4LP
Service: Psychosomatic medical investigation and treatment for individuals and couples with sexual difficulties
Area served: Northern Region HA
Referral: Health Practitioner
Training of workers: Dr R Freedman is a member of the Institute of Psychosexual Medicine
Code of Ethics: IPM
Management by: NHS
Fees: None

BODY POSITIVE NORTH EAST LTD 091 232 2855
SIDA Centre, 12 Princes Square, NEWCASTLE-UPON-TYNE NE1 8EG
Service: Support, information, counselling and advice for those living with HIV, their carers, families and friends
Area served: Newcastle upon Tyne, Tyneside, Gateshead, Northumberland
Referral: Self or others
Training of workers: Basic counselling skills and specialist HIV/AIDS training
Management by: Board of Directors
Fees: None

NEWCASTLE COUNCIL FOR THE DISABLED
091 284 0480, Fax 091 213 0910
The Dene Centre, Castle Farm road, NEWCASTLE-UPON-TYNE NE3 1PH
Service: Counselling for people with a disability or illness and for their carers. This covers all aspects of counselling, not necessarily disability
Area served: Borders, N Yorkshire, Cumbria (Northern Region)
Referral: Self, Health/Soc Work Professional
Training of workers: Training in psychotherapy, Member of Nat Council of Psychotherapy. 2nd Counsellor has passed a BAC Rec Course
Code of Ethics: BAC, NCHP
Management by: Mr Kevin Durkin (Director)
Fees: None

NEWCASTLE FAMILY PLANNING AND WELL WOMAN SERVICE
091 273 9560
4 Graingerville North, Westgate Road, NEWCASTLE-UPON-TYNE NE4 6UJ
Service: Psychosexual counselling
Area served: Newcastle
Referral: Self
Training of workers: Psychosexual medicine training, Balint seminars
Code of Ethics: GMC
Management by: Newcastle Family Planning Well Woman Service
Fees: None

Tyne & Wear

NORTHERN ASSOCIATION FOR ANALYTICAL PSYCHOTHERAPY
Sec 091 522 6913, chair 0661 842727
Secretary, 10 West Lawn, Ashbrooke, SUNDERLAND SR2 7HW
Service: Aims to provide a PG forum for the cont growth & interest in analytical psychotherapy thro' seminars, lectures, confs. Meetings on 1st & 3rd Mons each month when papers are read.
Training of workers: Candidates would normally have background in caring profs. Min personal therapy 2 yrs; weekly supervision of 2 patients seen weekly for a period of 2 yrs
Code of Ethics: NAAP, UKCP

Individual Practitioners
*Each individual is a **member of** one or more organisations eligible for entry into this directory. BAC Accredited Counsellors and Recognised Supervisors are shaded.*

GEATER Kathy   091 273 8336
77 Dunholme Road, Grainger Park, NEWCASTLE-UPON-TYNE NE4 6XD
Member of: BAC
Quals/training: Adv Dip Couns (Durham) 1995; MA Couns
Personal Therapy: Yes
Supervision: Ongoing
Counselling offered: Stress management, Bereavement, Sexual abuse, Addiction, Women's issues, Relationship
Service for: Individuals, Groups, Organisations
Specific to: Survivors of sex abuse
Theoretical Approach: Person-centred, Eclectic
Fees: £15 - £25

COULING Jo   091 504 0060
7 Littleburn Close, HOUGHTON-LE-SPRING DH4 5HJ
Member of: BAC
Quals/training: MA Guidance & Counselling; RELATE trained
Personal Therapy: Yes
Supervision: Ongoing
Counselling offered: General, Relationship, Bereavement
Service for: Individuals, Couples
Theoretical Approach: Person-centred
Fees: £25

BIANCARDI Jenny   091 281 6243
Jenny Biancardi Consultancy, 94 St George's Terrace, NEWCASTLE-UPON-TYNE NE2 2DL
Member of: BAC Acc, BPA, Member of UKCP Register
Quals/training: BAC Acc; RMN; Primary Trainer for BPA
Personal Therapy: Yes
Supervision: Ongoing
Counselling offered: General, Drama therapy
Service for: Individuals, Couples, Organisations
Theoretical Approach: Client-centred, Psychodrama
Fees: £20 - £35

Tyne & Wear

BIRCHALL Patricia 091 281 4846
202 Jesmond Dene Road, Jesmond, NEWCASTLE-UPON-TYNE NE2 2NL
Member of: BAC
Quals/training: 4 year training in Person-Centred Therapy 1984-7; advanced training 1987-90; MA(Ed) Couns & Guidance (Durham Univ) pending
Personal Therapy: Yes
Supervision: Ongoing
Counselling offered: General, Psychotherapy
Service for: Individuals
Theoretical Approach: Person-centred
Fees: £25

FREEDMAN Roland 091 285 6156
1 The Grove, Gosforth, NEWCASTLE-UPON-TYNE NE3 1NU
Member of: Institute of Psychosexual Medicine
Quals/training: 1947 medical doctor with psychosexual training
Personal Therapy: No
Supervision: Ongoing
Counselling offered: Psychosomatic, Psychosexual, Analysis
Service for: Individuals, Couples
Theoretical Approach: Freudian
Fees: £15 - £60 sliding scale

WINTERNITZ Robert 091 285 4643
17 Brookfield, Westfield, Gosforth, NEWCASTLE-UPON-TYNE NE3 4YB
Member of: BAC
Quals/training: Dip Couns(Eigenwelt); MA Phil(Oxon); UKPCA Network: Careline
Personal Therapy: Ongoing
Supervision: Ongoing
Counselling offered: General
Service for: Individuals
Specific to: People with disabilities
Theoretical Approach: Person-centred, Rogerian
Fees: Negotiable

HIGDON Juliet 091 413 4016
The Old Rectory, RYTON NE40 3QP
Member of: BAC
Quals/training: MA; qualified Social Worker; RELATE trained counsellor; trained in psychodynamic approach at TC and TIMS
Personal Therapy: Yes
Supervision: Ongoing
Counselling offered: General, Marital, Bereavement
Service for: Individuals, Couples, Groups
Specific to: Ethnic minorities, Managers, Helping professions
Theoretical Approach: Psychodynamic
Fees: £15 - £30 sliding scale

Tyne & Wear

MORRIS Vivienne 091 511 0397
25 Tunstall Vale, SUNDERLAND SR2 7HP
Member of: BAC Acc
Quals/training: BAC Acc; BA; MA Couns; PhD; Dip Ed; Dip Couns; Additional training in Adv Hypnotherapy, Groupwork, Metaphor therapy, Psychodrama; AHP
Personal Therapy: Ongoing
Supervision: Ongoing
Counselling offered: **General, Incest, Child abuse, Psychotherapy, Occupational, Supervision**
Service for: Individuals, Groups, Organisations
Specific to: Creative people, Health care professionals
Theoretical Approach: Person-centred, Eclectic
Fees: Negotiable

YOUNG Louise 091 522 8487
38 Manston Close, Moorside, SUNDERLAND SR3 2RR
Member of: BAC, BPS
Quals/training: BSc(Hons) Psychol; MA(Ed) Guidance & Couns
Personal Therapy: Ongoing
Supervision: Ongoing
Counselling offered: **General, Crisis, Psychotherapy**
Service for: Individuals
Theoretical Approach: Integrative
Fees: £35 negotiable

LLOYD-WILLIAMS Kathleen 091 416 7324
125 Westernmoor, Hawthorn Park, WASHINGTON NE37 1LT
Member of: BAC, ANLP (PCS)
Quals/training: NCPHR 1983-88; Full Memb NCP; Trained in sexuality and Disability
Personal Therapy: Yes
Supervision: Ongoing
Counselling offered: **General, Psychotherapy, Hypnotherapy, Disability, Crisis**
Service for: Individuals
Theoretical Approach: Rogerian, RET
Fees: £25

FERRY Pat 091 251 0684
5 Clovelly Gardens, WHITLEY BAY NE26 1PZ
Member of: BAC, ANLP (PCS)
Quals/training: CQSW; Cert Master Practitioner NLP; Master Hypnotist & Hypnotherapist; Memb BCHE
Personal Therapy: Unknown
Supervision: Ongoing
Counselling offered: **Psychotherapy, Hypnotherapy, Anxiety, Stress**
Service for: Individuals, Couples
Theoretical Approach: Eclectic, Rogerian, Egan, NLP
Fees: £20

Warwickshire

Organisations

ASHBY TRUST
c/o 19A New Street, Cubbington, LEAMINGTON SPA CV32 7LA
Service:	The Trust provides financial support to people who need counselling and would otherwise be unable to afford the full cost
Area served:	Coventry, Warwickshire, expanding into W Midlands
Referral:	Self
Training of workers:	Own recognition procedure
Code of Ethics:	Varies with professional seen
Management by:	Management Committee answerable to Board of Trustees
Fees:	What the client can afford

ROSEMARY CLARKE & BARRIE HINKSMAN, PSYCHOTHERAPISTS
0926 832312
67 Cubbington Road, Lillington, LEAMINGTON SPA CV32 7AQ
Service:	Psychotherapy in individual or group sessions
Area served:	No restriction
Other languages:	French, German
Referral:	Self or others
Training of workers:	Trained Midlands psychotherapists with experience of personal therapy; regular supervision
Code of Ethics:	Agency's own code
Management by:	Partners
Fees:	£22 - £42 by arrangement, concessions

NORTH WARWICKSHIRE CLINICAL PSYCHOLOGY SERVICE
0203 35011
George Eliot Hospital, College Street, NUNEATON CV10 7DJ
Service:	Full range of psychological therapy & counselling for a wide range of problems eg anxiety, depression, marital, sexual, relationship. Mental health (all ages), learning disability
Area served:	North Warks Nuneaton & Bedworth
Referral:	Health Practitioner, Health/Soc Work Professional
Training of workers:	GPs, consultants, medical, nursing & social services staff
Code of Ethics:	BPS
Management by:	North Warks NHS Trust
Fees:	None

OASIS COUNSELLING AND TRAINING
0926 491291
15 High Street, WARWICK CV34 4AP
Service:	General counselling including divorce, loss, personal, relationship, sexual
Area served:	No restriction
Referral:	Self
Training of workers:	RELATE training including counselling couples with sexual problems
Code of Ethics:	BAC
Management by:	Partners - Jan Le Tocq & Gill Frost
Fees:	£25; £30 evening

Warwickshire

Individual Practitioners
*Each individual is a **member of** one or more organisations eligible for entry into this directory. BAC Accredited Counsellors and Recognised Supervisors are shaded.*

HILL Brenda   **0789 773192**
93 High Street, Bidford on Avon, ALCESTER B50 4BD
Member of:	BAC, BASMT
Quals/training:	BA; RELATE trained inc Couns & Sexual Therapy; Divorce Mediation training (Family Mediation Assoc)
Personal Therapy:	No
Supervision:	Ongoing
Counselling offered:	**General, Marital, Sexual**
Service for:	Individuals, Couples
Theoretical Approach:	Eclectic
Fees:	£25

AINSWORTH Janet   **0926 851065**
12 New Street, KENILWORTH CV8 2EZ
Member of:	BAC Acc
Quals/training:	BAC(Acc); BA; CQSW; NMGC trained '82; trained WPF Associate '86-'88
Personal Therapy:	Yes
Supervision:	Ongoing
Counselling offered:	**General**
Service for:	Individuals, Couples
Theoretical Approach:	Psychodynamic
Fees:	£15 - £20

TE VELDE Johanna   **0926 311298**
0 Deaconsfield Street, LEAMINGTON SPA CV31 1DT
Member of:	BAC
Quals/training:	Higher Vocational Training Sociology/Pedagogy; CQSW, trained in Gestalt Psychotherapy (EGI)
Personal Therapy:	Yes
Supervision:	Ongoing
Counselling offered:	**Psychotherapy**
Service for:	Individuals
Specific to:	Women
Theoretical Approach:	Gestalt
Other languages:	Dutch, French, German
Fees:	£23 - £29 sliding scale, no-one refused

MYERS Marion   **0926 425403**
44 St Mary's Road, LEAMINGTON SPA CV31 1JP
Member of:	BAC Acc, WMIP
Quals/training:	BAC Acc; Psychiatric Social Worker 1970 LSE; Training in Family & Marital Therapy IGA '74; Trainee BAP 1992.
Personal Therapy:	Ongoing
Supervision:	Ongoing
Counselling offered:	**General, Marital, Long-term, Supervision**
Service for:	Individuals, Couples
Theoretical Approach:	Psychodynamic
Fees:	£24 Concessions negotiable

Warwickshire

BECKER Renate 0926 336905
16 Radford Road, LEAMINGTON SPA CV31 1LX
Member of: BAC
Quals/training: 1974 BA Social Studies & Psychology; 1984-7 Gestalt therapy (Gestalt Training Services UK)
Personal Therapy: Ongoing
Supervision: Ongoing
Counselling offered: Psychotherapy, Supervision
Service for: Individuals, Groups
Specific to: Women
Theoretical Approach: Gestalt
Other languages: German, French
Fees: £26 - £36 negotiable

RENFREW Denise 0926 883645
211 Rugby Road, LEAMINGTON SPA CV32 6DY
Member of: BAC
Quals/training: Qualified Gestalt Psychotherapist GTS (UK) '84-87
Personal Therapy: Yes
Supervision: Ongoing
Counselling offered: General, Psychotherapy
Service for: Individuals
Theoretical Approach: Gestalt
Fees: Negotiable

HINKSMAN Barrie 0926 832312
67 Cubbington Road, Lillington, LEAMINGTON SPA CV32 7AQ
Member of: BAC
Quals/training: Trained in Clinical Pastoral Care(CTA)1961-70; Group Dynamics(C of E Board of Education)1967-79; NMGC training 1967-70; Gestalt(London Gestalt Centre)1973-78
Personal Therapy: Yes
Supervision: Ongoing
Counselling offered: Psychotherapy
Service for: Individuals, Groups
Theoretical Approach: Gestalt
Other languages: French
Fees: £28 - £44 negotiable

SHAW Sue 0926 336319
32 Hadrian Close, LEAMINGTON SPA CV32 7ED
Member of: BAC
Quals/training: Cert Ed; RELATE 1980-82; Gestalt training 1983-87 (GTS Midlands) in Psychotherapy
Personal Therapy: Yes
Supervision: Ongoing
Counselling offered: Psychotherapy
Service for: Individuals
Theoretical Approach: Gestalt
Fees: £19 - £29 sliding scale

Warwickshire

JAMES Patricia 0203 326441
52 Lutterworth Road, NUNEATON CV11 4LF
Member of: BAC Acc, WMIP
Quals/training: BAC Acc; RSA Cert Couns 1987; WPF Training; Assoc WMIP
Personal Therapy: Ongoing
Supervision: Ongoing
Counselling offered: **General, Marital, Personal growth**
Service for: Individuals, Couples
Theoretical Approach: Psychodynamic, Analytical
Fees: £23 negotiable

HOLMES Dorothy 0203 340864
1 Quarry Lane, NUNEATON CV11 6QB
Member of: BAC, WMIP
Quals/training: Cert Couns Studies (Leicester Univ); 2 yr training (WPF Associate); Jungian Analytical Course on going (WMIP)
Personal Therapy: Ongoing
Supervision: Ongoing
Counselling offered: **Psychotherapy**
Service for: Individuals
Theoretical Approach: Analytical, Jungian
Fees: £20 - £25

MARSHALL Beth 0203 384616
11 Quarry Lane, NUNEATON CV11 6QB
Member of: BAC
Quals/training: Cert Ed; WPF Affiliate trained
Personal Therapy: Ongoing
Supervision: Ongoing
Counselling offered: **General, Bereavement, Relationship, Psychotherapy**
Service for: Individuals, Couples
Theoretical Approach: Psychodynamic, Client-centred
Fees: £20 - £25 negotiable

DAY Christine ansaphone 0788 547516
163 Clifton Road, RUGBY CV21 3QN
Member of: BAC
Quals/training: NNEB 1973; Cert Couns Skills (East Warwickshire College) 1993
Personal Therapy: No
Supervision: Ongoing
Counselling offered: **General**
Service for: Individuals, Couples, Families, Groups, Organisations
Specific to: Children
Theoretical Approach: TA, Integrative
Fees: £18

Warwickshire

DAY Roger   ansaphone 0788 547 516
163 Clifton Road, RUGBY CV21 3QN
Member of:	BAC
Quals/training:	Cert Couns Skills (East Warwickshire College)1992; Dip Couns 1993
Personal Therapy:	Ongoing
Supervision:	Ongoing
Counselling offered:	**General, Redundancy**
Service for:	Individuals, Couples, Families, Groups, Organisations
Specific to:	Children
Theoretical Approach:	Integrative
Fees:	£18

BECHHOFER Susi   0788 576925
193 Lower Hillmorton Road, RUGBY CV21 3TR
Member of:	BAC
Quals/training:	Dip Couns - 1 yr Pastoral Studies at B'ham Univ; Counsellor in General Practice; Dip Eircksonian Hypnotherapy/NLP
Personal Therapy:	Yes
Supervision:	Ongoing
Counselling offered:	**Stress management, Loss, Bereavement**
Service for:	Individuals, Couples, Groups
Theoretical Approach:	Eclectic, Integrative
Fees:	£15 - £25 sliding scale (free if nec.)

BURNS Alex   071 435 5369
RUGBY CV21
Member of:	BAC, IPSS
Quals/training:	BA(Hons); Dip Psychotherapy (IPSS)
Personal Therapy:	Ongoing
Supervision:	Ongoing
Counselling offered:	**Psychotherapy**
Service for:	Individuals, Couples, Families, Groups
Theoretical Approach:	Psychodynamic
Fees:	£28 - £35

DALE Irene   0788 537809
31 Albert Street, RUGBY CV21 2SG
Member of:	BAC
Quals/training:	MSc Couns Psych; BA(Hons) Psych; Cert Ed; RELATE Trained; trained Counselling Psychologist
Personal Therapy:	Yes
Supervision:	Ongoing
Counselling offered:	**General, Relationship, Marital**
Service for:	Individuals, Couples
Theoretical Approach:	Integrative
Fees:	£20

Warwickshire

CASEMORE Roger   0788 814727
57 Long Furlong, RUGBY CV22 5QT
Member of: BAC
Quals/training: BA Psychology'65; Diploma in Counselling (London Univ)'69; MEd (Nottingham Univ)'83
Personal Therapy: Yes
Supervision: Ongoing
Counselling offered: General, Crisis, Drugs, Incest, Relationship, HIV, AIDS, Conciliation
Service for: Individuals, Families
Theoretical Approach: Rogerian
Fees: £30 negotiable

KNIGHT-ADAMS Christa   0564 784110
Clover Hill, Old Warwick Road, Lapworth, SOLIHULL B94 6LD
Member of: BAC, BPS
Quals/training: BSc (Hons) Psychol; Dip Couns; RELATE trained
Personal Therapy: Yes
Supervision: Ongoing
Counselling offered: General, Relationship, Marital
Service for: Individuals, Couples
Theoretical Approach: Client-centred, Psychodynamic, Behavioural
Other languages: German
Fees: £20 - £30 sliding scale

WALL MORRIS Katherine   0789 292524
Harlyn House, Manor Road, STRATFORD-UPON-AVON CV37 7EA
Member of: BAC
Quals/training: RELATE trained; training in Psychosexual therapy
Personal Therapy: No
Supervision: Ongoing
Counselling offered: General, Relationship
Service for: Individuals, Couples
Theoretical Approach: Psychodynamic, Rogerian
Fees: £25

HOOPER Robert   0926 490140
1 Lakin Road, WARWICK CV34 5BU
Member of: BAC Acc
Quals/training: BAC(Acc); MA; B Phil Couns in Education(Exeter Univ)'78
Personal Therapy: Yes
Supervision: Ongoing
Counselling offered: General
Service for: Individuals, Couples, Families, Groups
Theoretical Approach: Rogerian
Fees: £20 initial session, then by negotiation

Warwickshire

SHILLITO-CLARKE Carol   0926 494174
25 Emscote Road, WARWICK CV34 5QE
Member of: BAC Acc
Quals/training: BAC Acc; RELATE trained; BA (Hons) Psychology 1984; memb BPS; C Psychol (Counselling)
Personal Therapy: Ongoing
Supervision: Ongoing
Counselling offered: **General, Personal growth, Relationship, Loss**
Service for: Individuals, Couples, Groups
Theoretical Approach: Integrative, Gestalt
Fees: £25 - £35

RUGBY PROFESSIONAL COUNSELLING SERVICE   0604 891436
47 Bedford Road, Brafield on the Green, NORTHAMPTON NN7 1BD
Service: General, bereavement, relationship, anxiety management and psychotherapy for individuals, couples and families; groupwork available
Area served: Warwickshire and adjacent areas
Referral: Self or others
Training of workers: Fully trained counsellors and therapists; regular supervision
Code of Ethics: Varies with professional seen
Management by: 3 partners: L Bunn, F Bishop, S Thorpe
Fees: £25 - £50 negotiable

Warwickshire

West Midlands

Organisations

LIFELINE PREGNANCY COUNSELLING AND CARE 021 233 1641
1st Floor, Corporation Street, BIRMINGHAM B4 6RP
Service:	Non directive, non judgemental counselling service for any woman of childbearing age, including post abortion counselling and choice counselling
Area served:	Greater Birmingham
Referral:	Self, GP, Health/Soc Work Professional
Training of workers:	Aims to employ trained counsellors plus twice yearly training in related areas. Supervision
Code of Ethics:	BAC
Management by:	Local Management Committee
Fees:	Free but donations encouraged

CARRS LANE COUNSELLING CENTRE 021 643 6363
Carrs Lane Church Centre, Carrs Lane, BIRMINGHAM B4 7SX
Service:	Short or long term counselling & support at times of distress, breakdown or sadness. General, family, marital, psychosexual for individuals and couples
Area served:	Greater Birmingham area
Referral:	Self or others
Training of workers:	Basic counselling skills course & at least 8 in-service training sessions annually. Regular supervision
Code of Ethics:	Agency's own code
Management by:	Executive Committee; Director Liz Doggart
Fees:	None

FRIEND - WEST MIDLANDS 021 622 7351
PO Box 2405, BIRMINGHAM B5 4AJ
Service:	Counselling, befriending & information to those who are homosexual, bisexual or uncertain of their sexuality. Including some AIDS crisis counselling
Area served:	West Midlands & surrounding counties
Referral:	Self
Training of workers:	Basic training in counselling skills and sensitivity
Code of Ethics:	BAC
Management by:	Management Committee and Counselling Committee
Fees:	None

ST BASIL'S CENTRE 021 772 2483/8540
Heathmill Lane, Deritend, BIRMINGHAM B9 4AX
Service:	Information, advice & crisis counselling to the homeless & potentially homeless. Some personal counselling
Area served:	West Midlands
Referral:	Self or others
Training of workers:	Regular supervision
Code of Ethics:	-
Management by:	Voluntary Board of Directors
Fees:	None

West Midlands

HIGHGATE CENTRE FOR COMMUNITY HEALTH, PSYCHOSEXUAL CLINIC　　021 440 2422
St Patricks Centre, Highgate Street, BIRMINGHAM B12 0YA
Service:　　　　　　　Psychosomatic medical investigation and treatment including hypnotherapy where appropriate for people with sexual difficulties
Area served:　　　　　West and South Birmingham
Referral:　　　　　　　Self or others
Training of workers:　Institute of Psychosexual Medicine
Code of Ethics:　　　　Institute of Psychosexual Medicine
Management by:　　　NHS
Fees:　　　　　　　　　None

KEYS: COUNSELLING & PSYCHOTHERAPY　　021 449 8122
131a Alcester Road, Moseley, BIRMINGHAM B13 8JP
Service:　　　　　　　Individual counselling and psychotherapy. Person-centred and psychodynamic approaches
Area served:　　　　　West Midlands
Referral:　　　　　　　Self
Training of workers:　Various, as well as personal therapy and ongoing supervision
Code of Ethics:　　　　BAC
Management by:　　　Laurence Kingsley
Fees:　　　　　　　　　£23 (£25 after 6pm)

DEPARTMENT OF PSYCHOLOGICAL THERAPY - UFFCULME CLINIC
Uffculme Clinic, Queensbridge Road, Moseley, BIRMINGHAM B13 8QD
Service:　　　　　　　General psychotherapy & couns service & specialist service for people with previous mental health difficulties, short & long term couns & psychotherapy for indivs, couples, groups
Area served:　　　　　South Birmingham
Referral:　　　　　　　Self or others
Training of workers:　Appropriate professional qualifications and additional psychotherapy/counselling training. Regular supervision
Code of Ethics:　　　　BAC, WMIP, Therapists' Professional body
Management by:　　　South Birmingham HA
Fees:　　　　　　　　　None

COUNSELLING & PSYCHOTHERAPY ASSOCIATES　　021 449 2308
6 Clarence Road, Moseley, BIRMINGHAM B13 9SX
Service:　　　　　　　Psychoanalytic psychotherapy & counselling for relationships sexual functioning and sexual identity for indivs & couples. Service also for disabled people with sexual problems
Area served:　　　　　Anywhere
Referral:　　　　　　　Self or others
Training of workers:　Diploma in Counselling (Aston), training with Tavistock, personal therapy, group and individual supervision
Code of Ethics:　　　　BAC, BASMT, WMIP
Management by:　　　The Associates
Fees:　　　　　　　　　£24 - £40

West Midlands

BIRMINGHAM SOCIAL SERVICES   021 443 3571, 021 444 7020
Windsor House, 11A High Street, Kings Heath, BIRMINGHAM B13 9TY
Service:	Counselling for all aspects of HIV/AIDS plus practical services; counselling for children around HIV testing. HIV training
Area served:	Birmingham
Other languages:	Mainly Asian, Others arranged
Referral:	Self
Training of workers:	CSS/ CQSW, post qualifying courses. Supervision
Code of Ethics:	BASW
Management by:	Local Authority
Fees:	None

BIRMINGHAM BROOK ADVISORY CENTRE   021 455 0491
9 York Road, BIRMINGHAM B16 9HX
Service:	Contraceptive advice and supplies; help with personal, emotional and sexual problems in confidence
Area served:	West Midlands and beyond
Referral:	Self or others
Training of workers:	Appropriate training and regular supervision
Code of Ethics:	Therapists' Professional body
Management by:	Executive Committee
Fees:	According to service

YEWCROFT MENTAL HEALTH RESOURCE CENTRE   021 428 2323
Court Oak Road, Harborne, BIRMINGHAM B17 9AB
Service:	Short and long term counselling and psychotherapy; group work; art therapy
Area served:	Edgbaston, Harborne, Quinton (Birmingham)
Referral:	GP, Health/Soc Work Professional
Training of workers:	Psychology, nursing, social work, art therapy, occupational therapy, some extra psychotherapy/couns training
Code of Ethics:	BAC, WMIP, Therapists' Professional body
Management by:	Sue Stennett
Fees:	None

DUDLEY ROAD HOSPITAL PSYCHOSEXUAL CLINIC   021 3801 x 4584
Outpatients Department, Dudley Road Hospital, BIRMINGHAM B18 7QH
Service:	Psychosomatic medical investigation and treatment including hypnotherapy where appropriate for people with sexual difficulties
Area served:	Birmingham
Referral:	Health Practitioner
Training of workers:	Institute of Psychosexual Medicine
Code of Ethics:	Institute of Psychosexual Medicine
Management by:	NHS
Fees:	-

West Midlands

WHAT? STOURBRIDGE YOUNG PERSON'S ADVICE INFORMATION & COUNSELLING CENTRE
34 Lower High Street, STOURBRIDGE DY8 1TA
Service: General counselling for 16-25 year olds
Area served: Stourbridge, Dudley area
Referral: Self or others
Training of workers: Selection then in-service training; ongoing supervision
Code of Ethics: Agency's own code
Management by: Annually elected Management Committee of 16
Fees: None

COUNSELLING ASSOCIATES 0384 896792
102 Cementery Road, Lye, STOURBRIDGE DY9 8AE
Service: Counsellors offering a personal counselling service to individuals, couples & families & an effective counselling provision for management & staff in commerce & industry
Area served: Mainly West Midlands/South England
Referral: Self, Organisations, GP
Training of workers: All have Postgraduate Diploma from Reading Univ plus ongoing training, personal therapy and supervision
Code of Ethics: BAC
Management by: Regular supportive, informal business meetings
Fees: £25

WALSALL COMMUNITY HEALTH TRUST PSYCHOSEXUAL CLINIC
0922 20209
Town Centre Clinic, 18/20 Hatherton Road, WALSALL WS1 1TE
Service: Psychosomatic medical investigation and treatment including hypnotherapy where appropriate for people with sexual difficulties
Area served: Walsall and area
Referral: Self or others
Training of workers: Member of Institute of Psychosexual Medicine
Code of Ethics: Institute of Psychosexual Medicine
Management by: Walsall Community Health Trust
Fees: -

BIRMINGHAM COUNSELLING CENTRE 021 429 1758
62 Lightwoods Hill, Bearwood, WARLEY B67 5EB
Service: Confidential counselling for individuals
Area served: Midlands
Referral: Self
Training of workers: BCC 4 year couns training programme including personal therapy & ongoing supervision
Code of Ethics: BAC, AHPP
Management by: Deb Williams and Bob Smith
Fees: £20 negotiable, some low cost

West Midlands

Individual Practitioners
Each individual is a **member of** one or more organisations eligible for entry into this directory.
BAC Accredited Counsellors and Recognised Supervisors are shaded.

FOX Barbara   021 472 8571
52 Jacoby Place, Priory Road, Edgbaston, BIRMINGHAM B5 7UN
Member of:	WMIP
Quals/training:	ALAM: Cert Probation & Approved Social Work; trained in family therapy; trained in Psychotherapy (WMIP)
Personal Therapy:	Unknown
Supervision:	Ongoing
Counselling offered:	**Psychotherapy, Relationship, Family, Eating disorders**
Service for:	Individuals, Couples
Specific to:	Women
Theoretical Approach:	Dynamic, Cognitive
Other languages:	French
Fees:	£25 negotiable

JOHNSON Judy   021 449 4760
5 Geoffrey Road, Sparkhill, BIRMINGHAM B11 4HU
Member of:	WMIP, AFT
Quals/training:	BA; MA; CQSW; Training in Family Therapy (Uffculme, Birmingham Univ); Advanced training Psychoanalytic Psychotherapy (WMIP); BASW; Full Memb WMIP
Personal Therapy:	Yes
Supervision:	Ongoing
Counselling offered:	**General, Family, Relationship**
Service for:	Individuals, Couples, Families
Theoretical Approach:	Psychodynamic
Fees:	Negotiable

SPEED Bebe   021 449 8503
BIRMINGHAM
Member of:	BASMT, WMIP
Quals/training:	BA Sociology; Dip Psychiatric Social Work; CQSW; Dip Psychotherapy; 10 yrs working at Family Inst Cardiff
Personal Therapy:	Yes
Supervision:	Ongoing
Counselling offered:	**Psychotherapy**
Service for:	Individuals, Couples, Families
Theoretical Approach:	Systemic, Psychodynamic
Fees:	£35 - £50

KINGSLEY Laurence   021 449 8122
Keys Counselling Service, 131a Alcester Road, Moseley, BIRMINGHAM B13 8JP
Member of:	BAC, BPS, WMIP
Quals/training:	BSc (Hons); CPsychol; currently training in Psychoanalytical Psychotherapy (WMIP)
Personal Therapy:	Ongoing
Supervision:	Ongoing
Counselling offered:	**General, Psychotherapy**
Service for:	Individuals
Theoretical Approach:	Psychodynamic, Person-centred
Fees:	£22 - £35

West Midlands

BUTTERS Steve 021 449 9701
34 Salisbury Road, Moseley, BIRMINGHAM B13 8JT
Member of: BAC
Quals/training: MA Employment Studies; Memb Inst Personal Management
Personal Therapy: No
Supervision: Ongoing
Counselling offered: Career, EAP, Midlife
Service for: Individuals, Groups, Organisations
Theoretical Approach: Eclectic
Fees: On application

DANIELS Lois 0869 241387
Sycamore Beech, 1 Holders Lane, Moseley, BIRMINGHAM B13 8NL
Member of: BAC
Quals/training: CQSW 1978; Dip Family Therapy (Birmingham); 1982 Acc Counselling Cal-USA (Santa Cruz); Victim Support Group Scheme Consultant
Personal Therapy: No
Supervision: Ongoing
Counselling offered: General, Loss, Relationship, Stress, Family
Service for: Individuals, Couples, Families, Groups
Theoretical Approach: Behavioural
Fees: £20 sliding scale

COLE Martin 021 449 0892
40 School Road, Moseley, BIRMINGHAM B13 9SN
Member of: BAC, BABCP, BASMT
Quals/training: Training at Kinsey Inst 1974; Masters & Johnson Inst 1975; Memb BASMT 1976
Personal Therapy: Ongoing
Supervision: Ongoing
Counselling offered: General, Relationship, Sexual
Service for: Individuals, Couples
Theoretical Approach: Cognitive, Behavioural, Eclectic
Fees: £20 - £25 negotiable

COOPER Grahame Dr 021 449 2308
6 Clarence Road, Moseley, BIRMINGHAM B13 9SX
Member of: BAC, BASMT, WMIP
Quals/training: PhD; Dip Couns 1975 (Aston Univ); BASMT Acc; additional training at Tavistock Institute
Personal Therapy: Ongoing
Supervision: Ongoing
Counselling offered: Psychotherapy, Sexual, Relationship
Service for: Individuals, Couples
Specific to: People with disabilities
Theoretical Approach: Psychoanalytic
Fees: £24 - £40

West Midlands

HARVEY Tricia   021 449 2308
6 Clarence Road, Moseley, BIRMINGHAM B13 9SX
Member of: BAC, WMIP, ACP
Quals/training: BA; M Phil; Dip Couns (Aston Univ) '76; training with ACP
Personal Therapy: Ongoing
Supervision: Ongoing
Counselling offered: Psychotherapy
Service for: Individuals
Theoretical Approach: Psychoanalytic
Fees: £24 - £34 sliding scale

BROWN Douglas   021 449 3710
28 Greenend Road, Moseley, BIRMINGHAM B13 9TJ
Member of: BAC
Quals/training: RELATE trained; NHS trained; trained in relationship, anxiety management, hypnotherapy and AIDS & bereavement couns
Personal Therapy: Ongoing
Supervision: Ongoing
Counselling offered: General, Personal growth, Relationship, Work
Service for: Individuals, Couples, Groups
Specific to: Helping professions, High achievers
Theoretical Approach: Rogerian, Cognitive/Behavioural, Gestalt
Fees: £15 - £25 negotiable; £35 in-company

STOKES Jenny   021 444 0627
68 Springfield Road, Kings Heath, BIRMINGHAM B14 7DY
Member of: BAC Acc, WMIP, Guild of Psychotherapists
Quals/training: BAC Acc; B Hons Social Science; Dip Couns (Aston Univ); Redwood Training
Personal Therapy: Ongoing
Supervision: Ongoing
Counselling offered: General, Psychotherapy
Service for: Individuals, Couples, Groups
Theoretical Approach: Psychodynamic
Fees: On application

NAGEL Beatrice   021 440 2157
24 Spring Road, Edgbaston, BIRMINGHAM B15 2HA
Member of: BAC, BPS
Quals/training: BA; MEd; Memb Brit Educational Research Assoc
Personal Therapy: No
Supervision: Ongoing
Counselling offered: General
Service for: Individuals, Couples
Theoretical Approach: Cognitive
Other languages: German
Fees: £20 - £30 sliding scale

West Midlands

COLE Jonathan   **021 429 4593**
12 Willow Avenue, Edgbaston, BIRMINGHAM B17 8HD
Member of: BAC, BPS, WMIP
Quals/training: BSc(Hons) Psychol (Leicester Univ); Dip Careers Guidance (Manchester Poly); Adv Cert Psychodynamic Couns (WPF)
Personal Therapy: Ongoing
Supervision: Ongoing
Counselling offered: General, Vocational
Service for: Individuals, Organisations
Theoretical Approach: Psychodynamic
Fees: £15 - £25

HARRIS Pamela   **021 429 4593**
12 Willow Avenue, Edgbaston, BIRMINGHAM B17 8HD
Member of: BAC
Quals/training: 2 yr training (CCP); 10 week course (Carrs Lane); 2.5 yrs training in Psychodynamic Couns (WPF)
Personal Therapy: Ongoing
Supervision: Ongoing
Counselling offered: General
Service for: Individuals
Theoretical Approach: Person-centred, Psychodynamic
Fees: £15 - £25

WAY Jean   **021 429 3307**
4 Carisbrooke Road, Edgbaston, BIRMINGHAM B17 8NW
Member of: BAC Acc, WMIP, Member of UKCP Register
Quals/training: BAC Acc; SRN; Dip Soc Work (Birmingham Univ) 1969; Memb APPNHS, PCS
Personal Therapy: Yes
Supervision: Ongoing
Counselling offered: Psychotherapy, Supervision
Service for: Individuals
Theoretical Approach: Psychoanalytic
Fees: Negotiable

CROWDER Rachel   **021 427 2308**
28 Croftdown Road, Harborne, BIRMINGHAM B17 8RB
Member of: BAC, WMIP
Quals/training: BA; SRN; Adv Cert in Psychodynamic Couns (Beginagen - WPF Associated Centre); CTA
Personal Therapy: Ongoing
Supervision: Ongoing
Counselling offered: General
Service for: Individuals
Theoretical Approach: Psychodynamic
Fees: £10 - £20 sliding scale

West Midlands

DOGGART Elizabeth 021 427 7292
49 Wood Lane, Harborne, BIRMINGHAM B17 9AY
Member of: BAC, AFT
Quals/training: Dip Couns; Dip Rational Emotive Therapy; SEN (M); Memb Assoc for Rational Emotive Therapy; Acc practitioner in RET (MARET); currently Dip Addiction Studies
Personal Therapy: Yes
Supervision: Ongoing
Counselling offered: **General, Addiction, Anxiety, Assertiveness, Stress**
Service for: Individuals, Couples, Families, Groups, Organisations
Theoretical Approach: Eclectic, RET
Fees: £20 - £35 negotiable

YAPP Robin 021 427 7292
49 Wood Lane, Harborne, BIRMINGHAM B17 9AY
Member of: BAC
Quals/training: Member Inst Personnel Management; AREBT Accredited RET Practitioner; ITD(Assoc); Cert Couns; Cert RET; Dip RET & Couns; trained in Rogers & Egan; Memb Int Stress Man Assoc
Personal Therapy: Yes
Supervision: Ongoing
Counselling offered: **General, Anxiety, Stress management, Psychotherapy**
Service for: Individuals
Theoretical Approach: Cognitive, RET
Fees: Negotiable

TOD Victoria 021 472 7523
84 Witherford Way, Selly Oak, BIRMINGHAM B29 4AS
Member of: BAC
Quals/training: BSc Soc Sci (Birmingham); Grad Dip Social Work
Personal Therapy: No
Supervision: Ongoing
Counselling offered: **General, Bereavement, Crisis, Terminal illness**
Service for: Individuals, Couples, Families, Groups, Organisations
Theoretical Approach: Psychodynamic
Fees: £10 - £20 Sliding scale

MATE Helen 021 443 2422
177 Pineapple Road, Kings Norton, BIRMINGHAM B30 2SY
Member of: BAC, WMIP
Quals/training: BA (Arts); RELATE; psychoanalytical psychotherapy
Personal Therapy: Yes
Supervision: Ongoing
Counselling offered: **General, Anxiety, Depression, Relationship, Cross/multi-cultural**
Service for: Individuals, Couples
Theoretical Approach: Analytical, Psychodynamic
Fees: £20 - £30

West Midlands

BLAKEY Angela   021 475 3948
170 Hole Lane, Northfield, BIRMINGHAM B31 2DD
Member of: BAC, WMIP
Quals/training: MA; CQSW; RELATE trained counsellor
Personal Therapy: Yes
Supervision: Ongoing
Counselling offered: General, Relationship
Service for: Individuals, Couples
Theoretical Approach: Psychodynamic
Fees: £25

TWEED Brenda   021 477 2420
148 Sir Hiltons Road, West Heath, BIRMINGHAM B31 2NW
Member of: BAC, WMIP
Quals/training: BA; Memb Assoc Psychiatric Social Workers, EATA, BASW; Clinical Teaching Member & Provisional Supervising Memb ITAA
Personal Therapy: Ongoing
Supervision: Ongoing
Counselling offered: Psychotherapy
Service for: Individuals, Couples, Families, Groups
Theoretical Approach: TA
Fees: £25

PRICE Jacqueline   021 426 6673
266 Court Oak Road, Harborne, BIRMINGHAM B32 2EE
Member of: BAC, WMIP
Quals/training: RGN; Couns Theory & Practice (ENB)
Personal Therapy: Yes
Supervision: Ongoing
Counselling offered: General, Loss, Bereavement, Relationship, Marital
Service for: Individuals, Couples
Theoretical Approach: Rogerian, Psychodynamic
Fees: £20 - £30 sliding scale

IZZARD Sue   021 443 1580
The Well, 87 Drayton Road, Kings Heath, BIRMINGHAM B14 7LP
Member of: BAC, WMIP
Quals/training: BA (Hons); BA (Hons); PGCE; MEd (Counselling)
Personal Therapy: Ongoing
Supervision: Ongoing
Counselling offered: General
Service for: Individuals
Theoretical Approach: Psychodynamic
Fees: £25

West Midlands

DICKINSON Colin 021 749 1565
11 Biggin Close, Castle Vale, BIRMINGHAM B35 6BU
Member of: BAC
Quals/training: PGD Industrial Psychology; training in Christian couns
Personal Therapy: Ongoing
Supervision: Ongoing
Counselling offered: **General, Trauma, Crisis**
Service for: Individuals, Groups
Specific to: Helping professions, Religious
Theoretical Approach: Egan, Rogerian, Christian
Other languages: Welsh
Fees: None made

CAMPBELL Hazel 0203 685776
11 Bideford Road, Wyken, COVENTRY CV2 3LD
Member of: BAC
Quals/training: BA (Hons) Sociology; CQSW 1973; Gestalt Psychotherapy (EGI)
Personal Therapy: Yes
Supervision: Ongoing
Counselling offered: **Psychotherapy**
Service for: Individuals
Theoretical Approach: Gestalt
Fees: £22.50-£32.50

MIERVALDIS Gundega 0203 448091, 0203 456987
4 Ashdown Close, Ernsford Grange, COVENTRY CV3 2PT
Member of: NRHP
Quals/training: RGN; Dip Counselling (Univ Warwick)
Personal Therapy: Yes
Supervision: Ongoing
Counselling offered: **General, Addiction, Bereavement, Crisis, Hypnotherapy**
Service for: Individuals, Couples, Families
Specific to: Adolescents, Young people, Women
Theoretical Approach: Eclectic
Other languages: Latvian
Fees: Negotiable

WALTON Andrew 0203 410001
Blenheim Keep, 279 Leamington Road, COVENTRY CV3 6NB
Member of: BPS
Quals/training: BA Psychol; Dip Psychotherapy & Hypnotherapy '81; Practitioner Couns Psychol(BPS); Fellow RSH; Reg Psychologist; Memb Psychol Soc of Ireland
Personal Therapy: Yes
Supervision: Ongoing
Counselling offered: **General, Relationship, Psychotherapy, Hypnotherapy**
Service for: Individuals, Couples, Families
Specific to: Women, Professionals, Managers
Theoretical Approach: Eclectic
Fees: Negotiable

West Midlands

FARRELL Anita   0203 711275
61 Rochester Road, Earlsdon, COVENTRY CV5 6AF
Member of:	BPS
Quals/training:	MSc Clinical Psychology (Surrey); BSc Psychol (Warwick)
Personal Therapy:	Ongoing
Supervision:	Ongoing
Counselling offered:	General, Sexual, Medical
Service for:	Individuals, Couples, Families
Specific to:	Elderly
Theoretical Approach:	Eclectic
Fees:	Negotiable

SUNDERLAND Cynthia   0203 335204
25 Glentworth Avenue, Keresley, COVENTRY CV6 2HU
Member of:	BAC
Quals/training:	Trained in Gestalt Psychotherapy (English Gestalt Inst) 1987
Personal Therapy:	Ongoing
Supervision:	Ongoing
Counselling offered:	Psychotherapy
Service for:	Individuals
Theoretical Approach:	Gestalt
Fees:	£20 - £25

BALLINGER Liz   0676 535441
340 Kenilworth Road, Balsall Common, COVENTRY CV7 7ER
Member of:	BAC
Quals/training:	RELATE trained Counsellor; education trainer for RELATE
Personal Therapy:	Yes
Supervision:	Ongoing
Counselling offered:	General, Relationship
Service for:	Individuals, Couples
Theoretical Approach:	Client-centred
Fees:	£25

DOHERTY Nora   0926 339744
22 Friars Road, COVENTRY CV1 2LL
Member of:	BAC
Quals/training:	BA; MSc; Licence in Acupuncture; Memb Traditional Acupuncture Soc; training in couns & stres management
Personal Therapy:	Ongoing
Supervision:	Ongoing
Counselling offered:	General, Self-esteem, Relationship, Stress management
Service for:	Individuals, Groups
Theoretical Approach:	Eclectic
Fees:	£25 Practice also in Leamington

West Midlands

WILDAY Greville 0384 280016
The Hollies, St Johns Close, Swindon, DUDLEY DY3 4PQ
Member of: BAC
Quals/training: BSc(Hons); MSc; Dip Ed; currently MA/Dip Psych Couns
Personal Therapy: Ongoing
Supervision: Ongoing
Counselling offered: Career, Personal growth, Psychotherapy, Relationship, Stress
Service for: Individuals, Couples, Organisations
Specific to: Professionals, Managers
Theoretical Approach: Integrative
Fees: £25 - £60

NICHOLAS Geraldine 021 745 7666
36 Halifax Road, Shirley, SOLIHULL B90 2BT
Member of: BAC
Quals/training: Cert Skills & Therapy (CAC); ongoing training Person-Centred Therapy (FDI); RGN
Personal Therapy: Yes
Supervision: Ongoing
Counselling offered: General, Bereavement, Crisis, Crit. incident debriefing, PTSD
Service for: Individuals, Organisations
Specific to: Women, Managers
Theoretical Approach: Rogerian
Fees: Negotiable

DAVIES Bozena 021 704 1451
Solihull Parkway Hospital, SOLIHULL B91 2PP
Member of: Institute of Psychosexual Medicine
Quals/training: 1959 Qualified Dr (MB ChB); Member IPM
Personal Therapy: No
Supervision: Ongoing
Counselling offered: Psychosomatic, Sexual
Service for: Individuals
Fees: £60

MALLEY John 021 742 9610
99 Ulleries Road, Olton, SOLIHULL B92 8DY
Member of: BAC
Quals/training: Trained in Couns SW London College 1983-5; MA Chicago 1987
Personal Therapy: Yes
Supervision: Ongoing
Counselling offered: General, Bereavement, Stress, Pastoral
Service for: Individuals, Couples
Theoretical Approach: Psychodynamic, Egan
Fees: £12 - £30 negotiable

West Midlands

WILSON Mary 0384 877121
Coxgreen, Enville, STOURBRIDGE DY7 5LG
Member of: BAC Acc
Quals/training: BAC(Acc); BSc Soc; NMGC trained; Dip CTP
Personal Therapy: Ongoing
Supervision: Ongoing
Counselling offered: General, Psychotherapy
Service for: Individuals
Theoretical Approach: Psychodynamic, Transpersonal
Fees: £25

GARDINER Alison 0384 373586
Claremont, 66 Worcester Street, STOURBRIDGE DY8 1AY
Member of: BAC
Quals/training: Dip Social Work (USP Fiji); Dip Community Work (Birmingham Univ); Combined Cert Couns Skills & Theory (CSCT); Dip Couns (CSCT)
Personal Therapy: Yes
Supervision: Ongoing
Counselling offered: General, Bereavement, Crisis, Personal growth
Service for: Individuals, Groups, Organisations
Specific to: Women, Young adults
Theoretical Approach: Rogerian
Fees: £15 - £25 sliding scale

JEVONS Sheilagh 0384 390639
129 Heath Lane, STOURBRIDGE DY8 1BB
Member of: BAC Acc
Quals/training: BAC (Acc); BPhil Counselling
Personal Therapy: Ongoing
Supervision: Ongoing
Counselling offered: General, Short-term, Long-term, Psychosexual, Supervision
Service for: Individuals, Couples, Groups
Specific to: Women
Theoretical Approach: Psychodynamic, Humanistic
Fees: £15 - £25 Sliding Scale

MORGAN-BRYANT Linda 0384 379141
The Creative Health Centre, 52 Hagley Road, STOURBRIDGE DY8 1QD
Member of: NSHAP
Quals/training: Trained with NSHAP, CRAH
Personal Therapy: Ongoing
Supervision: Ongoing
Counselling offered: General, Hypnotherapy, Anxiety, Relaxation, Self-esteem, Sexual abuse
Service for: Individuals, Groups, Organisations
Specific to: Women
Theoretical Approach: NLP, Humanistic, Client-centred
Fees: £25

West Midlands

MALE David 0384 278761
81 Belle Vue, Wordsley, STOURBRIDGE DY8 5DB
Member of: WMIP
Quals/training: RMN; RMN Child Psychiatry; Deliberate Self-harm counsellor; Major disaster counsellor; APP(NHS) Assoc
Personal Therapy: Ongoing
Supervision: Ongoing
Counselling offered: General, Bereavement, Crisis, Psychotherapy
Service for: Individuals, Couples, Families
Theoretical Approach: Psychoanalytic, Freudian
Fees: £20 - £30

BRAY Jillyan 021 354 2403
26 Maney Hill Road, SUTTON COLDFIELD B72 1JL
Member of: BAC, WMIP
Quals/training: BA(Hons); 1970-3 CTA; '75-76 CMAC; '81-82 Psychotherapy (Uffculme Clinic); '85-88 Psychotherapeutic Community
Personal Therapy: Yes
Supervision: Ongoing
Counselling offered: General, Psychotherapy, Women's issues, Spiritual
Service for: Individuals
Theoretical Approach: Psychodynamic, Eclectic
Fees: On Application

TILNEY Tony 021 354 4042
63 Victoria Road, SUTTON COLDFIELD B72 1SN
Member of: BAC Acc, BPS
Quals/training: BAC Acc; BA(Hons) Psychol; 1984 Cert in cognitive aspects of counselling (Aston Univ); Memb CTA, ITAA & EATA
Personal Therapy: Yes
Supervision: Ongoing
Counselling offered: General, Marital, Psychotherapy
Service for: Individuals, Couples, Families, Groups
Theoretical Approach: TA, RET, Cognitive
Fees: £25

HARRISON Diane 021 345 3449
96 The Boulevard, Wylde Green, SUTTON COLDFIELD B73 5JG
Member of: NRHP
Quals/training: NRHP (Assoc); Reg & Community nurse (Mental Handicap); Behaviour modification techniques (Assoc for Psychological Therapies)
Personal Therapy: Yes
Supervision: Ongoing
Counselling offered: General, Hypnotherapy, Psychotherapy, Bereavement, Psychosexual
Service for: Individuals, Couples
Specific to: People with learning difficulties, Children, Women, Professionals
Theoretical Approach: Eclectic, Behavioural, RET
Fees: Negotiable

West Midlands

HARRIS Gerald 021 355 5278
77 Highbridge Road, SUTTON COLDFIELD B73 5QE
Member of: NRHP
Quals/training: Cert Hypnosis & Psychotherapy National College; 39 yrs experience of hypnosis
Personal Therapy: No
Supervision: Yes
Counselling offered: General, Psychotherapy, Addiction, Bereavement
Service for: Individuals, Couples
Theoretical Approach: Eclectic
Fees: £15 per hour

EAST Gillian 021 355 8250
85 Park Road, SUTTON COLDFIELD B73 6BT
Member of: BAC
Quals/training: MA in Couns Studies
Personal Therapy: Ongoing
Supervision: Ongoing
Counselling offered: General, Bereavement
Service for: Individuals, Couples
Theoretical Approach: Eclectic, Integrative
Fees: £15 - £25 Sliding scale

DOUGLAS-MAUL Jean
PP Counselling Centre, 84 Thornhill Road, SUTTON COLDFIELD B74 3EW
Member of: BAC
Quals/training: 1980 training in counselling at Carrs Lane Counselling Centre, Birmingham
Personal Therapy: Yes
Supervision: Ongoing
Counselling offered: General, Marital, Sexual, Bereavement, Career, Work
Service for: Individuals, Groups, Organisations
Theoretical Approach: Jungian, Psychodynamic
Other languages: French
Fees: £10 - £20 sliding scale

PARKES Val 021 308 4803
16 Little Sutton Road, Four Oaks, SUTTON COLDFIELD B75 6QU
Member of: BAC
Quals/training: BSc(Hons) Psychol; Dip Couns (Aston Univ) 1984
Personal Therapy: Yes
Supervision: Ongoing
Counselling offered: General, Psychotherapy
Service for: Individuals, Couples
Theoretical Approach: Psychodynamic, Cognitive/Behavioural
Fees: £20 negotiable

West Midlands

ROY Geraldine　　　　　　　　　　　　　　　　　　　　021 351 1651
174 Walmley Road, SUTTON COLDFIELD B76 8PY
Member of:	**BAC Acc, WMIP**
Quals/training:	BAC Acc; Adv Cert Couns (Leicester Univ) 1988; Family Therapy (Charles Burns Clinic B'ham) 1984; Psychotherapy Course (Uffculme Clinic) 1980-82
Personal Therapy:	Ongoing
Supervision:	Ongoing
Counselling offered:	**General, Bereavement, Psychotherapy**
Service for:	Individuals
Specific to:	Adoptees, Adoptors, Parents
Theoretical Approach:	Psychodynamic
Fees:	£20 sliding scale

SMITH Bob　　　　　　　　　　　　　　　　　　　　021 429 1758
62 Lightwoods Hill, Bearwood, WARLEY B67 5EB
Member of:	**BAC, AHPP**
Quals/training:	MEd Human Relations; Dip Couns; Dip Couns & Guidance; GRTA
Personal Therapy:	Ongoing
Supervision:	Ongoing
Counselling offered:	**General**
Service for:	Individuals, Groups
Theoretical Approach:	Humanistic
Fees:	£18 - £25

KEELING Doreen　　　　　　　　　　　　　　　　　　　　021 552 3184
9 St Katherines Road, Oldbury, WARLEY B68 9TT
Member of:	**WMIP, BAC**
Quals/training:	Adv Cert Psychodynamic Couns (Beginagen)
Personal Therapy:	Ongoing
Supervision:	Ongoing
Counselling offered:	**General**
Service for:	Individuals
Theoretical Approach:	Psychodynamic, Person-centred
Fees:	£10 adults only

McDONALD James　　　　　　　　　　　　　　　　　　　　0902 893512
20 Greenfields Road, Wombourne, WOLVERHAMPTON WV5 0HP
Member of:	**BAC, WMIP**
Quals/training:	Post Grad Cert in Psychotherapy; MSc Applications in Psychology
Personal Therapy:	Yes
Supervision:	Ongoing
Counselling offered:	**General, Bereavement, Loss, Retirement**
Service for:	Individuals, Groups
Specific to:	Elderly
Theoretical Approach:	Psychodynamic
Fees:	£20 negotiable

West Midlands

RENTOUL Robert 0902 758504
Woodhill, Ormes Lane, Tettenhall Wood, WOLVERHAMPTON WV6 8LL
Member of: BAC, WMIP, BPS
Quals/training: Training Analysis, Seminars & Supervision; MA; BSc; Cert Theol; C Psychol; AFBPsS
Personal Therapy: Yes
Supervision: Ongoing
Counselling offered: Psychotherapy
Service for: Individuals
Theoretical Approach: Psychoanalytic, Self-psychology (Kohut)
Fees: On application

STIBBE Paul 0902 743231
8 Churchill Road, Tettenhall, WOLVERHAMPTON WV6 9AT
Member of: BAC
Quals/training: Trained at Carrs Lane CC 1987; Cert Couns Skills (Westhill Coll) 1991
Personal Therapy: Ongoing
Supervision: Ongoing
Counselling offered: General
Service for: Individuals
Theoretical Approach: Psychodynamic, Humanistic
Fees: £25 negotiable

FOX Fiona 0902 850269
Chillington Farm, Codsall Wood, WOLVERHAMPTON WV8 1RB
Member of: BAC, WMIP
Quals/training: NMGC Acc; trained Psychotherapist WMIP; CTP Dip
Personal Therapy: Yes
Supervision: Ongoing
Counselling offered: Psychotherapy, Relationship, Bereavement
Service for: Individuals, Couples
Theoretical Approach: Psychodynamic, Eclectic
Fees: £25 sliding scale

Wiltshire

Organisations

SWINDON COUNSELLING SERVICE   **0793 514550**
23 Bath Road, SWINDON SN1 4AS
Service: General counselling for individuals and groups
Area served: Wiltshire and border counties of Oxon and Glos
Referral: Self or others
Training of workers: WPF Affiliated Centre for training; counsellors are fully trained; regular supervision
Code of Ethics: BAC, WPF
Management by: Trustees and an Executive Committee
Fees: Contributions

Individual Practitioners

*Each individual is a **member** of one or more organisations eligible for entry into this directory. BAC Accredited Counsellors and Recognised Supervisors are shaded.*

LONSDALE-DEIGHTON Mrs Perry   **0249 813188**
Sunnycroft, Mile Elm, CALNE SN11 0NE
Member of: BAC
Quals/training: Dip Psychotherapy/Hypnotherapy 1985; ICM Reg Complementary Therapist (Hypnotherapy); Memb NAHP, ISMA(UK) & BCMA (Reg)
Personal Therapy: Yes
Supervision: Ongoing
Counselling offered: **General, Hypnotherapy, Psychotherapy, Stress management, Relaxation**
Service for: Individuals, Organisations
Theoretical Approach: Jungian, Adlerian, Ericksonian, Holistic, Transpersonal
Fees: £30

VOELCKER Cara   **0249 720202**
Avils Farm, Lower Stanton, CHIPPENHAM SN14 6DA
Member of: BAC, BCP
Quals/training: RELATE trained; Transpersonal psychology course '85-7; Psychotherapist in training (BCPC)
Personal Therapy: Ongoing
Supervision: Ongoing
Counselling offered: **General, Relationship, Bereavement, Psychotherapy**
Service for: Individuals, Couples
Fees: £20

WILSON Tony   **0225 858766**
Moonshine Cottage, The Rocks, Ashwicke, CHIPPENHAM SN14 8AW
Member of: BAC
Quals/training: 10 yrs leading groups & training co-counsellors (CCI); 5 yrs career couns; 4 yrs business ethics; trainer in motivation, personal skills, qual management; completing MSc Couns & Sup
Personal Therapy: Yes
Supervision: Ongoing
Counselling offered: **General, Work, Career, Change, Cross/multicultural, Supervision**
Service for: Individuals, Couples, Groups
Specific to: People with disabilities, Ethnic minorities, Work teams
Theoretical Approach: Humanistic, Existential
Fees: £25 negotiable

Wiltshire

ELTON WILSON Jenifer   **0225 743081**
The Bakehouse, Thickwood, Colerne, CHIPPENHAM SN14 8BN
Member of: BAC RSup, BPS
Quals/training: MSc Couns Psychol '87; Psychotherapy training (metanoia, St George's Hospital); C Psychol; BAC Recognised Supervisor
Personal Therapy: Ongoing
Supervision: Ongoing
Counselling offered: **General, Marital, Eating disorders, Psychotherapy, Supervision**
Service for: Individuals, Couples, Groups, Families
Theoretical Approach: Psychoanalytic, Existential, Humanistic
Fees: £25 negotiable

MELLETT Jane   **0225 742163**
16 Tutton Hill, Colerne, CHIPPENHAM SN14 8DN
Member of: BCPC
Quals/training: BSc; CQSW 1974; in final year Dip Humanistic & Integrative Psychotherapy (BCPC); Memb AHP(B)
Personal Therapy: Ongoing
Supervision: Ongoing
Counselling offered: **General, Bereavement, Psychotherapy**
Service for: Individuals
Theoretical Approach: Humanistic, Integrative
Fees: £18 negotiable for unwaged

KING Paul   **0380 859200**
2 Holbrook, ST Edith's Marsh, Bromham, CHIPPENHAM SN15 2DH
Member of: ANLP (PCS)
Quals/training: Master Practitioner NLP 1986
Personal Therapy: Yes
Supervision: Ongoing
Counselling offered: **General, Stress, Personal growth, Bodywork**
Service for: Individuals, Organisations
Theoretical Approach: Eclectic, Humanistic, Systemic
Fees: Negotiable

HANCOCK Patricia
1 Hocketts Close, Lyneham, CHIPPENHAM SN15 4QX
Member of: BAC
Quals/training: Cert Ed; Cert Residential Work with Children & Young People; Trainee Psychotherapist (SIP)
Personal Therapy: Yes
Supervision: Ongoing
Counselling offered: **Psychotherapy**
Service for: Individuals
Theoretical Approach: Psychodynamic, Analytical
Fees: £12 - £25 sliding scale

Wiltshire

JOHNSON Dione 0672 512577
9 Kingsbury Street, MARLBOROUGH SN8 1HU
Member of: BAC, AFT
Quals/training: MA (Oxford) Psychol & Philos; RELATE Trained (Acc) 1987; ongoing training at Centre for Transpersonal Psychology
Personal Therapy: Yes
Supervision: Ongoing
Counselling offered: General, Relationship, Marital, Supervision, Consultation
Service for: Individuals, Couples
Specific to: Adolescents
Theoretical Approach: Psychodynamic, Transpersonal
Other languages: French
Fees: £22

BOWIE Joan 0672 870410
The Grove, Shalbourne, MARLBOROUGH SN8 3QD
Member of: BAC
Quals/training: RELATE trained 1984; Family Mediators Assoc 1991
Personal Therapy: Yes
Supervision: Ongoing
Counselling offered: General, Marital, Relationship, Bereavement
Service for: Individuals, Couples, Groups
Theoretical Approach: Person-centred, Psychodynamic
Fees: £20 negotiable

ENGLISH Wendy 0722 321323
87 Greencroft Street, SALISBURY SP1 1JF
Member of: BAC Acc, LCP
Quals/training: BAC Acc; BA; LCP Associate; Cert in Psychodynamic Counselling Supervision (WPF)
Personal Therapy: Yes
Supervision: Ongoing
Counselling offered: General, Bereavement, Crisis, Psychotherapy
Service for: Individuals
Theoretical Approach: Eclectic, Psychoanalytic
Fees: £10 - £25 Sliding scale

POCOCK Olga 0722 320093
104 Tollgate Road, SALISBURY SP1 2JW
Member of: BAC, LCP, SIP
Quals/training: BA Oxon; Dip Ed: Lambeth Dip Theology; Trained Psychotherapist LCP:
Personal Therapy: Yes
Supervision: Ongoing
Counselling offered: General, Psychotherapy
Service for: Individuals
Theoretical Approach: Analytical, Psychodynamic
Other languages: French, German, Russian
Fees: £10 - £25 Negotiable

Wiltshire

PERRY Pamela   **0722 336262 x 3093**
SALISBURY
Member of: BAC
Quals/training: PG Dip AT; RATh 1983; BAAT; Cert in Pschodynamic Counselling Supervision (WPF) 1993; CRUSE training 1987; CRUSE supervisor
Personal Therapy: Yes
Supervision: Ongoing
Counselling offered: General, Psychotherapy, Art therapy, Bereavement, Supervision
Service for: Individuals, Groups
Theoretical Approach: Jungian, Kleinian
Fees: £15 - £30 dependent on income

GRACIE Anthony   **0793 695 235**
53 Ashford Road, SWINDON SN1 3NS
Member of: BAC Acc
Quals/training: BAC Acc; CTA Trained 1996; Trained at LCP 1982-4
Personal Therapy: Yes
Supervision: Ongoing
Counselling offered: General, Marital, Sexual, Psychotherapy
Service for: Individuals, Couples, Groups
Theoretical Approach: Analytic, Object relations
Other languages: French
Fees: £20 - £28 negotiable

GRACIE Jane   **0793 695 235**
53 Ashford Road, SWINDON SN1 3NS
Member of: BAC RSup, AGIP, SIP
Quals/training: BAC RSup; Full Memb AGIP; CQSW; RELATE Trained
Personal Therapy: Yes
Supervision: Ongoing
Counselling offered: Psychotherapy, Supervision
Service for: Individuals, Groups
Theoretical Approach: Analytic
Fees: £20 - £28 negotiable

HOARE Ian   **0793 536577**
Quarry Steps, Quarry Road, SWINDON SN1 4EW
Member of: BAC, AHPP, BCPC
Quals/training: Dip Applied Behavioural Sciences '70-'73; trained with BCPC '85-'86; Dip Humanistic Integrative Psychotherapy '90; Memb Inst Training/Development
Personal Therapy: Ongoing
Supervision: Ongoing
Counselling offered: General
Service for: Individuals, Couples, Groups
Theoretical Approach: Humanistic, Holistic, Integrative
Fees: £25 sliding scale

Wiltshire

WONNACOTT Ian   **0793 431060**
New Dimensions, Pinehurst People's Centre, Beech Avenue, SWINDON SN2 1JT
Member of:	BAC
Quals/training:	Dip Couns(CSCT)1992; Cert RET (Centre for Stress Management) 1992; ongoing training in Integrative Couns & RET
Personal Therapy:	Ongoing
Supervision:	Ongoing
Counselling offered:	General, Anxiety, Depression, Personal growth, Relationship, Stress, Crisis
Service for:	Individuals
Theoretical Approach:	Integrative, Psychodynamic, RET
Fees:	Negotiable

SOFRONIOU Andreas   **0793 538586, 0225 840751**
33 Marlborough Road, SWINDON SN3 1PH
Member of:	BAC Acc
Quals/training:	BAC Acc; Dip Psychol & Dr Psychol (USA); PhD Psychol; Certs in Mental Health, Couns, Children's Art Therapy; Dip Hypnotherapy (Inst Psychol & Parapsychol), ICM Reg
Personal Therapy:	Ongoing
Supervision:	Ongoing
Counselling offered:	General, Sexual, Hypnotherapy, Psychotherapy, Work, Educational, Medical
Service for:	Individuals, Couples, Groups, Families
Theoretical Approach:	Holistic, Rogerian, Analytical, Behavioural
Other languages:	Greek
Fees:	Negotiable dependent on income

WHITWELL John   **0285 861694**
The Old Farmhouse, Cotswold Community, Ashton Keynes, SWINDON SN6 6QU
Member of:	BAC, LCP
Quals/training:	BSc Econ; LCP Acc; GAS Assoc; Senior Cert in Residential Care of Children & Young People '77
Personal Therapy:	Ongoing
Supervision:	Ongoing
Counselling offered:	Psychotherapy
Service for:	Individuals, Groups
Specific to:	Therapeutic communities
Theoretical Approach:	Psychoanalytic
Fees:	Negotiable

MOSLEY Jennifer   **0225 767157**
8 Westbourne Road, TROWBRIDGE BA14 0AJ
Member of:	BAC, BPS
Quals/training:	MEd (Couns & Guidance) Bristol Univ; Registered Drama-therapist; Memb BADTh
Personal Therapy:	Yes
Supervision:	Ongoing
Counselling offered:	General
Service for:	Individuals, Couples, Groups
Specific to:	People with learning difficulties, Mentally ill
Theoretical Approach:	Humanistic
Fees:	£15 - £35 sliding scale

Wiltshire

HEWITT Val   **0985 216691**
Carbury Cottage, 35 South Street, WARMINSTER BA12 8DZ
Member of: **BAC Acc**
Quals/training: BAC Acc; trained with Wessex Counselling Service (WPF Aff) 1985-90
Personal Therapy: Ongoing
Supervision: Ongoing
Counselling offered: **General**
Service for: Individuals
Theoretical Approach: Psychodynamic
Fees: £20 - £25

Yorkshire - North

Organisations

TUKE CENTRE FOR PSYCHOTHERAPY & COUNSELLING 0904 430370
Garrow Bank, 28 Green Dykes Lane, YORK YO1 3HH
Service:	Psychotherapy & counselling for personal, emotional & relationship problems; individual & group
Area served:	York & environs
Referral:	Self or others
Training of workers:	Recognised course of minimum 3 years leading to diploma. All paid staff have UKCP accredited qualifications
Code of Ethics:	BAC, UKCP
Management by:	Retreat Committee of Management
Fees:	£5 - £30 sliding scale

YORK PSYCHOSEXUAL CLINIC 0904 645165
Clifton Hospital, YORK YO3 6RD
Service:	Marital, sexual counselling, treatment of psychosexual disorders for individuals and couples
Area served:	York NHS Trust
Referral:	Health Practitioner, GP, Consultant
Training of workers:	Qualified clinical psychologists
Code of Ethics:	BPS
Management by:	York NHS Trust
Fees:	-

YORK DISTRICT CLINICAL PSYCHOLOGY SERVICES 0904 645165
Clifton Hospital, Shipton Road, YORK YO3 6RD
Service:	Clinical Psychology Service for assessment and treatment of psychological problems for all age groups
Area served:	York NHS Trust
Referral:	Health Practitioner
Training of workers:	Post graduate clinical psychology; regular supervision
Code of Ethics:	BPS
Management by:	York NHS Trust
Fees:	None

COUNSELLING AND CONSULTANCY UNIT 0904 616680
University College of Ripon &, York St John, Lord Mayor's Walk, YORK YO3 7EX
Service:	Counselling, supervision, training and consultancy for both individuals and organisations
Area served:	Local and National through a professional network
Referral:	Self or others
Training of workers:	All are trained counsellors in regular supervision with recognised qualifications to Diploma and Masters level
Code of Ethics:	BAC
Management by:	The Unit
Fees:	£20 - £30 per hour, negotiable

Yorkshire - North

YORK DISTRICT HOSPITAL SOCIAL WORK DEPT   0904 631313 x 3411
Wigginton Road, YORK YO3 7HE
Service: Individual face to face and telephone counselling for all aspects of HIV/AIDS. 1 counsellor specialises in ante-natal & women. Occasional training in HIV/AIDS
Area served: South part of N Yorks into Humberside
Other languages: Please enquire
Referral: Self
Training of workers: Approved courses - RHA - 6 day course & NACTU
Code of Ethics: BASW
Management by: Social Service Dept
Fees: None

YORK COUNSELLORS   0904 744422
The Maltings, Appleton Roebuck, YORK YO5 7DG
Service: Marital, relationship and personal counselling
Area served: York, N Yorkshire and Humberside
Referral: Self or others
Training of workers: RELATE trained; bereavement training
Code of Ethics: BAC
Management by: Executive Committee
Fees: £18 (£20 couples) negotiable

Individual Practitioners
*Each individual is a **member of** one or more organisations eligible for entry into this directory. BAC Accredited Counsellors and Recognised Supervisors are shaded.*

DUNCAN Ursula   0423 569 640
18 Mayfield Grove, HARROGATE HG1 5HB
Member of: BAC, ITA
Quals/training: BSc (Hons); Adv Dip Couns; MEd; currently in training as a transactional analyst with clinical speciality
Personal Therapy: Ongoing
Supervision: Ongoing
Counselling offered: General, Bereavement, Stress management
Service for: Individuals, Groups, Organisations
Theoretical Approach: Humanistic, Psychodynamic, TA
Fees: £18 - £22

HYMAS Mary   0423 503917
1 The Grove, HARROGATE HG1 5NN
Member of: BAC
Quals/training: BA; RELATE Couns; sex therapist; training in education
Personal Therapy: No
Supervision: Ongoing
Counselling offered: PTSD, Stress management, Assertiveness
Service for: Individuals, Couples, Groups
Theoretical Approach: Behavioural
Fees: £30 inds; £50 groups

Yorkshire - North

LEVINE Julie 0423 504856
6 East Park Road, HARROGATE HG1 5QT
Member of:	BAC, YAPP
Quals/training:	RELATE trained; Groupwork training (York Univ); Post Trauma work
Personal Therapy:	Yes
Supervision:	Ongoing
Counselling offered:	General, Marital, Crisis, Psychotherapy
Service for:	Individuals, Couples, Groups, Organisations
Theoretical Approach:	TA, Gestalt
Fees:	£15 - £30 sliding scale

HOUSLEY Rosemary 0423 879157
3 Leadhall Gardens, HARROGATE HG2 9NQ
Member of:	BAC, YAPP
Quals/training:	RELATE trained; State Reg Occupational Therapist
Personal Therapy:	Yes
Supervision:	Ongoing
Counselling offered:	General, Bereavement, Relationship, Sexual abuse, PTSD
Service for:	Individuals, Couples, Families
Theoretical Approach:	Eclectic
Fees:	£20 - £25 sliding scale

BANNISTER Dorothy 0423 780736
Birch Hill Farm, Dacre Banks, HARROGATE HG3 4EE
Member of:	BAC
Quals/training:	Cert Couns (RSA); Cert in Humanistic & Psychodynamic Couns AIDMA (teaching); in service (Mental Health) Social Services Dramatherapy; currently in Couns Sup Cert course
Personal Therapy:	Yes
Supervision:	Ongoing
Counselling offered:	General, Bereavement, Loss, Stress, Drama therapy
Service for:	Individuals, Couples, Groups, Organisations
Theoretical Approach:	Humanistic, Psychodynamic
Other languages:	Sign Language
Fees:	£18 Negotiable

CROUCH Ann 0423 868196
The Old Smithy, Scriven Green, KNARESBOROUGH HG5 9EA
Member of:	BAC
Quals/training:	Cert Ed; BA Psychol & Sociology '72; basic training Couns (Durham Univ)'82; Advanced Couns Cert (Stockton Psychotherapy Centre)'89
Personal Therapy:	Ongoing
Supervision:	Ongoing
Counselling offered:	General, Mental health
Service for:	Individuals
Theoretical Approach:	Rogerian
Fees:	Up to £20

Yorkshire - North

GREENING Sarah 0609 776680
Prospect House, Thornton Le Beans, NORTHALLERTON DL6 3SW
Member of: BAC, ITA
Quals/training: BA(Hons); Dip Hum Couns(Stockton PTI); 4 yrs of clinical training in TA
Personal Therapy: Ongoing
Supervision: Ongoing
Counselling offered: General, Assertiveness
Service for: Individuals, Couples, Groups
Specific to: Students
Theoretical Approach: TA, Person-centred
Fees: £15 - £20 sliding scale

FARMER Eddie 0748 86500
Rowleth Edge, Gunnerside, RICHMOND DL11 6JP
Member of: IPC
Quals/training: BSc; 1981 full member IPC/WPF in Individual Psychotherapy & Groupwork
Personal Therapy: Yes
Supervision: Ongoing
Counselling offered: Spiritual, Psychotherapy, Supervision, Consultation
Service for: Individuals, Couples, Groups, Organisations
Theoretical Approach: Psychodynamic, Existential
Fees: £25 negotiable

CREDLAND Jean 0904 629024
Rainbows, 7 Baile Hill Terrace, YORK YO1 1HF
Member of: BAC
Quals/training: Dip Hypnosis & Psychotherapy National College 1981
Personal Therapy: Yes
Supervision: No
Counselling offered: General, Hypnotherapy, Psychotherapy
Service for: Individuals, Couples, Groups, Families
Fees: £18 - £26 sliding scale

WOODBURN Latilla Dr 0904 658861
3 Crosslands Road, Off Broadway, Fulford, YORK YO1 4JD
Member of: BAC
Quals/training: BA(Hons); D Phil Psycholinguistics; RSA Cert Couns; Cert & Extended Cert Couns (South Manchester College)
Personal Therapy: Yes
Supervision: Ongoing
Counselling offered: General, Depression, Anxiety, Bereavement
Service for: Individuals
Specific to: Women, Adolescents
Theoretical Approach: Rogerian, Integrative
Fees: £12 negotiable Free 1st interview

Yorkshire - North

DAVIDOFF Suzanne   0904 621866
18 Broadway West, Fulford, YORK YO1 4JJ
Member of: BAC, NRHP
Quals/training: BA (Hons); PCGE; Dip Couns WPF 1983; IPSS 1985; NRHP (Assoc) 1988
Personal Therapy: Yes
Supervision: Ongoing
Counselling offered: Hypnotherapy, Addiction, Relationship, Stress, Phobias, Anxiety
Service for: Individuals, Couples
Specific to: Children
Theoretical Approach: Hypnotherapy, Psychodynamic
Fees: £25 reduced for unemployed & OAPs

MARTIN Gill   0904 87329
Foldyard House, Naburn, YORK YO1 4RU
Member of: BAC Acc RSup
Quals/training: BAC Acc & Rec Supervisor; MA; CQSW; Trained psychotherapist; (Minster Centre)
Personal Therapy: Yes
Supervision: Ongoing
Counselling offered: General, Relationship, Psychotherapy, Adoption, Fostering
Service for: Individuals, Families
Specific to: Women
Theoretical Approach: Psychodynamic
Other languages: French
Fees: £22 negotiable

THATCHER Betsy   0904 647893
10 Gray Street, Scarcroft Green, YORK YO2 1BN
Member of: BAC Acc, ITA
Quals/training: BAC Acc; BA; Dip Hum Couns (Stockton PTI); completed 4 yrs training in Transactional Analysis; Memb EATA & ITAA
Personal Therapy: Ongoing
Supervision: Ongoing
Counselling offered: General
Service for: Individuals, Couples, Groups
Theoretical Approach: Humanistic, TA
Fees: £25 negotiable

GOMEZ Anthea   0904 641043
22 Millfield Road, YORK YO2 1NQ
Member of: BAC, YAPP
Quals/training: Dip Couns; currently in further training (WFP North)
Personal Therapy: Yes
Supervision: Ongoing
Counselling offered: General, Relationship
Service for: Individuals
Theoretical Approach: Psychodynamic
Fees: £16 - £20

Yorkshire - North

KENNETT Christine 0904 638623
38 Millfield Road, YORK YO2 1NQ
Member of:	BAC, GPTI
Quals/training:	BA; MEd Couns/Human Relations; RELATE Training; currently in Adv Gestalt Psychotherapy Training (GPTI); Massage training (Assoc of Natural Medicines)
Personal Therapy:	Yes
Supervision:	Ongoing
Counselling offered:	**General, Abuse, Psychotherapy, Relationship, Stress**
Service for:	Individuals, Couples, Groups
Specific to:	Adult survivors of abuse, Health care professionals
Theoretical Approach:	Gestalt, Integrative
Fees:	£18 - £30 Sliding Scale

TILLS Lynne 0904 796455
97 Carr Lane, Acomb, YORK YO2 5HN
Member of:	BAC, YAPP
Quals/training:	RSA Cert in Couns; Dip in Practice of Couns & Management of Change
Personal Therapy:	Ongoing
Supervision:	Ongoing
Counselling offered:	**General, Career, Relationship, Stress**
Service for:	Individuals, Couples, Groups
Specific to:	Women
Theoretical Approach:	Integrative, Psychodynamic
Fees:	£18 - £40 sliding scale

SHANNON Jan 0904 794378
The Villa, The Green, Upper Poppleton, YORK YO2 6DF
Member of:	BAC, YAPP
Quals/training:	RELATE trained; ongoing course at Tavistock Clinic '
Personal Therapy:	Ongoing
Supervision:	Ongoing
Counselling offered:	**General, Relationship**
Service for:	Individuals, Couples
Theoretical Approach:	Psychodynamic
Other languages:	French
Fees:	£18 (£20 for couples)

ALLISON Tricia 0347 810978
Seniors Cottage, Sutton on the Forest, YORK YO6 1DW
Member of:	BAC
Quals/training:	BA Hons; PG Dip Social Work(Univ of Edinburgh)
Personal Therapy:	Yes
Supervision:	Ongoing
Counselling offered:	**General, Marital, Work, PTSD, Psychotherapy, Supervision**
Service for:	Individuals, Couples, Organisations
Theoretical Approach:	Eclectic, Psychodynamic
Fees:	£30 (£50-£75 organisations)

Yorkshire - North

HESTER Bridget   0347 21593
The Old Rectory, Crayke, YORK YO6 4TA
Member of: **BPS, YAPP**
Quals/training: BA; PhD Psychol; Dip Psychotherapy (Liverpool Univ); C Psychol; RELATE trained marital/sex therapist; family mediator training
Personal Therapy: Yes
Supervision: Ongoing
Counselling offered: **General, Relationship, Sexual, Psychotherapy, Divorce, Mediation, Cross/multi-cultural**
Service for: Individuals, Couples, Families, Groups
Theoretical Approach: Psychodynamic, Systemic, Behavioural
Fees: £30

LOCKSTONE Colleen   0947 603966
Cherry Garth, Stakesby Vale, WHITBY YO21 1JZ
Member of: **BAC, YAPP**
Quals/training: RGN; RHV; Dip N (London); Cert Ed; RSA Cert Couns Skills; Dip Practice of Couns & the Management of Change
Personal Therapy: Ongoing
Supervision: Ongoing
Counselling offered: **General, Bereavement, Relationship, Crisis**
Service for: Individuals, Couples
Theoretical Approach: Psychodynamic, Eclectic
Fees: £15 - £18

LAWRENCE Yvonne   0947 603496
Shannon House, 13 York Terrace, WHITBY YO21 1PT
Member of: **BAC, ITA**
Quals/training: BA(Hons); PGCE: MSW; CQSW; Dip Hum Couns; Ongoing training in TA since 1990 (Stockton PTI)
Personal Therapy: Ongoing
Supervision: Ongoing
Counselling offered: **General**
Service for: Individuals, Groups
Theoretical Approach: TA, Rogerian, Gestalt
Fees: £15

Yorkshire - North

Yorkshire - South

Organisations

BARNSLEY COMMUNITY & PRIORITY SERVICES NHS TRUST
0226 730000 x 3460
CLINICAL PSYCHOLOGY SERVICES, 11/12 Keresforth Close, Off Broadway, BARNSLEY S70 6RS

Service:	1. A full range of psychotherapy & counselling services for individuals, couples, groups & families. 2. Counselling service & workshops for staff groups at competitive rates.
Area served:	Barnsley
Referral:	Self, Agencies
Training of workers:	Postgraduate Clinical Psychology followed by dynamic psychotherapy/counselling training
Code of Ethics:	BAC, BPS
Management by:	Manager - Psychology Services (NHS Trust)
Fees:	None except for 2 above

SHEFFIELD COMMUNITY UNIT FAMILY PLANNING SERVICE
0742 768885
Central Health Clinic, Mulberry Street, SHEFFIELD S1 2PJ

Service:	Psychosexual counselling for men & women. Cllg for marital difficulties, problems relating to sex & women's health; AIDS prevention; counselling clinics for menopause
Area served:	Sheffield & District
Referral:	GP, Health Practitioner, Self
Training of workers:	Medical training & Institute of Psychosexual Medicine; ongoing seminars
Code of Ethics:	Institute of Psychosexual Medicine
Management by:	Health Authority
Fees:	-

SHARE PSYCHOTHERAPY AGENCY
0742 682883
176 Crookesmoor Road, SHEFFIELD S6 3FS

Service:	Psychotherapy for emotional, personality and relationship problems
Area served:	Sheffield
Referral:	Self
Training of workers:	Four year training course. Regular supervision
Code of Ethics:	Agency's own code
Management by:	Management Committee
Fees:	£2 minimum

CHURCH ARMY COUNSELLING SERVICE NORTH
0742 585 360/521
41 Bannerdale Road, SHEFFIELD S7 2DJ

Service:	Individual counselling for emotional & spiritual problems, depression and marital difficulties, in strict confidence for those of any creed or none
Referral:	Self or others
Training of workers:	Professional counsellors, BAC Accred, qualified psychotherapist
Code of Ethics:	BAC
Management by:	Church Army
Fees:	£20 negotiable

Yorkshire - South

SHEFFIELD UNIVERSITY, PSYCHOLOGICAL CLINIC
0742 756600/752349, Fax 0742 727206
Social & Applied Psychol Unit, Department of Psychology, University of Sheffield, SHEFFIELD S10 2TN
Service: Individual psychotherapy for people suffering stress at work. The clinic is funded for research into the effectiveneess of psychotherapy
Area served: Travelling distance of Sheffield
Referral: Self, GP, Health Practitioner, Psychiatrist
Training of workers: Postgraduate clinical psychology training
Code of Ethics: BPS
Management by: Medical Research Council/University of Sheffield
Fees: None

SHEFFIELD MARITAL & SEXUAL DIFFICULTIES CLINIC
0742 852222/309502
Whiteley Wood Clinic, Woofindin Road, SHEFFIELD S10 3TL
Service: Marital & sexual therapy
Area served: Sheffield and surrounding districts
Referral: GP, Health Practitioner
Training of workers: Appropriate qualifications; BASMT accredited; regular supervision
Code of Ethics: GMC, BASMT
Management by: Health Authority
Fees: -

LODGE MOOR HOSPITAL SOCIAL WORK DEPARTMENT 0742 630222
Redmires Road, SHEFFIELD S10 4LH
Service: Individual face to face counselling for all aspects of HIV/AIDS
Area served: Sheffield
Referral: Self, Health Practitioner
Training of workers: Social work and NACTU
Code of Ethics: BASMT
Management by: Social Services Dept
Fees: None

Individual Practitioners
Each individual is a **member of** one or more organisations eligible for entry into this directory. BAC Accredited Counsellors and Recognised Supervisors are shaded.

CLIFFORD Alice   0226 730658
2 Park Road, Worsbrough, BARNSLEY S70 5AW
Member of: BAC
Quals/training: Cert Adult Ed; Ass memb Inst of Training & Development; Cert Couns Skills
Personal Therapy: No
Supervision: Ongoing
Counselling offered: General, Educational
Service for: Individuals
Specific to: Adolescents
Theoretical Approach: Rogerian
Fees: £5 free if unwaged

Yorkshire - South

RAINE Margaret   0302 327963
69 Thorne Road, DONCASTER DN1 2EX
Member of:	BAC
Quals/training:	RMN 1988; RSA Cert Couns (Sheffield Univ)
Personal Therapy:	Yes
Supervision:	Ongoing
Counselling offered:	Bereavement, Relationship, Anxiety, Stress, Self-esteem
Service for:	Individuals
Theoretical Approach:	Client-centred
Fees:	£20

DRAPER Joyce   0302 322554
21 Lawn Road, DONCASTER DN1 2JF
Member of:	BAC
Quals/training:	RSA Cert Couns 1986; Psychosexual Couns & Therapy London Inst for Study of Human Sexuality 1986-88
Personal Therapy:	Yes
Supervision:	Ongoing
Counselling offered:	General, Marital, Sexual, Psychotherapy, Depression, Bereavement
Service for:	Individuals, Couples
Specific to:	Survivors of sex abuse, Transsexuals, Transvestites
Theoretical Approach:	Rogerian, Eclectic
Fees:	None stated, negotiable

SMITH Eileen   0977 642481
First Floor Flat,, The Hall, Hooton Pagnell, DONCASTER DN5 7BW
Member of:	BAC, HIP, Member of UKCP Register
Quals/training:	MEd; PhD; Dip Ed Psychol 1952
Personal Therapy:	Yes
Supervision:	Ongoing
Counselling offered:	General, Bereavement, Crisis
Service for:	Individuals, Groups
Theoretical Approach:	Person-centred, Psychodynamic
Fees:	Negotiable, usually £1 per £1000 income.

BROWN Linda   0302 752675
Wedgwoods, Doncaster Road, Tickhill, DONCASTER DN11 9JD
Member of:	BAC
Quals/training:	Cert Couns Skills; Adv Cert Couns Theory
Personal Therapy:	No
Supervision:	Ongoing
Counselling offered:	General, Bereavement, Crisis, Drugs, Dependency, Stress management
Service for:	Individuals, Couples, Families, Groups, Organisations
Specific to:	Women
Theoretical Approach:	Humanistic, Behavioural, Rogerian
Other languages:	Sign Language
Fees:	£15 Sliding scale

Yorkshire - South

HARDWICK Barbara   0709 554795
26 Admirals Crest, Keppel Gardens, Scholes, ROTHERHAM S61 2SU
Member of:	BAC, BASMT
Quals/training:	BA (Hons); PGCE (FE); Cert Marital & Relationship Therapy (RELATE) to be awarded 1993; RELATE trained Supervisor & Counsellor
Personal Therapy:	Yes
Supervision:	Ongoing
Counselling offered:	**General, Bereavement, Crisis, Marital, Relationship**
Service for:	Individuals, Couples, Groups, Organisations
Theoretical Approach:	Eclectic
Fees:	£15 - £30 sliding scale

PARKER Cath   0742 449940
SHEFFIELD S5
Member of:	BAC
Quals/training:	BA(Hons); Cert Social Service; training in Dip Couns (Sherwood PTI)
Personal Therapy:	Yes
Supervision:	Ongoing
Counselling offered:	**General, Bereavement, Loss**
Service for:	Individuals
Theoretical Approach:	Humanistic, Person-centred
Fees:	£10

ELLIOTT Mary   0742 334934
168 Carr Road, SHEFFIELD S6 1WZ
Member of:	BAC
Quals/training:	BA; Dip Couns
Personal Therapy:	Yes
Supervision:	Ongoing
Counselling offered:	**General**
Service for:	Individuals
Specific to:	Women
Theoretical Approach:	Rogerian, Psychodynamic
Fees:	£15 - £20 negotiable

CANNY Patricia   0742 341284
7 Church Street, Stannington, SHEFFIELD S6 6DB
Member of:	BAC
Quals/training:	RMN; CAC Cert in Counselling Skills
Personal Therapy:	No
Supervision:	Ongoing
Counselling offered:	**General, Addiction, Relationship, Psychotherapy, Sexual abuse**
Service for:	Individuals, Couples, Groups
Specific to:	Women
Theoretical Approach:	Cognitive/Behavioural
Fees:	£10 - £30 sliding scale

Yorkshire - South

COLVER Stephen 0742 585521
41 Bannerdale Road, SHEFFIELD S7 2DJ
Member of: BAC, Guild of Psychotherapists, YAPP
Quals/training: Psychoanalytic Psychotherapist (Guild of Psychotherapists): 1 yr intro course in Group Psychotherapy (IGA)
Personal Therapy: Yes
Supervision: Ongoing
Counselling offered: Psychotherapy, Supervision
Service for: Individuals, Couples
Theoretical Approach: Psychoanalytic, Eclectic
Fees: £20 negotiable

FLETCHER Brian 0742 585 360
Chruch Army Counselling North, 30 Montrose Road, SHEFFIELD S7 2EE
Member of: BAC Acc
Quals/training: BAC Acc; Various Short Courses & Workshops 1977-81; Guidance, Couns & Pastoral Care Salford College 1979
Personal Therapy: Ongoing
Supervision: Ongoing
Counselling offered: General, Psychotherapy
Service for: Individuals, Couples
Theoretical Approach: Rogerian, Eclectic, Person-centred
Fees: £18 negotiable

PERRETT Angelina 0742 365973
53 Endowood Road, SHEFFIELD S7 2LY
Member of: BAC
Quals/training: BA(Hons) Social Science; Cert Youth & Community Work; trained Psychotherapist (SCOPE - Sheffield Analytic School); Marital & Sexual Difficulties Course (Sheffield)
Personal Therapy: Ongoing
Supervision: Ongoing
Counselling offered: Psychotherapy, Sexual, Marital, Eating disorders
Service for: Individuals, Couples
Specific to: Survivors of sex abuse
Theoretical Approach: Psychoanalytic, Psychodynamic
Fees: £20

LOXLEY David 0742 305602
193 Crimicar Lane, SHEFFIELD S10 4EH
Member of: BAC, BPS, AFT
Quals/training: BA Psychol; Dip Psychotherapy (Sheffield); C Psychol; FBPsS
Personal Therapy: Ongoing
Supervision: Ongoing
Counselling offered: Psychotherapy, Psychometric testing
Service for: Individuals, Groups, Families, Organisations
Theoretical Approach: Psychodynamic, Cognitive/Behavioural, Eclectic
Fees: Negotiable

Yorkshire - South

BROUGHTON Vivian 0742 686963
84 Glenalmond Road, SHEFFIELD S11 7GX
Member of: BAC, GPTI
Quals/training: Dip Couns (metanoia); training in Gestalt (metanoia) 1987
Personal Therapy: Yes
Supervision: Ongoing
Counselling offered: General, Psychotherapy
Service for: Individuals, Couples, Groups
Theoretical Approach: Rogerian, Gestalt
Fees: £22 - £30 Sliding scale unemployed neg

HAWLEY Thomas A ansaphone 0742 682661
32 Rossington Road, SHEFFIELD S11 8SA
Member of: BAC, BASMT
Quals/training: Cert in Psychiatric Social Work; Cert in Rational-Emotive Therapy; Dip in Hypnosis & Hypnotherapy
Personal Therapy: Yes
Supervision: Ongoing
Counselling offered: General, Marital, Sexual, Stress, Hypnotherapy
Service for: Individuals, Families
Specific to: Mentally ill, Families of
Theoretical Approach: Eclectic, Cognitive, RET
Fees: £20

GARVIN-CROFTS Pauline 0742 368307
Tether's End, 630 Abbey Lane, Whirlow, SHEFFIELD S11 9NA
Member of: NRHP
Quals/training: DHP(NC); MFTCom; Cert Ed; trained in couns, NLP, etc
Personal Therapy: Ongoing
Supervision: Ongoing
Counselling offered: General, Psychotherapy, Relationship, Sexual, Bereavement, Assertiveness, Supervision
Service for: Individuals, Couples, Families, Groups
Theoretical Approach: Eclectic
Fees: £20 negotiable

Yorkshire - West

Organisations

BRADFORD PSYCHOTHERAPY & COUNSELLING SERVICE
0274 641152
505a Otley Road, Undercliffe, BRADFORD BD2 4QL
Service: Psychotherapy for individuals, counselling for individuals and couples, supervision, personal development workshops and training courses
Area served: Nationwide
Referral: Self
Training of workers: Training in Humanistic and Psychodynamic approaches
Code of Ethics: BAC
Management by: Steve Page and Geoff Pelham
Fees: £23; £12 initial meeting

CAIRNS PERSONAL COUNSELLING SERVICE
0274 394822
8 Surrey Grove, West Bowling, BRADFORD BD5 7EJ
Service: Personal, marital, loss through divorce, abortion and bereavement counselling
Area served: West Yorkshire
Training of workers: BAC(Acc); NMGC trained; BSc(Hons) Behavioural Sciences; ongoing supervision
Code of Ethics: BAC
Management by: Jean Cairns
Fees: £20

LEEDS HA, CLINICAL PSYCHOLOGY SERVICE
0943 876151
High Royds Hospital, Menston, ILKLEY LS29 6AQ
Service: General counselling and therapy for all types of emotional, sexual and relationship difficulties
Area served: Leeds District
Referral: GP, Self
Training of workers: Post Graduate Clinical Psychology
Code of Ethics: BPS
Management by: Leeds Community & Mental Health Services
Fees: None

AIREDALE GENERAL HOSPITAL DEPT OF CLINICAL PSYCHOLOGY
0535 652511 x 2841
Steeton, KEIGHLEY
Service: Assessment and treatment of all forms of psychological problem. Counselling, psychotherapy, behaviour therapy for individuals, couples, families and groups
Area served: Airedale NHS Trust
Other languages: Gujerati, Hindi, Urdu
Referral: GP, Consultant
Training of workers: Post Grad Clinical Psychology, Counselling
Code of Ethics: BAC, BPS
Management by: Airedale NHS Trust
Fees: None for NHS patients

Yorkshire - West

WOMEN'S COUNSELLING & THERAPY SERVICE LTD 0532 455725
Oxford Chambers, Oxford Place, LEEDS LS1 3AX
Service: Individual and group analytic psychotherapy and counselling for women, training and supervision from a feminist analytic perspective
Area served: Leeds
Referral: Self or others
Training of workers: Selection by interview, two year course or experience, including personal therapy; regular supervision
Code of Ethics: Agency's own code
Management by: Management Committee
Fees: Donations encouraged

WPF COUNSELLING NORTH 0532 450303
Westminster Pastoral Foundation, St Peter's House, Kirkgate, LEEDS LS2 7DJ
Service: Individual counselling for a wide range of emotional difficulties including depression, anxiety and problems of relationship
Area served: West Yorkshire
Referral: Self
Training of workers: Couns qualification or significant in-service training inc personal therapy. Centre offers weekly professional supervision
Code of Ethics: BAC
Management by: Local Management Group
Fees: £5 - £15 negotiated & paid weekly

YORKSHIRE ASSOCIATION FOR PSYCHODYNAMIC PSYCHOTHERAPY 0532 439000
Dept Psychotherapy, Southfield House, 40 Clarendon Road, LEEDS LS2 9PJ
Service: YAPP is an organisation for promoting psychodynamic psychotherapy. It considers professional issues such as potential accreditation of membs. Membs in public/private sectors.
Area served: Yorkshire
Referral: Self or others
Training of workers: The organisation will only recommend trained & qualified psychotherapists though some members are not trained
Code of Ethics: YAPP
Management by: Committee
Fees: Variable (Public Sector Free)

LEEDS CRISIS CENTRE 0532 755898
3 Spring Road, LEEDS LS6 1AD
Service: Short term (up to 12 weeks) intensive counselling for people at times of stress or personal catastrophe, inc emotional or relationship difficulties, trauma
Area served: Metropolitan District of Leeds
Referral: Self or others
Training of workers: Dip SW or equivalent with experience in counselling; ongoing in-house training; personal therapy; regular supervision
Code of Ethics: Agency's own code
Management by: Leeds City Council Dept of Social Services
Fees: None

Yorkshire - West

EAST LEEDS FAMILY SERVICE UNIT 0532 484847
15 Lavender Walk, LEEDS LS9 8TX
Service:	Family social work & group work for parents and children 'at risk' or under stress
Area served:	Leeds 7,8,9,14, & 15
Referral:	Self or others
Training of workers:	CQSW
Code of Ethics:	BASMT
Management by:	Family Service Unit & local management committee
Fees:	None

WEST YORKSHIRE MS THERAPY CENTRE LTD 0532 504528
Leeds Road, Rawdon, LEEDS LS19 6JY
Service:	Counselling for MS sufferers, their families and carers
Area served:	West Yorkshire
Referral:	Self or others
Training of workers:	Appropriate training & qualifications
Code of Ethics:	BAC
Management by:	ARMS
Fees:	According to means

Individual Practitioners
*Each individual is a **member of** one or more organisations eligible for entry into this directory. BAC Accredited Counsellors and Recognised Supervisors are shaded.*

TREPKA Chris 0274 560311 x 2281
The Yorkshire Clinic, Bradford Road, BINGLEY BD16 1TW
Member of:	BPS
Quals/training:	BA Psychol; M Phil Clinical Psychol; Cognitive Therapy Training; CPsychol
Personal Therapy:	No
Supervision:	Ongoing
Counselling offered:	Mental health, Stress, Eating disorders, Anxiety, Depression, Phobias, Obsessions
Service for:	Individuals
Theoretical Approach:	Cognitive
Fees:	£45 - £55 sliding scale

PAGE Steve 0274 641152, 0422 354100
Bradford Couns & Psychotherapy, 505a Otley Road, Undercliffe, BRADFORD BD2 4QL
Member of:	BAC Acc
Quals/training:	BAC Acc; BA; RF Senior Staff Training 1976-9; Dip Humanistic Psychol (IDHP Leeds) 1984-6; MEd Couns 1992
Personal Therapy:	Ongoing
Supervision:	Ongoing
Counselling offered:	General, Crisis, Psychotherapy
Service for:	Individuals, Couples, Groups, Families
Theoretical Approach:	Psychodynamic, Humanistic
Fees:	£23; 1st = £12, also in Halifax

Yorkshire - West

CAIRNS Jean   **0274 394822**
8 Surrey Grove, West Bowling, BRADFORD BD5 7EJ
Member of: BAC Acc
Quals/training: BAC(Acc); RELATE trained; BSc (Hons) Behavioural Sciences
Personal Therapy: Yes
Supervision: Ongoing
Counselling offered: General, Marital, Divorce, Abortion, Bereavement
Service for: Individuals, Couples
Theoretical Approach: Humanistic, Eclectic
Fees: £20

WRIGHT Anne   **0274 672334**
44 Larch Hill, Odsal, BRADFORD BD6 1DP
Member of: BAC
Quals/training: BA; Person-centred Couns(Bradford Cancer Support Centre)
Personal Therapy: Yes
Supervision: Ongoing
Counselling offered: General, Bereavement, Crisis, Relationship
Service for: Individuals, Couples
Theoretical Approach: Rogerian
Fees: £10 - £15 negotiable

AINSWORTH Peter   **0274 544807**
St Saviour's Vicarage, Ings Way, Fairweather Green, BRADFORD BD8 0LU
Member of: BAC
Quals/training: NMGC trained; CTA affiliated
Personal Therapy: Yes
Supervision: Ongoing
Counselling offered: General, Relationship
Service for: Individuals, Couples, Groups
Theoretical Approach: Rogerian
Fees: £5 - £25 by negotiation

HILLIER Shirley   **0274 499707**
28 Milford Place, Heaton, BRADFORD BD9 4RU
Member of: BAC Acc, YAPP
Quals/training: BAC Acc; CQSW 1975; CTA 1978; MSc Mental Health (Univ of Leeds) 1981; RELATE trained 1987; Cert Couns Supervision (Univ of Leeds)
Personal Therapy: Yes
Supervision: Ongoing
Counselling offered: General, Relationship, Psychotherapy, Sexual, Supervision
Service for: Individuals, Couples
Theoretical Approach: Psychodynamic
Fees: £18 - £30 negotiable

Yorkshire - West

HEENAN Colleen
BRADFORD BD9
0274 4931254

Member of:	YAPP
Quals/training:	RMN; BA Psychol/Soc; Intro Dip Group Analysis; MSc Psychotherapy; 10 yrs supervised practice
Personal Therapy:	Ongoing
Supervision:	Ongoing
Counselling offered:	General, Psychotherapy, Eating disorders, Relationship, Supervision
Service for:	Individuals
Specific to:	Women, Lesbians
Theoretical Approach:	Analytic, Feminist
Fees:	£25

HEDLEY David
Moorfield, Baldwin Lane, Clayton, BRADFORD BD14 6PN
0274 880354

Member of:	BAC
Quals/training:	1985 NMGC trained
Personal Therapy:	Yes
Supervision:	Ongoing
Counselling offered:	General, Relationship, Sexual, Psychotherapy
Service for:	Individuals, Couples, Families, Groups
Theoretical Approach:	Client-centred
Fees:	£20

LOMAX Pauline
Long Fallas, 2 Knowles Road, BRIGHOUSE HD6 3RN
0484 712210

Member of:	BAC
Quals/training:	Adv Dip Couns (Leeds); Cert Couns (CSCT)
Personal Therapy:	No
Supervision:	Ongoing
Counselling offered:	General, Crisis, Bereavement, Sexual abuse
Service for:	Individuals, Couples, Families, Groups, Organisations
Specific to:	Survivors of child abuse
Theoretical Approach:	Rogerian, Gestalt
Fees:	£15

MARSHALL Pauline
BRIGHOUSE HD6
0484 710210

Member of:	BAC
Quals/training:	Adv Dip Guidance & Couns; Dip Ed; Cert Ed; Currently studying for MEd Couns & HRM; training in Gestalt, TA, Co-Counselling
Personal Therapy:	Yes
Supervision:	Ongoing
Counselling offered:	General, Bereavement, Psychotherapy, Relationship, Stress
Service for:	Individuals, Groups, Organisations
Theoretical Approach:	Person-centred, Gestalt
Fees:	£15 - £25 Sliding Scale

Yorkshire - West

SILLETT Angie 0274 878727
4 Dewsbury Road, Gomersal, CLECKHEATON BD19 4LD
Member of:	BAC
Quals/training:	Dip Couns; RSA Cert Couns in Work Settings, training in marital couns & family therapy
Personal Therapy:	Yes
Supervision:	Ongoing
Counselling offered:	**General, Bereavement, Sexual abuse, Supervision**
Service for:	Individuals, Couples, Families
Specific to:	Women
Theoretical Approach:	Rogerian, Egan
Fees:	£15 - £30 sliding scale

HONEY Barbara 0422 883971
Woodbank West, Burnley Road, Luddendenfoot, HALIFAX HX2 6AH
Member of:	BAC
Quals/training:	BA Gen Arts; PCGE; RELATE trained 1987; tutor for GSCT; counsellor for Schools Psychological Service; Memb BICA
Personal Therapy:	Yes
Supervision:	Ongoing
Counselling offered:	**General, Relationship, Infertility, Redundancy**
Service for:	Individuals, Couples, Families
Theoretical Approach:	Psychodynamic, Person-centred
Other languages:	French
Fees:	£20

BARKER Christine 0422 354100
3 Beverley Place, Boothtown, HALIFAX HX3 6LR
Member of:	BAC
Quals/training:	RMN; Dip Humanistic Psychol; working with Sexual Abuse training
Personal Therapy:	Ongoing
Supervision:	Ongoing
Counselling offered:	**General, Relationship, Abuse**
Service for:	Individuals, Couples
Specific to:	Survivors of sex abuse
Theoretical Approach:	Humanistic
Fees:	£23; £12 initially, also Bradford

WEBB Felicity 0484 540829
Fieldhead Surgery, Leymoor Road, Golcar, HUDDERSFIELD HD7 4QQ
Member of:	BAC
Quals/training:	BSc(Hons); PGCE; Adv Dip Couns
Personal Therapy:	Ongoing
Supervision:	Ongoing
Counselling offered:	**General, Bereavement, Loss, Depression, Relationship, Sexual abuse**
Service for:	Individuals, Couples, Groups
Theoretical Approach:	Humanistic, Psychodynamic
Fees:	£20

Yorkshire - West

CHANDLER Kevin — ansaphone 0484 861702
Springfield Mill, Norman Road, Denby Dale, HUDDERSFIELD HD8 8TH
Member of:	BAC Acc RSup
Quals/training:	BAC(Acc); RELATE trained; Certificated; Advanced Dip Guidance & Couns (Teeside Poly); BAC Recognised Supervisor
Personal Therapy:	Yes
Supervision:	Ongoing
Counselling offered:	**General, Marital, Sexual, Bereavement, Loss**
Service for:	Individuals, Couples
Theoretical Approach:	Integrative, Psychodynamic, Person-centred, Behavioural
Fees:	£35

JACKSON Sharon Ruth — 0484 864 824
Highdale Cottage, 217 Barnsley Road, Denby Dale, HUDDERSFIELD HD8 8TS
Member of:	BPS, CPCP
Quals/training:	C Psychol; AFBPsS; BA(Hons); Dip Adv Couns Psychol; Dip PCP Therapy & Research; Honourary Lecturer, Leeds University
Personal Therapy:	Ongoing
Supervision:	Ongoing
Counselling offered:	**Psychotherapy**
Service for:	Individuals, Groups
Specific to:	Children, Adolescents, Young adults
Theoretical Approach:	PCP
Fees:	£30

O'DONNELL Maire — 0943 830926
Whynbrae, Heathness Road, Addingham, ILKLEY LS29 0JP
Member of:	BAC
Quals/training:	RGN; Adv Dip Couns
Personal Therapy:	No
Supervision:	Ongoing
Counselling offered:	**General, Bereavement, Loss**
Service for:	Individuals
Theoretical Approach:	Integrative, Person-centred, Egan
Fees:	Negotiable

RHODES Thelma — 0943 608 917
5 Wilton Road, ILKLEY LS29 9PG
Member of:	BAC
Quals/training:	MA: Post Grad Dip Social Administration; PGCE: RELATE training in counselling/sex therapy; BASMT
Personal Therapy:	No
Supervision:	Ongoing
Counselling offered:	**General, Marital, Psychotherapy, Sexual dysfunction**
Service for:	Individuals, Couples
Theoretical Approach:	Psychodynamic, Client-centred, Behavioural
Fees:	£25

Yorkshire - West

WAKEFIELD Peter　　　　　　　　　　　　　　　　0535 634593
4 North View, Cononley, KEIGHLEY BD20 8JS
Member of: BAC
Quals/training: Dip Couns; Cert in Couns Supervision
Personal Therapy: Yes
Supervision: Ongoing
Counselling offered: General, Supervision
Service for: Individuals, Couples
Theoretical Approach: Person-centred
Fees: £20

TYAS Barbara　　　　　　　　　　　　　　　　0535 642839
7 Low Bank, Oakworth, KEIGHLEY BD22 7SD
Member of: BAC
Quals/training: BA; Dip in Couns; Cert in Education
Personal Therapy: Yes
Supervision: Ongoing
Counselling offered: General, Relationship, Bereavement, Women's issues
Service for: Individuals, Couples
Theoretical Approach: Rogerian, Psychodynamic
Fees: £15 - £20 negotiable

DALE Heather　　　　　　　　　　　　　　　　0274 566555
BRADFORD, KEIGHLEY
Member of: BAC Acc, ITA, YAPP
Quals/training: BAC Acc; BA; 1981 Couns Cert (SW London College)
Personal Therapy: Ongoing
Supervision: Ongoing
Counselling offered: General, Assertiveness, Psychotherapy
Service for: Individuals, Couples, Groups
Specific to: Women, Lesbians
Theoretical Approach: TA
Fees: £25 reduced in cases of need

BISHOP Maggie　　　　　　　　　　0532 307560, 0482 587868
5 Beechwood Walk, LEEDS LS4 2LZ
Member of: BAC
Quals/training: MA; CQSW; Dip Couns; training in Therapeutic Massage
Personal Therapy: Ongoing
Supervision: Ongoing
Counselling offered: General, Relationship, Bereavement, Miscarriage
Service for: Individuals, Couples, Groups
Theoretical Approach: Humanistic, Person-centred
Fees: £18 - £30 Negotiable

McGUIRE Alec　　　　　　　　　　ansaphone 0532 400336
34 Gledhow Wood Road, LEEDS LS8 4BZ
Member of: BAC Acc, YAPP
Quals/training: BAC Acc; BA; MA; Fellow RSH; Full memb ASSP
Personal Therapy: Yes
Supervision: Ongoing
Counselling offered: Psychotherapy
Service for: Individuals
Theoretical Approach: Jungian
Fees: £15 - £30 sliding scale

Yorkshire - West

MATTHEWS Catriona   0532 744817
20 Heathfield Terrace, off Cottage Road, LEEDS LS6 4DE
Member of:	**BAC, YAPP**
Quals/training:	BA(Hons); Dip Manamement Studies; Dip Couns, extensive theoretical & experiential training since 1975
Personal Therapy:	Yes
Supervision:	Ongoing
Counselling offered:	**General, Bereavement, Change, Personal growth, Psychotherapy, Relationship, Stress management**
Service for:	Individuals, Couples, Groups, Organisations
Theoretical Approach:	Integrative, Humanistic, Gestalt, Behavioural
Fees:	£25

WEBB Joan   0532 623766
23 Henconner Lane, Chapel Allerton, LEEDS LS7 3NX
Member of:	**BAC Acc, YAPP, HIP**
Quals/training:	BAC Acc; Hallam Inst Psychotherapy Acc; Dip Psychotherapy; CQSW
Personal Therapy:	Yes
Supervision:	Ongoing
Counselling offered:	**Psychotherapy, General, Relationship**
Service for:	Individuals, Couples
Theoretical Approach:	Psychodynamic
Fees:	£25

TYNDALE-BISCOE Mrs. Savi   0532 663401
43 The Drive, Roundhay, LEEDS LS8 1JQ
Member of:	**BAC**
Quals/training:	SRN; Adv Dip Couns & Guidance; Cert Supervision (WPF)
Personal Therapy:	Yes
Supervision:	Ongoing
Counselling offered:	**General, Relationship, Bereavement, Loss**
Service for:	Individuals, Groups
Theoretical Approach:	Person-centred, Psychodynamic
Fees:	£10 - £25 Sliding scale

NEWTON Janie   evenings 0532 323270
13 Oakwood Drive, LEEDS LS8 2JB
Member of:	**BAC Acc**
Quals/training:	BAC Acc; MA Couns; Cert Ed; RELATE counsellor
Personal Therapy:	Yes
Supervision:	Ongoing
Counselling offered:	**General, Relationship, Bereavement, Supervision**
Service for:	Individuals, Couples
Specific to:	Students, Ethnic minorities
Theoretical Approach:	Person-centred, Analytical, Behavioural
Fees:	£20 - £30 sliding scale

Yorkshire - West

JOY Janet   0532 667631
Fairfield, 68c Glendhow, Wood Road, LEEDS LS8 4DH
Member of:	BAC, BPS
Quals/training:	BEd(Hons) Psychol; Dip Ericksonian Hypnosis (BHR); NLP (St George's Hospital)
Personal Therapy:	Ongoing
Supervision:	Ongoing
Counselling offered:	Psychotherapy, Hypnotherapy, Depression, Bereavement, Phobias, Personal growth
Service for:	Individuals
Theoretical Approach:	Rogerian, Ericksonian
Fees:	£15 - £30 sliding scale

ROMAINE Stephanie   0532 709021
1 Crossland Terrace, LEEDS LS11 6EU
Member of:	BAC
Quals/training:	Dip in Couns
Personal Therapy:	Ongoing
Supervision:	Ongoing
Counselling offered:	General
Service for:	Individuals, Couples
Theoretical Approach:	Psychodynamic
Fees:	£20 negotiable

LAWTON Barbara   0532 554582
10 Luther Street, Rodley, LEEDS LS13 1LU
Member of:	BAC
Quals/training:	BEd(Hons)(Keele); Adv Dip Couns (Leeds Univ)
Personal Therapy:	Yes
Supervision:	Ongoing
Counselling offered:	General, Bereavement, Child abuse, Eating disorders, Relationship, Stress
Service for:	Individuals
Theoretical Approach:	Psychodynamic
Fees:	£20

GLOVER Jean   0532 576202, 0302 325598
27 Hough End Lane, Bramley, LEEDS LS13 4EY
Member of:	BASMT
Quals/training:	RELATE trained; BA; RGN; Dip Human Sexuality; short courses in Gestalt, Groupwork
Personal Therapy:	Yes
Supervision:	Ongoing
Counselling offered:	Sexual, Relationship
Service for:	Individuals, Couples
Theoretical Approach:	Eclectic
Fees:	35 initial, £25-£30 thereafter

Yorkshire - West

WATTIS Libby   0532 736076
8 Compton Mount, LEEDS LS9 7BT
Member of:	BAC Acc RSup
Quals/training:	BAC Acc & Recog Supervisor; BA(Hons); RGN; CTA Seminars '76-'79; RELATE trained '84; Dip Humanistic Psychol '88; Dip Psychotherapy (Liverpool) '92
Personal Therapy:	Ongoing
Supervision:	Ongoing
Counselling offered:	General, Marital, Bereavement, Psychotherapy, Supervision
Service for:	Individuals, Couples
Theoretical Approach:	Psychodynamic
Fees:	£12 - £27

HAMILTON PAGE Steve   0532 788515
30 West Park Drive, West Park, LEEDS LS16 5BL
Member of:	BAC, YAPP
Quals/training:	Adv Dip Couns(Park Lane Coll); 1 yr course in Therapeutic Groupwork(York Univ); various trainings in Family Therapy, Family Mediation & counselling Young People
Personal Therapy:	Yes
Supervision:	Ongoing
Counselling offered:	General, Short-term, Long-term, Anxiety, Stress, Bereavement, Relationship
Service for:	Individuals, Couples, Families, Groups, Organisations
Specific to:	Victims of violence, Survivors of sex abuse
Theoretical Approach:	Psychodynamic
Fees:	£20

ELEY Frances Ann   0532 610515
31b Grove Farm Crescent, LEEDS LS16 6BZ
Member of:	BAC, YAPP
Quals/training:	BA (Open) Psychol, Sociology & Technology; Dip Couns 1990; training in NLP - Foundation Skills Cert
Personal Therapy:	Yes
Supervision:	Ongoing
Counselling offered:	General, Bereavement, Relationship, PTSD
Service for:	Individuals, Couples
Theoretical Approach:	Eclectic
Fees:	£30 org, £22.50 ind £17.50 unwaged

COLDRICK Judith   0532 610538
LEEDS LS16
Member of:	BAC
Quals/training:	Groupwork; Mental Health & Therapy (Leeds Met. Univ); RSA Couns Cert
Personal Therapy:	Yes
Supervision:	Ongoing
Counselling offered:	General, Relationship, HIV, AIDS, Sexuality
Service for:	Individuals, Couples, Groups, Families
Specific to:	Lesbians, Gays
Theoretical Approach:	Person-centred
Fees:	£22

Yorkshire - West

ROWE Carolyn 0532 842567
Low Meadow, Hall Drive, Bramhope, LEEDS LS16 9JF
Member of: BAC
Quals/training: BA (Hons); PCGE; Dip Psychotherapy (Sheffield University)
Personal Therapy: Yes
Supervision: Ongoing
Counselling offered: General, Eating disorders
Service for: Individuals
Theoretical Approach: Psychodynamic, Cognitive, Integrative
Fees: £15 - £25

QUATE Monty 0532 662060
545 Shadwell Lane, LEEDS LS17 8AP
Member of: BAC
Quals/training: MSc; Cert Ed; Dip Psychol; Dip Sociology:
Personal Therapy: Yes
Supervision: Ongoing
Counselling offered: General, Sexual, Psychotherapy, Crisis, Stress, Depression, Anorexia, Children's problems
Service for: Individuals, Couples, Families
Theoretical Approach: Rogerian, Analytical, Behavioural
Fees: £25 Depends on length of treatment

HEATON-ROSS Sheila 0532 584411
33 Outwood Lane, Horsforth, LEEDS LS18 4JB
Member of: BAC Acc
Quals/training: BAC Acc; NMGC trained '81; Registered Dramatherapist; Cert Ed; trained in Gestalt, TA, Creative Therapy
Personal Therapy: Yes
Supervision: Ongoing
Counselling offered: General, Psychotherapy, Marital, Bereavement
Service for: Individuals, Couples, Groups
Theoretical Approach: Person-centred, Transpersonal
Fees: £27 - £35

SYME Gabrielle 0532 505700
Mount Farm House, Town Street, Rawdon, LEEDS LS19 6QJ
Member of: BAC Acc, BAC RSup
Quals/training: BAC Acc; BSc; PhD; BAC Recog Supervisor
Personal Therapy: Ongoing
Supervision: Ongoing
Counselling offered: General, Bereavement, Psychotherapy
Service for: Individuals, Couples, Families
Theoretical Approach: Psychodynamic
Fees: £32

Yorkshire - West

POTTER Keith **0532 503989**
1 Haw Lane, Yeadon, LEEDS LS19 7XQ
Member of: BAC
Quals/training: Courses in Clin Theol '60 '65 '91/2; Cert Soc Stud (Psychol) Leeds; MA Psychol Therapies (Bradford); CPE (USA & Eire); TA Gestalt & other courses; Supervision training '89-90:
Personal Therapy: Yes
Supervision: Ongoing
Counselling offered: General, Marital, Family, Pastoral, Psychotherapy
Service for: Individuals, Couples, Families, Groups
Theoretical Approach: Person-centred, Psychodynamic
Fees: £10 - £22 Sliding Scale

SYKES Vernon **0532 533494**
3 Troy Road, Morley, LEEDS LS27 8JH
Member of: BAC
Quals/training: PhD (Psychol & Health Sciences); Fellow of RSH; Member Nat Counc of Psycho, Internat Stress Management Assoc, European Soc Medical Hypnosis; Cons Hypno; Reg Comp Practitioner(ICM)
Personal Therapy: Yes
Supervision: Ongoing
Counselling offered: General, Hypnotherapy, Psychotherapy, Stress management
Service for: Individuals
Theoretical Approach: Hypnotherapy
Fees: £21

GREEN Anthea **0924 279728**
12 Fearnley Avenue, OSSETT WF5 9ET
Member of: BAC Acc, YAPP
Quals/training: BAC Acc; RELATE Trained 1981
Personal Therapy: Yes
Supervision: Ongoing
Counselling offered: General, Marital, Bereavement
Service for: Individuals, Couples
Specific to: Parents
Theoretical Approach: Psychodynamic, Person-centred
Fees: £28

KITWOOD Tom **0274 590524**
11 Wellington Crescent, SHIPLEY BD18 3PH
Member of: BAC, BPS
Quals/training: PhD Social Psychol 1980; Dip Natural Therapeutic Massage; RSA Cert Couns Skills in Work Setting 1985; Gestalt Foundation 1990
Personal Therapy: No
Supervision: Ongoing
Counselling offered: General
Service for: Individuals
Specific to: Carers
Theoretical Approach: Eclectic
Fees: £25 60-90 min sessions

Yorkshire - West

MORVILLE Laraine   0706 818770
821a Burnley road, Carnholme, TODMORDEN OL14 7EF
Member of: BAC
Quals/training: RELATE trained
Personal Therapy: Unknown
Supervision: Ongoing
Counselling offered: **General, Relationship**
Service for: Individuals, Couples
Theoretical Approach: Psychodynamic
Fees: Negotiable

COOK Rose   0937 572527
Woodbank House, Harewood Road, Collingham, WETHERBY LS22 5BY
Member of: BAC
Quals/training: MEd Advanced Dip in Couns, York
Personal Therapy: Yes
Supervision: Ongoing
Counselling offered: **General, Relationship, Career, Change**
Service for: Individuals, Couples
Theoretical Approach: Integrative
Fees: £20 - £35

Scotland

National Organisations

FAMILY MEDIATION SCOTLAND 031 220 1610
127 Rose Street, South Lane, EDINBURGH EH2 4BB
Service: Assistance by an impartial mediator to separating and divorcing couples to help them reach agreement over arrangements for the future care of the children
Area served: Scotland
Referral: Self, Health/Soc Work Professional
Training of workers: Includes theory and practice of mediation, legal, social and emotional aspects of divorce, conflict management
Code of Ethics: Agency's own code
Management by: Executive Committee
Fees: Donations requested

GARNETHILL CENTRE LTD 041 333 0730
28 Rose Street, GLASGOW G3 6RE
Service: General counselling and individual psychotherapy for adults. Analytic therapy groups
Area served: Scotland
Other languages: French
Referral: Self
Training of workers: Professionally trained counsellors, psychotherapists, CPNs or social workers. Regular supervision
Code of Ethics: BAC
Management by: Board of Governors
Fees: Individually negotiated

PCT SCOTLAND ASSOCIATION FOR PERSON-CENTRED THERAPY SCOTLAND 041 332 6888
Service throughout Scotland, 40 Kelvingrove Street, GLASGOW G3 7RZ
Service: General counselling & psychotherapy
Area served: Scotland
Referral: Self
Training of workers: Most are graduates or staff of PCT Britain (BAC Rec course)
Code of Ethics: BAC
Management by: Network of Association Members
Fees: £20 - £40 negotiable

Scotland

Borders

Individual Practitioners
Each individual is a **member of** one or more organisations eligible for entry into this directory.
BAC Accredited Counsellors and Recognised Supervisors are shaded.

LINN Iris ansaphone 089 682 2469
Laneside, Main Street, Newstead, MELROSE
Member of:	NRHP
Quals/training:	Trained at NCHP & by W Mids Area HA, courses on AIDS & bereavement (East Birmingham Hosp)
Personal Therapy:	No
Supervision:	No
Counselling offered:	Hypnotherapy, Psychotherapy, Stress management
Service for:	Individuals, Couples
Theoretical Approach:	Cognitive
Fees:	£20 (Assessment £25)

Central

Individual Practitioners
Each individual is a **member of** one or more organisations eligible for entry into this directory.
BAC Accredited Counsellors and Recognised Supervisors are shaded.

KILBORN Mary 0786 833332
Hillhead, 12 Well Road, Bridge of Allan, STIRLING FK9 4DR
Member of:	BAC Acc
Quals/training:	BAC Acc; 1974-76 Marriage Guidance Trained & assessed; Dip Psychotherapy with PCT (Britain); memb Assoc for Person-centred Therapy
Personal Therapy:	Yes
Supervision:	Ongoing
Counselling offered:	General, Relationship
Service for:	Individuals, Couples
Theoretical Approach:	Person-centred
Other languages:	French, German, Spanish
Fees:	£15 - £40

Dumfries & Galloway

Organisations

DEPT OF PSYCHOLOGICAL SERVICES & RESEARCH 0387 55301 x 2271
Crichton Royal, DUMFRIES DG1 4TG
Service:	A range of personal approaches to psychotherapy; behaviour therapy; sexual counselling; for a wide range of clients family work.
Area served:	Dumfries & Galloway
Referral:	GP, Agencies, Self
Training of workers:	Postgraduate Clinical Psychology and continuing training in therapeutic psychology
Code of Ethics:	BPS
Management by:	Dumfries & Galloway HB
Fees:	None

Scotland

Individual Practitioners
*Each individual is a **member of** one or more organisations eligible for entry into this directory. BAC Accredited Counsellors and Recognised Supervisors are shaded.*

CAMPBELL Colin 046 16 288
Scaleridge Cottage, Waterbeck, LOCKERBIE DG11 3EU
Member of: BAC Acc, ITA, NRHP
Quals/training: BAC(Acc); Cert Hynotherapy & Psychotherapy; NRHP(Assoc); Transactional Analyst in clinical training; Cert Anatomy & Physiology; ITEC
Personal Therapy: Ongoing
Supervision: Ongoing
Counselling offered: General, Relationship, Psychotherapy, Massage
Service for: Individuals, Couples, Groups
Theoretical Approach: TA, Gestalt, Rogerian, Ericksonian, Hypnotherapy
Fees: £15 - £30 sliding scale

Fife

Individual Practitioners
*Each individual is a **member of** one or more organisations eligible for entry into this directory. BAC Accredited Counsellors and Recognised Supervisors are shaded.*

HASLAM-EVANS James 0592 743185
160 Piper Drive, Collydean, GLENROTHES KY7 6TF
Member of: NRHP
Quals/training: Cert Hypnotherapy & Psychotherapy (NCHP); NRHP (Assoc)
Personal Therapy: Yes
Supervision: Ongoing
Counselling offered: General, Psychotherapy, Anorexia, Bereavement, Hypnotherapy, Marital
Service for: Individuals, Couples
Specific to: Children, Adolescents, Women, Nurses, Managers
Theoretical Approach: Rogerian, Eclectic
Fees: £15 - £20

TURNER Allan 0382 542772
57 Bay Road, Wormit, NEWPORT-ON-TAY DD6 8LW
Member of: BAC Acc
Quals/training: BAC Acc; 1985-8 Dip FDI; memb Assoc for Person-Centred Therapy (Scotland) & BAPCA
Personal Therapy: No
Supervision: Ongoing
Counselling offered: General, Supervision
Service for: Individuals, Couples
Theoretical Approach: Client-centred
Fees: £15 - £40

Scotland

LEWCZUK Zinaida   0334 74745
88 Hepburn Gardens, ST. ANDREWS KY16 9LN
Member of:	BAC Acc
Quals/training:	BAC Acc; MA; PhD 1984; Dip Person-centred Couns & Psychotherapy (FDI) 1988
Personal Therapy:	No
Supervision:	Ongoing
Counselling offered:	**General, Crisis, Transition, Psychotherapy**
Service for:	Individuals, Couples
Theoretical Approach:	Person-centred
Other languages:	Polish
Fees:	£15 - £25 sliding scale

Grampian

Organisations

LIFELINE PREGNANCY COUNSELLING AND CARE   0224 640266
Margaret House, 132 Huntley Street, ABERDEEN AB1 1SU
Service:	**Non directive, non judgemental counselling service for any woman with pregnancy related problems, including post abortion counselling**
Area served:	Grampian Region
Referral:	Self, Health/Soc Work Professional, GP
Training of workers:	Aims to employ trained counsellors plus twice yearly training in related areas. Supervision
Code of Ethics:	BAC
Management by:	Local Management Committee
Fees:	Donations welcomed

Individual Practitioners

*Each individual is a **member of** one or more organisations eligible for entry into this directory. BAC Accredited Counsellors and Recognised Supervisors are shaded.*

BAIRD Phyllis   0224 620919
24 Union Wynd, ABERDEEN AB1 1SL
Member of:	BAC
Quals/training:	Dip Psychotherapy (Aberdeen) 1983; Scottish MGC Training 1963-5
Personal Therapy:	Yes
Supervision:	Ongoing
Counselling offered:	**Psychotherapy, Marital, Family**
Service for:	Individuals, Couples, Groups, Families
Theoretical Approach:	Psychodynamic, Rogerian, Behavioural, Object relations
Fees:	£20 - £30

Scotland

KOHLER Christiane 0224 781747
51 Cairngrassie Circle, Portlethen, ABERDEEN AB1 4TZ
Member of:	NSHAP, CRAH
Quals/training:	Dip Therapeutic Hypnosis & Psychotherapy (NSHAP); Past Life Regression (Atkinson-Ball Coll of Hypnotherapy & Hypno- healing)
Personal Therapy:	Yes
Supervision:	Ongoing
Counselling offered:	**General, Relationship, Crisis, Hypnotherapy, Psychotherapy, Regression therapy, Stress, Imaging**
Service for:	Individuals
Specific to:	Women
Theoretical Approach:	Humanistic
Other languages:	German
Fees:	£20 - £30

BUCHAN Roberta 0224 641331, 0467 24888
ABERDEEN AB2
Member of:	BAC
Quals/training:	RMN; trained by Scottish Council on Alchohol
Personal Therapy:	Ongoing
Supervision:	Ongoing
Counselling offered:	**General, Short-term, Long-term, Anxiety, Depression, Loss, Stress**
Service for:	Individuals, Couples, Groups
Theoretical Approach:	Phenomenological
Fees:	£25 sliding scale

HUDSON Fiona 0224 633583
55 Short Loanings, ABERDEEN AB2 4TA
Member of:	BAC
Quals/training:	Post Grad Dip in Couns (Aberdeen Univ); Aberdeen Counselling & Information Service couns training
Personal Therapy:	Yes
Supervision:	Ongoing
Counselling offered:	**General**
Service for:	Individuals
Theoretical Approach:	Person-centred
Fees:	£20 (£10 1st assessment interview)

McNULTY Geoff 0330 24673
11 Wilson Road, BANCHORY AB31 3UY
Member of:	BAC Acc
Quals/training:	BAC Acc; Post grad Dip Couns (Aston); BEd(Hons); MEd Human Relations
Personal Therapy:	Yes
Supervision:	Ongoing
Counselling offered:	**General**
Service for:	Individuals, Groups, Organisations
Theoretical Approach:	Integrative
Fees:	Negotiable

Scotland

CLARK David Findlay 0261 812624
Glendeveron, 8 Deveron Terrace, BANFF AB45 1BB
Member of: BPS
Quals/training: MA; PhD; C Psychol
Personal Therapy: Yes
Supervision: No
Counselling offered: General, Sexual, Marital, Stress, Bereavement, Psychotherapy, Anxiety, Disaster
Service for: Individuals, Couples, Families
Theoretical Approach: Cognitive/Behavioural, Eclectic
Fees: £40 sliding scale

YOUNG Courtenay 0309 690251
c/o Findhorn Foundation, The Park, FORRES IV36 0TZ
Member of: AHPP, Member of UKCP Register
Quals/training: Dip Biodynamic Psychotherapy & Massage '83; Dip Psychol '85; Full Memb AHPP
Personal Therapy: Ongoing
Supervision: Ongoing
Counselling offered: General, Crisis, Psychotherapy, Spiritual
Service for: Individuals, Couples, Families, Organisations
Specific to: Children
Theoretical Approach: Humanistic
Fees: £25 sliding scale (=/- £5)

Highland

Individual Practitioners
Each individual is a **member of** one or more organisations eligible for entry into this directory. BAC Accredited Counsellors and Recognised Supervisors are shaded.

TREVELYAN Jane 047 022306
Kensalroag House, DUNVEGAN IV55 8GZ
Member of: BAC
Quals/training: Dip Adult Couns'87; Dip Transpersonal Perspectives & Skills in Couns & Psychotherapy(CTP)'92
Personal Therapy: Ongoing
Supervision: Ongoing
Counselling offered: General, Bereavement, Crisis, Stress, Personal growth, Sexuality
Service for: Individuals, Groups
Specific to: Women, Ethnic minorities
Theoretical Approach: Person-centred, Transpersonal
Fees: £20

Scotland

DOBSON Gill ansaphone 0381 620176
INVERNESS
Member of: BAC
Quals/training: Counsellor with Scottish Marriage Counselling Services since '82; Dip in Couns & Psychotherapy(FDI & PCT Britain)
Personal Therapy: Yes
Supervision: Ongoing
Counselling offered: **General, Addiction, AIDS, Bereavement, Relationship, Marital, Sexual, Psychotherapy, Supervision**
Service for: Individuals, Couples, Families, Groups
Theoretical Approach: Person-centred
Fees: £25 - £40 sliding scale

THOMAS Georgette 0667 55050
Inverwick House, Albert Street, NAIRN IV12 4HE
Member of: BAC, GPTI
Quals/training: MA Couns Ed & Licensed Counsellor (CA, USA); Adv Trainee (GPTI), Adv Trainee, Bonny Method of Guided Imagery & Music
Personal Therapy: Yes
Supervision: Ongoing
Counselling offered: **General, Child abuse, Music therapy**
Service for: Individuals, Couples, Families, Groups
Specific to: Survivors of child abuse, Health care professionals
Theoretical Approach: Person-centred, Gestalt
Fees: £20 - £25 Sliding scale

Lothian

Organisations

LIFELINE PREGNANCY COUNSELLING AND CARE 031 557 2060
7a Albany Street, EDINBURGH EH1 3PY
Service: Non directive, non judgemental counselling service for women of childbearing age, including post abortion counselling, choice counselling & all aspects of pregnancy
Area served: Lothian region, Fife and the Borders
Referral: Self, GP, Health/Soc Work Professional
Training of workers: Employs trained counsellors and twice yearly training and attendance at weekly training courses (Ed Past C). Supervision
Code of Ethics: BAC
Management by: Local Management Committee
Fees: Donations for pregnancy tests

EDINBURGH ASSOCIATION FOR MENTAL HEALTH 031 225 8508
40 Shandwick Place, EDINBURGH EH2 4RT
Service: Open-ended service for adults presenting with wide range of problems, depression, anxiety, long-term mental health problems etc
Area served: Lothian, parts of Fife and Borders
Referral: Self
Training of workers: All are trained but from a variety of backgrounds - SIHR NMGC, IPC. Required to attend regular supervision
Code of Ethics: BAC
Management by: Committee, comprising appointees with specialist knowledge, and counsellors
Fees: None, donations welcome

Scotland

WELLSPRING   **031 553 6660**
13 Smiths Place, EDINBURGH EH6 8NT
Service: Couns & psychotherapy inc analytical, person-centred & art therapy, psychosynthesis, dreamwork, Heimler hum soc funct, therapeutic massage & other comp therapies for inds/grps
Area served: Scotland
Referral: Self
Training of workers: All are qualified in their field, have had personal therapy and make own arrangements for supervision
Code of Ethics: BAC
Management by: Management Committee
Fees: Dependent on income

Individual Practitioners

*Each individual is a **member of** one or more organisations eligible for entry into this directory. BAC Accredited Counsellors and Recognised Supervisors are shaded.*

MORRISON Jean   **031 449 6859**
45 Corslet Road, CURRIE EH14 5LZ
Member of: BAC Acc
Quals/training: BAC Acc & Recog Supervisor; Dip College of Ed; Deaconess in Church of Scotland; Certified Transactional Analyst (Ed)
Personal Therapy: Yes
Supervision: Ongoing
Counselling offered: General, Relationship, Bereavement, Spiritual
Service for: Individuals, Couples
Specific to: Christians, Clergy/priests
Theoretical Approach: TA, Eclectic
Fees: £15 - £25 Negotiable

SHEWAN Alistair   **031 225 6537**
3 Castle Wynd North, EDINBURGH EH1 2NQ
Member of: NRHP
Quals/training: BA (Hons); training in Hypnotherapy
Personal Therapy: Ongoing
Supervision: Ongoing
Counselling offered: General, Hypnotherapy
Theoretical Approach: Rogerian
Fees: Sliding scale

HARRIS Jenny   **031 332 1890**
19 Balmoral Place, EDINBURGH EH3 5JA
Member of: BAC
Quals/training: Dip SW; Dip Health Educ; training in Gestalt Psychotherapy (Gestalt Training Scotland) 1988-93; Marriage Counselling Scotland Registered
Personal Therapy: Yes
Supervision: Ongoing
Counselling offered: General, Transition, Relationship, Psychotherapy
Service for: Individuals, Couples
Theoretical Approach: Gestalt
Fees: £17

Scotland

BURNS Jo   Ansaphone 031 332 2316
16 St Bernards Row, Stockbridge, EDINBURGH EH4 1HW
Member of: BAC
Quals/training: MSc in Mental Health (Surrey Univ); Dip in Person-Centred Couns & Psychotherapy; (Person-Centred Therapy {Britain] in assoc with the Norwich Centre)
Personal Therapy: Ongoing
Supervision: Ongoing
Counselling offered: **General, Psychotherapy, Long-term, Sexuality, Personal growth, Consultation, Supervision**
Service for: Individuals, Groups, Organisations
Theoretical Approach: Person-centred
Fees: £20 - £35 negotiable for low/unwaged

SHOEMARK Alison   031 661 1648
23 Spring Gardens, EDINBURGH EH8 8HU
Member of: BAC Acc
Quals/training: BAC Acc; Dip Couns & Psychotherapy; RGN;
Personal Therapy: Yes
Supervision: Ongoing
Counselling offered: **General, Psychotherapy**
Service for: Individuals, Groups
Theoretical Approach: Person-centred
Fees: £20 negotiable

BEASLEY Ronald   24 hours 031 317 3252, 031 229 8383
37 Warrender Park Terrace, EDINBURGH EH9 1EB
Member of: BAC
Quals/training: Dip Pastoral Studies '70; SIHR (Associate); Memb COSCA, ASC and American Assoc of Pastoral Counsellors; ASC Acc
Personal Therapy: Yes
Supervision: Ongoing
Counselling offered: **General, Bereavement, Crisis, Relationship, Long-term**
Service for: Individuals, Couples, Families
Specific to: Young people
Theoretical Approach: Psychodynamic
Fees: £15 negotiable

BUCHAN Diana   031 668 2429
28 Blackford Bank, EDINBURGH EH9 2PR
Member of: BAC
Quals/training: MA; Dip Person-Centred Counselling & Psychotherapy (Person-Centred Therapy [Britain]); Memb Assoc Person-centred Therapists (Scotland)
Personal Therapy: Yes
Supervision: Ongoing
Counselling offered: **General, Bereavement, Crisis, Personal growth, Stress, Relationship, Depression, Psychotherapy**
Service for: Individuals, Couples
Theoretical Approach: Person-centred
Fees: £20 - £30 also in E Lothian & Berwicks.

Scotland

FEWELL Judith   031 447 2597
33a Colinton Road, EDINBURGH EH10 5DU
Member of:	BAC
Quals/training:	BEd(Hons), Couns in Education; Dip Couns & Human Relations, & Psychoanalytical Psychotherapy training (SIHR); Training in group work; Assoc Memb SIHR
Personal Therapy:	Ongoing
Supervision:	Ongoing
Counselling offered:	**General, Psychotherapy, Anxiety, Depression**
Service for:	Individuals, Couples
Specific to:	Lesbians
Theoretical Approach:	Psychodynamic, Person-centred
Fees:	£20 - £30 sliding scale

GARDINER Morag   031 447 5416
10 St Clair Terrace, Morningside, EDINBURGH EH10 5NW
Member of:	BAC
Quals/training:	Adv Cert Couns (Eigenwelt)1989-91; DipCouns (Jesmond Centre for Humanistic Therapy) 1991-92; Couns Supervision Course (Birmingham Univ) 1993
Personal Therapy:	Ongoing
Supervision:	Ongoing
Counselling offered:	**General**
Service for:	Individuals
Theoretical Approach:	Person-centred
Fees:	£15 - £35 sliding scale

FAULKNER Ann   031 447 0564
54/2 Craighouse Gardens, EDINBURGH EH10 5TZ
Member of:	BAC, BPS
Quals/training:	O Psychol; MA Psychol Edinburgh Univ; MSc Educ Psychol (Strathclyde Univ); Dip Ed; Dip EHPNLP; Memb BSECH
Personal Therapy:	Ongoing
Supervision:	Ongoing
Counselling offered:	**General, Psychotherapy, Hypnotherapy**
Service for:	Individuals, Couples, Families, Groups
Theoretical Approach:	Ericksonian, Cognitive, Rogerian, TA
Fees:	£30

JARVIE Margaret   031 334 7821
5 Traquair Park West, EDINBURGH EH12 7AN
Member of:	BAC
Quals/training:	MA; MPhil; Scottish Marriage Guidance trained 1960; MEd Human Relations (Nottingham) 1984; Memb BAPCA & COSCA
Personal Therapy:	Yes
Supervision:	Ongoing
Counselling offered:	**General**
Service for:	Individuals, Couples, Groups, Families
Theoretical Approach:	Rogerian
Fees:	£20 negotiable for low incomes

Scotland

### BOWES Peter	031 443 8969
24 Craiglockhart Terrace, EDINBURGH EH14 1AJ
Member of:	BAC Acc
Quals/training:	BAC Acc; BSc; BD
Personal Therapy:	Yes
Supervision:	Ongoing
Counselling offered:	**General**
Service for:	Individuals, Couples
Theoretical Approach:	Psychodynamic, Eclectic
Fees:	£15 - £25 Sliding scale

### KIRKWOOD Colin	031 667 4273
159 Dalkeith Road, EDINBURGH EH16 4HQ
Member of:	BAC
Quals/training:	MA; MSc Adult Education & Community Development; Cert Human Relations & Couns (SIHR); currently trianing as Psychoanalytic Psychotherapist
Personal Therapy:	Ongoing
Supervision:	Ongoing
Counselling offered:	**General, Psychotherapy**
Service for:	Individuals, Couples
Theoretical Approach:	Object relations
Other languages:	Italian
Fees:	£25 - £30

### DOBSON Gill	ansaphone 031 332 2316
16 St Bernards Row, Stockbridge, EDINBURGH EH4 1HW
Member of:	BAC
Quals/training:	Counsellor with Scottish Marriage Counselling Services since '82; Dip in Couns & Psychotherapy (FDI & PCT Britain)
Personal Therapy:	Yes
Supervision:	Ongoing
Counselling offered:	**General, Addiction, AIDS, Bereavement, Relationship, Marital, Sexual, Psychotherapy, Supervision**
Service for:	Individuals, Couples, Families, Groups
Theoretical Approach:	Person-centred
Fees:	£25 - £40 sliding scale

Scotland

Strathclyde
Organisations

WOMEN'S COUNSELLING & RESOURCE SERVICE 041 227 6006/6020
1st Floor, McIver House, Cadogan Street, GLASGOW G2
Service: Face to face counselling for pregnancy, post abortion, rape, incest; telephone counselling also possible
Area served: Strathclyde
Referral: Self or others
Training of workers: CQSW, one has sex therapy training; regular supervision
Code of Ethics: Agency's own code
Management by: Strathclyde Social Work Dept
Fees: None

TOM ALLAN CENTRE (CHURCH OF SCOTLAND) 041 221 1535
23 Elmbank Street, GLASGOW G2 4PD
Service: Individual, family & group counselling for people of all denominations & faiths & of none; back-up & consultative facilities for ministers, laity & social workers
Referral: Self, Agencies, Health/Soc Work Professional
Training of workers: Psychodynamic couns training over 2 years including personal therapy; ongoing supervision
Code of Ethics: Agency's own code
Management by: Church of Scotland Board of Social Responsibility
Fees: Negotiable

ARGYLL & CLYDE HB CLINICAL PSYCHOLOGICAL SERVICE
0475 33777 x 5270
Ravenscraig Hospital, GREENOCK PA16 9HA
Service: Behavioural psychotherapy, dynamic psychotherapy, family therapy; for individuals, couples, groups and families
Area served: Inverclyde (also Bute & Cowal for children)
Referral: GP
Training of workers: Postgraduate clinical psychology training; training in dynamic psychotherapy & family therapy
Code of Ethics: BPS
Management by: Argyll & Clyde Health Board
Fees: None

RENFREW PRIORITY SERVICES UNIT PSYCHOLOGY DEPT
041 884 5122
Psychology Dept, Dykebar Hospital, Grahamston Road, PAISLEY PA2 7DE
Service: Cognitive & behavioural therapy, individual & group psychotherapeutic work, addictions counselling, family therapy
Area served: Renfrew & district
Referral: Health/Soc Work Professional, GP
Training of workers: Postgraduate clinical psychology
Code of Ethics: BPS
Management by: Argyll & Clyde HB
Fees: None

Scotland

Individual Practitioners
*Each individual is a **member of** one or more organisations eligible for entry into this directory. BAC Accredited Counsellors and Recognised Supervisors are shaded.*

SMITH Alicia　　　　　　　　　　　　　　　　　　0292 281793
17 Fotheringham Road, AYR KA8 0EY
Member of:　　　　　　BAC
Quals/training:　　　　　　BA Psychol; CHP
Personal Therapy:　　　　　No
Supervision:　　　　　　　Ongoing
Counselling offered:　　General, Hypnotherapy
Service for:　　　　　　　Individuals, Couples
Theoretical Approach:　　　Eclectic
Fees:　　　　　　　　　　£15 - £23

McQUEEN David　　　　　　　　　　　　　　　　0236 737946
6 Gainburn Court, Condorrat, CUMBERNAULD
Member of:　　　　　　NRHP
Quals/training:　　　　　　Cert Hypnosis & Psychotherapy (NCHP Assoc); Cert Residential Care Children & Young Persons; BA Community Studies
Personal Therapy:　　　　　Yes
Supervision:　　　　　　　Ongoing
Counselling offered:　　General, Hypnotherapy
Service for:　　　　　　　Individuals, Couples, Families, Groups, Organisations
Specific to:　　　　　　　Adolescents, Young adults
Theoretical Approach:　　　Rogerian, Cognitive
Fees:　　　　　　　　　　£20

CARRUTHERS Barbara　　　　　　　　　　　　　041 357 3371
115 Dowanhill Street, GLASGOW G12 9EQ
Member of:　　　　　　BAC, AHPP, BPS
Quals/training:　　　　　　MEd Psychol (Glasgow Univ)'82; MSc Educational Psychol '86; (Univ of Strathclyde); Dip Humanistic Psychol (Surrey Univ) '89; C. Psychol
Personal Therapy:　　　　　Yes
Supervision:　　　　　　　Ongoing
Counselling offered:　　Personal growth, Life planning, Regression therapy, Sexual abuse, MS
Service for:　　　　　　　Individuals, Couples, Groups
Theoretical Approach:　　　Humanistic, Regression & integration
Fees:　　　　　　　　　　£20 or less according to means

GOWANS Alasdair　　　　　　　　　　　　　　　041 334 9001
114 Novar Drive, Hyndland, GLASGOW G12 9SX
Member of:　　　　　　BAC Acc
Quals/training:　　　　　　BAC(Acc); MA Psychol '78; Dip Couns '90; 4 yrs clinical training in TA(metanoia)
Personal Therapy:　　　　　Ongoing
Supervision:　　　　　　　Ongoing
Counselling offered:　　General
Service for:　　　　　　　Individuals
Theoretical Approach:　　　Rogerian, TA
Fees:　　　　　　　　　　£25 negotiable

Scotland

RUTHERFORD Morna   041 946 9750
57 Fergus Drive, GLASGOW G20 6AH
Member of:	BAC Acc
Quals/training:	BAC Acc; BSc Soc Sci/Nursing; Dip in Couns & Psychotherapy (Person-centred Therapy, Britain)
Personal Therapy:	Yes
Supervision:	Ongoing
Counselling offered:	General, Bereavement, Relationship, Transition, Psychotherapy, Supervision
Service for:	Individuals, Couples, Families, Groups
Theoretical Approach:	Person-centred
Fees:	£25 negotiable for low/un-waged

HALLIBURTON Anne   041 946 5426
259 Garrioch Road, GLASGOW G20 8QZ
Member of:	BAC
Quals/training:	MA 1968; Dip Ed 1973; CQSW 1978
Personal Therapy:	No
Supervision:	Ongoing
Counselling offered:	General, Relationship, Psychotherapy
Service for:	Individuals, Couples
Theoretical Approach:	Eclectic
Fees:	£25

COIA Grace   041 632 6663
10 Carment Drive, GLASGOW G41 3PP
Member of:	NCHP, Member of UKCP Register
Quals/training:	MA; Cert Ed; DHP (NCHP) 1991
Personal Therapy:	Yes
Supervision:	Ongoing
Counselling offered:	General, ME
Service for:	Individuals
Theoretical Approach:	Person-centred, Eclectic
Other languages:	French, Italian
Fees:	£10 - £25

SIMPSON James   041 883 0365
73 Leithland Road, GLASGOW G53 5AX
Member of:	NRHP
Quals/training:	RMN; RGN; Cert Hypnotherapy & Psychotherapy (NCHP)
Personal Therapy:	No
Supervision:	No
Counselling offered:	General, Hypnotherapy, Psychotherapy
Service for:	Individuals, Couples
Specific to:	Nurses
Theoretical Approach:	Eclectic
Fees:	Negotiable

Scotland

MACPHERSON Christine　　　　　　　　　　　　　　　　041 942 3508
2 Thomson Drive, Bearsden, GLASGOW G61 3NU
Member of:	**BAC, BPS**
Quals/training:	MA; BA (Hons) Psychol; Dip Couns (Board of Social Responsibility, Church of Scotland); Memb COSCA
Personal Therapy:	Ongoing
Supervision:	Ongoing
Counselling offered:	**General, Social skills**
Service for:	Individuals, Couples, Families, Groups
Theoretical Approach:	Person-centred, Rogerian
Fees:	£15 - £25

GRANT John　　　　　　　　　　　　　　　　　　　　　041 942 1210
6 Ledcameroch Crescent, Bearsden, GLASGOW G61 4AD
Member of:	**BAC**
Quals/training:	CTA authorised tutor 1981
Personal Therapy:	Ongoing
Supervision:	Ongoing
Counselling offered:	**General, Bereavement, Crisis, Work**
Service for:	Individuals, Couples, Groups
Theoretical Approach:	Rogerian
Fees:	None

EVANS John　　　　　　　　　　　　　　　　　　　　　0360 312122
4 Archibald Terrace, Milton of Campsie, GLASGOW G65 8JW
Member of:	**BAC**
Quals/training:	Dip in Hypnosis Hypnotherapy, Psychology, Psychotherapy (NCHP) 1986
Personal Therapy:	Yes
Supervision:	Ongoing
Counselling offered:	**General, Hypnotherapy, Psychotherapy, Imaging**
Service for:	Individuals, Couples
Specific to:	Children, Deaf
Theoretical Approach:	Eclectic
Fees:	£25

HARKNESS Margaret　　　　　　　　　　　　　　　　　041 644 4600
7 Springhill Road, Clarkston, GLASGOW G76 7XJ
Member of:	**BAC**
Quals/training:	Scottish Marriage Guidance trained; Dip from Person-Centred Therapy (Britain)
Personal Therapy:	Yes
Supervision:	Ongoing
Counselling offered:	**General, Marital, Addiction, Supervision**
Service for:	Individuals, Couples, Groups
Theoretical Approach:	Person-centred
Fees:	£15 - £30 sliding scale

Scotland

Tayside

Individual Practitioners

*Each individual is a **member of** one or more organisations eligible for entry into this directory.
BAC Accredited Counsellors and Recognised Supervisors are shaded.*

TREWARTHA Robin 082 622 337
Maywood, Main Street, Longforgan, DUNDEE DD2 5EP
Member of:	BAC, ITA
Quals/training:	BSc Econ 1968; CQSW 1969; MEd 1987; Memb BASW
Personal Therapy:	No
Supervision:	Ongoing
Counselling offered:	**General, Problem solving, Work, Supervision**
Service for:	Individuals, Groups, Organisations, Families
Theoretical Approach:	Egan, TA
Fees:	£15 - £25 £25- £35 supervision

BAGNALL Carol 0382 533291
24 Well Street, Monifieth, DUNDEE DD5 4AT
Member of:	BAC
Quals/training:	MA Psychol; Cert Couns Skills (Durham Univ); Dip Couns (Jesmond Centre for Humanistic Therapy)
Personal Therapy:	Ongoing
Supervision:	Ongoing
Counselling offered:	**General, Sexual abuse, Psychotherapy, Bereavement**
Service for:	Individuals, Couples
Specific to:	Women, Lesbians
Theoretical Approach:	Person-centred
Fees:	£20 sliding scale

Wales

Clwyd

Individual Practitioners
*Each individual is a **member of** one or more organisations eligible for entry into this directory. BAC Accredited Counsellors and Recognised Supervisors are shaded.*

HOOD Jane   **0745 832178**
Afalon, Tan-Y-Fron Road, ABERGELE LL22 9BA
Member of:	BAC
Quals/training:	CASE (Liverpool)
Personal Therapy:	Yes
Supervision:	Ongoing
Counselling offered:	General, Bereavement, Psychotherapy, Relationship, Sexual
Service for:	Individuals, Couples, Families
Theoretical Approach:	Person-centred, RET
Fees:	£20

ELAND Ann   **049 082 448**
Gaeddren, Cerrig-y-drudion, CORWEN LL21 9TE
Member of:	BAC
Quals/training:	Member of British Institute of Management
Personal Therapy:	Yes
Supervision:	Ongoing
Counselling offered:	General, Bereavement, Crisis, Stress, Sexual abuse
Service for:	Individuals, Couples, Groups
Specific to:	Young people, People with disabilities
Theoretical Approach:	Eclectic
Fees:	£20 per hour, or by negotiation

COTTRELL Steve   **0745 816992**
54 Love Lane, DENBIGH LL16 3LU
Member of:	BAC
Quals/training:	RMN; Cert Clinical Psychodrama, Creative Therapies; currently training in TA
Personal Therapy:	Ongoing
Supervision:	Ongoing
Counselling offered:	General, Psychotherapy
Service for:	Individuals, Groups, Couples, Organisations
Theoretical Approach:	Humanistic
Fees:	£20 sliding scale

STEVENS Jean   **0745 342544**
Holmlea, Kinmel Bay, RHYL LL18 5HH
Member of:	NRHP
Quals/training:	Dip Hypnotherapy & Psychotherapy NCHP; Dip IAH; Memb Brit Register Complementary Practitioners (Hypnotherapy); Psychotherapeutic NLP
Personal Therapy:	Yes
Supervision:	Ongoing
Counselling offered:	General, Stress management, Unwanted habits
Service for:	Individuals, Couples, Families
Theoretical Approach:	Eclectic
Fees:	£25 - £45

Wales

COUPAR Alan 0745 730571
The Clock Tower, Llannerch Park, ST. ASAPH LL17 0BD
Member of:	BPS
Quals/training:	BA(Hons) Psychol; MSc Clinical Psychol; C Psychol; Dip Hypnotherapy
Personal Therapy:	Yes
Supervision:	Ongoing
Counselling offered:	General, Relationship, Sexual, Weight, Supervision
Service for:	Individuals, Couples, Groups
Theoretical Approach:	Eclectic, Cognitive
Fees:	£30 - £60 sliding scale

HECTOR Viv 0987 362383
NSPCC, 11 Grosvenor Road, WREXHAM LL11 1SD
Member of:	BAC
Quals/training:	Dip Social work; CQSW; Cert Family Protective Social Work; trained in Family Therapy & Marital Counselling
Personal Therapy:	Yes
Supervision:	Ongoing
Counselling offered:	Sexual abuse, Child abuse
Service for:	Individuals, Couples, Families, Groups
Specific to:	Survivors of sex abuse
Theoretical Approach:	Eclectic
Fees:	No charge, NSPCC Officer

BURNETT Brian 097 888 442
Nant Yr Hafod Cottage, Hafod Bilston, Llandegla, WREXHAM LL11 3BG
Member of:	NRHP
Quals/training:	BA General Science inc Psychol; Cert in Hypnosis & Psychotherapy (NCHP); Cert Ed
Personal Therapy:	Unknown
Supervision:	No
Counselling offered:	General, Hypnotherapy, Psychotherapy, Massage, Stress management
Service for:	Individuals, Families, Groups
Fees:	£20 - £25 per session

FORRESTER Barry 0978 853744
Lane End, 33 Wynnstay Lane, Marford, WREXHAM LL12 8LF
Member of:	BAC
Quals/training:	Ad Dip Couns, Wigan; training in marital therapy and pain management
Personal Therapy:	No
Supervision:	Ongoing
Counselling offered:	General, Marital, Relationship, Pain, Psychosexual, Stress management
Service for:	Individuals, Couples, Families, Groups
Specific to:	Counsellor has disability
Theoretical Approach:	Rogerian, Egan, Psychodynamic
Fees:	Negotiable

Wales

Dyfed

Individual Practitioners
*Each individual is a **member of** one or more organisations eligible for entry into this directory. BAC Accredited Counsellors and Recognised Supervisors are shaded.*

HARRISON Donald   09747 376
Ffynnonwen Natural Therapy, Centre, Llangwyryfon, ABERYSTWYTH SY23 4EY
Member of:	BAC, BPS
Quals/training:	BA (Hons); BSc; Dip Hypnosis & Psychotherapy; Memb Royal Pharm Soc
Personal Therapy:	Yes
Supervision:	Ongoing
Counselling offered:	**General, Psychotherapy, Sexual, Hypnotherapy**
Service for:	Individuals, Couples
Theoretical Approach:	Eclectic, Reichian
Fees:	£25

GIBBIN Jane   0994 427319
Mapsland, Laugharne, CARMARTHEN SA33 4QP
Member of:	BAC, BASMT
Quals/training:	RELATE Trained; RELATE Sex Therapist
Personal Therapy:	Yes
Supervision:	Ongoing
Counselling offered:	**General, Relationship, Sexual, Psychotherapy, Marital, Abuse**
Service for:	Individuals, Couples, Groups
Theoretical Approach:	Psychodynamic, Object relations
Fees:	£25 negotiable

BOWEN Elizabeth   0348 837714
2 Penrhyn, Llanreithan, Mathry, HAVERFORDWEST SA62 5LH
Member of:	NRHP
Quals/training:	BA; Dip Ed; Cert HP (NC); Cert Couns
Personal Therapy:	Yes
Supervision:	Ongoing
Counselling offered:	**General, Depression, Phobias, Hypnotherapy, Psychotherapy**
Service for:	Individuals, Couples, Families
Theoretical Approach:	Eclectic
Fees:	£20 Negotiable

JAMES Jeanette
LLANELLI SA15 1LS
Member of:	NRHP
Quals/training:	Dip (NCHP) 1988; Memb ISMA
Personal Therapy:	Yes
Supervision:	Ongoing
Counselling offered:	**Psychotherapy, Hypnotherapy, Personal growth, Stress management**
Service for:	Individuals
Theoretical Approach:	Holistic
Other languages:	Welsh
Fees:	Negotiable

Wales

Gwent

Individual Practitioners
*Each individual is a **member of** one or more organisations eligible for entry into this directory. BAC Accredited Counsellors and Recognised Supervisors are shaded.*

HILLMAN Jan   **0600 715717**
The Darlin, Llangattock-Vibon-Avel, MONMOUTH NP5 4NG
Member of: BAC, BASMT
Quals/training: RELATE trained inc sex therapy
Personal Therapy: Yes
Supervision: Ongoing
Counselling offered: **General, Relationship, Psychotherapy, Psychosexual, Sexual**
Service for: Individuals, Couples
Theoretical Approach: Eclectic
Fees: £25 - £35

MORGAN Jo   **0633 420847**
6 Silver Birch Close, Roman Reach, Caerleon, NEWPORT NP6 1RX
Member of: BAC, CRAH
Quals/training: Dip Couns (Univ of Wales); Dip Ericksonian Hypnosis & NLP
Personal Therapy: Ongoing
Supervision: Ongoing
Counselling offered: **General, Stress management, Bereavement, Eating disorders, Psychotherapy, Hypnotherapy**
Service for: Individuals, Groups, Organisations
Theoretical Approach: NLP
Fees: £25 Negotiable

GILL Vilma   **0633 243269**
Flat 3, 36 Ombersley Road, NEWPORT NP9 3EE
Member of: BAC
Quals/training: Dip Pastoral Care, Guidance & Couns (Gwent Coll) 1990; CRUSE/ Rape Crisis training
Personal Therapy: Yes
Supervision: Ongoing
Counselling offered: **Anxiety, Relationship, PTSD**
Service for: Individuals
Theoretical Approach: Rogerian, Eclectic, TA, Cognitive/Behavioural
Fees: £18

Wales

Gwynedd

Individual Practitioners
Each individual is a **member of** one or more organisations eligible for entry into this directory.
BAC Accredited Counsellors and Recognised Supervisors are shaded.

EPHRAIM Nona 0407 840706
Plas Paradwys, BODORGAN LL62 5PE
Member of:	BAC
Quals/training:	BA; Dip Soc Sci; IPSS 1985-7; RELATE 1988; currently - MA in Counselling Studies (Keele)
Personal Therapy:	Yes
Supervision:	Ongoing
Counselling offered:	General, Relationship, Psychotherapy, Women's issues
Service for:	Individuals, Couples
Theoretical Approach:	Integrative, Psychodynamic, Person-centred
Other languages:	Welsh
Fees:	£23

TAYLOR Lissie 0286 880143
Siop Y Fron, Upper Llandwrog, CAERNARFON LL54 7BS
Member of:	BAC
Quals/training:	Dip Couns, BA Humanities
Personal Therapy:	Yes
Supervision:	Ongoing
Counselling offered:	General, Bereavement, Crisis, Personal growth, Stress, Terminal illness
Service for:	Individuals, Groups, Organisations
Theoretical Approach:	Gestalt, Transpersonal
Fees:	£30 Negotiable

Powys

Individual Practitioners
Each individual is a **member of** one or more organisations eligible for entry into this directory.
BAC Accredited Counsellors and Recognised Supervisors are shaded.

HOWES Kathleen 0874 623638
Y Bwthyn, Battle, BRECON LD3 9RN
Member of:	BAC
Quals/training:	RGN; RELATE training; FE Teaching Cert; Rational Emotive Behaviour Therapy
Personal Therapy:	Yes
Supervision:	Ongoing
Counselling offered:	General, Crisis, Stress management
Service for:	Individuals, Couples, Groups
Theoretical Approach:	Eclectic, Integrative
Fees:	£30 negotiable

Wales

BUCKLEY Anne 0547 528425
Highway Cottage, Knucklas, KNIGHTON LD7 1PR
Member of:	BAC Acc
Quals/training:	BAC Acc; BEd Care & Couns 1985; Dip in Psychosynthesis Counselling/Therapy 1990
Personal Therapy:	Yes
Supervision:	Ongoing
Counselling offered:	**General, Bereavement, Transition, Spiritual, Relationship, Psychotherapy, Midlife**
Service for:	Individuals
Specific to:	Adolescents
Theoretical Approach:	Person-centred, Transpersonal, Christian
Fees:	£15 - £25 negotiable

SMITH Pam 0686 412 708
18 Short Bridge Street, LLANIDLOES SY18 6AD
Member of:	BPS
Quals/training:	Training in educational, social & cognitive psychology
Personal Therapy:	Ongoing
Supervision:	Ongoing
Counselling offered:	**General, Bereavement**
Service for:	Individuals, Families
Theoretical Approach:	Eclectic, Humanistic
Fees:	Nil

THOMPSON Hilary 0686 630626
The Coachhouse, Dolforwyn Hall, Abernule, MONTGOMERY SY15 6JG
Member of:	BAC Acc
Quals/training:	BAC Acc; MA; Dip Couns & Psychotherapy (IP) 1981
Personal Therapy:	Unknown
Supervision:	Ongoing
Counselling offered:	**General, Supervision**
Service for:	Individuals, Couples, Groups
Theoretical Approach:	Integrative, Psychosynthesis, Alice Miller, John Bowlby
Fees:	25 - £30

BIGGS Julie 0686 623216
12 Crescent Street, NEWTOWN SY16 2HB
Member of:	NRHP, NCHP
Quals/training:	Dip Hypnosis & psychotherapy (NCH); training in Psych Couns (Roehampton Inst); general training in Couns & NLP
Personal Therapy:	Yes
Supervision:	Ongoing
Counselling offered:	**General, Crisis, Psychotherapy**
Service for:	Individuals, Couples, Groups
Specific to:	People with language problems
Theoretical Approach:	Cognitive, Hypnotherapy
Fees:	£20

Wales

South Glamorgan

Organisations

FAMILY INSTIUTE BARNARDOS   **0222 226532**
Ben Kennedy, 105 Cathedral Road, CARDIFF CF1 9PH
Service:	Unit within Barnardos. Free accessible service for individuals, couples, families, difficulties with adolescents, young children, marital problems, psychiatric
Area served:	Unlimited
Referral:	Self or others
Training of workers:	Professionally qualified & experienced therapists; peer supervision
Code of Ethics:	AFT
Management by:	Barnardos
Fees:	Donations optional

PENARTH PASTORAL FOUNDATION   **0222 709358**
Albert Road Methodist Church, Community Centre, Albert Road, PENARTH CF6
Service:	Long term general, marital & bereavement counselling for those in need, regardless of age, sex or religion. (Affiliated to WPF)
Area served:	South East Wales
Referral:	Self or others
Training of workers:	18 months part time Foundation course - Welsh Joint Educat Committee PGCE 1 & 2 Adv Cert Couns (Gwent Coll of Higher Educ) 2 years (In-service courses)
Code of Ethics:	BAC
Management by:	Director & Management Committee
Fees:	Donations

Individual Practitioners

*Each individual is a **member of** one or more organisations eligible for entry into this directory. BAC Accredited Counsellors and Recognised Supervisors are shaded.*

ROWLANDS Helen   **0446 740517**
32 Kingsland Crescent, BARRY CF6 6JQ
Member of:	MPTI
Quals/training:	BA (Hons); MSc Econ; Post Grad Cert Ed; currently training Integrative psychotherapy
Personal Therapy:	Yes
Supervision:	Ongoing
Counselling offered:	**General, Psychotherapy**
Service for:	Individuals, Couples
Specific to:	Women
Theoretical Approach:	Integrative
Fees:	Negotiable

Wales

TRICKEY Veronica   **0222 231849**
6 Plasturton Avenue, Pontcanna, CARDIFF CF1 9HH
Member of: BAC
Quals/training: BA; NMGC trained including sex therapy
Personal Therapy: Yes
Supervision: Ongoing
Counselling offered: General, Marital, Sexual
Service for: Individuals, Couples
Specific to: Survivors of sex abuse
Theoretical Approach: Person-centred
Fees: £20 with concessions

LANE Betty   **0222 498209/220019**
3 Tydfil Place, Roath Park, CARDIFF CF2 5HP
Member of: BAC
Quals/training: BSc(Hons) Social Psychol (Univ of Wales); Cert Couns (Gwent CFE); WPF Affiliate trained; PGCE (FE)
Personal Therapy: Yes
Supervision: Ongoing
Counselling offered: General, Relationship
Service for: Individuals, Couples, Groups
Theoretical Approach: Person-centred, Rogerian
Fees: £5 - £20 sliding scale

SELIGMAN Philippa   **0222 561491**
22 West Orchard Crescent, Llandaff, CARDIFF CF5 1AR
Member of: AFT
Quals/training: CQSW 1972 (Cardiff)
Personal Therapy: Yes
Supervision: Yes
Counselling offered: General, Marital, Relationship
Service for: Individuals, Couples, Families
Theoretical Approach: Systemic
Fees: £35

LOWE Julie   **0222 340376**
32 Victoria Park Road East, Canton, CARDIFF CF5 1EH
Member of: BAC
Quals/training: MA Psychol of Therapy & Couns; currently training in Existential Psychotherapy (Regent's College)
Personal Therapy: Yes
Supervision: Ongoing
Counselling offered: General
Service for: Individuals
Theoretical Approach: Psychodynamic
Fees: £20 Unwaged negotiable

Wales

West Glamorgan

Individual Practitioners

*Each individual is a **member of** one or more organisations eligible for entry into this directory. BAC Accredited Counsellors and Recognised Supervisors are shaded.*

HALE Sue   **0792 234176**
Beaumont, Sandy Lane, Pennard, SWANSEA SA3 2ER
Member of:	BAC
Quals/training:	BSc; CQSW; PGCE; Dip Couns
Personal Therapy:	Yes
Supervision:	Ongoing
Counselling offered:	**General, Crisis, Psychotherapy**
Service for:	Individuals, Couples, Groups
Specific to:	Women, Children
Theoretical Approach:	Eclectic, Gestalt, TA, Regression & integrationOther languages:
Fees:	Sliding scale

HALLETT Jane   **0792 896656**
25 Taliesin Place, Loughor, SWANSEA SA4 3GJ
Member of:	BAC Acc
Quals/training:	BAC Acc; Dip Couns (Reading Univ) 1985; currently training in Gestalt Psychotherapy (metanoia)
Personal Therapy:	Ongoing
Supervision:	Ongoing
Counselling offered:	**General**
Service for:	Individuals, Couples
Theoretical Approach:	Person-centred, Gestalt
Fees:	£20 - £30 according to income

Wales

Northern Ireland

Individual Practitioners
Each individual is a **member of** one or more organisations eligible for entry into this directory.
BAC Accredited Counsellors and Recognised Supervisors are shaded.

BROWN Avril   Ansaphone 0232 312942
113 University Street, BELFAST BT7 1HP
Member of:	BASMT
Quals/training:	Dip Psychol; training in sex therapy, marital therapy, psychotherapy; BASMT Acc
Personal Therapy:	Yes
Supervision:	Ongoing
Counselling offered:	**Sexual, Psychosexual, Marital, Sexual dysfunction**
Service for	:Individuals, Couples
Theoretical Approach:	Eclectic, Integrative, Behavioural
Other languages:	Spanish
Fees:	£20 - £30 negotiable

McDONALD Dick   0232 666737
76 Osborne Drive, BELFAST BT9 6LJ
Member of:	BAC Acc
Quals/training:	BAC Acc; NMGC trained, including Sexual Dysfunction; Acc by Assoc for Couples in Marriage Enrichment (USA)
Personal Therapy	:No
Supervision:	Ongoing
Counselling offered:	**General, Marital**
Service for	:Individuals, Couples
Theoretical Approach:	Rogerian
Fees:	£25 waived in cases of need

BEATTIE Heather   0232 768556
13 Cedar Grove, HOLYWOOD BT18 9QG
Member of:	BAC
Quals/training:	Dip Pastoral & Clinical Couns; Cert Social Welfare Studies (inc 2 years couns); Cert Biblical Couns
Personal Therapy:	Yes
Supervision:	Ongoing
Counselling offered:	**General, Bereavement, Crisis, Relationship**
Service for	:Individuals, Couples
Specific to:	People with disabilities, Counsellor has disability
Theoretical Approach:	Rogerian, Christian
Fees:	Negotiable

Northern Ireland

Channel Islands

Guernsey

Individual Practitioners
Each individual is a **member of** one or more organisations eligible for entry into this directory.
BAC Accredited Counsellors and Recognised Supervisors are shaded.

LEWIS Helen   0481 39874, mobile 0860 741 019
Justesse, Forest Road, St Martin, GUERNSEY
Member of:	BAC, NRH, Member of UKCP Register
Quals/training:	DHP(NC); Psychology Foundation Courses 1 & II; currently undertaking NLP training (John Seymour Assocs)
Personal Therapy:	Yes
Supervision:	Ongoing
Counselling offered:	General, Psychotherapy, Hypnotherapy, Stress management, Relationship
Service for:	Individuals, Couples, Families, Groups, Organisations
Theoretical Approach:	Cognitive, NLP, Rogerian, Gestalt
Fees:	£35

Jersey

Organisations

JERSEY WOMEN'S AID RAPE COUNSELLING SERVICE   0534 68368
PO Box 708, ST HELIER
Service:	Some 4 qualified counsellors, usually in full employment or retired, are retained to respond to the needs of rape or trauma victims as incidents occur. They remain anonymous
Area served:	Jersey, Channel Islands
Referral:	Police
Training of workers:	Various previous to joining the scheme
Code of Ethics:	Check with counsellor
Management by:	Management Committee
Fees:	None

Individual Practitioners
Each individual is a **member of** one or more organisations eligible for entry into this directory.
BAC Accredited Counsellors and Recognised Supervisors are shaded.

LUCAS Rosemarie   0534 862467
Perry Farm, Rue Des Servais, St Lawrence, JERSEY JE3 1HL
Member of:	BAC
Quals/training:	Dip Ed; 5 years' experience in Private Practice
Personal Therapy:	Ongoing
Supervision:	Ongoing
Counselling offered:	General
Service for:	Individuals, Couples, Families, Groups, Organisations
Theoretical Approach:	Cognitive, Analytic
Fees:	Negotiable

Index of Organisations

42ND STREET COMMUNITY 327
ACT: PSYCHOLOGY SERVICE
FOR SEXUAL HEALTH 572
ADFAM NATIONAL 15
ADLERIAN COUNSELLING CENTRE 97
ADLERIAN SOCIETY FOR INDIVIDUAL
PSYCHOLOGY 7
AIDSAHEAD 15
AIDSLINE 58
AIREDALE GENERAL HOSPITAL
DEPT OF CLINICAL PSYCHOLOGY 631
ALBANY TRUST 1
ALBANY ASSOCIATES 184
ALDER CENTRE 431
ALED RICHARDS TRUST 209
ALTON COUNSELLING SERVICE 339
ANNA FREUD CENTRE 93
ARC 477
ARGYLL & CLYDE HB CLINICAL
PSYCHOLOGICAL SERVICE 656
ARK THERAPY CENTRE 519
ASHBROOK COUNSELLING
SERVICE 299
ASHFORD COUNSELLING SERVICE 389
ASHBY TRUST 585
ASHLEY CAREER COUNSELLING 1
ASIAN FAMILY COUNSELLING
SERVICE 183
ASIAN COUNSELLING SERVICE 95
ASSOCIATION FOR ANALYTIC
& BODYMIND THERAPY/TRAINING 55
ASSOCIATION FOR NEURO-
LINGUISTIC PROGRAMMING 7
ASSOCIATION FOR PSYCHOTHERAPY
IN EAST LONDON (APEL) 38
ASSOCIATION FOR RATIONAL-
EMOTIVE THERAPISTS 7
ASSOCIATION OF COGNITIVE
ANALYTIC THERAPISTS 8
ASSOCIATION OF HUMANISTIC
PSYCHOLOGY PRACTITIONERS 8
ASSOCIATION OF SHORT-TERM &
STRATEGIC PSYCHOTHERAPISTS 7
ASSOCIATION OF WOMEN
PSYCHOTHERAPISTS 97
ASSOCIATION OF INDEPENDENT
PSYCHOTHERAPISTS 54
AVALON, SOMERSET NHS TRUST 491
AYLESBURY VALE NHS TRUST 239
BACUP 15
BAKER-VAUGHAN COUNSELLING
SERVICES 419
BARKING, HAVERING &
BRENTWOOD H.A. 300
BARNET HEALTHCARE NHS
TRUST 39, 363
BARNSLEY COMMUNITY &
PRIORITY SERVICES NHS TRUST 625
BATH CENTRE FOR PSYCHOTHERAPY
& COUNSELLING 209
BEAUMONT TRUST 15
BEDFORD PSYCHOSEXUAL
COUNSELLING CLINIC 223

BENFLEET OPEN DOOR SERVICE 299
BEREAVEMENT COUNSELLING
SERVICE FOR GAYS & LESBIANS 478
BIOENERGETIC PARTNERSHIP 95
BIRMINGHAM COUNSELLING CENTRE 596
BIRMINGHAM BROOK ADVISORY
CENTRE 595
BIRMINGHAM SOCIAL SERVICES 595
BISHOP R O HALL CHINESE CENTRE ... 25
BLACKPOOL AND FYLDE
COUNSELLING CENTRE 411
BOARDING SCHOOL SURVIVORS 16
BODY POSITIVE NORTH EAST LTD 581
BOTTLEFED 96
BRADFORD PSYCHOTHERAPY &
COUNSELLING SERVICE 631
BRANDON CENTRE 93
BRIDGE COUNSELLING CENTRE 541
BRITISH ASSOCIATION OF
ANALYTICAL BODY THERAPY 8
BRITISH ASSOCIATION OF SEXUAL &
MARITAL THERAPY 9
BRITISH ASSOCIATION OF
PSYCHOTHERAPISTS 9
BRITISH PREGNANCY ADVISORY
SERVICE 16
BRITISH PSYCHODRAMA ASSOCIATION . 9
BRITISH PSYCHOLOGICAL SOCIETY 9
BROADWAY LODGE 210
BROMSGROVE & REDDITCH DEPT
OF CLINICAL PSYCHOLOGY 357
BURY PRACTICE FOR COUNSELLING
& PSYCHOTHERAPY 501
CAIRNS PERSONAL COUNSELLING
SERVICE 631
CAMBRIDGE PASTORAL GROUP 249
CAMBRIDGE SOCIETY FOR
PSYCHOTHERAPY 249
CAMBRIDGE BODY
PSYCHOTHERAPY PRACTICE 249
CAMBRIDGE GROUP WORK 249
CAMBRIDGESHIRE CONSULTANCY
IN COUNSELLING 250
CAMDEN PSYCHOTHERAPY UNIT 185
CAMDEN BEREAVEMENT SERVICE 185
CANCER HELP CENTRE BRISTOL 1
CARE CONCERN 58
CAREASSIST GROUP LTD 1
CAREER AND EDUCATIONAL
COUNSELLING 2
CARELINE 300
CAROLE SPIERS ASSOCIATES 2
CARRS LANE COUNSELLING CENTRE 593
CASSEL CENTRE 129
CATHOLIC MARRIAGE ADVISORY
COUNCIL 16
CENTRE FOR COUNSELLING &
PSYCHOTHERAPY EDUCATION 10, 182
CENTRE FOR HEALTH & HEALING 184
CENTRE FOR STRESS MANAGEMENT 127
CENTRE FOR TRANSPERSONAL
PSYCHOLOGY 10
CHELMSFORD RAPE & SEXUAL
ABUSE COUNSELLING CENTRE 299

• CPRD 1994 •

I

CHICHESTER COUNSELLING SERVICE ... 571
CHILD & CHILCOTT - EMPLOYEE COUNSELLING PROGRAMMES ... 2
CHILD DEATH HELPLINE ... 16
CHILD GROWTH FOUNDATION ... 17
CHILDLINE ... 17
CHIRON CENTRE FOR HOLISTIC PSYCHOTHERAPY ... 181
CHOICE FWA (Islington) ... 25, 57
CHURCH ARMY COUNSELLING SERVICE ... 96
CHURCH ARMY COUNSELLING SERVICE NORTH ... 327, 625
CLAPHAM COMMON CLINIC ... 151
CLINICAL PSYCHOLOGY SERVICES 471
CLINICAL THEOLOGY ASSOCIATION 10
COMMUNICARE COUNSELLING SERVICE ... 439
COMMUNITY COUNSELLING SERVICE ... 328
COMPASS ... 431
COMPASSIONATE FRIENDS ... 17
CONCERN COUNSELLING SERVICE 520
CONFIDE, SHROPSHIRE COUNSELLING SERVICE ... 487
CONNEXIONS ... 519
CORNERSTONE ... 183
COT DEATH RESEARCH ... 17
COUNSELLING & ADVISORY SERVICE FOR NURSES ... 18
COUNSELLING & PSYCHOTHERAPY SERVICES ... 300
COUNSELLING ASSOCIATES ... 596
COUNSELLING IN NORTH LONDON ... 55
COUNSELLING AND CONSULTANCY UNIT ... 617
COUNSELLING CONSULTANCY ... 389
COUNSELLING SERVCE LEAGUE OF JEWISH WOMEN ... 58
COUNSELLING & PSYCHOTHERAPY ASSOCIATES ... 594
COUNSELLING PARTNERSHIP (LONDON) ... 184
CROYDON YOUTH COUNSELLING SERVICE ... 509
CROYDON PASTORAL FOUNDATION .. 509
CRUSE ... 18
DAPAS ... 279
DARLINGTON CLINICAL PSYCHOLOGY DEPT ... 297
DEPT OF PSYCHOLOGICAL THERAPY - UFFCULME CLINIC ... 594
DEPT OF CLINICAL & COMMUNITY PSYCHOLOGY ... 283
DEPT OF PSYCHOLOGICAL SERVICES & RESEARCH ... 646
DERBY AIDSLINE ... 279
DERWENT RURAL COUNSELLING SERVICE ... 279
DEVON PASTORAL COUNSELLORS 283
DOVER COUNSELLING CENTRE ... 390
DRUG ADVICE & TREATMENT PROJECT ... 385
DUDLEY ROAD HOSPITAL PSYCHOSEXUAL CLINIC ... 595
DYMPNA CENTRE ... 18
EALING HOSPITAL NHS TRUST (PASTEUR SUITE) ... 438
EAR EMPLOYEE ADVISORY RESOURCE ... 2
EAST BERKSHIRE PSYCHOLOGICAL SERVICES ... 229
EAST LEEDS FAMILY SERVICE UNIT ... 633
EAST DORSET CLINICAL PSYCHOLOGY SERVICE ... 291
EATING DISORDERS ASSOCIATION ... 18
EDINBURGH ASSOCIATION FOR MENTAL HEALTH ... 651
ELM THERAPISTS, The ... 152, 519
ENTERPRISE COUNSELLING SERVICES ... 182
EQUILIBRIUM COUNSELLING SERVICES ... 128
EQUILIBRIUM CENTRE ... 153
FAMILY INSTIUTE BARNARDOS ... 667
FAMILY MEDIATION SCOTLAND ... 645
FAMILY PLANNING ASSOCIATION ... 19
FAMILY SERVICES UNIT ... 19
FAREHAM & GOSPORT PSYCHOSEXUAL CLINIC, OSBORN CLINIC ... 339
FELLOWSHIP CHARITABLE FOUNDATION ... 438
FELTHAM OPEN DOOR PROJECT LTD. 437
FLEET COUNSELLING SERVICE ... 539
FRIEND - WEST MIDLANDS ... 593
GARNETHILL CENTRE LTD ... 645
GENDER DYSPHORIA TRUST INTERNATIONAL ... 19
GESTALT STUDIO ... 94
GESTALT CENTRE LONDON ... 25
GLOUCESTERSHIRE COUNSELLING SERVICE ... 321
GODALMING COUNSELLING SERVICES ... 3
GREENWICH MIND NETWORKS ... 128
GROUP ANALYTIC NETWORK ... 54
GROVE NATURAL THERAPY CENTRE . 340
GUILD OF PSYCHOTHERAPISTS ... 10
GUILDFORD COUNSELLING RESOURCE CENTRE ... 540
GUILDFORD CENTRE & SOCIETY FOR PSYCHOTHERAPY ... 539
HAMPSTEAD COMMUNITY COUNSELLING ... 96
HARROW & WEMBLEY COUNSELLING FOUNDATION ... 437
HASLEMERE COUNSELLING SERVICE ... 540
HASTINGS & ROTHER NHS TRUST, DEPT OF CLINICAL PSYCHOLOGY ... 559
HEALING CENTRE ... 93
HEATHSIDE COUNSELLING SERVICE ... 94
HELP ADVISORY CENTRE ... 183
HELPFULNESS ... 501
HERONBROOK HOUSE INTERNATIONAL THERAPEUTIC CENTRE FOR CLERGY 3

HERTS & BEDS PASTORAL FOUNDATION 223, 363
HIGHGATE CENTRE FOR COMMUNITY HEALTH, PSYCHOSEXUAL CLINIC 594
HIGHGATE COUNSELLING CENTRE 55
HIGHLIGHT TRUST 321
HILLINGDON HOSPITAL, DEPT OF CLINICAL PSYCHOLOGY 439
HIV/AIDS TESTING & COUNSELLING SERVICE 540
HOBBS-GORDON COUNSELLING 181
HOLISTIC PSYCHOTHERAPY 363
HOLMWOOD COUNSELLING SERVICE 539
HORSHAM CITIZENS ADVICE BUREAU & BEREAVEMENT SERVICE 571
HOUNSLOW YOUTH COUNSELLING SERVICE 437
HULL HA, DEPARTMENT OF CLINCAL PSYCHOLOGY 385
HUMAN PERSPECTIVE LTD 3
ICAS LTD 3
IDENTITY COUNSELLING SERVICE 4
INDEPENDENT PSYCHOLOGY SERVICE 57
INSIGHT - PROFESSIONAL FAMILY THERAPY 487
INSIGHT COUNSELLING & CONSULTANCY 466
INSTITUTE OF FAMILY THERAPY 11
INSTITUTE OF PSYCHOTHERAPY & SOCIAL STUDIES 11
INSTITUTE OF PSYCHOSEXUAL MEDICINE 11
ISIS COUNSELLING & THERAPY SERVICE 129
ISIS CENTRE 477
ISLE OF WIGHT YOUTH TRUST 339
ISLINGTON WOMEN'S COUNSELLING CENTRE 57
ISSUE 19
JERSEY WOMEN'S AID RAPE COUNSELLING SERVICE 673
JEWISH BEREAVEMENT COUNSELLING SERVICE 53
JUST ASK ADVISORY & COUNSELLING SERVICE 37
KATIE MARIE STRESS & CANCER SURVIVAL CHARITY 465
KENT COUNSELLING SERVICE 390
KEYS: COUNSELLING & PSYCHOTHERAPY 594
LAMBOURN COURT INTERNATIONAL 4
LANCASTER HD, DEPT OF CLINICAL PSYCHOLOGY 411
LAPIS FELLOWSHIP 300
L A S COUNSELLING SERVICE 539
LEAS CENTRE FOR COUNSELLING & COMPLEMENTARY THERAPIES 301
LEEDS CRISIS CENTRE 632
LEEDS HA, CLINICAL PSYCHOLOGY SERVICE 631
LEICESTER COUNSELLING CENTRE ... 419
LESBIAN & GAY CENTRE 54
LESBIAN & GAY CHRISTIAN HELPLINE .. 20
LICHFIELD COUNSELLING SERVICE ... 497
LIFE 20
LIFELINE PREGNANCY COUNSELLING AND CARE 559, 593, 648, 651
LINK PSYCHOTHERAPY CENTRE 98
LODDON NHS TRUST, PSYCHOLOGY SERVICES 339
LODGE MOOR HOSPITAL SOCIAL WORK DEPARTMENT 626
LONDON ASSOCIATION OF PRIMAL THERAPISTS 11
LONDON CENTRE FOR PSYCHOTHERAPY 12
LONDON IRISH WOMEN'S CENTRE 56
LONDON CLINIC OF PSYCHOANALYSIS 25
LONDON ASSOCIATION OF BEREAVEMENT SERVICES 94
LONDON THERAPY CO-OPERATIVE 129
MAGDALEN CENTRE TRUST FOR GROUP PSYCHOTHERAPY 364
MAIDSTONE COUNSELLING SERVICE 390
MALE SURVIVORS GROUP 478
MANCHESTER INSTITUTE FOR INTEGRATIVE PSYCHOTHERAPY 328
MANCHESTER CENTRE FOR COUNSELLING 328
MARGATE HOSPITAL - AIDS/ HAEMOPHILIA CENTRE 389
MATCH 20
MAUDSLEY HOSPITAL, PSYCHOSEXUAL CLINIC 127
MEDIATION UK 20
MEDWAY DISTRICT CLINICAL PSYCHOLOGY SERVICE 390
MERSEYSIDE BROOK ADVISORY CENTRE 431
MERSEYSIDE PRIVATE COUNSELLING ... 4
MERTON FAMILY LINKS 153
METANOIA 12
MID-SUFFOLK MIND 501
MID-SUSSEX COUNSELLING CENTRE 571
MILTON KEYNES PASTORAL FOUNDATION 239
MIND IN HARINGEY, COUNSELLING SERVICE 54
MIND TAMESIDE & GLOSSOP 327
MIND NORTH STAFFS 497
MING WAH ASSOCIATION 25
MINSTER CENTRE 12
MORDEN PASTORAL COUNSELLING CENTRE 510
MYATTS COMMUNITY COUNSELLING PROJECT 151
NATIONAL ASSOCIATION FOR GIFTED CHILDREN 21
NATIONAL COUNCIL OF PSYCHOTHERAPISTS 12
NATIONAL FRIEND 21
NATIONAL REGISTER OF HYPNO- THERAPISTS & PSYCHOTHERAPISTS ... 13
NATIONAL SCHOOL OF HYPNOSIS & PSYCHOTHERAPY 53
NE LONDON PSYCHOTHERAPY & COUNSELLING ASSOCIATION 56

• CPRD 1994 •

III

Entry	Page
NETWORK FOR PSYCHOTHERAPY & CONSULTATIVE SERVICES	98
NETWORK 6 COUNSELLING & THERAPY	94
NETWORK FOR PSYCHOTHERAPY & CONSULTATIVE SERVICES	97
NEWCASTLE COUNCIL FOR THE DISABLED	581
NEWCASTLE FAMILY PLANNING AND WELL WOMAN SERVICE	581
NEWCASTLE PSYCHOSEXUAL CLINIC	581
NO 5	229
NORCAP	21
NORTH SURREY COUNSELLING	520
NORTH LONDON PSYCHOTHERAPY & COUNSELLING ASSOCIATION	57
NORTH LONDON COUNSELLING PRACTICE	437
NORTH LINCOLNSHIRE HA DISTRICT DEPT OF CLINICAL	427
NORTH END ROAD PRACTICE	97
NORTH BEDS DISTRICT PSYCHOLOGY SERVICE	223
NORTH LONDON PERSONAL CONSULTATION PRACTICE	53
NORTH MIDDLESEX HOSPITAL PSYCHOSEXUAL CLINIC	56
NORTH LONDON CENTRE FOR GROUP THERAPY	56
NORTH WARWICKSHIRE CLINICAL PSYCHOLOGY SERVICE	585
NORTHAMPTON PASTORAL COUNSELLING SERVICE	465
NORTHERN ASSOCIATION FOR ANALYTICAL PSYCHOTHERAPY	582
NOTTING HILL CENTRE FOR COUNSELLING & CONSULTATION	182
OASIS COUNSELLING AND TRAINING	585
OFF THE RECORD, THANET	391
OFFINGTON COUNSELLING SERVICE	571
OPENINGS	209
OUTSIDERS CLUB	21
OXFORD CHRISTIAN INSTITUTE FOR COUNSELLING	477
PARENTLINE	22
PARENTS' FRIEND	22
PCT SCOTLAND ASSOCIATION FOR PERSON-CENTRED THERAPY	645
PELLIN CENTRE	151
PENARTH PASTORAL FOUNDATION	667
PERSON TO PERSON	438
PERSONAL COUNSELLING CENTRE	412
PERSONAL DEVELOPMENT CENTRE	250
PETERSFIELD COUNSELLING SERVICE	340
PHILADELPHIA ASSOCIATION LTD (PA)	94
PINK PRACTICE, THE	185
POST ABORTION COUNSELLING SERVICE	182
POST ADOPTION CENTRE	22
POST GREEN PASTORAL CENTRE	291
PREGNANCY ADVISORY SERVICE	22
PRESTON PSYCHOTHERAPY CENTRE	411
PRINCESS ROYAL HOSPITAL DEPT OF GUM, TELFORD	487
PROJECT FOR ADVICE, COUNSELLING & EDUCATION,	54
PSYCHOSYNTHESIS & EDUCATION TRUST (PET)	13, 127
PSYCHOTHERAPY & COUNSELLING SERVICE	261
PSYCHOTHERAPY REFERRAL SERVICE SOUTH & WEST LONDON	129
RAPHAEL CLINIC	4
RAPHAEL CENTRE	93
RE•VISION	13
RED ADMIRAL PROJECT	151
REDHILL COUNSELLING CENTRE	541
RELATE	23
RENFREW PRIORITY SERVICES UNIT PSYCHOLOGY DEPT	656
RICHMOND TWICKENHAM & ROEHAMPTON HEALTH CARE NHS TRUST	152
RICHMOND COUNSELLING CENTRE	519
RICKMANSWORTH COUNSELLING SERVICE	363
ROLE MANAGEMENT LTD	5
ROMFORD COUNSELLING SERVICE	301
ROSEMARY CLARKE & BARRIE HINKSMAN, PSYCHOTHERAPISTS	585
ROTHER COUNSELLING SERVICE	391, 560
ROYAL LONDON PSYCHOLOGY DEPT	37
ROYAL LONDON HOSPITAL SEXUAL PROBLEMS CLINIC	37
RUGBY PROFESSIONAL COUNSELLING SERVICE	465, 591
S.A.M.S. (SEXUAL ABUSE MUMS SUPPORT)	301
SAINT ANNE'S	357
SAMARITANS	23
SEAHORSE SOCIETY	23
SEVEN TREES PSYCHOSEXUAL CLINIC	283
SEVERNSIDE INSTITUTE FOR PSYCHOTHERAPY (SIP)	209
SHARE PSYCHOTHERAPY AGENCY	625
SHARE (NCH) COUNSELLING SERVICES	491
SHEFFIELD MARITAL & SEXUAL DIFFICULTIES CLINIC	626
SHEFFIELD UNIVERSITY, PSYCHOLOGICAL CLINIC	626
SHEFFIELD COMMUNITY UNIT FAMILY PLANNING SERVICE	625
SHERWOOD PSYCHOTHERAPY TRAINING INSTITUTE	471
SOCIETY FOR PRIMARY CAUSE ANALYSIS	13
SOUTH WORCESTERSHIRE HYPNOTHERAPY CENTRE	357
SOUTH LONDON PSYCHOTHERAPY GROUP	153
SOUTH LONDON PSYCHOTHERAPY CENTRE	128
SOUTH HUMBERSIDE H A, DEPT CLINICAL PSYCHOLOGY	385

SOUTH EAST LONDON COUNSELLING ... 128
SOUTH WEST DURHAM HA, DISTRICT PSYCHOLOGY SERVICE ... 271
SOUTH LONDON NETWORK FOR COUNSELLING & PSYCHOTHERAPY ... 510
SOUTHAMPTON PASTORAL COUNSELLING SERVICE ... 340
SOUTHSIDE COUNSELLORS ... 152
SPECTRUM ... 53
ST MARY'S CENTRE(SEXUAL ASSAULT REFERRAL CENTRE) ... 327
ST GEORGE'S COUNSELLING CENTRE ... 510
ST BARNABAS COUNSELLING CENTRE ... 457
ST MARYLEBONE HEALING & COUNSELLING CENTRE ... 96
ST BASIL'S CENTRE ... 593
STEPFAMILY ... 23
STOCKTON PSYCHOTHERAPY TRAINING INSTITUTE ... 271
STOCKWELL CENTRE PRACTICE ... 300
STRESS AT WORK FOUNDATION ... 465
SUDBURY COUNSELLING & THERAPY PRACTICE ... 501
SURREY COUNSELLORS ... 520
SURVIVORS (BEDFORDSHIRE) ... 223
SUTTON BEREAVEMENT SERVICE ... 509
SUTTON PASTORAL FOUNDATION ... 510
SWALE COUNSELLING PRACTICE ... 391
SWANAGE COUNSELLING SERVICE ... 291
SWINDON COUNSELLING SERVICE ... 611
TAVISTOCK CLINIC ... 14
TAVISTOCK INSTITUTE OF MARITAL STUDIES ... 14
TENOVUS - CANCER INFORMATION CENTRE ... 5
THAMES PSYCHOLOGY & COUNSELLING CENTRE ... 153
THAMESIDE COUNSELLING ASSOCIATES ... 520
TOM ALLAN CENTRE (CHURCH OF SCOTLAND) ... 656
TOWER HAMLETS YOUTH COUNSELLING SERVICE ... 37
TUKE CENTRE FOR PSYCHOTHERAPY & COUNSELLING ... 617
TUNBRIDGE WELLS COUNSELLING CENTRE ... 391
UNITED KINGDOM COUNCIL FOR PSYCHOTHERAPY ... 14
UNIVERSITY OF EAST LONDON DEPARTMENT OF PSYCHOLOGY ... 38
UNIVERSITY COLLEGE HOSPITAL PSYCHOSEXUAL CLINIC ... 186
VECTOR CENTRE FOR EATING DISORDERS ... 5
VICTIM SUPPORT ... 24
VICTIMS HELPLINE ... 24
WALSALL COMMUNITY HEALTH TRUST PSYCHOSEXUAL CLINIC ... 596

WALTHAM FOREST HIV/AIDS COUNSELLING SERVICE ... 38
WALTHAM FOREST YOUTH COUNSELLING SERVICE ... 38
WALWOOD FAMILY CONSULTATION SERVICE ... 509
WANDSWORTH HA FAMILY PLANNING PSYCHOSEXUAL CLINIC ... 152
WANTAGE COUNSELLING SERVICE ... 477
WARREN BROWNE UNIT ... 559
WATERLOO COMMUNITY COUNSELLING PROJECT ... 127
WATERS & WINTERSTEIN ASSOCIATES ... 438
WELBECK COUNSELLING SERVICE ... 184
WELL WOMAN CENTRE ... 411
WELLSPRING ... 652
WESSEX COUNSELLING SERVICE ... 491
WEST SUSSEX & SURREY COUNSELLORS GROUP ... 540
WEST LONDON COUNSELLING & PSYCHOTHERAPY GROUP ... 183
WEST HAMPSTEAD PSYCHOTHERAPY ... 95
WEST YORKSHIRE MS THERAPY CENTRE LTD ... 633
WEST LONDON FAMILY SERVICE UNIT ... 181
WESTMINSTER BEREAVEMENT SERVICE ... 181
WESTMINSTER PASTORAL FOUNDATION ... 14
WHAT? ... 596
WHITEHOUSE TRUST ... 5
WINNICOTT CLINIC OF PSYCHOTHERAPY ... 6
WINCHESTER DISTRICT PSYCHOLOGY SERVICES ... 340
WOKING COUNSELLING SERVICE ... 541
WOKINGHAM & DISTRICT COUNSELLING SERVICE ... 229
WOMEN'S COUNSELLING & RESOURCE SERVICE ... 656
WOMEN'S COUNSELLING & THERAPY SERVICE LTD ... 632
WOMEN'S THERAPY CENTRE ... 55
WOMENS THERAPY LINK ... 95
WOODS PLACE CENTRE FOR COUNSELLING AND THERAPY ... 559
WPF COUNSELLING NORTH ... 632
WRITTLE PASTORAL FOUNDATION ... 299
YEWCROFT MENTAL HEALTH RESOURCE CENTRE ... 595
YORK PSYCHOSEXUAL CLINIC ... 617
YORK COUNSELLORS ... 618
YORK DISTRICT CLINICAL PSYCHOLOGY SERVICES ... 617
YORK DISTRICT HOSPITAL SOCIAL WORK DEPT ... 618
YORKSHIRE ASSOCIATION FOR PSYCHODYNAMIC PSYCHOTHERAPY ... 632
YOUTH INFORMATION SERVICE ... 239

Index of Individual Practitioners

AARON WALKER Jean 413
ACKET Marijke 562
ACKROYD Rosemary 268
ADAM Madeleine 292
ADAMS Martin 43
ADDENBROOKE Mary 576
ADDIE Georgia 408
ADKINS Dee 377
ADLER Eve 227
AGAR James 454
AHRENDS Liz 99
AINSWORTH Peter 634
AINSWORTH Janet 586
AITKENS Judy 524
ALBERY Nicholas 102
ALBERY-SPEYER Josephine 26
ALDER Judith 221
ALLEN Joanne 383
ALLEN Mrs Regina 178
ALLEN, Kay 322
ALLEN Caroline 233
ALLEN Patricia 483
ALLISON Jo 281
ALLISON Tricia 622
ALLMAN David 135
AMBROSE Tony 26
AMBROSE Sheila 397
ANDERMAN Margaret 524
ANDERS-RICHARDS Donald 488
ANDERS-RICHARDS Judith 488
ANDERSON James 388
ANDERSON Jackie 230
ANDERSON Julie 302
ANDERSON Jette 570
ANDERSON Judith 476
ANDERSON Jackie 237
ANDERSON Linda 120
ANDREW Elizabeth 178
ANDREWS Robert 273
ANGEL Rita 51
ANKER Ofra 71
ARMITAGE Jan 564
ARNOLD Lynn 203
ARNOLD Susan 489
ARTHUR Andrew 107
ARUNDALE Rita 271
ARZOUMANIDES Yiannis 201
ASHBY Susan 543
ASHBY Jean 459
ASHLEY Anne 514
ASHLEY Owen 345
ASHMORE Anne 568
ASHWELL Veronica 362
ASHWORTH Freda 330
ASSEILY Alexandra 207
ASSITER Shelley 204
ATKINSON Laura 280
AUBREY Christine 577
AUSTIN Adela 403
BACHA Claire 334
BAGENAL Beauchamp 384
BAGNALL Carol 660
BAILEY Lyn 318

BAILEY Dr Roy 241
BAIRD Phyllis 648
BAKER Celia 82
BAKER Jan 196
BAKER Yvonne 265
BALFOUR Joan 69
BALLINGER Liz 604
BANKS Mary 395
BANKS Liz 233
BANNELL Liz 542
BANNERMAN Afrakuma 83
BANNISTER Gill 40
BANNISTER Dorothy 619
BARKER Jocelyn 42
BARKER Christine 636
BARKER Gina 87
BARKHAM (STURT) Alison 266
BARNETT Ruth 113
BARNS Michael 295
BARON Yvonne 61
BARTYS Anita 475
BATCHELOR Carol 535
BATTERSBY Elaine 148
BATY Ted 256
BAUGHAN Richard 74
BAWS Helen 162
BAYNES Leila 490
BEAK Richard 422
BEALE Diana 561
BEARMAN Patricia 469
BEASLEY Ronald 653
BEATTIE Heather 671
BEATTIE Lilian 240
BEAUMONT Caroline 467
BEAZLEY RICHARDS Joanna 565
BECHHOFER Susi 589
BECK Carol 263
BECKER Renate 587
BEELEY Linda 358
BELL Angela 45
BELL Linda 396
BELLRINGER Helen 573
BENNETT Valerie 224
BENNETT Ross Ms 348
BENNETT Ross 352
BENNION Jean 534
BENSON Rosemary 569
BENTLEY Charles 26
BERG Richard 293
BERG Morris L 548
BERGER Jocelyn 176
BERGER Iris 365
BERGER Noemi 69
BERMAN Linda 262
BERNACCA Tony 565
BERNSTEIN Samuel 313
BESTFORD Jan 297
BETTS Toni 343, 344
BIANCARDI Jenny 582
BIGGS Julie 666
BIRCHALL Patricia 583
BISHOP Maggie 638
BISHOP Patricia 132

BLACK Sandra 142	BROIDO Isabelle 124
BLACK Margaret 159	BROOKE Penelope 529
BLACKLOCK Neil 170	BROOKS Gill 305
BLAKE Adrian 405	BROOKS Carole 401
BLAKE Raymond 454	BROOKS Bernard 305
BLAKE Nancy 387	BROOKS Louise 266
BLAKE Christy 244	BROOKS-CARLISLE Allan 413
BLAKEY Angela 602	BROUGHTON Vivian 630
BLAMPIED Annette 265	BROWN Revd Ian B 27
BLATCH Chrissi 332	BROWN Ursula 83
BLEACH Andrew 424	BROWN Douglas 599
BLEASDALE Roz 397	BROWN Eileen 447
BLISS Sonia 489	BROWN Linda 627
BLOCH Sue 371	BROWN Dee 332
BLOMFIELD Val 137	BROWN Avril 671
BLOOMFIELD Robert 401	BRUCE Ann 149
BOATWRIGHT Christine 507	BRUMWELL Pauline 441
BODDINGTON Daphne 346	BRUNO Virginia 205
BODGENER Sue 121	BRUNT Clare 455
BOHL Yvonne 132	BUCHAN Diana 653
BOLLINGER Charmain 26	BUCHAN Roberta 649
BOLLINGHAUS Elaine 242	BUCHANAN Gill 355
BOLSOVER Dr G N 386	BUCHANAN Dr Sarah-Jill 528
BOMMER Herman 207	BUCHANAN-DUNNE Kevin 489
BONNEFIN Valerie 98	BUCKERIDGE Shane 338
BONSER Wendy 423	BUCKLEY Miranda 157
BORSIG Su 194, 212	BUCKLEY Anne 666
BOSTOCK Elizabeth 442	BUCKROYD Julia 145
BOULTON Anthony John 39	BUDGELL Rosemary 228
BOURNE Ruth 81	BULL Sonia 553
BOWDEN Mandy 286	BULL Martin 255
BOWEN Elizabeth 663	BULL Graham 316
BOWER Margaret 545	BULLEN-SPICER Robert 475
BOWES Ann 215	BULLER Jemima 308
BOWES Peter 655	BULMAN Brian 69
BOWIE Joan 613	BUNN Jeanne 401
BRADLEY Lorne Natalie 482	BURKE Dorothy 456
BRADSHAW Norma 259	BURKE Terry 333
BRADY Kate 161	BURL Emma 231
BRADY Kate 39	BURNES David 267
BRAIN Sara 123	BURNETT Brian 662
BRAITHWAITE Dana 324	BURNETT Mrs Joan 168
BRANKIN Irene 302	BURNETT-STUART Sarah 367
BRANSON Clare 469	BURNS Alex 102, 589
BRATERMAN Eleanor 65	BURNS Jo 653
BRAVE Anna 70	BURSTON Helen 359
BRAY Jillyan 607	BURTON Mary 379
BRAY Michael 148	BURTT Lucy 198
BRAZIER John 245	BUSH Sandra 83
BREWER Caroline 224	BUSS Heather 345
BREWER Madelyn 482	BUTCHER Barbara 241
BRICKELL John 227	BUTLER Ruth 224
BRICKMAN Louisette 197	BUTLER Catherine 166
BRIDGMAN Michelle 242	BUTLER John 161
BRIGGS Margarete 310	BUTLER Todd 193
BRIGGS Dr Andrew 312	BUTTERFIELD Janet 525
BRIND William 306	BUTTERFIELD Janet 156
BRINTON Patricia 341	BUTTERS Steve 598
BRION Marion 42	BUTTERWICK Marcia 369
BRISTOW Margot Hogan 453	BYFORD Annette 350
BROADBENT Faith 462	CAHN Albert 154, 527
BROADLEY Richard 472	CAHN Malka 154, 527
BROCK Sue 342	CAIRNS Jean 634

CALDWELL Annee	505	CLARK Jean	460
CALLAGHAN Joan	421	CLARK Jackie	352
CALVERT Jane	475	CLARK Margaret	304
CAMERON Katherine	317	CLARK David Findlay	650
CAMERON Mary	187	CLARK Isobel	507
CAMERON Angela	253	CLARKE Wendela	242
CAMPBELL Hazel	603	CLARKE Christine	273
CAMPBELL Colin	647	CLARKE Catherine	235
CAMPBELL Robbi	578	CLAXTON Brenda	515
CAMPBELL Colin	277	CLAYTON Maureen	379
CAMPBELL Julia	172	CLAYTON Zena	125
CAMPBELL Elizabeth	106	CLEAL Robin	296
CANNAN Philippa	568	CLEGG Adrienne	349
CANNY Patricia	628	CLEGG Alison	499
CANTER Anita	432	CLEMENTS Judith	262
CARAPETIAN Rosemarie	113	CLEMENTS Pip	215
CARDEW Patricia	516	CLEMINSON Dorel	133
CARDEW David	516	CLIFFORD Andrea	343
CARR Jean	218	CLIFFORD Alice	626
CARRINGTON Norah	154, 527	CLIFTON Elaine	161
CARRUTHERS Barbara	657	CLOUGH Rosemary	554
CARSLEY Carol	393	CLOUGH Andrea	133
CARTER Paula	323	CLOUTTE Penny	71
CARTER Ursula	284	CLOWES Brenda	51, 303
CARTER Paula	322	COBBAN Joy	566
CARUANA Charles	139	CODD Anne Marie	226
CASEMORE Roger	590	COFFEY V (Ms)	523
CASSIDY Janis	27, 445	COGHAN Tony	99
CASTLE Steve	349	COHEN Renee	61
CATTLE Liese	478	COHEN Michael	517
CAVENDISH Jean	338	COHEN Ruth	62
CAWLEY Tony	431	COIA Grace	658
CECIL Yvette	484	COLCLOUGH Pam	176
CERNER Ruth	440	COLDRICK Judith	641
CHADWICK Anne	547	COLE Rosemary	398
CHADWICK Kay	434	COLE Laurence	451
CHALK Caroline	529	COLE Martin	599
CHAMLEE-COLE Laurena	74	COLE Jonathan	600
CHANCER Anne	167	COLE Sara	577
CHANDLER Diana	146, 513	COLEBY Nik	167, 294
CHANDLER Kevin	637	COLLIS June	169, 551
CHANDLER David	240	COLLIS Elizabeth	214
CHANDLER Stanley	448	COLMAN Greta	549, 574
CHANDWANI Lilian	124	COLVER Stephen	629
CHANEY Gerry Alide	531	COMBER Philippa	460
CHANNON Michael T	530	CONDER Sue	160
CHAPMAN Maureen	198, 308	CONRADI Prue	461
CHAPMAN Trudy	145	CONROY Ruth	118
CHARLETON Mary	552	CONSTANTINOU Lydia	79
CHARNOCK Donald	432	CONWELL James	104
CHESSELL Susan Tak Chiu	517	CONYERS Maria	302
CHEVALLIER Thelma Ann	232	CONYNGHAM Laura	284
CHEVERTON Gordon	425	COOK Rose	289, 644
CHEW Alex	378	COOKSON Diana	402
CHEW Elisabeth	40	COOPER Howard	62
CHILTON Barbara	566	COOPER Cassie	443
CHISWELL JONES Susan	562	COOPER Dawn	444
CHITTY Kenneth	378	COOPER Sara	62
CHIVERTON-HUNT Ann	382	COOPER Suzanne	447
CHRISTIAN Janet	498	COOPER Grahame Dr	598
CHRISTOPHER Elphis Dr	77	COOPER Sandra	484
CLARE John	191	COOPER Cassie	120
CLARE Louise	225	COOPER Jacqueline	488

COOPER Margaret 271	DALTON Helen 137
COPELAND Sue 265	DANBURY Hazel 528
COPEMAN Ann 111	DANIELS Frank 475
COPLESTON Nora 311	DANIELS Lois 598
COPPENHALL Kate 267	DARLING Nick 45
CORBETT Michael 415	DAUBENSPECK Viv 533
CORBETT Marjorie 538	DAVENPORT Hilary 549
CORDER Francisca 244	DAVID Ann 63
CORKER Enid 498	DAVIDOFF Suzanne 621
COTTRELL Steve 661	DAVIES Pam 385
COTTRELL Sue 141	DAVIES Peggy 397
COULING Jo 582	DAVIES Vera 268
COULSON Christopher J 507	DAVIES Elizabeth 210
COUMONT Val 165	DAVIES Lisa 434, 488
COUPAR Alan 662	DAVIES Dominic 474
COURTAULT Susie 165	DAVIES Jennifer 235
COURTNEY Joy 337	DAVIES Joy 48
COUSSENS Kay 316	DAVIES Bozena 605
COWEN Lynne 542	DAVIES Ruth 572
COWLING Sue 77	DAVIS Janet 174
COWPER JOHNSON Dinah 284	DAVIS Josephine 452
COX Philip 50	DAVIS Patricia 311
COX Margaret 500	DAVIS James 331
COX George 344	DAVISON Judith 533
COX David 554	DAVY Antonia Sybil 275
CRACE Gay 81	DAY Roger 589
CRADDOCK Jenny 200	DAY Lesley 453
CRAIB Ian 506	DAY Christine 588
CRAIGEN Jenny 220	de Vos Maggie 569
CRAN Ros 414	DE BERKER Patricia 550
CRAWFORD Audrey 27	DE IONNO Christine 144
CREAMER Mary 136	DE BERKER Paul 550
CREDLAND Jean 620	DE BERTODANO Joanna 146
CRICK Jill 525	DE LA COUR Gill8 382
CRIDDLE Felicity 73	DEACON David 371
CROMWELL Sheila 318	DEACON Jerry 474
CROSBY Simon 27, 567	DEAN Paul 455
CROSS Vara 76	DEAN Sally 455
CROUAN Michele 331	DEAN Harry 393
CROUCH Ann 619	DEANS Guy 422
CROUCH Anthony 493	DEARDEN Padmini, Ms 293
CROUCHMAN Tinky (Ms) 379	DEBNEY Jacqueline 529
CROWDER Rachel 600	DEERING Christine 447
CROWTHER Ann 568	DELL Jacqueline 254
CULLISS Andrew 154	DELL Judith 123
CUMMINS Eddie 513	DELLER William 233
CUNNINGHAM Valerie 407	DELROY Dr Sandra 63
CURRA Jenny 28, 530	DEMETER Katherine 213
CURTIS JENKINS Graham 449	DEMPSEY Aileen 551
CURTIS Jill 169	DENING Sarah 162
CUSSINS Anne 158	DENNET Annette 536
DAGLEISH John 514	DENNIS JONES Kathleen 405
DAHLE Josephine 350	DENSHAM Deborah 337
DAINTREE Jean 261	DENT Peter 419
DAINTRY Penelope 551	DESSAUER Helga 244
DALAL Farhad 85	DICKINSON Colin 603
DALE John 412	DICKSON Carole 236
DALE Peter 569	DIDSBURY Patricia 416
DALE Irene 589	DIETZ Doreen 376
DALE Marjorie 578	DIMMOCK Cherryll 247
DALE Heather 638	DIX Francoise 219
DALTON Frances 386	DIXON-NUTTALL Rosemary 566
DALTON Peggy 189	DOBBS Wendy 111

DOBSON Gill	651, 655
DOGGART Elizabeth	601
DOGMETCHI Geraldine	111
DOHERTY Nora	604
DOHERTY Prue	560
DOMLEO Jill	536
DONINGTON Laura	163
DONOVAN Louise	506
DONOVAN Marlyn	138
DOOLEY Patricia	543
DOOLEY Patricia	511
DOREY Mary	376
DOUGLAS Hazel	483
DOUGLAS Sue	484
DOUGLAS Carolyn	202
DOUGLAS-MAUL Jean	608
DOWNER Yvonne	575
DRABBLE Sarah	551
DRAPER Joyce	627
DRIVER June	528
DRIVER Christine	65
DRUMMOND Mary	388
DRYDEN Windy	117
DUCKWORTH Moira	187
DUDLEY Valerie	517
DUFFELL Nicholas	73
DUFFELS Catharina	446
DUFFY Maria Bento	534
DUIGNAN K	512
DUNCAN Ursula	618
DUNKLEY Gillian	288
DUNN Elizabeth	499
DUNN Nicola	104
DUNSTAN Gina	379
DUPONT-JOSHUA Aisha	346
EAST Gillian	608
EASTON Simon	349
EATOCK John	417
ECCLES Susan Mrs	407
EDEN Glenis	220
EDGE Jon	134
EDGELL Marjory	157
EDMONDS Jean	522
EDRIDGE Maren	552
EDWARDS John	234
EDWARDS Jennifer Jane	396
EDWARDS Mary	190
EDWARDS Dagmar	444
EDWARDS Linda	133
EDWARDS Lyn	372
EGGELING Celia	177
EISEN Susan	85
ELAND Ann	661
ELDER Mary	450
ELDER Penny	75
ELDERTON John	485
ELDRIDGE Rodney	348
ELEY Frances Ann	641
ELLIOT Patricia	178
ELLIOT Beryl	556
ELLIOTT Mary	628
ELLIOTT Lea K	321
ELLIS Mary Lynne	111
ELLIS Roger	429
ELLWOOD Jane	51
ELMS Gill	432
ELSON Melinda	73
ELSWORTH Gillian	336
ELTON WILSON Jenifer	612
ELVIN Gillian	163
EMANUEL Kay	480
ENCKE Jochen	189
ENCKE Ulrike	189
ENGEL-MADISON Rachel	76
ENGLISH Wendy	613
ENTWISTLE Christine-Anne	28
ENTWISTLE Paul Andrew	28, 434
EPHRAIM Nona	665
ERICKSON Margaret	246
ERRINGTON Richard	298
ERSKINE Angela	368
ESKENAZI Irene	295
ETHERINGTON Kim	493
EVAN Rod	259
EVANS Jane	392
EVANS John	659
EVANS Len	575
EXALL Jean	399
FABIAN Carole	308
FADER John	541
FAGIN Anthony	78
FAIRHURST Irene	28, 313
FAITH Patricia	245
FAIZ Nasim	198
FARMER Eddie	157, 620
FARRELL Anita	604
FARRELL William	264
FARUKI Shirley	51
FAULKNER Ann	654
FAWCETT Jane	113
FELDSCHREIBER Lyn	531
FELL Angela	192
FELLOWS Ruth	448
FENTON Judy	91
FERNANDES Jennie	87
FERNIE Ann Mrs	553
FERNS Patricia	497
FERRARA Linda	232
FERRY Pat	584
FEWELL Judith	654
FIRTH Gail	507
FIRTH David	354
FISHER Suze	176
FISHER Maggie	574
FISHMAN Paul	313
FISZER Mike	419
FITTON Freda	263
FITZGERALD Maura	106
FITZGERALD-BUTLER Albina	446
FITZSIMMONS Janet	366
FLATMAN Brian	330
FLETCHER Brian	629
FLEWETT Dave	565
FLINSPACH Elisabeth	66, 466
FORD Eileen	359
FORD Mandy	353

FORRESTER Barry	662
FORSTER Kay	43
FORSYTH Tom	108
FOX Joshua	141
FOX Barbara	597
FOX Fiona	610
FOX Susan	87
FRANCIS Pippa	577
FRANKEL Joyce	514
FRANKHAM Hans	450
FRANKLYN Frank	110
FRANSELLA Fay, Dr	275
FREEDMAN Roland	583
FREEMAN CARTWRIGHT John	361
FREEMAN Ruth	381
FREEMAN CARTWRIGHT Josephine	361
FREEMAN Martin	186
FREESTONE Eileen	245
FRENCH Jean	393
FRENCH Jeannie	275
FRIEDMAN Elizabeth	245
FROST Charles	576
FRY Caroline	206
FULLER Dianne	359
FURNEAUX Anne	193
GABELL Yvonne	463
GABLE Judith	100
GAIRDNER Wendy	170
GALANT Irene	214
GALE Derek	314
GALLOP Margaret	479
GALLOWAY Jan	243
GANDY Rus	162
GARDINER Alison	606
GARDINER Margaret	130
GARDINER Morag	654
GARLINGE Margaret	399
GARNER Janet	295
GARRARD Patricia	203
GARROD Nigel	450
GARRY Lesley	387
GARVIN-CROFTS Pauline	630
GASKELL Judy Ms	356
GATTI-DOYLE Fiorella	156
GAUSDEN Chris	409
GAVIN Lorraine	268
GAYTON Maria	565
GEATER Kathy	582
GEE Ann	360
GEER Carol	570
GERRARD Jackie, Mrs	368
GIBBIN Jane	663
GIBSON Melanie	199
GILBERT Maria	194
GILBERT Sharon	312
GILDEBRAND Katarina	63
GILES Gail	414
GILL Vilma	664
GILMORE Ian	140
GLADSTONE Guy	29
GLAISYER Alison	568
GLASSPOOL Patricia	344, 355
GLOGER Estela	114
GLOVER Jan	577
GLOVER Jean	640
GODDARD Moira	338
GODDEN Mary	402
GOLDENBERG Harriett	109
GOLDZWEIG Jack	62
GOMEZ Lavinia	114
GOMEZ Anthea	621
GOOD Patricia	342
GOODACRE David	469
GOODARE Heather	575
GOODCHILD Angela	407
GOODMAN Helen	365
GOODMAN Diana	107
GOODRICH Diana	73
GORDON Paul	117
GORDON Mrs Loekie	59
GORDON Sheila	147
GORDON Leila	254
GORDON-GRAHAM Vivienne	555
GORNEY Carry	29
GORTON Patricia	404
GORTON Elisabeth	378
GOSLING Peggy	88
GOSS Diana	352, 353
GOTTSCHALK Margaret	142
GOUGH Tony	421
GOUGH Cathy	303
GOUGH Anna	370
GOULD Jean	448
GOULD Geraldine	424
GOULDING Barbara	331
GOWANS Alasdair	657
GRACE Carole	188
GRACIE Anthony	614
GRACIE Jane	614
GRAFF Avril	365
GRAHAM Hilary	281, 472
GRANGE Jean	315
GRANOWSKI Margaret	89
GRANT Yvonne Shirley	310
GRANT Karen	325
GRANT John	659
GRANT Nigel	140
GRANVILLE Marion	100
GRAY Nigel	72
GRAYSON Juliet	526
GREATOREX Christopher	326
GREEN Fiona	29
GREEN June	446
GREEN Jennifer	573
GREEN Fiona	286
GREEN Anthea	643
GREENBERG Harry	112
GREENING Sarah	620
GREENSLADE Josephine	324
GREGORY Heather	307
GREGORY Christine	567
GRIFFITHS Thelma	233
GRILLET Kate	252
GRIMSEY Alan	502
GROTE Janie	85
GROVE-WHITE Helen	414

GRUNDY Mary	546	HARVEY Tricia	599
GUEST Hazel	256	HASLAM Deidre	41
GULIAN-MINSHULL Edith	252	HASLAM Wendy	494
GULLIVER Pamela	168	HASLAM-EVANS James	647
GUTHRIE Claire	557	HASLOP Rosemary	256
HALE Sue	669	HASTINGS Jon	213
HALES Jonathan	564	HATSWELL Valerie	341
HALL Kelvin	326	HAWKES Kim	537
HALL Jan	145	HAWKINS Jan	40
HALL June	325	HAWLEY Thomas A	630
HALL June	211	HAWORTH Ann	328
HALL Cherrie	348	HAYFIELD Elaine	409, 511
HALLETT Jane	669	HAYMAN Penny	476
HALLIBURTON Anne	658	HAYWARD Marie-Louise	548
HAMILTON PAGE Steve	641	HAYWOOD Rachel	499
HAMILTON Irene	125	HEADON Christopher	30, 408
HAMILTON Nigel	203	HEAL Christianne	252
HAMILTON Mr Kim	383	HEAL Felicity	347
HAMILTON-WILSON Dr Adrian	227	HEATON-ROSS Sheila	642
HAMMERSLEY Diane	358	HECTOR Viv	662
HAMMOND Margaret	449	HEDLEY David4	635
HAMNETT Jennifer	217	HEENAN Colleen	635
HAMORY Eva	423	HEMMING Judith	68
HAMPTON Charles	482	HENDERSON Pauline	85
HAMPTON Wendy	456	HENDRY Devam Mrs	311
HANCHEN Tomasz	138	HENLEY Philippa	220
HANCOCK Patricia	612	HENRIQUES Marika	161
HANCOCK Alan	105	HENSON Tricia	526
HANNEMAN Janet	573	HERMAN Yvette	383
HANSON Anne	521	HERSHMAN Claire Odeon	67
HARDAKER Susan	406	HESSEL Susan	74
HARDEN Bev	334, 337	HESTER Bridget	623
HARDING Celia	47	HEUER Gottfried	187
HARDWICK Barbara	628	HEUER Birgit	187
HARDY Liz	250	HEWETT Rachael	531
HARDY Jennifer	329	HEWITT Eva	564
HARE Lesley	247, 372	HEWITT Val	616
HARGADEN Helena	144	HEWSON Jean	366
HARKNESS Margaret	659	HEWSON Julie	289
HARLEY Ki	63	HEWSON Jan Ms	66
HARLING Biljana	41	HEYWOOD TAYLOR Beatrice	555
HARNESS Jennifer	61	HICKLING Sally	294
HARPER Suzanne	29, 199	HICKMAN Barbara	202
HARRINGTON Elizabeth	188	HIGDON Juliet	583
HARRIS Debra	467	HIGGINBOTHAM Maggie	281
HARRIS Michael	110	HIGHAM Debbrah	536
HARRIS Jonathon	484	HIGHLEY John	280
HARRIS Jenny	652	HILDEBRAND Miki Mrs	110
HARRIS Rowena	81	HILL Joanne	172
HARRIS Richard	386	HILL Jenny	360
HARRIS Cynthia	361	HILL Brenda	586
HARRIS Gerald	608	HILL Lorna	452
HARRIS Pamela	600	HILLIER Shirley	634
HARRISON MAYOR Susan	384	HILLMAN Christine	544
HARRISON Donald	663	HILLMAN Jan	664
HARRISON Diane	607	HINDMARSH Roland	252
HARRISON Jenny	459	HINKSMAN Barrie	587
HARRISON Eileen	412	HIPPS Hilary	170
HART Azina	545	HITCHINGS Paul	188
HART Paul	502	HOANG Astrid	49
HART Chris	130, 463	HOARE Ian	614
HARTLEY Fiona	555	HOBBES Robin	329
HARVEY Anna	335	HOBBS Sandra	218

Name	Page
HOBBS Anita	445
HOBBS Janet	92
HODSON Phillip	103
HOLBORN Julie	480
HOLLANDERS Henry	415
HOLLIDAY Rebecca	398
HOLLINGS Avril	64
HOLLOWAY Roberta	304
HOLMES Dorothy	588
HOLMES Elizabeth	292
HOLMES Phyllis	394
HOLT Alan	422
HONEY Barbara	636
HOOD Jane	661
HOOPER Robert	590
HOPE Joyce	67
HOPKINS Eric	461
HOPKINS Barbara	428
HOPKINS John	258
HOPKINS Ian	220
HOPPE Maggie	578
HOPWOOD Jean	553
HORDER Daphne	30
HORNBY Garry Dr	388
HORROCKS Roger	207
HORROCKS Pam	265
HORROCKS Mary	269
HORTON David	218
HOUGHTON Christine	442
HOUSLEY Rosemary	619
HOWARD David	440
HOWARD Angela	119
HOWARD Heather	131
HOWARD Susan	551
HOWE Kenneth	270
HOWE Patti	492
HOWES Kathleen	665
HOWTONE Christina	316
HUDSON Fiona	649
HUDSON Rosmy	400
HUDSON Marjorie	523
HUGGINS Alan	304
HUGHES Linda	502
HUISH Margot	59
HULME Kendall	354
HUMPHREYS Jacky	214
HUMPHREYS Lorraine	371
HUMPHRIES Tamsin	481
HUNT Bruce	476
HUNT Ruth	285
HUNT Kathleen	288
HUNTER Lynne	314
HUNTER Norma	109
HURFORD Patricia	380
HUXTABLE Pamela	41
HYMAS Mary	618
ILJON FOREMAN Elaine	101
INSKIPP Francesca	570
IRVINE Barbara	469
ISAACS Joy	166
ISAACSON Zelda	116
ISAAKS Cath	60
ISON Mary	217
IZOD Karen	550
IZZARD Sue	602
JACKSON Roderick	30
JACKSON Diana	124
JACKSON Roderick	105
JACKSON Gerry	237
JACKSON Jennifer	533
JACKSON Val	118
JACKSON Barbara	371
JACKSON Sharon Ruth	637
JACOB Emily	165
JACOBS Marion	380
JACQUES Glenys	44
JAMES Ken	210
JAMES Jeanette	663
JAMES Patricia	588
JAMES-GARDINER Christina	270
JANE Melanie	155
JANE-PATMORE Tanya	30
JANI Marian	526
JARVIE Margaret	654
JARVIS Cecilia	206
JEFFREY Joy	502
JELFS Martin	47
JENNINGS Anne	39
JESSON Alison	543
JEVONS Sheilagh	606
JOFFE Riva	116
JOHNSON Jannette	298
JOHNSON Joan	244
JOHNSON Dione	613
JOHNSON Judy	597
JOHNSON Duncan B	226
JOHNSON Elaine	416
JOHNSTON Candice	246
JOHNSTONE Janice	317
JONATHAN Arthur Dr	516
JONES Mel Mrs	293
JONES Judith	436
JONES Sue	140
JONES David	163
JONES Heather	439
JONES Veronica	305
JONES David	45
JONES Monica	206
JONES Alan	516
JONES Cerys Ms	42
JORDAN Pauline	429
JORDAN Ruth	549
JOY Janet	640
JUSTICE Patricia	48
KABERRY Sue	336
KADISH Faigie, Mrs	101
KALISCH David	284
KANE Janine	572
KAPLAN Myron	99
KEELING Doreen	609
KEELING David	59
KEENE Margy	288
KEENE Linda	42
KEENES Susan	452
KEITH Nina	532
KELL Christine	373

KELLY Michael	66	LE DUC-BARNETT Roger	141
KELLY Kathleen	123	LEA Claire J	92
KENNEDY Caroline	462	LEDER Catherine	114
KENNEDY Des	436	LEDERMANN Eric	31
KENNEDY Tony	521	LEE Terry	315
KENNETT Christine	622	LEES Gordon	272
KENNY Brigid	86	LEFTON Mildred	108
KENNY Angela	84	LEGG Christopher	376
KEOGH Kate	263	LEITMAN Norman	193
KERKHAM Pat	458	LENDRUM Susan	332
KERLOGUE Margaret	341	LEROY Eric	59
KERR Anna	131	LESLIE Jenny	247
KESHET-ORR Judi	78	LESTER Frances	366
KETCHELL Helen	264	LESTER Anne	219
KIERNAN Ursula	578	LETHBRIDGE CLEGG Sue	347
KILBORN Mary	646	LETO Daphne Anne	160
KILBURN Andrew	132	LEVENE Tricia	374
KILGOUR Mimi	258	LEVIEN Myra	290
KILICH-WALPOLE Suna	382	LEVINE Julie	619
KILMARTIN Nuala Sister	550	LEVITSKY Patricia	243
KINDER Diana	193	LEVY Colette	119
KING Paul	612	LEVY Sipora	171
KINGSLEY Laurence	597	LEWCZUK Zinaida	648
KIRBY Babs	157	LEWIN Susan	80
KIRK Ruth	424	LEWIN Ann	368
KIRKLAND Jean-Pierre	262	LEWIN Elisabeth	355
KIRKWOOD Colin	655	LEWINSOHN Joan	156
KIRSON Paula	512	LEWIS Jean	268
KIRTON Myrtle	201	LEWIS Gretl	346
KITWOOD Tom	643	LEWIS Penny	556
KLEANTHOUS Dina	88	LEWIS Kenneth	264
KLEIN Valentina	80	LEWIS Maggie	483
KLINEFELTER Polly	397	LEWIS Helen	673
KNIGHT-ADAMS Christa	590	LEWIS David	31
KNIGHT-EVANS Alison	179, 547	LEWIS Penny	445
KNOWLES Christine	298	LEYGRAF Bernd	134
KNOWLES Gwen	285	LIDSTER Wendy	563
KOHLER Christiane	649	LIGHTOWLER Peter	228
KOWSZUN Graz	139	LILLIE Mr Francis	31
KUBEL Patricia	82	LING Felicity	457
KUYPERS Birgit	409	LINN Iris	646
KWEI Daniel	303	LINTERN Fran	513
KYRKE-SMITH Susan	286	LISTER Patricia	66
KYTE Elizabeth	314	LITMAN Gloria Dr	200
LA TOURELLE Maggie	112	LITTLE Ray	191
LACEY Frances	326	LLEWELYN Billie	324
LAMPRELL Michael	46	LLOYD Patricia	31
LAND Patricia	88	LLOYD-JONES Judy	524
LANE Corinne	231	LLOYD-WILLIAMS Kathleen	584
LANE Judy	216	LOBB Brian	400
LANE Betty	668	LOBEL Sydney	333
LANGDON Monica	138	LOBEL Sandra	333
LANGRAN Michael	257	LOCKSTONE Colleen	623
LANSBERRY Christopher	515	LOEWE Eva	109
LAPWORTH Phil	212	LOGAN Faith	487
LARGE Wendy A	427	LOGIE Robin	413
LAURET Marti	287	LOMAC Gina	319
LAW Heather	383	LOMAX Maggie	349
LAW Susan	173	LOMAX Pauline	635
LAWLEY James	200	LOMAX Carol	266
LAWRENCE Yvonne	623	LOMOND Marsha	310
LAWTON Barbara	640	LONCELLE Marie-Jose	89
LAWTON Margaret	287	LONG Audrey	405

LONSDALE-DEIGHTON Mrs Perry 611	MARTIN Peter 351
LOOMS Suzanne 147	MARTIN Margaret 40
LORD Anne 285	MARTIN Deidre 562
LORIMER Angela 554	MARTINO Barbara A 323
LOUDON Julia 298	MARX Philippa 84
LOVE Jacqui 164	MASON Richard 32
LOWE Julie 668	MASON Lindy 98
LOWINGER Leah 346	MASON Ann 498
LOWSON Helen 292	MATE Helen 601
LOXLEY David 629	MATTAR Greta 449
LUCAS Rosemarie 673	MATTHEWS Frances 269
LUCAS Tina 453	MATTHEWS Catriona 639
LUCKS Cecilia 114	MATTHEWS Carol 196
LUMSDEN Barbara 43	MAUGER Benig 80
LUNT William 479	MAXWELL Brian 521
LUSTY Robert 135, 396	MAYBANK Alison 553
LUTHY Barbara 325	MAYHEW David 310
LYNCH Dian 522	MAYHEW Richard 382
LYONS Gill 412	MAYNES Paddy (Ms) 65
MABERLEY Diana 230	McCLEMENT Shirley 373
MABEY Judith 373	McCLINTOCK Jane 457
MACALEVEY Mike 567	McCORMCK Helen 264
MACALISTER Eileen 336	McDERMOTT Olive 188
MACDONALD Laurie 47	McDONALD James 609
MACDONALD Marsali 474	McDONALD Dick 671
MACHADO Danuza 104	McDONNELL Frances 330
MACINTYRE Theresa 528	McDONNELL Fokkina 335
MACKAY Mel, Mrs 254	McGEE Colin 92, 126
MACKINNON Sylvia 236	McGINNIS Sylvia 113
MACKRODT Kathleen 261	McGRATH Kevin 489
MACPHERSON Christine 659	McGREGOR Tony 231
MADDEN Felicity 425	McGUIRE Alec 638
MAHABIR Joel 196	McKENNELL Vivienne 103
MAKIN Anne 329	McKENZIE Jemma 316
MALE David 607	McLEOD John 497
MALKIN Julius 48	McMAHON Gladeana 131
MALLARD Monica 495	McMINNIES Patricia 574
MALLEY John 605	McNAB Stuart 270, 436
MALONE Ronald 532	McNAMARA Jennifer 273
MANDER Gertrud 99	McNEILL Rab 319
MANN David 84	McNULTY Geoff 649
MANN Angela 372	McQUEEN David 657
MANN Elizabeth 324	MEABY Katy 572
MANSFIELD Jacqui 306, 461	MEADEN Rosaleen 175
MARCH SMITH Rosie 294	MEIGS Melinda 136, 176
MARCHANT Paul 312	MEISE Linda 395
MARINER Gail 408	MELBOURNE Benita 306
MARKHAM Sonia 173	MELLETT Jane 612
MARKS Lesley 64	MENEZES Evette 101
MARLER Sally 481	MEPSTED Anne, Mrs 514
MARNELL Rose 435	MEREDEEN Shirley 67
MARQUIEGUI Asun de 158	MERRICKS Belinda 400
MARSDEN Patricia 175	METCALF Pamela 259
MARSH Carol 272	MHLONGO Anne 65
MARSHALL Antoinette 76	MICHAELIS Rae 402
MARSHALL Janet 537	MICHAUD-LENNOX Suzanne 440
MARSHALL Beth 588	MICKELBOROUGH Peter 414
MARSHALL Hazel MEd 423	MIDDLETON Alice 387
MARSHALL Pauline 635	MIDDLETON Suzanne 301
MARSTON-WYLD Joanna 213	MIDGLEY David 272
MARTIN Edward 145	MIERVALDIS Gundega 603
MARTIN Anne 110	MILLAR Anthea 255
MARTIN Gill 621	MILLER Geraldine 315

Name	Page
MILLER Alison	104
MILLER Morris	375
MILLER John Andrew	107
MILLER Margaret	417
MILLER Janet	444
MILLER Bonnie	255
MILLETT Hugh Rev	360
MILLS David	309
MILTON Thelma	215
MOBSBY Sue	493
MOGGRIDGE Cass	324
MOHAN Terry	503
MOJA-STRASSER Lucia	115
MOLE Elizabeth	386
MOLNOS Angela	160
MONJACK Carol	374
MONSON Janet	458
MONTUSCHI Olivia	69
MONYPENNY Helen	147
MOORE Jill	289
MOORE Joan	199
MORDECAI Aslan	75
MORDECAI Kay	75
MORGAN Katina	442
MORGAN Jo	664
MORGAN-BRYANT Linda	606
MORRIS Peter	560
MORRIS Elizabeth	364
MORRIS Vivienne	584
MORRISON Jean	652
MORRISON Barbara	44
MORRISON Philippa	158
MORVILLE Laraine	644
MOSLEY Jennifer	615
MOTH Lenise	405
MOTHERSOLE Geoff	44
MOUQILET Françoise	317
MOUNTAIN Sylvia	330
MOUNTJOY Lesleen	546
MOXLEY Kurt	483
MUGRIDGE Helle	351
MUIR Margaret	138
MUIR Liz	333
MUIR Margaret	170
MULLINS Daphne	227
MUMFORD Susan	137, 173
MUNT Stephen	167
MURDOCH Edna	567
MURPHY Val	573
MURPHY Pam	404
MURPHY Antonia	473
MURPHY Maureen	503
MURRAY Chris	266
MURRAY Cecil Dr	174
MURTON Jean	403
MUSKETT Florence	381
MYERS Marion	586
MYERS Dania	136
NAGEL Beatrice	599
NAIK Raman	79
NAISH Julia	68
NASH Mallory	478
NATHAN Lesley	517
NAYLOR-SMITH Alan	370
NEEDS-GARDINI Liliana	197
NELSON Denise	49
NELSON Margaret	257
NETTE-THOMAS Katy	505
NEUSTEIN David	142
NEVILLE-SMITH Graeme	229
NEWBERY Christopher	296
NEWBERY Christine	545
NEWBIGIN Alison	140
NEWBOLD Linda M	309
NEWMAN Margaret	257
NEWNHAM Elizabeth	548
NEWSOME Marjorie	103
NEWSON Mary	109, 456
NEWTON Janie	639
NEWTON Don	287
NEWTON Angela	377
NEWTON Jeanne	558
NEY Judy	169
NICHOLAS Geraldine	605
NICHOLLS Stephen	423
NICHOLLS Sylvie	286
NIGHTALL Celia	88
NIGHTINGALE Eileen	70, 407
NKUMANDA Rachel	141
NOBLE Katina	214
NOBLE Jane	72
NORMIE Shirley	270
O'BRIEN Jane	192
O'CALLAGHAN Lesley	121
O'CONNOR Noreen	72
O'DELL Tricia	521
O'DONNELL Maire	637
O'GORMAN Mary Pat	106
O'HALLORAN Mike	164
O'NEILL James	158
O'NEILL Teresa	357
OAKLEY Madeleine	60
OCHIENS Samuel	479
OKIN Sandra	120
OLIVER Jenny	358
OLLEY Margaret	427
OPENSHAW Pamela Diana	219
OPPENHEIMER Diana	90
ORLANS Vanja	124
ORWIN Judith	576
OSBORNE Lynda	545
OVERTON David	79, 365
OWEN Christopher	112
OWEN Dave	290
OWEN Angela	436
PAGE Steve	633
PAIN Jean	257
PALLENBERG Susan	159, 380
PALMER Stephen	131
PALMER Helen	84
PALMER-BARNES Fiona	71
PANTALL Marlis Mrs	262
PAPE Maureen	225
PARAMOUR Anabelle	225
PARFITT Will	492
PARKER Cath	628

PARKER Mary	155
PARKES Val	608
PARKINSON Diana	242, 372
PARKINSON Pamela	525
PARKINSON Frank	479
PARKS Val	64
PARLETT Malcolm	215
PARR John	232
PARRITT Simon	171
PARROTT Heather	458
PASSER Sadie	81
PASSINGHAM Carol	466
PATERSON Sheila	32
PAUL Sandra	146
PAVEY Rosemary	303
PAYNE Jean	358
PAYNE Helen	377
PAYNE Martin	457
PEARCE Gerald	228
PEARCE Peter	144
PEARCE Mel	281
PEARMAN Cathy	557
PEARSON Althea	396
PEART Mary	228
PEGLAR Graham	251
PENN Joyce	317
PENN-TAPLIN Pam	326
PENNINGTON Adrian	49
PERMAN KERR Lesley	378
PERREN Mary	384
PERRETT Angelina	629
PERRIN Jane	525
PERRY Janet	420
PERRY Pamela	352, 614
PERSIGHETTI Teresa	49
PETERS Sheila	147
PETHICK Ursula	569
PHELPS Margaret	524
PHILLIPS Sue	476
PHILLIPS Wendy	123
PHILLIPS Richard	466
PHILLIPS Mary	544
PHILLIPS Marian	108
PHILLIPS Laurie	294, 542
PHILLIPS Dot	198
PHILLIPS Leonard	259
PICKETT Alan	392
PICKSTOCK Keith	86
PIERCE Graham	269
PIGOTT Sheila	472
PIMENTEL Allan	204
PITCAIRN Richard	373
PITCEATHLY Hamish	515
PITT Rosemary	353
PIXNER Stef	44
PLATT Sue	118
PLATT John	460
PLOTEL Angela	195, 205
PLOWMAN Polly	130
POCKLINGTON Michael	459
POCOCK Olga	613
POLLOCK Josephine Seton	234
POOLE Robert	204
POPE Alan	205
POPKIN Jennifer	570
POPPLEWELL Sue1	428
PORTER Danny	331
PORTSMOUTH Francziska	243
POTTER Val	119
POTTER Keith	643
POWE Roger	560
POWELL Glyn	451
POWER Lilian	505
POWER Anne	416
PRABATANI Kala	304
PRATT Sheila	552
PRATT John	280
PRATT Stephen	498
PREISINGER Kristiane	100
PRESANT Fern	86
PRICE Jacqueline	602
PRICE Kit	32
PRICE Wendy	544
PRINGLE Diana	490
PRITCHETT Ruth	323
PROCTER Ann	494
PROSSER Susan	355
PROUD Sylvia	542
PRYOR Tim	166
PUCKETT Jane	139
PULLEN Denise, Dr	579
PULLIN Andrew	492
PURDY Meg	280
PURKISS Jane	213
PURTON Campbell	462
QUATE Monty	642
QUINLAN Jennifer	221
QUINN Asher	32, 292
RABE Marie-Louise	512
RAE Frances	408
RAINE Margaret	627
RAM Elizabeth	74
RAMAGE Margaret	33
RANDALL Rosemary	250
RANDALL Sebastian	307
RANDELL Peter	557
RANDLE Rosalind	264
RANDOLPH Jenefer	392
RATOFF Tamar Ms	47
RAWSON Penny	205
RAYMENT Jenny	461
RAYMOND Caroline	178
RAYMOND Liz	409
READ Jane	192
REBUCK Gerald	33
REDFERN Neil	279
REDGRAVE Kenneth	267
REDMAN Christopher	155
REDMILL-SORENSEN Bernice	370
REDPATH Robert	241
REECE Rosalind	122
REES Susan	206
REES-ROBERTS Diane	455, 535
REEVE Gill	164
REEVE Jean	421
REGIS Steve	79

REID Rosamund	558
RENFREW Denise	587
RENTOUL Robert	493, 610
RENTOUL Lynette	77
RENWICK John	50
REUVID Jennie	163
REX Imogen	474
RHODES Thelma	637
RIBET Oonagh	445
RICHARDS Diana	117
RICHARDSON Madeleine	563
RICHARDSON Maureen	472
RICHARDSON Susan	462
RICHARDSON Naomi	359
RICHARDSON Elizabeth	384
RICKABY Susan	297
RICKARD Pamela	557
RICKETT Marion	371
RIDDELL Caroline	174
RIDGEWAY Christopher	230
RIDGEWELL Margaret	420, 481
RIES Paul	254
RIMMER Annie	148
RIMMER Janet	443
RINK Jane	549
RIPPON Lynda	177
RITCHIE Ann	342
RITTER Sandie	46
ROBBINS Peter	219
ROBERT Leslie	186
ROBERTS Sheila	148
ROBERTS Laurence	43
ROBERTS Pauline	394
ROBERTS Ellie	433, 481
ROBERTSON Judith	103
ROBERTSON Ewa	101
ROBERTSON L Hattie	308
ROBERTSON David	546
ROBINS Jane	218
ROBINS Julia	33
ROBINSON Louise	494
ROBINSON Hazel	116
ROBINSON Lisa	255
ROBINSON Martin	291
ROBINSON Fran	235
ROBINSON Gerald	579
ROBSON Ian	302
ROBSON Barbara	130
ROCKLIFFE Elizabeth	531
RODGER Hilary	202
RODGERS Susan	172
RODKOFF Lesley	314
ROE Peter	277
ROGERS Brenda	395
ROGERS Anne	224
ROGNERUD Tove	90
ROHRIG Angelika	142
ROMAINE Stephanie	640
ROSE Suzanna	134, 235
ROSE-NEIL Wendy	171
ROSENFIELD Maxine	61
ROSS Vicky	203
ROSSETER Bill	246
ROTH Ruth	102
ROWE Carolyn	642
ROWLANDS Helen	667
ROWLEY Jill	443
ROY Geraldine	609
RUDNICK Joan	433
RUIJTERMAN Caroline	579
RUSSELL Dorothy	345
RUSSELL Hazel	221
RUSSELL Valerie	395
RUTHERFORD Morna	658
RUTLEDGE Joan	197
RYDE Judith	211
RYLEY Brigitte	143
RYVES Meg	350
SADEGHIAN Arsalan	48
SAGGERS Andrew	41
SAGOE Vanessa	503
SALFIELD Angela	375, 441
SALMON Cindy	307
SALTER Gill	351
SALTER E Alan	458
SAMARI Samandar Mr	194
SAMUELS Carole	60
SANDELSON Adam	45
SANDERS Susie	204
SANDERS Cheryl	195
SANDERSON Adelheid	394
SANDERSON Lesley	473
SANSOM Lavender	523
SAUNDERS Christina	186
SAUNDERS Dr Chris	482
SAUNDERSON Adrienne	311
SAWARD Stephanie	534
SAWERS Martin	217
SCARLETT Jean	102
SCHAPIRA Sylvie	171
SCHAVERIEN Joy	258, 425
SCHEMBRI Veronica	341
SCHILD Maureen	117
SCHMID Doria	199
SCHMUCKER Rosemarie	156
SCHOFIELD Caroline	155
SCHULTZ Evelyn	201
SCOTCHMAN Susan	305
SCOTT Mary	416
SCOTT Lena	532
SCOTT Mary	332
SCOTT Ann	258
SCOTT Judy	494
SCOTT Catherine	415
SCOTT-MCCARTHY Brian	400
SCRIMSHAW George	435
SEABORN-JONES Glyn	78
SEAL Raymond	505
SEALE Donna	89
SEAMAN Daphne	443
SEEAR Louise	139
SEGAL Julia	121
SELBY Anne	211
SELBY-BOOTHROYD Judith	243
SELIGMAN Philippa	668
SEMPLE Beryl	406

SERPELL Vivienne	253
SEYMOUR CLARK Vivienne	290
SHAER Madeleine	78
SHANNON Jan	622
SHANNON Betty	537
SHAPIRO Ilona	77
SHAPLEY Bernard	92
SHARMAN Roslyn	135
SHARON Linda	82
SHARP Linda	272
SHARPLES Geraldine	334
SHATTOCK Avril	58, 364
SHAW Sue	587
SHAW Maureen	447
SHAW Marion	446
SHEARMAN Christine	46
SHELDRICK Linda	293
SHEMIS Kamilia	527
SHEPHERD David	318
SHEPHERD Jane	210
SHEWAN Alistair	652
SHILLITO-CLARKE Carol	591
SHOEMARK Alison	653
SHORT Ruth	563
SHORT Deborah	473
SHRIMPTON David	309
SICHEL David	191
SIDHU Frankie	561
SIGNPOST	185
SILKE Phillipa	451
SILLETT Angie	636
SILLS Charlotte	196
SILVER-LEIGH Vivienne	159
SILVERSTONE Liesl	122
SIM Wendy	442
SIMMONDS Gail	70
SIMMONS Peg	225
SIMMONS Gloria	90
SIMMONS Diana	504
SIMMONS Rochelle	118
SIMON Gail	83
SIMONS Timothy	415
SIMONS William	467
SIMPSON Rosie	322
SIMPSON James	658
SINCLAIR Ilse	217
SINGER Sidney	440
SINGH Tony	64
SIVYER John	492
SKINNER Vivienne	530
SKINNER Alan	295
SKONE Carolyn	444
SMALL Juliette	144
SMALLACOMBE Ruth	177
SMALLE Sarah	544
SMITH Jonathan	70
SMITH Phyllis	177
SMITH Christine	121
SMITH Eileen	627
SMITH Gordon	467
SMITH Ann	315
SMITH Thomas	406
SMITH Alicia	657
SMITH Pam	666
SMITH Margaret	433
SMITH Kathleen	367
SMITH Carole	115
SMITH Bob	609
SMITH Patsy	195
SMITH Lionel	168
SMITHURST June	535
SMYTHE Ronald	506
SNYDER Maggie	380
SOBERS Marlene	120
SOFRONIOU Andreas	615
SOMERVILLE Jenny	167
SONN Gillian	312
SORENSEN Barbara	547
SOUTHGATE John	105
SPEED Bebe	597
SPEIRS John	496
SPENCER Mary	369
SPENCER Susan	296
SPENCER Fiona	543
SPIERS Carole	450
SPOOR Lin	239
SPRINGALL Lynn	534
SPURR Pamela	34
SPY Terri	179
SQUIRE Sheila	137
ST JOHN AUBIN Beverley	33
STACEY Linda	368
STANTON Andrew	374
STEDMAN John	366, 561
STEEL Sandra	376
STEIN Avril	91
STEINER Monika	89
STELL Peter PhD	434
STEMBRIDGE David	515
STEPHENS Elyan P	143
STERN James	420
STEVEN Hilary	216
STEVENS Jean	661
STEWARD Jill	480
STEWART Lisa	179
STEWART June	435
STIBBE Paul	610
STIMPSON Quentin	344
STOCK Pauline	226
STOKES Anne	342
STOKES Jenny	599
STOKES Tania	90
STOKES Jean	175
STOLZENBERG Jenny	80
STONE Rosalind	91
STONE Anthony	122
STONE Miriam	105
STOTT Joan	381
STOTT Ken	197
STOVELL Joy	91
STRASSER Dr Freddie	107
STRAWBRIDGE Sheelagh	387
STRIBBLING Judith	547
STRUTHERS Cassandra	34
STUART Lilly	136
STYLE Hinda	34

SUFFOLK Toni	512	TOLEMAN Olive	351
SUGARMAN John	125	TOMAN Ann	574
SULLIVAN Mary	132	TOMPKINS Penny	200
SUMMERFIELD Solharra Gene	432	TONGE Dr Anne	404
SUNDERLAND Cynthia	604	TOPOLSKI Denise	558
SUSS Lawrence	562	TOUT William	288
SUSSMAN Susan	448	TOWERS Anne	343
SUTCLIFFE Patricia	234	TOWNSEND Angela	361
SUTTON Carole	421	TOWNSEND Mrs Clare	518
SUTTON Janet	348	TOYNE Joy K	406
SVIRSKY Orit	116	TRAN Van, Mr	473
SWEENEY Margaret	321	TREPKA Chris	633
SWEENEY Catherine	511	TREVELYAN Jane	650
SWINBANK Doris	230	TREVIS Geoffrey	232
SYKES Vernon	643	TREWARTHA Robin	660
SYME Gabrielle	642	TREWHELLA John	275
TARJAN Claire	441	TRICKEY Veronica	668
TARSH Helen	529	TRUSTAM Gillian	226
TAUSSIG Hanna	253	TUCKER Alison	201
TAYLOR Sylvia	338	TUCKER Frances	323
TAYLOR Meg	86	TUNE David	146
TAYLOR Donald	350	TUNNICLIFFE Michael	283
TAYLOR Mary	112	TURNBULL Peter	485
TAYLOR Lesley	441	TURNER Mary	360
TAYLOR Lissie	665	TURNER Allan	647
TE VELDE Johanna	586	TURNER Pauline	50
TELLING Susan	393	TWEED Brenda	602
TEMPLE Susannah	287	TWEEDALE Beryl	337
TEPER Mrs Gay	106	TWELVETREES Heidy	399
THACKER Rose	273	TYAS Barbara	638
THACKRAY Ms Dayle	189	TYLEE Susan	523
THATCHER Betsy	621	TYLLSEN Ken	277
THISTLE Roger	511	TYNDALE-BISCOE Mrs. Savi	639
THOLSTRUP Margaret	169	TYRWHITT Stephen	135
THOMAS Madeleine	491	ULLMANN Jacqueline	125
THOMAS Diana	533	UNWIN Toni	480
THOMAS Georgette	651	UPCHURCH Ms Terry	309
THOMAS Mary	143	UPTON Sonia	504
THOMAS Clive	460	VAIZEY Phillipa	504, 506
THOMAS Peter	143	VAL BAKER Jess	115
THOMAS Clive	322	VALENTINE Christine	211
THOMASON June	398	VALLINS Yvonne	556
THOMPSON Jean	394	VARNEY Peter	459
THOMPSON Joan	318	VAUGHAN Katherine	555
THOMPSON Hilary	666	VELLACOTT Julia	60
THOMPSON Sholto	165	VENEMA Ashen	546
THORMAN Chris	369	VENNER Ruth	564
THORNE Angela	401	VERNEY Juliet	354
THORNE Heather	234	VICKERS Kate	100
THORNE-JONES Angela	538	VINE Francis	216
THORNHILL Daphne	281	VOELCKER Cara	611
THORNTON Susanne	522	VOLLANS Audrey	552
THORP Cherry	334	VON BUHLER Jose	345
THROWER Gillian	173	VORA Valerie	329
TILLER Brenda Leo	76	WADDELL Susie	449
TILLS Lynne	622	WADE Gloria	504
TILNEY Tony	607	WAGSTAFF Sheila	231
TIMBER Jennifer	68	WAIN Mary	566
TIMMERMAN Robert	172	WAITE Barbara	282
TIMS Patricia	307	WAKEFIELD Peter	638
TINSLEY Maureen	251	WAKELING Linda	377
TITMAN Ann	354	WALKER Pat	436
TOD Victoria	601	WALKER Jane	225

WALKER Jillian	367
WALKLEY Stuart	325
WALL MORRIS Katherine	590
WALLACE Anthea	251
WALLBANK Susan	453
WALLIS Simon	575
WALSH Frieda	548
WALSH Eileen	190
WALSH Aine	164
WALTON Patricia	50
WALTON Andrew	603
WANLESS Peter	115
WARD Shona	454
WARD Roy	149
WARDE Janet	319
WARDEN Rita	468
WARING Judith	216
WARNER Kerri	236
WARRELL Jon	503
WARREN Jeanne	535
WARREN Steven	34, 289
WARREN Madeline	119
WARWICK Heather	253
WATERFIELD Ruth	313
WATERS Sue	451, 452
WATKINS Jean	347
WATKINS SEYMOUR Eileen	122
WATTIS Libby	641
WAUMSLEY Elizabeth	240
WAY Jean	600
WAYMARK TRUST	389
WEAVER Martin	191
WEAVER Daphne	398
WEBB Felicity	636
WEBB Joan	639
WEBSTER Annie	403
WEIGHT Dawn	403
WEITZ Philippa	522
WELCH Rosie	468
WELLER Alan	375
WELLER Celia	435
WELLS Penny	495
WELLS Roger	495
WENHAM Peter	240
WENHAM Franklin	561
WENHAM Jane	190
WESSON Peter	413
WEST John	256
WEST Antonia	35
WESTLAKE Robert	179
WESTON Sarah	454
WEXLER Jean	194
WHISTLER Jennifer Mrs	175
WHITE John	530
WHITE Mary	35
WHITESON Riva	58, 364, 439
WHITTAKER Lesley	499
WHITTAKER Ann	433
WHITTAM Enid	263
WHITTLE Lorna	251
WHITTLE Alan	513
WHITWELL John	615
WHITWORTH Patricia	424
WHYTE Elizabeth	133
WICKER Jane	554
WIDDICOMBE Howard	556
WIDLAKE Bernard	168
WIGHAM Avril	68
WILD Sue	576
WILDASH Sheila	296
WILDAY Greville	605
WILKINSON Linda	82
WILKINSON Margaret	404
WILLCOCK Pamela	306
WILLETT Eleanor	166
WILLIAMS Christopher	285
WILLIAMS Royston	362
WILLIAMS Diana	149
WILLIAMS Nigel	495
WILLIAMS Jane	336
WILLIAMS Ann	353
WILLIAMS Tony	202
WILLIAMS Sherly	422
WILLIAMSON Derrick	428
WILLINGSON Tom	236
WILLIS Sally	532
WILLISON Sandra	46
WILLSON Sheila	162
WILMERS Kath	417
WILMOT Victoria	536
WILSON Mary	606
WILSON Sally	134
WILSON Tony	611
WILSON Veronica	392
WILSON Mick	347
WILTON Angela	159
WINDISCH Thelma	456
WINKWORTH Maggie	190
WINMILL Martin	526
WINTER Pamela	335
WINTERNITZ Robert	583
WINTERSTEIN Mani	192
WISEMAN Anna	381
WITHERS Jane	563
WITKIN Colleen	108
WOLF-PHILLIPS Lisa	367
WOMPHREY Jenny	246
WONNACOTT Ian	615
WOOD Judith	269
WOOD Richard	420
WOOD Anne	362
WOOD Pam	428
WOOD Christine	195
WOODBRIDGE Gill	212
WOODBURN Latilla Dr	620
WOODER Bernie	87, 369
WOODHEAD Chez Ms	471
WOODLEY Jan	212
WOOLFENDEN Jennifer	71
WRIGHT Patricia	35
WRIGHT Regina	399
WRIGHT Marsha	267
WRIGHT Anne	634
WYATT Gill	471
WYNN PARRY Charlotte	174
WYNNE-JONES Christa	343

YALLOP Melanie 537	YOUNG Mary 402
YAPP Robin 601	YOUNG Courtenay 650
YATES Ann 335	YOUNG Anne 375
YENDELL Bridget 75	YOUNG Margot 67
YOUNG Delia 241	YOUNG Louise 374, 584
YORKE Kathy 72	ZINOVIEFF Victoria 160
YOUNG Louise 370	